T0192049

# Lecture Notes in Computer Science 11799

More information about this series at http://www.springer.com/series/7409

Antoine Doucet · Antoine Isaac ·
Koraljka Golub · Trond Aalberg ·
Adam Jatowt (Eds.)

# Digital Libraries for Open Knowledge

23rd International Conference on Theory and Practice
of Digital Libraries, TPDL 2019
Oslo, Norway, September 9–12, 2019
Proceedings

 Springer

*Editors*
Antoine Doucet
University of La Rochelle
La Rochelle, France

Antoine Isaac
VU University Amsterdam
Amsterdam, The Netherlands

Koraljka Golub
Linnaeus University
Växjö, Sweden

Trond Aalberg 🆔
OsloMet – Oslo Metropolitan University
Oslo, Norway

Adam Jatowt 🆔
Kyoto University
Kyoto, Japan

ISSN 0302-9743          ISSN 1611-3349  (electronic)
Lecture Notes in Computer Science
ISBN 978-3-030-30759-2          ISBN 978-3-030-30760-8  (eBook)
https://doi.org/10.1007/978-3-030-30760-8

LNCS Sublibrary: SL3 – Information Systems and Applications, incl. Internet/Web, and HCI

This Springer imprint is published by the registered company Springer Nature Switzerland AG
The registered company address is: Gewerbestrasse 11, 6330 Cham, Switzerland

# Preface

We are happy and proud to present to you the papers accepted for presentation at the 23rd International Conference on Theory and Practice of Digital Libraries (TPDL 2019), which was held at OsloMet – Oslo Metropolitan University, Norway, during September 9–12, 2019.

The TPDL conference brings together researchers, developers, and data experts in the field of digital libraries. This year's theme was "Connecting with Communities." Digital libraries and repositories store, manage, represent, and disseminate rich and heterogeneous data that are often of enormous cultural, scientific, educational, artistic, and social value. Serving as digital ecosystems they provide unparalleled opportunities for novel knowledge extraction and discovery. To become especially useful to the diverse research and practitioner communities, digital libraries need to consider special needs and requirements for effective data utilization, management, and exploitation. TPDL 2019 attempted to facilitate establishing connections and convergences between diverse research communities such as Digital Humanities, Information Sciences, and others that could benefit from (and contribute to) ecosystems offered by digital libraries and repositories.

Our two keynote speakers have embodied this year's focus: Sally Chambers from the University of Ghent has played a key role in the setup of digital humanities infrastructure, while Krisztian Balog from the University of Stavanger is a leading researcher on intelligent information access.

From the 75 papers submitted to the conference, the Program Committee selected 16 long papers and 12 short papers. In addition, 18 posters and demonstrations were presented, as an attempt to showcase the diversity of ongoing efforts and encourage more cross-community discussions.

This year's workshops also illustrate our community outreach efforts, with the 5th International Workshop on Computational History (HistoInformatics 2019) and the 19th European Networked Knowledge Organisation Systems (NKOS) Workshop. The conference program also included a doctoral consortium and a tutorial on the Memento Tracer Framework for Scalable High-Quality Web Archiving.

The success of TPDL 2019 was a result of the teamwork of many individuals. We would like to thank the Program Committee members for their careful assessment of submitted contributions, Ricardo Campos and Mickaël Coustaty (poster and demonstration chairs), Jose Borbinha, Avishek Anand and Nils Pharo (doctoral consortium chairs), Milena Dobreva and Giannis Tsakonas (workshop chairs), and the local organization team. In addition, we warmly acknowledge the financial support of our sponsors and all of the support we have received from Oslo Metropolitan University.

September 2019

Antoine Doucet
Antoine Isaac
Koraljka Golub
Trond Aalberg
Adam Jatowt

# Organization

## General Chairs

Trond Aalberg      Oslo Metropolitan University, Norway
Adam Jatowt      Kyoto University, Japan

## Program Chairs

Antoine Doucet      University of La Rochelle, France
Koraljka Golub      Linnæus University, Sweden
Antoine Isaac      Europeana, VU University Amsterdam,
         The Netherlands

## Poster and Demonstration Chairs

Ricardo Campos      Ci2 – Polytechnic Institute of Tomar, INESC TEC,
         Portugal
Mickaël Coustaty      Lab L3I, University of La Rochelle, France

## Doctoral Consortioum Chairs

Avishek Anand      Leibniz University, L3S Research Center, Germany
Jose Borbinha      NESC-ID, University of Lisbon, Portugal
Nils Pharo      Oslo Metropolitan University, Norway

## Workshop Chairs

Milena Dobreva      University College London Qatar, Qatar
Giannis Tsakonas      University of Patras, Greece

## Program Committee

### Senior Program Committee Members

Maristella Agosti      University of Padua, Italy
David Bainbridge      University of Waikato, New Zealand
George Buchanan      The University of Melbourne, Australia
Milena Dobreva      UCL Qatar, Qatar
Nicola Ferro      University of Padova, Italy
Edward Fox      Virginia Tech, USA
Norbert Fuhr      University of Duisburg-Essen, Germany
Richard Furuta      Texas A&M University, USA

| | |
|---|---|
| Sarantos Kapidakis | Ionian University, Greece |
| Laszlo Kovacs | MTA SZTAKI, Hungary |
| Clifford Lynch | CNI, USA |
| Wolfgang Nejdl | L3S, University of Hannover, Germany |
| Michael Nelson | Old Dominion University, USA |
| Erich Neuhold | University of Vienna, Austria |
| Christos Papatheodorou | Ionian University, Greece |
| Edie Rasmussen | The University of British Columbia, Canada |
| Mário J. Silva | Universidade de Lisboa, Portugal |
| Hussein Suleman | University of Cape Town, South Africa |
| Giannis Tsakonas | University of Patras, Greece |
| Pertti Vakkari | University of Tampere, Finland |
| Maja Žumer | University of Ljubljana, Slovenia |

## Program Committee Members

| | |
|---|---|
| Hamed Alhoori | Northern Illinois University, USA |
| Robert Allen | Independent affiliation |
| Vangelis Banos | Aristotle University of Thessaloniki, Greece |
| Valentina Bartalesi | ISTI-CNR, Italy |
| Maria Manuel Borges | University of Coimbra, Portugal |
| Pável Calado | INESC-ID, University of Lisbon, Portugal |
| Vittore Casarosa | ISTI-CNR, Italy |
| Lillian Cassel | Villanova University, Canada |
| Songphan Choemprayong | Chulalongkorn University, Thailand |
| Sally Jo Cunningham | Waikato University, New Zealand |
| Theodore Dalamagas | IMIS – Athena R.C., Greece |
| Boris Dobrov | Research Computing Center of Moscow State University, Russia |
| Shyamala Doraisamy | University Putra Malaysia, Malaysia |
| Fabien Duchateau | Université Claude Bernard Lyon 1, LIRIS, France |
| Maud Ehrmann | EPFL, DHLAB, Switzerland |
| Nuno Freire | INESC-ID, Portugal |
| Manolis Gergatsoulis | Ionian University, Greece |
| Marcos Gonçalves | Federal University of Minas Gerais, Brasil |
| Sergiu Gordea | AIT Austrian Institute of Technology GmbH, Austria |
| Jane Greenberg | Drexel University, USA |
| Mark Michael Hall | Martin-Luther-Universität Halle-Wittenberg, Germany |
| Andreas Henrich | University of Bamberg, Germany |
| Frank Hopfgartner | The University of Sheffield, UK |
| Perla Innocenti | University of Northumbria at Newcastle upon Tyne, UK |
| Jaap Kamps | University of Amsterdam, The Netherlands |
| Ioannis Karydis | Ionian University, Greece |
| Roman Kern | Graz University of Technology, Austria |

| | |
|---|---|
| Kimmo Kettunen | National Library of Finland, University of Helsinki, Finland |
| Claus-Peter Klas | GESIS – Leibniz Institute for Social Sciences, Germany |
| Martin Klein | Los Alamos National Laboratory, USA |
| Stefanos Kollias | National Technical University of Athens, Greece and University of Lincoln, UK |
| Monica Landoni | University of Lugano (USI), Switzerland |
| Hyowon Lee | Singapore University of Technology and Design, Singapore |
| Suzanne Little | Dublin City University, Ireland |
| Ying-Hsang Liu | The Australian National University, Australia |
| Penousal Machado | University of Coimbra, Portugal |
| Joao Magalhaes | Universidade NOVA de Lisboa, Portugal |
| Yannis Manolopoulos | Open University of Cyprus, Cyprus |
| Zinaida Manžuch | Vilnius University, Lithuania |
| Jani Marjanen | University of Helsinki, Finland |
| Bruno Martins | INESC-ID, University of Lisbon, Portugal |
| Philipp Mayr | GESIS – Leibniz Institute for Social Sciences, Germany |
| Cezary Mazurek | IChB PAN – PCSS, Poland |
| Robert H. Mcdonald | University of Colorado Boulder, USA |
| Dana Mckay | The University of Melbourne, Australia |
| Andras Micsik | SZTAKI, Hungary |
| Jean-Philippe Moreux | Bibliothèque nationale de France, France |
| Agnieszka Mykowiecka | IPI PAN, Poland |
| Heike Neuroth | University of Applied Sciences Potsdam, Germany |
| David Nichols | University of Waikato, New Zealand |
| Ragnar Nordlie | Oslo and Akershus University College, Norway |
| Kjetil Nørvåg | Norwegian University of Science and Technology, Norway |
| Nils Pharo | Oslo Metropolitan University, Norway |
| Francesco Piccialli | University of Naples Federico II, Italy |
| Dimitris Plexousakis | Institute of Computer Science, FORTH, Greece |
| Andreas Rauber | Vienna University of Technology, Austria |
| Cristina Ribeiro | INESC TEC, University of Porto, Portugal |
| Thomas Risse | University Frankfurt, University Library J. C. Senckenberg, Germany |
| João Rocha Da Silva | University of Porto, Portugal |
| Irene Rodrigues | Universidade de Evora, Portugal |
| Heiko Schuldt | University of Basel, Switzerland |
| Michalis Sfakakis | Ionian University, Greece |
| Frank Shipman | Texas A&M University, USA |
| Gianmaria Silvello | University of Padua, Italy |
| Nicolas Spyratos | University of Paris South, France |
| Shigeo Sugimoto | University of Tsukuba, Japan |

| Cyrille Suire | Université Paris-Saclay, UVSQ, France |
| Tamara Sumner | University of Colorado Boulder, USA |
| Atsuhiro Takasu | National Institute of Informatics, Japan |
| Mikko Tolonen | University of Helsinki, Finland |
| Diana Trandabat | Alexandru Ioan Cuza University of Iasi, Romania |
| Theodora Tsikrika | Information Technologies Institute, CERTH, Greece |
| Chrisa Tsinaraki | European Commission – Joint Research Center, Italy |
| Douglas Tudhope | University of South Wales, Australia |
| Yannis Tzitzikas | University of Crete, FORTH-ICS, Greece |
| Stefanos Vrochidis | Information Technologies Institute, CERTH, Greece |
| Michele Weigle | Old Dominion University, USA |
| Marcin Werla | Qatar National Library, Qatar |
| Iris Xie | University of Wisconsin-Milwaukee, USA |
| Marcia Zeng | Kent State University, USA |

## Additional Reviewers

| George Bruseker | Institute of Computer Science, FORTH, Greece |
| Danielle Caled | INESC-ID, Portugal |
| Serafeim Chatzopoulos | IMIS – Athena R.C., Greece |
| Erika Fabris | University of Padua, Italy |
| Gustavo Gonçalves | Universidade NOVA de Lisboa, Portugal |
| Christos Iliou | Information Technologies Institute, CERTH, Greece |
| Ilias Kanellos | IMIS – Athena R.C., Greece |
| Thanasis Vergoulis | IMIS – Athena R.C., Greece |
| Jouni Tuominen | University of Helsinki, Finland |

# Contents

# Long and Short Papers

# Coner: A Collaborative Approach for Long-Tail Named Entity Recognition in Scientific Publications

Daniel Vliegenthart[1,2], Sepideh Mesbah[1(✉)], Christoph Lofi[1],
Akiko Aizawa[2], and Alessandro Bozzon[1]

[1] Delft University of Technology,
Van Mourik Broekmanweg 6, 2628 XE Delft, The Netherlands
{d.vliegenthart,s.mesbah,c.lofi,a.bozzon}@tudelft.nl
[2] National Institute of Informatics Tokyo,
Chome-1-2 Hitotsubashi, Chiyoda, Tokyo 100-0003, Japan
aizawa@nii.ac.jp

**Abstract.** Named Entity Recognition (NER) for rare long-tail entities as e.g., often found in domain-specific scientific publications is a challenging task, as typically the extensive training data and test data for fine-tuning NER algorithms is lacking. Recent approaches presented promising solutions relying on training NER algorithms in an iterative weakly-supervised fashion, thus limiting human interaction to only providing a small set of seed terms. Such approaches heavily rely on heuristics in order to cope with the limited training data size. As these heuristics are prone to failure, the overall achievable performance is limited. In this paper, we therefore introduce a collaborative approach which incrementally incorporates human feedback on the relevance of extracted entities into the training cycle of such iterative NER algorithms. This approach, called Coner, allows to still train new domain specific rare long-tail NER extractors with low costs, but with ever increasing performance while the algorithm is actively used in an application.

## 1 Introduction

With the increasing amount of scientific publications, there is a growing need for methods that facilitate the exploration and analysis of a given research field in a digital library collection [9], but also for techniques which can provide effective retrieval and search experiences. To this end, *"deep meta-data"* extracted from scientific publications allows for novel exploration capabilities [10].

Domain-specific typed named entities [11] such as *datasets* used in a given publication; the *methods* applied to the data or used in implementation are representative examples of deep meta-data. However, extracting and typing named entities for this scenario is hard, as most entities relevant to a specific scientific domain are very rare, i.e. they are part of the *entity long-tail*. Most current state-of the art Named Entity Recognition (NER) algorithms focus on high-recall

© Springer Nature Switzerland AG 2019
A. Doucet et al. (Eds.): TPDL 2019, LNCS 11799, pp. 3–17, 2019.
https://doi.org/10.1007/978-3-030-30760-8_1

named entities (e.g., person and location) [7], as they rely on extensive manually curated training and test data. Due to the rare nature of long-tail entity types, training data is scarce or non-available. Some approaches addressed this problem by relying on bootstrapping [18] or entity expansion [3,6] techniques, achieving promising performance. However, how to train high-performance *long-tail* entity extraction and typing with minimal human supervision remains an open research question.

Recently, TSE-NER [12] was presented, an iterative approach for entity extraction in scientific publications. The approach starts with a small seed set of known entity instances; for each type it is sufficient to have one or two domain experts denote between 5 to 50 known entities. These sets are then heuristically expanded and annotated to generate training data to train a new traditional NER classifier, and heuristically filtered to remove likely false positives to create the entity set for the next iteration. As results of experiments in [12] have shown, this approach is hampered by the simplicity and unreliability of the heuristics used for expanding, but especially by those used for filtering the current iteration's entity set. Nonetheless, the approach promises a lot of potential if these heuristics can be improved by bringing intelligently human judgment in the loop.

**Original Contribution.** In this paper we extend TSE-NER with incremental, collaborative feedback from human contributors to support the heuristic filters. The core goal of this paper is to further the understanding of *how far does human feedback confirm or conflict with TSE-NER heuristics* and *how does incorporating human feedback into the TSE-NER filtering step improve the overall performance with respect to precision, recall, and F-measures*. For this we introduce `Coner`, an approach that allows the users of our system to continuously provide easy-to-elicit low-effort feedback on the semantic fit and relevance of extracted entities. Also, new entities may be added that they deem relevant for a specific facet/type. This feedback is then exploited to support the heuristic expansion and filter phases of the TSE-NER algorithm. The human-in-the-loop approach allows us to still maintain the advantages of the initial design of TSE-NER (i.e., training a NER algorithm cheaply, only relying on a small seed set, and providing an immediate result to users with acceptable extraction quality), while exploiting the human feedback into the next NER training iteration. Coner allows the TSE-NER system to improve its performance over time by benefiting from additional human intelligence in the training process. Coner is available as an open-source project.[1]

We performed two experiments to evaluate our approach on a collection of 11,589 data science publications from ten conference series: (1) an exploratory experiment performed on 10 papers and with 10 users showing that by utilizing human feedback, up to **94.3%** of false positives can be detected for the *dataset* entity type and **57.9%** for the *method* entity type; (2) similar to experiment (1) but receiving only human feedback on entities with high expected information gain in order to maximize the impact of user feedback. This resulted in an average per-entity annotation time of just above 15 s and an increase of precision of up to 4% by boosting the filtering step of TSE-NER.

---

[1] https://github.com/vliegenthart/coner_interactive_viewer.

# 2    TSE-NER: An Iterative Approach for Long-Tail Entity Extraction

In this section we will summarize TSE-NER, an iterative five-step low-cost approach for training NER/NET classifiers for long-tail entity types. For more detailed information on this approach, refer to [12]. The approach is summarized in the following five steps:

1. For *Training Data Extraction*, a set of *seed terms* is determined, which are known named entities of the desired type. The *seed terms* are then used to identify a set of sentences containing the term.
2. *Expansion strategies* are used to automatically expand the set of seed terms of a given type, and the training data sentences.
3. The *Training Data Annotation* step is used to automatically annotate the expanded *training data* using the expanded seed terms.
4. A new *Named Entity Recognizer* (NER) will be trained using the annotated training data for the desired type of entity.
5. The *Filtering step* refines the list of extracted named entities by heuristically removing those entities which are most likely false positives. The set of remaining entities is treated as a seed set for the next iteration. This step is the focal point of this paper.

## 2.1    Heuristic Filtering

In this final step of TSE-NER, which is also the focus of this work, the trained NER model is used to annotate the whole corpus and consider all the positively annotated terms as candidate terms for the next round of iteration. As the training data for training the NER is noisy, the list of entities extracted by the NER contains many items which are not specifically related to the entity type of interest. Therefore, the goal of this last step is to filter out all terms which are most likely not relevant using the following basic heuristics:

**Wordnet + Stopwords (WS).** To preserve only the domain-specific terms and exclude the general English terms we filter out the stopwords (e.g. something) and concepts coming from "common" English language (e.g., "dataset", "software") that could be found in Wordnet[2].

**Similar Terms (ST).** The idea is to keep only the entities which are semantically similar to the seed terms of a given entity type. While there can be many implementations for capturing semantic relatedness, word embeddings [13] have shown to perform this task particularly well. In this step we cluster entities based on their embedding feature using K-means clustering, and keep only the entities that appear in the cluster that contains a seed term.

**Pointwise Mutual Information (PMI).** This filtering heuristic is inspired by Hearst Patterns [14]. We measure the number of times two given keywords appear

---

[2] http://wordnet.princeton.edu/.

together in a *sentence* in our corpus. As an example the word SVM appears mostly with the word Method in sentences, which is an indicator of being a method entity type. In this step, we filter out the entities having a PMI measure lower than a threshold.

**Knowledge Base Lookup (KBL).** Excluding entities that have a reference in the DBpedia knowledge base under the assumption that, if they are mentioned in DBpedia, then they are not long-tail domain-specific entities.

**Ensemble Majority Vote (EMV).** Preserving the entities that are passed through two out of three selected filtering strategies.

Interested readers can refer to [12] for detailed explanation. As those heuristics are rather basic in their nature, we discuss in the next section if filtering can be supported by human feedback.

## 3   Collaborative Crowd Feedback

As outlined in the previous section, a core design feature of TSE-NER is the heuristic filter step in each iteration, which is designed to filter out named entities which are most likely misrecognized (this can easily happen as the used training data is noisy due to the strong reliance on heuristics). While it was shown in [12] that this filter step indeed increases the precision of the overall approach, it does also impact the recall negatively. For example, this could happen by filtering out *true positives*, i.e. entities which have been correctly identified by the newly trained NER extractor but are filtered out by the heuristic. This could for example happen if a domain-specific named entity is part of common English language. More importantly, the heuristic filter often does not reach its full potential by not filtering all *false positives*, i.e. entities which are incorrectly classified as being of the type of interest, and should have been filtered out by the heuristics but were missed. Also, for the expansion phase, the heuristics often miss relevant entities which should be added.

These shortcomings are addressed in this paper by introducing an additional layer on top of the basic TSE-NER training cycle described in Sect. 2. Instead of treating the algorithm only in isolation, we also consider the surrounding production system and its users (in most cases, this would be a digital library repository with search, browsing, and reading/downloading capabilities). When the production system is set-up, a NER algorithm is trained for each entity type of interest (e.g., datasets, methods, and algorithms for data science) using the TSE-NER workflow until training converges towards stable extraction performance. Then, the resulting trained NER algorithm is applied to all documents in the repository, annotating their full-texts. Users then can interact with the recognized entities, providing feedback.

For this, we introduce novel Coner modules:

1. **Coner Document Analyser (CDA)**: This module serves two purposes; analyse documents to extract "deep metadata" and intelligently select entities for annotation. In an user experiment like the one presented in this paper,

the CDA selects the documents and entities where user feedback would be most effective (see Sect. 4). In a real-life deployed version of Coner, users would continuously provide feedback on documents they are currently reading as part of their normal consumption workflow, so no document selection is necessary.

2. **Coner Interactive Document Viewer (CIDV)**: Online interactive viewer that renders PDF documents and visualises automatically annotated entities. The CIDV allows users to interact with entities by giving feedback on existing annotations, or adding new typed named entities.

3. **Coner Feedback Analyser (CFA)**: Analyzes the entity type labels for each entity that received human feedback, and also decides which labels should be considered valid and which ones are irrelevant. This feedback is then incorporated into the iterative TSE-NER training.

### 3.1   Coner Document Analyser CDA

This module selects representative papers from the document corpus based on being published at a higher-level conference, having average length, high citation counts, and an average number of distinct recognized typed entities in their full texts. In addition we employ a heuristic smart named entity selection (HSES) mechanism that solely selects entities with high potential knowledge gain about the entity's relevance. A traditional approach to implement this is to use merely active learning techniques to select the most useful examples (e.g. based on informativeness) [15] for labeling and add the labeled example to training set to retrain the NER model. However the reliability of active learning (AL) techniques suffers when dealing with noisy training data generated in a semi-automatic fashion as AL techniques are heavily influenced by the quality of the initial labeled examples. For this reason we designed the heuristic smart entity selection mechanism specific for long-tail entities in our document collection (i.e. where there is an overlap of semantic spaces between the different facets). HSES exclusively selects heuristic filtered entities that were doubly classified; recognised as a relevant entity and kept by the TSE-NER filter for multiple facet NERs. Doubly classified entities clearly indicate an overlap of semantic spaces between NERs for different facets, because in reality, it is extremely unlikely that a single named entity describes a *dataset* and a *method* name.

### 3.2   Coner Interactive Document Viewer CIDV

We introduce an *interactive document viewer*, rendering PDF documents and highlighting recognized named entities. The viewer is based on the NII PDFNLT [1,2], which already included a basic viewer and a sentence annotation tool. One of our design goals for the interactive viewer component was to impose as little cognitive load on the users as possible, thus only very simple feedback mechanisms have been considered. During our proof of concept testing phase, we recruited 10 lab student of graduate or post-graduate level to stress test and give feedback on the viewer. Based on the feedback of these users, we opted for

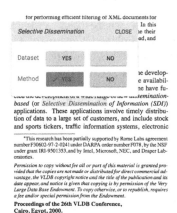

**Fig. 1.** Coner Interactive Document Viewer with highlighted entities

a system design allowing for simple YES/NO relevance feedback for recognized entities. Furthermore, users can add new typed entities by selecting n-grams in the document and assigning an entity type (Fig. 1). For other users, these manually added entities are also highlighted, and additional user feedback can be provided for them.

### 3.3   Coner Feedback Analyser CFA

The purpose of the feedback analyzer is to aggregate collected user feedback on entities, and decide which new entities to finally add and which entities to label as incorrectly typed. In the current version of the feedback analyzer, this is realized with a simple majority vote on the user feedback.

However, like with any crowd-sourcing task, the feedback analyzer can be further extended to cope with common crowd-sourcing problems like spam, malicious indent, or incompetent users. For example, while for our prototype system maliciousness was not an issue, we could already see that some users were significantly more reliable than others. This also reflects in their time investment: more reliable users took much longer to provide feedback on a document, while some users provided feedback in a time frame which should not be sufficient for even reading the paragraphs surrounding an entity. Here, more complex user and task models should help to increase the reliability of aggregated user annotations. As a minimalist step towards this, we only consider users who provided feedback on at least 10 entities per publication, and only considered majority votes with at least 3 votes.

As described in Sect. 2.1, TSE-NER filters the current set of terms every iteration. Coner boosts this process by adding or removing entities from the iterations. Filtering heuristics can be used individually or in an ensemble. Ensemble filtering was shown to have the best, but still limited performance [12]. Coner overwrites the filtering heuristics by ensuring that entities which were labeled by users as irrelevant for a type are always removed during filtering, and entities labeled as relevant are always retained.

## 4   Evaluation

To evaluate the effectiveness of incorporating crowd feedback into the NER training process, we focus on the following two research questions:

RQ1 What are the properties of obtained user feedback? Especially, in how far does human feedback confirm or conflict with TSE-NER heuristics?

RQ2 How does incorporating human feedback into the TSE-NER filtering step improve the overall performance with respect to precision, recall, and F-measures?

To answer these research questions we conducted two user experiments. We focus on the two entity types *dataset* and *method* in data science publications. We had corpus of 11,589 papers from 10 conferences on data science available (this is the same corpus as used by [12]). We conducted the user interaction with the Coner system in a lab setting, recruiting graduate-level/post-graduate-level volunteers who are knowledgeable in the data science domain.

The first experiment, as described in Sect. 4.1, focuses on answering RQ1 by asking users to give feedback or add to unfiltered extracted entities (i.e., on the output of TSE-NER using expansion but no filtering heuristics). By comparing crowd-based filtering to the different filter heuristics, we can obtain insights into their relative performance.

As we only had a limited number of volunteers available for this evaluation, we selected papers from our corpus using the Coner Document Analyser CDA (without the heuristic smart entity selection mechanism HSES) for which the expected impact of additional annotations is representative for the whole collection.

Furthermore, for the second experiment in Sect. 4.2, instead of relying on our users to decide themselves on which entity to provide feedback, we actively steer this process towards entities for which human feedback would have a significant expected impact and use the HSES mechanism. In particular, we focus on entities which were classified as both *dataset* and *method*. This happened quite often in our collection (i.e. 22% of all the detected entities in the whole corpus), and in nearly all cases, at least one classification is incorrect. We divert the decision which of the two types (if any) is correct for the entity to our system's users.

### 4.1   Experiment 1: Human Feedback on Unfiltered Entities

In this section, we look into the properties of user feedback itself, and also evaluate how it conflicts or supports TSE-NER heuristics.

**Documents and Evaluators:** Ten papers were selected from multiple conferences of interest using the Document Analyzer. We selected from the following conferences: The Web Conference (3 papers), ACL (3 papers), ICWSM

**Table 1.** Comparison of false positive rates, resulting from majority vote on relevance of unfiltered extracted entities for both user added and NER extracted entities

|                | Dataset (FP%) | Method (FP%) |
|----------------|---------------|--------------|
| User added     | 25.9%         | 11.7%        |
| NER extracted  | 94.3%         | 57.9%        |
| Total          | **80.4%**     | **27.4%**    |

(2 papers) and VLDB (2 papers). The selected documents contain overall 255 distinct recognised *dataset* entities before filtering, and 85 distinct recognized *method* entities before filtering. The average number of times each selected paper has been cited is 581. The 10 human evaluators are randomly and uniformly assigned to the documents such that each document is processed by at least 3 evaluators. Note that users could add new entities, increasing the number of distinct entities. The evaluators showed quite varying task completion times for giving feedback on all entities contained in a document, with an average of 7:57 min to provide feedback for a single document, while the fastest evaluator only needed 3:14 min and the slowest 19:38 min.

**Entities and Agreement:** The evaluators were not forced to rate all occurrences of recognized entities (the assignment was: "provide feedback on the recognized entities as you see fit."). The average percentage of recognized entities (highlighted in the Coner Viewer) each evaluator gave feedback on is 65.9%. There were no discernible differences between *dataset* and *method* entities. After the experiment we interviewed the evaluators on their reasons for skipping feedback: First, ambiguous meanings of the same entities annotated in different sections and contexts caused doubt about type relevance (e.g. the named entity `Microsoft` can reference a dataset created by Microsoft or the actual company itself). Second, some bigram or trigram *method* entities were recognized with additional useless trailing words (e.g. *question taggings have*), therefore also not receiving feedback from some evaluators.

Table 1 compares the percentage of *dataset* and *method* entities that where considered correct by the TSE-NER classifier (i.e. without the filtering step) or manually added by an evaluator, but judged as incorrect by the majority of evaluators. The false positive rates in Table 1 indeed show the effectiveness of collaborative feedback on TSE-NER. Interestingly, not all of the named entities added by users were rated as relevant for their intended type; for user added entities, we observe a false positives rate of 25.9% for *dataset* and 11.7% for *method*. This means that it is crucial to also receive user feedback from evaluators on entities other users added to ensure the quality of human feedback. Evaluators differ in skill, expertise, and also effort they put into feedback, which clearly influences their decision making.

We calculated the average Cohen's Kappa between the 10 evaluators for each entity type. On average, Cohen's Kappa for *dataset* entities is 0.51, while for *method* entities it is 0.63.

**Table 2.** Comparison of entity retention rate between Coner and TSE-NER filter techniques (315 entities for *dataset* and 198 entities for *method*). Filtering acronyms: Pointwise Mutual Information (PMI), Wordnet + Stopwords (WS), Similar Terms (ST), Knowledge Base Look-up (KBL), Ensemble Majority Vote (EMV), Filtering Coner Boost (FCB): EMV + Coner Human Filtering

|         | PMI  | WS    | ST    | KBL   | EMV   | FCB   |
|---------|------|-------|-------|-------|-------|-------|
| Dataset | 9.0% | 86.9% | 34.4% | 90.7% | 35.0% | 19.5% |
| Method  | 9.4% | 73.7% | 69.0% | 81.2% | 41.6% | 52.2% |

**Table 3.** Percentage of false positives in the remaining filtered entity sets of TSE-NER filtered heuristics compared to Coner human filtered entities. Filtering acronyms same as Table 2

|         | PMI   | WS    | ST    | KBL   | EMV   | FCB  |
|---------|-------|-------|-------|-------|-------|------|
| Dataset | 38.7% | 73.9% | 79.7% | 79.4% | 76.7% | 8.8% |
| Method  | 25.0% | 28.2% | 40.3% | 37.7% | 37.7% | 3.9% |

**Comparison Filtering Techniques: Coner vs TSE-NER**

Table 2 compares the performance of Coner human feedback filtering and different filtering heuristic setups for TSE-NER in terms of retention rate; the percentage of unfiltered extracted entities kept by each filter. The different filtering techniques were performed on the complete set of entities that received feedback from at least three evaluators in the 10 selected papers; 315 *dataset* and 198 *method* entities. As illustrated in Table 2, the Coner Boost (FCB) filtering technique described in this paper is more strict than Ensemble Majority Vote originally used by TSE-NER for the *dataset* type, but less strict for the *method* type. This can be explained by the larger percentage of user added named entities for the *method* type compared to the *dataset* type, with user added named entities having a much lower average false positive rate compared to NER extracted entities (Table 1).

To get a better insight into the filtering performances, we compared the false positives rate for each filtering technique with regards to the set of entities determined to be relevant by human evaluators (Table 3); if an entity is kept by a filter for a type, but was voted as irrelevant for a type by the majority of evaluators, then it is considered a false positive instance. For most of the TSE-NER filtering setups the average false positives rate for both facets is above 50% (only PMI has a lower false positive rate, because it is much more selective in its retention of entities). This means there are a significant number of entities that were recognised as irrelevant for a type by human judgement, but TSE-NER heuristic filtering was unable to do so.

We also considered the false negatives which were excluded by the filtering techniques but were labelled as relevant by majority of evaluators (Table 4). The PMI filtering as explained in [12] achieved the highest precision among the TSE-NER filtering techniques in their evaluation. Table 4 clearly indicates a major shortcoming of the PMI filtering heuristic; it filters out on average 82.2% of Coner viewer entities that were rated as true positives by Coner human feedback. Even for the EMV filtering heuristic, which is regarded as most effective in terms of F-score by [12], the average false negatives rate is 60.8%. Also, in Table 3 we see that KBL has the highest average retention rate of named entities, which also translates in a high false positive rate and lower false negatives rate.

Finally, Tables 3 and 4 demonstrate that the FCB filtering approach results in the lowest false positives and false negatives rates compared to Coner human filtering; this is good for the quality of filtered entities, because more relevant named entities overlap with the Coner human filtering (regarded as true positives), but it also means it difficult to scale this approach with a significantly larger number of named entities.

**Table 4.** Percentage of false negatives in the remaining filtered entity sets of TSE-NER filtered heuristics with regards to Coner filtered entities.

|         | PMI   | WS   | ST    | KBL   | EMV   | FCB  |
|---------|-------|------|-------|-------|-------|------|
| Dataset | 76.2% | 3.8% | 70.0% | 20.0% | 65.0% | 0.0% |
| Method  | 88.2% | 4.6% | 30.9% | 15.1% | 56.6% | 1.3% |

**Qualitative Entity Inspection:** When there is a user consensus, Coner removes or adds entities to the TSE-NER expansion and filter phases, effectively overwriting the heuristics. We manually inspected some of these entities to obtain an intuition on what entities the TSE-NER heuristics usually fail at. Table 5b shows some randoms sample entities which have been consensually labeled as wrong with respect to the recognized type, while Table 5a shows entities which are labeled as correct. Table 6 shows some samples which failed to obtain user consensus and obtained a mix of positive and negative labels.

**Table 5.** Examples of *Dataset* and *Method* entities annotated as correct or incorrect.

| Dataset | digg, flickr, wikipedia, datasets |
|---------|-----------------------------------|
| Method  | hybrid multimodal method, similarity search, reinforcement learning, logistic regression, acyclic subgraph |

(a) Correct

| Dataset | digg interfaces, logistic regression, acyclic subgraph |
|---------|--------------------------------------------------------|
| Method  | digg, flickr, wikipedia, dynamic programming, system description signed clustering |

(b) Incorrect

For example users seem to be uncertain and fail to reach consensus when entities are related to a type but are too generic, e.g. signed networks, news article, news feed, data base for *dataset* and algorithm, decision rule and used search algorithm for *method* entity type. This could be explained by a difference in domain expertise or interpretation of what belongs to a certain type between evaluators. This shows that even for humans, reliably typing entities is hard as there is quite some room for subjective interpretation.

Also, during our inspection, we encountered frequently entities which are classified both as *method* and *dataset* by TSE-NER like digg, flickr, wikipedia, logistic regression, acyclic subgraph. Most of these double classifications are wrong, and we will further investigate this double classification phenomenon in Sect. 4.2.

**Table 6.** Sample of *Dataset* and *Method* annotated without clear user consensus

| Dataset | signed networks, slash, data base<br>news article, news feed |
|---|---|
| Method | 10-foldcross validation, algorithm,<br>decision rule, used search algorithm,<br>vldb, web services |

## 4.2  Experiment 2: NER Performance

We picked 28 papers from 4 conferences in our document corpus, similarly to our document selection described in Sect. 4.1; 13 papers from VLDB, 9 papers from The Web Conference, 4 from SIGIR and 2 from ICWSM.

We recruited 15 graduate-level/post-graduate-level volunteers and instructed them to focus their efforts on judging entities recognized in these papers. However, for this experiment we want to make sure that user feedback is as effective as possible to use our human annotators time efficiently. As a heuristic we focus on entities which have been double-classified as both *dataset* and *method*, and thus one of the types is nearly guaranteed to be wrong. As mentioned before, double classifications between *dataset* and *method* are quite common. This can be explained by the relative similarity of these two types: both types appear in similar contexts and/or sentence structures, and are much closer to each other than typical entities types considered in NER like *location* and *person*. Thus, distinguishing between *dataset* and *method* can be considered a very hard task for an automatic classifier. Cases like these is when user feedback are the most valuable.

In order to measure the effect of human feedback into the TSE-NER filtering, we repeat the experiments described in [12] and use the same test set, measuring the F-score, precision, and recall with and without the Coner feedback. We used the output of the experiment and the TSE-NER to train the NER model. For training we used 71,292 and 103,568 (i.e, *dataset* and *method* entity type) sentences for TSE-NER and 25,819 and 53,200 (i.e, *dataset* and *method* entity type) sentences for Coner and employed the SE strategy. For testing, 3149 sentences were used for dataset and 1097 sentences for method entity type.

Table 7 compares the performance of TSE-NER with and without Coner feedback focused on double-classified entities in terms of precision, recall and F-score. As shown in Table 7 there is an increase in precision for both *dataset* and *method* type classifiers when incorporating user feedback with Coner, while recall and F-score remains stable. Naturally, providing feedback on recognized entities as part of the filter step cannot increase recall, but only affect precision by removing *false positives*. Overall, the test dataset covered 555 unique entities, and we obtained user feedback on 29 unique entities of the test set. Nonetheless, this shows that by focusing user feedback on parts which are in doubt, like the double-classified entities, even a smaller number of user feedback can make a difference, i.e. by obtaining feedback on only 0.05% of the entities in the test set we could increase the precision by 4%. This significant increase in precision is mainly due to the fact that user feedback improves the quality of the input data for each training iteration of TSE-NER, thus the effect of each feedback is greatly magnified. In a scenario where Coner is constantly running in the background, we expect notable increases both for precision and recall (due to allowing users to suggest new entities).

**Table 7.** Comparison of performance of *TSE-NER* and *Coner* in terms of Precison/Recall/F-score for two type of doubly filtered entities: *Dataset* and *Method*

|          | Dataset (P/R/F)     | Method (P/R/F)       |
|----------|---------------------|----------------------|
| TSE-NER  | 0.66/0.60/0.63      | 0.56/**0.21**/0.30   |
| Coner    | **0.70**/0.60/**0.65** | **0.59**/0.20/0.30 |

## 5   Related Work

A considerable amount of literature published in recent years addressed the *deep analysis* of text such as topic modelling, domain-specific entity extraction, etc. Common approaches for *deep analysis* of publications rely on techniques such as dictionary-based [17], rule-based [4], machine-learning [16] or hybrid (combination of rule-based and machine-learning) [19] techniques. Despite its high accuracy, a major drawback of dictionary-based approaches is that they require an exhaustive dictionary of domain terms. These dictionaries are often too expensive to create for less relevant domain-specific entity types. The same holds for rule-based techniques, which rely on formal languages to express rules and require comprehensive domain knowledge and time to create. The lack of large collections of labelled training data and the high cost of data annotation for a given domain is one of the main issues of machine-learning approaches. Many attempts have been made to reduce annotation costs such as bootstrapping [18] and entity set expansion [3,6] which rely only on a set of seed terms provided by the domain expert. Unfortunately, this reliance on weak supervision just providing seed terms limited also the maximal achievable performance with respect to precision, recall, and F-scores.

Active learning (AL) is another technique that has been proposed in the past few years, asking users to annotate a small part of a text for various natural language processing approaches [5,15,20] or generating patterns used to recognize entities [8]. With active learning, the unlabelled instances are chosen intelligently by the algorithm (e.g. least confidence, smallest margin, informativeness, etc.) for annotation. However the AL techniques are heavily influenced by the quality of the previous labeled examples and its reliability suffers when dealing with noisy training data generated in a semi-automatic fashion. Our approach on the other hand relies on training NER algorithms for long-tail entities in a weakly-supervised fashion which incrementally incorporates human feedback on the relevance of extracted entities with high expected information gain into the training cycle. In addition, in contrast to [5] where the authors just present bibliographic sentences to Amazon Mechanical Turk annotators for labelling, our work focuses on the annotation of long-tail entities which relies on the occurrence context for easier annotation. We incorporate collaborative user feedback on type relevance of classified entities and annotation of new entities to continuously support the sentence expansion and entity filtering steps of the iterative TSE-NER algorithm [12]. Newly annotated relevant domain specific entities are added to the seed set in the expansion step, to fetch additional relevant training sentences and terms to increase the number of true positive occurrences in the training data. Furthermore, we allow to filter out irrelevant entities in the filtering step, to reduce the number of false positives detected by the noisy NER.

# 6   Conclusion and Future Work

In this work we focused on augmenting the filter step of TSE-NER by incorporating user feedback into the NER training process. Our lab experiments showed that 94.3% for *dataset* and 57.9% for *method* of entities detected by partial TSE-NER without heuristic filtering were indeed false positives. We observed that by using different filtering heuristics we can reduce the number of false positives up to 38.7% for *dataset* and 25% for *method* (i.e. using the PMI filtering heuristic) which also results in higher false negatives rate as shown in Table 4. In order to reduce the number of false positives as well as false negatives we proposed incorporating user feedback into filtering which resulted in the lowest false positives (i.e. 8.8% for *dataset* and 3.9% for *method*) and false negatives (i.e. 0.0% for *dataset* and 1.3% for *method*). Furthermore we showed that by obtaining feedback on only 0.05% of the entities in the test set (and others outside the set), we could increase the precision by 4% while keeping recall and f-score stable.

For future work, we can leverage Coner's full potential by integrating it into an existing production system, like a large scale digital library. In this case we can receive continuous feedback from the system's users on a number of papers magnitudes bigger than our private lab experiment conducted so far and improve the performance of the NER models over time. Likely, user feedback techniques usable for term expansion will require a heavier toll, and thus need further investigation. To a certain extend, this could be offset using appropriate *incentivation* techniques: by motivating user to be willing to contribute feedback (for example by means of gamification), even more elaborate feedback mechanisms could be employed without degrading user satisfaction.

# References

1. Abekawa, T., Aizawa, A.: SideNoter: scholarly paper browsing system based on PDF restructuring and text annotation. In: COLING (Demos), pp. 136–140 (2016)
2. Aizawa, A.: PDFNLT (2018). https://github.com/KMCS-NII/PDFNLT
3. Brambilla, M., Ceri, S., Della Valle, E., Volonterio, R., Acero Salazar, F.X.: Extracting emerging knowledge from social media. In: Proceedings of the 26th International Conference on World Wide Web, pp. 795–804. International World Wide Web Conferences Steering Committee (2017)
4. Eftimov, T., Seljak, B.K., Korošec, P.: A rule-based named-entity recognition method for knowledge extraction of evidence-based dietary recommendations. PLoS One **12**(6), e0179488 (2017)
5. Goldberg, S.L., Wang, D.Z., Kraska, T.: CASTLE: crowd-assisted system for text labeling and extraction. In: First AAAI Conference on Human Computation and Crowdsourcing (2013)
6. Kejriwal, M., Szekely, P.: Information extraction in illicit web domains. In: Proceedings of the 26th International Conference on World Wide Web, pp. 997–1006. International World Wide Web Conferences Steering Committee (2017)
7. Lample, G., Ballesteros, M., Subramanian, S., Kawakami, K., Dyer, C.: Neural architectures for named entity recognition. In: Proceedings of NAACL-HLT, pp. 260–270 (2016)
8. Marrero, M., Urbano, J.: A semi-automatic and low-cost method to learn patterns for named entity recognition. Nat. Lang. Eng. **24**, 1–37 (2017)
9. Mathew, G., Agarwal, A., Menzies, T.: Trends in topics at SE conferences (1993–2013). arXiv preprint arXiv:1608.08100 (2016)
10. Mesbah, S., Fragkeskos, K., Lofi, C., Bozzon, A., Houben, G.-J.: Facet embeddings for explorative analytics in digital libraries. In: Kamps, J., Tsakonas, G., Manolopoulos, Y., Iliadis, L., Karydis, I. (eds.) TPDL 2017. LNCS, vol. 10450, pp. 86–99. Springer, Cham (2017). https://doi.org/10.1007/978-3-319-67008-9_8
11. Mesbah, S., Fragkeskos, K., Lofi, C., Bozzon, A., Houben, G.-J.: Semantic annotation of data processing pipelines in scientific publications. In: Blomqvist, E., Maynard, D., Gangemi, A., Hoekstra, R., Hitzler, P., Hartig, O. (eds.) ESWC 2017. LNCS, vol. 10249, pp. 321–336. Springer, Cham (2017). https://doi.org/10.1007/978-3-319-58068-5_20
12. Mesbah, S., Lofi, C., Torre, M.V., Bozzon, A., Houben, G.-J.: TSE-NER: an iterative approach for long-tail entity extraction in scientific publications. In: Vrandečić, D., et al. (eds.) ISWC 2018. LNCS, vol. 11136, pp. 127–143. Springer, Cham (2018). https://doi.org/10.1007/978-3-030-00671-6_8
13. Mikolov, T., Sutskever, I., Chen, K., Corrado, G.S., Dean, J.: Distributed representations of words and phrases and their compositionality. In: Advances in Neural Information Processing Systems, pp. 3111–3119 (2013)
14. Seitner, J., et al.: A large database of hypernymy relations extracted from the web. In: LREC (2016)

15. Shen, D., Zhang, J., Su, J., Zhou, G., Tan, C.L.: Multi-criteria-based active learning for named entity recognition. In: Proceedings of the 42nd Annual Meeting on Association for Computational Linguistics, p. 589. Association for Computational Linguistics (2004)
16. Siddiqui, T., Ren, X., Parameswaran, A., Han, J.: FacetGist: collective extraction of document facets in large technical corpora. In: International Conference on Information and Knowledge Management, pp. 871–880. ACM (2016)
17. Song, M., Yu, H., Han, W.S.: Developing a hybrid dictionary-based bio-entity recognition technique. BMC Med. Inform. Decis. Mak. **15**(1), S9 (2015)
18. Tsai, C.T., Kundu, G., Roth, D.: Concept-based analysis of scientific literature. In: Proceedings of the 22nd ACM International Conference on Conference on Information and Knowledge Management, pp. 1733–1738. ACM (2013)
19. Tuarob, S., Bhatia, S., Mitra, P., Giles, C.L.: AlgorithmSeer: a system for extracting and searching for algorithms in scholarly big data. IEEE Trans. Big Data **2**(1), 3–17 (2016)
20. Wang, A., Hoang, C.D.V., Kan, M.Y.: Perspectives on crowdsourcing annotations for natural language processing. Lang. Resour. Eval. **47**(1), 9–31 (2013)

# An Unsupervised Method for Concept Association Analysis in Text Collections

Pavlo Kovalchuk[1,2]([✉]) [iD], Diogo Proença[2] [iD], José Borbinha[1,2] [iD], and Rui Henriques[1,2] [iD]

[1] Instituto Superior Técnico, Universidade de Lisboa, Lisbon, Portugal
[2] INESC-ID, Lisbon, Portugal
{pavlo.kovalchuk,diogo.proenca,jlb,rmch}@tecnico.ulisboa.pt

**Abstract.** This paper addresses the challenge of content categorization to support document navigation and retrieval. The work is motivated by the need to categorize all legislation of a country, where the existing metadata for each document is not sufficient for effective categorization, as concepts vary considerably among documents, resulting in highly sparse vector-space models. To address this challenge, we survey recent related work and propose a solution that integrates currently dispersed principles in a new unsupervised knowledge discovery process combining principles from topic modeling and formal concept analysis, thus not requiring prior domain knowledge to be applied in large document collections. The results confirm the potential of the proposed approach.

**Keywords:** Unsupervised knowledge discovery · Topic Modeling · Formal concept analysis · Concept associations · Large digital libraries

## 1 Introduction

This work is motivated by the need to support search and navigation in *Diário da República Eletrónico* (DRE)[1], the official on-line publication journal of the Portuguese state. DRE is a digital library updated in continuum, publishing laws, regulations and legal acts. Resource discovery is supported by browsing and search in metadata and full-text, which is effective and efficient for tasks with the objective finding specific documents. However, when the task is knowledge discovery, with the purpose of learning what the collection can hide behind the metadata, the service is not efficient. Given the diversity of topics, DRE.PT results in a very sparse vector-space model, thus motivating the development of a knowledge discovery in text (KDT) process for document categorization. However, generic and fully unsupervised methods for document categorization and KDT are still in demand [37]. Despite the need to support the search and navigation within DRE and digital repositories alike, there are still limitations hampering the user experience. First, existing text mining approaches for the

---

[1] https://dre.pt/.

© Springer Nature Switzerland AG 2019
A. Doucet et al. (Eds.): TPDL 2019, LNCS 11799, pp. 18–32, 2019.
https://doi.org/10.1007/978-3-030-30760-8_2

unsupervised categorization of documents are mostly driven by clustering algorithms that take in consideration basic aspects of the documents, such as word relative frequency and overall content similarity, ignoring more complex relations in documents. In addition, these approaches typically map documents into a vector-space model, representing each document as a high-dimensional vector of weights, hampering clustering performance. Second, most of the existing alternatives for document categorization are based on supervised techniques where the categories for a given document collection are well known [17,25]. Third, in the domain of (Portuguese) legal documents, there is no related work for the topic of document categorization based on concept associations (although a few contributions have been recently proposed in the context of legal repositories [6,30], they focus on single-specific aspects of the overall KDT process).

The aim of this work is to propose a unsupervised approach for document categorization and KDT, centered on associations between topics and concepts extracted from document collections. The proposed method combines recent findings from the application of state-of-art techniques on topic modeling and formal concept analysis. As such, it comprehensively tackles all aspects of the KDT process. All the methods proposed in this work will not consider any category for the documents, the entire collection will be treated as equal, and all the document relations and concepts are extracted using automatic methods. The target approach aims at facilitating three major applications of interest: (1) support navigation between documents through the use of hyperlinks; (2) facilitate categorization; and (3) enable summarizing and the comprehensive taxonomic understanding of a set of documents.

This work is organized as follows. Section 2 introduces fundamental topics and theoretical principles behind the methods in the context of the target problem. Section 3 surveys the relevant related work, covering publications that make use of various methods and techniques for the purpose of analyzing textual data. Section 4 describes in detail the solution briefed in Sect. 3. Section 5 presents some results. Section 6 details the evaluation method for the proposed solution. Finally, Sect. 7 presents conclusions and future work.

## 2  Background

We define here KDT as a composition of principles from information retrieval, topic modeling, and concept analysis, aiming at finding relevant relations in a collection of documents $D = \{d_1, .., d_n\}$ in order to provide the necessary knowledge to support document categorization for search and navigation.

To preserve a sound terminology ground, *topic* denotes a semantically related set of *terms*, and *concept* is a (putative) association between terms or topics.

**Core Concepts.** Representing unstructured documents as sets of terms supports their subsequent retrieval by specifying queries on those terms. The *vector space model* represents documents as weighted vectors, $d_i = (w_{i1}, w_{i2}, w_{i3}, ..., w_{im})$ where $w_{ij} \in \mathbb{R}$ and $w_{ij} \geq 0$, so $w_{ij}$ is the frequency of term $t_j$ in document $d_i$. The weights can be alternatively computed using the classic term frequency-inverse document frequency (Tf-idf) metric [31]. Document similarity can be easily computed over a vector space model using metrics such as the cosine of the angle between document vectors.

**Topic Modeling.** The dimensionality of vector space models can be reduced to facilitate subsequent mining tasks while preserving as much useful information as possible.

*(A) Principal Component Analysis* (PCA). Singular value decomposition (SVD), and the centered PCA variant, are traditional algebraic methods to reduce dimensionality (number of terms) by projecting the original data space in a new data space along the directions where the data varies the most [20]. These directions are determined by the eigenvectors, defining a linear composition of original terms, $w'_{ij} = \sum_k^m \alpha_k w_{ik}$. Although this way of reducing data is effective since only a few directions are commonly needed to capture most data variability, the semantic relations between terms $t_j$ are lost.

*(B) Latent Semantic Analysis.* In natural language processing and distributional semantics, Latent Semantic Analysis (LSA) is widely applied for extracting and analyzing the semantic relations between documents of a given collection. This extraction does not rely on any manually constructed dictionaries or semantic networks. The introduced vector space model assumes that terms in a given text document are conceptually independent of each other, which in real-world problems is not always true. Most terms in a document are linked to each other by underlying, unobserved topics, and the main focus of the LSA algorithm is to identify those topics. The LSA process starts by representing a document as a matrix where each entry represents the frequency of a term (row) in a text passage (column). Depending on the objective of the problem, text passages can be paragraphs, sets of terms or entire documents. For each entry, LSA applies a set of preliminary transformations considering both the term's importance in a particular passage and the degree to which the term carries information in the universe of discourse in general [24]. In order to reduce the number of rows without loosing important information, the LSA applies SVD to obtain a lower dimensional matrix where each feature is a combination of previous values.

*(C) Latent Dirichlet Allocation.* In contrast to LSA, Latent Dirichlet Allocation (LDA) produces topics with a probabilistic frame from a given document by assuming documents with similar topics will use similar groups of terms. Documents are thus defined as a probability distribution over latent topics, and the topics are probability distributions over terms. As defined in [26], the LDA process breaks down a large corpus of documents into three levels: the corpus level, the document level and the term level. At the corpus level, for each topic $z_k$ from a Dirichlet distribution with prior parameter $\beta$, LDA generates a topic-terms multinominal distribution $\phi_{z_k}$. At the document level, for each document $d_i$ from a Dirichlet distribution with prior parameter $\alpha$, it generates a document-topics multinominal distribution $\theta_{d_i}$. At the term level, LDA first generates a topic assignment $z_k$ from the document-topics multinominal distribution $\theta_{d_i}$, and for each term $t_j$ in document $d_i$ a term assignment $w_{ij}$ from the topic-terms

distribution $\phi_{z_k}$ is generated. Accordingly, for a given parameterizable number of $K$ topics,

$$p(w_{i1},...,w_{im}|\alpha,\beta) = \int_{\theta} \left( \prod_{j=1}^{m} \sum_{k=1}^{K} p(z_k|\theta)p(w_{ij}|z_k,\beta) \right) p(\theta,\alpha) \, d\theta \ . \qquad (1)$$

*(D) Hierarchical Dirichlet Processes.* Hierarchical Dirichlet Processes (HDP) provide a non-parametric way to discover topics in text data, where each document is interpreted as a set of distributions over topics, and the topics are distributions over terms. Unlike the LDA process, where the number of topics is as a parameter, the HDP infers the number of topics from the data.

**Formal Concept Analysis (FCA).** The theory of FCA, first introduced by Rudolf Wille [41], became a popular method for knowledge representation [15]. Given a collection of objects (documents), formal concept analysis aims to capture associations between objects (documents) based on the shared attributes (terms or topics). The relationships among objects and attributes can be represented as a concept lattice (also called Galois lattice) where each group of objects can be hierarchically grouped together based on common attributes, from most specific concepts (with fewer objects and more attributes) to less specific ones (concepts grouping many objects but sharing few attributes). A *formal context* is a triplet $(D,T,I)$, where $D$ is the set of documents, $T$ is the set of terms and/or topics, and $I \subseteq D \times T$ is a relation between $D$ and $T$ called an incidence relation. A *formal concept* is a pair $(A,O)$ of a formal context $(D,T,I)$, where $A$ objects (extent) is the set of documents that share $O$ attributes (intent). A *concept lattice*, $\mathfrak{B}_{(D,T,I)}$, is the set of all formal concepts in a formal context.

Fuzzy Formal Concept Analysis (FFCA) [29] incorporates fuzzy logic into FCA to represent vague information. Traditional FCA is suitable for conceptual clustering and the generated lattices disclose relevant information about a given domain. However, information uncertainty may occur in a given domain which results in some attributes being more relevant than others. In order to represent information in these domains, a formal concept's relation between objects and attributes is represented using memberships between 0 and 1, and a confidence threshold placed to eliminate relations that have low membership values.

## 3   Survey on Unsupervised Analysis of Digital Collections

Figure 1 provides a compacted version of our proposed unsupervised method. Relevant related work per step is surveyed in the next subsections, and the underlying design principles and validation described in Sects. 4 and 6 accordingly.

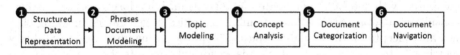

**Fig. 1.** Compact version of the overall pipeline of the proposed solution.

### 3.1  Related Work

**Step 1: Structured data representation.** Among diverse work [19,35], Gonçalves et al. [13] assessed the impact of different representations and pre-processing procedures – including data reduction and term weighting schema – on the categorization of two collections of legal documents (PAGOD, the Portuguese Attorney General's Office dataset, and Reuters). Singh et al. [34] explored the impact of placing different data representations (with/without stop words, with/without stemming), schemes (term frequency, Tf-idf and Boolean), clustering algorithms (K-means, Heuristic K-means and Fuzzy C-means) and algorithmic variants (different heuristics for initial seed selection) to categorize documents from Reuters-21578, Classic-7095 and 20 Newsgroups collections. Fuzzy C-means, unlike K-means, provides a degree of membership of each document for each cluster. Using Residual Sum of Squares (RSS) and Purity metrics, it was concluded that the Tf-idf scheme with stemming is the best setup to represent documents, that heuristic K-means produced better results than the standard K-means, and Fuzzy C-means proves to be the most robust clustering algorithm.

**Step 2: Phrases document modeling.** Modeling word order and phrases can be used to enrich term representations based on the classic bag-of-words assumption. Wang et al. [40] presented a topical $n$-gram model, an extension of unigram models, to this purpose and extraction of topics and topical phrases.

**Step 3: Topic modeling.** In [30], we find an approach to organize legal judgments from topics obtained using LDA aiming at minimizing distances between topics and documents (so each cluster of documents relates to a given topic). Using legal judgments manually categorized, this work aimed improving retrieval by finding topics using LDA and then computing the cosine similarity between each document and the extracted topics to find the closest topic for each document. In [39], the authors compared LDA and HDP, concluding HDP shows better results. In addition to the traditional document categorization methods, [8] presents a survey of several probabilistic topic models with soft clustering abilities and their applications for knowledge discovery in text corpora.

**Step 4: Concept analysis.** FCA has been both applied on terms and topics. In [5], a method for topic detection based on FCA is proposed, guided by both internal clustering quality metrics (Davies-Bouldin Index [9], Dunn Index [10], Silhouette coefficient [32] and The Calinski-Harabasz Index [22]) and external metrics (Reliability, Sensitivity and F-measure [2]). The experimental analysis used a collection of 2200 manually labeled tweets from 61 entities, where the binary attributes associated with terms, named entities, references and URLs. To produce a smaller and denser formal context maintaining the relevant relations, attributes with high frequency were removed. Afterwards, the concept lattice are computed with the Next Neighbours [4] algorithm. Each formal concept is here considered a topic. Still, a large number of topics is generated, meaning that not all concepts are meaningful topics. The authors thus propose the Stability metric [23] to extract the most promising formal concepts. From the obtained results the authors concluded that, if considering the external evaluation, FCA demonstrates a more homogeneous performance than the LDA and Hierarchic Agglomerative Clustering (HAC), obtaining better overall results independent of the parameter setting. In [28], we find an application of FCA for web document categorization. Tf-idf was used to extract the relevant terms to build the formal context, and a threshold considered to capture the absence or presence of a given attribute (term) in a specific object (document). Several text mining techniques were applied on the frequent term-sets of the given domain to analyse the relations among terms and documents. Concept lattices and clusters of formal concepts were further discovered to support the analysis of results.

**Step 5: Document categorization.** In [21] three approaches for document clustering (HAC [11], K-means and the bisecting K-means) are compared over the datasets Reuters-21578, WebAce and TREC. Each document is represented using a vector-space model based on term frequency. Results collected using entropy, F-measure and overall similarity based on a weighted cosine formula (to measure cluster cohesiveness) indicate that bisecting K-means is better than the standard K-means and as good or better than the hierarchical approach.

A cluster-based approach is proposed in [7] to browse large document collections (Scatter/Gather). It starts to scatter the collection into a small number of documents clusters, presenting short summaries of the obtained results to the user. Clusters can be selected, gathered together to form a sub-collection and clustered to generate smaller clusters. This is repeated until the groups of documents become small enough. Results produced on 5000 articles posted on the New York Times News Service during August of 1990 show that the Scatter/Gather method can be an effective.

In [27], an inter-passage approach for text document clustering is proposed based on the discovery of multiple topic segments per document. The method removes stop-words, applies stemming, and computes a score based on the Tf-idf and SentiNetWord for each word in each topic segment per document. The word with the highest score in a segment will be treated as representative keyword for that segment. Once having the representative keyword for each segment, the overall segment score is computed by averaging the score of all words in a segment. Finally, segments are clustered together by applying the K-means algorithm. The result are clusters of segments that relate to a given topic, and the original document associated to each segment.

An improved K-means algorithm combined with Particle Swarm Optimization (POS) [33] is proposed in [16] for efficient web document clustering. POS is considered to obtain the best initial cluster centroids for the K-means algorithm. This method was tested against other clustering methods on various text document collections[2], consistently showing lower ADDCC values (mean distance between documents and the clusters centroid).

Krill Herd (KH) algorithms for efficient text document clustering is presented in [1]. KH [12] is a nature-inspired clustering method aiming at finding the minimum distance of krill individuals (documents) from foods (centroids) with

---

[2] http://trec.nist.gov/data.html.

the highest density. The performance of KH algorithms are compared against standard K-means on four Labic datasets and show superior Purity and Entropy.

**Step 6: Document navigation.** The Concept Chain Queries (CCQ) is defined in [18] as a text mining technique focused on detecting links between topics across text documents. It generates a Concept Association Graph (CAG) where the nodes correspond to concepts and the links to associations. Queries are interpreted as finding the most meaningful evidence trails across documents. A cross-document knowledge discovery solution is proposed in [26] using Semantic Concept Latent Dirichlet Allocation (SCLDA) and Semantic Concept Hierarchical Dirichlet Process (SCHDP) methods, where documents are represented

**Table 1.** Overview on the different contributions and limitations on surveyed works.

| Ref. | Contributions | Limitations |
|---|---|---|
| **(1) Structured Data Representation** | | |
| [13] | Analysis on representation and preprocessing procedure for Portuguese legal documents | Overlook of syntactical and semantic information on the representation of documents |
| [34] | Performance comparison of different representations and hard versus soft clustering algorithms | Document categorization based on the overall content similarity |
| **(2) Phrases Document Modeling** | | |
| [40] | Topic modeling integrated with $n$-grams models | Topic quality not compared with standard metrics (Coherence or Perplexity) |
| **(3) Topic Modeling** | | |
| [30, 39] | Document categorization based on topic modeling techniques | Tests on small document collection where overall domains are known; hard clustering type results |
| **(4) Concept Analysis** | | |
| [5] | FCA as a topic modeling method; formal context reduction; external and internal topic quality metrics | No comparison with other well known topic modeling methods namely, HDP or LSA |
| [28] | FCA applied in the context of IR; Concept-based document categorization | Non-exhaustive exploration of different attributes for the documents in the formal context |
| **(5) Document Categorization** | | |
| [21] | Overview on several clustering algorithms and their performance on document categorization | Fairly basic clustering algorithms |
| [7] | Cluster-based method to support document search in large collections of documents | No cluster quality measures; no comparison with other clustering methods |
| [27] | Document categorization based on text segments related to a specific topic | Non-exhaustive exploration of different methods for text segmentation |
| [16] | Improved K-means algorithm with POS approach | Hard clustering type results; non-exhaustive quality comparison with other clustering algorithms |
| [1] | KH algorithm applied for document categorization | The KH algorithm require a large number of iterations not suitable for large collections of documents |
| **(6) Document Navigation** | | |
| [18] | Combining text retrieval and link analysis for KDT; exploring the concept of CCQ for topic associations | No clear evidence for the scalability of the proposed method; no explicit description on the tools used |
| [26] | New topic modeling methods based on the principle of BOC; exploring different preprocessing methods | No direct comparison of topic quality based on standard metrics |

as meaningful Bag-of-Concepts, rather than words. The methods were applied to the CCQ problem, where the objective is to discover new relations between concepts across documents. Tests on 9/11 counter-terrorism data show superior performance over other LDA and HDP-based approaches.

## 3.2 Concluding Remarks

Table 1 synthesizes the contributions and limitations of the surveyed work over each step of our proposed pipeline. Most methods only consider standard vector based representations, overlooking conceptual aspects of the documents. The methods that take into consideration concept associations within documents either rely on prior knowledge, omit relevant specifics to guarantee a generic and implementable KDT process, or do not guarantee the scalability of the proposed approach for large collections.

## 4    The Proposed Unsupervised KDT Process

The proposed unsupervised method, first depicted in Fig. 1, is here detailed. The extended pipeline of our proposed solution is presented in Fig. 2. Figure 2 depicts each stage of the pipeline, detailed throughout this section.

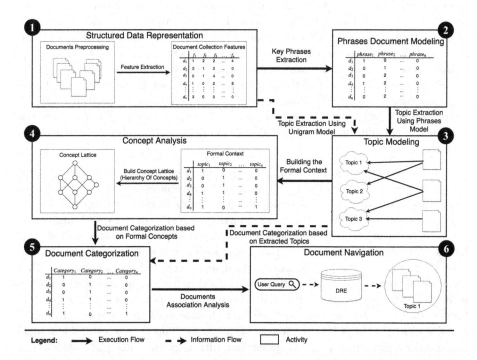

**Fig. 2.** Extended pipeline for the proposed solution.

**(1) Structured Data Representation.** Each document in the collection is preprocessed, and words not carrying relevant information removed, including stop words, punctuation, alphanumeric words, numbers, and highly frequent words. Then, each document is converted into a vector representation based on BOW-word for the subsequent extraction of features. Each document is represented as an entry in a real-valued matrix, offering a high-dimensional and structured representation of the corpus.

**(2) Phrases Document Modeling.** In the next step, a representation combining BOW and keyphrases (BOW-phrase) is produced for each document using PKE, a keyphrase extraction method presented by Boudin and Florian [3].

**(3) Topic Modeling.** Using representations based on BOW-word (step 1) and the BOW-phrase (step 2), different sets of topics can be extracted using LSA, LDA and HDP methods for topic modeling. The topics produced from the different approaches can be combined and subsequently mapped into a formal context. If topics are to be readily used for the aimed categorization end, topics with highly overlapping terms should be merged or removed.

**(4) Concept Analysis.** This step starts by creating a formal context based on a fuzzy FCA frame, where objects correspond to documents and attributes correspond to the set of topics obtained in step 3. The relations between documents and topics are represented by a membership value between $[0, 1]$ that corresponds to the likelihood of a given document being characterized by a specific topic. In order to avoid meaningless formal concepts in the next step, all entries from the formal context that do not satisfy a membership threshold can be binarized and the AddIntent algorithm [38] (or equivalent) applied over the reduced formal context. To facilitate interpretation, the obtained formal concepts can be organized in a concept lattice that corresponds to a hierarchical structure based on a generalization-specialization relationship, where those at the top (bottom) of the concept lattice will represent general (specific) topics. To guarantee the relevance of the obtained formal concepts, an additional pruning procedure (step 5) is required.

**(5) Document Categorization.** The quality of each topic or formal concept can be measured using Stability, a metric of cohesiveness [5]. Stability is used to remove from the concept lattice the formal concepts that do not represent cohesive groups of documents. The pruned lattice provides an organized and informative view over the document collection, where each document is categorized by the hierarchy of topics where it appears. In other words, the entire collection is factorized into groups of documents that are correlated in accordance with a given set of topics that can be interpreted as a general concept. Unlike hard clustering algorithms described in the literature, the proposed method adequately tackles the difficulty of learning from high-dimensional and sparse data structures, and further enables the identification of overlapping groups of documents by allowing a given document to appear in multiple groups. The possibility to not only rely on concepts, but to augment these with the original topics extracted in stage **3** (Fig. 2) guarantees that all potentially relevant content is considered, enabling a comprehensive characterization and full traceability of document categories from concepts, topics, and phrases.

**(6) Document Navigation.** Once the document collection is organized by topics and concepts, searching and browsing can be narrowed to the groups of documents that share identical contents (step 5), instead of the entire collection.

## 5    Results

This section presents initial results gathered from 5000 legal documents mentioning the Ministry of Agriculture ("Ministério da Agricultura", in Portuguese). Following the pipeline presented in Sect. 4, in step 1 each document was preprocessed to remove uninformative words (including words that are not noun phrases or proper nouns) and frequent words on most documents. Next, in step 2 all phrases per document were extracted and used to convert each document into a BOW-phrase vector representation. In step 3, topic modeling was applied using the six setups described in Sect. 4 (recalling: LSA, LDA and HDP, each with BOW-word and BOW-phrase representations). Both LSA and LDA take as input the number of topics $k$ to be extracted from the document collection. Figure 3 measures the impact of $k$ on the topic's coherence [36]. The best $k$ corresponds to 82 topics (coherence of 0.43) for setup (A), 82 topics (coherence of 0.32) for setup (B), 113 topics (coherence of 0.51) for setup (C), and 3 topics (coherence of 0.56) for setup (D). HDP extracts a total of 150 topics for both setups (E) and (F) (coherence of respectively 0.474 and 0.627), a constant regardless of $k$.

In Table 2 we compare the results for the six setups, considering for each the 10 most frequent topics. In the upper side we can see, on the left, the total number of documents assigned to each topic, and on the right, the number of unique

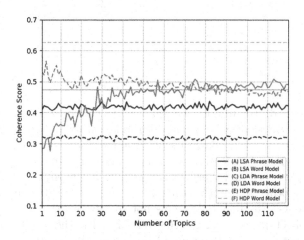

**Fig. 3.** Comparison of the Coherence Score for the Different Models.

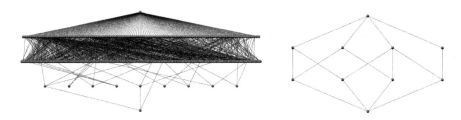

**Fig. 4.** Example of a reduced concept lattices from the LDA-phrase model (left) and for the document **3535010**, contained in that concept lattices (right).

**Table 2.** Documents assigned to each topic for the 10 most frequent topics, counting the total of documents (left) and unique documents (right).

| | HDP | | LDA | | LSA | | HDP | | LDA | | LSA | |
|---|---|---|---|---|---|---|---|---|---|---|---|---|
| # | Word | Phrase | Word | Phrase | Word | Phrase | Word | Phrase | Word | Phrase | Word | Phrase |
| 1 | 4489 | 3768 | 1696 | 690 | 1192 | 1369 | 2191 | 2387 | 466 | 288 | 1192 | 1369 |
| 2 | 1385 | 732 | 1508 | 628 | 1096 | 1163 | 93 | 170 | 347 | 71 | 1096 | 1163 |
| 3 | 751 | 382 | 1014 | 588 | 716 | 313 | 152 | 46 | 134 | 308 | 716 | 313 |
| 4 | 513 | 302 | 968 | 577 | 413 | 233 | 47 | 149 | 109 | 104 | 413 | 233 |
| 5 | 358 | 258 | 955 | 570 | 324 | 142 | 3 | 47 | 93 | 90 | 324 | 142 |
| 6 | 234 | 213 | 886 | 568 | 177 | 106 | 8 | 73 | 139 | 87 | 177 | 106 |
| 7 | 221 | 166 | 838 | 553 | 90 | 80 | 14 | 14 | 45 | 91 | 90 | 80 |
| 8 | 139 | 150 | 770 | 519 | 84 | 80 | 3 | 23 | 90 | 85 | 84 | 80 |
| 9 | 119 | 134 | 747 | 507 | 81 | 77 | 0 | 23 | 50 | 154 | 81 | 77 |
| 10 | 85 | 132 | 733 | 481 | 80 | 76 | 0 | 21 | 71 | 251 | 80 | 76 |
| 1 | 90% | 75% | 34% | 14% | 24% | 27% | 49% | 63% | 27% | 42% | 100% | |
| 2 | 28% | 15% | 30% | 13% | 22% | 23% | 7% | 23% | 23% | 11% | | |
| 3 | 15% | 8% | 20% | 12% | 14% | 6% | 20% | 12% | 13% | 52% | | |
| 4 | 10% | 6% | 19% | 12% | 8% | 5% | 9% | 49% | 11% | 18% | | |
| 5 | 7% | 5% | 19% | 11% | 6% | 3% | 1% | 18% | 10% | 16% | | |
| 6 | 5% | 4% | 18% | 11% | 4% | 2% | 3% | 34% | 16% | 15% | | |
| 7 | 4% | 3% | 17% | 11% | 2% | 2% | 6% | 8% | 5% | 16% | | |
| 8 | 3% | 3% | 15% | 10% | 2% | 2% | 2% | 15% | 12% | 16% | | |
| 9 | 2% | 3% | 15% | 10% | 2% | 2% | 0% | 17% | 7% | 30% | | |
| 10 | 2% | 3% | 15% | 10% | 2% | 2% | 0% | 16% | 10% | 52% | | |

documents assigned. To support the analysis, in the lower side of the table we see the same information but normalized in relation to the size of the collection (5000 documents). We can realize LDA is the methods that creates topics that are assigned to groups of documents of more uniform sizes (ranging from 15% to 30% for BOW-word and, very impressing, from an 10% to 14% for BOW-phrase). On the other side, LSA assures, by its nature, that each topic has only unique documents. Finally, HDP seems not so interesting, at least considering the specific collection we used for this test. Finally, the AddIntent algorithm is used to extract the formal concepts from a formal context, maintaining only the formal concepts with high stability. In Fig. 4 we can see the example of the resulted concept lattices over the topics resulted from the LDA-phrase model, and the concepts for the document $3535010^3$ (The *Lattice Visualization*[4] tool was used for this purpose). This way, we are able to categorize each document based on its related topics and formal concepts, as well as link it to documents with similar concepts (to support document navigation, for example).

## 6    Principles for Quality Assessment of the Pipeline

Our future work must now research how the best way to make use of each method, eventually resulting in a solution combining the best of each (or at least from LSA and LDA). In addition to well-known clustering metrics (such as accuracy-based views in the presence of ground truth on document categories or cohesion-separation views) that can be considered at the end of pipeline to assess document categorization, we suggested additional metrics to test the adequacy of the proposed unsupervised KDT process over a given document collection. Motivated by the results in [5] that show internal clustering measures are adequate to estimate the quality of topic modeling methods, the performance of each setup in step 3 should be promptly assessed using: coherence [36] to measure the degree of similarity between high scoring words in a topic; Dunn index [10] to measure how dense and well-separated are the obtained topics; and Calinski-Harabasz index [22], a ratio between topic variance and the overall within-topic variance. These measures should be applied to estimate the optimal number of topics in LSA and LDA procedures. Measures of homogeneity and quality should be applied to evaluate formal concepts in step 4. For example, the amount of tolerated noise (fraction of 0), and statistical tests based on the Bernoulli distribution can be placed to access if a formal concept is statistically significant (i.e. it deviates from expectations) [14]. To evaluate how closely related are the documents in a formal concept, the cohesion metric is suggested.

## 7    Conclusion and Future Work

This work addressed the problem of creating a structured and categorized view of a collection of documents without background knowledge. Accordingly an unsupervised KDT process is proposed to support document indexing for retrieval and general navigation in the entire collection of documents. Relevant related work was surveyed to this end, and their limitations and contributions identified. Building upon these findings, the principles underlying the target KDT process were introduced. The results demonstrate the applicably and the potential of our proposed method. In future work, we aim to use alternative collections of legal documents to study the adequacy of the proposed approach and the impact of selecting alternative document representations and topic modeling approaches; explore different ways of preprocessing Portuguese legal documents

---

[3]  https://dre.pt/web/guest/home/-/dre/3535010/details/maximized.

[4]  http://latviz.loria.fr/.

in order to overcome some linguistic barriers present in the Portuguese language that may reduce the quality of the extracted topics; and also to further analyze the obtained hierarchy of term associations to dynamically infer an ontology, which can then be considered to support content categorization.

**Acknowledgement.** This work was supported by Imprensa Nacional Casa da Moeda (INCM) and national funds through Fundação para a Ciência e a Tecnologia (FCT) with reference UID/CEC/50021/2019.

# References

1. Abualigah, L.M., Khader, A.T., Al-Betar, M.A., Awadallah, M.A.: A krill herd algorithm for efficient text documents clustering. In: 2016 IEEE Symposium on Computer Applications and Industrial Electronics (ISCAIE), pp. 67–72. IEEE (2016)
2. Amigó, E., Gonzalo, J., Verdejo, F.: A general evaluation measure for document organization tasks. In: Proceedings of the 36th International ACM SIGIR Conference on Research and Development in Information Retrieval, pp. 643–652. ACM (2013)
3. Boudin, F.: Pke: an open source python-based keyphrase extraction toolkit. In: COLING, Osaka, Japan, pp. 69–73 (2016)
4. Carpineto, C., Romano, G.: Concept Data Analysis: Theory and Applications. Wiley, Hoboken (2004)
5. Castellanos, A., Cigarrán, J., García-Serrano, A.: Formal concept analysis for topic detection: a clustering quality experimental analysis. Inf. Syst. **66**, 24–42 (2017)
6. Chen, Y.L., Liu, Y.H., Ho, W.L.: A text mining approach to assist the general public in the retrieval of legal documents. IJ Am. Soc. Inf. Sci. Technol. **64**(2), 280–290 (2013)
7. Cutting, D.R., Karger, D.R., Pedersen, J.O., Tukey, J.W.: Scatter/Gather: a cluster-based approach to browsing large document collections. In: ACM SIGIR, pp. 318–329. ACM (1992)
8. Daud, A., Li, J., Zhou, L., Muhammad, F.: Knowledge discovery through directed probabilistic topic models: a survey. Front. Comput. Sci. China **4**(2), 280–301 (2010)
9. Davies, D.L., Bouldin, D.W.: A cluster separation measure. IEEE Trans. Pattern Anal. Mach. Intell. **PAMI-1**(2), 224–227 (1979)
10. Dunn, J.C.: Well-separated clusters and optimal fuzzy partitions. J. Cybern. **4**(1), 95–104 (1974)
11. El-Hamdouchi, A., Willett, P.: Comparison of hierarchic agglomerative clustering methods for document retrieval. Comput. J. **32**(3), 220–227 (1989)
12. Gandomi, A.H., Alavi, A.H.: Krill herd: a new bio-inspired optimization algorithm. Commun. Nonlinear Sci. Numer. Simul. **17**(12), 4831–4845 (2012)
13. Gonçalves, T., Quaresma, P.: Evaluating preprocessing techniques in a text classification problem. SBC-Sociedade Brasileira de Computação, São Leopoldo, RS, Brasil (2005)
14. Henriques, R., Madeira, S.C.: BSig: evaluating the statistical significance of biclustering solutions. Data Min. Knowl. Discov. **32**, 124–161 (2017)

15. Ignatov, D.I.: Introduction to formal concept analysis and its applications in information retrieval and related fields. In: Braslavski, P., Karpov, N., Worring, M., Volkovich, Y., Ignatov, D.I. (eds.) RuSSIR 2014. CCIS, vol. 505, pp. 42–141. Springer, Cham (2015). https://doi.org/10.1007/978-3-319-25485-2_3

16. Jaganathan, P., Jaiganesh, S.: An improved k-means algorithm combined with particle swarm optimization approach for efficient web document clustering. In: ICGCE, pp. 772–776. IEEE (2013)

17. Jiang, S., Pang, G., Wu, M., Kuang, L.: An improved k-nearest-neighbor algorithm for text categorization. Expert Syst. Appl. **39**(1), 1503–1509 (2012)

18. Jin, W., Srihari, R.K., Ho, H.H., Wu, X.: Improving knowledge discovery in document collections through combining text retrieval and link analysis techniques. In: ICDM, pp. 193–202 (2007)

19. Kadhim, A.I., Cheah, Y.N., Ahamed, N.H.: Text document preprocessing and dimension reduction techniques for text document clustering. In: 2014 4th International Conference on Artificial Intelligence with Applications in Engineering and Technology, pp. 69–73. IEEE (2014)

20. Kalman, D.: A singularly valuable decomposition: the SVD of a matrix. Coll. Math. J. **27**(1), 2–23 (1996)

21. Karypis, M.S.G., Kumar, V., Steinbach, M.: A comparison of document clustering techniques. In: IW on Text Mining at SIGKDD (2000)

22. Kozak, M.: "A dendrite method for cluster analysis" by Caliński and Harabasz: a classical work that is far too often incorrectly cited. Commun. Stat.-Theory Methods **41**(12), 2279–2280 (2012)

23. Kuzuetsov, S.: Stability as an estimate of the degree of substantiation of hypotheses derived on the basis of operational, similarity (1990)

24. Landauer, T.K., Foltz, P.W., Laham, D.: An introduction to latent semantic analysis. Discourse Process. **25**(2–3), 259–284 (1998)

25. Li, C.H., Yang, J.C., Park, S.C.: Text categorization algorithms using semantic approaches, corpus-based thesaurus and wordnet. Expert Syst. Appl. **39**(1), 765–772 (2012)

26. Li, X., Jin, W.: Cross-document knowledge discovery using semantic concept topic model. In: ICMLA, pp. 108–114. IEEE (2016)

27. Mishra, R.K., Saini, K., Bagri, S.: Text document clustering on the basis of inter passage approach by using k-means. In: IC on Computing, Communication and Automation, pp. 110–113. IEEE (2015)

28. Myat, N.N., Hla, K.H.S.: Organizing web documents resulting from an information retrieval system using formal concept analysis. In: Asia-Pacific Symposium on Information and Telecommunication Technologies, pp. 198–203. IEEE (2005)

29. Quan, T.T., Hui, S.C., Cao, T.H.: A fuzzy FCA-based approach to conceptual clustering for automatic generation of concept hierarchy on uncertainty data. In: CLA, pp. 1–12 (2004)

30. Raghuveer, K.: Legal documents clustering using latent dirichlet allocation. IAES Int. J. Artif. Intell. **2**(1), 34–37 (2012)

31. Rajaraman, A., Ullman, J.D.: Data Mining, pp. 1–17. Cambridge University Press, Cambridge (2011)

32. Rousseeuw, P.J.: Silhouettes: a graphical aid to the interpretation and validation of cluster analysis. J. Comput. Appl. Math. **20**, 53–65 (1987)

33. Shi, Y., Eberhart, R.C.: Parameter selection in particle swarm optimization. In: Porto, V.W., Saravanan, N., Waagen, D., Eiben, A.E. (eds.) EP 1998. LNCS, vol. 1447, pp. 591–600. Springer, Heidelberg (1998). https://doi.org/10.1007/BFb0040810

34. Singh, V.K., Tiwari, N., Garg, S.: Document clustering using k-means, heuristic k-means and fuzzy c-means. In: IC on Computational Intelligence and Communication Networks, pp. 297–301. IEEE (2011)
35. Srividhya, V., Anitha, R.: Evaluating preprocessing techniques in text categorization. Int. J. Comput. Sci. Appl. **47**(11), 49–51 (2010)
36. Stevens, K., Kegelmeyer, P., Andrzejewski, D., Buttler, D.: Exploring topic coherence over many models and many topics. In: Joint Conference on Empirical Methods in NLP and Computational Natural Language Learning, pp. 952–961. Association for Computational Linguistics (2012)
37. Tan, P.N.: Introduction to Data Mining. Pearson Education, Delhi (2018)
38. van der Merwe, D., Obiedkov, S., Kourie, D.: AddIntent: a new incremental algorithm for constructing concept lattices. In: Eklund, P. (ed.) ICFCA 2004. LNCS (LNAI), vol. 2961, pp. 372–385. Springer, Heidelberg (2004). https://doi.org/10.1007/978-3-540-24651-0_31
39. Venkatesh, R.K.: Legal documents clustering and summarization using hierarchical latent Dirichlet allocation. IAES Int. J. Artif. Intell. **2**(1) (2013)
40. Wang, X., McCallum, A., Wei, X.: Topical n-grams: phrase and topic discovery, with an application to information retrieval. In: ICDM, pp. 697–702. IEEE (2007)
41. Wille, R.: Restructuring lattice theory: an approach based on hierarchies of concepts. In: Rival, I. (ed.) Ordered Sets. ASIC, vol. 83, pp. 445–470. Springer, Dordrecht (1982). https://doi.org/10.1007/978-94-009-7798-3_15

# Linking Semantic Fingerprints of Literature – from Simple Neural Embeddings Towards Contextualized Pharmaceutical Networks

Janus Wawrzinek[✉] , José María González Pinto ,
and Wolf-Tilo Balke

IFIS TU-Braunschweig, Mühlenpfordstrasse 23, 38106 Brunswick, Germany
{wawrzinek, pinto, balke}@ifis.cs.tu-bs.de

**Abstract.** The exponential growth of publications in medical digital libraries requires new access paths that go beyond term-based searches, as these increasingly lead to thousands of results. An effective approach for this problem is to extract important pharmaceutical entities and their relations to each other in order to reveal the embedded knowledge in digital libraries. State-of-the-art approaches in the field of neural-language models (NLMs) enable progress in learning and predicting such relations in terms of semantic quality, scalability, and performance and already now make them valuable for important research tasks such as hypothesis generation. However, in the field of pharmacy a simple list of (predicted) associations is often challenging to interpret because, between typical pharmaceutical entities, such as active substances, diseases, and genes, complex associations will exist. A *contextualized network* of pharmaceutical entities can support the exploration of these associations and will help to assess and interpret predicted relationships. On the other hand, the prerequisite for building meaningful entity networks is an answer to the question: *When is an NLM-learned entity relation meaningful?* In this paper, we investigate this question for important pharmaceutical entity relations in the form of drug-disease associations (DDAs). To do so, we present a *new methodology* to determine entity-specific thresholds for the existence of associations. Such entity-specific thresholds open-up the possibility of automatically constructing (meaningful) embedded pharmaceutical networks, which can then be used to explore and to explain learned relationships between pharmaceutical entities.

**Keywords:** Digital libraries · Information extraction · Neural embeddings

## 1 Introduction

The increased quantity of publications in Digital Libraries challenges users that need to collect, understand, and integrate a broad range of relevant and related knowledge to design new hypotheses. As a good example, consider entity-based searches in scientific digital libraries. The keyword search for the disease "*Ovarian Neoplasms*" in the PubMed medical library leads to a result set of over 96,000 documents. One of the most effective ways to address this problem is to extract important pharmaceutical entities such as active ingredients, diseases, and genes plus their mutual relationships to reveal

© Springer Nature Switzerland AG 2019
A. Doucet et al. (Eds.): TPDL 2019, LNCS 11799, pp. 33–40, 2019.
https://doi.org/10.1007/978-3-030-30760-8_3

the embedded knowledge contained in such massive collections. In this context state of the art Neural Language Models (NLMs) can be used not only to extract known relationships, but also to predict new relationships [6] such as Drug-Disease Associations (DDAs). A DDA exists when (a) a drug helps against a particular disease (cures, prevents, alleviates) or (b) a drug induces a disease in the sense of a side effect [3]. Such DDAs are important to explore, for instance, because they are possible candidates for drug-repurposing [5]. Indeed, pharmaceutical research often focuses on well-known and proven active substances against other diseases, as this generally leads to lower risk in terms of adverse side effects. The question is how can we support users in the exploration and assessment of predicted Drug-Disease-Associations? In this context, network views constructed using k-nearest-neighbour (kNN) sets can help users to understand complex entity associations [1] better. For instance, extracting k-nearest-disease sets for each drug and using them for building a drug-disease network could give users an overview of all embedded drug-disease associations learned by the NLM and thus may support users in formulating new hypothesises for predicted associations. *How to build such k*-nearest-neighbour *sets?* Using similarity thresholds for the extraction of the *kNN* sets is error-prone, because threshold-based approaches are hard to estimate and to interpret [6, 8, 9] and may vary for different entities, time-periods, and corpus sizes [6, 10]. Thus, as a prerequisite for building meaningful drug-disease networks, we have first to answer the question: *How to find a meaningful k for each embedded drug-entity?*

In this paper, we present a *new literature-based methodology* which enables us to predict how many k-Nearest-Disease-Neighbors (k-NDNs) we should extract per drug-entity from the embedding space, and this stays relatively stable for different corpora sizes, time-periods, and document lengths. Even if our research focuses on a specific task, we believe that our investigations lead to a general better understanding of state-of-the-art Neural Language Models like Word2Vec. This is a short version of our extended study. Thus for the interested reader, we have our full technical report available [10]. The paper is organized as follows: Sect. 2 revisits related work accompanied by our extensive investigation of entity-specific thresholds in Sect. 3. We close with conclusions in Sect. 4.

## 2   Related Work

Research in the field of digital libraries has been dealing with semantically meaningful similarities for entities and their relations for a long time. For the investigation of semantic relations between words, Neural Language Models (NLMs) like Word2Vec are currently the state-of-the-art approaches [4]. Word2Vec models can also be divided into the categories Continuous Bags of Words (CBOW) and the Skip-gram model. The difference here is how word-embeddings are learned; for example, CBOW tries to predict the matching word with a word context, while Skip-gram tries to predict a word context with a word. An important aspect here is that the Skip-gram model is better suited for semantic tasks [4]. Therefore, in our investigation, we will rely on the Word2Vec Skip-Gram model implementation from the open source

Deep-Learning-for-Java[1] library. With the increasing popularity of predictive models, interest in the study of the semantic meaning of distance in high-dimensional spaces is growing. Elekes et al. [8] investigated the influence of hyperparameters and document corpus size to the similarity of word pairs. In their investigation, they compare word pair distances in the embedding space with a WordNet Similarity. They also point out that similarity of words in natural language is blurred and therefore problematic to measure. In contrast to natural language, the word pairs we are investigating feature rather a binary than a blurred relation to each other (a drug $x$ affects disease $y$ or not [3]). In our investigation, we measure the quality of this binary relation in the word embedding space. The next question is whether meaningful similarity thresholds exist for semantically associated word pairs. However, similarity thresholds are difficult to calculate and can vary for different models and corpora [6, 8]. Therefore, we do not determine the thresholds with a similarity comparison but use corpus information in order to determine how many neighbors we should extract from the embedding space.

## 3 Experimental Investigation

We will first describe our pharmaceutical text corpus and experimental set-up decisions. Afterward, we investigate for various time-periods the general correlation between embedded DDAs and corpora-statistics (Sect. 3.1). We continue our correlation analysis involving predicted DDAs (Sect. 3.2) and propose a method for entity-specific thresholds. Finally, we compare the efficiency of our entity-specific k-NDNs thresholds (Sect. 3.3) with two conventional approaches (fixed k-NDNs, Similarity-Threshold). As shown in [6] on the one hand DDA predictions are possible, but on the other hand, the majority of existing DDAs cannot be extracted from the embedding space. Therefore, we focus on precision as the main quality-measure.

### Experimental Setup

*Evaluation Corpus.* PubMed[2] is with more than 29 million document citations, the largest and most comprehensive digital library in the biomedical field. Since full-text access is not available for the most publications, we used only abstracts for our evaluation corpus (More details about the corpus can be found here [10]).

*Time Period Evaluation Corpora.* In order to calculate the change in different time periods as well as on different corpus sizes, we divide our evaluation corpus into four corpora: **1900–1988, 1900–1998, 1900–2008, 1900–2018**. Each corpus contains only the documents for the respective time period.

*Query Entities.* As query entities for the evaluation, we randomly selected 350 drugs from the *DrugBank*[3] collection, which is a 10% sample of all approved drugs. Thus, our final document set for evaluation contains $\sim 2.5$ million abstracts for 350 drugs.

---

[1] https://deeplearning4j.org/.

[2] https://www.ncbi.nlm.nih.gov/pubmed/.

[3] https://www.drugbank.ca/.

**Experiment Implementation and Parameter Settings**

1. *Text Preprocessing.* Stop-word removal and stemming were performed using a *Lucene*[4] index. For stemming we used Lucene's *Porter Stemmer* implementation. We considered all words contained in more than half of the indexed abstracts as stop-words. Here we made sure that the drug and disease identifiers were not affected.
2. *Word Embeddings.* After pre-processing, word embeddings were created with DeepLearning4J's *Word2Vec*[5] implementation.
3. *Hyperparameter-Tuning.* Larger window-sizes may affect association learning quality [7]. Based on the extended experiments described in our technical report [10], we will investigate the effect of a default window-size setting ($w = 5$) as well as with a higher window-size ($w = 50$) in our correlation-experiments.
4. *Similarity-Measure.* As the similarity measure between the drug/disease embeddings, we choose cosine similarity in all experiments. A value of 1 between two vectors means a perfect similarity (vectors match perfectly) and the value 0 means a maximum dissimilarity (vectors are orthogonal to each other).

### 3.1 Relationship Between Corpus-Data and Existing-DDAs

In our first experiment we clarify if there exists always, and to which extent, a general correlation between *corpus data* and the number of *existing* DDAs (DDA appears in at least three abstracts) to be extracted from the embedded space. As *corpus data,* we use the following data sets:

1. **Document-Count (Doc-Count)**: We count all abstracts per drug entity in which the drug is present.
2. **DDA-Count**: For each drug, we count the number of all DDAs existing in the abstracts. Here, we count only DDAs which are present in at least three abstracts.

*Evaluation Implementation.* In our experiment, we extract for each drug-entity 20-NDNs from the embedding space and measure the AVG-Precision of the *existing* DDAs occurring in literature. For our experiment, we sorted the two data set lists per drug-entity in ascending order and divided them into ten percentile groups. We have performed this grouping in order to ensure a better overview and comparability in the presentation. Therefore, for example, the first group contains the first 10% of all drug-entities with the lowest document counts or DDA counts, and the 10th group the 10% of drug-entities with the highest counts. As window size, we have chosen $w = 50$ and set the number of dimensions to 200. We experiment with the four corpora already introduced: 1900–1988, 1900–1998, 1900–2008, 1900–2018.

What we can see is that with increasing amounts of data (higher group) as well as in all corpora, the precision increases (Fig. 1a, b). Therefore, as expected, the more data available per drug-entity, the more *existing*-DDAs can probably be extracted. For the corpora 1900–2008 and 1900–2018 the values are almost the same.

---

[4] https://lucene.apache.org/.

[5] https://deeplearning4j.org/word2vec.

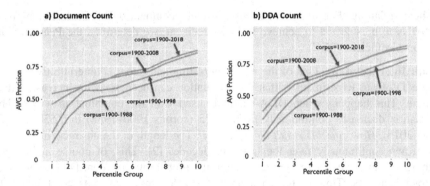

**Fig. 1.** AVG precision values reached for different corpora and percentile groups with Document-Count (a) and DDA-Count (b).

Thus, from a certain amount of data, there seems to be no substantial improvement in precision. The curves for the DDA-Count (Fig. 1b) seem to be more similar in shape and course than the Document-Count curves (Fig. 1a). This could indicate that DDA-Count data correlation is more stable over periods and corpora. This experiment has shown us that a certain correlation between data volume and individual entity probably exists. We will investigate this possible correlation, its expression, and stability in more detail in our subsequent experiments to determine entity thresholds.

## 3.2   Relationship Between Corpus-Data and Predicted DDAs

Given our findings of the previous section, here we investigate how we can find possible thresholds if DDA predictions are involved and that we are precision-oriented. In other words, how do we choose a *meaningful* precision value for our further investigations? If we set the precision $p$ too high ($p > 95\%$) we have fewer chances of making predictions. If we set the precision too low ($p < 50$), the majority of DDAs are not meaningful at a current point in time. In order to choose a meaningful precision value, we have made a ***majority assumption***: If the majority (here in AVG-$p$ $\sim 67\%$) of the DDAs exists - each DDA occurs in at least three abstracts - then there is a probability that the remaining minority is also meaningful and represents DDA predictions. Based on this majority assumption and the determination of a *meaningful* precision value, we customize our correlation analysis: What is the number $k$, of NDNs we need to extract to achieve AVG (*existing*)-DDA precision of $\sim 67\%$? Moreover, how strong does $k$ correlate with the amount of data $d$, where $d$ = Document-Count or $d$ = DDA-Count? If there is a strong linear correlation, we can, for example, train a regression model and for a given amount of data $d$ of a drug $x$, to determine the number $k$ of NDNs leading probably to the desired DDA-precision of $\sim 67\%$.

*Evaluation Implementation.*  To measure changes in the correlation over time, we train the models again on the four corpora: 1900–1988, 1900–1998, 1900–2008, and 1900–2018. Besides, we train the models with 200 dimensions, with the best window size ($w = 50$) and the default setting ($w = 5$) to determine the influence of the window size on the correlations. For all combinations between Document-/DDA-Count and number of NDNs to be selected to achieve ~67% precision, we determine the Pearson Correlation Coefficient (PCC).

**Result Interpretation.** One of the more interesting and rather counterintuitive results (Table 1) of our experiment is that the correlation can decrease with increasing data volume. This happens when DDA-Count is used with the combination $w = 5$. The correlation decreases continuously from 0.725 (corpus 1900–1988) to 0.530 (corpus 1900–2018). *How can this result be explained?* The length of the abstracts in PubMed has grown continuously over the last four decades [2]. This, of course, affects the training, because with increasing text length the probability for more DDAs within an abstract increases. This, in turn, means that smaller entity contexts combined with longer texts potentially contain fewer DDAs, and thus the correlation decreases. This thesis is supported by the fact that this effect does not occur with larger entity contexts (DDA count with $w = 50$). This leads to two insights for larger entity contexts in combination with DDA-Count: (a) The correlation is always strong (AVG PCC = 0.744) and (b) is hardly influenced by the size of the corpus as well as by the abstract length (SD = 0.018). Thus, there is a chance that we can train a regression model based on the DDA-Count and at a window size of 50 and this independent of corpus size and document length. Besides the described properties, this finding can be useful in the historical analysis of drugs. The results for Document-Count (Table 1) confirm the hypothesis that with increasing data also learning quality improves, and this leads to increasing correlation values. On the other hand, only weak AVG correlation can be achieved with Document-Count (AVG PCC < 0.5). In general, the correlation with a DDA-Count is always stronger compared to Document-Count. Therefore, it would be probably advantageous to use only documents with contained DDAs for training.

**Table 1.** PCCs for different window sizes and data counts. Best values in bold (SD = Standard Deviation).

| Corpus | DDA-Count | | Doc-Count | |
|---|---|---|---|---|
| | (w = 50) | (w = 5) | (w = 50) | (w = 5) |
| 1900–2018 | **0.763** | 0.530 | 0.590 | 0.453 |
| 1900–2008 | **0.732** | 0.634 | 0.509 | 0.448 |
| 1900–1998 | **0.726** | 0.640 | 0.444 | 0.386 |
| 1900–1988 | **0.756** | 0.725 | 0.439 | 0.434 |
| Mean: | **0.744** | 0.632 | 0.495 | 0.431 |
| SD: | **0.018** | 0.079 | 0.070 | 0.030 |

### 3.3   Learning Dynamic Thresholds for K-NDNs

Now it has to be tested if a predicted $k$-NDN-threshold approach is more efficient than, e.g., sing a fixed $k$ or determining a specific similarity value. How do we compare the performance of these thresholds? A comparison with precision values is less meaningful, because the fewer NDNs we choose per drug entity, the higher the precision, the lower the recall and probably fewer DDA predictions are possible. Efficient in our case means that with a given precision ($\sim 67\%$) we can achieve a higher recall.

*Experimental Evaluation.* We investigate the efficiency of our thresholds again for different periods using the four corpora already introduced. First, we train the embedding models with a window size of $w = 50$ and a dimension size of $d = 200$ with the respective corpora. Then we train a regression model to determine the $k$-NDNs. For this, we use the DDA-Count and the number of k-NDNs which lead to an AVG DDA precision of 67%. We perform 10-fold cross-validation and train with 90% of the data and test with 10% of the remaining data. The recall is always determined in the current period. Therefore, for example, in 1900–1988, we can determine 8% of all DDAs existing at that time (Table 2).

**Table 2.** Recall values for the different approaches and corpora. Precision is fixed in all approaches to $\sim 67\%$. Best values in bold.

| Time periods | Predicted threshold | Fixed k-NDNs | Similarity threshold |
|---|---|---|---|
| 1900–2018 | **0.07** | 0.03 | 0.04 |
| 1900–2008 | **0.07** | 0.04 | 0.06 |
| 1900–1998 | **0.07** | 0.03 | 0.04 |
| 1900–1988 | **0.08** | 0.02 | 0.04 |

*Comparative Approaches.* We perform a comparison with two conventional approaches (fixed $k$-NDNs, Similarity-Threshold). First, we determine the fixed number of k-NDNs, which lead to a DDA AVG precision of $\sim 67\%$. As an example, 6-NDNs must be extracted from the embedding space per drug-entity in the period 1900–1988 in order to achieve a DDA AVG precision of 67%. For further comparison, we determine a similarity value which leads to an AVG DDA precision of $\sim 67\%$. Where a Similarity value of 0 means maximum inequality and a value of 1 means maximum equality. For example, the Similarity value in the period 1900–1998 is $\sim 0.38$ to reach an AVG precision of $\sim 67\%$.

As presented in Table 2, our approach leads to improved recall values. On average, the recall increases by about 61% compared to Similarity-Threshold and 142% compared to a fixed-k-NDNs approach. Thus, we can extract more DDAs from the embedded space. The recall is *relatively* stable for the different time-periods and corpora. Thus, we can rely on certain value-stability.

## 4   Conclusions

State-of-the-art approaches in the field of Neural Language Models (NLMs) enable progress in learning and predicting entity associations in terms of semantic quality, scalability, and performance. In this context, network views constructed using $k$-nearest-neighbour sets can help users to understand better complex entity associations

[1] contained in literature and thus help to explain *why* an NLM has learned or predicted a certain entity association. On the other hand, learning quality varies per entity and (default) approaches like fixed-$k$-NN or Similarity-Thresholds are less meaningful for the extraction of $k$-nearest-neighbour sets from the embedded space. In this paper, we presented a novel literature based method to learn entity-specific thresholds for pharmaceutical entities. This enables us to become independent from the difficult to determine $k$-NN or Similarity-Thresholds and opens up the possibility to develop a more meaningful contextualized drug-disease network using $k$-nearest-neighbour sets.

# References

1. Greene, D., Cunningham, P.: Producing a unified graph representation from multiple social network views. In Proceedings of the 5th Annual ACM Web Science Conference, pp. 118–121. ACM, May 2013
2. MEDLINE®/PubMed® Data Element (Field) Descriptions. (U.S. National Library of Medicine). https://www.nlm.nih.gov/bsd/mms/medlineelements.html#ab. Accessed 4 Apr 2019
3. Zhang, W., et al.: Predicting drug-disease associations based on the known association bipartite network. In: 2017 IEEE International Conference on Bioinformatics and Biomedicine (BIBM), pp. 503–509. IEEE, November 2017
4. Mikolov, T., Chen, K., Corrado, G., Dean, J.: Efficient estimation of word representations in vector space. arXiv preprint arXiv:1301.3781 (2013)
5. Dudley, J.T., Deshpande, T., Butte, A.J.: Exploiting drug–disease relationships for computational drug repositioning. Briefings Bioinform. **12**(4), 303–311 (2011)
6. Wawrzinek, J., Balke, W.-T.: Measuring the semantic world – how to map meaning to high-dimensional entity clusters in PubMed? In: Dobreva, M., Hinze, A., Žumer, M. (eds.) ICADL 2018. LNCS, vol. 11279, pp. 15–27. Springer, Cham (2018). https://doi.org/10.1007/978-3-030-04257-8_2
7. Hill, F., Reichart, R., Korhonen, A.: SimLex-999: Evaluating semantic models with (genuine) similarity estimation. Comput. Linguist. **41**(4), 665–695 (2015)
8. Elekes, Á., Schäler, M., Böhm, K.: On the various semantics of similarity in word embedding models. In 2017 ACM/IEEE Joint Conference on Digital Libraries (JCDL), pp. 1–10. IEEE, June 2017
9. Al-Natsheh, Hussein T., Martinet, L., Muhlenbach, F., Rico, F., Zighed, D.A.: Metadata enrichment of multi-disciplinary digital library: a semantic-based approach. In: Méndez, E., Crestani, F., Ribeiro, C., David, G., Lopes, J.C. (eds.) TPDL 2018. LNCS, vol. 11057, pp. 32–43. Springer, Cham (2018). https://doi.org/10.1007/978-3-030-00066-0_3
10. Wawrzinek, J., Pinto, J.M., Balke, W.T.: Linking semantic fingerprints of literature – from simple neural embeddings towards contextualized pharmaceutical networks (supplement) (2019). http://www.ifis.cs.tu-bs.de/sites/default/files/wawrzinek-pinto-balke-Technical-Report.pdf. Accessed 18 June 2019

# Learning to Rank Claim-Evidence Pairs to Assist Scientific-Based Argumentation

José María González Pinto$^{(\boxtimes)}$ ⓘ , Serkan Celik,
and Wolf-Tilo Balke ⓘ

IFIS TU-Braunschweig, Mühlenpfordstrasse 23, 38106 Braunschweig, Germany
{pinto,balke}@ifis.cs.tu-bs.de, s.celik@tu-bs.de

**Abstract.** We consider the novel problem of learning to rank claim-evidence pairs to ease the task of *scientific argumentation*. Researchers face daily scientific argumentation when writing research papers or project proposals. Once confronted with a sentence that requires a citation, they struggle to find the manuscript that can support it. In this work, we call such sentences claims – a natural language sentence – that needs a citation to be credible. *Evidence* in our work refers to a paper that provides *credibility* to its corresponding claim. We tackle the scientific domain where the task of matching claim-evidence pairs is hindered by complex *terminology variations* to express the same concept and also by the *unknown* characteristics beyond *content* that makes a paper worth to be cited. The former calls for a suitable *representation* capable of dealing with the challenge of content-based matching considering domain knowledge, whereas the latter implies a need to propose *semantic features* of suitable characteristics to guide the learning task. To this end, we test the scope and limitation of a deep learning model tailored to the task. Our experiments reveal what specific attributes can guide the learning task, the impact of using domain knowledge in the form of concepts and also the assessment of which metadata of a document, e.g., 'background', 'conclusion', 'method', 'objective', or 'results' should be considered to achieve better results.

**Keywords:** Learning to rank · Scientific claims · Scientific arguments

## 1 Introduction

Our work considers the problem of claim-evidence matching as a learning to rank problem whose goal is to find *evidence* in the form of a paper to make a natural language sentence, hereafter a *claim,* credible. Our notion of claim-evidence pairs draws motivation from the Argumentation Mining community. In particular, we build on the argument model established in Computational Linguistics [1]. An argument refers to a topic and consists of two components: a claim defined as a 'general concise statement that directly supports or contests a topic' while evidence is 'a text segment that directly supports a claim in the context of a given topic'. Consider for example our user Anna, a post-doc researcher, currently writing a research proposal regarding the role of 'Lycopene' in human health. She writes the following claim: *'research has been not sufficient to establish whether lycopene consumption has a positive or a negative*

© Springer Nature Switzerland AG 2019
A. Doucet et al. (Eds.): TPDL 2019, LNCS 11799, pp. 41–55, 2019.
https://doi.org/10.1007/978-3-030-30760-8_4

*effect on human health'*. Anna considers submitting her claim as a query to a curated Digital Library such as PubMed to rely on high-quality content. However, among the possible papers that exist in the Digital collection, which specific paper would be needed here for Anna? Beyond the content matching capabilities of a modern retrieval system behind PubMed, what other attributes are needed? Perhaps Anna would need a paper that is highly cited, or that is published in a high-impact Journal, or a paper by a highly cited author? Is it possible to accurately learn a model that can assist users such as Anna in the difficult task of *scientific argumentation*?

In general, scientific argumentation is a complex information need and a hard-task: we will show in our experiments (Sect. 4) that treating a claim as query terms to measure the relevance of those query terms occurring in documents leads to an inadequate solution. Hence, we promote a learning to rank strategy tailored to the specific needs of claim-evidence pairs targeting as our main use case biomedical paper citations.

Moreover, we promote the citations on the Wikipedia archive as a *valuable* source for our novel problem because the crucial role that *citations* play in Wikipedia, i.e., valid citations provide *credibility* to Wikipedia's content. Moreover, credibility makes the task of claim-evidence ranking a challenge. How can we account for *credibility*?

To answer the question, perhaps we can gain insights from Wikipedia itself. For instance, consider Wikipedia citing sources page[1] that states: 'Wikipedia's verifiability policy requires inline citations for any material challenged or likely to be challenged and for all quotations, anywhere in article space'. Moreover, in Wikipedia's verifiability page[2] we find that 'verifiability means that other people using the encyclopedia can check that the information comes from a reliable source. Verifiability, no original research and neutral point of view are Wikipedia's core content policies'.

Given these observations, we investigate whether it is possible to learn from existing citations of biomedicine in Wikipedia, content and non-content-based patterns, to automatically rank research papers to ease scientific-based argumentation. In summary, the questions that guided our research were the following:

1. How different is claim-evidence ranking from content-based ranking?
2. How relevant is domain knowledge, given that we are targeting the biomedical field?
3. Can we gain performance improvement if the models are aware of rhetorical parts of documents? By rhetorical parts in this work, we mean metadata such as 'objective', 'methods', 'conclusions', 'background' or 'methods'.

In a nutshell, our goal is to design and implement a learning to rank model based on the novel task of learning to rank claim-evidence pairs. To this end, we characterize current citations to device semantic properties (Sects. 3.3 and 3.4), introduce a proper representation of the claim-evidence pairs (Sect. 3.2) and test different versions of our proposed model (Sect. 4) to assess its scope and limitations. In Sect. 2 we provide

---

[1] https://en.wikipedia.org/wiki/Wikipedia:Citing_sources.

[2] https://en.wikipedia.org/wiki/Wikipedia:Verifiability.

relevant related work, and finally, in Sect. 5, we conclude with a summary and outlook of our findings.

## 2 Related Work

In this section, we discuss related work on research efforts using models based on deep learning techniques in information retrieval and recent efforts to account for Argumentative machines: information systems aiming at helping users to retrieve arguments from corpora.

Information Retrieval like many other fields where machine learning is a core part of solving problems, has seen many efforts based on the Renaissance of neural networks. In particular, deep neural architectures. We refer the reader to a recent overview of various neural ranking models [17]. As first proposed in [5] neural ranking approaches can be classified as early and late combination models. Some examples of the first category are DRMM [9] that uses histogram analysis between query and document contents to model their interaction. The idea behind DRMM is to include matching signals between the query and document pairs using word embeddings as a fundamental block of transfer learning. Afterward, DRMM uses a deep learning architecture to learn latent patterns to compute the relevance score. Another example is the work of [15] that instead of representing query and document pairs as vectors, they model sequence to sequence interactions of objects. In other words, the model tries to accurately detect which parts of the pairs have an impact on the ranking.

An example of the second category of models is the work of [21] that uses Convolutional Neural Networks first to learn a latent representation of query and document pairs. Then using max-pooling to retain the most relevant features of the model, a relevance score between query and document pairs is computed using the cosine similarity.

Another instance of this category is the recent work of [23] that differs fundamentally to previous models in one relevant aspect: they proposed to learn sparse latent representations for each query and document pair. The latent sparsity representation of the proposed model showed that sparsity in neural information retrieval systems could have a positive impact. All these models demonstrated how to model meaningful interactions between query and document pairs.

One particular work that also accommodates for additional features beyond semantic matching between query and document pairs is the work of [20]. The model that the authors proposed used a Convolutional Neural Network representation of query and document pairs to model their interactions. In addition to that, they proposed to include at the end of the deep learning architecture the inclusion of features that account for relatedness between the query and document pairs. For instance, they considered word overlap and IDF-weighted word overlap between all words and only non-stopwords. These are lexical features that boost the learning to rank task as it was shown in the paper.

In contrast in our work, we proposed to include claim-evidence features that can help our claim-evidence proposed task. In particular, to include prestige and domain knowledge features. Prestige features are particularly relevant for our problem because they allow us to model 'credibility' when assessing a match between claim-evidence pairs. The inclusion of domain knowledge allows us to answer one of our research questions to assess the impact of medical concepts in our learning to rank task.

Research efforts to perform claim-oriented document retrieval includes the work of [19], where researchers introduced a specific retrieval task focused on controversial topics. This pioneering work aims at Argumentative machines: enabling information systems to have a notion of arguments that need the support of one or more relevant claims [13]. Claims, as defined by [13], are concise statements that directly support or contest a discussed topic. Their work focused on the retrieval of controversial topics using Wikipedia. To do so, they relied on state-of-the-art retrieval models and developed a set of features in the form of a 'controversial lexicon' to re-rank their models.

## 3   Approach and Problem Formulation

In this section, we provide definitions to accomplish our goal: learning to rank claim-evidence pairs; then, we describe the model that we used in our attempt to answer our research questions. Finally, we describe in details the features used to help our learning models.

### 3.1   Problem Formulation

We follow the terminology introduced in [14] and thus refer the reader for a detailed exposition of the different ranking models that have been proposed and studied. Learning to Rank is a task to automatically construct a ranking model using training data such that the model can determine the degree of relevance or importance of a set of objects for a given query. Learning to Rank relies on machine learning algorithms to accomplish its goal.

We denote $Q$ the set of queries and $D$ the set of documents. We are given a set of retrieved lists where each $q_i \in Q$ has its own list of candidate documents $D_i = \{d_{i1}, \ldots d_{in}\}$ and for each document $\in D_i$ a relevancy judgement is also given. Documents that are relevant for the query $q_i$ have judgements equal to 1 or 0 otherwise. The goal is the following: build a model that for each query $q_i$ and its candidate list $D_i$ delivers a ranking $R$ such that relevant documents appear at the top of the list.

More formally, because learning to rank is a supervised learning task, we have training and testing sets to measure the success of a ranking model. Thus a training set consists of $n$ training queries $q_i (i = 1..n) \in Q$, their associated documents represented by feature vectors $x^{(i)} = \left\{x_j^{(i)}\right\}_{j=1}^{m^{(i)}}$ where $m^{(i)}$ is the number of documents associated with the query $q_i$ and the corresponding relevant judgments. Then, a specific learning algorithm is used to learn the ranking model such that the output can predict the ground truth in the training set as accurately as possible. The learned model is then applied to new unseen queries to rank the relevance of the documents. Finally, the hypothesis space that defines the function mapping the input space to the output space in learning to rank is as follows:

$$h(w, \psi(q_i, D_i)) \rightarrow \mathcal{R}$$

where $\psi(\cdot)$ plays a key role in the task because it models the que-document matching pairs in the feature space and learns a suitable weighted vector $w$ during the training phase. In what follows we define what we mean by claim-evidence pairs and how these terms fit the general setting of query-document pairs.

**Definition 1.** *Claim*: a claim in this work is a natural language sentence in Wikipedia that needs or has a specific paper as a citation. Each claim represents a query $q_i$ in our setting.

**Definition 2.** *Evidence*: evidence in this work is a paper that could be paired with a claim to provide credibility. Thus, each evidence represents a document in $\mathcal{D}$.

**Learning to Rank Approach.** In our work we focus on a pointwise approach to provide insights on two core aspects of the problem (a) what type of representation is needed: content and non-content semantic features (b) what specific rhetoric part of a document better suits the ranking task: 'background', 'conclusion', 'methods', 'objective' or 'results'. To that end, we implemented and tested deep learning models with our proposed features. In pointwise, the training instances are triples of the form $(q_i, d_{ij}, r_{ij})$ and one can train a classifier to achieve the task.

## 3.2   Model

In this section, we describe the model used for our learning to rank task. To learn a content match between claim-evidence pairs, we apply a learning to rank model that uses a convolutional deep learning architecture [20]. The model is an instance of a feed-forward multi-input model commonly used in Deep Learning. In particular, the model accounts for the two main inputs that correspond to our task: claim and evidence pairs. Moreover, the model also accommodates for the inclusion of a set of 'non-trainable attributes' that guide the learning to rank process. In what follows we describe the five core components of the model.

**Claim-Evidence Matching.** We represent each claim and evidence as sequences. Their resulting vector representations are $x_c$ and $x_e$. These sequences are learned using Convolutional Neural Networks [10, 12]. The goal of having $x_c$ and $x_e$ is to compute a claim-evidence similarity score. One way to perform such a computation is the one introduced by [4] that defines the similarity between $x_c$ and $x_e$ as follows:

$$sim(x_c, x_e) = x_c^T M x_e$$

The role of the similarity matrix $M \in \mathbb{R}^{d \times d}$ is to find the closest document to the input query $x_c$. The model learns during training the similarity matrix $M$ as another parameter.

**Non-trainable Attributes.** The idea behind 'non-trainable attributes' is to guide the learning task to find an optimal hypothesis. What we want to do is to accommodate for situations where the model needs to learn attributes beyond claim-evidence matching. In our case, we introduce the idea of 'prestige' relevant to our task. Thus, we hypothesized that a paper to be cited needs to have a certain degree of 'prestige'.

**Join Layer.** The 'Join layer' concatenates the latent representations of $x_c$ and $x_e$, the similarity score and the 'non-trainable attributes'. Up to this point, the model has not yet computed interactions between the different attributes. To accomplish the computation of the interactions, the model uses a hidden layer.

**Hidden Layer.** The hidden layer computes the following transformation:

$$\alpha(w_h \cdot x + b)$$

Where $w_h$ is the weight vector of the hidden layer and $\alpha$. is a non-linearity function to explore more complex hypotheses. What this layer attempts is to capture possible interactions between the attributes (latent and 'non-trainable') previously computed.

**Softmax Layer.** Finally, the model is ready to compute a fully connected softmax layer. Formally, the model computes the probability distribution over the labels:

$$p(y = j|x) = \frac{e^{x^T \theta_j}}{\sum_{k=1}^{K} e^{x^T \theta_k}}$$

$\theta_k$ is the weighted vector of the $k - th$ class.

In our work we will show how we exploit and contrast the use of two different representations of the claim-evidence pairs: firstly, as sequences of tokens. Secondly, we also model them as a sequence of medical concepts using the UMLS. Furthermore, we incorporate in our models the notion of 'prestige' (details in Sect. 3.4) to measure the credibility of a paper that may influence the decision of being included as evidence given a claim.

In what follows, we provide the details of the domain knowledge that we used in our models and the prestige features that we considered.

### 3.3   Domain Knowledge

We rely on the Unified Medical Language System (UMLS) to incorporate into our models a representative set of biomedical entities. We used SemMedDB [11] database that uses SemRep [18] a specialized tool that given a natural language sentence returns a triple representation with the unique CUI ids and concepts from the UMLS. In particular, for this task, we used the table named PREDICATION that contains for each document, a sentence id and all the triples that SemRep identified.

Consider the following example to clarify what domain knowledge means in our case (taken from the SemRep web site)

Input: natural language sentence, for instance: "We used hemofiltration to treat a patient with digoxin overdose that was complicated by refractory hyperkalemia".

Output:
Hemofiltration-TREATS-PatientsDigoxin
overdose-PROCESS_OF-Patients
hyperkalemia-COMPLICATES-Digoxin overdose
Hemofiltration-TREATS(INFER)-Digoxin overdose

The subject and object arguments of each predication are concepts from the UMLS Metathesaurus and their relationship shown in uppercase is a relation from the UMLS Semantic Network. Thus, for each claim and each evidence in our dataset, we extracted these concepts to measure their impact in our task.

### 3.4   Prestige Representation

In this section, we describe the prestige attributes that we used given our particular setting. We hypothesized that our claim-evidence rank needs a notion of relevance beyond content-matching. Thus, we will consider the following attributes:

- Impact Factor (IF): The "Impact Factor" (IF) is the primary indicator of the scientific importance of journals [8]. IF is calculated annually by the Institute for Scientific Information (ISI). Despite its widespread acceptance in the scientific world, IF has been criticized recently on many accounts as mentioned in [6]: lack of quality assessment of the citations, the influence of self-citation, or English language bias.
- Eigenfactor score (ES) is another index of scientific journal impact which uses a similar algorithm like Google's PageRank [3]. For calculating ES an iterative method is used, and journals are considered to be influential if they are cited more often by other prestigious journals [3].
- The Normalized Eigenfactor Score is the Eigenfactor score normalized, by rescaling the total number of journals in the JCR each year, so that the average journal has a score of 1. Journals can then be compared and influence measured by their score relative to 1. For example, if a journal has a Normalized Eigenfactor Score of 5, that journal is considered to be five times as influential as the average journal in the JCR.
- SCImago journal rank indicator (SJR) is another index which uses a similar method as the ES. However, this index is based on SCOPUS database which has much broader indexed journals compared to ISI [6].

### 3.5   Papers Rhetoric's

To account for specific metadata of a biomedical paper, we rely on SemMedDB database. Particularly relevant for our purposes is the table named SENTENCE that contains for each paper in MEDLINE: the pmid identifier for a paper, the sentence and the rhetorical category that corresponds to a given sentence. There are five of these rhetorical categories in the data: 'methods', 'conclusions', 'results', 'background', 'objective'.

Unfortunately, not all the documents contain these valuable metadata. Thus, to account for this aspect of the papers, we had to introduce a machine learning task to learn a function that can perform the mapping: from a natural language sentence to one of the rhetorical categories. We present the results of this classification task in Sect. 4.2.

### 3.6  Embeddings

In this section, we describe our primary strategy to enhance our model's performance: embeddings. In particular, we use word embeddings in two different ways. Firstly, to improve our tokenized representations of our collection of claim-evidence. Secondly, to improve our UMLS-based claim-evidence representation.

We relied on distributional representations of words as our first step to account for deep semantics. To do so, we trained a word2vec [16] model on PubMed Central to account for a vocabulary size of 4,361,948, dimension size of 300, using a windows size of five and a minimum count of five as the parameters of the model. To train our word2vec model we used a random sample of 200 Million sentences from PubMed Central. The model trained here is the Skip-gram model using Hierarchical softmax.

To represent the medical concepts with a similar semantic representation, we used the model trained by [22]. The model that we used here is the one trained on OHSUMED: a collection of 348,566 MEDLINE medical journal abstracts used in TREC 2000 Filtering Track. To accomplish the task, researchers first transformed the free-text representation into UMLS concept identifiers. After that, they trained word2vec by Mikolov using hierarchical softmax, see [22] for more details.

## 4  Experimental Setup

In this section, we will empirically evaluate learning to rank models to answer our research questions. First, we will describe the datasets used in our experiments. Next, we will discuss the results of the models used to perform the automatic rhetoric classification of sentences. Then, we will discuss the performance of the ranking models.

### 4.1  Data Description

In this section, we will describe the dataset used in our experiments. We used the Wikipedia dump from the work of Fetahu et al. [7]. We limited our work to the citations that correspond to biomedical papers. To generate our data, we considered as ground truth the citations that currently exist on Wikipedia and divided the data in training, validation, and testing sets randomly.

We had to omit some of the claim-evidence pairs because we could not retrieve 'prestige' attributes of some of them. We show in Table 1 a summary of the dataset used for our experiments. To generate our claim-evidence pairs with relevant and non-relevant samples, we proceeded as follows: we indexed the abstracts of the entire PubMed up to the date of the Wikipedia dataset using Solr (hereafter SolrBM25). Then, we submitted each claim as a query to our index and retrieved up to the top ten (training and validation datasets) and 20 (testing dataset) documents in addition to the ground truth from Wikipedia. Thus, each model is trained assuming that the notion of 'relevance' from our SolrBM25 can be improved by learning a valuable latent space to re-rank the result set.

*Preprocessing.* As part of the preprocessing of the data, we need to consider that most of the claims and documents differ in their lengths, posing a problem to most algorithms since they are not able to work on variable length but fixed-length sequences. One way to solve this problem is to use padding. Padding means inserting a constant in the beginning or after the sequence. Thus, for instance, all the claims are padded to the length of the longest query. The same process is applied to the documents. This approach, in general, works well if the majority of the claims, for instance, is close to the longest claim. However, if they differ, then applying padding will cause unnecessarily high memory consumption and will make the models take much time to train. In our case, this is important to investigate because we aim at optimizing the models' architecture through Bayesian optimization and a wrong decision regarding padding will make it harder for an algorithm to learn. Therefore, we investigated the balance between padding data and real data.

Unfortunately, most of the claim lengths of the corpus are far from the maximum as our analysis revealed. We observed some outliers with claims that are very long with more than 200 words. Thus, we decided to try different values until we reach a good trade-off between models' performance and computational resources. In summary, we used the following lengths to represent our queries and documents: query length is 100; document length is 1,345; document length using UMLS concept representation is 231, and vocabulary size of 50,000.

## 4.2    Results and Discussion

In this section, we will show the results of our experiments. Firstly, we start with the results of the 'rhetoric' classification task, and then we introduce each learning to rank model used to answer our research questions. To account for reproducibility of our results, we will be providing on request all the datasets used and the source code of all the models trained in our website.

**Rhetoric Classification Task.** To put the task into perspective, Table 2 shows the statistics of the metadata that we refer to as 'rhetoric' class. We can observe more than 20 Million documents that do not have this critical information. Moreover, none of the documents used in our datasets contained the metadata. Thus, we used a sample of documents from SemMedDB to learn a function that at the sentence level can determine a rhetoric category. We randomly sampled 200 thousand sentences per class. We have then divided the data using 80% as training data and 20% for testing.

For this task, we compared two machine learning approaches: naïve Bayes and Support Vector Machine both using Bag of Words to represent each sentence. In Table 3, we show the results for this task where we can see that the SVM outperforms NB by a small but significant margin of 6%.

Moreover, in Table 4, we show the results per class for the SVM. We can observe a fair balance between the F1 scores among the classes. The classes 'Results' 'Methods' and 'Conclusions' were more straightforward for the model to distinguish. Furthermore, the 'Objective' class was the most challenging performing with very high precision but at the cost of the lowest recall. Afterward, we used our machine learning model to annotate each sentence of each document present in our dataset.

**Table 1.** Summary of the dataset

| Data | #queries | #relevant documents | #irrelevant documents |
|---|---|---|---|
| Training | 18,512 | 19,450 | 83,678 |
| Validation | 2,317 | 2,614 | 11,350 |
| Testing | 2,296 | 2,579 | 44,030 |

**Table 2.** Documents in SemMedDB with rhetoric classes

| Data | #documents |
|---|---|
| Background | 1,717,959 |
| Conclusions | 3,640,469 |
| Methods | 3,285,462 |
| Objective | 2,388,024 |
| Results | 3,469,876 |
| With no rhetoric | 27,851,118 |

**Table 3.** Results of the rhetoric classification task

| Model | Precision | Recall | F1 |
|---|---|---|---|
| NB-BOW | 0.76 | 0.76 | 0.76 |
| SVM-BOW | 0.82 | 0.82 | 0.82 |

**Table 4.** Results of the SVM-BOW

| Class | Precision | Recall | F1 |
|---|---|---|---|
| Background | 0.75 | 0.75 | 0.75 |
| Conclusions | 0.86 | 0.86 | 0.86 |
| Methods | 0.81 | 0.88 | 0.85 |
| Objective | 0.87 | 0.73 | 0.79 |
| Results | 0.80 | 0.87 | 0.83 |

**Table 5.** Results models using abstracts

| Model | MAP | NDCG |
|---|---|---|
| CNNRank-Content | 0.2800 | 0.4415 |
| CNNRank-UMLS | 0.2374 | 0.4043 |
| CNNRank-Content-Prestige | **0.3605** | **0.5068** |
| CNNRank-UMLS-Prestige | 0.3154 | 0.4693 |
| CNNRank-Cont-UMLS-Prestige | 0.3306 | 0.4821 |

**Table 6.** Results models using rhetoric

| Model | MAP | NDCG |
|---|---|---|
| CNN-Background-Pres | 0.3227 | 0.4749 |
| CNN-Conclusions-Pres | 0.2807 | 0.4388 |
| CNN-Methods-Pres | 0.2943 | 0.4506 |
| CNN-Objective-Pres | 0.3295 | 0.4785 |
| CNN-Results-Pres | 0.3156 | 0.4676 |

**Table 7.** Summary of Datasets per Rhetoric

| Data | # queries | #relevant documents | #irrelevant documents |
|---|---|---|---|
| *Background* | | | |
| Training | 16,092 | 18,039 | 80,460 |
| Validation | 2,062 | 2,330 | 10,310 |
| Testing | 2,043 | 2,314 | 35,830 |
| *Conclusions* | | | |
| Training | 12,894 | 14,145 | 64,470 |
| Validation | 1,525 | 1,685 | 7,625 |
| Testing | 1,573 | 1,717 | 22,099 |
| *Methods* | | | |
| Training | 15,255 | 17,009 | 76,275 |
| Validation | 1,841 | 2,071 | 9,205 |
| Testing | 1,892 | 2,109 | 31,081 |
| *Objective* | | | |
| Training | 12,782 | 14,049 | 63,910 |
| Validation | 1,571 | 1,744 | 7,855 |
| Testing | 1,559 | 1,720 | 21,770 |
| *Results* | | | |
| Training | 15,402 | 17,148 | 77,010 |
| Validation | 1,970 | 2,221 | 9,850 |
| Testing | 1,939 | 2,153 | 32,377 |

We noticed that in some cases, our model did not detect some of the rhetoric classes in some documents. Thus, we decided to build new training, validation, and testing sets. We report in Table 7 the statistics of the number of queries, relevant and irrelevant documents per rhetoric category.

**Claim-Evidence Rank Task.** Herein we show the results of the different variations of the models used in our ranking task.

We report two metrics to evaluate the models and answer our research questions. Normalized Discounted Cumulative Gain (NDCG) and Mean Average Precision (MAP). To calculate both metrics, we used the official *trec_eval* tool. To validate the differences between the models we used the Wilcoxon signed-rank test considering a two-sided hypothesis with significance level of 0.95%.

We show in Table 5 the results of each model that we implemented. In the table, 'CNNRank-Content' stands for a model that uses tokenized versions of the claim and the document pairs to learn a relevance score. 'CNNRank-UMLS' stands for a model that uses domain knowledge –UMLS concepts as the representation for each document. 'CNNRank-Content-Prestige' is a model similar to 'CNNRank-Content' but incorporates the 'prestige' attributes. 'CNNRank-UMLS-Prestige' is a model that incorporates our proposed 'prestige' attributes and uses domain knowledge to represent documents. Finally, 'CNNRank-Cont-UMLS-Prestige' is a model that uses the prestige attributes, the tokenized versions of the documents, and the domain knowledge representation of them.

To find the hyperparameters of each model's architecture, we used Bayesian optimization [2]. In what follows, we discuss the results regarding our research questions.

**RQ1: How different is claim-evidence ranking from content-based ranking?**
To address our first research question, we compare the performance differences between the models using only content-based matching and the models that incorporate 'prestige'. Thus, we refer here to the models 'CNNRank-Content' and 'CNNRank-UMLS' as the models using only content-based matching and compare them with its corresponding counterparts incorporating 'prestige'.

We can observe that in both cases, content-based matching models are significantly outperformed with statistical significance according to Wilcoxon Test (both cases with a p-value $< 2.2\text{e}{-}16$ using MAP and NDCG). This finding indicates that the neural models can profit from the notion of 'prestige' to achieve a better notion of 'relevance' beyond what is implied by the semantics of the matching between the claim and evidence pairs. This finding supports our hypothesis that claim-based ranking requires the inclusion of features that can represent the notion of 'prestige' to decide between papers that have similar semantics but with a different degree of 'prestige'.

**RQ2: How relevant is domain knowledge, given that we are targeting the biomedical field?**
The complexity of the terminology in the biomedical field motivated us to account for models where documents are sequences of medical concepts using the UMLS. Thus, to answer our second research question, we compare here the performance of the models using tokenized versions of the documents with the models using medical concept versions of the documents.

To our surprise, the tokenized versions of the documents outperformed the medical concept-based representation with statistical significance according to Wilcoxon Test (p-value $3.369\text{e}{-}13$ for MAP and p-value $2.418\text{e}{-}13$ for NDCG). Furthermore, we can observe the same behavior in the models that incorporated the 'prestige' attributes (p-value of $4.721\text{e}{-}14$ for MAP, p-value of $3.3\text{e}{-}14$ for NDCG).

Given the results obtained, word embeddings at the tokenized label outperformed the UMLS embeddings. This is probably due to the semantics behind word embeddings that account to some degree for different representations of related and similar terms. In contrast, UMLS concept embeddings are an abstraction of the documents that for our task cannot guide the models as efficient as their word embeddings counterparts.

In summary, given the results of the experiments we have conducted, we have to conclude that for our task, domain knowledge is not needed. This finding indicates that we can disregard domain knowledge.

**RQ3: Can we gain performance improvement if the models are aware of rhetorical parts of documents? By rhetorical parts in this work, we mean meta-data such as 'objective', 'methods' 'conclusions', 'background', or 'methods'?**

In Table 6, we show the results of our models looking at the specific rhetoric of the documents' abstracts. In particular, we used our tailored trained SVM to classify each sentence of an abstract as being of one of the five classes that we have learned from a vast collection from SemMedDB: 'background', 'conclusions', 'methods', 'objective' and 'results'.

The idea here is to discover if specific metadata of documents could benefit our models to uncover claim-evidence relevance. We can see that our best running model performed somewhat stable among all the different datasets. We can observe that no matter in which 'rhetorical' part of a document our model focuses on, the differences across the datasets are negligible. This finding indicates that the model can generate a latent representation of a biomedical paper regardless of the presence or absence of specific rhetoric parts.

We also investigated whether the models are making the same mistakes or if they could somehow be combined to build a stronger model using, for example, majority vote. Thus, we proceeded as follows: we looked at the results of each model and computed the Jaccard coefficient to measure the similarity between the models regarding the correct queries (queries where the models could find the relevant document) and incorrect queries.

After our analysis, we decided to combine the 'CNNRank-Content-Prestige' with the 'CNNRank-UMLS' because they had the lowest Jaccard coefficient regarding correct queries (0.13). Then we computed a weighted sum of the predictions of the models as follows: $\alpha * \text{pred}_1 + \beta * \text{pred}_2$. Where $\alpha$ and $\beta$ are the accuracy of 'CNNRank-UMLS' and 'CNNRank-Content-Prestige' respectively and $\text{pred}_1$ and $\text{pred}_2$ are the predictions of the corresponding models. Unfortunately, we got inferior results compare to 'CNNRank-Content-Prestige' alone. Thus, this simple combination cannot lead to better performance.

## 5   Summary and Outlook

In this paper, we motivated the novel problem of learning to rank claim-evidence pairs to assist scientific argumentation.

Our results showed that to successfully rank claim-evidence pairs, a model should account for other semantic properties beyond content-matching. In particular, the inclusion of features that can guide the learning process considering the 'prestige' of a paper. In our case, 'prestige' included external properties of the papers that we hypothesized could approximate better the ground truth. We have also provided empirical evidence that in our proposed solution, including domain knowledge in the form of UMLS concepts surprisingly resulted in inferior performance.

Moreover, we showed that our best-tailored model exhibits a stable performance even when it focuses on a specific rhetoric part of a document such as 'background' or 'conclusions', instead of using the whole abstract. As a future line of work, we will explore listwise approaches to improve our results.

# References

1. Aharoni, E., et al.: A benchmark dataset for automatic detection of claims and evidence. In: Proceedings of COLING 2014, the 25th International Conference on Computational Linguistics, pp. 1489–1500. Dublin City University and Association for Computational Linguistics, Dublin (2014)
2. Bergstra, J., et al.: Algorithms for hyper-parameter optimization. In: Proceedings of the 24th International Conference on Neural Information Processing Systems, pp. 2546–2554. Curran Associates Inc., Lake Tahoe (2011)
3. Bergstrom, C.T.: Eigenfactor: measuring the value and prestige of scholarly journals. Coll. Res. Libr. News. **68**(5), 314–316 (2007)
4. Bordes, A., Weston, J., Usunier, N.: Open question answering with weakly supervised embedding models. In: Calders, T., Esposito, F., Hüllermeier, E., Meo, R. (eds.) ECML PKDD 2014. LNCS (LNAI), vol. 8724, pp. 165–180. Springer, Heidelberg (2014). https://doi.org/10.1007/978-3-662-44848-9_11
5. Dehghani, M., et al.: Neural ranking models with weak supervision. In: Proceedings of the 40th International ACM SIGIR Conference on Research and Development in Information Retrieval, pp. 65–74. ACM, New York (2017)
6. Falagas, M.E., et al.: Comparison of SCImago journal rank indicator with journal impact factor. FASEB J. **22**(8), 2623–2628 (2008)
7. Fetahu, B., et al.: Finding news citations for Wikipedia. In: Proceedings of the 25th ACM International on Conference on Information and Knowledge Management, pp. 337–346. ACM, Indianapolis (2016)
8. Garfield, E.: The history and meaning of the journal impact factor. J. Am. Med. Assoc. **295**(1), 90–93 (2006)
9. Guo, J., et al.: A deep relevance matching model for ad-hoc retrieval. In: Proceedings of the 25th ACM International on Conference on Information and Knowledge Management, pp. 55–64. ACM, Indianapolis (2016)
10. Kalchbrenner, N., et al.: A convolutional neural network for modelling sentences. In: Proceedings of the 52nd Annual Meeting of the Association for Computational Linguistics, pp. 655–665. Association for Computational Linguistics, Baltimore (2014)
11. Kilicoglu, H., et al.: SemMedDB: a PubMed-scale repository of biomedical semantic predications. J. Bioinform. **28**(23), 3158–3160 (2012)
12. Kim, Y.: Convolutional neural networks for sentence classification. In: Proceedings of the 2014 Conference on Empirical Methods in Natural Language Processing (EMNLP), pp. 1746–1751. Association for Computational Linguistics, Doha (2014)
13. Levy, R., et al.: Context dependent claim detection. In: Proceedings of COLING 2014, the 25th International Conference on Computational Linguistics, pp. 1489–1500. Dublin City University and Association for Computational Linguistics, Dublin (2014)
14. Liu, T.-Y.: Learning to rank for information retrieval. Found. Trends Inf. Retr. **3**(3), 225–331 (2009)

15. Lu, Z., Li, H.: A deep architecture for matching short texts. In: Proceedings of the 26th International Conference on Neural Information Processing Systems, vol. 1, pp. 1367–1375. Curran Associates Inc., Lake Tahoe (2013)
16. Mikolov, T., et al.: Distributed representations of words and phrases and their compositionality. In: Proceedings of the 26th International Conference on Neural Information Processing Systems, pp. 3111–3119. Curran Associates Inc., Lake Tahoe (2013)
17. Mitra, B., Craswell, N.: An introduction to neural information retrieval. Found. Trends Inf. Retr. **13**(1), 1–126 (2018)
18. Rindflesch, T.C., Fiszman, M.: The interaction of domain knowledge and linguistic structure in natural language processing: interpreting hypernymic propositions in biomedical text. J. Biomed. Inform. **36**, 462–477 (2003)
19. Roitman, H., et al.: On the retrieval of Wikipedia articles containing claims on controversial topics. In: Proceedings of the 25th International Conference Companion on World Wide Web, pp. 991–996 International World Wide Web Conferences Steering Committee, Montreal (2016)
20. Severyn, A., Moschitti, A.: Learning to rank short text pairs with convolutional deep neural networks. In: Proceedings of the 38th International ACM SIGIR Conference on Research and Development in Information Retrieval, pp. 373–382. ACM, Santiago (2015)
21. Shen, Y., et al.: Learning semantic representations using convolutional neural networks for web search. In: Proceedings of the 23rd International Conference on World Wide Web, pp. 373–374. ACM, New York (2014)
22. De Vine, L., et al.: Medical semantic similarity with a neural language model. In: Proceedings of the 23rd ACM International Conference on Information and Knowledge Management, pp. 1819–1822. ACM, New York (2014)
23. Zamani, H., et al.: From neural re-ranking to neural ranking: learning a sparse representation for inverted indexing. In: Proceedings of the 27th ACM International Conference on Information and Knowledge Management, pp. 497–506. ACM, Torino (2018)

# The OpenAIRE Research Community Dashboard: On Blending Scientific Workflows and Scientific Publishing

Miriam Baglioni[1], Alessia Bardi[1], Argiro Kokogiannaki[2], Paolo Manghi[1(✉)],
Katerina Iatropoulou[2], Pedro Principe[3], André Vieira[3], Lars Holm Nielsen[4],
Harry Dimitropoulos[2], Ioannis Foufoulas[2], Natalia Manola[2], Claudio Atzori[1],
Sandro La Bruzzo[1], Emma Lazzeri[1], Michele Artini[1], Michele De Bonis[1],
and Andrea Dell'Amico[1]

[1] Consiglio Nazionale delle Ricerche, Istituto di Scienza e Tecnologie
dell'Informazione "A. Faedo", Pisa, Italy
{miriam.baglioni,alessia.bardi,paolo.manghi,sandro.labruzzo,
emma.lazzeri,michele.artini,michele.bonis,andrea.amico}@isti.cnr.it
[2] Department of Informatics and Telecommunications,
National and Kapodistrian University of Athens, Athens, Greece
{argirok,kiatrop,harryd,i.foufoulas,natalia}@di.uoa.gr
[3] Universidade do Minho, Braga, Portugal
{pedroprincipe,andrevieira}@sdum.uminho.pt
[4] CERN IT Department, Geneva, Switzerland
lars.holm.nielsen@cern.ch

**Abstract.** Despite the hype, the effective implementation of Open Science is hindered by several cultural and technical barriers. Researchers embraced digital science, use "digital laboratories" (e.g. research infrastructures, thematic services) to conduct their research and publish research data, but practices and tools are still far from achieving the expectations of transparency and reproducibility of Open Science. The places where science is performed and the places where science is published are still regarded as different realms. Publishing is still a post-experimental, tedious, manual process, too often limited to articles, in some contexts semantically linked to datasets, rarely to software, generally disregarding digital representations of experiments.

In this work we present the OpenAIRE Research Community Dashboard (RCD), designed to overcome some of these barriers for a given research community, minimizing the technical efforts and without renouncing any of the community services or practices. The RCD flanks digital laboratories of research communities with scholarly communication tools for discovering and publishing interlinked scientific products such as literature, datasets, and software. The benefits of the RCD are show-cased by means of two real-case scenarios: the European Marine Science community and the European Plate Observing System (EPOS) research infrastructure.

© Springer Nature Switzerland AG 2019
A. Doucet et al. (Eds.): TPDL 2019, LNCS 11799, pp. 56–69, 2019.
https://doi.org/10.1007/978-3-030-30760-8_5

**Keywords:** Open science · Scholarly communication ·
Research infrastructures · Research communities

# 1   Introduction

Research communities are increasingly operating under the hat of *Research Infrastructures* (RIs), intended as initiatives of governance where scientists and organizations can define common policies, recommend best practices, and deliver and maintain digital services to leverage better scientific workflows and foster innovation. Within RIs researchers can assemble their *digital laboratory* by selecting the services, tools and resources they need, and perform digital science according to common scientific workflows and sharing of scientific results. Digital laboratories are the place where researchers perform their digital experiments, share and find scientific products, track their lineage and provenance and, where possible, enable their fully-fledged re-use. In fact, based on the degree of maturity of a digital laboratory, researchers may find the $R^*$ conditions to repeat ("same research activity, same lab"), replicate ("same research activity, different lab"), reproduce ("same research activity, different input parameters"), or re-use ("using a product of a research activity into another research activity") the digital experiment, thereby maximizing transparency and exploitation of scientific findings [6].

Still, although digital science and digital laboratories facilitate the way to Open Science, a number of cultural and technical barriers are to be overcome before this vision will be effectively achieved. One of the grand challenges is the clear cultural and technical separation between digital laboratories and the scholarly communication ecosystem, intended as the environment used by science stakeholders (e.g. researchers, organizations, funders, academic societies, publishers) to publish, review, find, evaluate, and monitor science.

The mission of the OpenAIRE initiative[1], one of the pillars of the European Open Science Cloud (EOSC)[2], is to address this challenge at both cultural and technical level, by providing training, dissemination, and technical services to incept Open Science publishing practices into the research life-cycle. In this work, we shall present the OpenAIRE Research Community Dashboard (RCD), a service conceived to provide research communities with transparent bridges between their digital laboratory and the scholarly communication ecosystem. The RCD provides tools for scientists to discover, interlink and manually or automatically publish all kinds of research products and for officers to monitor the Open Science, Open Access, scientific trends and statistics of the community. This complements the mission of research infrastructure services, minimizing the cost of publishing, while respecting community practices and relative scientific workflows. Two use-cases will be presented to illustrate the RCD functionalities,

---

[1] OpenAIRE: www.openaire.eu.

[2] EOSC: https://www.eosc-portal.eu.

relative to the European Plate Observing System (EPOS) infrastructure[3] and the European Marine research community[4].

*Outline.* Section 2 describes the barriers to Open Science publishing identified in the gap between digital laboratories and scholarly services. Section 3 describes the disseminaton, training, and technical solutions to such challenges proposed by the OpenAIRE infrastructure, while Sect. 4 describes the Research Community Dashboard and its functionalities. Finally, Sect. 5 reports on the real-case scenarios of RCD adoption for the community of European Marine Science and the EPOS Research Infrastructure. Related work is illustrated in Sect. 6, while Sect. 7 concludes the paper and discusses future work.

## 2   Digital Laboratories and Scholarly Communication Ecosystem: The Gap

According to Open Science (OS) principles [7,8], all scientific products generated by research activities (e.g. scientific literature, research data, software, experiments) should be as open access as possible ( "as closed as necessary"), made available as soon as possible, and "under terms that enable reuse, redistribution and reproduction of the research and its underlying data and methods".[5] To implement this vision, scientists should follow OS publishing workflows while being technically and properly supported by digital laboratories, whose services and tools should not only allow for scientific processes to be carried out, but also for the resulting digital products to be published via scholarly/scientific communication services. The European Open Science Cloud is pro-actively promoting this vision and supporting communities and research infrastructures at implementing it, but still the overall level of technical and cultural maturity across RIs is rarely sufficient to achieve the $R^*$ conditions. Surveying RI experiences in collaboration with OpenAIRE (see Sect. 5), we can observe common lacks:

- *Article-centric publishing*: many research communities still show poor interest in publishing research products beyond the scientific article; when other products are published, research data is the focus, with links to articles, while software publishing (preservation, DOIs, etc) is still largely overlooked, and digital experiment publishing (e.g. methods, workflows, research objects) is an exception;
- *Article-centric scientific reward practices*: poor or absent support for scientific reward systems that take into account all kinds of research products;
- *Fragmentation of research products*: products are often published into community-independent data sources, where they lose their "community flavour"; identifying the collection of products of one community across such sources is in many cases not straightforward or requires manual/technical high costs;

---

[3] European Plate Observing System (EPOS): https://www.epos-ip.org.

[4] EuroMarine: https://www.euromarinenetwork.eu.

[5] FOSTER definition of Open Science: https://www.fosteropenscience.eu/foster-taxonomy/open-science-definition.

- *Manual publishing cost*: publishing is mostly a manual action, there is poor or absent support for on-demand, automated publishing of research objects produced via services of RIs;
- *Static publishing*: publishing occurs at the end of the research activity, as an act of "freezing" the products by deposition onto scholarly communication data sources; any event taking place after publishing to the products (e.g. citation, new version, usage in another experiment) is not dynamically reflected/materialized in the data sources with proper semantic links.

In the following we shall present the solutions undertaken by the OpenAIRE infrastructure in trying to blend these two worlds.

## 3 The OpenAIRE Infrastructure

For a sustainable and smooth implementation of Open Science publishing, the places where research is performed, i.e. the digital laboratories, and the place where research is published, i.e. the scholarly communication ecosystem, should be bridged. The mission of the OpenAIRE initiative, one of the pillars of the European Open Science Cloud (EOSC), is to address this challenge at both cultural and technical level, by providing training, dissemination, and technical services to incept Open Science publishing practices into the research life-cycle. OpenAIRE is a Legal Entity representing a partnership of more than 50 institutions, working to shape and implement effective Open Access and Open Science policies in support of FAIR research, reproducible science, transparent assessment and omni-comprehensive evaluation.

**OpenAIRE Networking Services.** OpenAIRE supports the implementation and alignment of Open Science policies at the international level by developing and promoting the adoption of global open standards and interoperability guidelines[6] to realize a sustainable, participatory, trusted, scholarly communication ecosystem, open to all relevant stakeholders (e.g. research communities and organizations, funders, project coordinators) and capable of engaging society and foster innovation. The network of 34 National Open Access Desks (NOADs)[7], present in every European country (and beyond) increases the awareness at the local and national level, reaching out to researchers, project coordinators and policy makers with training and support activities like workshops and webinars.

**OpenAIRE Technical Services.** The monitoring of Open Science publishing trends is supported by a big data service infrastructure. The core of such technical infrastructure consists of metadata aggregation services that collect metadata records relative to digital research products (literature, dataset, software, and others) from more than 13,000 scholarly data sources world-wide, for a current

---

[6] OpenAIRE Guidelines for Content Providers: https://guidelines.openaire.eu.

[7] OpenAIRE National Open Access Desks: https://www.openaire.eu/contact-noads.

total of more than 30 million metadata records. Aggregated metadata records are represented in the form of a directed labelled graph where each record is a node (with properties) and each semantic link is a labelled edge, where the label expresses the semantics of the relationship (e.g. the dataset is *supplement to* a journal article, the publication is *funded by* a project). The graph is also processed by algorithms to (*i*) find and merge metadata records that describe the same object [2], (*ii*) apply inference techniques on the metadata records and full-texts of Open Access publications to add new properties and new semantic relationships [11].

The resulting graph is called the OpenAIRE Research Graph, on top of which added-value services are built to serve different scholarly communication stakeholders. The Research Graph data model is described in details in [12] and depicted in Fig. 1. The main entities of the model are:

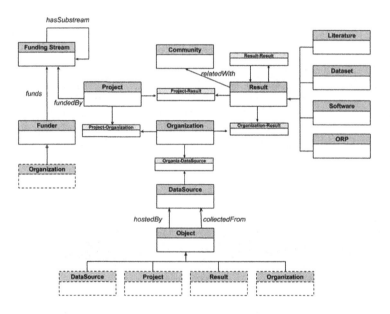

**Fig. 1.** OpenAIRE data model

**Results:** outcome of research activities, which in OpenAIRE are of four classes *Datasets, Software, Literature* and *Other Research Products* (ORP). They are related to *Projects, Organizations, Communities,* and other *Results.*

**Funders:** *Organizations* (e.g. European Commission, Wellcome Trust, FCT Portugal, Australian Research Council) responsible for a list of *Funding Streams* (e.g. FP7 and H2020 for the EC).

**Funding Streams:** identify the strands of investments managed by a *Funder* and can be nested to form a tree of sub-funding streams (e.g. FP7-IDEAS, FP7-HEALTH).

**Projects:** are research projects under a *Funding Stream* of a *Funder*. *Projects* are associated to the *Results* produced under their activities and grants.

**Data sources:** web sources from which OpenAIRE collects the metadata (and the full-texts, if possible) of the objects in the graph. Each object is associated to the *Data source* from which the metadata was collected and to the one where the object is hosted; e.g. articles whose metadata is collected from DOAJ[8] have PDFs hosted by specific journals.

**Communities:** include *research communities* and *research infrastructures*. Research communities are intended as communities of practice in a research field, willing to share and discover scientific results among the community itself and beyond. Research infrastructures are intended as service providers of research communities that are willing to monitor their impact in terms of results produced thanks to their existence.

The Research Graph is openly available under CC-BY license[9] to programmatic clients via the DEVELOP API and to humans via the EXPLORE portal (https://explore.openaire.eu). Funders, officers of research initiatives, project coordinators and policy makers can use the functionality of the MONITOR portal (https://monitor.openaire.eu) to access statistics about the scientific production, monitor the uptake of Open Science publishing practices and use tools that support official reporting. The PROVIDE dashboard (https://provide.openaire.eu) target data source managers (e.g. repository managers) by offering tools to register data sources in OpenAIRE, validate their metadata records against the OpenAIRE guidelines, subscribe to other OpenAIRE added-value services like the OpenAIRE Usage Statistics[10] and to the Catch-all Broker [1]. Finally, via the CONNECT portal (https://connect.openaire.eu) research communities and infrastructures can request the Research Community Dashboard, which offers a set of Open Science tools described in details in Sect. 4.

## 4   The OpenAIRE Research Community Dashboard

The RCD has been realized in the context of the EC H2020 OpenAIRE-Connect project, in collaboration with a number of research communities, which provided requirements and tested the service for improvement and usability. It has been designed to address the challenges identified in Sect. 2 by means of the following strategies: (*i*) building a single entry point, called Community Gateway, where scientists can find all research products and links between them; (*ii*) provide community researchers with customizable Open Science publishing tools; (*iii*) enabling the customization of the criteria to be applied by the OpenAIRE mining and tagging algorithms to associate products in the OpenAIRE Research

---

[8] DOAJ (Directory of Open Access Journals).

[9] Some data sources aggregated by OpenAIRE do not allow to re-distribute metadata in CC0; the availability of another version of the graph including only information that can be redistributed in CC0 is in OpenAIRE's plans.

[10] Guide about the OpenAIRE Usage Statistics Service: https://www.openaire.eu/guides-usage-statistics.

Graph to the community; (*iv*) providing APIs for research infrastructure services, part of digital laboratories, to automatically publish research products (e.g. datasets, software, digital experiments) in Zenodo, the OpenAIRE "catchall" repository, and associate them to the community thanks to the concept of Zenodo community, a "container" of deposited products of the community[11]. The RCD can serve two types of customers: research infrastructures in need of tools for monitoring and reporting the outcome of the science they support and research communities willing to find a scientific gateway for their Open Science publishing needs.

**For Scientists.** The gateway offers a discovery portal where users can search within the research products relative to their community. Moreover, then find publishing-oriented tools to: (*i*) manually deposit and get a persistent identifer (DOI) for research products of any kind (e.g. datasets, software, literature, methods, workflows, research packages) via Zenodo; (*ii*) interlink existing research products, e.g. link a dataset to the software that produced it; (*iii*) claim (i.e. assert) that a given research product, currently available in the OpenAIRE Research Graph, but not in the community gateway, is relevant for the community. Via such tools, researchers populate and access an open, participatory scholarly communication graph of interlinked objects through which they can share any kind of products in their community, maximise re-use and reproducibility of science, and outreach the scholarly communication at large.

**For RCD Managers.** An RCD is managed by a set of *RCD managers*, which can configure the mining and tagging algorithms used by the OpenAIRE infrastructure to assign scientific products in the OpenAIRE Research Graph to the community. OpenAIRE algorithms analyze the research graph to identify all products that are relevant for the community (e.g. products with relevant subjects, deposited in thematic or community specific repositories and archives, linked to domain-specific projects). In particular, RCD managers can perform the following actions (in any order):

- Select projects (among those available in OpenAIRE) that are related to the community: all research products linked to those projects will be automatically discoverable via the gateway.
- Select data sources (among those available in OpenAIRE) that are relevant for the community: all research products collected from such sources will automatically be discoverable via the gateway.
- Select Zenodo communities related to the community: research products in the given Zenodo communities will be discoverable via the gateway.
- Specify keyword/subject terms related to the community: all the research products whose metadata matches such terms will be discoverable via the gateway.

---

[11] Zenodo communities: https://zenodo.org/communities/.

– Define full-text mining rules: all publications whose full-text matches the rules will automatically be discoverable via the gateway; e.g., some research infrastructures mandate specific acknowledgment statements when research was supported by infrastructure services.

In addition, RCD managers can also:

– Manage end-users' claims: researchers can via UIs assert that a given product is relevant to the community. The RCD manager can confirm or reject those claims, acting as a "community moderator".
– Configure statistics and charts: OpenAIRE makes available a number of stats for the community (e.g. percentage of Open Access publications and data, number of publications linked to data and to software, growth of Open Access publishing through the years). The RCD managers can decide which stats are public and which are private, for internal monitoring.

**For RI Services.** Cultural barriers represent one of the major obstacles to the implementation of Open Science publishing. Digital products may well be generated by scientists via RI services, but still remain unpublished due to "lack of scientific reward" and "manual publishing cost". In such cases, the OpenAIRE RCD can be used to support the RI at overcoming its current limits with minimal efforts and without renouncing any of its services or current practices. RI services can interact with the RCD to deposit scientific products through the Zenodo APIs, hence publish them as scholarly communication first-citizens, with attribution/citation metadata and a DOI. Community-specific metadata can be included in the deposition, so that researchers of the same domain can better interpret the scientific product, reproduce the activity or re-use the published results.

## 5    Real-Case Scenarios

The RCD is a BETA service (https://beta.connect.openaire.eu) supporting community gateways for 6 research communities (European Marine Science, Neuroinformatics, Digital Humanities and Cultural Heritage, Fisheries and Aquaculture Management, Sustainable Development Solutions Network Greece, Agricultural and Food Sciences) and 7 research infrastructures and initiatives (CLARIN, EGI, DARIAH-EU, ELIXIR-GR, Instruct-ERIC, Research Data Alliance, EPOS-IT), whose members actively contributed to its testing, both in terms of functionality and GUI usability.[12] The RCD operates on the BETA OpenAIRE Research Graph, which aggregates today (June 2019) +400Mi metadata objects, counting, once deduplicated, +90Mi literature records, 8Mi dataset records, 140k software records, and 350Mi links between them objects (https://beta.explore. openaire.eu).

---

[12] Some of gateways are still in private mode and cannot be accessed.

In the following we report the experience with two use-cases of RCD adoption: an Open Science gateway for the European Marine Science community and a Open Science monitoring gateway for the EPOS research infrastructure that implements on-demand publishing functionality.

## 5.1    The European Marine Science RCD Gateway

In Europe, the marine science community uses public and commercial infrastructures and services to publish and share their research products, mainly literature and data. These include about 150 scientific journals, a network of 45 national oceanographic data centres (e.g. SeaDataNet), a European Marine Observation and Data portal (EMODnet), operational data access services (e.g. Copernicus), geographic and taxonomic registers (e.g. MarineRegions and WoRMS), and thematic data archives that work closely with the research community (e.g. PANGAEA, EMBL-EBI and ICES).[13] Efforts to connect and link these resources are growing, but they remain poorly known or used by the research community. Additionally, there is an important lack of infrastructure to store and share research methods such as model codes, model outputs, scientific reports and outreach/training material.

The European Marine Science RCD (https://beta.mes.openaire.eu) offers to the community of the EuroMarine network (a consortium of 56 research and academic organisations) the set of Open Science-oriented functionalities they need. Thanks to the community gateway, researchers have one single entry point where they can find all the research products relevant to their research discipline. Today (June 2019), they have access to more than 120,000 research products among publications, datasets, software and other research products associated to the community with no effort but the configuration process. The European Marine Science gateway has been configured to include products from about 50 Zenodo communities, 600 projects funded by the European Commission and Fondation Tara Expéditions[14], some of the most relevant data sources for the community including PANGAEA and DRYAD, and finally a set of generic keywords in order to minimize the number of false negatives (i.e. results that are supposed to be in the gateway but they are not).

The RCD manager also decided to publicly show all available statistics and charts, even though numbers and pictures should be considered provisional because the configuration of the OpenAIRE algorithms has not yet

---

[13] Relevant resources for the Marine Science community: SeaDataNet (https://www.seadatanet.org), EMODnet (http://www.emodnet.eu/), Copernicus (https://www.copernicus.eu), MarineRegions (http://www.marineregions.org/), World Register of Marine Species (WoRMS) (http://www.marinespecies.org/), PANGAEA. Data Publisher for Earth and Environmental Science (https://www.pangaea.de/), European Bioinformatics Institute (EMBL-EBI, https://www.ebi.ac.uk/), International Council for the Exploration of the Sea (ICES, https://www.ices.dk), DRYAD (https://datadryad.org).

[14] Fondation Tara Expéditions: https://oceans.taraexpeditions.org.

been finalised. Figure 2 shows some screenshots of the GUI for European Marine
Science RCD managers.

**Fig. 2.** RCD managers user interfaces

The European Marine Science RCD was initially created as a pilot in the
context of the H2020 project OpenAIRE-Connect to show to researchers in the
EuroMarine network the potential and the benefit of Open Science publishing
practices. Thanks to the successful pilot, plans for the future include the deployment of additional RCDs for monitoring research infrastructures in the domain
(e.g. EMBRC[15] and EMSO-ERIC[16]) and advisory boards (e.g. ICES[17]).

### 5.2 The EPOS Research Infrastructure RCD Gateway

The European Plate Observing System (EPOS) is the pan-European distributed
Research Infrastructure for solid Earth science to support a safe and sustainable
society. Through the integration of National research infrastructures and data,
EPOS will allow scientists to make a step change in developing new geo-hazards
and geo-resources concepts and Earth science applications to help address key
societal challenges. The ESA's Geohazards Exploitation Platform (GEP) is a

---

[15] European Marine Biological Resource Centre (EMBRC): http://www.embrc.eu/.
[16] European Multidisciplinary Seafloor and water column Observatory (EMSO):
http://emso.eu.
[17] The International Council for the Exploration of the Sea (ICES): https://www.ices.
dk.

system that offers as-a-service to EPOS scientists a number of scalable and parallel processing/analysis tools to be run as parallel jobs on a public/private cloud over user-identified satellite big datasets (e.g. from Copernicus). GEP tracks the history of execution of the algorithms and stores in a local database the output, in such a way past executions, i.e. GEP experiments, can be subsequently re-executed by GEP users.

According to Open Science publishing, the GEP should offer scientists the possibility to publish GEP experiments (i.e. algorithms, parameters, links to input data) as well as the digital results. In a collaboration with EPOS, between the EOSC-Hub and OpenAIRE-Advance projects, OpenAIRE will offer an RCD for EPOS and provide support for GEP on-demand publishing [13] for the specific use-case of the CNR-IREA EPOSAR tool in GEP.

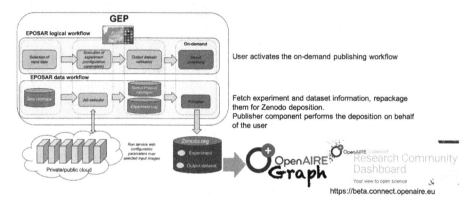

**Fig. 3.** EPOSAR workflow integrated with OpenAIRE RCD (Color figure online)

Figure 3, shows how the current EPOSAR workflow implemented in GEP can be extended with an on-demand publishing process. The red boxes in Fig. 3 represent the steps that are missing to bridge the researchers' digital laboratory and the scholarly communication ecosystem. The EPOSAR GUI will be modified to prompt the researcher with the authorization to publish. GEP will be equipped with a publishing component capable of fetching experiment and dataset information from the local databases and deposit them as products (via APIs) in Zenodo.org under the EPOS community, on behalf of the EPOSAR authorized service. Such products will be given a DOI, described by citation/attribution metadata, reciprocally linked, equipped with semantic links to other products (e.g. the DOI of the articles describing the EPOSAR algorithms). As a consequence, scientists will publish all their scientific products if needed, and, as a consequence of being deposited in Zenodo under the EPOS community, be discoverable/browsable through the OpenAIRE EPOS RCD. When extended to all GEP algorithms, the EPOS infrastructure will be able via the RCD to monitor/report all scientific products mature enough to be published. Moreover, experiments will reach out other scientists via the scholarly communication ecosystem, allowing them to access GEP and reproduce GEP experiments, as well as citing their authors when this is the case.

# 6  Related Work

The call for the implementation of Open Science principles generated a number of tools that facilitate their adoption.

SDSC ScienceGateways [14], VRE4EIC [10], and D4Science [4] are platforms for the deployment of Scientific Gateways or Virtual Research Environments (VREs), intended as web-based working environments where researchers of a community of practice can find services to perform their research activities and share intermediate and final results by guaranteeing ownership, provenance and attribution. [5] The VRE managers can select the tools and resources available in the platform that should be accessible in the VRE. Researchers use the VRE as their digital laboratory, as a single entry point to the resources relevant for their community, and as a dissemination means for their (ongoing) research activities. VREs typically focus on the OS principle of open collaboration and on the $R^*$s of the scientific process [3]. In the majority of the cases, VREs are decoupled from the scholarly communication infrastructure and must be flanked with tools like the Research Community Dashboard.

Another platform that supports the deployment of community-specific gateways for discovery and re-use purposes is SciCrunch[18]. SciCrunch was "designed to help communities of researchers create their own portals to provide access to resources, databases and tools of relevance to their research areas". [9] It offers a high degree of customization of community portals in terms of content, look and feel and services. Communities can select relevant data sources from a registry of 250+ data repositories and 13,000 research resources in the biomedical domain. New sources can also be added and those become available for selection to all other communities using the platform. The look and feel and the search functionality of the community can be configured to exploit community-specific ontologies.

The approach of SciCrunch is very similar to the one of the OpenAIRE RCD. Both are designed to provide a single entry point to all research resources the researchers of a given community many need. This information is selected by community managers from a set of available sources that may change over time, enabling the possibility to include new community-specific sources. The main differences among SciCrunch and the RCD are to be found in the underlying content they are built upon and in the functionality offered to their users. SciCrunch works on biomedical data and can offer a higher degree of customization of the gateways, since it serves different communities related to the same high-level discipline. The OpenAIRE RCD, instead, is built on top of the OpenAIRE research graph and can potentially be used to deploy gateways for research communities of any disciplines. Since the OpenAIRE research graph is not specific for any disciplines, the RCD offers more advanced configuration options in terms of

---

[18] SciCrunch: https://scicrunch.org/.

content: the selection of the relevant data sources is only one of the options that the RCD managers can configure to include research products in their gateways. In addition, the RCD offers Open Science publishing tools that allows researchers to "interact" with the scholarly communication ecosystem from within the gateway in such a way the data sources responsible for the products can get notified about the new links they add (via the OpenAIRE Broker service).

## 7    Conclusions and Future Work

In this paper we have presented the OpenAIRE Research Community Dashboard (RCD) as a toolkit to support the shift of research communities towards Open Science publishing. The RCD has already passed two functional and usability testing phases to which members of different research communities and infrastructures have participated and is now ready for production. Future developments include (*i*) a general re-styling of the GUIs to improve the user experience; (*ii*) the possibility for RCD managers to configure gateway pages to provide community-specific recommendations for the adoption of OS principles (e.g. preferred repositories, publishing practices); (*iii*) the addition of the *tagging propagation mode*, allowing RCD managers to opt for research products to be associated to the community if they are semantically linked to products of the community; e.g. if an article is associated to the community and linked to a dataset with a *supplementedBy* realtionship, then also the dataset can be associated to the community; and (*iv*) the integration with the Search and Link Wizard of ORCID, to allow ORCID users logged in the system to add OpenAIRE products to their ORCID Curriculum.

**Acknowledgements.** This work is partly funded by the OpenAIRE-Advance H2020 project (grant number: 777541; call: H2020-EINFRA-2017) and the OpenAIRE-Connect H2020 project (grant number: 731011; call: H2020-EINFRA-2016-1). Moreover, we would like to thank our colleagues Michele Manunta, Francesco Casu, and Claudio De Luca (Institute for the Electromagnetic Sensing of the Environment, CNR, Italy) for their work on the EPOS infrastructure RCD; and Stephane Pesant (University of Bremen, Germany) for his work on the European Marine Science RCD.

## References

1. Artini, M., Atzori, C., Bardi, A., La Bruzzo, S., Manghi, P., Mannocci, A.: The OpenAIRE literature broker service for institutional repositories. D-Lib Mag. **21**(11/12), 1 (2015). https://doi.org/10.1045/november2015-artini
2. Atzori, C., Manghi, P., Bardi, A.: GDup: de-duplication of scholarly communication big graphs. In: 2018 IEEE/ACM 5th International Conference on Big Data Computing Applications and Technologies (BDCAT), pp. 142–151. IEEE (2018). https://doi.org/10.1109/BDCAT.2018.00025
3. Barker, M., et al.: The global impact of science gateways, virtual research environments and virtual laboratories. Future Gener. Comput. Syst. **95**, 240–248 (2019). https://doi.org/10.1016/j.future.2018.12.026

4. Candela, L., Castelli, D., Pagano, P.: D4Science: an e-infrastructure for supporting virtual research environments. In: Agosti, M., Esposito, F., Thanos, C. (eds.) Post-proceedings of the Fifth Italian Research Conference on Digital Libraries - IRCDL 2009, Padova, Italy, 29–30 January 2009, pp. 166–169. DELOS: An Association for Digital Libraries/Department of Information Engineering of the University of Padua (2009). http://www.dei.unipd.it/%7Eagosti/ircdl/atti-ircdl2009-finale.pdf
5. Candela, L., Castelli, D., Pagano, P.: Virtual research environments: an overview and a research agenda. Data Sci. J. **12**, GRDI75–GRDI81 (2013). https://doi.org/10.2481/dsj.GRDI-013
6. De Roure, D.: The future of scholarly communications. Insights **27**(3), 233–238 (2014). https://doi.org/10.1629/2048-7754.171
7. European Commission: Validation of the results of the public consultation on Science 2.0: Science in Transition. Technical report, European Commission (2015). http://ec.europa.eu/research/consultations/science-2.0/science_2_0_final_report.pdf
8. European Commission: Open innovation, open science and open to the world. Technical report, European Commission's Directorate-General for Research & Innovation (2016). https://ec.europa.eu/digital-single-market/en/news/open-innovation-open-science-open-world-vision-europe
9. Grethe, J.S., et al.: SciCrunch: a cooperative and collaborative data and resource discovery platform for scientific communities. Front. Neuroinform. (69) (2014). https://doi.org/10.3389/conf.fninf.2014.18.00069
10. Jeffery, K.G., et al.: A reference architecture for virtual research environments. In: Everything Changes, Everything Stays theSame? Understanding Information Spaces, Proceedings of the 15th International Symposium of Information Science (ISI 2017), pp. 76–88 (2017). https://doi.org/10.18452/1448
11. Kobos, M., Bolikowski, Ł., Horst, M., Manghi, P., Manola, N., Schirrwagen, J.: Information inference in scholarly communication infrastructures: the OpenAIRE-plus project experience. Procedia Comput. Sci. **38**, 92–99 (2014). https://doi.org/10.1016/j.procs.2014.10.016
12. Manghi, P., et al.: The OpenAIRE research graph data model (2019). https://doi.org/10.5281/zenodo.2643199
13. Manghi, P., et al.: Enabling open science publishing for research infrastructures via OpenAIRE: the EPOS use-case (2018). https://doi.org/10.5281/zenodo.1412509
14. Moore, R.L., et al.: Gateways to discovery: cyberinfrastructure for the long tail of science. In: Proceedings of the 2014 Annual Conference on Extreme Science and Engineering Discovery Environment, XSEDE 2014, pp. 39:1–39:8. ACM, New York (2014). https://doi.org/10.1145/2616498.2616540

# A Framework for Citing Nanopublications

Erika Fabris[1(✉)] [ID], Tobias Kuhn[2] [ID], and Gianmaria Silvello[1] [ID]

[1] Department of Information Engineering, University of Padua, Padua, Italy
{erika.fabris,gianmaria.silvello}@unipd.it
[2] Department of Computer Science, VU University Amsterdam,
Amsterdam, The Netherlands
t.kuhn@vu.nl

**Abstract.** In this paper we discuss the role of the Nanopublication (nanopub) model for scholarly publications with particular focus on the citation of nanopubs.

To this end, we contribute to the state-of-the-art in data citation by proposing: the *nanocitation* framework that defines the main steps to create a text snippet and a machine-readable citation given a single nanopub; an *ad-hoc* metadata schema for encoding nanopub citations; and, an open-source and publicly available citation system.

**Keywords:** Nanopublication · Data citation · DisGeNET

## 1 Introduction

Nowadays, the role of data in scientific research is central and the transition to the fourth paradigm of science marks a change even in academic publications. New concepts of data scholarship [5] and data-intensive research [16] have now become extremely important to the world of science. Experimental and observational data along with scientific models pertain mainly to a digital domain. Scholarly publications and credit attribution processes are increasingly considering this trend. Data can thus be regarded as first-class subjects of the system of sciences and, in many cases, are becoming scholarly publications in their own right [22]. Moreover, data publication is regarded as a prerequisite for data sharing and reuse, often through data journals that mirror the scientific publication model [7].

In this context, the connection between scientific claims and the underlying data that lead to their definition or discovery should be explicit and evident. As generally known, "we must respect the connection between the articles and the [underlying] data and value both appropriately" and that "*de novo* claims and the supporting data should be exchanged in machine-readable [and] unambiguous format" [22].

To this end, the Nanopublication (nanopub) model has been proposed as a means to represent scientific statements and results and make them uniquely

© Springer Nature Switzerland AG 2019
A. Doucet et al. (Eds.): TPDL 2019, LNCS 11799, pp. 70–83, 2019.
https://doi.org/10.1007/978-3-030-30760-8_6

identifiable, accessible, attributable, citable and reusable [14]. A nanopub is normally represented as three Resource Description Framework (RDF) graphs: the main one containing the scientific assertion; the second, the assertion source—e.g., where the assertion comes from and how it has been defined; the third one, called publication information, contains metadata of the nanopub indicating who curated the assertion and when the nanopub was created. A nanopub is a self-contained entity associated with a persistent identifier that can be used to explicitly connect articles with underlying data.

The use of nanopubs is becoming more popular, especially in the domain of life sciences where a growing dataset of more than 10 million nanopubs comes from heterogeneous sources such as DrugBank[1], DisGeNET[2], Global biotic interactions[3] and others [20]. Nanopubs are also increasingly prominent within the domain of digital humanities where they are used for philosophical[4], archaeological [12] and music notation[5] purposes. The use of nanopub is also found in the context of Europeana as a format for data on humanities[6].

The potential of nanopubs in scholarly publications is expanding since they enable article-data connections and credit attribution to data creators and curators. Their role is however limited to the identification, representation, and access to scientific assertions, but there is no generally-agreed method to cite them at a specific and general level of aggregation. Nanopubs are generally cited at the dataset level and not at the single statement level, which is the very purpose on the nanopub model [20]. This limits the chance to attribute credit to data creators and curators and estimate the impact of data themselves.

The aim of our work is to define a model for single nanopubs citations and provide a system to automatically create references to cite nanopubs. A data citation system has to meet some basic requirements [1,10,25]: (i) identification (with variable granularity) of the cited data; (ii) access to the cited data in the form they were cited; (iii) create human-readable citation text snippets to be used as reference in the articles; (iv) develop machine-readable citations/references to enable interoperability. The nanopub model and its supporting services guarantee data identification and access, we therefore focus on the definition and creation of human- and machine-readable citations at the single nanopub level.

The citation text snippet has to address the trade-off between completeness of the information it reports and its length. A dataset usually has hundreds of creators, curators, and contributors who cannot be exhaustively reported in a scientific paper due to space limitations. On the other hand, every contributor counts and should get credit. For this reason, we define the citation text snippet based on custom citation policies, established by data curators or database

---

[1] https://www.drugbank.ca/.

[2] http://www.disgenet.org.

[3] https://www.globalbioticinteractions.org/.

[4] http://emto-nanopub.referata.com/wiki/EMTO_Nanopub.

[5] https://mith.umd.edu/research/enhancing-music-notation-addressability/.

[6] https://dm2e.eu/open-humanities-awards-early-modern-european-peace-treaties-online-final-update/.

administrators, aimed at finding the best trade-off between completeness and length of the citation text snippet. Moreover, the citation system we propose, together with the citation text snippet, returns a web landing page containing all the information regarding the cited nanopub and the citation itself.

**Contributions** of this work include:

1. a general framework (i.e. the *nanocitation* framework) that defines the main steps to create a citation text snippet and a machine-readable citation given a single nanopub;
2. an *ad-hoc* metadata scheme for encoding nanopub citations;
3. an open-source nanopub citation system and a publicly available WebApp that given a nanopub identifier, returns a text snippet and a web landing page.

**Outline.** The other part of the paper is organized as follows: Sect. 2 discusses related work about data citation and nanopubs. Section 3 introduces a use case based on DisGeNET gene-disease association data and a running example used throughout the paper. Section 4 presents the nanocitation framework and the metadata scheme. Section 5 describes how the citation system is realized, and finally, Sect. 6 draws some final remarks and outlines for future work.

## 2    Background

*Linked Open Data and RDF.* The Linked Open Data (LOD) paradigm [15] refers to a set of best practices for the publication of data on the Web, based on a standardized data model, RDF [17]. RDF is designed to represent information in a minimally constraining way. It is based on the following building blocks: graph data model, IRI-based vocabulary, data types, literals, and several serialization syntaxes. The basic structural construct of RDF is a triple: subject, predicate, and object. It can be represented in a graph where subjects and objects are the nodes and the predicates the arcs. An RDF dataset is a collection of RDF graphs composed of a default RDF graph and a set of named graphs [8]. The latter are pairs consisting of an IRI (i.e. the name of the graph) and an RDF graph.

*Nanopublication.* Nanopubs are "the smallest unit of publishable information: an assertion about anything that can be uniquely identified and attributed to its author"[7]. The nanopub model was introduced to overcome the increasing difficulties to retrieve, exchange and connect scientific results with the underlying data as a consequence of an ever-growing amount of scientific papers and datasets [14]. A nanopub is a publication itself that carries all the information to be understood and re-used by humans and machines.

The key idea behind the nanopub model is that a scientific result can be divided into individual atomic statements—i.e., assertions—represented as RDF triples. A nanopub comprehends all the information related to a single assertion

---

[7] http://nanopub.org/.

which is structured into three main named graphs: (i) the *assertion* graph containing the information related to the main scientific statement of the nanopub; (ii) the *provenance* graph containing information on the origin and creation process of the assertion; and (iii) the *publication info* graph including the metadata about the creation and publication of the nanopub. The above three graphs are interconnected by means of an additional graph: the *head* graph.

The main goals of the nanopub model are to promote interoperability among scientific results, data integration and trustworthiness, to ease the access to a scientific statement and to enable the citation of atomic statements allowing for fine-grained citation metrics on the level of individual claims [11,14,19].

The nanopub model has been used to represent data and content of sources from different fields, so far mainly in biomedicine and bioinformatics, e.g. WikiPathways[8], DisGeNET, and neXtProt[9]. In general, there are currently more than 10M nanopubs publicly accessible [20] at http://npmonitor.inn.ac/ and mirrored on 13 different server instances.

*Data Citation.* Citations are a cornerstone for the diffusion of knowledge in science and a pivotal tool to assess the quality of research as well as to direct investments in science. In this transition phase towards the fourth paradigm of science, data are as vital to scientific progress as traditional publications. For this reason, data are considered as first-class subjects of the system of sciences and data citation is gaining ground in all scientific fields [27].

Until now, data citation has been studied from two main perspectives: defining core principles and developing computational solutions. Two major international initiatives have focused on defining the core principles for data citation: CODATA, which published a report on data citation principles [1]; and FORCE 11, which published a list of principles summarising the ideas of a number of working groups [10]. The principles not only highlight the idea that data is a research object that should be citable, giving credit to data curators, but they also identify the criteria that a citation should follow: (i) the identification of and access to the cited data; (ii) the persistence of data identifiers as well as related metadata; (iii) the completeness of the reference, thus data citation that contains all the necessary information to interpret and understand the data; and, (iv) the interoperability of citations, thus interpretable both by humans and machines.

Data citation has been recently defined also as a computational problem [6] and some solutions to automatically generate data citations have been proposed in the literature [3,9,26,29]. Most of the solutions proposed focus on relational and graph databases where a citation for a given query must be provided, exploiting database views to build a viable reference. In [25] a system to store user queries is defined and these queries are treated as proxies of cited data, but it does not provide a solution to produce human- and machine-readable references. In general, none of the existing solutions can be easily applied to nanopubs. Whenever a scientific assertion is central, information from named graphs must automatically be extracted and no user query or views can be leveraged on.

---

[8] https://www.wikipathways.org.
[9] https://www.nextprot.org.

Although one of the main goals of nanopubs is to enable the citation of atomic scientific statements, no solution to automatically build human- and machine-readable nanopub citations has been found so far.

## 3  Use Case: DisGeNET

We consider the biomedical platform DisGeNET (ver. 4.0.0) as a use case and we employ it as a running example throughout the paper.

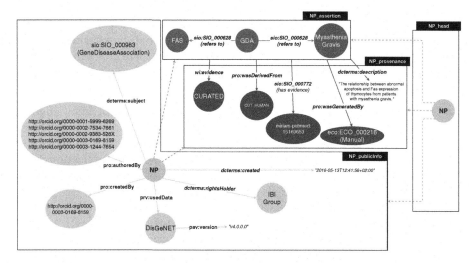

**Fig. 1.** Running example: A simplified graphical representation of DisGeNET nanopub.

DisGeNET is an open discovery platform containing comprehensive information on gene-disease associations (GDA) and variant-disease associations (VDAs) gathered through extraction and text-mining procedures from expert curated databases, catalogues and the scientific literature [23]. DisGeNET is widely used in several domains because it provides: free access to one of the most comprehensive collections of GDAs and VDAs (i.e. 430K GDAs, linking 17K genes to 15K diseases, and 72K VDAs), access to heterogeneous resources and external datasets, a web interface with search functionalities, an automatic generator of customized scripts, suitable tools to visualize and explore GDAs networks, and machine-readable version of the data as RDF. Moreover, DisGeNET is one of the foremost sources providing access to its data as nanopubs [24].

Figure 1 shows a simplified graphic representation of a typical DisGeNET nanopub used as a running example in the paper. It consists of three named graphs linked together by a fourth named graph called "head graph". The publication info graph provides all the information related to the publication of the DisGeNET nanopubs such as creation date, owner rights, names of creators and contributors. Worth noting that all the DisGeNET nanopubs are authored by five contributors and one creator. They target one general assertion topic—i.e., gene-disease association. The provenance graph contains all the information about the origin of the assertion and its generation process—i.e., the identifier of the scientific paper containing the evidence of the assertion, classification derivation and the way the assertion was created, either automatically or manually. The assertion graph maps the details about the gene-disease association. In Fig. 1 the assertion consists on the relationship (i.e., GDA) between the gene Myasthenia Gravis and the disease FAS. Currently, in DisGeNET all nanopubs have the same structure and number of triples.

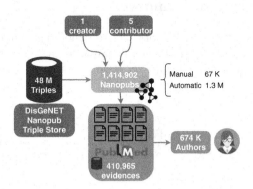

**Fig. 2.** DisGeNET nanopubs v. 4.0.0 statistics.

In Fig. 2, some basic statistics about DisGeNET and its nanopubs are provided. There are 1,414,909 nanopubs for a total of about 48M of triples. The majority of nanopubs are automatically created – 1.3M – and nanopubs refer to 410K PubMed evidences (citations and abstracts for biomedical literature) written by a total of 674K authors.

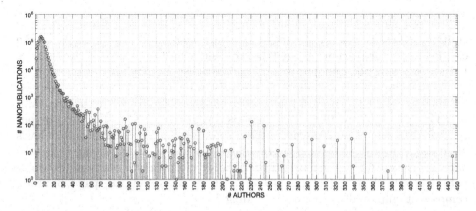

**Fig. 3.** Number of nanopubs grouped by the same number of evidence authors (y-axis is log-based) – e.g., ~150K nanopubs are based on an evidence with 6 authors.

Two key facts are therefore worth highlighting: (i) many nanopubs are based on the same evidence and a nanopub can be based on several evidences; and, (ii) many nanopubs refer to evidences written by a large number of authors.

Figure 3 reports the number of nanopubs that share the same number of evidence authors. As can be seen, there are thousands of nanopubs with dozens of evidence authors and that in general, almost all nanopubs have more than ten evidence authors. For this reason, all the evidence authors in the text snippet of a nanopub cannot be reported properly.

## 4   The Nanocitation Framework

We propose *nanocitation*, a framework to cite nanopubs composed of four main components that takes the URI of a single nanopub and a set of citation policies as inputs and returns a reference (i.e. text snippet) and a web landing page as outputs.

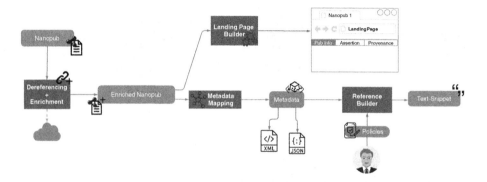

**Fig. 4.** Framework schema for nanopub citation.

Figure 4 shows the main components of the nanocitation framework. The citation process is created starting from a raw nanopub – i.e., the object of the citation. The `Dereferencing and Enrichment` component dereferences all the URIs composing the nanopub triples and searches for relevant information on the Web to enrich the nanopub. Afterwards, the enriched nanopub is mapped into metadata that encode all the necessary information to create the text snippet. The metadata can also be serialized as XML or JSON files. The text snippet is created by selecting and transforming some fields of metadata, on the basis of citation procedures defined by the database administrator or the nanopubs curator. The output of the `reference builder` component is the final text snippet. Moreover, the enriched nanopub is the input of the `landing page builder` component employed to create the landing page.

***Enriched nanopub.*** An enriched nanopub is a human-readable version of the nanopub where all the URIs have been dereferenced by accessing external sources such as: ORCID[10] to get the nanopub creators and curators names, PubMed to get evidence of the assertion; relevant ontologies such as ProteinAtlas[11] and NCBI[12] to get details on assertion terms on genes, diseases and proteins. The enriched nanopub contains more information than the original one: it offers the list of evidence-authors extracted from PubMed, detailed and related information on genes and diseases found in the assertion.

*Metadata.* Human-readable information composing the enriched nanopub are structured as metadata. For data citation several metadata formats are proposed by the literature [4,13,28]. DataCite [2], the most recent and widely recognized metadata format proposal for citing data, provides a common set of fifteen fields. Nevertheless, the DataCite format cannot be used to cite a nanopub since several data within the enriched nanopub do not find any correspondent field or lead to field overload as reported in Table 1.

Hence, a custom metadata scheme was defined as a Dublin Core Application Profile. Table 1 illustrates the core terms of this scheme and a concrete metadata instance based on the running example reported above. All literal terms are formatted strings based on standards that depend on the entity they represent – i.e. W3CDTF standard for date types, RFC3986 syntax for URIs or identifiers. Other terms refer to non-literal customized types. These are: `creator` and `contributor`, defined as `person` type (composed of `givenName`, `familyName` and `personID` string-fields) or `organisation` type (composed of a string field `orgName`), `evidenceAuthor`, defined as `person` type and `content`, defined as set of pairs `subject-assertion(s)` (there may exist multiple assertions associated to a single subject).

The metadata description set and the XML/JSON scheme are publicly available from the homepage of the *nanocitation* WebApp.

*Policies.* To create the text snippet some relevant metadata fields need to be selected and transformed. This process is controlled by the database administrator or the nanopub creator using a set of predefined data citation policies. Data citation policies are constituted by a set of operations on the metadata fields.

Let us consider the instance in Table 1, a viable citation policy is:

**Selection and ordering:** `creator`, `contributor`, `creationDate`, `rightsHolder`, `content`, `platform`, `version`, `evidenceAuthor`, `landingpageUrl`.
**Operations:**
- `creator`, `contributor` and `evidenceAuthor`: select `givenName` and `familyName` of the first element and, in the case of more than one creator (curator), affix "et al." followed by brackets containing the total number of creators (curators).
- `creationDate`, `rightsHolder`, `platform`, `version` and `landingpageUrl`: use the content field as it is.

---

[10] https://orcid.org/.
[11] https://www.proteinatlas.org/.
[12] https://www.ncbi.nlm.nih.gov/.

**Table 1.** Nanopublication metadata schema and a description of its use based on the running example.

| Term | Min-Max | Lit. | Instance | DataCite |
|---|---|---|---|---|
| NanopubIdentifier | 1-1 | l | http://rdf.disgenet.org/resource/nano pub/NP14146.RALnE6gfq0eJ45bgXk mCLy3rV9GT2VSRUMfRYS9qR8KQk | Identifier |
| Creator | 1-∞ | non-l | [(Núria, Queralt Rosinach, http://orcid. org/0000-0003-0169-8159)] | Creator |
| Contributor | 0-∞ | non-l | [(Álex, Bravo Serrano, http://orcid.org/ 0000-0001-5999-6269), (Ferran, Sanz, http://orcid.org/0000-0002-7534-7661), (Laura I., ...] | Contributor |
| CreationDate | 0-1 | l | 2016-05-13 | Date |
| RightsHolder | 0-1 | l | IBIGroup | Contributor |
| Content | 1-1 | non-l | [(gene-disease association (gene-disease biomarker association), FAS Fas cell surface death receptor - Myasthenia Gravis)] | – |
| Platform | 0-1 | l | Disgenet | – |
| Version | 0-1 | l | v4.0.0.0 | Version |
| EvidenceReference | 0-∞ | l | [http://identifiers.org/pubmed/ 15169653] | RelatedIdentifier |
| EvidenceAuthor | 0-∞ | non-l | [(Y, Du, -), (QY, Zhang, -), (LR, Ruan, -), (CC, Liang, -), (W, He, -)] | Contributor |
| LandingpageUrl | 1-1 | l | nanocitation.dei.unipd.it/landingpage/ RALnE6gfq0eJ45bgXkmCLy3rV9GT2V SRUMfRYS9qR8KQk | RelatedIdentifier |

- **content**: select the **subject** followed by a colon and the **assertions** separated by comma.

**Presentation:** Separate text-snippet elements with a comma.

The *selection and ordering* component defines the list of fields that are selected from the metadata and the order in which they appear in the text snippet. The *operations* component defines the operations to be performed on the single selected fields, and the *presentation* component defines how the field's content is rendered in the text snippet. For sake of clarity, we have not presented the specific syntax that define the operations over the fields, but have focused on the idea of citation policy at a higher abstraction level. By applying this policy to the metadata reported in Table 1 the following text-snippet is obtained:

Queralt Rosinach Núria, Piñero Janet et al. (5), 2016-05-13, IBIGroup, gene-disease association (gene-disease biomarker association): FAS Fas cell surface death receptor - Myasthenia Gravis, disgenet, v4.0.0, Du Y et al. (6). nanocitation.dei.unipd.it/landingpage/RALnE6gfq0eJ45bgXkm CLy3rV9GT2VSRUMfRYS9qR8KQk

Worth noting that the text-snippet contains all the information that allows the reader to easily identify the authors and contributors who provided the data, the date of creation, the publish information of the source, the general content and the authors' evidence of the content, alongside the link to the landing page where more information is provided. Text-snippets may vary in length, depending on the policies applied: the above example is concise enough to be included in the reference list of a paper.

## 5   The Nanocitation System

We implemented the nanocitation framework as a WebApp accessible at the URL: nanocitation.dei.unipd.it

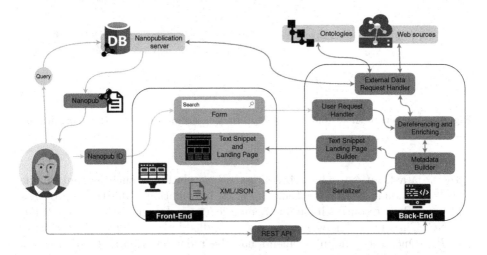

**Fig. 5.** Nanopublication citation system architecture.

Figure 5 illustrates the overall structure of the nanocitation system composed of a front-end and a back-end component.

The front-end provides a user interface which takes the identifier of the nanopub to be cited as input, returning the landing page of the citation. The landing page is structured as shown in Fig. 6. It provides the citation text-snippet, the link to the nanopub and three main collapsible elements where all the information contained in the nanopub (named graphs) and the additional information added in the enrichment phase are reported. From the landing page, the user can access external sources containing a more detailed definition or further data related to the nanopub. For instance, the authors are connected to their ORCID pages, and the assertion elements are connected to their ontological definitions. The landing page offers the possibility to download the XML and JSON serialization of the citation metadata.

The back-end comprises six main components. The *User Request Handler* receives the identifier requested by the user and activates the citation mechanism by calling the *Dereferencing and Enrichment* component. This component

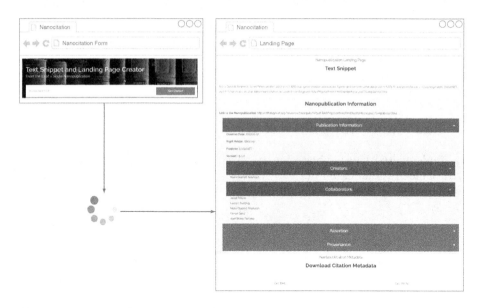

**Fig. 6.** Two screen-shots showing the primary user interfaces of the nanocitation system.

gathers data from external web sources – i.e., platforms such as Linked Life Data[13], National Center for Biotechnology Information (NCBI)[14], ontologies and vocabulary resources including SemanticScience Integrated Ontology (SIO) and NCI Thesaurus. The whole process is handled by an *External Data Request Handler*. Once the nanopub elements have been dereferenced and enriched, the *Metadata Builder* component creates the metadata object as defined above. The *Text Snippet/Landing Page Builder* component creates the text snippet and the landing page by applying the policies specified by the database administrator or the data curator. As a result, the landing page provides additional data and references on the aforementioned nanopub in a readable format for both users who do not know the structure of nanopub as well as for informed users.

Moreover, a RESTful API enables programmatic requests of the citation text snippet, the citation landing page and the XML or JSON serialization of the citation metadata.

The back-end component is implemented in Java 8 and relies on the `nanopub-java` external library [18]. The WebApp runs on an Apache Tomcat ver. 9 web server based on the Spring MVC framework ver. $5^{15}$ and on Thymeleaf ver. $3^{16}$. The code is available as open-source at: https://github.com/erikafab/nanocitation/.

---

[13] http://linkedlifedata.com.
[14] https://www.ncbi.nlm.nih.gov.
[15] https://spring.io/.
[16] https://www.thymeleaf.org/.

We tested the system by randomly sampling 1000 DisGeNET nanopubs, recording the time needed to generate the text snippet, the number of empty fields in the text snippets and in the citation metadata. On average, text snippets are 335-characters long; this length is comparable to a conference bibliographic citation. The average generation time is 10 s, due mainly to the delay time to get data from external resources. The percentage of citation metadata with missing fields is 2% of the total, where the only missing field is `evidenceAuthor` due to nanopubs without explicit reference to an evidence paper.

## 6    Conclusion and Future Work

In this paper we discuss the nanopub model in the context of scholarly publications highlighting the importance of data citation for credit attribution at the data level. As contribution to the research in the field of data citation, we propose the *nanocitation* framework for citing single nanopubs and an open-source system that enables the automatic creation of citation text snippets and landing pages. Until now, the nanopublications were referenced at the datasets level or just by the means of their identifiers; with our system researchers can create references to the specific nanopubs used or mentioned in their works. In addition, our work offers a system for in-depth exploration of their content (landing page) that is missing in the current state of the art in nanopubs.

The proposed nanocitation framework meets data citation requirements discussed in the Background section, namely: (i) identification and access of the cited data; (ii) persistence of data ids and related metadata; (iii) completeness of the citation; and, (iv) interoperability. In fact, a nanopub is uniquely identified by its URL and the citation landing page is uniquely connected to it because its URL includes the identifier of the nanopub. This guarantees that a landing page is always associated with one and only one nanopub. Moreover, given a nanopub identifier, the nanocitation system always returns the same landing page and citation metadata (the text snippet depends on the specific citation policy). Currently, the page and the metadata are generated dynamically, so they rely on the availability of the nanopub and external information. Nevertheless, without weakening the general framework and avoiding any significant changes, the landing page and the citation metadata can be dumped and stored in a database to guarantee their availability even beyond the nanopub lifespan.

Nanopubs persistence is guaranteed by the nanopub specification and the storage system put in place to deal with fixity of nanopubs, as described in [19]. When a nanopub is updated, a new nanopub is minted or a versioning system based on the creation date is activated [21]. In the first case, the citation produced by the nanocitation system always refers to the initially cited nanopub; whereas, in the second case, the creation date of the nanopub stored in the citation metadata refers to the initially cited nanopub. In the latter case, we cannot rely on a dynamic citation system, and all citation metadata at creation time must be dumped and stored.

The completeness of the citation text snippet depends on the citation policy. Nevertheless, the citation metadata contains all the available information about the nanopub and related resources. Consequently, with adequate citation policies (i.e., selection and operations over the metadata fields) the text snippet can be correctly interpreted by the users.

What guarantees interoperability is the nanocitation system which returns a human-readable text snippet and a landing page as well as a machine-readable serialized version of the citation metadata. The metadata can be automatically processed by bibliometric systems to count citations or to calculate other relevant metrics.

As future work we intend to extend the citation framework and the citation system of nanopub aggregation with variable granularity and to provide a language to define citation policies.

**Acknowledgments.** The work was partially funded by the "Computational Data Citation" (CDC) STARS-StG project of the University of Padua. The work was also partially funded by the EXAMODE (contract n. 825292) part of the H2020-ICT-2018-2 call of the European Commission.

# References

1. Out of Cite, Out of Mind: The Current State of Practice, Policy, and Technology for the Citation of Data, vol. 12. CODATA-ICSTI Task Group on Data Citation Standards and Practices, September 2013
2. DataCite Metadata Schema Documentation for the Publication and Citation of Research Data, Version 4.0. Technical Report, DataCite Metadata Working Group (2016)
3. Alawini, A., Davidson, S.B., Silvello, G., Tannen, V., Wu, Y.: Data citation: a new provenance challenge. IEEE Data Eng. Bull. **41**(1), 27–38 (2018)
4. Altman, M., King, G.: A proposed standard for the scholarly citation of quantitative data. D-Lib Mag. **13**(3/4) (2007)
5. Borgman, C.L.: Big Data, Little Data, No Data. MIT Press, Cambridge (2015)
6. Buneman, P., Davidson, S.B., Frew, J.: Why data citation is a computational problem. Commun. ACM (CACM) **59**(9), 50–57 (2016)
7. Candela, L., Castelli, D., Manghi, P., Tani, A.: Data journals: a survey. J. Assoc. Inf. Sci. Technol. **66**(9), 1747–1762 (2015)
8. Carroll, J., Bizer, C., Hayes, P., Stickler, P.: Semantic web publishing using named graphs. In: Proceedings of the ISWC 2004 Workshop on Trust, Security, and Reputation on the Semantic Web. CEUR Workshop Proceedings, vol. 127. CEUR-WS.org (2004)
9. Davidson, S.B., Buneman, P., Deutch, D., Milo, T., Silvello, G.: Data citation: a computational challenge. In: Proceedings of the 36th ACM Symposium on Principles of Database Systems, PODS 2017, pp. 1–4. ACM Press (2017)
10. FORCE-11: Data Citation Synthesis Group: Joint Declaration of Data Citation Principles. FORCE11, San Diego, CA, USA (2014)
11. Gibson, A.P., van Dam, J.C.J., Schultes, E., Roos, M., Mons, B.: Towards computational evaluation of evidence for scientific assertions with nanopublications. In: Proceedings of the 5th International Workshop on Semantic Web Applications and Tools for Life Sciences (2012)

12. Golden, P., Shaw, R.: Period assertion as nanopublication: the PeriodO period gazetteer. In: Proceedings of the 24th International Conference on World Wide Web, WWW 2015 Companion, pp. 1013–1018. ACM Press (2015)
13. Green, T.: We need publishing standards for datasets and data tables. Technical report. OECD Publishing (2010)
14. Groth, P., Gibson, A., Velterop, J.: The anatomy of a nanopublication. Inf. Serv. Use **30**(1–2), 51–56 (2010)
15. Heath, T., Bizer, C.: Linked Data: Evolving the Web into a Global Data Space. Synthesis Lectures on the Semantic Web: Theory and Technology. Morgan & Claypool Publishers, San Rafael (2011)
16. Hey, T., Tansley, S., Tolle, K. (eds.): The Fourth Paradigm: Data-Intensive Scientific Discovery. Microsoft Research, Redmond (2009)
17. Klyne, G., Carroll, J.J.: Resource description framework (RDF): concepts and abstract syntax. Technical report W3C (2004)
18. Kuhn, T.: nanopub-java: a Java library for nanopublications. In: Proceedings of the 5th Workshop on Linked Science 2015 co-located with (ISWC 2015). CEUR Workshop Proceedings, vol. 1572, pp. 19–25. CEUR-WS.org (2015)
19. Kuhn, T., et al.: Decentralized provenance-aware publishing with nanopublications. PeerJ Comput. Sci. **2**, e78 (2016)
20. Kuhn, T., et al.: Nanopublications: a growing resource of provenance-centric scientific linked data. In: 14th IEEE International Conference on e-Science, pp. 83–92. IEEE Computer Society (2018)
21. Kuhn, T., Willighagen, E., Evelo, C., Queralt-Rosinach, N., Centeno, E., Furlong, L.I.: Reliable granular references to changing linked data. In: d'Amato, C., et al. (eds.) ISWC 2017. LNCS, vol. 10587, pp. 436–451. Springer, Cham (2017). https://doi.org/10.1007/978-3-319-68288-4_26
22. Mons, B., et al.: The value of data. Nat. Genetics **43**(4), 281–283 (2011)
23. Piñero, J., et al.: DisGeNET: a comprehensive platform integrating information on human disease-associated genes and variants. Nucleic Acids Res. **45**(D1), D833–D839 (2017)
24. Queralt-Rosinach, N., Piñero, J., Bravo, À., Sanz, F., Furlong, L.: DisGeNET-RDF: harnessing the innovative power of the semantic web to explore the genetic basis of diseases. Bioinformatics **32**(14), 2236–2238 (2016)
25. Rauber, A., Ari, A., van Uytvanck, D., Pröll, S.: Identification of reproducible subsets for data citation, sharing and re-use. Bull. IEEE Techn. Comm. Digit. Libr. Spec. Issue Data Cit. **12**(1), 6–15 (2016)
26. Silvello, G.: Learning to cite framework: how to automatically construct citations for hierarchical data. J. Assoc. Inf. Sci. Technol. (JASIST) **68**(6), 1505–1524 (2017)
27. Silvello, G.: Theory and practice of data citation. J. Assoc. Inf. Sci. Technol. (JASIST) **69**(1), 6–20 (2018)
28. Starr, J., Gastl, A.: isCitedBy: a metadata scheme for DataCite. D-Lib Mag. **17**(1/2) (2011)
29. Wu, Y., Alawini, A., Davidson, S.B., Silvello, G.: Data citation: giving credit where credit is due. In: Proceedings of the 2018 International Conference on Management of Data, SIGMOD Conference 2018, pp. 99–114. ACM Press (2018)

# Analysis of Transaction Logs from National Museums Liverpool

David Walsh[1,2]([✉]) [iD], Paul Clough[2,4] [iD], Mark M. Hall[3] [iD],
Frank Hopfgartner[2] [iD], Jonathan Foster[2] [iD], and Georgios Kontonatsios[1] [iD]

[1] Edge Hill University, Ormskirk, Lancashire, UK
walshd@edgehill.ac.uk
[2] University of Sheffield, Sheffield, UK
[3] Martin Luther University Halle-Wittenberg, Halle, Germany
[4] Peak Indicators, Chesterfield, UK

**Abstract.** The websites of Cultural Heritage institutions attract the
full range of users, from professionals to novices, for a variety of tasks.
However, many institutions are reporting high bounce rates and therefore
seeking ways to better engage users. The analysis of transaction logs can
provide insights into users' searching and navigational behaviours and
support engagement strategies. In this paper we present the results from
a transaction log analysis of web server logs representing user-system
interactions from the seven websites of National Museums Liverpool
(NML). In addition, we undertake an exploratory cluster analysis of users
to identify potential user groups that emerge from the data. We compare
this with previous studies of NML website users.

**Keywords:** Digital cultural heritage · Museum website · Users ·
Survey · Transaction log analysis · Cluster analysis

## 1 Introduction

The analysis of transaction logs provides insight into users' searching and browsing behaviours and is a common activity in the design and evaluation of search
and website interfaces [1,2]. Although there is extensive literature on transaction log analysis of user-system interaction logs, such as Online Public Access
Catalogues (OPAC's) [3,4], less attention has been given to digital cultural heritage websites, especially those containing a collection archive. However, with
high website bounce rates being reported by cultural heritage institutions [5,6],
there is clearly a need for deeper investigation to be undertaken.

An example of such a cultural heritage institution is the National Museums Liverpool (NML). The NML website[1] is a collection of seven separate sites
that cover a wide range of areas from art galleries to natural/world history,
maritime and slavery museums. Similar to previous studies of Digital Cultural

---

[1] http://www.liverpoolmuseums.org.uk/.

© Springer Nature Switzerland AG 2019
A. Doucet et al. (Eds.): TPDL 2019, LNCS 11799, pp. 84–98, 2019.
https://doi.org/10.1007/978-3-030-30760-8_7

Heritage (DCH) website usage [5, 7], data from NML transaction logs indicates that approximately 60% of users leave within ten seconds (i.e., a high bounce rate). In 2017, Walsh et al. [7] undertook a large-scale online survey of users visiting the NML website to better understand uses of the website from multiple perspectives. The study investigated characteristics of users with respect to atypical groups that visitors assigned themselves (e.g., student, professional, hobbyist, etc). In this work we continue to study the behaviours of NML website visitors utilising web server logs (weblogs) and transaction log analysis. NML forms an appropriate case study given their wide spread of heritage subject areas leading to a wide range of museum visitors in both physical and online spaces. To the best of our knowledge, this is the first in-depth study of web server logs from National Museums Liverpool. Insights into user groups gained from this study, especially given the multi-site nature of the NML website, may be equally applicable to other digital cultural heritage sites.

The remainder of this paper is structured as follows: Sect. 2 describes related work in categorising users of digital cultural heritage and transaction log analysis. Section 3 describes the study undertaken. Sections 4 and 5 present and discuss results of the transaction log analysis and presents results of the exploratory cluster analysis. Finally, Sect. 6 concludes the paper and offers directions for future work.

## 2    Related Work

### 2.1    Background of This Study

In previous research we identified distinct categories of online NML user based on visitor answers to a large-scale online user survey [6, 7]. We found that user groups could be distinguished by aspects, such as motivation, task, engagement, search strategy, domain knowledge and location. Results showed that the frequently understudied 'general public' and 'non-professional' groups made up the majority of users (approximately 77% of survey respondents). In this research we seek to further our understanding of NML visitor behaviours through the analysis of user-system interactions, where possible automatically deriving characteristics and categories of users. Whilst we are unable to extract log traces of survey respondents directly, we use transaction logs that cover the same time period as the survey was live, thereby offering complementary information. Analysing how people engage with websites and search systems can help identify what information people require, how they find it and potential findability issues [8]. For NML, understanding and identifying user groups will help support users' needs, such as developing personalised and adaptive user interfaces [9].

### 2.2    Cultural Heritage User Groups

Cultural heritage institutions have made significant efforts to understand visitors to its physical sites. Previous studies have used multiple methods and considered visitors from various perspectives, such as motivation [10]; engagement [11]; role adopted during the visit [12]; user expertise and profession [13,14]; information needs [15,16]; or the chances of wandering in [7]. Similar findings have emerged from studying online users of DCH websites. Clough et al. [17] studied the users of Europeana[2] via an online survey to better understand their search tasks. They devised a scheme for categorising users' search motives and further actions. Walsh et al. [7] conducted a survey on the NML website where existing user groups were identified with five distinguishing characteristics [6]: Motivation, Domain or CH Knowledge, Task, Location and Frequency of visit. The most common group was the "general user" or "general public." This contrasts with much of the prior work that has focused on more specific groups, such as museum professionals, academics, students, and hobbyists.

### 2.3  Transaction Log Analysis

Whenever users interact with online services their requests are logged in server logs (or weblogs), which can help to provide insights into users' search and navigation behaviours, such as the pages accessed, time spent on pages, and patterns of use [18] (e.g., sequential pages accessed [19] or search queries entered and reformulated [20]). Previous work on transaction log analysis typically relies on grouping requests into *sessions*: all concurrent requests from the same IP address and User-Agent, often within some cut-off period (e.g., 30 min). Jones et al. [1] undertook a manual analysis of a digital library log and were able to identify user demographics and the searches and search patterns the users adopted. Chen et al. [21] found a user session could be characterised, based on 47 variables from a library catalogue log, these were grouped into six clusters which characterised users' interactions (mostly reflecting domain knowledge and technical knowledge).

Wang et al. [22] identified clusters of "similar" users by partitioning a similarity graph (where nodes are users and edges are weighted by click stream similarity). The partitioning process leverages iterative feature pruning to capture the natural hierarchy within user clusters to visualise and understand user behaviours. An unsupervised learning method is used to build interaction behaviour models from click stream data. Zhang and Kamps [23] use search logs to identify searcher stereotypes of novice and expert users. By manually analysing user query terms, session lengths, session duration and repeat visits (i.e., frequency of visit), they were successfully able to establish that further groups discovered shared traits with that of the two groups. However, Stenmark [24] states that in order to capture the variety in behaviour known to exist amongst searchers, an automatic clustering technique (based on self-organising maps and search log data) is required. Overall, they identified six clusters and condensed them into three groups: casual seekers (fact seekers - intranet users looking for quickly retrieved answers); a more holistic group (longer sessions

---

[2] https://www.europeana.eu/portal/en.

and more reading time); and information-seeking-savvy employees who formulate longer queries and browse through more documents than other groups.

## 3   Methodology

In this study three months of weblogs from NML (Sect. 3.1) are analysed. Although Google Analytics provides similar data, for deeper analysis web server logs are needed. To identify potential users groups, cluster analysis is used on features derived from the server logs (Sect. 3.2). Relationship between the user-system interactions and the groups is also investigated. Clustering is performed on a re-structured version of the logs where each row represents users and features that capture interactions averaged across user sessions.

### 3.1   Analysing the Logs

Initially logs were gathered from the Microsoft IIS web server hosting the NML sites. All interactions are logged, including those from 'real' users and those from robots (also known as crawlers or spiders). IIS logs can store referrer details, but this feature has not been enabled for the NML website. The format of logs is standard IIS format:

> *Example log entry*: 2015-07-08 00:00:00 172.17.101.21 GET
> /onlineshop/graphics/product/thumbnails/sewing-box-new-thumb.jpg - 80 - 66.249.64.146
> Googlebot-Image/1.0 304 0 0 15

The logs were prepared by extracting entries for the period of the user survey $+/-1$ month (1 Jan - 30 Mar 2017). Using logs for this period allows comparisons between the survey findings and the log analysis to be made. Next, bots, crawlers and developer validation tools (e.g. link checkers etc) were removed using existing seed lists. The location (country, county and city levels) of requests was identified based on the IP address and using the IP2location library[3]. The next stage was *sessionisation* - segmenting entries into user sessions based on IP address, User-Agent and a 30 min time cut-off, which ensured the full activity for the session was captured (as outlined in [25]). With entries grouped into sessions log data were fully anonymised - all potential user identifying data (e.g., names, emails, credit card numbers, etc.) were removed, IP addresses randomly hashed. Next, data were cleaned: entries without a 200 HTTP status code (successfully displayed pages) were removed; entries that were not GET requests removed; and requests for background files (e.g., images; CSS, JavaScript, font and Adobe Flash files; XML data and linked PDF files) removed. Finally, sessions were grouped by user based on IP address and User-Agent.

---

[3] https://lite.ip2location.com/ip-address-ranges-by-country.

## 3.2   Clustering the Logs

Previous studies have clustered user sessions [18,26]; however, in this paper we wanted to establish if potential user groups could be identified from the logs. Therefore, we focus on clustering *users*. To enable this all sessions containing the same IP address and User-Agent were grouped together and features derived from the logs were used to infer user groups (see Table 1). K-means clustering was applied using the features that are likely to distinguish user groups[4].

**Table 1.** Mapping user group characteristics to log data

| User group characteristic | Log data |
| --- | --- |
| Motivation | Starting level page |
| Domain/CH knowledge | Page type and queries |
| Task | Page type and possibly queries |
| Location | IP (reversed) identifying country, region and city |
| Frequency of visits | Repeat visits (sessions), queries, length of session |

Features used to characterise users were based on the findings of prior work [6,7] and can be divided into 3 main categories: *Locational* (country, region and city); *Behavioural* (#sessions; total page requests; #page requests for museum overview, collection overview, item, event, shop and general information page; #museums accessed; average interactions/session); and *Knowledge* (total queries; average queries/session). We also experimented with clustering using the location and session count columns; however, results for both features in all clusters did not result in clear clusters.

As previously mentioned, cluster analysis was used to derive user groupings from the data rather than relying on pre-defined groups. The commonly used k-means algorithm, well-suited to numeric data, was used. Prior to clustering variable values were scaled and to choose the appropriate number of clusters $k$, the elbow method was used [27]. This identified the suitable number of clusters between 6 and 8. To ensure the number of clusters was valid and stable we repeatedly ran the cluster analysis with different values of $k$ (between 5–9), with $k = 7$ producing the most stable results.

## 4   Findings

### 4.1   Website Interactions

Server logs for this study comprised 586,868 rows, each representing a page request. After pre-processing and sessionisation (Sect. 3), the data reduced to

---

[4] Alternative algorithms such as k-modes (k-prototypes) and DBScan were also tested, but no stable clusters emerged.

321,174 rows representing user sessions. Page requests come from 213 different countries[5], with February being the most accessed month across all sites. This aligned to the time period our online survey was running (see Fig. 1). Tuesday and Wednesday are the most frequently accessed days with least usage at the weekends (see Table 2). The increased access that can be seen in Fig. 1 during February relates to collections that are ending and new ones being announced. This period is also the local school holidays and could explain the increase in accesses for the general information pages.

**Table 2.** Visits per day (Jan-Mar 2017)

| Day | Mon | Tue | Wed | Thur | Fri | Sat | Sun | Total |
|---|---|---|---|---|---|---|---|---|
| Requests | 81,450 | 100,325 | 101,314 | 97,311 | 85,603 | 54,967 | 65,898 | 586,868 |
| Percentage | 13.88% | 17.09% | 17.26% | 16.58% | 14.59% | 9.37% | 11.23% | 100% |

**Table 3.** Requests by Museum

| Museum | Requests |
|---|---|
| ISM | 97,686 |
| Other pages | 92,433 |
| WML | 86,516 |
| Walker | 73,194 |
| Maritime | 68,912 |
| Events | 58,273 |
| MOL | 54,697 |
| Ladylever | 24,607 |
| Shop | 21,740 |
| Sudley | 8,810 |
| Total | **586,868** |

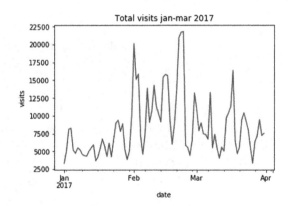

**Fig. 1.** Total visits (Jan-Mar 2017)

### 4.2   Museum and Gallery Access

The International Slavery Museum (ISM) is the most accessed site of the NML website with 97,686 requests. This is followed by the World Museum Liverpool, Walker art gallery, Maritime Museum, Museum of Liverpool, Ladylever art gallery and lastly Sudley House. The overall request breakdown between the main sections of the website can be seen in Table 3.

---

[5] Based on the **IP2Location** IP4 allocated IP address ranges; however, it is noted that the United Nations only identifies 195.

## 4.3   Page-Level Access

Throughout the NML website(s), there are 8 main types of pages: **General** pages (G), which include the highest level NML home page, about page, visit pages, floor plans, policy pages and contact pages etc; the individual **Museum/gallery** home pages and the general overview pages (M); the **Collection overview** pages (C), which introduce the collections the museum is displaying on the site; the **Item** pages (I), which contain item/artefact detail pages for collections; the **Archive** pages (A) for the maritime museum only, separate to the collections but act as a more traditional archive of artefacts; the **Events** (E) pages, including 'Whats-on' pages regarding attractions visitors can view/book; the **Kids** (K) pages, which is a dedicated children's area; and **Undefined** pages: pages that do not fit other categories or occasional pages in new sections, such as Christmas e-cards or 'picture-of-the-month'. The general pages are the most requested (31%), followed by the item pages (24%) - see Table 4. The most frequent (requested) page is the NML homepage (/) with 44,247 requests, followed by the world museum home page (/wml/) with 27,015 requests. The next is (/wml/collections/zoology/herptile/item.aspx) with 23,788 requests.

**Table 4.** Page type usage

| Page type | Count | Percentage |
|---|---|---|
| General | 182,185 | 31% |
| Item | 139,163 | 24% |
| Event | 58,273 | 10% |
| Museum overview | 56,675 | 10% |
| Collection overview | 40,573 | 7% |
| Undefined | 40,546 | 7% |
| Kid | 36,694 | 6% |
| Shop | 21,740 | 4% |
| Archive | 11,019 | 2% |

With the page types extracted from the `cs-uri-stem` (uristem) we see that the UK provides the most visitors to the website (see Table 5). We also note that the top two page types are the general pages and the item pages. Surprisingly, the events pages are third (and less surprising is the shop, which is the lowest accessed page type). When exploring only the UK page requests, the general pages are still the most requested with the events a close second. The events pages seem to be high for a number of the more local areas to Liverpool. This might be an indication of a possible physical visit. For those areas outside of the Northwest UK the pattern of requests focuses more on the general pages and the item pages (see Table 6).

Findings also show that single page visits occur when users leave the site, without exploring more than the initial page. There are 586,868 total requests over the 3 months with 238,061 (40.56%) of the requests for single page accesses (a breakdown of this can be seen in Table 7). The country with least accesses is Denmark (2.75%); the highest Brazil (70.73%). Looking at the UK's single page request, which is the largest proportion of requests, the majority of requests are from areas within the locality of physical museums in Liverpool (see Table 8).

**Table 5.** Page types by country

| Countries | G | M | C | I | S | E | Requests | Queries |
|---|---|---|---|---|---|---|---|---|
| United Kingdom | **45,242** | 35,799 | 16,972 | 38,500 | 9,235 | 43,245 | 307,347 | 181,903 |
| United States | 12,658 | 6,033 | 3,768 | **14,153** | 6,132 | 2,768 | 120,584 | 43,062 |
| Denmark | 2,279 | 491 | 546 | **17636** | 3,111 | 599 | 32,012 | 9,098 |
| Germany | **5,158** | 833 | 934 | 3,036 | 291 | 488 | 16,878 | 7,846 |
| Australia | **731** | 250 | 171 | 507 | 86 | 48 | 15,805 | 4,012 |
| Ireland | 1,177 | 447 | 620 | 1,384 | 557 | **7,018** | 15,306 | 5,527 |
| France | **2,484** | 961 | 447 | 1,802 | 454 | 732 | 11,671 | 5,630 |
| Canada | **979** | 256 | 190 | 896 | 417 | 168 | 6,418 | 3,592 |
| ... | ... | ... | ... | ... | ... | ... | ... | ... |
| Grand total | **84,133** | 49,849 | 25,974 | **87,712** | 21,740 | 58,273 | 586,868 | 297,492 |

**Table 6.** Page types by UK city

| UK City/Town | G | M | C | I | S | E | Requests | Queries |
|---|---|---|---|---|---|---|---|---|
| Manchester | 5,157 | 4,661 | 2,405 | **5,590** | 1,375 | **5,899** | 40,992 | 20,696 |
| Liverpool | **7,304** | 4,146 | 2,173 | 4,278 | 1,242 | **7,383** | 37,804 | 23,014 |
| London | **3,656** | 2,784 | 1,304 | **3,557** | 778 | 2,600 | 26,513 | 14,798 |
| Runcorn | 1,398 | 1,220 | 698 | 1,200 | 275 | **1,994** | 10,070 | 6,468 |
| Sheffield | **973** | **838** | 324 | **889** | 207 | 738 | 7,151 | 4,473 |
| Birmingham | **1,014** | **908** | 302 | 804 | 198 | 831 | 7,148 | 4,132 |
| Warrington | **940** | **905** | 364 | 616 | 193 | 844 | 6,114 | 3,974 |
| Chesterfield | **1,043** | **852** | 294 | 634 | 137 | 681 | 5,097 | 2,743 |
| ... | ... | ... | ... | ... | ... | ... | ... | ... |
| Grand total | **45,242** | 35,799 | 16,972 | 38,500 | 9,235 | **43,245** | 307,347 | 181,903 |

**Table 7.** Single page sessions

| Country | Single sessions | Total requests | Percentage |
|---------|----------------|----------------|------------|
| United Kingdom | 130,017 | 307,347 | 42.30% |
| United States | 50,493 | 120,584 | 41.87% |
| Germany | 11,133 | 16,878 | **65.96%** |
| Australia | 5,174 | 15,805 | 32.74% |
| France | 4,086 | 11,671 | 35.00% |
| Canada | 2,874 | 6,418 | 44.78% |
| Ireland | 2,623 | 15,306 | 17.14% |
| Italy | 2,049 | 5,822 | 35.19% |
| ... | ... | ... | ... |

**Table 8.** Single page session by UK city

| UK City/Town | G | M | C | I | S | E | Total | Queries |
|--------------|------|------|------|------|------|------|--------|---------|
| Liverpool | 1,714 | 1,257 | 936 | 1,452 | 222 | **1,951** | 7,532 | 11,934 |
| Manchester | **1,491** | 1,242 | 798 | 1,381 | 164 | 1,279 | 6,355 | 10,566 |
| London | 1,287 | 868 | 512 | **1,271** | 158 | 638 | 4,734 | 8,300 |
| Runcorn | 479 | 381 | 342 | 434 | 54 | 570 | 2,260 | 3,584 |
| Warrington | 388 | 303 | 160 | 283 | 45 | 237 | 1,416 | 2,367 |
| Sheffield | 367 | 280 | 147 | 370 | 42 | 232 | 1,438 | 2,658 |
| Birmingham | 358 | 277 | 118 | 289 | 40 | 204 | 1,286 | 2,255 |
| Chesterfield | 257 | 198 | 100 | 163 | 34 | 193 | 945 | 1,407 |
| ... | ... | ... | ... | ... | ... | ... | ... | ... |
| Grand total | **14,915** | 11,092 | 7,020 | 13,562 | 1,782 | 10,998 | 59,369 | 99,398 |

### 4.4   Sessions

A total of 321,174 sessions were identified when the 30 min cut-off time limit was applied (265,776 sessions without applying the cut-off). Looking at sessions comprising single pages, we see general pages (G) are accessed the most (see Table 8). These are closely followed by item pages (I). In the case of NML item level pages, bounces are likely cases when the visitor has obtained the information needed or desired. Also the item level pages do not promote other items; rather highlight the collection that the item belongs (but the links are not obvious).

**Session Entry Pages:** Understanding users' entry points can offer insights regarding how a site is used, as well as the level of knowledge being sought. The logs show that the NML group homepage (G) and the item pages (I) are the most initially requested pages. This is followed by the museum homepages, the collection overview pages, the event pages and then the kids area pages, the shop and only a small number for the archive pages (see Table 9).

**Session Exit Pages:** Just as interesting, and potentially as informative as entry pages, are the exit pages. The closeness of the entry and exit results clearly highlight the amount of single page sessions (see Table 9). There is an indication of some movement around the site from the Museum overview pages and some of the undefined pages to all other page types, from which they then leave.

**Length of Session:** Results show that 246,643 sessions ended within 10 s, only 7,637 of these sessions ended within 10 s after visiting more than one page - a 43% drop-out within the 10 s period. Google Analytics reports a 52.6% bounce rate for the same period. The drop-out rates over time clearly identify that there are very few users during this three month period who spend significant time on the site (see Table 10).

## 5   Discussion

The results clearly show that the majority of pages accessed by users fall under the categories of general and item (see Table 4). This aligns with the findings identified in [6] for understanding users' purposes for using the website, which showed that the major reason for visiting by the general public and non-professional users was to prepare for a visit.

The high number of single page sessions (see Tables 7 and 8) may indicate that users are being provided with the correct information to meet their needs (e.g., finding a known-item). These numbers also align with [6], where the majority of users (especially the general public and non-professional users) were visiting for the first time. Linking to the number of sessions that end within 10 s (Table 10) and little movement around the site indicated by session entry and exit pages (Table 9) highlights limited engagement with the site(s).

**Table 9.** Session entry and exit pages

| Page type | Entry | Exit |
|---|---|---|
| General | 110,322 | 114,884 |
| Item | 62,576 | 65,922 |
| Museum overview | 37,698 | 28,432 |
| Undefined | 29,478 | 28,840 |
| Collection overview | 26,322 | 26,418 |
| Event | 25,856 | 26,647 |
| Kids | 14,125 | 14,087 |
| Shop | 7,950 | 8,983 |
| Archive | 6,847 | 6,961 |

**Table 10.** Session drop-out rates

| Length | Count | Percentage |
|---|---|---|
| <10 s | 246,643 | 76.8% |
| <20 s | 252,239 | 78.5% |
| <30 s | 256,571 | 79.9% |
| <1 min | 265,991 | 82.8% |
| 30 min | 321,174 | 100% |

The rareness of search results (only 7,121 from 586,868 requests) also aligns with the [6] study where the survey identified that the use of navigational links was the preferred method of access by the majority of users (general public and non-professionals). A 2015 survey conducted by NML also indicated that only a small fraction of visitors were museum professionals or academics. Taking into consideration their higher CH and domain knowledge levels this could indicate that the searchers of known-items or collections are from these user groups.

The NML websites are being accessed from all over the world (Table 5). When IP addresses are reversed we see the largest number of visits are from the UK (52.3%). Whilst this is not as high as the survey results from [6] indicate (75%), it is still the largest proportion of requests. The bulk (12.7%) of these UK users are local to the Liverpool area (Table 6) and thus are within in a reasonable distance to physically visit the museums/galleries. This also aligns with findings of [6]: location is a good indicator of user group. In our case the high number of local users could indicate general public (pre-visit) users.

### 5.1 Clustering Results

The logs provide a data set of 225,796 total users, which reduces to 225,730 when reducing the noise in the clusters by removing rows with over 100 in the columns of Museum overview pages (M), Collection overview pages (C), artefact Item pages (I), Event pages (E), Shop pages (S), General information pages (G), and queries.

**Table 11.** Cluster results with assigned labels

| Cluster | # Users | M | C | I | E | S | G | Queries | Label |
|---|---|---|---|---|---|---|---|---|---|
| 1 | 172,692 (76.6%) | 0.17 | 0.09 | 0.21 | 0.15 | 0.04 | 0.00 | 1.07 | Single page viewers |
| 2 | 46 (0.02%) | 2.02 | 4.33 | 31.48 | 9.91 | 26.85 | 11.04 | 56.91 | High all round searchers |
| 3 | 4,162 (2.1%) | 0.80 | 0.30 | 0.34 | 3.77 | 0.15 | 0.57 | 3.39 | Event visitors |
| 4 | 45,282 (20%) | 0.20 | 0.05 | 0.07 | 0.08 | 0.02 | 1.29 | 1.15 | Single query general page visitors |
| 5 | 292 (0.1%) | 1.10 | 3.48 | 23.35 | 4.73 | 7.48 | 5.90 | 21.84 | Deep level browsers |
| 6 | 290 (0.1%) | 4.96 | 1.69 | 2.02 | 1.68 | 0.76 | 17.58 | 3.78 | General museum visitors |
| 7 | 2,966 (0.8%) | 0.42 | 0.63 | 4.57 | 0.37 | 1.11 | 0.74 | 5.25 | Known-item searchers |

## 5.2   Describing the Clusters

As discussed previously 7 groups of users were identified from the cluster analysis and assigned labels, based on their characteristics (see Table 11):

**Cluster 1:** The cluster labelled "Single page viewers" is by far the largest grouping (76.6%). This cluster is comprised of users who look at only one page and then leave. The pages are at various levels (general to detailed item pages) and on average the users issue 1–2 queries.

**Cluster 2:** The smallest cluster (0.02%) we label as "High all round searchers" as they view high numbers of all level pages and also issue many queries. Hobbyists have been identified as undertaking research for personal reasons, but are very knowledgeable in their particular areas of interest and as such are able to use search successfully. They are also interested in both the overview as well as the deeper item level pages [28–30].

**Cluster 3:** This cluster (2.1% of users) are labelled as "Event visitors" and reflect users who predominantly visit event pages and tend to query for them.

**Cluster 4:** The second biggest cluster (20%) of users has been labelled as "Single query general page visitors" with the pages mostly being viewed being general and museum overview pages. This aligns with Booth's [15] findings of the general user - someone seeking general information about opening hours, prices, facilities, etc.

**Cluster 5:** This cluster (0.1% of users) we label as "Deep level browsers" as they commonly use queries, view many item level pages, but very few general or museum overview pages. Similarities can be drawn with Vilar et al. [13] who define professional users (museum staff) as those who have good knowledge of the task, are trained in the systems and have deep understanding of the context.

**Cluster 6:** This cluster (0.1% of users) is labelled as "General museum visitors" who mostly view general and museum overview pages, with the occasional "deep dive". This aligns with Booth's [15] general user.

**Cluster 7:** This cluster (0.8% of users) we label as "Known item searchers" who view only item level pages and query frequently. This behaviour may arise as the majority of item level pages in the NML site(s) can only be accessed by the search feature. This behaviour aligns with Marchionini et al.'s [16] professional user (including academics) who are described as being highly motivated, having high domain knowledge, system knowledge, time available and focus.

The differences in cluster profiles can be clearly seen from the example polar/spider charts shown in Fig. 2. The differences in the shapes and the scales are some of the most striking differences.

Some of the clusters produced as part of this study show some potential as being candidates for mapping to the known user groups. The potential candidates are shown in Table 12.

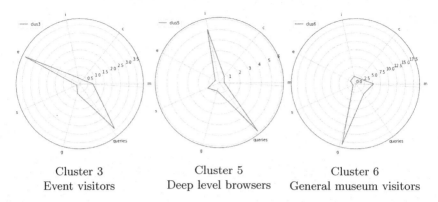

Cluster 3
Event visitors

Cluster 5
Deep level browsers

Cluster 6
General museum visitors

**Fig. 2.** Example user cluster sub-figures

**Table 12.** Clusters mapped to potential user groups

| Cluster | # Users | Label | Potential user group |
|---|---|---|---|
| 1 | 172,692 | Single page viewers | Currently un-documented user-group called "Bouncers" |
| 2 | 46 | High all round searchers | Non-professionals (hobbyists) |
| 3 | 4,162 | Event visitors | Teachers/General Public |
| 4 | 45,282 | Single query general page visitors | General public (Pre-visit)/Teachers |
| 5 | 292 | Deep level browsers | Museum Staff |
| 6 | 290 | General museum visitors | General public/Students |
| 7 | 2,966 | Known item searchers | Academics (experts)/Non-professionals |

## 6    Conclusions and Future Work

In this paper we have extended prior work on studying users of the National Museums Liverpool (NML) websites through the use of transaction log analysis on web server logs. The analysis has identified a number of documented activities in the server logs that align with known user group activities and behaviours. Using only the types of pages visited as features for cluster analysis the resulting groups are similar to user categories previously discovered in the literature and previous studies of NML users based on user surveys. In future work we plan to further analysis the session data and cluster the logs using additional features of user-system interaction and user characteristics.

**Acknowledgements.** We would like to thank National Museums Liverpool for providing access to the web server transaction logs.

# References

1  Jones, S., Cunningham, S.J., McNab, R., Boddie, S.: A transaction log analysis of a digital library. Int. J. Digit. Libr. **3**(2), 152–169 (2000)
2  McKay, D., Buchanan, G., Chang, S.: It ain't what you do, it's the way that you do it: design guidelines to better support online browsing. Proc. Assoc. Inf. Sci. Technol. **55**(1), 347–356 (2018)
3  Peters, T.A.: The history and development of transaction log analysis. Library Hi Tech **11**(2), 41–66 (1993)
4  Jansen, B.J., Spink, A., Saracevic, T.: Real life, real users, and real needs: a study and analysis of user queries on the web. Inf. Process. Manag. **36**(2), 207–227 (2000)
5  Ciber: Europeana 2012–2013: usage and performance update. Technical report, CIBER Research, July 2013
6  Walsh, D., Hall, M.M., Clough, P., Foster, J.: Characterising online museum users: a study of the National Museums Liverpool museum website. Int. J. Digit. Libr. (2018). https://doi.org/10.1007/s00799-018-0248-8
7  Walsh, D., Hall, M., Clough, P., Foster, J.: The ghost in the museum website: investigating the general public's interactions with museum websites. In: Kamps, J., Tsakonas, G., Manolopoulos, Y., Iliadis, L., Karydis, I. (eds.) TPDL 2017. LNCS, vol. 10450, pp. 434–445. Springer, Cham (2017). https://doi.org/10.1007/978-3-319-67008-9_34
8  Farrell, S.: Search-log analysis: the most overlooked opportunity in web UX research, July 2017. https://www.nngroup.com/articles/search-log-analysis/. Accessed 14 Mar 2019
9  Eirinaki, M., Vazirgiannis, M.: Web mining for web personalization. ACM Trans. Internet Technol. (TOIT) **3**(1), 1–27 (2003)
10  Falk, J.H.: Identity and the Museum Visitor Experience. Left Coast Press, Walnut Creek (2009)
11  Templeton, C.A.: Museum visitor engagement through resonant, rich and interactive experiences (2011)
12  Spellerberg, M., Granata, E., Wambold, S.: Visitor-first, mobile-first: designing a visitor-centric mobile experience. In: Museums and the Web (2016)
13  Vilar, P., Šauperl, A.: Archival literacy: different users, different information needs, behaviour and skills. In: Kurbanoğlu, S., Špiranec, S., Grassian, E., Mizrachi, D., Catts, R. (eds.) ECIL 2014. CCIS, vol. 492, pp. 149–159. Springer, Cham (2014). https://doi.org/10.1007/978-3-319-14136-7_16
14  Pantano, E.: Virtual cultural heritage consumption: a 3D learning experience. Int. J. Technol. Enhanc. Learn. **3**(5), 482–495 (2011)
15  Booth, B.: Understanding the information needs of visitors to museums. Mus. Manag. Curatorship **17**(2), 139–157 (1998)
16  Marchionini, G., Plaisant, C., Komlodi, A.: The people in digital libraries: multifaceted approaches to assessing needs and impact. In: Social Practice in Design and Evaluation, Digital Library Use, pp. 119–160 (2003)

17 Clough, P., Hill, T., Paramita, M.L., Goodale, P.: Europeana: what users search for and why. In: Kamps, J., Tsakonas, G., Manolopoulos, Y., Iliadis, L., Karydis, I. (eds.) TPDL 2017. LNCS, vol. 10450, pp. 207–219. Springer, Cham (2017). https://doi.org/10.1007/978-3-319-67008-9_17

18 Russell-Rose, T., Clough, P.: Mining search logs for usage patterns. In: Text Mining and Visualization: Case Studies using Open-Source Tools, vol. 40 (2016)

19 Kachhadiya, B.C., Patel, B.: A survey on sequential pattern mining algorithm for web log pattern data. In: 2018 2nd International Conference on Trends in Electronics and Informatics (ICOEI), pp. 1269–1273. IEEE (2018)

20 Lau, T., Horvitz, E.: Patterns of search: analyzing and modeling web query refinement. In: Kay, J. (ed.) UM99 User Modeling. CICMS, vol. 407, pp. 119–128. Springer, Vienna (1999). https://doi.org/10.1007/978-3-7091-2490-1_12

21 Chen, H.M., Cooper, M.D.: Using clustering techniques to detect usage patterns in a web-based information system. J. Am. Soc. Inf. Sci. Technol. **52**(11), 888–904 (2001)

22 Wang, G., Zhang, X., Tang, S., Zheng, H., Zhao, B.Y.: Unsupervised clickstream clustering for user behavior analysis. In: Proceedings of the 2016 CHI Conference on Human Factors in Computing Systems, pp. 225–236. ACM (2016)

23 Zhang, J., Kamps, J.: Search log analysis of user stereotypes, information seeking behavior, and contextual evaluation. In: Proceedings of the Third Symposium on Information Interaction in Context, pp. 245–254. ACM (2010)

24 Stenmark, D.: Identifying clusters of user behavior in intranet search engine log files. J. Am. Soc. Inf. Sci. Technol. **59**(14), 2232–2243 (2008)

25 He, D., Göker, A.: Detecting session boundaries from web user logs. In: Proceedings of the BCS-IRSG 22nd Annual Colloquium on Information Retrieval Research, pp. 57–66 (2000)

26 Bogaard, T., Hollink, L., Wielemaker, J., Hardman, L., van Ossenbruggen, J.: Searching for old news: user interests and behavior within a national collection. In: Proceedings of the 2019 Conference on Human Information Interaction and Retrieval, pp. 113–121. ACM (2019)

27 Bholowalia, P., Kumar, A.: EBK-means: a clustering technique based on elbow method and k-means in wsn. Int. J. Comput. Appl. **105**(9), 17–24 (2014)

28 Skov, M., Ingwersen, P.: Exploring information seeking behaviour in a digital museum context. In: Proceedings of the Second International Symposium on Information Interaction in Context, IIiX 2008, pp. 110–115. ACM, New York (2008)

29 Skov, M.: The reinvented museum: exploring information seeking behaviour in a digital museum context. Ph.D. thesis, Københavns Universitet'Københavns Universitet', Faculty of Humanities, School of Library and Information Science, Royal School of Library and Information Science (2009, unpublished thesis)

30 Elsweiler, D., Wilson, M.L., Lunn, B.K.: Chapter 9 understanding casual-leisure information behaviour. In: New Directions in Information Behaviour. Library and Information Science, vol. 1, pp. 211–241. Emerald Group Publishing Limited (2011)

# Knowledge Graph Implementation of Archival Descriptions Through CIDOC-CRM

Inês Koch[iD], Nuno Freitas[✉][iD], Cristina Ribeiro[iD], Carla Teixeira Lopes[iD], and João Rocha da Silva[iD]

INESC-TEC, Faculty of Engineering, University of Porto, Porto, Portugal
up201403153@letras.up.pt, up201404739@fe.up.pt, mcr@fe.up.pt, ctl@fe.up.pt, joaorosilva@gmail.com

**Abstract.** Archives have well-established description standards, namely the ISAD(G) and ISAAR(CPF) with a hierarchical structure adapted to the nature of archival assets. However, as archives connect to a growing diversity of data, they aim to make their representations more apt to the so-called linked data cloud. The corresponding move from hierarchical, ISAD-conforming descriptions to graph counterparts requires state-of-the-art technologies, data models and vocabularies. Our approach addresses this problem from two perspectives. The first concerns the data model and description vocabularies, as we adopt and build upon the CIDOC-CRM standard. The second is the choice of technologies to support a knowledge graph, including a graph database and an Object Graph Mapping library. The case study is the Portuguese National Archives, Torre do Tombo, and the overall goal is to build a CIDOC-CRM-compliant system for document description and retrieval, to be used by professionals and the public. The early stages described here include the design of the core data model for archival records represented as the ArchOnto ontology and its embodiment in the ArchGraph knowledge graph. The goal of a semantic archival information system will be pursued in the migration of existing records to the richer representation and the development of applications supported on the graph.

**Keywords:** Archival description · CIDOC-CRM ·
Torre do Tombo National Archives · Knowledge graph

## 1 Introduction

The Portuguese National Archives, Torre do Tombo (ANTT) hold a vast collection of unique cultural objects and provide diverse services to the community, from support to scientific research to the access to legal documents. Given the huge effort invested in the creation of millions of document records, it is essential

This work is financed by National Funds through the Portuguese funding agency, FCT—Fundação para a Ciência e a Tecnologia within project DSAIPA/DS/0023/2018.

© Springer Nature Switzerland AG 2019
A. Doucet et al. (Eds.): TPDL 2019, LNCS 11799, pp. 99–106, 2019.
https://doi.org/10.1007/978-3-030-30760-8_8

to keep them in representations that are interoperable both within archives and across other knowledge sources. The archives are therefore exploring alternative representations to the traditional hierarchical standards [1].

This work is running as part of the EPISA project[1] (Entity and Property Inference for Semantic Archives). The project will define a new data model for the archives and a prototype knowledge graph to support applications for professionals and for the public. The model and the knowledge graph will be tested on a selection of archival records. To populate the graph, the contents of the records will be explored with automatic methods to extract entities and their relationships, enriching the graph with information in the existing records. The prototype knowledge graph and corresponding user interfaces will support the development of a new archival information system, for which the identification of requirements is also ongoing.

We describe our approach to move from hierarchical, ISAD-conforming descriptions to their graph counterparts. The problem is addressed from two perspectives. The first concerns the data model and description vocabularies and the second relates to the construction of an information system based on a knowledge graph.

## 2    Description Models for Cultural Heritage

To build a new data model for the archives it is essential to analyze the archival description standards in use at the ANTT and also to go into the details of CIDOC-CRM, selected as the foundation for the new model. It is also important to look at cases in which the CIDOC-CRM has been applied, to take into account their experience.

ISAD(G)—General International Standard Archival Description—provides general guidance on the preparation of archival descriptions and is the basis for the existing records [5]. The standard is based on uniform, multi-level description, and assumes the inheritance of descriptor content down the hierarchy. This provides contextual information for items even in case it is infeasible to describe them individually. Although appropriate for archives, ISAD(G) is based on archival concepts and does not favour relations to data from other sources.

The CIDOC-CRM [4] is being developed by the International Committee for Documentation (CIDOC) of the International Council of Museums (ICOM) to provide the museum community with good practice and technologies for documentation. The model is based on events and has at its core Temporal Entities, i.e., things that happened in a specific period of time. Only Temporal Entities can be linked to time and have Time Spans. On the other hand, the Objects (Conceptual Object and Physical Thing), Actors/People and Places, rather than being linked to time, are linked via an event—a Temporal Entity. A Place is a physical location, and it can be geographically referenced [6].

The CIDOC-CRM originated in museums and we can find applications mainly in this domain. The Museo del Prado, in Madrid, is an example of a

---

[1] http://episa.inesctec.pt/.

museum using the ontology in its Knowledge Graph[2]. The main entities of the Prado semantic network (Artwork, Author, Exhibition and Activity) are represented according to the CIDOC-CRM standard. For other kinds of entities not available on the CIDOC-CRM their model adopted concepts from FRBR (Functional Requirements for Bibliographic Records) and other vocabularies widely used in semantic web projects. The British Museum also uses the CIDOC-CRM, asserting that they were the first arts organization in the UK to publish their collection semantically[3].

The CIDOC-CRM has also been applied outside the museum environment, namely to represent archival metadata. These experiments were based on the EAD (Encoded Archival Description) representation of ISAD, taking into account the concepts of archival records and their components, as well as the main concepts of the archival description, namely the hierarchical structure and the inheritance of information down the hierarchy of the levels of description [2].

# 3   The CIDOC-CRM Ontology in Archives

The design of a flexible data model for the archives led to the analysis of the CIDOC-CRM, version 6.2[4]. This has shown that the CIDOC-CRM is powerful, and specific enough for the description of cultural objects in museums, but obviously lacks concepts that are present in the existing archival models and may not be discarded.

Building on the existing representations for the CIDOC-CRM, our model is represented as an ontology and follows the entities and properties of the CIDOC-CRM where applicable. The first challenge with this ontology is its detail and wide scope. The CIDOC-CRM defines a large number of classes and properties that required an in-depth analysis with the help of the existing documentation. Given that we intend to design a model for archives, we used a sample of 14 archival records, from two different sources, DigitArq (the DGLAB record database)[5] and the Guidelines for Archival Description (ODA) [3]. This allowed us to perform a first selection of the classes and properties based on features from actual records.

The second challenge was that most of the available properties are Object Properties, which relate individuals. Given that archive records include many literal fields with specific semantics, using only the available Data Properties proved insufficient to keep the semantics of the base content of archival records, that only requires basic datatypes, without creating artificial objects just to capture those values.

The CIDOC-CRM only defines eight Data Properties (namely P3 has note, P57 has number of parts, P79 beginning is qualified by, P80 end is qualified by, P81 ongoing throughout, P82 at some time within, P90

---

[2] https://www.museodelprado.es/modelo-semantico-digital/modelo-ontologico.
[3] https://www.britishmuseum.org/.
[4] http://new.cidoc-crm.org/Version/version-6.2.
[5] https://digitarq.arquivos.pt/.

has value and P168 place is identified by), so the ontology needs to be complemented to represent the semantics of the descriptors used in our archival records.

We therefore added several sub-properties to property P3 has note, to allow that distinction while retaining interoperability with CIDOC-CRM. Using the properties in Table 1, we keep the semantics associated to the existing descriptions in archival objects, while taking advantage of the CIDOC-CRM entity where they can aggregate. In our extension of CIDOC-CRM, named ArchOnto, new properties have prefix "ARP" and new entities prefix "ARE".

**Table 1.** ISAD(G) to CIDOC-CRM and extensions

| ISAD(G) | CIDOC-CRM | CIDOC-CRM extension |
| --- | --- | --- |
| Administrative/biographical history | P3 has note | ARP1 has administrative history |
| Archival history | P3 has note | ARP2 has archival history |
| Scope and content | P3 has note | ARP3 has scope |
| Conditions governing access | P3 has note | ARP4 has access conditions |

In addition to these Data Properties, new Object Properties were also introduced. They capture the hierarchy of levels of description in ISAD(G). Table 2 shows the two properties used to represent the relations between levels of description. The properties are the inverse of each other, and their instances capture the relations between levels. For example, a Fonds is the top of the hierarchy and can relate to a Sub-fonds via ARP9 lower level, but not to a upper level. Similarly, a document can have a Series as an upper level, or a Process.

**Table 2.** ISAD(G) to CIDOC-CRM - new object properties

| Description | CIDOC-CRM extension |
| --- | --- |
| Representation of upper level | ARP8 upper level |
| Representation of lower level | ARP9 lower level |

A new class was also introduced to represent the level of description, ARE1 Level of Description. This class, a subclass of E55 Type, is instantiated with the description levels used in the archives, that actually provide a type to each of the archival objects.

The new properties and entities presented here are a sample of what has been proposed for the ArchOnto model[6].

---

[6] OWL version available on GitHub: https://github.com/feup-infolab/archontology.

# 4   A Prototype CIDOC-CRM Knowledge Graph

We carried out an in-depth analysis and prototyping in order to design an architecture for the information system that will implement the CIDOC-CRM compliant knowledge graph[7]. For this purpose, we have decided to adopt a graph database because they have a simpler, more interoperable model that naturally integrates in the LOD cloud, one of the chief requirements of the whole endeavour. If we chose a relational database instead, and kept the plain semantic web model, there would be a systematic need for complex queries requiring costly `JOIN` operations, as the database would most likely degenerate into a very large table for the edges of the graph.

Additionally, the fact that CIDOC-CRM was designed according to object-oriented programming (OOP) [6] principles makes the model suitable to the application of an Object-Graph Mapping (OGM). This technology resembles Object-Relational Mapping for relational databases, and makes basic CRUD (Create-Read-Update-Delete) operations transparent to the programmer.

The ANTT specified the requirement that all components of the system should be free from any licensing costs and adopt open-source licenses. With this in mind, our database of choice was Neo4j, because of its open-source license (GPLv3), wide adoption, support for ACID transactions and most importantly a mature OGM library[8] that runs on the Java Virtual Machine (JVM). This makes the solution cross-compatible with any operating system, enabling the ANTT to adopt Linux-based servers for its archival information system.

## 4.1   Multiple Inheritance: the Diamond Problem

One of the first issues encountered when attempting to interface with the graph through an OGM was the fact that the CIDOC-CRM defines a complex set of classes and subclasses, where there are many cases of multiple inheritance. In OOP, this is a classic problem known as the "Diamond Problem"—when a class inherits from two or more other classes.

To maintain a clear code organization as close to the CIDOC-CRM concepts as possible, we needed a programming language capable of supporting multiple inheritance in an elegant way, while also supporting the Neo4j OGM, which is designed to run on Java. Our choice was Groovy, a modern language mostly compatible with Java syntax, which approaches the diamond problem through the use of "traits": sets of methods and fields akin to Java interfaces, which can be added to one or more classes to represent multiple inheritance. The Groovy compiler resolves method naming conflicts by using the method last declared when multiple other traits are extended. However, should one wish to use the same named method from a trait that was not the last declared one, this is still possible through additional configuration options.

---

[7] Prototype available on GitHub: https://github.com/feup-infolab/archgraph.
[8] Documentation: https://neo4j.com/docs/ogm-manual.

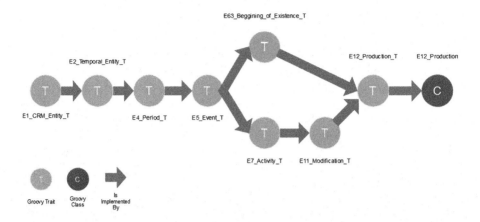

**Fig. 1.** Implementation of the traits for class E12 Production

The diagram in Fig. 1 is a graphical representation of the implementation of traits in class **E12 Production**. Several Groovy traits are created for each CIDOC-CRM class, and then combined at will to represent the multiple inheritance cases: in the example, **E12 Production** is a subclass of both **E11 Modification** and **E63 Beginning Of Existence**, both modelled as traits. Every trait contains its own **rdf:type** and its own methods. In this case the **E12 Production** "leaf" class is the only one that is to be instantiated. When an instance is created, it automatically gains all the methods in its trait hierarchy. When it is persisted to the Neo4j database, all **rdf:type** will be recorded, from **E12 Production** up to **E1 CRM Entity**.

## 4.2  Validation Trade-Offs

In theory, a graph data model should comply with an ontology and therefore be validated for consistency on every update, ensuring consistency with the model. In an operational system, however, such operations are not feasible due to their high computational cost. As a result, while developing the database and utilizing the OGM, one of the major concerns was to make sure that the model required as little external validation for consistency as possible. Using CIDOC-CRM and the OGM from Neo4j, we try to carry out most validation by enforcing, for each entity, the type induced by the corresponding class and ensuring that the relationships have the proper domains and ranges as defined for their properties. This includes making sure that the domains and ranges are subclasses of the classes specified as such on the CIDOC-CRM.

To further alleviate the validation effort, we decided to create extensions to the CIDOC-CRM, specifically for the software implementation of data properties and of ternary associations, which in CIDOC-CRM are denoted as properties of properties.

The new data properties were created with the prefix "ARP" and ternary associations were implemented by creating node entities that represent the property and have the prefix "PC", then creating properties `ARP01 has domain` and `ARP02 has range`. This allows the implementation of ternary relationships without any further validation besides compile-time verification.

Figure 2 is an example of a sub-graph showing an archival record for the Portuguese law that made the adoption of the Gregorian calendar official. This graphical representation is generated directly by Neo4j as an output of the existing version of our software and data model.

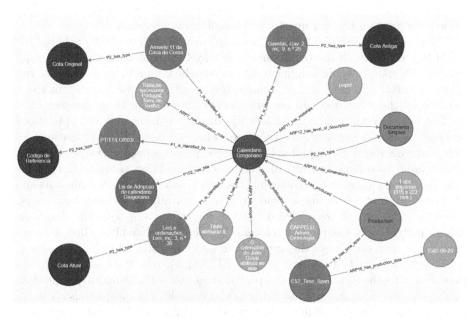

**Fig. 2.** The Portuguese law for the adoption of the Gregorian Calendar, as a graph (Color figure online)

This graph represents the neighbourhood of the "Calendário Gregoriano" resource (Gregorian Calendar). It represents the law that passed the adoption of the Gregorian calendar in Portugal. The Gregorian Calendar record is at the center, in blue. It is linked to the physical material of the record ("papel" or paper), as well as publication notes, the title scopes, general notes, dimensions and level of description. Several objects of assertions for `P2 has type` (in red) are the original, the previous and the current call number for the record. Finally, the record holds a reference code and is linked to its production date.

## 5   Conclusions

In this paper, we present several challenges behind the implementation of a knowledge graph at the Portuguese National Archives. Balancing the expressiveness of the graph model and the demand for high performance in an operational system, while ensuring elegant code organization, have led us to complement the existing CIDOC-CRM with new classes and properties and to adopt the Neo4j graph database, the Groovy programming language and the Grails framework.

The initial approach to the archival model and corresponding knowledge graph allowed us to identify issues that will be addresses in the next steps and have to do with graph traversal, querying and searching the database and user interfaces.

Cypher, the Neo4j query language, is currently being used mostly for testing. In the future, the OGM will handle CRUD operations, traversals and searching, while a few custom Cypher queries will handle complex cases.

Query and traversal modules are not implemented and tested yet; should the OGM fail to satisfy all the requirements, it may be complemented with a graph traversal Domain-Specific Language such as Apache Gremlin, more suited to run graph traversal and thus act as a connector for the machine learning modules required by the migration and information extraction tasks in the project.

The user interfaces have to satisfy the diverse requirements of applications and end users. For applications, the graph must provide CRUD operations, as well as the display of sub-graphs. Users can be professionals (archivists creating new records), or other users and all need to access the information on the records in an intuitive manner, while traversing the graph based on archival contents and relationships. For the business logic we will use Grails as the web framework, which in turn uses Groovy, already in use for interacting with the database. Additionally, Grails has plugins that can be used with Neo4J to allow a better integration with the rest of the application, and can also share the same server.

This work is part of a larger project, EPISA, where a systematic migration from ISAD to the new model is expected, together with domain-specific data mining on the extensive textual fields in the records. The project also aims to satisfy requirements from different stakeholders: archivists who need a convenient environment for description; scholars who use the archives as their main data source; and laypeople who explore the archives for various purposes.

# References

1. de Almeida, M.J., Runa, L.: ICON project: content integration in Portuguese national archives using CIDOC-CRM. In: 2018 CIDOC Annual Conference (2018)
2. Bountouri, L., Gergatsoulis, M.: Mapping encoded archival description to CIDOC CRM. In: First Workshop on Digital Information Management, Corfu, Greece (2010)
3. Direcção Geral de Arquivos, Grupo de Trabalho de Normalização da Descrição em Arquivo: Orientações para a Descrição Arquivística, 2nd edn. Direção Geral de Arquivos, Lisboa (2007)
4. ICOM/CIDOC CRM Special Interest Group: Definition of the CIDOC Conceptual Reference Model. ICOM, 6.2.2 edn. (2017)
5. International Council on Archives: ISAD(G) Second Edition. ICA (2000)
6. Oldman, D.: The CIDOC Conceptual Reference Model (CIDOC-CRM): PRIMER. CRM Labs (2014)

# Investigating Correlations of Inter-coder Agreement and Machine Annotation Performance for Historical Video Data

Kader Pustu-Iren[1,2]([✉])([iD]), Markus Mühling[3], Nikolaus Korfhage[3],
Joanna Bars[4], Sabrina Bernhöft[4], Angelika Hörth[4], Bernd Freisleben[3]([iD]),
and Ralph Ewerth[1,2]([iD])

[1] TIB – Leibniz Information Centre for Science and Technology, Hannover, Germany
{kader.pustu,ralph.ewerth}@tib.eu
[2] L3S Research Center, Hannover, Germany
[3] Department of Mathematics and Computer Science,
University of Marburg, Marburg, Germany
{muehling,korfhage,freisleb}@informatik.uni-marburg.de
[4] German Broadcasting Archive (DRA), Potsdam, Germany
{joanna.bars,sabrina.bernhoeft,angelika.hoerth}@dra.de

**Abstract.** Video indexing approaches such as visual concept classification and person recognition are essential to enable fine-grained semantic search in large-scale video archives such as the historical video collection of the former German Democratic Republic (GDR) maintained by the German Broadcasting Archive (DRA). Typically, a lexicon of visual concepts has to be defined for semantic search. But the definition of visual concepts can be more or less subjective due to individually differing judgments of annotators, which may have an impact on training data quality for supervised machine learning methods. In this paper, we analyze the inter-coder agreement on historical TV data of the former GDR for visual concept classification and person recognition. The inter-coder agreement is evaluated for a group of expert as well as non-expert annotators. Furthermore, correlations between visual recognition performance and inter-annotator agreement are measured. In this context, information about training dataset size and agreement are used to predict average precision for concept classification. Finally, the impact of expert vs. non-expert annotations on person recognition is analyzed.

**Keywords:** Inter-coder agreement · Historical videos ·
Visual concept classification · Person identification ·
Performance prediction

## 1 Introduction

Automatic indexing is an important prerequisite to enable semantic search in large video archives. In particular, visual concept classification and person recognition play an essential role to provide fine-grained access to large image and

ⓒ Springer Nature Switzerland AG 2019
A. Doucet et al. (Eds.): TPDL 2019, LNCS 11799, pp. 107–114, 2019.
https://doi.org/10.1007/978-3-030-30760-8_9

video databases like the historical video collection of the German Broadcasting Archive (DRA). The DRA maintains the cultural heritage of television (TV) broadcasts of the former German Democratic Republic (GDR) and thus grants access to researchers who are interested in German-German history. Semantic search through pre-defined lexicons of visual concepts and personalities associated with the former GDR can support the investigation of specific research questions and be a starting point for further analyses and scientific studies. Typically, such a lexicon has to be defined in advance. However, in order to allow for such a fine-grained search by automatically indexing the video collection, a huge manual effort for initializing this process is necessary. A large amount of manually labeled keyframes and shots is necessary to train or fine-tune deep learning based video indexing approaches. While the number of training images is known to matter for these approaches, the quality of manually annotated data also affects video indexing performance. In this context, visual concepts in images and video frames are not always perceived objectively. As shown in previous work [3,7,13], human annotators can have different understandings and judgments and the inter-coder agreement can noticeably vary for different visual concepts. Therefore, the precise definition of such concepts and consequently carefully labelled data are crucial for system success.

In this paper, we investigate the inter-coder agreement for annotations of historical TV data of the former GDR for experts and non-experts. The quality of the manually labeled keyframes is assessed for visual concept classification and person recognition (Sect. 3). Furthermore, correlations between inter-coder agreement and system performance by means of average precision results on these two tasks are analyzed (Sect. 4). Our hypothesis is that besides the amount of available training data, the agreement is correlated with the performance of video indexing methods based on supervised learning. Moreover, we suppose that inter-coder agreement might form an upper bound for such methods. In this regard, some first experiments are presented to predict average precision using support vector regression based on inter-coder agreement and training data size (also Sect. 4). Finally, the influence of image annotation quality induced by experts vs. non-experts on person recognition performance is investigated (Sect. 5).

## 2    Related Work

In the field of computational linguistics, a considerable number of articles addressed inter-coder agreement on text corpora in the past [1]. Snow et al. [11] evaluated non-expert annotations by means of crowd workers for natural language tasks. Among other experiments, they observed that annotations of four non-experts are needed to rival the annotation quality of one expert annotator. Furthermore, they have trained machine learning classifiers on expert as well as non-expert annotations and reported better system performance for non-experts due to high annotation diversity reducing the annotator bias. In this context, Bodorff and Richter-Levin [2] observed that annotators' viewpoints in the field of politics cause diverging term assignments. Reidsma and Caletta [8] demonstrated that annotation-dependant noise can be handled by machine learning algorithms and argue that machine learning performance cannot be predicted through agreement. However, these findings were exclusively made for annotating text. Besides further studies for indexing graphic materials [13], Nowak and Rüger [7] presented an inter-coder agreement study for image annotation by both crowd workers and experts. The annotators had to label 99 images with respect to 22 partially mutually exclusive images. The authors measured higher agreement for experts, but argued that majority voting filters out noise in non-expert annotations and closes the gap to expert annotations of higher quality. Another study [3] dealt with the question whether machines perform better than humans in visual concept classification. Human performance by means of inter-coder agreement was measured via Krippendorff's $\alpha$, and human-level performance of deep learning models was reported for 20 common PASCAL VOC concepts.

# 3   Inter-coder Agreement Study (Concepts and Persons)

In this section, we compare the reliability of expert vs. non-expert annotations for historical TV data in terms of inter-coder-agreement. For this purpose, we collected annotations of experts as well as students (Sect. 3.2) for a selected set of concepts and persons (Sect. 3.1) following the experimental design described in Sect. 3.3. Agreement results are discussed in Sect. 3.4.

## 3.1   Dataset of Historical Concepts and Personalities

In previous work, we developed a video retrieval system for historical GDR television data. For this purpose, a GDR specific lexicon of 100 classes (91 concepts and nine persons) has been defined [6]. The concept classification was based on a CNN approach using a GoogleNet architecture [12]. Person recognition was performed using FaceVACs[1]. For evaluation, the respective Top-200 retrieval results in terms of mean average precision based on 2,500 h of video data have been manually labeled by an expert [6]. In the current study, 20 concepts and 9 persons have been chosen from the GDR-specific lexicon such that categories with high, medium, and low retrieval quality are evenly represented. The images for the study have been randomly sampled from the Top-200 retrieval results. Altogether, 744 positive images for concepts and 199 positive images of persons have been acquired. The dataset includes additional archive images for rarely occurring classes and an extra person ("Mikhail Gorbachev"). To further enlarge the dataset, 257 images with negative labels are randomly chosen from the Top-200 retrieval results. These images tend to be similar to one of the concepts or persons, making the manual labeling process more difficult. Finally, the image annotation study comprises 1200 images. The following 20 concepts and 10 persons are used in our study: {*Apartment Construction, Automotive*

---

[1] http://www.cognitec.com.

*Industry, Banner, Camping, Kindergarten, Microelectronics, Military Parade, Mining, Narrow-gauge Railway, Open-pit Mining, Panel Building, Playground, Prison, Ship Launching, Shipyard, Shopping Mall, Textile Factory, Theater Performance, Unrefurbished House, Waiting Line, Christa Wolf, Erich Honecker, Fritz Cremer, Hermann Henselmann, Hilde Benjamin, Siegmund Jaehn, Stephan Hermlin, Walter Ulbricht, Werner Tuebke, Mikhail Gorbachev*}.

### 3.2  Study Participants

Five experts and five non-experts participated in our study. The group of experts consisted of DRA employees, who are in a general sense very familiar with the historical material we used in our study. In particular, experts are fully trained archivists and information specialists with a mean age of 40 ($\pm$10) years and work experiences ranging from 3 to 28 years. The non-expert group was composed of Master students in computer science with a mean age of 26 ($\pm$3) years, who have not worked with the material previously. Students were rewarded 30 Euro.

### 3.3  Experimental Design

Participants were asked to label the images based on the 20 concept as well as 10 person categories. They were allowed to assign no label, a single label, or multiple labels to an image. Participants were provided with annotation instructions. For concept categories we provided formal descriptions and for each of the personalities we provided three images showing the person in different appearance and age. Prior to the study, the participants were allowed to look up concepts and persons on the Web in case of uncertainties. To measure inter-coder agreement between different sets of annotators, we used Krippendorff's alpha (K's $\alpha$) coefficient [5]. We chose K's $\alpha$, since it is not affected by the number of coders [4] and reliability can be compared for groups of asymmetric size.

### 3.4  Results

While experts and non-experts agree almost equally strong on the concept categories (0.8 vs. 0.79 across all concepts), expert annotations seem to be more homogeneous for the GDR personalities (0.83 vs. 0.71 across all personalities). According to Krippendorff [5], an $\alpha > 0.8$ indicates reliable annotations. Thus, annotations on concepts can be considered reliable for both groups of experts and students. For persons, greater differences between experts and non-experts can be observed suggesting that experts are better annotators for this task. Except for commonly known personalities such as *Erich Honecker* larger uncertainty and disagreement can be observed among non-experts. In order to measure how well non-experts and experts agree on the categories, we also calculated the combined agreement among both groups. Overall, an averaged joint agreement of 0.78 on concepts and 0.76 on persons was measured. The overall concept agreement in the inter-group scenario is lower than the agreement for the weaker non-expert annotators. This could suggest that archivists and students may have different understandings for some concepts which causes diverging annotations.

We assume that a high agreement is an indicator for an accurate set of annotations. For the set of visual concepts, experts and non-experts were found to be equally accurate annotators. In the next section, we analyze to which extent agreement contributes to video indexing performance and investigate the opportunity of performance prediction. We found that experts are more accurate labelers when it comes to historically relevant persons of the GDR. However, judgments of different groups may have different biases as also reasoned for the concept categories. In Sect. 5, we exemplary analyze for different sets of personality annotations whether high agreement on training images implies higher system performance for person recognition.

# 4 Predicting Concept Classification Performance

In this section, we discuss correlations between original average precision results and inter-coder agreements as well as training data size. The highest correlations were measured for AP results on concepts. While the correlation with expert agreement (0.64) was slightly higher than with non-expert agreement (0.62), also a significant correlation between AP values and the number of training images was measured (0.78). We noticed only moderately high correlations for AP on persons as well as for total AP results. For this reason, we exploit *the high correlations observed for concepts* to perform performance prediction based on both inter-coder agreement and training data size for concept classification.

We used support vector regression (SVR) [10] based on a linear kernel to estimate AP for our concepts given the corresponding training data sizes and agreement values as input. SVR is performed separately for expert and student agreement. According to leave-one-out cross validation, utilizing expert agreement yielded a mean absolute error of 13.95% (±12.3%) in predicting AP. Using non-expert agreement as input instead, yielded a slightly higher error of 14.55% (±10.6%). In order to determine the individual impact of the number of training images and annotation quality on predicting the AP on concepts, we also trained SVR with training data size and expert agreement as separate inputs. The mean absolute error for using solely training data size as input was 20.0% (±10.8%). AP prediction based on the agreement achieved only an error of 21.1% (±14.6%). In comparison, the error of a random baseline using prediction by chance is around 33.1%. Figure 1 shows errors for the individual concepts of the different performance prediction approaches. It can be seen that the combined input significantly reduced the error for some of the concepts and overall led to lower errors for most of the concepts. Overall, estimation results suggest that the AP performance on the historical concepts can be approximated by using both the number of training images and inter-coder agreement. Using expert agreement and performing SVR on all concepts as training samples (i.e., no leave-one-out setting), AP can be *exemplarily* approximated by the following function:

$$\hat{P}_A^T = 0.379 \cdot \alpha' + 0.698 \cdot t' + 0.018 \tag{1}$$

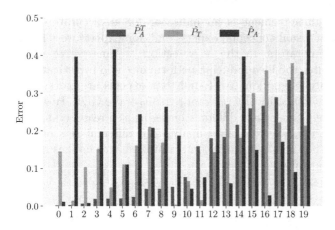

**Fig. 1.** Errors of concepts' AP estimates trained with (1) both agreement and training data size ($\hat{P}_A^T$), solely with (2) training data size ($\hat{P}_T$), or (3) agreement ($\hat{P}_A$) as input.

where $\alpha'$ corresponds to agreement K's $\alpha$ and $t'$ to the training data size, both normalized (min-max) to $\in [0, 1]$. $\hat{P}_A^T$ have to lie within $[0, 1]$ for valid estimates, i.e., results for $\hat{P}_A^T > 1.0$ are set to 1.0.

# 5   Impact of Annotation Quality on Person Identification

In this section, we evaluate person identification performance based on different sets of expert and non-expert annotations acquired in the inter-coder annotator study (Sect. 3). In particular, we create classifiers dependent on different annotations following a face matching approach and evaluate systems based on single participant's vote as well as majority vote for both experts and non-experts.

## 5.1   Experimental Setup

For the identification of the introduced 10 personalities associated with GDR, we employed a basic face matching approach, in which comparisons rely on deep feature representations. In order to build a lexicon of facial representations, each personality is represented by the mean of their embeddings which are generated from a ground truth set of face images. Thus, an unknown face is considered a person of the dictionary, if the cosine similarity between its embedding and a dictionary embedding is sufficiently high according to a threshold. In order to extract facial features, we utilized a FaceNet [9] implementation[2]. We used a cosine similarity threshold of 0.67 from the FaceNet implementation code.

---

[2] ResNet v1 trained on VGGFace2: https://github.com/davidsandberg/facenet.

We used the judgments on the GDR personalities of the different annotators from the annotation study as input data for the described person identification approach. Following the described approach, we independently built a training dataset for each of the expert and non-expert study participants based on their annotations. This allows us to directly compare the system's person identification performance for different sets of annotators. After evaluating classification accuracy based on each participant's training data individually, we averaged the estimated performances for experts and non-experts, respectively. Furthermore, we generated ground truth labels considering the majority vote of the five experts and also evaluated the performance for this training dataset. For the non-experts, majority vote is used accordingly. For testing, we utilize further archive data from DRA as well as additional images crawled from Google. After detecting faces and manually deleting irrelevant faces, we obtain a test set with 350 face images in total.

## 5.2 Results

The averaged single expert system yielded an overall accuracy of 81.0%, whereas the averaged non-expert system had an accuracy of 79.4%. For only three of the 10 personalities non-expert systems could keep up with or outperform those of experts. For the other seven personalities expert training images led to a relative improvement of up to 5% in accuracy. As expected, annotations based on the majority vote of respectively five participants led to better results for both experts and non-experts in comparison to individual judgments. The majority vote results in more accurate labels and acts as a filter for noise such as individual incorrect judgments or accidental false annotations. However, non-expert majority voting (accuracy of 80.9%) is still inferior to that of the expert voting (82.0%). The correlation between the number of training images and person identification accuracy is rather low (0.3 on average). Presumably, performance differences are not caused by training data size but by incorrectly annotated images.

## 6 Conclusions

In this paper, we have presented an inter-coder agreement study for the annotation of historical TV data involving both experts and non-experts. We demonstrated that non-experts are as reliable annotators as experts for common as well as GDR specific concepts. However, in identifying historical personalities, non-experts were more uncertain. In an attempt to identify the importance of inter-coder agreement for the performance of visual concept classification, we measured correlations between AP results, training data size, and inter-coder agreement. Using support vector regression, we modeled AP prediction for visual concepts by the number of training images and inter-coder agreement. For the task of face recognition, we showed that expert systems on average slightly outperformed systems based on single non-expert annotation sets. In this context, we argue that differences in performance may even rise in a more complex real-world task that would involve more personalities with even more persons who are not well known (anymore). It turned out that majority voting corrects erroneous annotations and thus positively affects system performance. However, when it comes to annotating large-scale data that current deep learning methods require, it is usually not plausible to annotate several times. Also, crowd workers for co-annotating may not be as accurate annotators as the German students, who had fair domain knowledge and were considered as non-experts in our case.

**Acknowledgements.** This work is funded by the Deutsche Forschungsgemeinschaft (DFG, German Research Foundation) - project number 388420599.

# References

1. Artstein, R., Poesio, M.: Inter-coder agreement for computational linguistics. Comput. Linguist. **34**(4), 555–596 (2008)
2. Bodoff, D., Richter-Levin, Y.: Viewpoints in indexing term assignment. J. Assoc. Inf. Sci. Technol. 1–12 (2019). https://doi.org/10.1002/asi.24246
3. Ewerth, R., Springstein, M., Phan-Vogtmann, L.A., Schütze, J.: "Are machines better than humans in image tagging?" - a user study adds to the puzzle. In: Jose, J.M., et al. (eds.) ECIR 2017. LNCS, vol. 10193, pp. 186–198. Springer, Cham (2017). https://doi.org/10.1007/978-3-319-56608-5_15
4. Hayes, A.F., Krippendorff, K.: Reliability in content analysis. Hum. Commun. Res. **30**(3), 411–433 (2004)
5. Krippendorff, K.: Answering the call for a standard reliability measure for coding data. Commun. Methods Meas. **1**(1), 77–89 (2007)
6. Mühling, M., et al.: Content-based video retrieval in historical collections of the German broadcasting archive. In: Fuhr, N., Kovács, L., Risse, T., Nejdl, W. (eds.) TPDL 2016. LNCS, vol. 9819, pp. 67–78. Springer, Cham (2016). https://doi.org/10.1007/978-3-319-43997-6_6
7. Nowak, S., Rüger, S.: How reliable are annotations via crowdsourcing? A study about inter-annotator agreement for multi-label image annotation. In: International Conference on Multimedia Information Retrieval, pp. 557–566 (2010)
8. Reidsma, D., Carletta, J.: Reliability measurement without limits. Comput. Linguist. **34**(3), 319–326 (2008)
9. Schroff, F., Kalenichenko, D., Philbin, J.: FaceNet: a unified embedding for face recognition and clustering. In: Conference on Computer Vision and Pattern Recognition, pp. 815–823 (2015)
10. Smola, A.J., Schölkopf, B.: A tutorial on support vector regression. Stat. Comput. **14**(3), 199–222 (2004)
11. Snow, R., O'Connor, B., Jurafsky, D., Ng, A.Y.: Cheap and fast - but is it good? Evaluating non-expert annotations for natural language tasks. In: Conference on Empirical Methods in Natural Language, pp. 254–263 (2008)
12. Szegedy, C., et al.: Going deeper with convolutions. In: Conference on Computer Vision and Pattern Recognition, pp. 1–9 (2015)
13. Vaughan Hughes, A., Rafferty, P.: Inter-indexer consistency in graphic materials indexing at the national library of wales. J. Doc. **67**(1), 9–32 (2011)

# Who is Mona L.? Identifying Mentions of Artworks in Historical Archives

Nitisha Jain$^{(\boxtimes)}$ and Ralf Krestel

Hasso Plattner Institute, University of Potsdam, Potsdam, Germany
{nitisha.jain,ralf.krestel}@hpi.de

**Abstract.** Named entity recognition (NER) plays an important role in many information retrieval tasks, including automatic knowledge graph construction. Most NER systems are typically limited to a few common named entity types, such as person, location, and organization. However, for cultural heritage resources, such as art historical archives, the recognition of titles of artworks as named entities is of high importance. In this work, we focus on identifying mentions of artworks, e.g. paintings and sculptures, from historical archives. Current state of the art NER tools are unable to adequately identify artwork titles due to the particular difficulties presented by this domain. The scarcity of training data for NER for cultural heritage poses further hindrances. To mitigate this, we propose a semi-supervised approach to create high-quality training data by leveraging existing cultural heritage resources. Our experimental evaluation shows significant improvement in NER performance for artwork titles as compared to baseline approach.

**Keywords:** Named entity recognition · Cultural heritage data

## 1 Artwork Mentions in Historical Archives

Named entity recognition (NER) is a key component for information extraction pipelines that aims to identify the named entities in text and classify them into pre-defined categories. NER serves as an important step for various semantic tasks, such as knowledge base creation, text based search, relation extraction and question answering, among many others. There is a large body of existing work on improving its performance, with the recent approaches based on machine learning techniques. However, most efforts have focused only on some common categories of named entities, i.e., person, organization, location, and date. Moreover, state of the art NER systems are trained on a few well-established corpora available for the task such as the CoNNL datasets [8] or OntoNotes [5]. Although these systems attain good results for generic tasks, their performance and utility is essentially limited due to the specific training. Thus, it comes as no surprise that it has been a challenge to adapt NER systems for identifying domain-specific named entity categories with reasonable accuracy [6].

This is especially true for cultural heritage data where the cultural artefacts serve as one of the most important named entity categories. Recently, there has

© Springer Nature Switzerland AG 2019
A. Doucet et al. (Eds.): TPDL 2019, LNCS 11799, pp. 115–122, 2019.
https://doi.org/10.1007/978-3-030-30760-8_10

been a surge in the availability of digitized cultural data with the principles of linked open data[1] gaining momentum in the cultural heritage domain [11]. Initiatives such as OpenGLAM[2] and flagship digital library projects such as Europeana[3] aim to enrich open knowledge graphs with cultural heritage data by improving the coverage of the topics related to the cultural domain. Efforts have been made to digitize historical as well as recent art related texts such as auction catalogues, art books and exhibition catalogues [3]. In such resources, cultural objects, mainly artworks, are often described with help of unstructured text narratives. The identification and extraction of the mentions of artworks from such text descriptions can serve various important use cases, such as facilitate search and browsing in digital resources, help art historians with tracking of provenance of artworks and enable wider semantic text exploration for digital cultural resources.

In this paper, we refer to the named entities depicting the titles of artworks to be of type *title*. These titles could have been assigned by artists, by collectors, art historians, or other domain experts. Due to the ambiguities that are inherent in artwork titles, their identification from texts is a challenging task. As an example, consider the painting titled *'Girl before a mirror'* by famous artist Pablo Picasso. This title merely describes in an abstract manner what is being depicted in the painting and thus, it is hard to identify it as a named entity without knowing the context of its mention. Yet, such descriptive titles are common in the art domain, as are abstract titles such as *'untitled'*. In this work, we focus on identifying mentions of artworks from unstructured text in art historical archives. Due to the innate complexity of this task, NER models need to be trained with domain-specific named entity annotations. As such, the unavailability of high-quality training data for the cultural heritage domain is one of the biggest hindrances for this task. We address this gap by proposing techniques for generating annotations for NER via a semi-automated approach from a large corpus of art related documents, while leveraging existing art resources that are integrated in popular knowledge bases, such as Wikidata [12].

## 2   Named Entity Recognition for Artworks

Identification of mentions of artworks seems, at first glance, to be no more difficult than detecting mentions of persons or locations. But the special characteristics of artwork titles makes this a complicated task which requires significant domain expertise. This section illustrates three types of errors that arise when trying to recognize artwork mentions in practice.

*Incorrectly Missed Named Entity Mention.* Many artwork titles contain generic words that can be found in dictionary. This poses difficulties in the recognition of titles as named entities. E.g., a painting titled *'A pair of shoes'* by Van Gogh can

---

[1] Linked Open Data: http://www.w3.org/DesignIssues/LinkedData.

[2] OpenGLAM: http://openglam.org.

[3] Europeana: http://europeana.eu.

be easily missed while searching for named entities in unstructured text. Such titles can only be identified if they are appropriately capitalized or highlighted, however this cannot be guaranteed for all languages and in noisy texts.

*Incorrect Named Entity Boundary Detection.* Often, artworks have long and descriptive titles, e.g., a painting by Van Gogh titled *'Head of a peasant woman with dark cap'*. If this title is mentioned in text without any formatting indicators, it is likely that the boundaries may be wrongly identified and the named entity be tagged as *'Head of a peasant woman'*, which is also the title of a different painting by Van Gogh. In fact, Van Gogh had created several paintings with this title in different years. For such titles, it is common that location or time indicators are appended to the titles (by the collectors or curators of museums) in order to differentiate the artworks. However, such indicators are not a part of the original title and should not be included within the scope of the named entity.

*Incorrect Named Entity Type Tagging.* Even when the boundaries of the artwork titles are identified correctly, they might be tagged as the wrong entity type. This is especially true for portraits and self-portraits. The most well-known example is that of *'Mona Lisa'*, which refers to the person as well as the painting by Da Vinci that depicts her. Numerous old paintings are portraits of the prominent personalities of those times and are named after them such as *'King George III'*, *'Queen Anne'* and so on—such artwork titles are likely to be wrongly tagged as the *person* type in the absence of contextual clues. Apart from names of persons, paintings may also be named after locations such as *'Paris'*, *'New York'*, *'Grand Canal, Venice'* and so on and may be incorrectly tagged as type *location*.

## 3  Related Work

In the absence of manually curated NER annotations, the adaptation of existing NER solutions to the art and cultural heritage domain faces multiple challenges, some of them being unique to this domain. Van Hooland et al. [10] discuss some of these difficulties and compare the performance of several NER tools on descriptions of objects from the Smithsonian Cooper-Hewitt National Design Museum in New York. In [7], Rodriquez et al. discuss the performance of several available NER services on a corpus of mid-20th-century typewritten documents and compare their performance against manually annotated test data having named entities of types people, locations, and organizations. On similar lines, Ehrmann et al. [4] offer a diachronic evaluation of various NER tools for digitized archives of Swiss newspapers. However, none of the existing works have focused on the task of identifying artwork titles that are highly relevant as a named entity type for the art domain. Moreover, previous works have merely compared the performance of existing NER systems, whereas in this work, we aim to improve the performance of NER systems for cultural heritage with the help of domain-specific high-quality training data.

Although there is increasing effort to publish cultural heritage collections as linked data [2,3,9], to the best of our knowledge, there is no annotated dataset available for facilitating NER in this domain yet. This work proposes techniques to generate a high-quality training corpus in a scalable and semi-supervised manner and demonstrates that NER systems can be trained to identify mentions of artworks with notable performance gains.

## 4    Annotating Complex Named Entity Types

**NER Model.** None of the existing NER systems can identify titles of artworks as named entities out of the box. The closest NER category to artwork titles was found in the SpaCy[4] library as *work_of_art*, which refers not only to artworks such as paintings and sculptures, but also covers a large variety of others cultural heritage objects such as movies, plays, books, songs etc. Although the pre-trained SpaCy model performed poorly for cultural heritage domain, we have used this as a naive baseline for the lack of better alternatives. In order to improve the identification of named entities of type *title*, training on high-quality annotated training datasets is imperative and for this purpose, the baseline SpaCy NER model was leveraged for domain-specific re-training. Due to the steep costs and efforts of manual annotations, we aimed to generate a large corpus of annotated data in a semi-automated fashion from our dataset. It is to be noted that the proposed techniques for improving the quality of NER training data are independent of the NER model used for the evaluation. Thus, SpaCy can be substituted with any other re-trainable NER system.

**Training Dataset.** The underlying dataset for this work is a large collection of art historical documents that have been recently digitized. The collection consists of different types of documents—auction catalogues, full texts of art books related to particular artists or art genres, catalogues of art exhibitions and other documents. A sample document[5] is shown in Fig. 1a. The auction and exhibition catalogues contain semi-structured and unstructured texts that describe artworks on display, mainly paintings and sculptures. Art books may contain more unstructured text about the origins of artworks and their creators. Figure 1c shows the distribution of the different types of documents in the dataset. The pages of these catalogues and books were scanned with OCR and each page was converted to an entry stored within a search index. Due to the limitations of OCR, the dataset suffers from noise and does not retain its rich original formatting information which would have been quite useful for analysis. The dataset consists of texts in a number of different languages, which adds additional complexity to the NER task. English, French, German and Italian account for the majority of the languages as shown in Fig. 1b, while Dutch, Spanish, Swedish

---

[4] SpaCy: https://spacy.io/, version 2.1.3.
[5] from the exhibition catalogue "Lukas Cranach: Gemälde, Zeichnungen, Druckgraphik" (https://digi.ub.uni-heidelberg.de/diglit/koepplin1974bd1/0084).

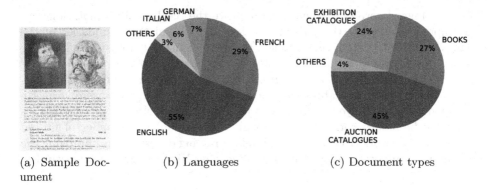

(a) Sample Document     (b) Languages     (c) Document types

**Fig. 1.** Dataset characteristics

and Danish were also recognized in a sizeable number of entries. In this work, however, we avoid the multi-lingual analysis for the sake of simplicity and focus on the NER task for English documents. After initial pre-processing including the removal of non alpha-numeric characters, the dataset consisted of a total of 117,912 entries in English, which was then transformed into annotated NER data.

**Named Entity Annotations with High Precision.** In order to match and correctly tag the artwork titles present in our dataset as named entities of type *title*, we leveraged cultural resources that have been integrated into popular knowledge bases. As a first step, available resources from Wikidata were collected to generate a large entity dictionary or *gazetteer* of titles of artworks. Integrating other sources, such as art-related ontologies or lists from museums is also possible. To generate the entity dictionary for titles, Wikidata was queried with the Wikidata Query Service[6] for names of artworks, specifically for names of paintings and sculptures. In order to match the original non-English titles of artworks, titles belonging to other major languages present in our dataset were also added. Many of the titles were highly generic, for instance, *'Italian'*, *'Winter'*, *'Landscape'* etc., therefore, the titles consisting of only one word filtered out. Since quite a few artwork titles were identical to location names that could lead to incorrect name entity type tagging, such titles were also ignored. A combined list of approximately 15,000 titles in different languages were obtained, with the majority of them being in English.

**Named Entity Annotations with High Recall.** As discussed in Sect. 2, partial matching of artwork titles can lead to ambiguities. Due to the limitations of the naive NER model there were several instances where only a part of the full title of artwork was recognized as a named entity from the text, thus it

---

[6] https://query.wikidata.org/.

was not tagged correctly as such. To improve the recall of the annotations, we attempted to identify the partial matches and extend the boundaries of the named entities to obtain the complete and correct titles. For example, from the text *"..the subject of the former is not Christ before Caiaphas, as stated by Birke and Kertész, but Christ before Annas.."*, the named entities *'Christ'*, *'Caiaphas'* and *'Annas'* were separately identified initially. However, they were correctly updated to *'Christ before Caiaphas'* and *'Christ before Annas'* as *title* entities after the boundary corrections. Through this technique, a number of missed mentions of artwork titles were added to the training dataset, thus improving the recall of the annotations and in turn, influencing NER performance positively.

## 5  Evaluation

**Experimental Setup.** In order to evaluate the impact on NER performance with improvements in quality of the training data, we trained the baseline NER model for the new entity type *title* on different variants of training data:

- *High-precision*: Annotations obtained by matching Wikidata titles.
- *High-recall*: Additional annotations from named entity boundary corrections.

The number of annotations (training set size) for each of the datasets are shown in Table 1. An NER model was obtained by training with the above datasets for 10 epochs, with the training data batched and shuffled before every iteration. The performance of the trained NER models was compared with the *Baseline* NER model i.e. the pre-trained SpaCy model without any specific annotations for artwork titles. In the absence of a gold standard dataset for NER for artwork titles, we performed manual annotations to obtain a test dataset for evaluation.

**Manual Annotations for Test Dataset.** For generating a test dataset, a set of texts were chosen at random from the dataset, while making sure that this text was representative of the different types of documents in our corpus. This test data consisted of 544 entries (with one or more sentences per entry) and was carefully excluded from the training dataset. The titles of paintings and sculptures mentioned in this data were then manually identified and tagged as named entities of type *title*. The annotations were performed by two non-expert annotators independently of each other in 3–4 person hours with the help of Enno[7] tool. The inter-annotator agreement in terms of the Fleis-kappa and Krippendorf-kappa scores were calculated to be $-1.86$ and $0.61$ respectively. The poor inter-annotator agreement reflected by these scores reaffirmed that the task of annotating the artwork titles is difficult, even for humans. In order to obtain the gold standard test dataset for the evaluation of NER models, the disagreements were manually sorted out with the help of web search, resulting in a total of 144 entities being positively tagged as *title*.

---

[7] https://github.com/HPI-Information-Systems/enno

**Table 1.** Performance of NER models trained on different annotated datasets

| Train dataset | Size | Strict | | | Relaxed | | |
|---|---|---|---|---|---|---|---|
| | | P | R | F1 | P | R | F1 |
| Baseline | – | .14 | .06 | .08 | .22 | .08 | .12 |
| High-precision | 226,801 | .20 | .12 | .15 | .32 | .20 | .25 |
| High-precision + High-recall | 413,932 | **.23** | **.22** | **.23** | **.39** | **.41** | **.40** |

**Evaluation Metrics.** The performance of NER systems is generally measured in terms of precision, recall and F1 scores. The correct matching of a named entity involves the matching of the boundaries of the entity (in terms of character offsets in text) as well as the tagging of the named entity to the correct category. The strict F1 scores for NER evaluation were used in the CoNNL 2003 shared task [8], where the entities' boundaries were matched exactly. The MUC NER task [1] allowed for relaxed evaluation based on the matching of left or right boundary of an identified named entity. In this work, the evaluation of NER was performed only for entities of type *title* and therefore, it was sufficient to check only for the boundary matches of the identified entities. We evaluated the NER models with both strict metrics based on exact boundary match, as well as the relaxed metrics based on partial boundary matches. The relaxed metrics allowed for comparison of the entities despite errors due to wrong chunking of the named entities in the text (Sect. 2).

**Results and Discussion.** The results shown in Table 1 demonstrate significant improvement in performance for the NER models that were re-trained with relevant annotated data as compared to the baseline performance. Since the relaxed metrics allowed for flexible matching of the boundaries of the identified titles, they were consistently better than the strict matching scores for all cases. With the benefit of domain-specific and entity-specific annotations generated from the Wikidata entity dictionaries, the high-precision NER model was able to correctly identify many artwork titles. The performance was further boosted after including the high-recall dataset having additional annotations obtained with the help of boundary corrections. This illustrates the importance of quality of the NER training data for challenging domains. Our approach to generate high-quality annotations in semi-automated manner from a domain-specific corpus is an important contribution towards this direction.

## 6 Conclusion

In this work we proposed an approach to identify artwork mentions from art historic archives. We motivated the need for NER training on high-quality annotations and proposed techniques for generating the relevant training data for this task in semi-automated manner. Experimental evaluations showed that the NER performance can be significantly improved by training on high-quality training data generated with our methods. This indicates that even for noisy datasets, such as digitized art historical archives, supervised NER models can be trained to perform well. Furthermore, our approach is not limited to the cultural heritage domain but can be adapted for other domain-specific NER tasks, where there is also shortage of annotated training data. As future work we would like to apply our techniques for named entity recognition to other important entities and perform entity-centric text exploration for cultural heritage resources.

**Acknowledgements.** We thank the Wildenstein Plattner Institute[8] for providing the corpus used in this work.

# References

1. Chinchor, N.: Overview of MUC-7. In: Proceedings of the Seventh Message Understanding Conference (MUC-7) (1998)
2. de Boer, V., et al.: Supporting linked data production for cultural heritage institutes: the Amsterdam museum case study. In: Simperl, E., Cimiano, P., Polleres, A., Corcho, O., Presutti, V. (eds.) ESWC 2012. LNCS, vol. 7295, pp. 733–747. Springer, Heidelberg (2012). https://doi.org/10.1007/978-3-642-30284-8_56
3. Dijkshoorn, C., et al.: The Rijksmuseum collection as linked data. Semant. Web **9**(2), 221–230 (2018)
4. Ehrmann, M., Colavizza, G., Rochat, Y., Kaplan, F.: Diachronic evaluation of NER systems on old newspapers. In: Proceedings of the 13th Conference on Natural Language Processing (KONVENS 2016), pp. 97–107 (2016)
5. Pradhan, S., et al.: Towards robust linguistic analysis using OntoNotes. In: Proceedings of the Seventeenth Conference on Computational Natural Language Learning, pp. 143–152 (2013)
6. Prokofyev, R., Demartini, G., Cudré-Mauroux, P.: Effective named entity recognition for idiosyncratic web collections. In: Proceedings of the 23rd International Conference on World Wide Web (WWW), pp. 397–408. ACM (2014)
7. Rodriquez, K.J., Bryant, M., Blanke, T., Luszczynska, M.: Comparison of Named entity recognition tools for raw OCR text. In: Konvens, pp. 410–414 (2012)
8. Sang, E.F.T.K., De Meulder, F.: Introduction to the CoNLL-2003 shared task: language-independent named entity recognition. Development **922**, 1341 (1837)
9. Szekely, P., et al.: Connecting the smithsonian american art museum to the linked data cloud. In: Cimiano, P., Corcho, O., Presutti, V., Hollink, L., Rudolph, S. (eds.) ESWC 2013. LNCS, vol. 7882, pp. 593–607. Springer, Heidelberg (2013). https://doi.org/10.1007/978-3-642-38288-8_40
10. Van Hooland, S., De Wilde, M., Verborgh, R., Steiner, T., Van de Walle, R.: Exploring entity recognition and disambiguation for cultural heritage collections. Digit. Sch. Humanit. **30**(2), 262–279 (2013)
11. Van Hooland, S., Verborgh, R.: Linked Data for Libraries, Archives and Museums: How to Clean, Link and Publish Your Metadata. Facet Publishing, London (2014)
12. Vrandečić, D., Krötzsch, M.: Wikidata: a free collaborative knowledge base. Commun. ACM **57**(10), 78–85 (2014). https://doi.org/10.1145/2629489

---

[8] https://wpi.art.

# Gatekeeper: Quantifying the Impacts of Service to the Scientific Community

Spyke Krepshaw[✉] and Dongwon Lee[✉]

The Pennsylvania State University, State College, PA, USA
{spyke,dongwon}@psu.edu

**Abstract.** Academic scholars have several duties, including teaching, research, and service to the community and society. While a scholar's research impacts can be reasonably measured and tracked via citation analysis in existing digital libraries, to our best knowledge, there has been no system that systematically collects and quantifies a scholar's impacts of *service* to the scientific community. In particular, we are interested in measuring scholars' impacts as "gatekeepers," who play a key role in the spread of research findings and new knowledge via the accept/reject decisions of research articles. In this work, toward this goal, we present a prototype digital library, Gatekeeper, that crawls, extracts, and quantifies the impacts of service based on one's roles in the technical program committees of Computer Science conferences.

**Keywords:** Service impact · Citation analysis · $h$-index

## 1 Introduction

Being able to model and quantify the impacts of a scholar's service to the society has many utilities in applications–e.g., hiring and promoting scholars, or finding experts for service based committees. Yet, it is inherently subjective and ambiguous to quantify the impacts of one's service. Unlike quantifying one's research impacts that has been well studied and implemented by means of citation analysis, the term "service" itself has broad interpretations with discipline-specific definitions and examples. For instance, a scholar's service may include diverse activities such as participating in conference organization/technical committees, serving in editorial boards of journals, delivering talks/keynotes in events, reviewing books, serving in funding related panels, or interviewing with press and media. To our best knowledge, there is currently no digital library that collects scholars' service related activities and quantifies the impacts of service. In this work, therefore, we aim to address this gap and present the prototype digital library, named as Gatekeeper.

As the initial attempt, we first focus on one type of scholars' service activity– i.e., serving in the technical program committees (TPC) of Computer Science (CS) conferences for several reasons: (1) As well noted, CS is a unique discipline where conferences play a major role in disseminating significant findings.

© Springer Nature Switzerland AG 2019
A. Doucet et al. (Eds.): TPDL 2019, LNCS 11799, pp. 123–135, 2019.
https://doi.org/10.1007/978-3-030-30760-8_11

There is a well maintained digital library such as DBLP that shows a comprehensive list of CS conferences and their past websites; (2) Often, CS conference websites list detailed membership information of organization and program committees, along with their full names and identifying information (e.g., email or homepage) often available for easy extraction; and (3) As TPC members critically review research articles and contribute to the decision of accepting/rejecting the articles, thereby acting as a "gatekeeper" of new knowledge into the scientific community, collecting and quantifying their impacts of service is critically important.

Even with the focus on the service activities only in TPC, there are several challenges to address, including: (1) how to extract and differentiate different roles in TPC (e.g., program chair vs. area chair vs. senior program committee vs. program committee); (2) how to contrast the impacts of service across conferences or sub-disciplines (e.g., TPC in TPDL vs. TPC in AAAI); (3) how to factor in the size of TPC (e.g., TPC of 20 vs. TPC of 200); and (4) how to deal with the quality of conference in quantifying the impacts of service (e.g., TPC in a top CS venue vs. TPC in an obscure venue). Note that answers to all these challenges may vary as they are subjective in nature. In this paper, therefore, we present an approach that we took and a prototype that demonstrates the proof-of-concept.

## 2 Related Work

There are few works on quantifying the impacts of service, but abundant works on evaluating the impacts of research or scholars thereof.

### 2.1 Quantifying the Impacts of Research

Although journal articles are normally viewed more significant than conference articles in many disciplines, a culture in CS is radically different such that majority of major findings are reported in the form of conference articles. With such an abundance of articles being submitted to conferences, it has naturally become increasingly important to be able to discern the quality of conferences [11]. However, being able to understand the importance of a particular conference is not always immediately available. In the following, we review several representative methods to rate the quality of venues.

The (Journal) Impact Factor (IF) [6] was originally intended to assist in the selection of journals. It is calculated by taking the number of citations received in a specific year, adding the number of articles published in that journal during the two preceding years, and dividing by the total number of articles published in that journal during the two preceding years [7]. It is important to note that comparing IF scores between journals across disciplines is in general not useful. The idea of IF can be equally applied to conferences. In general, despite some pitfalls, IF scores are still one of the most popular indicators to assess the qualities of venues [10]. Applying the idea of PageRank [2] to a citation graph, one can infer impactful articles such that articles with more incoming citations, especially those from other impactful articles are viewed more impactful [3]. Similarly, other popular website ranking algorithms such as HITS [9] can be also applied to a citation graph, yielding hubs and authorities of research articles. When applied to a set of conferences and TPC list of those conferences, methods such as HITS can naturally identify important conferences and TPC members.

Other lesser-known research into ranking conferences includes ranking by way of TPC characteristics [13]. The idea of measuring TPC characteristics looks at the number of members, number of publications by members, average number of authors and so forth. Using this method, results have shown a high accuracy rate of classifying conferences. Unlike the previously mentioned methods, this model of ranking can be achieved without citation-based analysis. Conceptually related to PageRank, [12] takes an approach of *browser-based measure*, which takes the reader's behavior into consideration. This new method determines quality based on how a reader might "jump" from paper to paper. Such jumps could occur by looking for other papers with the same author(s), or finding a paper which was cited int he original.

## 2.2  Quantifying the Impacts of Scholars

One of the most popular methods to quantify the research impacts of a scholar is the $h$-index [8] that measures both the productivity (i.e., how many articles) and impact (i.e., how many citations) of one's research articles. In order words, a scholar receives an $h$-index score of $h$ if she has published at least $h$ articles have been cited at least $h$ times. While capturing both the productivity and impact of one's research well, the $h$-index method fails to recognize scholars who have made seminar findings with a small number of publications as they will have a low number of $h$. To improve on this shortcoming, the $g$-index method [4] further modifies the $h$-index such that a scholar receives a $g$-index score of $g$ if she has published at least $g$ articles that have been cited "collectively" at least $g^2$ times. This change has the effect of allowing highly-cited articles to effectively assist the low-cited articles in the calculation.

## 3  Quantifying the Impacts of Service

To quantify one's impacts of service, we apply both $h$-index and $g$-index ideas to our context and propose several "Gatekeeper"-index methods. Just like both $h$-index and $g$-index attempted to capture both productivity and impact of research concurrently, we aim to capture both productivity (i.e., how many TPC a scholar has served) and impact (i.e., how good a conference is) of service. Therefore, a scholar $A$ whose has served in 100 TPCs is deemed to have a higher service impact than a scholar $B$ who has served in 10 TPCs. Similarly, a scholar $C$ who has served in 10 TPCs of top CS venues may be deemed to have a higher service impact than a scholar $D$ who has served in 15 TPCs of obscure venues.

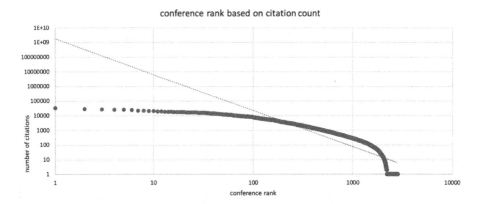

**Fig. 1.** A power-law like distribution of conference citations.

Further, to capture how good a conference is, we leverage on the well-studied citation analysis. Figure 1 illustrates a power-law like distribution (in a log-log plot) between the number of citations and the rank of conferences. That is, a small fraction of conferences accrue a large number of citations while a lot of conferences receive only a small number of citations. Using a total number of citations per conference as a measure of the goodness of a conference, then, we propose our first Gatekeeper-index as follows:

**Definition 1 ($G_1$-index).** *A scholar has the $G_1$-index score of N if she has served in N conferences as TPC and each conference has accrued at least a total of $f(N)$ citations, where $f()$ is a normalization function.*

For $f()$, for instance, one may simply use $\sqrt{}$ or $\sqrt[3]{}$ to oppress the influence of the large number of the total citation of a conference. In practice, due to a wide range of citation count per conference and delay of data collection, one may have to use a customized normalization function to have more realistic $G_1$-index scores. Table 1 shows a list of conferences where Bruce Worthman has served in TPC and their corresponding citation counts using the Microsoft Academic Graph (MAG)[1] digital library. Note that citation counts of many recent conferences have not been collected yet and there is a huge number of differences in citations between conferences.

For a scholar to have the $G_1$-index score of 10, for instance, she has to serve in at least 10 TPCs of conferences, where each conference has received at least a total of $\sqrt{100}$ or $\sqrt[3]{1000}$ citations. The $G_1$-index is intuitive and relatively easy to compute. However, as it uses the collective number of citations of a conference, it would disproportionately favor a large conference with many articles (thus larger total citations). To address this shortcoming, next, we use an average number of citations per article in a conference, instead of a total number of citations of a conference, to capture the quality of a conference.

---

[1] https://www.microsoft.com/en-us/research/project/microsoft-academic-graph/.

**Table 1.** A listing of conferences served by Bruce Worthman.

| Conference title | Citation count | Conference title | Citation count |
|---|---|---|---|
| WCNC 2019 | 0 | HPSR 2015 | 70 |
| IM 2019 | 0 | IM 2015 | 0 |
| VNC 2018 | 10 | INFOCOM 2015 | 4,150 |
| CNS 2018 | 0 | WCNC 2015 | 1,811 |
| ICC 2018 | 268 | GLOBECOM 2014 | 9,725 |
| MobiSec 2018 | 0 | ICC 2014 | 8,921 |
| GLOBECOM 2017 | 450 | NOMS 2014 | 1,792 |
| Healthcom 2017 | 29 | ICC 2013 | 10,040 |
| SECON 2017 | 50 | ICC 2012 | 13,279 |
| CISS 2017 | 95 | VNC 2011 | 582 |
| IM 2017 | 17 | PIMRC 2011 | 2,749 |
| INFOCOM 2017 | 722 | INFOCOM 2011 | 14,230 |
| WCNC 2017 | 482 | INFOCOM 2010 | 17,310 |
| GLOBECOM 2016 | 2,305 | IM 2009 | 1,424 |
| CNS 2016 | 0 | WCNC 2008 | 5,706 |
| IEEE PIMRC 2016 | 536 | IEEE SECON 2005 | 0 |
| SECON 2016 | 194 | INFOCOM 2004 | 28,439 |
| ISPLC 2016 | 54 | INFOCOM 2003 | 33,133 |
| GLOBECOM 2015 | 954 | | |

**Definition 2 ($G_2$-index).** *A scholar has the $G_2$-index score of $N$ if she has served in $N$ conferences as TPC and an article of each conference has accrued on average at least $N$ citations.*

Using the $G_2$-index formula, a scholar who has served in many TPCs, or who has served in impactful conferences, whose articles have high citations on average, is likely to have a high $G_2$-index score. Next, applying the $g$-index idea to our context, we propose our third Gatekeeper-index as follows:

**Definition 3 ($G_3$-index).** *A scholar has the $G_3$-index score of $N$ if she has served in TPC of top-$N$ conferences (sorted in descending order of citations) that have collectively received at least $N^2$ citations: i.e., $\sum_{N \geq i} C_i \geq N^2$, where $C_i$ is the citation count of a conference among top-$N$ conferences.*

Equivalently, $G_3$-index can be defined as the largest number $N$ of highly cited conferences (whose TPCs a scholar has served) for which the average number of citations is at least $N$. A scholar who has served in many highly-cited impactful conferences is likely to have a higher $G_3$-index score.

## 4    Data Collection

As indicated throughout this document, the need for a model to measure the impact of a gatekeeper's service is evident. To accomplish this task, various types of data from several sources are needed. The data which is required is that of conferences, the scholars who serve as the TPC members at the conferences, and their metadata. Unfortunately, widely renowned data resources such as DBLP or Google Scholar do not offer this specific type of data. Therefore, a further solution needs to be sought out. A block diagram of the data collection workflow can be seen in Fig. 2.

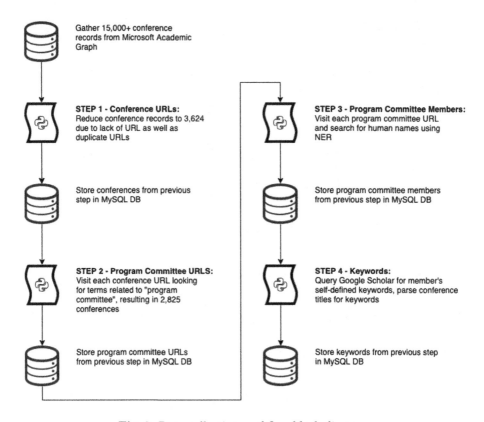

**Fig. 2.** Data collection workflow block diagram.

### 4.1    STEP 1: Finding Conference Websites

Initially, the data collection will start out by focusing on conferences in Computer Science. A valuable resource with a multitude of conference listings which is frequently updated can be viewed using the Microsoft Academic Graph (MAG). At the time of this writing, the MAG boasts over 15,000 conferences. The following attributes have been retrieved for each conference record from the MAG:

- `ConferenceInstanceId`: Unique MAG identifier for each conference
- `NormalizedName`: Full conference title
- `DisplayName`: Shorthand conference title
- `ConferenceSeriesId`: Determines if conference is part of a series
- `Location`: Geographic location of conference
- `OfficialUrl`: URL of conference website
- `StartDate/EndDate`: Start and end date of conference
- `PaperCount`: Number of papers accepted at conference
- `CitationCount`: Total number of citations for papers accepted at conference

The calculation of the aforementioned $G_1$-index uses the `CitationCount` while that of $G_2$-index uses the `PaperCount` in addition. The `OfficialUrl` attribute, if not null, readily provides the location of conference websites. When it is null, one can still attempt to locate the URLs of conferences using other means such as search engines.

## 4.2  STEP 2: Finding TPC Webpages

A conference website many have hundreds of webpages underneath. Among these webpages, in this step, we need to identify a set of webpages that list the TPC member information (i.e., gatekeepers). Essentially, we implemented a simple pattern-matching based detection (e.g., using a set of relevant keywords or phrases {program committee, TPC, reviewers, ...}). However, one can also build a more sophisticated machine learning model using features from contents of webpages and structures of websites.

## 4.3  STEP 3: Scraping Gatekeepers

Once TPC webpages are found, next, we attempt to scrape gatekeeper information from the webpages. This scraping is a non-trivial task due to varying and disagreeing formats that conference websites use. For instance, Fig. 3 shows four example TPC webpages, where gatekeeper information is listed in vastly different formats. Despite their differences in formats, however, we can derive a few heuristic rules: (1) Gatekeepers' information is displayed in some type of repeating pattern such as "list," and (2) Gatekeepers have human-like names. Therefore, we wrote a script to detect human-like names in a repeating fashion in the given webpage. The script goes through the entire HTML page, tokenizing each tag, and apply Stanford NER (Name Entity Recognizer) package[2] to identify each gatekeeper's name and additional accompanying information such as email, homepage URL, and affiliation (if one exists). The recent study [1] revealed that Stanford NER outperformed other NER packages such as Illinois NET, OpenCalais NER WS, and Alias-i LingPipe. All encountered unique human names are kept in an underlying database, forming many-to-many relationships between conferences and gatekeepers. At the end, we have scraped 56,187 gatekeepers serving at 2,825 computer science conferences.

---

[2] https://nlp.stanford.edu/software/CRF-NER.html.

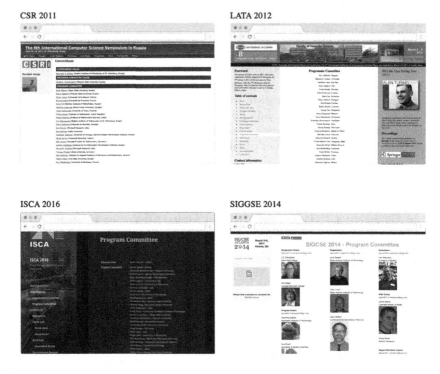

**Fig. 3.** Example TPC webpages with varying formats of gatekeeper information.

### 4.4   STEP 4: Scraping Research Keywords

Conference and gatekeeper information are the primary data to be collected, however, research keywords are also being collected. Research keywords are usually relevant words to either the topic/genre of a conference or research interests of a gatekeeper. These keywords can aid users in searching for specific gatekeepers or conferences. We first considered to run a topic model method such as LDA over the contents of conference websites or a collection of (titles of) articles authored by gatekeepers. However, by connecting gatekeepers to their corresponding pages in Google Scholar, where scholars often voluntarily pick a small number of research areas or keywords, we were able to scrape a list of self-defined research keywords of gatekeepers.

The summary of data statistics in our current prototype is listed in Table 2.

## 5   Prototype Gatekeeper

We have built a prototype digital library, Gatekeeper, with a limited number of conferences and gatekeepers. The backend of Gatekeeper is operating on a MySQL database. Using a combination of PHP and HTML, a frontend interface allows users to query information from Gatekeeper. The entire Gatekeeper runs

**Table 2.** Summary of data statistics in the prototype.

| Data type | Count |
|---|---|
| Conferences | 2,825 |
| Gatekeepers | 56,187 |
| Edges/Connections | 87,368 |
| Years | 27 |

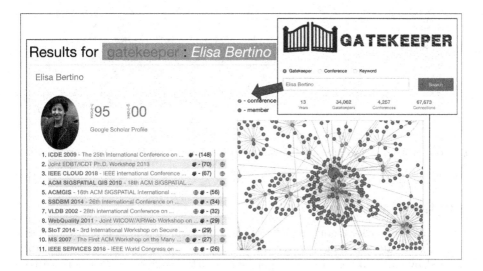

**Fig. 4.** Querying a gatekeeper "Elisa Bertino."

on an AWS (Amazon Web Services) Windows Server-based EC2 (Elastic Cloud
Computing) server. The system in its current state allows for users to browse a
list of top conferences (with respect to their research impacts) or top gatekeepers (with respect to their service impacts), or search by a gatekeeper name, a
conference name, or a research keyword.

## 5.1 Querying Gatekeepers

A query for a gatekeeper's name will produce a list of conferences served by the
gatekeeper, sorted in descending order with respect to one of Gatekeeper-index
scores. Users can switch among Gatekeeper-index methods to see different result.
For instance, Fig. 4 shows an example for a gatekeeper "Elisa Bertino." In the
conference list, next to each conference title will be an indicator of how many
gatekeepers have served at that particular conference. Lastly, a node-based graph
will represent the connections of the gatekeeper with their conferences. Viewing
larger served conferences or more servicing gatekeepers results in being able to
see the formation of clustering communities.

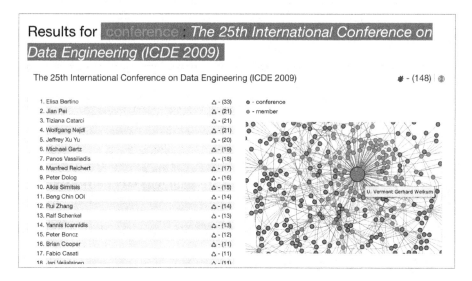

**Fig. 5.** Querying a conference "International Conference on Data Engineering/ICDE 2009."

## 5.2 Querying Conferences

Much like a query for a gatekeeper's name, a query for a conference title will produce a list of all matching records in the database. The returned list is currently ordered by the number of gatekeepers serving the conferences from greatest to least. After the calculation of the one of Gatekeeper-index methods, users will be offered multiple ways to sort the returned information. There is an indicator next to each conference title returned that identifies the number of gatekeepers who have served in the conference. Upon clicking on the conference, the conference detail page will show the list of gatekeepers who have served at the conference. For instance, Fig. 5 shows an example for a conference "International Conference on Data Engineering/ICDE 2009." Next to each gatekeeper name will be an indicator of how many conferences they have served. Lastly, a node-based graph will represent the connections of the conferences with their gatekeepers.

## 5.3 Querying Research Keywords

A query for a research keyword will produce a list of conferences (whose research themes match the keyword) or gatekeepers (whose research interests overlap the keyword). For instance, Fig. 6 shows an example for the keywords "artificial intelligence."

## 5.4 Other Applications of Gatekeeper

While not implemented yet, there are many useful applications of Gatekeeper that we plan to work in future.

**91 results for** keyword like: *artificial intelligence*

| | |
|---|---|
| 1. IBERAMIA 2018 - 16th Ibero-American Conference on Artificial Intelligence (IBERAMIA 2018) | △ - (108) ⊕ |
| 2. CSCI-ISAI - Symposium on Artificial Intelligence (CSCI-ISAI) | △ - (83) ⊕ |
| 3. ARIA-2015 - Second International Conference on Artificial Intelligence and Applications (ARIA-2015) | △ - (81) ⊕ |
| 4. AIPR2017 - The Fourth International Conference on Artificial Intelligence and Pattern Recognition (AIPR2017) | △ - (54) ⊕ |
| 5. MDAI 2018 - Modeling Decisions for Artificial Intelligence (MDAI 2018) | △ - (49) ⊕ |
| 6. AIME - 12th Conference on Artificial Intelligence in MEdicine (AIME) | △ - (47) ⊕ |
| 7. JELIA 2016 - 15th European Conference on Logics in Artificial Intelligence (JELIA 2016) | △ - (46) ⊕ |
| 8. MDAI 2016 - 13th International Conference on Modeling Decisions for Artificial Intelligence (MDAI 2016) | △ - (43) ⊕ |
| 9. MDAI 2015 - 12th International Conference on Modeling Decisions for Artificial Intelligence (MDAI 2015) | △ - (42) ⊕ |
| 10. MDAI 2017 - The 14th International Conference on Modeling Decisions for Artificial Intelligence (MDAI 2017) | △ - (42) ⊕ |
| 11. MDAI 2014 - 11th Int. Conf. on Modeling Decisions for Artificial Intelligence (MDAI 2014) | △ - (39) ⊕ |
| 12. MDAI 2010 - 7th Int. Conference on Modeling Decisions for Artificial Intelligence (MDAI 2010) | △ - (37) ⊕ |
| 13. MDAI 2012 - 9th Int. Conference on Modeling Decisions for Artificial Intelligence (MDAI 2012) | △ - (37) ⊕ |
| 14. AI and FL 2016 - Fourth International Conference of Artificial Intelligence and Fuzzy Logic (AI and FL 2016) | △ - (36) ⊕ |
| 15. AISE-IJCNN 2019 - Artificial Intelligence and Security (AISE-IJCNN 2019) | △ - (34) ⊕ |
| 16. AIAP-2015 - Second International Conference on Artificial Intelligence and Applications (AIAP-2015) | △ - (34) ⊕ |
| 17. AISCA 2018 - 2nd International Conference on Artificial Intelligence, Soft Computing and Applications (AISCA 2018) | △ - (32) ⊕ |
| 18. ICTAI 2018 - The 30th IEEE International Conference on Tools with Artificial Intelligence (ICTAI 2018) | △ - (32) ⊕ |
| 19. AAISC - The special Track on Applications of Artificial Intelligence in Smart Cities (AAISC) | △ - (32) ⊕ |
| 20. AIS 2018 - 4th International Conference on Artificial Intelligence and Soft Computing (AIS 2018) | △ - (30) ⊕ |
| 21. AIAPP 2018 - 5th International Conference on Artificial Intelligence and Applications (AIAPP 2018) | △ - (29) ⊕ |
| 22. ASAI - X Argentine Symposium on Artificial Intelligence (ASAI) | △ - (29) ⊕ |

**Fig. 6.** Querying a keyword "artificial intelligence."

First, consider an application that requires a group of experts in various settings. For instance, a program director at a funding agency may want to identify 20 experts to convene a review panel whose expertise closely match the theme of a program $X$. Similarly, a program chair of a new conference on a topic $Y$ may want to identify 30 scholars who can serve as TPC member. This is so-called the expert-finding problem [5]. By ranking gatekeepers with particular research keywords, then, one can easily find a group of experts for such settings. In addition, such tasks can be also solved by modeling it as a graph-based community detection or a recommendation problem on top of a bipartite graph between gatekeepers and conferences.

Second, by solving the link prediction problem in a graph of gatekeepers, one can recommend new service collaboration among gatekeepers. If two gatekeepers have not served in the TPC of the same conferences in past, but have neighboring gatekeepers in common, then such gatekeepers can be put into the same service collaboration in future.

## 5.5 Future Work

As the prototype currently covers only TPC members of Computer Science conferences, it needs to be significantly expanded to cover other types of gatekeepers (e.g., journal editors), other disciplines (e.g., Physics), and differentiate the roles of services (e.g., TPC member vs. Senior TPC member vs. Track Chair). This requires the development of a more sophisticated web crawling and entity/attribute scraping algorithm.

In addition, to have meaningful distributions of Gatekeeper-index scores, the dataset needs to be significantly expanded to cover a larger number of conferences over a more comprehensive period across multiple disciplines.

Also, we intend to use the Wayback Machine to explore conferences with identical year-to-year website URLs. Use of the Wayback Machine may be able to provide us with previous TPC committee lists.

Finally, we plan to conduct user studies to understand Gatekeeper-index methods better. For instance, we need to study the following questions: Among three variants, which method's scores are more likely to be in sync with scholars' impressions? Do the score distributions of Gatekeeper-index methods make sense?

## 6  Conclusion

In this work, we have presented an early attempt to design and implement a digital library to assess the impacts of service to the scientific community. To quantify the impacts of service in serving as TPC members of computer science conferences, we proposed three Gatekeeper-index methods that capture both productivity as well as impact of service.

## References

1. Atdağ, S., Labatut, V.: A comparison of named entity recognition tools applied to biographical texts. In: International Conference on Systems and Computer Science (2013)
2. Brin, S., Page, L.: The anatomy of a large scale hypertextual Web search engine, published version. In: Computer Networks and ISDN Systems (1998)
3. Chen, P., Xie, H., Maslov, S., Redner, S.: Finding scientific gems with Google's PageRank algorithm. J. Informetr. **1**, 8–15 (2007)
4. Egghe, L.: Theory and practise of the g-index. Scientometrics **69**, 131–152 (2006)
5. Fang, H., Zhai, C.X.: Probabilistic models for expert finding. In: Amati, G., Carpineto, C., Romano, G. (eds.) ECIR 2007. LNCS, vol. 4425, pp. 418–430. Springer, Heidelberg (2007). https://doi.org/10.1007/978-3-540-71496-5_38
6. Garfield, E.: Citation indexes for science. Science **122**, 108–111 (1955)
7. Garfield, E.: The history and meaning of the journal impact factor (2006)
8. Hirsch, J.E.: An index to quantify an individual's scientific research output. Proc. Natl. Acad. Sci. U S A **102**, 16569–16572 (2005)
9. Kleinberg, J.M.: Authoritative sources in a hyperlinked environment. J. ACM **46**, 604–632 (1999)
10. Li, X., Rong, W., Shi, H., Tang, J., Xiong, Z.: The impact of conference ranking systems in computer science: a comparative regression analysis. Scientometrics **116**(2), 879–907 (2018)
11. Sidiropoulos, A., Manolopoulos, Y.: A new perspective to automatically rank scientific conferences using digital libraries. Inf. Process. Manag. **41**, 289–312 (2005)

12. Yan, S., Lee, D.: Toward alternative measures for ranking venues: a case of database research community. In: 7th ACM/IEEE-CS Joint Conference on Digital Libraries (JCDL), pp. 235–244. ACM, New York (2007)
13. Zhuang, Z., Elmacioglu, E., Lee, D., Giles, C.L.: Measuring conference quality by mining program committee characteristics. In: 7th ACM/IEEE-CS Joint Conference on Digital Libraries (JCDL) (2007)

# A Study on the Readability of Scientific Publications

Thanasis Vergoulis[1]([✉]), Ilias Kanellos[1,2], Anargiros Tzerefos[3],
Serafeim Chatzopoulos[1,3], Theodore Dalamagas[1], and Spiros Skiadopoulos[3]

[1] IMSI, Athena Research and Innovation Center, 15125 Athens, Greece
{vergoulis,ilias.kanellos,schatz,dalamag}@athenarc.gr
[2] School of Electrical and Computer Engineering, NTUA, 15780 Athens, Greece
[3] Department of Informatics and Telecommunications, University of the Peloponnese,
22100 Tripoli, Greece
{dit13139,spiros}@uop.gr

**Abstract.** Several works have used traditional readability measures to investigate the readability of scientific texts and its association with scientific impact. However, these works are limited in terms of dataset size, range of domains, and examined readability and impact measures. Our study addresses these limitations, investigating the readability of paper abstracts on a very large multidisciplinary corpus, the association of expert judgments on abstract readability with traditional readability measures, and the association of abstract readability with the scientific impact of the corresponding publication.

**Keywords:** Readability · Scientific impact · Text analysis

## 1 Introduction

Reporting scientific issues with clarity in publications is a fundamental part of the scientific process, since it aids the comprehension of research findings and establishes the foundation for future research work. In addition, well-written scientific texts help the comprehension of research findings and scientific knowledge by journalists, educators, science enthusiasts, and the public, in general, preventing the dissemination of inaccuracies and misconceptions.

For these reasons, measuring and studying the readability in academic writing is of great importance and many studies have been conducted to investigate relevant issues. Most of the studies rely on traditional readability measures originally introduced to help in selecting appropriate teaching materials [21], or quantify the minimum required educational level for a text to be understood.

In this work, we focus our investigation on the readability of scientific paper abstracts. In particular, we focus on the following research questions:

– RQ1: How does the readability of publication abstracts, as calculated by traditional readability measures, evolve over time?

A. Doucet et al. (Eds.): TPDL 2019, LNCS 11799, pp. 136–144, 2019.
https://doi.org/10.1007/978-3-030-30760-8_12

– RQ2: To what extent are these measures associated with what is considered by domain experts as a well-written scientific text?
– RQ3: To what extent is the readability of a publication abstract associated with the scientific impact of the corresponding publication?

Existing literature investigates some of the previous research questions to a limited extent only, e.g., most works only focus on particular scientific domains, use small datasets, or examine only few readability and impact measures (details in Sect. 2). Our contributions are the following:

– We investigate readability over time on a multidisciplinary corpus an order of magnitude larger than those used by previous studies ($\sim 12$M abstracts).
– To the best of our knowledge, this is the first work to examine the agreement of readability as it is perceived by domain experts, compared to that calculated by traditional readability measures. Additionally, we make our dataset of the expert judgments publicly available at Zenodo (see Sect. 3.1)
– We examine the association of readability, as measured both by traditional measures and expert judgements, to impact. We employ three different impact measures, capturing slightly different notions of scientific impact.

## 2   Related Work

Several studies investigated the readability of scientific texts (abstracts and/or full texts) over time and its association to paper impact. However, most studies investigate small datasets, restricted to a particular domain (e.g., management and marketing [1,4,16,18], psychology [9,10], chemistry [3], information science [11]). Only few studies investigated multiple disciplines [6,15].

Longitudinal studies examining readability of scientific texts report varying results. In [6] FRE was measured for 260,000 paper abstracts revealing no significant changes in readability over time. In [20] the 100 most highly cited neuroimaging papers were examined in terms of readability, using an average of five grade level readability formulas, showing no relationship between readability and the papers' publication years. In [11] FRE and SMOG were used on papers of the Information Science Journals, published in the span of a decade, reporting only a trivial decrease of abstract readability and a respective increase in full text readability. Another recent research, however, examined more than 700,000 abstracts from PubMed using the FRE and Dale-Chall measures, reporting a statistically significant decrease in readability over time [15]. The association of paper impact and readability has also been examined, with most studies reporting no significant association between readability and citation counts [6,11,20]. However, in [10], although no correlation between citation counts and FRE was found, the authors additionally consider existing curated selections of prestigious publications finding, in this case, that readability and impact did correlate.

Our work extends previous studies threefold: first, we use four measures to examine abstract readability over time on a larger corpus and time span, compared to previous work. Second, we investigate the association of readability measures to expert readability judgements on scientific abstracts. Finally, we study the association of readability and impact using three impact measures capturing different impact aspects.

## 3   Methods

### 3.1   Datasets

**Publication Abstracts and Impact (D1).** To study the readability of scientific publications over time (RQ1) and its correlation to scientific impact (RQ3), we used a large multidisciplinary collection of scientific texts. We gathered all publications (distinct DOIs) included in the OpenCitations COCI dataset[1]. We collected their abstracts and titles from the Open Academic Graph[2] [17,19] and the Crossref REST API[3], keeping only publications for which the abstract was available. Then, we performed basic cleaning by removing publications containing XML tags in the abstract and ignoring publications with abstracts containing less than three sentences[4]. This resulted in a dataset containing abstracts and citations for $12,534,077$ publications. Finally, we used this dataset to calculate citation counts and additionally gathered extra impact scores (i.e., PageRank and RAM) about all the collected publications using BIP! Finder's API[5].

**Domain Expert Readability (D2).** To investigate RQ2 and RQ3, we gathered judgments for the readability of publication abstracts from 10 data and knowledge management experts (PhD students or post-docs) through a Web-based survey. The abstracts were a subset of AMiner's DBLP citation dataset[6]. To guarantee that most of the abstracts would be relevant to the area of expertise of our experts, we only used abstracts containing the terms illustrated in Table 1. Each expert provided judgments for a small subset of these abstracts $(34-202)$. Upon reviewing a particular publication, an expert had to read its abstract and then, answer three questions relevant to different aspects of abstract readability. These questions were worded as shown in Table 2 and the allowed answers were based on a 5 point scale[7]. Each time an expert requested to review a new abstract, the system provided either an abstract already rated by other experts, or one unrated. To guarantee a substantive overlap between the sets of abstracts rated by each expert, we used the following procedure: an unrated abstract was provided to the expert only after rating 10 abstracts previously rated by others. Dataset D2 is openly available at Zenodo[8].

---

[1] http://opencitations.net/download (November 2018 Dump).
[2] https://www.openacademic.ai/oag/.
[3] https://www.crossref.org/services/metadata-delivery/rest-api/.
[4] This is a restriction imposed by the `textstat` library (see Sect. 3.2).
[5] http://bip.imsi.athenarc.gr:4000/documentation.
[6] https://aminer.org/citation.
[7] For each question, the interpretation of the extreme scale values (i.e., 1 and 5) were provided (actual wording is described in the dataset description page in Zenodo).
[8] https://doi.org/10.5281/zenodo.2651009.

**Table 1.** List of terms used to construct D2

| "database" | "machine learning" | "information retrieval" | "data management" |
|---|---|---|---|
| "cloud computing" | "data mining" | "algorithms" | "classification" |
| "query processing" | "networks" | "indexing" | "distributed systems" |

**Table 2.** The questions of the Web-based survey

| Q1 | "Please rate how well-written the abstract is" |
|---|---|
| Q2 | "Does the abstract contain linguistic errors?" |
| Q3 | "Please rate how clear the contribution of the paper is (based on the abstract)" |

### 3.2 Examined Readability and Impact Measures

In our experiments we examine abstract readability based on four measures: FRE [5], SMOG, [13], Dale-Chall (DC) [21], and Gunning Fog (GF) [8]. The former two use statistics such as sentence length and average number of syllables per word, while the latter two also take into account "difficult" words (e.g., based on syllable length, or dictionaries). For FRE a higher score indicates a more readable text, while the opposite holds for the other measures. All readability scores were calculated using the `textstat`[9] (release 0.5.6) Python library.

Additionally we calculate three scientific impact measures: citation counts, PageRank [14], and RAM [7]. Citation counts are the de facto measure used in evaluations of academic performance. PageRank differentiates citations, based on the paper making them, following the principle that "good papers cite other good papers". Finally, RAM considers recent citations as more important, aiming to overcome the citation bias against recently published papers.

## 4 Results and Discussion

### 4.1 Longitudinal Study of Readability

In this section we focus on research question RQ1. To examine temporal changes in readability, we calculated the FRE, SMOG, GF, and DC scores on dataset D1 and measured the yearly average scores (Fig. 1). We observe that, generally, abstract readability seems to be decreasing over time, based on all measures[10]. These findings are in agreement with the results of [11] which showed an insignificant downtrend in FRE on Information Science Journals, however they do not demonstrate as dramatic a drop in readability, as shown in [15] for PubMed papers. On the other hand, our findings contrast previous domain specific works that report relatively constant readability with time [6]. The trend of decreasing readability could be attributed, as previous works have stated, on factors such as the increased use of scientific jargon [15].

---

[9] https://github.com/shivam5992/textstat.

[10] Recall that FRE scores increase with readability, contrary to the other measures.

## 4.2    Readability Measures Vs Expert Judgments

Since traditional readability measures were initially introduced for testing the
readability level of school textbooks [21] their suitability for use in the context
of scientific articles (as conducted in previous studies) could be debatable. In
this section, we investigate this matter using dataset D2. For each abstract in D2
we calculated (a) its score based on each of the four readability measures used
in our study and (b) the average score it gathered for each question posed to
the experts. In our experiments, to avoid biases, we kept only abstracts judged
by at least four experts resulting in a set of 172 publication abstracts.

Table 3 illustrates the correlation (Spearman's $\rho$ and Kendall's $\tau$) of the
four readability measures to the average score for each question. Interestingly,
only extremely weak correlations were found. Although the dataset is relatively
small, following the reasoning in [2], if a true significantly stronger correlation
(e.g., $\tau > 0.3$) existed, we would expect to have measured greater values of

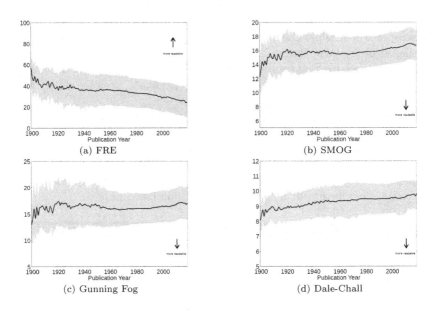

**Fig. 1.** Average scores per year (with st. deviation)

**Table 3.** Correlations of expert judgments to readability measures. FRE scores were
reversed for reasons of uniformity, i.e. readability decreases with score, for all measures.

|    | Spearman's $\rho$ | | | | Kendall's $\tau$ | | | |
|----|---------|---------|---------|---------|---------|---------|---------|---------|
|    | FRE | SMOG | DC | GF | FRE | SMOG | DC | GF |
| Q1 | −0.0776 | 0.0371 | −0.0372 | −0.0552 | −0.0509 | 0.0256 | −0.0275 | −0.0395 |
| Q2 | −0.0346 | −0.0100 | 0.0946 | 0.0794 | −0.0247 | −0.0135 | 0.0657 | 0.0542 |
| Q3 | −0.0884 | 0.0216 | −0.1033 | −0.0712 | −0.0584 | 0.0114 | −0.0741 | −0.0494 |

**Table 4.** Pairwise correlations ($\tau$) of expert judgments on question Q1. *Corr. coefficients significant at $p < 10^{-3}$. **Corr. coefficients significant at $p < 10^{-5}$.

| Q1 | E1 | E2 | E3 | E4 | E5 | E6 | E7 | E8 | E9 | E10 |
|---|---|---|---|---|---|---|---|---|---|---|
| E1 | 1.0 | | | | | | | | | |
| E2 | 0.27 | 1.0 | | | | | | | | |
| E3 | 0.05 | 0.51** | 1.0 | | | | | | | |
| E4 | 0.20 | 0.07 | 0.18 | 1.0 | | | | | | |
| E5 | 0.50* | 0.23 | 0.26 | 0.38 | 1.0 | | | | | |
| E6 | 0.31 | 0.37* | 0.42* | 0.09 | 0.35 | 1.0 | | | | |
| E7 | 0.20 | 0.27 | 0.46* | 0.23 | 0.35 | 0.48** | 1.0 | | | |
| E8 | 0.22 | 0.28 | 0.21 | 0.22 | 0.38 | 0.31* | 0.26 | 1.0 | | |
| E9 | 0.17 | 0.32* | 0.51** | 0.24 | 0.17 | 0.34* | 0.35* | 0.43** | 1.0 | |
| E10 | 0.28 | 0.60* | 0.68** | 0.45 | 0.47 | 0.50 | 0.68* | 0.33 | 0.40 | 1.0 |

correlation. This result may hint that mechanically applying classic readability measures in the context of scientific texts, a common practice in the literature, may not be entirely appropriate. While this is not to say that readability measures are entirely useless, it does point out the need for additional methods particularly tailored to measure readability in this context.

Another interesting subject for investigation is whether the notion of being "readable" is compliant between different experts and between the different questions of Table 2. Table 4 shows the correlation[11] between the average scores given by the experts to question Q1 for the abstracts in D2[12]. We observe that the answers of reviewers agree substantially only in few cases (e.g., $\tau = 0.68$ for researchers E3-E10) and overall expert responses do not seem to correlate at all (similar results were found for Q2 and Q3). These results indicate that each individual's idea of what defines a "well written" text may differ. The above may be to some degree reflected in the correlation of averages given to questions Q1-Q3. We found less than perfect correlation of these results to each other ($0.48 < \rho < 0.77$, and $0.34 < \tau < 0.59$ between averages for all pairs of Q1-Q3) which additionally hints that these questions indeed capture different semantics.

### 4.3 Abstract Readability vs Paper Impact

In this section we focus on research question RQ3, examining the association of publication readability and impact on dataset D1. First, we measure Spearman's $\rho$[13] between readability rankings (FRE, SMOG, GF, DC) and impact rankings (Citation Counts, PageRank, and RAM). Overall we report very weak

---

[11] Due to lack of space we omit $\rho$ values, however the results were similar.
[12] For this measurement, we used all overlapping D2 abstracts for each expert pair.
[13] We omit $\tau$ since it runs very slow on this dataset ($\sim$ 12M papers).

correlations between readability and impact measures (Table 5). This is in agreement with previous research which focused on particular domains [6,11,20]. An interesting observation is that, among the other impact measures, RAM achieves a significantly higher (but not moderate) correlation to the readability measures in comparison to Citation Counts and PageRank. This finding could be explained as follows: due to its de-bias mechanism, a large proportion of the top-ranked publications based on RAM are recently published articles. In addition, based on Figs. 1a–d, recent publications tend to have less readable abstracts. Therefore, since both RAM and readability scores favor recent publications, it is not surprising that we observe a higher correlation in this case.

**Table 5.** Correlations ($\rho$) of readability measures to impact measures (FRE scores reversed for uniformity, star notation same as in Table 4).

|                | FRE        | SMOG     | DC          | GF        |
|----------------|------------|----------|-------------|-----------|
| Citation count | −0.0525**  | 0.0656** | −0.0013**   | 0.03800** |
| PageRank       | 0.0001     | 0.0076** | −0.01635**  | 0.0011*   |
| RAM            | 0.1169**   | 0.1257** | 0.0397**    | 0.0837**  |

Since we generally found disagreements between traditional readability measures and expert judgments (Sect. 4.2), we also measure readability based on the averages of expert responses compared to impact measures. We note similar relative values for Spearman's $\rho$ and Kendall's $\tau$, that correspond to very weak and statistically insignificant correlations (Table 6). One conclusion based on the above is that readability does not seem to play a key role in whether a paper will be cited. Our results show that this holds regardless of whether we consider readability measures, or expert judgments. Along with discussion in [6] this counters claims that simple abstracts correlate with citation counts [12].

**Table 6.** Correlations of expert judgments to impact measures.

|     | Spearman's $\rho$ |        |        | Kendall's $\tau$ |        |        |
|-----|--------|--------|--------|--------|--------|--------|
|     | CC     | PR     | RAM    | CC     | PR     | RAM    |
| Q1  | 0.1925 | 0.1896 | 0.2242 | 0.1358 | 0.1286 | 0.1539 |
| Q2  | 0.1827 | 0.1433 | 0.1963 | 0.1273 | 0.0946 | 0.1366 |
| Q3  | 0.162  | 0.1285 | 0.2192 | 0.1139 | 0.0878 | 0.1526 |

## 5   Conclusion

In this work we investigated several issues regarding the readability of publications. First, we conducted a longitudinal study using ∼12M publication abstracts from many scientific disciplines. To the best of our knowledge, this is the largest collection of scientific texts analyzed in terms of readability so far. Our findings support the results of some earlier studies (e.g., [11,15]), that the overall readability of scientific publications tends to decrease. Second, we examine if the experts' opinion about the readability of scientific texts is compliant with the notion of readability captured by traditional measures. Our findings suggest that these measures are not in absolute agreement. This indicates that there is a need for new, specialized readability measures tailored for scientific texts. Finally, we examined how readability of publications (both as perceived by domain experts and as captured by traditional measures) associates with different aspects of scientific impact. Our results have shown no significant correlation of readability and impact.

**Acknowledgments.** We acknowledge support of this work by the project "Moving from Big Data Management to Data Science" (MIS 5002437/3) which is implemented under the Action "Reinforcement of the Research and Innovation Infrastructure", funded by the Operational Programme "Competitiveness, Entrepreneurship and Innovation" (NSRF 2014-2020) and co-financed by Greece and the European Union (European Regional Development Fund).

# References

1. Bauerly, R.J., Johnson, D.T., Singh, M.: Readability and writing well. Mark. Manag. J. **16**(1), 216–227 (2006)
2. Bonett, D.G., Wright, T.A.: Sample size requirements for estimating pearson, kendall and spearman correlations. Psychometrika **65**(1), 23–28 (2000)
3. Bottle, R.T., Rennie, J.S., Russ, S., Sardar, Z.: Changes in the communication of chemical information I: some effects of growth. J. Inf. Sci. **6**(4), 103–108 (1983)
4. Crosier, K.: How effectively do marketing journals transfer useful learning from scholars to practitioners? Mark. Intell. Plan. **22**(5), 540–556 (2004)
5. Flesch, R.: A new readability yardstick. J. Appl. Psychol. **32**(3), 221 (1948)
6. Gazni, A.: Are the abstracts of high impact articles more readable? Investigating the evidence from top research institutions in the world. J. Inf. Sci. **37**(3), 273–281 (2011)
7. Ghosh, R., Kuo, T.T., Hsu, C.N., Lin, S.D., Lerman, K.: Time-aware ranking in dynamic citation networks. In: 2011 IEEE 11th International Conference on Data Mining Workshops, pp. 373–380. IEEE (2011)
8. Gunning, R.: The Technique of Clear Writing. McGraw-Hill, New York (1952)
9. Hartley, J., Pennebaker, J.W., Fox, C.: Abstracts, introductions and discussions: how far do they differ in style? Scientometrics **57**(3), 389–398 (2003)
10. Hartley, J., Sotto, E., Pennebaker, J.: Style and substance in psychology: are influential articles more readable than less influential ones? Soc. Stud. Sci. **32**(2), 321–334 (2002)
11. Lei, L., Yan, S.: Readability and citations in information science: evidence from abstracts and articles of four journals (2003–2012). Scientometrics **108**(3), 1155–1169 (2016)
12. Letchford, A., Preis, T., Moat, H.S.: The advantage of simple paper abstracts. J. Informetr. **10**(1), 1–8 (2016)

13. Mc Laughlin, G.H.: Smog grading-a new readability formula. J. Read. **12**(8), 639–646 (1969)
14. Page, L., Brin, S., Motwani, R., Winograd, T.: The PageRank citation ranking: bringing order to the web. Technical report, Stanford InfoLab (1999)
15. Plavén-Sigray, P., Matheson, G.J., Schiffler, B.C., Thompson, W.H.: The readability of scientific texts is decreasing over time. Elife **6**, e27725 (2017)
16. Sawyer, A.G., Laran, J., Xu, J.: The readability of marketing journals: are award-winning articles better written? J. Mark. **72**(1), 108–117 (2008)
17. Sinha, A., et al.: An overview of Microsoft academic service (MAS) and applications. In: Proceedings of the 24th International Conference on World Wide Web, pp. 243–246. ACM (2015)
18. Stremersch, S., Verniers, I., Verhoef, P.C.: The quest for citations: drivers of article impact. J. Mark. **71**(3), 171–193 (2007)
19. Tang, J., Zhang, J., Yao, L., Li, J., Zhang, L., Su, Z.: ArnetMiner: extraction and mining of academic social networks. In: Proceedings of the 14th ACM SIGKDD, pp. 990–998. ACM (2008)
20. Yeung, A.W.K., Goto, T.K., Leung, W.K.: Readability of the 100 most-cited neuroimaging papers assessed by common readability formulae. Front. Hum. Neurosci. **12**, 308 (2018)
21. Zamanian, M., Heydari, P.: Readability of texts: state of the art. Theory Pract. Lang. Stud. **2**(1), 43–53 (2012)

# Interdisciplinary Collaborations in the Brazilian Scientific Community

Geraldo J. Pessoa Junior[1][(✉)], Thiago M. R. Dias[2], Thiago H. P. Silva[1], and Alberto H. F. Laender[1]

[1] Universidade Federal de Minas Gerais, Belo Horizonte, MG 31270-901, Brazil
{geraldo.pessoa,thps,laender}@dcc.ufmg.br
[2] Centro Federal de Educação Tecnológica, Divinópolis, MG 35503-822, Brazil
thiago@div.cefetmg.br

**Abstract.** Interdisciplinary collaborations have recently drawn the attention of scholars, since bridging academic relationships contributes to make scientific collaboration networks stronger. However, previous studies have focused on characterizing specific groups rather than on studying a complete and robust scientific community. In this paper, instead of analyzing particular scenarios, we characterize these collaborations with respect to the eight Brazilian scientific communities defined according to the upper level of a knowledge area classification scheme. Our results show that the Brazilian scientific collaboration network has grown, becoming especially interdisciplinary.

**Keywords:** Interdisciplinary collaborations ·
Scientific collaboration networks · Scientific communities ·
Lattes Platform

## 1 Introduction

Recent studies have addressed an important and broad issue involving the role of interdisciplinary collaborations in scientific coauthorship networks [1,7], since such collaborations contribute to strengthen the understanding of how science evolves. Indeed, this has drawn the attention of scholars and previous efforts have focused on external collaborations (e.g., cooperation among research groups [3], migration of researchers [4] and influence from distinct research areas [6]) as being an important factor in the evolution of scientific communities. However, such studies have mainly focused on characterizing specific research groups or areas [4], rather than on mining a complete and robust scientific community.

According to Sonnenwald [11], a scientific collaboration is the interaction between scientists with the purpose of sharing activities in order to achieve common goals as a final result. In this context, complex network analyses have been carried out to understand the meaning of such collaborations in different scenarios. In a pionieering work, Mena-Chalco et al. [7] conducted a study regarding major research areas within the Brazilian scientific community. In their study,

© Springer Nature Switzerland AG 2019
A. Doucet et al. (Eds.): TPDL 2019, LNCS 11799, pp. 145–153, 2019.
https://doi.org/10.1007/978-3-030-30760-8_13

they characterized the eight major areas that we address in this work, but only considering topological metrics. As a result, they contributed to a better understanding of how Brazilian researchers collaborate to each other.

In a recent work, Abramo et al. [1] reported the results of a study aiming at verifying the influence of multidisciplinarity among researchers from a same project and how scientific production can be affected by this type of collaboration. In their study, they analyzed the publications of all Italian faculty members, but covering a period of only five years, from 2004 to 2008. Like us, they also adopted a classification scheme and classified the Italian researchers according to their specialties in eight major areas. Their results show that scientific publications on specific topics are produced by researchers from the same area, while the most diversified ones come from multidisciplinary groups.

In this context, instead of analyzing particular scenarios of specific groups (e.g., a university, an academic department, a research area or research group), we move one step forward by constructing the global and the interdisciplinary coauthoship networks of an entire country, Brazil, using for this a specific data source, the Lattes Platform[1]. Maintained by the Brazilian National Council for Scientific and Technological Development (CNPq), this platform is an internationally renowned initiative [5] that provides a repository of researchers' curricula vitae and research groups, all integrated into a single system. Since all researchers in Brazil (from junior to senior) are required to keep their curricula updated in this platform, it provides a great amount of information about their research activities and scientific production. We stress that several studies tend to focus only on the global aspect of the collaboration networks, giving the same importance to all edges. We argue about the importance of mining more deeply interdisciplinary patterns to explore the strength of intra-links as a mechanism for revealing specific aspects of scientific collaborations [3,4].

In this paper, we analyze the interdisciplinary collaborations of the Brazilian scientific collaboration network based on a specific research area classification scheme. Particularly, we use the upper level of the CNPq knowledge area classification scheme[2], which considers the following eight major areas: *Agrarian Sciences, Biological Sciences, Health Sciences, Exact and Earth Sciences, Humanities, Applied and Social Sciences, Engineering*, and *Linguistics, Letters and Arts* (for more details, refer to [10]). Note that our effort involves the complete Brazilian academic collaboration network, comprising all scholars with a PhD degree (a total of 263,264 as for April, 2018). As we shall see, 35.2% of all collaborations in this network are interdisciplinary, i.e., they involve researchers from distinct major areas, which emphasizes the importance of interdisciplinary collaborations in a more interconnected world.

---

[1] Lattes Platform: http://lattes.cnpq.br.

[2] This classification scheme is organized into the following four levels (see http://bit. ly/1JM2j1k): *major area* (e.g., Exact and Earth Sciences), *area* (e.g., Computer Science), *subarea* (e.g., Theory of Computation) and *specialty* (e.g., Formal Languages and Automata).

In summary, the main contributions of this paper are twofold: (i) a characterization study of eight large Brazilian academic communities, considering its complete network and the interdisciplinary one, and (ii) an investigation of the intensity of the interdisciplinary collaborations across distinct communities.

The remainder of this paper is organized as follows. Section 2 describes how we acquired and prepared the data we use in our analysis. Section 3 summarizes the results of our analysis, highlighting the impact of the interdisciplinary collaborations in coauthorship networks. Finally, Sect. 4 presents our concluding remarks and some insights for future work.

## 2   Data Acquisition and Preparation

In this section, we describe our data acquisition and preparation process, before analyzing the properties of the interdisciplinary collaborations found in the Brazilian scientific network. As a profile analysis depends on high-quality data, we collected our data from the Lattes Platform, whose content provides an updated view of the Brazilian scientific production. We detail next the main steps carried out for building our dataset.

***Step 1: Electing the classification scheme.*** As already mentioned, we adopted the upper level of the CNPq knowledge area classification scheme, which considers the following eight major areas: *Agrarian Sciences, Biological Sciences, Health Sciences, Exact and Earth Sciences, Humanities, Applied and Social Sciences, Engineering,* and *Linguistics, Letters and Arts.*

***Step 2: Selecting the researchers.*** Since the Lattes Platform stores data from both young (e.g., undergraduate students) and more experienced researchers, in this work we considered only those researchers who hold a PhD degree. Thus, our goal was to emphasize only mature interdisciplinary collaborations, i.e., collaborations established by more experienced researchers. Note that our effort involves the complete Brazilian academic scientific collaboration network, which comprises a total of 263,264 researchers with a PhD degree that have some association with a research institution in Brazil.

***Step 3: Collecting the data.*** First, we collected from the Lattes Platform the XML versions of the curricula vitae of all elected researchers. Then, we transformed the respective XML documents into CSV files containing only those fields required to identify the researchers' scientific collaborations, thus reducing the amount of data required for further manipulation.

***Step 4: Identifying the collaborations.*** As data insertion on the Lattes Platform is done manually by the researchers themselves, there is no guarantee that the coauthors are properly identified in each registered publication. Given this drawback, we have processed all curricula in order to identify the collaborations by comparing the titles of the publications and their authors' names. To avoid processing all publications for all authors, we adopted the strategy proposed by Dias and Moita [2], which generates a kind of authorship identifier. This strategy first removes all special characters and stop words from the publication titles. Then, it stems each title word to its root form. Finally, it concatenates all generated tokens and adds the publication year to the final string, thus creating a hash key for each publication. The hash keys are then used as an identifier for the authors' collaborations. We notice that, for the purposes of the analyses carried out in this paper, we only consider collaborations that correspond to coauthorships identified from journal articles.

***Step 5: Building the networks.*** Once the collaborations were identified, we built two networks. The first one, called Global, includes a node for each one of the 263,264 researchers in our dataset, with an edge being created between two nodes whenever the respective researchers have at least one scientific collaboration. The second network, called Interdisciplinary, includes a node only for those researchers who have at least one collaboration with a researcher from a distinct major area, so that its edges represent only interdisciplinary collaborations.

Table 1 shows the final distribution of the number of researchers by major area in our dataset. As we can see, the number of researchers in each major area is quite uneven and basically reflects the popularity of each one of them.

**Table 1.** Distribution of researchers by major area.

| Major area | Researchers |
|---|---|
| Agrarian Sciences | 26,953 |
| Applied and Social Sciences | 29,146 |
| Biological Sciences | 36,356 |
| Engineering | 24,746 |
| Exact and Earth Sciences | 39,231 |
| Health Sciences | 45,990 |
| Humanities | 44,743 |
| Linguistics, Letters and Arts | 16,099 |
| Total | 263,264 |

## 3    Analysis of the Networks

In this section, we analyze the properties of the Brazilian Global and Interdisciplinary scientific collaboration networks, and depict how the nodes in these networks are interconnected by showing the intensity of the collaborations in each major area.

Table 2 shows the values for some usual metrics for both networks. First, we highlight that 35.2% of the collaborations (900,992 out of 2,563,017) correspond to interdisciplinary edges. This number is very expressive, since it refers to the network of an entire scientific community. In addition, the fact that a large number of edges in the giant component (maximal subgraph that includes a path

**Table 2.** Metric values of both networks.

| Metric | Global | Interdisciplinary |
|---|---|---|
| Number of nodes | 263,264 | 263,264 |
| Number of edges | 2,563,017 | 900,992 |
| Average degree | 11.9 | 6.8 |
| Size of the giant component | 207,583 | 167,324 |
| Nodes % in the giant component | 78.85% | 63.55% |
| Edges in the giant component | 2,447,681 | 791,161 |
| Network density | 3.98E−5 | 1.30E−5 |
| Network diameter | 15 | 18 |
| Average path length | 5.2 | 7.1 |
| Number of isolated components | 51,670 | 111,600 |

connecting each pair of nodes) of the Global network are kept in the Interdisciplinary network is very relevant, since 95.5% of the edges (2,447,681 out of 2,563,017) belong to the giant component. Moreover, this reinforces how closed and important such complex collaborations are in an academic context.

As expected, the number of edges and the average degree of the nodes have decreased in the Interdisciplinary network, whereas the total number of isolated components has increased. Despite that, the diameters (15 and 18) and the average path lengths (5.2 and 7.1) in both networks are very close. Regarding the density of the networks (i.e., the ratio between the number of existing edges and the number of possible edges), the Interdisciplinary one naturally tends to be less dense (1.30E−5 against 3.98E−5).

As mentioned earlier, we consider only PhD researchers as nodes, since our goal is to assess more consistent collaborations. On the other hand, in their pioneering study Mena-Chalco et al. [7] analyze a network that includes other kinds of nodes (i.e., researchers of all levels, ranging from undergraduate students to senior ones). Thus, for the sake of comparison with our results in Table 2, we report here some figures of their network: number of nodes equal to 1,131,912, average degree of 4.4, network density of 3.92E−6, average path length of 5.8 and percentage of nodes in the giant component equal to 35.4%. Although they do not report isolated nodes in their characterization, we believe that the differences observed with respect to these numbers are due to the presence of students and non-academic collaborators in their network. It is also noteworthy that their dataset was collected in May 2011, whereas ours is from April 2018. Such differences may also be explained by the natural evolution of the Brazilian scientific community. If we compare their network's density with ours, they differ by one order of magnitude (from 3.9E−6 to 5.8E−5), since their network includes all types of researcher, whereas ours includes only those holding a PhD degree.

It is worth mentioning that Mena-Chalco et al. [7] also performed a topological analysis of each major area network. More specifically, they observed different patterns across all of them, supporting their hypothesis that the entire Brazilian collaboration network presents a natural interdisciplinarity. De Souza Vanz and Stumpf [12] also showed that Brazilian major areas present different collaboration patterns. Such evidence shows the need for further analyses of these interdisciplinary collaborations, particularly to understand the researchers' motivation and the dynamics of their publication output.

Thus, in this paper we further investigate the characteristics of the interdisciplinary collaborations found in the Brazilian scientific collaboration network, considering the eight major areas defined according to the CNPq knowledge area classification scheme. Figure 1 shows the proportions of such collaborations for each major area. For example, *Agrarian Sciences* (first column) presents a collaboration distribution with respect to the other major areas of 53.1% (*Biological Sciences*), 19.2% (*Exact an Earth Sciences*), 13.0% (*Health Sciences*), 9.7% (*Engineering*), 2.4% (*Applied and Social Sciences*), 2.4% (*Humanities*) and 0.2% (*Linguistics, Letters and Arts*).

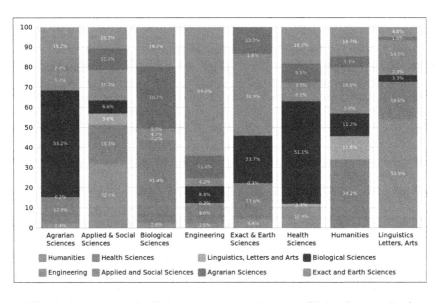

**Fig. 1.** Percentage of collaborations per major area. (Color figure online)

Looking at each major area, their most expressive interdisciplinary collaborations involve mainly the major areas *Biological Sciences* (gray bars), *Health Sciences* (pink bars), *Exact and Earth Sciences* (blue bars), and *Agrarian Sciences* (red bars). More specifically, the largest numbers of interdisciplinary collaborations occur between researchers from *Engineering* and *Exact and Earth Sciences* (64.0%), *Linguistics, Letters and Arts* and *Humanities* (53.9%), *Agrarian Sciences* and *Biological Sciences* (53.1%), and *Health Sciences* and *Biological Sciences* (51.2%).

Regarding collaboration diversity, the major areas of *Applied and Social Sciences* and *Humanities* can be highlighted as the most democratic ones among all, since their researchers tend to collaborate more evenly with colleagues from other areas. In contrast, researchers from *Agrarian Sciences, Health Sciences,* and *Linguistics, Letters and Arts* tend to concentrate their collaborations with those from a specific major area (*Biological Sciences, Biological Sciences* and *Humanities*, respectively).

Having provided some preliminary insights about the Global and the Interdisciplinary networks, we now analyze the researchers' collaborations from the viewpoint of the major areas involved, i.e., for each publication, we use the authors' area to establish edges between distinct major areas. Table 3 shows the collaboration figures for each major area in the Global and Interdisciplinary networks. For instance, the *Agrarian Sciences* presents 220,443 distinct collaborations (i.e., publications) that involves at least one coauthor from that specific major area, having 94,495 (42.9%) of those collaborations at least one coauthor from another major area. First of all, we note that the number of global collaborations does not necessarily reflect the size of the respective communities. For example, although *Exact and Earth Sciences* and *Humanities* are the second and third most populous major areas, they quite differ in terms of the number of global collaborations per researcher (respectively 5.3 and 2.0), which reinforces the fact that there are different collaboration patterns across the major areas.

**Table 3.** Collaborations by major area.

| Major area | Collaborations | |
|---|---|---|
| | Global | Interdisciplinary |
| Agrarian Sciences | 220,443 | 94,495 (42.9%) |
| Applied and Social Sciences | 68,409 | 33,125 (48.4%) |
| Biological Sciences | 255,572 | 164,084 (64.2%) |
| Engineering | 113,630 | 64,111 (56.4%) |
| Exact and Earth Sciences | 206,724 | 106,485 (51.5%) |
| Health Sciences | 340,933 | 131,303 (38.5%) |
| Humanities | 90,440 | 52,118 (57.6%) |
| Linguistics, Letters and Arts | 15,374 | 9,060 (58.9%) |

Regarding interdisciplinary collaborations, *Health Sciences*, which is the most populous major area, shows the lowest percentage (38.5%). As discussed earlier, this major area is one of those with the highest proportion of collaborations with other major areas. In contrast, *Applied and Social Sciences* shows a higher degree of interdisciplinarity, even though it presents a small number of researchers and collaborations, which endorses its diversified pattern. Overall, interdisciplinarity does not necessarily reflect the size of the respective communities, but reveals specific characteristics of their collaboration patterns.

# 4    Conclusions and Future Work

In this paper, we seek to emphasize the importance of interdisciplinary collaborations in scientific networks. For this, we have analyzed the Brazilian scientific network according to the eight major research areas defined by CNPq. Our results show that this network has grown consistently, becoming more interdisciplinary (i.e., 35.2% of all collaborations are interdisciplinary). They also show how integrated such major areas are, emphasizing the strength of the collaborations involving their respective researchers. Considering the interdisciplinary potential of the major areas, *Biological Sciences*, the third most populous one, stands out as the most democratic in terms of interdisciplinary diversity. However, it is important to note that the size of the major areas is not key for promoting interdisciplinarity.

When exploring the Interdisciplinary network considering the major research areas, we observe distinct profiles that demonstrate the dynamics and peculiarity of each one of them. In general, our study reinforces the idea that there is a clear effort to establish new collaborations, making the Brazilian scientific network more interconnected and robust.

As future work, we intend to analyze the formation of those researchers that tend to migrate to other regions in order to acquire more knowledge to disseminate to research groups in their own regions or to transmit to other areas through research collaborations [8]. Another perspective is to make explicit the strength of the collaborations by, for example, highlighting the main actors (researchers or groups of researchers) that make the collaboration networks more integrated, or even identifying those collaborations that give rise to new academic communities due to their strength [9]. In addition, it would be important to identify those researchers that are really relevant for knowledge sharing and, therefore, to promote the evolution of an academic network [4].

**Acknowledgements.** Work supported by individual grants from CAPES, CNPq and FAPEMIG. The first author thanks the Federal University of Viçosa for the leave granted for professional formation.

# References

1. Abramo, G., D'Angelo, C.A., Di Costa, F.: The effect of multidisciplinary collaborations on research diversification. Scientometrics **116**(1), 423–433 (2018)
2. Dias, T.M.R., Moita, G.F.: A method for the identification of collaboration in large scientific databases. Em Questão **21**(2), 140–161 (2015)
3. Freire, V.P., Figueiredo, D.R.: Ranking in collaboration networks using a group based metric. J. Braz. Comput. Soc. **17**(4), 255–266 (2011)
4. Kato, M., Ando, A.: The relationship between research performance and international collaboration in chemistry. Scientometrics **97**(3), 535–553 (2013)
5. Lane, J.: Let's make science metrics more scientific. Nature **464**, 488–489 (2010)
6. Lima, H., Silva, T.H.P., Moro, M.M., Santos, R.L.T., Meira Jr., W., Laender, A.H.F.: Aggregating productivity indices for ranking researchers across multiple areas. In: Proceedings of the 13th ACM/IEEE-CS Joint Conference on Digital Libraries, pp. 97–106 (2013)

7. Mena-Chalco, J.P., Digiampietri, L.A., Lopes, F.M., Cesar, R.M.: Brazilian bibliometric coauthorship networks. J. Assoc. Inf. Sci. Technol. **65**(7), 1424–1445 (2014)
8. Silva, T.H.P., Laender, A.H.F., Davis Jr., C.A., da Silva, A.P.C., Moro, M.M.: The impact of academic mobility on the quality of graduate programs. D-Lib Mag. **22**(9/10) (2016)
9. Silva, T.H.P., Laender, A.H.F., Vaz de Melo, P.O.S.: Social-based classification of multiple interactions in dynamic attributed networks. In: Proceedings of the IEEE International Conference on Big Data, pp. 4063–4072 (2018)
10. de Siqueira, G.O., Canuto, S.D., Gonçalves, M.A., Laender, A.H.F.: Automatic hierarchical categorization of research expertise using minimum information. In: International Conference on Theory and Practice of Digital Libraries - 21st International Conference on Theory and Practice of Digital Libraries, pp. 103–115 (2017)
11. Sonnenwald, D.H.: Scientific collaboration. Annu. Rev. Inf. Sci. Technol. **41**(1), 643–681 (2007)
12. de Souza Vanz, S.A., Stumpf, I.R.C.: Scientific output indicators and scientific collaboration network mapping in Brazil. Collnet J. Scientometr. Inf. Manag. **6**(2), 315–334 (2012)

# Exploring Scholarly Data by Semantic Query on Knowledge Graph Embedding Space

Hung Nghiep Tran[1]([⊠]) and Atsuhiro Takasu[2]

[1] SOKENDAI (The Graduate University for Advanced Studies), Tokyo, Japan
nghiepth@nii.ac.jp
[2] National Institute of Informatics, Tokyo, Japan
takasu@nii.ac.jp

**Abstract.** The trends of open science have enabled several open scholarly datasets which include millions of papers and authors. Managing, exploring, and utilizing such large and complicated datasets effectively are challenging. In recent years, the knowledge graph has emerged as a universal data format for representing knowledge about heterogeneous entities and their relationships. The knowledge graph can be modeled by knowledge graph embedding methods, which represent entities and relations as embedding vectors in semantic space, then model the interactions between these embedding vectors. However, the semantic structures in the knowledge graph embedding space are not well-studied, thus knowledge graph embedding methods are usually only used for knowledge graph completion but not data representation and analysis. In this paper, we propose to analyze these semantic structures based on the well-studied word embedding space and use them to support data exploration. We also define the semantic queries, which are algebraic operations between the embedding vectors in the knowledge graph embedding space, to solve queries such as similarity and analogy between the entities on the original datasets. We then design a general framework for data exploration by semantic queries and discuss the solution to some traditional scholarly data exploration tasks. We also propose some new interesting tasks that can be solved based on the uncanny semantic structures of the embedding space.

**Keywords:** Scholarly data · Data exploration · Semantic query · Knowledge graph · Knowledge graph embedding · Embedding space

## 1 Introduction

In recent years, digital libraries have moved towards open science and open access with several large scholarly datasets being constructed. Most popular datasets include millions of papers, authors, venues, and other information. Their large size and heterogeneous contents make it very challenging to effectively

© Springer Nature Switzerland AG 2019
A. Doucet et al. (Eds.): TPDL 2019, LNCS 11799, pp. 154–162, 2019.
https://doi.org/10.1007/978-3-030-30760-8_14

manage, explore, and utilize these datasets. The knowledge graph has emerged as a universal data format for representing knowledge about entities and their relationships in such complicated data. The main part of a knowledge graph is a collection of triples, with each triple $(h, t, r)$ denoting the fact that relation $r$ exists between head entity $h$ and tail entity $t$. This can also be formalized as a labeled directed multigraph where each triple $(h, t, r)$ represents a directed edge from node $h$ to node $t$ with label $r$. Therefore, it is straightforward to build knowledge graphs for scholarly data by representing natural connections between scholarly entities with triples such as *(AuthorA, Paper1, write)* and *(Paper1, Paper2, cite)*.

Notably, instead of using knowledge graphs directly in some tasks, we can model them by knowledge graph embedding methods, which represent entities and relations as embedding vectors in semantic space, then model the interactions between them to solve the knowledge graph completion task. There are many approaches [7] to modeling the interactions between embedding vectors resulting in many knowledge graph embedding methods such as ComplEx [8] and $CP_h$ [4]. In the case of word embedding methods such as word2vec, embedding vectors are known to contain rich semantic information that enables them to be used in many semantic applications [5]. However, the semantic structures in the knowledge graph embedding space are not well-studied, thus knowledge graph embeddings are only used for knowledge graph completion but remain absent in the toolbox for data analysis of heterogeneous data in general and scholarly data in particular, although they have the potential to be highly effective and efficient. In this paper, we address these issues by providing a theoretical understanding of their semantic structures and designing a general semantic query framework to support data exploration.

For theoretical analysis, we first analyze the state-of-the-art knowledge graph embedding model $CP_h$ [4] in comparison to the popular word embedding model word2vec skipgram [5] to explain its components and provide understandings to its semantic structures. We then define the *semantic queries on the knowledge graph embedding spaces*, which are algebraic operations between the embedding vectors in the knowledge graph embedding space to solve queries such as similarity and analogy between the entities on the original datasets.

Based on our theoretical results, we design a general framework for data exploration on scholarly data by semantic queries on knowledge graph embedding space. The main component in this framework is the conversion between the data exploration tasks and the semantic queries. We first outline the semantic query solutions to some traditional data exploration tasks, such as similar paper prediction and similar author prediction. We then propose a group of new interesting tasks, such as analogy query and analogy browsing, and discuss how they can be used in modern digital libraries.

## 2    Related Work

### 2.1    Knowledge Graph for Scholarly Data

Knowledge graph has gradually become the standard data format for hetero-geneous and complicated datasets [1]. There have been several attempts to build knowledge graph for scholarly data, either adopting the scholarly network directly [10], or deriving the knowledge graph from some similarity measures [6,9], or constructing the knowledge graph from survey papers [2]. However, they mostly focus on the data format or graph inference aspects of knowledge graph. In this paper, we instead focus on the knowledge graph embedding methods and especially the application of embedding vectors in data exploration.

### 2.2    Knowledge Graph Embedding

For a more in depth survey of knowledge graph embedding methods, please refer to [7], which defines their architecture, categorization, and interaction mecha-nisms. In this paper, we only focus on the semantic structures of the state-of-the-art model $CP_h$ [4], which is an extension of CP [3].

In CP, each entity $e$ has two embedding vectors $e$ and $e^{(2)}$ depending on its role in a triple as head or as tail, respectively. $CP_h$ augments the data by making an inverse triple $(t, h, r^{(a)})$ for each existing triple $(h, t, r)$, where $r^{(a)}$ is the augmented relation corresponding to $r$. When maximizing the likelihood by stochastic gradient descent, its score function is the sum:

$$\mathcal{S}(h,t,r) = \langle \boldsymbol{h}, \boldsymbol{t}^{(2)}, \boldsymbol{r} \rangle + \langle \boldsymbol{t}, \boldsymbol{h}^{(2)}, \boldsymbol{r}^{(a)} \rangle, \tag{1}$$

where $\boldsymbol{h}, \boldsymbol{h}^{(2)}, \boldsymbol{t}, \boldsymbol{t}^{(2)}, \boldsymbol{r}, \boldsymbol{r}^{(a)} \in \mathbb{R}^D$ are the embedding vectors of $h$, $t$, and $r$, respectively, and the trilinear-product $\langle \cdot, \cdot, \cdot \rangle$ is defined as:

$$\langle \boldsymbol{h}, \boldsymbol{t}, \boldsymbol{r} \rangle = \sum_{d=1}^{D} h_d t_d r_d, \tag{2}$$

where $D$ is the embedding size and $d$ is the dimension for which $h_d$, $t_d$, and $r_d$ are the scalar entries.

The validity of each triple is modeled as a Bernoulli distribution and its validity probability is computed by the standard logistic function $\sigma(\cdot)$ as:

$$P(1|h,t,r) = \sigma(\mathcal{S}(h,t,r)). \tag{3}$$

### 2.3    Word Embedding

The most popular word embedding models in recent years are word2vec variants such as word2vec skipgram [5], which predicts the context-words $c_i$ indepen-dently given the target-word $w$, that is:

$$P(c_i|w), \text{ where } i = 1, \dots, m. \tag{4}$$

In practice, the expensive softmax functions in these multinoulli distributions are avoided by approximating them with negative sampling and solve for the Bernoulli distributions by using the standard logistic function $\sigma(\cdot)$:

$$P(1|c_i, w) = \sigma(\boldsymbol{u}_{c_i}^{\top} \boldsymbol{v}_w), \text{ where } i = 1, \ldots, m, \tag{5}$$

where $\boldsymbol{u}_{c_i}$ is the context-embedding vector of context-word $c_i$ and $\boldsymbol{v}_w$ is the word-embedding vector of target-word $w$.

## 3  Theoretical Analysis

Word2vec skipgram and its semantic structures are well-studied both theoretically and empirically [5]. $CP_h$ is a new state of the art among many knowledge graph embedding models. We first ground the theoretical basis of $CP_h$ on word2vec skipgram to explain its components and understand its semantic structures. We then define semantic queries on knowledge graph embedding space.

### 3.1  The Semantic Structures of $CP_h$

We first look at Eq. 5 of word2vec skipgram and consider only one context-word $c$ for simplicity. We can write the probability in proportional format as:

$$P(1|c, w) \propto \exp\left(\boldsymbol{u}_c^{\top} \boldsymbol{v}_w\right). \tag{6}$$

Note that the context-word $c$ and target-word $w$ are ordered and in word2vec skipgram, the target-word is the central word in a sliding window, e.g., $w_i$ is the target-word and $w_{i-k}, \ldots, w_{i-1}, w_{i+1}, \ldots, w_{i+k}$ are context-words. Therefore, the roles in each word pair are symmetric over the whole dataset. When maximizing the likelihood by stochastic gradient descent, we can write the approximate probability of unordered word pair and expand the dot products as:

$$P(1|c, w; w, c) \propto \exp\left(\boldsymbol{u}_c^{\top} \boldsymbol{v}_w + \boldsymbol{u}_w^{\top} \boldsymbol{v}_c\right) \tag{7}$$

$$\propto \exp\left(\sum_{d=1}^{D} u_{cd} v_{wd} + \sum_{d=1}^{D} u_{wd} v_{cd}\right), \tag{8}$$

where $\boldsymbol{u}_c$ and $\boldsymbol{v}_c$ are the context-embedding and word-embedding vectors of $c$, respectively, $\boldsymbol{u}_w$ and $\boldsymbol{v}_w$ are the context-embedding and word-embedding vectors of $w$, respectively, and $u_{cd}, v_{cd}, u_{wd},$ and $v_{wd}$ are their scalar entries, respectively.

We now return to Eq. 1 of $CP_h$ to also write the probability in Eq. 3 in proportional format and expand the trilinear products according to Eq. 2 as:

$$P(1|h, t, r) \propto \exp\left(\langle \boldsymbol{h}, \boldsymbol{t}^{(2)}, \boldsymbol{r}\rangle + \langle \boldsymbol{t}, \boldsymbol{h}^{(2)}, \boldsymbol{r}^{(a)}\rangle\right) \tag{9}$$

$$\propto \exp\left(\sum_{d=1}^{D} h_d t_d^{(2)} r_d + \sum_{d=1}^{D} t_d h_d^{(2)} r_d^{(a)}\right), \tag{10}$$

where $\boldsymbol{h}, \boldsymbol{h}^{(2)}, \boldsymbol{t}, \boldsymbol{t}^{(2)}, \boldsymbol{r}, \boldsymbol{r}^{(a)}$ are knowledge graph embedding vectors and $h_d, h_d^{(2)}$, $t_d, t_d^{(2)}, r_d, r_d^{(a)}$ are the scalar entries.

Comparing Eq. 8 of word2vec skipgram and Eq. 10 of $CP_h$, we can see they have essentially the same form and mechanism. Note that the embedding vectors in word2vec skipgram are learned by aligning each target-word to different context-words and vice versa, which is essentially the same for $CP_h$ by aligning each head entity to different tail entities in different triples and vice versa, with regards to the dimensions weighted by each relation. This result suggests that the *semantic structures* of $CP_h$ are similar to those in word2vec skipgram and we can use the head-role-based entity embedding vectors, such as $\boldsymbol{e}$, for semantic applications similarly to word embedding vectors. The tail-role-based entity embedding vectors, such as $\boldsymbol{e}^{(2)}$, contain almost the same information due to their symmetric roles, thus can be discarded in semantic tasks, which justifies this common practices in word embedding applications [5].

## 3.2  Semantic Query

We mainly concern with the two following structures of the embedding space.

- *Semantic similarity structure:* Semantically similar entities are close to each other in the embedding space, and vice versa. This structure can be identified by a vector similarity measure, such as the dot product between two embedding vectors. The similarity between two embedding vectors is computed as:

$$sim(\boldsymbol{e}_1, \boldsymbol{e}_2) = \boldsymbol{e}_1^\top \boldsymbol{e}_2. \tag{11}$$

- *Semantic direction structure:* There exist semantic directions in the embedding space, by which only one semantic aspect changes while all other aspects stay the same. It can be identified by a vector difference, such as the subtraction between two embedding vectors. The semantic direction between two embedding vectors is computed as:

$$dir(\boldsymbol{e}_1, \boldsymbol{e}_2) = \boldsymbol{e}_1 - \boldsymbol{e}_2. \tag{12}$$

The algebraic operations, which include the above dot product and vector subtraction, or their combinations, can be used to approximate some important tasks on the original data. To do this, we first need to convert the data exploration task to the appropriate operations. We then conduct the operations on the embedding vectors and obtain the results. This process is defined as following.

**Definition 1.** *Semantic queries on knowledge graph embedding space* are defined as the algebraic operations between the knowledge graph embedding vectors to approximate a given data exploration task on the original dataset.

## 4    Semantic Query Framework

Given the theoretical results, here we design a general framework for scholarly data exploration by using semantic queries on knowledge graph embedding space. Figure 1 shows the architecture of the proposed framework. There are three main components, namely *data processing*, *task processing*, and *query processing*.

**Data processing:** with two steps, (1) *constructing the knowledge graph from scholarly data* by using the scholarly graph directly with entities such as *authors, papers, venues*, and relations such as *author-write-paper, paper-cite-paper, paper-in-venue*, and (2) *learning the knowledge graph embeddings* as in [7].

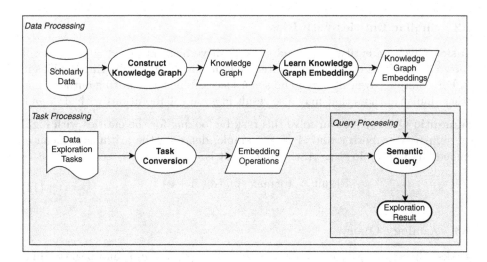

**Fig. 1.** Architecture of the semantic query framework. Eclipse denotes operation, parallelogram denotes resulting data.

**Task processing:** converting data exploration tasks to algebraic operations on the embedding space by following task-specific conversion templates. Some important tasks and their conversion templates are discussed in Sect. 5.

**Query processing:** executing semantic query on the embedding space and return results. Note that the algebraic operations on embedding vectors are linear and can be performed in parallel. Therefore, the *semantic query* is efficient.

Note that the proposed *semantic query framework* makes no assumption on the specific knowledge graph embedding models and the induced embedding spaces. Any embedding space that contains rich semantic information such as the listed *semantic structures* can be applied in this framework.

## 5    Exploration Tasks and Semantic Queries Conversion

Here we present and discuss the semantic queries for some traditional and newly proposed data exploration tasks on scholarly data.

## 5.1   Similar Entities

**Tasks.** Given an entity $e \in \mathcal{E}$, find entities that are similar to $e$. For example, given *AuthorA*, find authors, papers, and venues that are similar to *AuthorA*. Note that we can restrict to find specific entity types. This is a traditional tasks in scholarly data exploration, whereas other below tasks are new.

**Semantic Query.** We can solve this task by looking for the entities with highest similarity to $e$. For example, the first result is:

$$\text{Result} = \arg\max_{e_i \in \mathcal{E}} sim\left(\boldsymbol{e}_i, \boldsymbol{e}\right). \tag{13}$$

## 5.2   Similar Entities with Bias

**Tasks.** Given an entity $e \in \mathcal{E}$ and some positive bias entities $A = \{a_1, \ldots, a_k\}$ known as expected results, find entities that are similar to $e$ following the bias in $A$. For example, given *AuthorA* and some successfully collaborating authors, find other similar authors that may also result in good collaborations with *AuthorA*.

**Semantic Query.** We can solve this task by looking for the entities with highest similarity to both $e$ and $A$. For example, denoting the arithmetic mean of embedding vectors in $A$ as $\bar{A}$, the first result is:

$$\text{Result} = \arg\max_{e_i \in \mathcal{E}} sim\left(\boldsymbol{e}_i, \bar{A} + \boldsymbol{e}\right). \tag{14}$$

## 5.3   Analogy Query

**Tasks.** Given an entity $e \in \mathcal{E}$, positive bias $A = \{a_1, \ldots, a_k\}$, and negative bias $B = \{b_1, \ldots, b_k\}$, find entities that are similar to $e$ following the biases in $A$ and $B$. The essence of this task is tracing along a semantic direction defined by the positive and negative biases. For example, start with *AuthorA*, we can trace along the *expertise direction* to find authors that are similar to *AuthorA* but with higher or lower expertise.

**Semantic Query.** We can solve this task by looking for the entities with highest similarity to $e$ and $A$ but not $B$. For example, denoting the arithmetic mean of embedding vectors in $A$ and $B$ as $\bar{A}$ and $\bar{B}$, respectively, note that $\bar{A} - \bar{B}$ defines the semantic direction along the positive and negative biases, the first result is:

$$\text{Result} = \arg\max_{e_i \in \mathcal{E}} sim\left(\boldsymbol{e}_i, \bar{A} - \bar{B} + \boldsymbol{e}\right). \tag{15}$$

## 5.4   Analogy Browsing

**Tasks.** This task is an extension of the above analogy query task, by tracing along multiple semantic directions defined by multiple pairs of positive and negative biases. This task can be implemented as an interactive data analysis tool. For example, start with *AuthorA*, we can trace to authors with higher expertise, then continue tracing to new domains to find all authors similar to *AuthorA* with high expertise in the new domain. For another example, start with *Paper1*, we can trace to papers with higher quality, then continue tracing to new domain to look for papers similar to *Paper1* with high quality in the new domain.

**Semantic Query.** We can solve this task by simply repeating the semantic query for analogy query with each pair of positive and negative bias. Note that we can also combine different operations in different order to support flexible browsing.

## 6   Conclusion

In this paper, we studied the application of knowledge graph embedding in exploratory data analysis. We analyzed the $CP_h$ model and provided understandings to its semantic structures. We then defined the *semantic queries on knowledge graph embedding space* to efficiently approximate some operations on heterogeneous data such as scholarly data. We designed a general framework to systematically apply semantic queries to solve scholarly data exploration tasks. Finally, we outlined and discussed the solutions to some traditional and pioneering exploration tasks emerged from the semantic structures of the knowledge graph embedding space.

This paper is dedicated to the theoretical foundation of a new approach and discussions of emerging tasks, whereas experiments and evaluations are left for the future work. There are several other promising directions for future research. One direction is to explore new tasks or new solutions of traditional tasks using the proposed method. Another direction is to implement the proposed exploration tasks on real-life digital libraries for online evaluation.

**Acknowledgments.** This work was supported by "Cross-ministerial Strategic Innovation Promotion Program (SIP) Second Phase, Big-data and AI-enabled Cyberspace Technologies" by New Energy and Industrial Technology Development Organization (NEDO).

## References

1. Ehrlinger, L., Wöß, W.: Towards a definition of knowledge graphs. In: SEMANTICS 2016: Posters and Demos Track (2016)
2. Fathalla, S., Vahdati, S., Auer, S., Lange, C.: Towards a knowledge graph representing research findings by semantifying survey articles. In: Kamps, J., Tsakonas, G., Manolopoulos, Y., Iliadis, L., Karydis, I. (eds.) TPDL 2017. LNCS, vol. 10450, pp. 315–327. Springer, Cham (2017). https://doi.org/10.1007/978-3-319-67008-9_25
3. Hitchcock, F.L.: The expression of a tensor or a polyadic as a sum of products. J. Math. Phys. **6**(1–4), 164–189 (1927)
4. Lacroix, T., Usunier, N., Obozinski, G.: Canonical tensor decomposition for knowledge base completion. In: ICML 2018, June 2018
5. Mikolov, T., Sutskever, I., Chen, K., Corrado, G.S., Dean, J.: Distributed representations of words and phrases and their compositionality. In: NIPS 2013 (2013)

6.  Sadeghi, A., Lange, C., Vidal, M.-E., Auer, S.: Integration of scholarly communication metadata using knowledge graphs. In: Kamps, J., Tsakonas, G., Manolopoulos, Y., Iliadis, L., Karydis, I. (eds.) TPDL 2017. LNCS, vol. 10450, pp. 328–341. Springer, Cham (2017). https://doi.org/10.1007/978-3-319-67008-9_26
7.  Tran, H.N., Takasu, A.: Analyzing knowledge graph embedding methods from a multi-embedding interaction perspective. In: DSI4 at EDBT/ICDT 2019 (2019)
8.  Trouillon, T., Welbl, J., Riedel, S., Gaussier, E., Bouchard, G.: Complex embeddings for simple link prediction. In: ICML 2016 (2016)
9.  Vahdati, S., Palma, G., Nath, R.J., Lange, C., Auer, S., Vidal, M.-E.: Unveiling scholarly communities over knowledge graphs. In: Méndez, E., Crestani, F., Ribeiro, C., David, G., Lopes, J.C. (eds.) TPDL 2018. LNCS, vol. 11057, pp. 103–115. Springer, Cham (2018). https://doi.org/10.1007/978-3-030-00066-0_9
10. Wang, R., et al.: AceKG: a large-scale knowledge graph for academic data mining. In: CIKM 2018, July 2018

# The Memento Tracer Framework: Balancing Quality and Scalability for Web Archiving

Martin Klein[1]([✉]) [ID], Harihar Shankar[1] [ID], Lyudmila Balakireva[1] [ID],
and Herbert Van de Sompel[2] [ID]

[1] Los Alamos National Laboratory, Los Alamos, NM 87545, USA
{mklein,harihar,ludab}@lanl.gov
[2] Data Archiving and Networked Services,
Anna van Saksenlaan 51, 2593 HW The Hague, The Netherlands
herbert.van.de.sompel@dans.knaw.nl

**Abstract.** Web archiving frameworks are commonly assessed by the quality of their archival records and by their ability to operate at scale. The ubiquity of dynamic web content poses a significant challenge for crawler-based solutions such as the Internet Archive that are optimized for scale. Human-driven services such as the Webrecorder tool provide high-quality archival captures but are not optimized to operate at scale. We introduce the Memento Tracer framework that aims to balance archival quality and scalability. We outline its concept and architecture and evaluate its archival quality and operation at scale. Our findings indicate quality is on par or better compared against established archiving frameworks and operation at scale comes with a manageable overhead.

**Keywords:** Memento Tracer · Web archiving · Scholarly artifacts · Archival quality · Archiving at scale

## 1 Introduction and Motivation

The web archiving landscape has evolved significantly over the last twenty years. While the Internet Archive (IA) is the uncontested pioneer in this field and is to date by far the largest publicly available web archive, we are now able to freely access archived web resources from more than twenty web archives around the world[1]. Many national libraries and archives such as the National Library of Australia [15] and the UK National Archives [2] have begun to capture parts of the web and contribute to increased diversity. However, most of the current web archiving frameworks are optimized either to try to cope with the scale of the web or to provide high-quality archival captures. The IA, for example, generally crawls the web in a best-effort approach, capturing as many web resources as possible. This results in an ever-increasing number of URIs archived and available

---

[1] http://timetravel.mementoweb.org/.

© Springer Nature Switzerland AG 2019
A. Doucet et al. (Eds.): TPDL 2019, LNCS 11799, pp. 163–176, 2019.
https://doi.org/10.1007/978-3-030-30760-8_15

164    M. Klein et al.

(a) Internet Archive                (b) Webrecorder

**Fig. 1.** Replay of `cnn.com` Mementos

via the IA's Wayback Machine replay engine [10]. At the time of writing, this number stands at more than 731 billion URIs [11].

Regarding archival quality, web archiving has become increasingly challenging as a result of the proliferation of dynamic web content that only becomes available via activation of - typically JavaScript-based - affordances in pages. Web archiving dynamic web content is technically challenging and crawler-driven solutions that have been experimented with thus far are resource intensive, slowing down the crawling process [4,5]. As such, the IA, which focuses on scale, typically does not apply such techniques. The result of this focus on scale over quality is aptly illustrated by the fact that the `cnn.com` website has not been properly archived by the IA since November 2016 and can not be replayed correctly in the Wayback Machine [3]. The screenshot in Fig. 1a shows the replay of a `cnn.com` Memento (the archived copy) in the IA[2]. At the other end of the spectrum, the Webrecorder tool [13] has emerged, focusing on high-fidelity web archiving. Its value is evident in Fig. 1b showing a screenshot of the replay of a `cnn.com` Memento created with the Webrecorder tool[3]. However, Webrecorder achieves this level of quality via human interaction with the web resource that is to be archived and, as such, can not operate at a scale comparable to that of the IA's crawling processes. To date, approaches that can archive at scale and with high-fidelity remain elusive.

In this paper we introduce the Memento Tracer web archiving framework that aims to operate at web scale while also providing high-quality web captures. Memento Tracer is a result of the "Scholarly Orphans" project, a collaborative effort between the Prototyping Team of the Los Alamos National Laboratory Research Library and members of the Web Science and Digital Library group of the Old Dominion University Computer Science Department. The project is

---

[2] http://web.archive.org/web/20190417195948/https://www.cnn.com/.

[3] https://webrecorder.io/martinklein/tpdl_test_collection/20190417221002/https://www.cnn.com/.

focused on archiving scholarly artifacts, which are resources that scholars create or deposit in productivity portals such as GitHub, Slideshare, or Publons. Our contributions in this work are two-fold:

1. We outline the Memento Tracer concept, detail its architecture, and describe a pilot implementation.
2. We conduct an experimental evaluation of Memento Tracer regarding the scale and quality at which it can archive two resource types that present dynamic content challenges.

Despite the limited scope of the evaluation, we feel that our contributions reveal various attractive characteristics of Memento Tracer, which suggest the potential for it to evolve towards a web archiving approach that is able to capture web resources at scale and with high quality.

## 2  Related Work

The Internet Archive, in addition to its crawler-based web archiving services offers an archive-on-demand service called "Save page now". This service allows a user to submit a URI to the IA, which will be crawled immediately. Perma.cc and archive.today are two alternatives that offer very similar services, all of which come with strengths and weaknesses. Perma.cc, for example, requires a user login to pro-actively create Mementos of submitted URIs and charges a subscription fee that depends on the number of Mementos created per month. Little is publicly known about archive.today, their technology stack and institutional background but similar to the IA's "Save page now" service their capability to handle dynamic web content is limited. The IA has acknowledged this shortcoming and introduced a beta version of a more powerful archiving-on-demand service. This service is based on "brozzler" [8] and operates a Chromium browser to execute dynamic content and therefore, for example, discovers URIs that are generated by JavaScript. Our first tests did not return reliable results but once the service reaches a more stable state, it should be included in this comparative study.

Brunelle et al. [5] conducted a study to investigate the balance and implicit overhead between operating a "regular" web crawler such as Heritrix [9] and a headless browser such as PhantomJS [7] to more reliably execute dynamic content. They found that using the more sophisticated crawling approach based on a headless browser resulted in a spike of discovered URIs to crawl as well as vastly increased crawl time.

The Webrecorder tool is made for humans to interact with a web resource and record the interaction into an archival record. Dynamic content is typically handled very well and, as long as all essential parts of the resource are interacted with, the archival record represents a high-fidelity capture of the live web resource that can be played back, for example, with the Webrecorder Player [14]. While archiving with Webrecorder is a manual process, the tool's developers have made some initial steps towards automating certain interactions with individual web resources [12].

Brunelle et al. [6] proposed an automated method to assess the archived quality of web resources. Their algorithm assigns relative values to embedded resources and depending on the availability of these resources, determines a damage rating. The authors implemented a web service to assess Memento Damage[4] which we considered for our quality evaluation but since it does not compare two versions of the same resource but rather analyzes individual resources separately, it is not applicable for our study.

## 3    Memento Tracer Framework

We introduce a new collaborative approach to capture web publications for archival purposes with the Memento Tracer framework. The framework is inspired by existing capture approaches yet aims for a new balance between archiving at scale and quality of the resulting snapshots. The framework was developed as part of a project that focuses on capturing scholarly artifacts from productivity portals such as GitHub, Slideshare, Publons, Figshare, Wikipedia, and Stack Overflow. Similar to other existing web crawler approaches such as LOCKSS [17,18], it uses server-side processes that leverage the insight that web publications in a given portal are typically based on the same template and share features such as layout and interactive affordances.

Similar to the Webrecorder tool, a human helps achieve high quality captures and determines the boundary of the to be archived resource. However, with Memento Tracer, heuristics that apply to an entire class of web publications are recorded, not individual web publications. These heuristics can collaboratively be created by curators and deposited in a shared community repository. When the server-side capture processes come across a web publication of a class for which heuristics are available, they can be applied, yielding captures that are aligned with the curators' instructions.

### 3.1    Framework

Figure 2 visualizes the Memento Tracer concept and its three main components from left to right. Below we describe the framework in detail using the task of archiving slide decks from Slideshare as an example.

**A Browser Extension.** The first step in the framework begins when a curator navigates to a web page representative for a class of resources in that portal, for example the landing page of a Slideshare presentation, and activates the browser extension. By interacting with the web page (clicking through the slides, downloading the entire slide deck, etc), the curator creates a *trace* that, in an abstract manner, describes the artifact to be archived. The extension does not record actual resources or URLs that are traversed by the curator. Rather it captures interactions in terms that uniquely identify the page's elements that are being interacted with, for example by means of their class ID or XPath. The extension's recording of a page's elements is inspired by the Selenium IDE[5], which is an open

---

[4] http://memento-damage.cs.odu.edu/.
[5] https://www.seleniumhq.org/selenium-ide/.

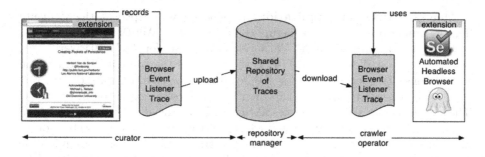

**Fig. 2.** Memento Tracer framework

source record and playback test automation suite for the web. Since all pages of the same class in the same portal are typically based on the same template, the resulting traces apply across all pages of the class rather than to a specific page only. In our example the created trace is valid for all slide decks in Slideshare. Currently, the extension is able to record simple mouse-clicks, clicks on all links in a certain user interface component, and repeated clicks. The latter is especially useful when navigating through all slides of a presentation or paginating through multi-page blog posts or manuals. The created trace also indicates the URL pattern to which the trace applies and provenance information including the resource on which the trace was created and the user agent used to create it. When the layout or affordances for a particular class of web publications change, a new trace needs to be recorded to ensure it is valid for all changed publications. In contrast to crawler-based approaches but similar to the Webrecorder concept, with Memento Tracer a curator is in charge of determining the desired components of a web resource that is to be archived. The fact that a trace can automatically be applied to all artifacts of the same class represents a major scalability advantage over other human-driven approaches such as Webrecorder. For each resource, even in the same class and portal, Webrecorder requires all interactions to be executed.

**A Shared Repository.** After a curator has successfully recorded a trace, she can share it with the community via a publicly accessible repository, thereby crowdsourcing the web curator task. The shared repository allows for reuse and refinement of existing traces. Hence, anyone in the community can utilize a trace created by another curator, for example the aforementioned Slideshare trace, to capture other slide decks. Since the perspective of what the essence of a web publication is may differ from one curator to the next [16], the repository supports multiple traces for a specific class of pages. Each can be unambiguously identified in the repository. In addition, since the layout of pages evolves over time, traces will need updating, making version support by the repository essential. Given these requirements, we consider GitHub a suitable host for the shared repository. Traces available to the community for reuse and refinement in addition to versioning in a shared repository further increases the scalability of the Memento Tracer approach.

**A Headless Browser Application.** To generate web captures, the Memento Tracer framework assumes a setup consisting of a WebDriver[6], a headless browser[7], and a capturing tool[8]. We developed a parser for the WebDriver (based on the Selenium WebDriver's API) that translates the content of a trace into instructions (JavaScript code) for the headless browser to emulate the interactions with the web resource as captured by the browser extension in the trace. The capturing tool writes resources navigated by the headless browser to WARC files [1]. When this fully automated capture setup comes across a web resource of a class for which a trace is available, the trace will be invoked to guide the capturing of the resource. This functionality of capturing resources based on traces guarantees high-fidelity archived resources, which is a major advantage over, for example, the IA's automated crawling approaches.

### 3.2   Pilot

We used a pilot implementation of the above described framework to capture artifacts deposited by 16 researchers in 11 productivity portals. We created a trace for a sample resource of each of the portals and used those traces to guide the capturing process of artifacts deposited in the respective portals by the researchers. The application at https://myresearch.institute provides an overview of artifacts captured since August 2018. The application offers different views on the collection of captured artifacts, such as by capture date, by researcher, and by productivity portal. A landing page per captured artifact[9] provides basic metadata about the artifact as well as links to the WARC file resulting from the capture and to a replay of the captured artifact. More information about the capture pipeline in which Memento Tracer was used is available via the About page[10].

## 4   Experiment Design

We evaluate our Memento Tracer framework in two dimensions: archival quality and scalability. To assess archival quality, we compare its performance against Mementos created with Webrecorder, the tool designed to create high-fidelity captures. To evaluate scalability, we conduct two experiments. The first assesses the extent to which Memento Tracer can generate quality captures for a large set of web resources. The second compares the time Memento Tracer and an automated crawling framework designed for scale require to create captures.

---

[6] Selenium WebDriver: https://www.seleniumhq.org/.

[7] Headless    Chrome:    https://chromium.googlesource.com/chromium/src/+/lkgr/headless/README.md.

[8] WarcProxy: https://github.com/internetarchive/warcprox.

[9] For    example:    https://myresearch.institute/event/e7e8fcc4e8c14392af1c264295d6268a/.

[10] https://myresearch.institute/about/.

Quality of archived web resources is not trivial to measure. Different replay systems of Mementos may vary in performance and individuals' perception of what the essence of a resource is and hence which part of the resource needs to be part of the archived record may differ [16]. Rather than trying to find a compromise between these arguably subjective aspects, we decided to focus our quality assessment on the extent to which URIs that should be captured according to curatorial decisions are actually captured. In order to create a baseline of the number of URIs we expect in a Memento, we analyze the live web version of each resource. We expect a high-quality archival record to contain at least the same number of URIs as its live web version. We are aware that this comparison may not capture all dimensions of quality. For example, a CSS that is missing from a captured resource may have a more detrimental impact on the "look and feel" of the replay than a missing image. However, this process enables us to automatically compare a dataset of live web resources with their corresponding Mementos.

## 4.1 Data Gathering

Memento Tracer is a result of our Scholarly Orphans project, where our focus is on archiving scholarly artifacts that researchers deposit in web productivity portals. We generated a dataset that consists of resources from two such portals selected because they present interesting web archiving challenges to analyze the performance of our novel web archiving framework. This dataset is applicable to investigate web archiving quality and scale. The first portal from which we obtained resources is GitHub. Its API does not offer the functionality to randomly select Github resources. We therefore decided to utilize the news and podcast platform https://changelog.com/ and its digest of GitHub repositories published daily since January 1st 2015. Changelog's digest consists of the most popular GitHub repositories on a given day as measured by the number of stars received. These repositories are further distinguished between popular overall, popular overall but making the list for the first time, and popular overall but newly created repositories. We focused on the latter two categories as this ensures we obtain established repositories, while also decreasing the chances of obtaining duplicates. Furthermore, newly created repositories are included. This mixture of GitHub repositories, while somewhat biased towards popularity (given the number of received stars or "likes"), serves as our sample set of resources. In total, we obtained 17,646 URIs of GitHub repositories. In order to conduct an accurate analysis of archiving quality, we need to ensure that our comparisons are based on the live web versions that were used to create Mementos, which, in fact, may no longer be the same version by the time we conduct our comparisons. We therefore use the GitHub API to identify the time-specific last commit URI of each repository and use these URIs, for which the repository content is fixed.

Our second dataset consists of resources from Slideshare. In order to obtain a random sample, we use the portal's Explore feature[11] to obtain a sample of slide

---

[11] https://www.slideshare.net/explore.

decks. Given this source, our dataset is clearly also biased towards popularity and Slideshare's selection algorithm. However, the algorithm to select slide decks and feature them on the Explore site is entirely opaque to us. In addition, this process guarantees a broad variety of subjects under which the slide decks are classified, making our sampling results an applicable dataset. Since Slideshare creates a new URI for each uploaded and updated slide deck, there is no concern that the resource on the live web will change throughout our experiment. In total, we obtain 12,280 URIs of distinct slide decks for this dataset.

### 4.2   Traces for Dataset Resources

We use the Memento Tracer Chrome extension to create a trace for GitHub repositories as well as for Slideshare slide decks. For this step we mimic the decision making of a curator and determine which parts of the resources are essential to be captured and archived. According to these curatorial decisions, the trace created for GitHub repositories includes all files and top level directories listed in the repository as well as the downloadable ZIP file containing the entire repository[12]. Guided by this trace[13], all GitHub repositories archived with Memento Tracer should therefore, when replayed, contain all repository files as well as the ZIP file. The trace created for Slideshare guides the capturing process to include all slides as well as all notes per slide deck[14].

These curatorial decisions allow us to precisely and automatically determine the number of URIs of interest contained in the live web version of each resource. For this purpose, our evaluation program loads the live web resource in a browser and interacts with it to count the number of URIs expected according to the curatorial decisions made. With this process we determine that each file and top-level directory in a GitHub repository as well as the Zip file has a distinct URI. Similarly, each slide in a Slideshare slide deck as well as its associated note has a unique URI.

## 5   Experiments and Results

### 5.1   Archival Quality

With our baseline of live web URIs in place, we can compare Mementos created with different archiving frameworks. We use the same evaluation program we used to assess the number of URIs from live web resources to assess the number of URIs in Mementos. To conduct this comparison, we create the following subsets derived from our dataset introduced in Sect. 4.1. We randomly pick 100 GitHub repositories and 100 Slideshare slide decks and use the Webrecorder tool to

---

[12] A screencast of the Memento Tracer Chrome extension and the interactions with a GitHub repository recorded into a trace is available at: https://doi.org/10.6084/m9.figshare.8049839.v1.

[13] The trace is available at: https://doi.org/10.6084/m9.figshare.8024612.

[14] The trace is available at: https://doi.org/10.6084/m9.figshare.8024615.

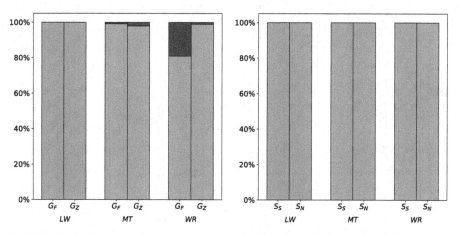

(a) GitHub URIs, each left bar represents file URIs, the right ZIP file URIs

(b) Slideshare URIs, each left bar represents slide URIs, the right notes URIs

**Fig. 3.** Relative number of URIs from live web, Memento Tracer, and Webrecorder Mementos. Green represents available, red unavailable resources. (Color figure online)

manually create respective Mementos. Being very familiar with the Webrecorder tool, we applied the same curatorial criteria that we used to record traces for the two productivity portals. For GitHub repositories, this means we click on every single file in a GitHub repository in order to capture these resources and the "Clone or Download" button in order to capture the ZIP file of the repository. For slide decks this means we click on the "Next" button as many times as necessary to capture all slides in the deck and on each of the included notes. Since this manual process is rather time consuming, we limit the size of this dataset to 100 repositories and 100 slide decks. In addition, with a trace recorded for GitHub repositories and for slide decks on Slideshare, we use the Memento Tracer framework to capture the same 100 GitHub repositories and 100 Slideshare slide decks.

Our first analysis is based on whether all expected URIs are contained in the archived record. We expect all URIs for files in GitHub repositories (each file has a distinct URI) and one URI for the repository ZIP file in addition to the URI of the repository itself. For Slideshare we expect all URIs for slides (each slide has a distinct URI) and all URIs for notes (each note has a distinct URI) plus the URI of the slide deck page itself. Since the URIs of the repositories and slide deck pages are all available on the live web and in all Mementos, we exclude them going forward and only focus on URIs of the component resources that are of interest according to our curatorial decisions.

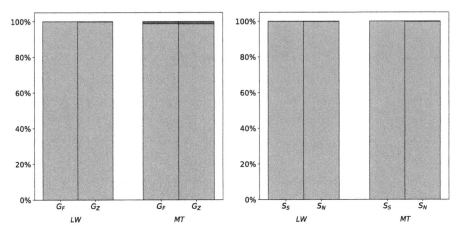

(a) GitHub URIs, files left, ZIP right    (b) Slideshare URIs, slides left, notes right

**Fig. 4.** Relative number of URIs from live web and Memento Tracer Mementos. Green represents available, red unavailable resources. (Color figure online)

Figure 3 displays the results of the analysis based on the total of 200 URIs sampled from the overall dataset. The relative numbers of URIs are represented on the y-axis and the corresponding sources (LW, MT, WR) are shown on the x-axis. The size of the green portion of a bar indicates the number of URIs available and the red portion shows unavailable URIs. Figure 3a displays the GitHub URIs where $G_F$ corresponds to repository file URIs and $G_Z$ to ZIP file URIs. Figure 3b shows the Slideshare URIs with $S_S$ representing URIs of slides and $S_N$ URIs of notes. We can immediately make a few observations from these graphs. As expected, the ratio of URIs in Webrecorder Mementos is very similar to the live web versions. Generally, more than 95% of URIs are available, which confirms the tool's reputation of delivering high-fidelity captures. We also notice very high ratios of available URIs for Mementos created with Memento Tracer. In fact, the ratio of available URIs in Memento Tracer Mementos is at times even higher than the ratio in Webrecorder Mementos. The drop in available URIs from Webrecorder GitHub repository file URIs can potentially be explained by observed network errors while creating the archival snapshots as well as possible human errors, for example forgetting to click on a file. Both points favor an automated framework to capture web resources. Such a process can detect network errors, try the capture again, and is not subject to human errors.

These findings strongly support our claim that Memento Tracer captures are of high quality, they are comparable to if not better than Webrecorder Mementos, and very closely align with their live web versions.

**Table 1.** Percentage of GitHub repositories with $x$ percent of available URIs from the corresponding repositories' live web version

|  | $x$ | 0 | 10 | 20 | 30 | 40 | 50 | 60 | 70 | 80 | 90 | 100 |
|---|---|---|---|---|---|---|---|---|---|---|---|---|
| GitHub | All | 0.64 | 99.36 | 97.18 | 96.92 | 96.86 | 96.83 | 96.7 | 96.36 | 95.91 | 94.81 | **92.83** |
|  | Files | 2.99 | 97.01 | 97.0 | 96.97 | 96.94 | 96.91 | 96.75 | 96.43 | 95.97 | 94.95 | **93.29** |
|  | ZIP | 1.3 | n/a | n/a | n/a | n/a | n/a | n/a | n/a | n/a | n/a | **98.7** |
| Slideshare | All | 0.15 | 99.85 | 99.85 | 99.85 | 99.85 | 99.83 | 99.71 | 99.71 | 99.7 | 99.65 | **98.67** |
|  | Slides | 0.1 | 99.9 | 99.9 | 99.9 | 99.9 | 99.9 | 99.9 | 99.9 | 99.9 | 99.9 | **99.9** |
|  | Notes | 0.28 | 99.72 | 99.71 | 99.71 | 99.71 | 99.71 | 99.68 | 99.65 | 99.62 | 99.56 | **98.58** |

## 5.2   Quality at Scale

Using our subset in previous experiments, we established that Memento Tracer Mementos are of very high quality, when compared to their live web versions (and Webrecorder Mementos). We are now interested in analyzing whether Memento Tracer keeps delivering quality when operating at scale. We use the framework to capture all resources in our dataset; 17,646 Memento Tracer Mementos of GitHub repositories as well as all 12,280 Memento Tracer Mementos of Slideshare slide decks. This translates to a dataset increase of more than two orders of magnitude (100 vs. 17,646 repositories and 100 vs. 12,280 slide decks). If we find a high level of similarity in terms of available URIs observed in the live web versions and Memento Tracer Mementos, we can confidently state that, even at scale, the Memento Tracer approach provides high-quality captures.

Figure 4 shows, in concept similar to Fig. 3, the results of this large-scale analysis. Figure 4a represents the GitHub URI ratios and Fig. 4b the Slideshare ratios. We can barely see a red portion in any of the bars, indicating that the same almost 100% of URIs available in live web versions are also available in the corresponding Memento Tracer Mementos.

Table 1 provides insight into the comparison between live web versions and Memento Tracer Mementos from the granularity level of GitHub repositories and Slideshare slide decks. The second row shows the percentage of Memento Tracer Memento GitHub repositories with $x$ percent (top row) of available URIs from the corresponding repositories' live web version. For example, we can see that 0.64 of Memento Tracer Memento repositories contain zero URIs from their live web version and 92.83% contain all 100% of available URIs. The third row shows the same data if we only consider repository file URIs and the fourth when only considering ZIP file URIs. Since there is only one ZIP file per repository, this data is binary. We can observe that Memento Tracer does very well overall, and slightly better for ZIP files (98.7% vs. 93.29%). The most likely reasons are that temporary network issues not caught by the automatic capture process prevented the Memento Tracer framework from archiving all file URIs. Rows five through seven show the same data for Slideshare slide decks. We find that Memento Tracer does even better there and almost perfect (99.9%) for slides. The percentage for notes is also very high, at 98.58%.

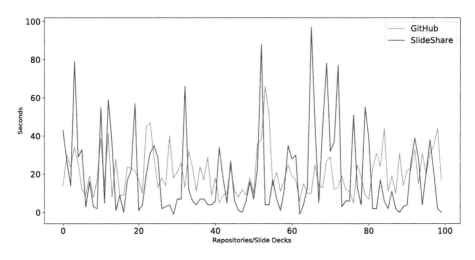

**Fig. 5.** Time deltas between Memento Tracer and a simple web crawler

These findings exceed our expectation and confirm that the Memento Tracer framework, even at large scale, archives web resources with high-quality.

### 5.3  Memento Tracer Overhead

We are further interested in the overhead of the WebDriver- and headless browser-based capture approach in the Memento Tracer framework. Simply comparing runtimes of Memento Tracer versus another automatic web archiving framework such as Heritrix would not be fair as a crawler would not discover the same URIs since it can not cope with some dynamic affordances. Instead, we extract all URIs captured by the Memento Tracer framework while creating Mementos of the initial subset of 100 GitHub URIs and 100 Slideshare URIs. This amounts to a total of 29,205 extracted URIs from the GitHub subset and 61,346 URIs from SlideShare and we crawl these URIs with a simple Python-based crawler. Our simple crawler builds on the popular Python `Requests` library to perform HTTP GET requests against the URIs and is configured to resemble a Chrome browser (specified user agent, set timeout values, etc). We also used 16 threads to parallelize these HTTP requests, speed up the crawling process, and emulate a production crawling framework operating at scale. The advantage of this process is that the crawler simply captures URIs and its runtime therefore provides the minimal time needed to capture the same resources as Memento Tracer. We compare both runtimes and present the delta in Fig. 5. All deltas (per GitHub and Slideshare URI) are positive (y-axis), which means Memento Tracer in all instances takes longer than the simple crawler. This finding is not surprising given Memento Tracer's overhead of running and controlling a browser for each URI. We see quite a variance from around 5 s to just under 100 s for Slideshare URIs. On average, based on our subset, GitHub URIs take 19.74 s longer to be captured with Memento Tracer and Slideshare URIs take 20.75 s longer. If we extrapolate this average to our entire dataset, the GitHub portion would take 97 h longer and Slideshare 71 h.

While this may sound like a lot, we highlight two arguments for why these numbers are reasonable; First, on average, the Memento Tracer framework is 10.17 times slower than the simple crawler. In contrast, Brunelle et al. [5] found their headless browser approach to be 38.9 times slower than a common crawler, so we see a significant decrease in crawl time. Second, simple automatic crawlers would not even discover a lot of the captured URIs, so speed is not the only factor. Runtimes can vary, depend on network speeds, and potential framework and crawler optimizations but objectively, these numbers provide insight into the cost (extra time) involved in automatic high-quality archiving.

## 6   Discussion and Future Work

Memento Tracer was developed as part of the Scholarly Orphans project, which focuses on artifacts that researchers deposit in a limited set of web productivity portals. Investigating the framework's applicability and merit beyond that scope remains for future work. We anticipate limitations imposed by the Chrome extension to create a trace for resources and limited value of the automated approach for web resources not based on common templates.

Traces created with our browser extension are currently expressed in a non-standardized manner. In order to enable interoperability between traces and other capture frameworks such as Puppeteer[15], a standard language needs to be devised to express interactions.

We are exploring alternate framework components to further stabilize our pilot implementation of the framework. Both the headless browser and the WarcProxy tool have proven unreliable at times.

## 7   Conclusion

In this paper we introduced Memento Tracer - a framework that provides high quality captures of web resources. Memento Tracer puts the curator in charge of determining the desired components of a to be archived web resource and takes advantage of frequently reused patterns in online productivity portals. We conducted experiments that show that Memento Tracer delivers high archival quality and that it can even outperform the Webrecorder tool that was designed for high fidelity captures. We have further shown that Memento Tracer captures web resources at high quality, even when operated at scale. The technical complexity of the framework, however, comes at a cost. In our experimental setup, compared to a simple crawling framework, Memento Tracer takes around 20 s longer to capture a single URI. Our findings prove the feasibility and highlight the potential of the Memento Tracer approach. As such, the contributions of this work should be considered a next step towards balancing quality and scalability for web archiving.

---

[15] https://github.com/GoogleChrome/puppeteer.

**Acknowledgement.** This work is supported in part by The Andrew W. Mellon Foundation grant 11600663.

# References

1. ISO 28500:2017 - information and documentation - WARC file format. https://www.iso.org/standard/68004.html
2. United Nations Archives: The National Archives. https://www.nationalarchives.gov.uk/
3. Berlin, J.: CNN.com Has Been Unarchivable Since November 1st, 2016. https://ws-dl.blogspot.com/2017/01/2017-01-20-cnncom-has-been-unarchivable.html
4. Berlin, J.A.: To relive the web: a framework for the transformation and archival replay of web pages. Master of Science (MS), Thesis, Computer Science, Old Dominion University (2018)
5. Brunelle, J.F., Weigle, M.C., Nelson, M.L.: Archival crawlers and Javascript: discover more stuff but crawl more slowly. In: 2017 ACM/IEEE Joint Conference on Digital Libraries (JCDL), pp. 1–10 (2017)
6. Brunelle, J.F., Kelly, M., SalahEldeen, H., Weigle, M.C., Nelson, M.L.: Not all mementos are created equal: measuring the impact of missing resources. In: Proceedings of the 14th ACM/IEEE-CS Joint Conference on Digital Libraries, pp. 321–330 (2014)
7. Hidayat, A.: PhantomJS. https://github.com/ariya/phantomjs
8. Internet Archive: Brozzler. https://github.com/internetarchive/brozzler
9. Internet Archive: Heritrix web crawler. https://github.com/internetarchive/heritrix3
10. Internet Archive: Wayback machine. http://web.archive.org/
11. Kahle, B.: Wayback rising!. https://twitter.com/brewster_kahle/status/1118172506777509890
12. Kreymer, I.: A prototype of automated web archiving, emulation and server preservation. https://blog.webrecorder.io/2018/08/28/automation-emulation-server-preserve.html
13. Kreymer, I.: Webrecorder. https://github.com/webrecorder/webrecorder
14. Kreymer, I.: Webrecorder player. https://github.com/webrecorder/webrecorder-player
15. National Library of Australia: Trove. https://trove.nla.gov.au/
16. Poursardar, F., Shipman, F.: How perceptions of web resource boundaries differ for institutional and personal archives. In: 2018 IEEE International Conference on Information Reuse and Integration (IRI), pp. 126–129 (2018)
17. Reich, V., Rosenthal, D.S.H.: LOCKSS: a permanent web publishing and access system. D-Lib Mag. **7**(6) (2001)
18. Rosenthal, D.S.H., Vargas, D.L., Lipkis, T.A., Griffin, C.T.: Enhancing the LOCKSS digital preservation technology. D-Lib Mag. **21**(9/10) (2015). https://doi.org/10.1045/september2015-rosenthal

# The Immigration Dilemma; Legal, Ethical and Practical Issues in Creating a Living, Growing Archive

Lisa Lamont[✉], Amanda Lanthorne, Arel Lucas, Katie Romabiles,
Christine Zielinski, Matthew Ferrill, Ivette Lorona, and Joseph Baker

San Diego State University, San Diego, CA, USA
mlamont@sdsu.edu

**Abstract.** Immigration is a widespread concern throughout the world and San Diego State University is located in the U.S.-Mexico border region, one of the most controversial areas. Also, located in this region is the Otay Mesa Detention Center which detains immigrants, asylum seekers, and undocumented persons seeking to cross legally into the U.S. With daily news stories about immigrants and border chaos, a group of concerned citizens, Detainee Allies, began to write and exchange letters with the detainees at the center in July 2018. The response from the detainees was immediate and continues to grow and the group quickly understood the import of the letters. They asked the SDSU library to archive, digitize, redact, and make the letters available to the public. This paper outlines a number of the legal and ethical issues surrounding this complex collection including the safety and privacy of the detainees, informed consent, the role of metadata, and the management of an archive growing in real time. Perhaps the collection will lead to a better understanding of the immigrants, or even help change public policy. At the very least the collection will be important for future research on immigration and the study of failed public policy.

**Keywords:** Digital archives · Legal and ethical concerns · Immigration

## 1 Background

Over the past few decades, civil unrest, ethnic cleansing, war, famine, and environmental crises have contributed to an ever-growing global migrant crisis. Millions of individuals have fled their home countries; many are still homeless while countless families remain separated. As a result, many nations are grappling with immigration issues, including the United States. The San Diego State University (SDSU), a diverse, Hispanic Serving Institution known for its cross-cultural research, is situated in one of the most controversial border regions in the United States. The city of San Diego lies next to Tijuana, Mexico, with SDSU just eighteen miles north of the US-Mexico border. San Diego's population is more than 33% Hispanic, and both English and Spanish are used and even mixed in conversation and business. In the past, the border was relatively porous with little or no documentation required to cross from one side to the other. The events of 9/11, coupled with recent government policies, have led to tighter border control. Still, a large number of workers commute every morning

A. Doucet et al. (Eds.): TPDL 2019, LNCS 11799, pp. 177–184, 2019.
https://doi.org/10.1007/978-3-030-30760-8_16

between Tijuana and San Diego, and many families consider themselves transborder making San Diego-Tijuana the busiest land border crossing in the Western Hemisphere and likely the world [1].

The Otay Mesa Detention Center (OMDC) is located on the U.S. side of the border with Mexico and houses asylum seekers, economic migrants and undocumented persons who are awaiting immigration hearings or parole. Many of the detainees are Spanish speakers from Central and South America along with others from China, Africa, the Middle East and Central Asia. Since the current U.S. government began its hard line on immigration and asylum, OMDC has reached its 1,500 capacity, with plans to expand. In 2018 the for-profit company administering the OMDC, CoreCivic, began requiring visitors, including non-profits, to sign nondisclosure agreements before entering the detention center. It also suspended its stakeholder tours. In October 2018, the company shut down a hotline, operated by Freedom for Immigrants, which allowed detainees to report inhumane conditions. Detainees are also unable to receive incoming calls, though they are able to make telephone calls for a fee. However, most of these persons used their savings for their journeys and the majority have few resources, often not enough for a telephone call or extra food from the commissary. Further complicating the situation, the Immigration and Customs Enforcement (ICE) agency has begun moving detainees to other detention centers and prisons across the US, including one in rural Alabama to alleviate overcrowding. These small, rural prisons are isolated and do not have the infrastructure or resources to assist migrants and asylum seekers.

In response to CoreCivic's actions and the increasingly hostile political atmosphere, a group of concerned San Diego State University faculty, researchers, and community members formed Otay Allies (recently renamed Detainee Allies) in July 2018. The Allies are a non-profit organization that "seeks to uphold standards of human decency and government accountability by communicating directly with detained refugees at Otay Mesa and SeaTac Detention Centers" [2]. The group regularly exchanges letters with detainees, who provide first-hand accounts of their experiences prior to detention and their path to seeking asylum. Many of the letter writers have fled torture, domestic violence, rape, LGBTQ persecution, drug cartels, gang violence, and political imprisonment. Not only do they describe these circumstances, but their journeys and routes to the United States as well, including migrant caravans. Many of the writers also document their experiences in the detention center(s), detailing wage theft, inadequate food and medical care, legal proceedings, family separations, and more. In addition to the letters, some detainees also send artwork such as drawings, crosses and baby booties made from candy wrappers, and even a dreamcatcher made of dental floss and pillow stuffing. These letters are one of the only ways for detainees to discuss their experiences and communicate with the outside world.

The Allies quickly realized the importance and impact of the correspondence. The group donated the ever-growing collection of letters to the SDSU Library in the hope that the Library would be able to make the letters available to a wide public audience via digitization. Through digitization and public access, the letters could potentially shape national immigration and asylum policy by providing first-hand accounts of how current policy is playing out. In February of 2019, Detainee Allies created a report documenting inhumane conditions at the OMDC, citing many of the letters as evidence [3]. Allies has distributed the report to the California Attorney General, numerous legislators, and the Department of Homeland Security's Office of Civil Rights and Liberties. Further mining of the letters from researchers outside of Detainee Allies may lead to other conclusions and/or reports not only on detention center conditions but also on national and international immigration and border policy(s). Many writers discuss why they sought asylum in the US, which could also serve to break down stereotypes about immigrants and asylum seekers, and promote empathy toward refugees and migrants.

## 2  Copyright and Consent

The Library began to receive, digitize and redact the letters in November of 2018. Although we attempted to locate similar archives to gather information on how to digitize and provide access to a real-time collection with serious privacy concerns, we found no comparable collections. We scan to .tif, and edit the files to enhance readability and remove any bleed through of the writing. We convert the files to .pdf and use Acrobat to redact. We open the completed redactions in several software packages to double check the reliability of the redactions.

While digitizing the collection is simple technologically, the complexity of archiving the collection and the legal and ethical considerations were evident from the start. The first major hurdle was copyright. Before the Library began digitizing the letters, we consulted with university counsel as well as an immigration lawyer to ensure that we were not compromising the safety of this vulnerable population, and that we were respectful of copyright and permissions. We recognize the inherent risk of providing public access to the digitized collection, but believe that the important content, and social and political weight of the letters outweigh the risks. The detainee correspondents hold copyright rights to their letters. While SDSU does not have their explicit written permission to post their letters online, we do believe we have implied consent.

Detainees receive an initial introduction letter in Spanish and English from Detainee Allies. Initially the letter included a vague statement about sharing the letters with others: "if you could tell us something about your story, it will be useful for us in educating other Americans about what is happening to immigrants like you. All of our volunteers have taken confidentiality training and understand how to treat your information in a safe and respectful manner." Detainee Allies recently made this language more explicit stating: "we have chosen to donate all of the letters we receive to the San Diego State University Library. Some of these letters are being included in a digital archive which is accessible online and open to the public. All letters posted in this online archive are redacted for privacy and confidentiality and we do our best to eliminate any identifying information. If you do not want your letters to be included in this public archive, please let us know. Your choice in this matter is entirely up to you and your choice will not affect your ability to receive commissary donations through our organization." With this new language, now featured on a separate page, detainees now have a way to opt in or out of the digital archive.

We also contemplated sending detainee correspondents formal permission forms from the library, but this was deemed logistically unfeasible for a variety of reasons including language barriers, findability (many writers have returned to their home countries or transferred to other detention centers with no forwarding information, effectively making their letters orphan works), and concern over detention center protocol. To further complicate the situation, many of the writers are not comfortable with written communication and several have noted that they are unable to write and that another detainee is writing for them. Given the inability for some writers to express themselves, can permission really be implied from their letters? Likewise, can detained authors freely and voluntarily give consent? Given the vulnerability of the detainees and the trauma of their journeys and incarceration it is arguable whether a yes to these statements can truly be considered permission.

This falls in line with Vannini, Gomez and Newell, who argue that privacy self-management (the detainee's ability to give consent) is insufficient, and detainees aren't always able to make informed decisions about consent because of their extreme circumstances [4]. In addition, the letter writers are often most interested in the immediate needs of obtaining legal and monetary support. The mention of online access and "telling your story" could raise hopes that their individual cases will be highlighted and resolved [5]. Also, agreeing to allow their letters to be exposed on the Internet could be seen as a requirement for obtaining assistance, despite the efforts of the Allies to make it clear that this is not true. Staff at the SDSU Library are unable to meet with individual letter writers in person to explain the digitization process, redaction, access, etc., or to show them the actual database, which means detainees have no way to ask about specifics or see their digitized letters before deciding whether or not to opt-in or out of the digital archive. Unfortunately for libraries, privacy self-management is often our main vehicle for obtaining permission to digitize and provide access to materials.

In several instances we have removed letters from the online archive because the writer has explicitly asked or made it clear that they do not wish to have their stories shared with the public. We address these situations by removing the redacted letter and noting in the metadata that the letter has been withdrawn at the request of the author. Most of the current writers state in their letters that they want their stories to be told. They have expressed this sentiment repeatedly to members of Detainee Allies. Again, we are interpreting this as *implied* consent, though we recognize that many writers might not fully understand how their stories are shared.

## 3    Privacy and Safety

In addition, as librarians and archivists we understand the need to respect privacy and at the same time provide access to a compelling and portentous collection. Other digitization projects have faced similar challenges. We consulted the IFLA guidelines for personal information in historical records [6]. Current best practices suggest that each sensitive collection will require its own well-planned guidelines and procedures that protect individuals and still allow access [7]. We have developed our own in-house procedures and redaction guidelines and we believe that we have managed to respect both the writers' privacy and their ownership of their stories.

Given that this collection documents ongoing current events, many of the correspondents remain in detention, are awaiting asylum trials, or have been returned to their home countries, and their privacy and safety are at risk. As a result, the physical unredacted letters have been embargoed until the year 2100, and the digitized letters are redacted to safeguard the identities of the writers.

Redaction is necessary for many reasons including to prevent the possibility of retaliation from detention center employees. We suspect that all outgoing letters are read by detention center staff and that the information in the letters is known to the staff. Still, having that information easily available on the Internet highlights practices at CoreCivic which they may not want publicly available. Also, the writers often site drug cartel violence or political persecution as the reasons for their journeys. Their identities must be protected in case they are deported and returned to the circumstances from which they fled. In order to maintain their anonymity the Library removes all identifying personal information such as: medical conditions, the use of medical devices, references to body art, physical features, names, names of family members, pets, small towns or neighborhoods, dates (such as the date of entry to the U.S. or court dates), commissary numbers, alien numbers, phone numbers, ages, and birthdates. In short, anything that could distinguish one detainee from another.

How much to redact is a constant concern. The desire to demonstrate the conditions and journeys and the need to keep the writer safe and not invade privacy are continually in balance. We revise our redaction guidelines often as new circumstances occur. For instance, as more letters arrived we discovered an interesting trend. Many writers use an initial letter as an introduction with a few general details about their journey or life in the detention center. As the writers become comfortable with the Allies, they use each following letter to include more details about their decisions to emigrate and their paths into detention. For several of these writers by the third or fourth letter they have described harrowing stories in so much detail that we have determined they are in serious danger and their locations should not be made evident on the Internet. Our policy is to immediately remove the earlier letters, determine whether more restrictive redacting is possible and, if not, embargo them along with the latest letter. We place a metadata record in the online database with no attached letter and a note in the description stating that the letter has been withdrawn from the online archive.

## 4   Metadata

Along with redaction, legal and ethical issues, the metadata has been a regular source of debate and is constantly evolving. We use MODS in our Islandora repository and fortunately, we have several Spanish speakers and readers among out staff. We have been able to locate translators for several other languages including Arabic and African dialects. For metadata creation, language was the first, but not the only consideration. We pondered which pronouns (if any) to use for transgendered persons. Also, if the gender of any person cannot be determined from the clues in the letter we try not to use a gender- defining pronoun in the metadata. We would like to add a geographic field to the metadata in order to map the journeys and show the flow of migration, however, because the correspondents sometimes come from small towns or travel through them we cannot add all the locations mentioned in the letters. We are still working through how best to address this issue. We want to include the letter writer's country of origin, though several authors have lived in the United States for most of their lives. For these writers we do not include a country of origin, but a country to which they may be deported.

We are now adding subjects terms according to a controlled vocabulary developed in consultation with Detainee Allies. The subject terms will aid researchers in locating letters addressing particular events or issues including complaints about food, water, medical neglect, family separations, and wages. The subjects will flag letters which include artworks and help identify persons who have been detained for longer than a year. We anticipate that the vocabulary will develop as more immigrants arrive and the public policy situation changes.

Our metadata, however, is in English while most of the letters are written in Spanish. Given the international scope of the collection, it is imperative to include bilingual metadata to enhance discoverability and access. We are working on how to leverage our Islandora installation to best represent two sets of metadata. Translation and transcription are also important for the project and will enhance discoverability. The letters are written in several different languages, though as noted earlier the majority are in Spanish. Translation has been fascinating, and researchers in linguistics or language studies may find the collection interesting. Some of the letter writers are well educated; the preponderance though are clearly uncomfortable with written communication. These writers spell phonetically and use little or no punctuation. Some letters have been written by a Spanish speaker for a detainee who speaks no English and little Spanish. Despite the challenges, we attempt to represent the writers' stories in their authentic voices through these translations and transcriptions as our brief summaries in a metadata description field do not do justice to the letters. Further, since U.S. citizens are not usually bilingual it is crucial to translate the letters to reach a wider audience.

Metadata and transcriptions should be in the language of the correspondent for ethical reasons as well [8]. In their letters, correspondents detail events and experiences in their home countries that should be made easily findable (via the Internet) for people in those countries, not just English-speakers in the United States. We have one bilingual staff member and a student working on translations and transcriptions. Both versions of the letters are being incorporated into our Islandora records.

## 5   Discussion

This is a complicated, time-consuming and risky project and yet we are committed to it for several reasons. First, as mentioned above, San Diego State University is a large public university located near the US-Mexico Border with a diverse student population representing all races, ethnicities, abilities, languages, sexualities, genders, religion, age, immigration status, socioeconomic backgrounds, military status, and other markers of identity. Many of our students are also DREAMers under the Deferred Action on Childhood Arrivals (DACA) program; persons who were brought to the country as children and have known no other life. San Diego also has one of the largest refugee populations in the United States. Documenting the stories of migrants helps to create an inclusive and supportive environment for DREAMers on the SDSU campus by providing relatable source material representing other undocumented persons. In this way, archives have the ability to empower students to question and dismantle oppressive structures and create their own narratives.

Secondly, the SDSU Library's collections are as diverse as our population and represent non-dominant histories and perspectives. As such, the SDSU Library strives to collect local and regional history documenting San Diego's local immigrant communities. Special Collections & University Archives has been working to collect the records of various underrepresented communities, including letters written by victims of torture. The Library has also collaborated with the Lambda Archives of San Diego to host its digital collection of LGBTQ material. The Otay Mesa Detention Center Detainee Letter Collection complements these collections by highlighting the migrant and asylum seeker experience.

Next, although border issues and immigration policy are daily headlines, the media frequently focus on ICE and the president, rather than the actual humans living in detention. In addition, the current US Administration regularly uses rhetoric that dehumanizes migrants and undocumented citizens. Through digitization, we hope to uplift the voices and stories of detainees, and highlight the lives of the real people involved. The digital collection gives migrants a voice despite attempts to silence them. The documentation and promotion of these overlooked and underrepresented perspectives may encourage empathy and get researchers, lawmakers, and the general public to think critically about the migrant crisis and our broken system.

Lastly, even if the collection does not reach the public consciousness or policy and law makers, it documents for future researchers the conditions brought about by public policy. The collection represents the plight of this marginalized population and will provide future researchers with a wealth of data and perspective. The letters contribute to a more accurate and complete historical record by documenting the experience of migration in the 21st century.

## 6   Conclusion

The growing collection contains over 1500 letters and other, similar organizations have contacted us to discuss archiving their correspondence and papers. Several SDSU classes are already using the letters including a qualitative methods class. In addition, a researcher is using the letters as an experiment in crowdsourced tagging, and we are in discussion with researchers at the University of California, San Diego who are also interested in incorporating the letters into the curriculum. Another university in the region has likewise expressed interested in exhibiting the redacted letters and creating related programming to engage students with the collection. In short, the letters are already proving valuable in the short term. Yet, it will be years before the true value of the collection is properly assessed. Daily we question whether we have made the correct legal and ethical decisions and whether the collection will truly bring awareness to the immigration dilemma.

Detainee Allies Letter Collection: https://digitallibrary.sdsu.edu/islandora/object/ sdsu%3AOtayMesaDetentionCenter.

# References

1. San Diego-Baja California Border Crossing and Trade Statistics. https://www.sandag.org/index.asp?classid=19&projectid=451&fuseaction=projects.detail. Accessed Apr 2019
2. Detainee Allies Homepage. http://www.detaineeallies.org/. Accessed Apr 2019
3. Otay Allies, Testimony from migrants and refugees in the Otay Mesa Detention Center. http://www.detaineeallies.org/report-for-policymakers/. Accessed Apr 2019
4. Vannini, S., Gomez, R., Newell, B.C.: Documenting the undocumented: privacy and security guidelines for humanitarian work with irregular migrants. In: Taylor, N.G., Christian-Lamb, C., Martin, M.H., Nardi, B. (eds.) iConference 2019: Information in Contemporary Society. LNCS, vol. 11420, pp. 236–244. Springer, Cham (2019). https://doi.org/10.1007/978-3-030-15742-5_23
5. Barber, R.: Research with vulnerable populations in humanitarian crises: ethical challenges and overlooked areas. In: PREA Conference. Ethics and Humanitarian Research: Generating Evidence Ethically, The Fawcett Event Center, The Ohio State University, Columbus, Ohio, 25–26 March 2019. Presentation, Session 13, Oral Presentations 4, Paper B (2019). http://hdl.handle.net/1811/87652
6. IFLA Statement on Access to Personally Identifiable Information in Historical Records. https://www.ifla.org/publications/ifla-statement-on-access-to-personally-identifiable-information-in-historical-records. Accessed Apr 2019
7. Manzuch, Z.: Ethical issues in the digitization of cultural heritage. J. Contemp. Arch. Stud. **4**, article 4 (2017)
8. Diekema, A.R.: Multilinguality in the digital library: a review. Electron. Libr. **30**(2), 165–181 (2012)

# Segmenting User Sessions in Search Engine Query Logs Leveraging Word Embeddings

Pedro Gomes[1]([✉]), Bruno Martins[1], and Luís Cruz[2]

[1] INESC-ID and Instituto Superior Técnico,
Universidade de Lisboa, Lisboa, Portugal
{pedro.almeida.gomes,bruno.g.martins}@tecnico.ulisboa.pt
[2] INESC-ID and Faculdade de Engenharia, Universidade do Porto, Porto, Portugal
luiscruz@fe.up.pt

**Abstract.** Segmenting user sessions in search engine query logs is important to perceive information needs and assess how they are satisfied, to enhance the quality of search engine rankings, and to better direct content to certain users. Most previous methods use human judgments to inform supervised learning algorithms, and/or use global thresholds on temporal proximity and on simple lexical similarity metrics. This paper proposes a novel unsupervised method that improves the current state-of-art, leveraging additional heuristics and similarity metrics derived from word embeddings. We specifically extend a previous approach based on combining temporal and lexical similarity measurements, integrating semantic similarity components that use pre-trained FastText embeddings. The paper reports on experiments with an AOL query dataset used in previous studies, containing a total of 10,235 queries, with 4,253 sessions, 2.4 queries per session, and 215 unique users. The results attest to the effectiveness of the proposed method, which outperforms a large set of baselines, also corresponding to unsupervised techniques.

**Keywords:** Analysis of search engine query logs ·
User session detection · String similarity metrics · Word embeddings

## 1 Introduction

In the context of user interactions with search engines, the notion of session is critical to the study of user habits and intentions when using these systems. In brief, a session is a sequence of activities followed by one individual to satisfy an information need, regardless of the elapsed time, number of interactions with the system, or the existence of interruptions on these interactions. Identifying user sessions is important to understand a search engine's effectiveness in suggesting content pointers for user searches, with several previous studies suggesting that by studying the properties of these sessions (e.g., clicks and dwell-time on search results) one can evaluate system quality and predict general user satisfaction [1–6].

© Springer Nature Switzerland AG 2019
A. Doucet et al. (Eds.): TPDL 2019, LNCS 11799, pp. 185–199, 2019.
https://doi.org/10.1007/978-3-030-30760-8_17

According to Hagen et al. [7], there are two possible scenarios where the identification of sessions can have a beneficial result: online, where it can help the search engine to present better results or to suggest queries that other users submitted in similar situations; and offline, where the identification of sessions within information collected from query logs gives information about the behavior of users, supporting the evaluation of their satisfaction. Typically, a session ends when the user has satisfied his information need, or when the user decided to stop (i.e., the user leaves the system or proceeds to a new information need). The correct identification of user sessions with search engines is still a challenging problem, which entails the following main issues:

– Session boundaries can be highly ambiguous. The most commonly used approach to identify user sessions involves grouping all interactions from the same user that happened within a constrained temporal interval. This approach is simple and efficient, having been reported to achieve a confidence level of approximately 70% on Web search logs [8]. However, this approach also introduces noise, since it does not take into account activity breaks or sessions that are very long. One of the difficulties in using a global temporal threshold is that true session intervals usually have a smooth distribution, and it is almost guaranteed that longer sessions will be handled incorrectly. Nonetheless, some previous proposals attempt to address this issue through variable thresholds depending on the user [9].
– It can be difficult to infer if two queries from the same user belong to the same session, e.g. when they do not have terms in common but correspond to the same underlying topic. For example, if one user searches for *iPhone* and then searches for *Apple*, there is no direct way to assess the similarity between these terms, although recent proposals have addressed this issue through semantic representations for the terms employed in user queries (e.g., through distributional semantics and word embeddings).
– Efficiency is a major concern, either in the context of timely online identification of user sessions, or in the processing of very large query logs for segmenting sessions boundaries. Depending on the circumstances, there is usually a trade-off between algorithm accuracy and efficiency.

Tackling the aforementioned challenges usually involves a combination of different carefully selected heuristics: temporal approaches (e.g., relying on a global threshold) have the advantage of simplicity and efficiency, although they also have problems with accuracy, whereas heuristics capturing lexical/topical similarity (e.g., methods based on distributional semantics) can have a high accuracy, although also a lower efficiency. By combining these general methods, we aim at achieving a useful trade-off between effectiveness and efficiency.

In this paper, we propose a new unsupervised method that improves upon a previous proposal by Gayo-Avello [10], which is based on a geometric interpretation for how temporal and lexical similarity measurements can be combined.

First, for comparing consecutive queries from the same user, our approach uses a geometric method to decide if the more recent query belongs to the same session, combining a user-specific temporal threshold with a lexical similarity value computed from $n$-gram overlaps. If a reliable decision cannot be made with this procedure, we compute separate semantic similarity measurements, e.g. with basis on pre-trained FastText embeddings [11]. The FastText approach represents tokens based on their character $n$-grams, and is capable of producing representations for query tokens that were not seen during model training.

We evaluated the proposed method against several alternative approaches, using a subset of the well-known 2006 AOL query log [12] that, despite the many privacy concerns[1], has frequently supported studies on user session identification. The entire dataset has 30 million queries from 650,000 different users, collected over a period of three months. From the entire dataset, Gayo-Avello [10] built a subset with ground-truth annotations for user sessions, containing 10,235 queries from 215 different users, where 4,253 sessions were manually identified.

On the AOL data subset from Gayo-Avello, our method achieved a precision of 88.19, a recall of 95.13, and an F1-score of 91.53, which is about 2.96% better than the unsupervised geometric method [10]. Ablation tests also confirmed the usefulness of the different components involved in the proposed method. As a side contribution, we deliver a reproducibility package[2] with all the scripts used in the evaluation experiments that are reported on this paper.

The rest of this paper is organized as follows: Sect. 2 surveys previous work in the area, while Sect. 3 details the proposed approach. Section 4 presents the experimental evaluation of the proposed method, detailing the dataset, the evaluation methodology, and the obtained results. Finally, Sect. 5 summarizes our main conclusions and presents possible directions for future work.

## 2   Related Work

Previous studies addressing user session identification have proposed methods (i) based only on temporal thresholds (i.e., the time gap between queries), (ii) based only on lexical heuristics (i.e., string similarity between queries, search patterns, etc.), and (iii) based on a combination of both these heuristics, either relying on supervised methods or completely unsupervised approaches.

The most common methods to identify user sessions are based on a global temporal threshold, in which two consecutive queries belong to the same session if the elapsed time is less than a pre-defined threshold. Previous studies have considered limits of 5 [13], 10–15 [14], or 30 min [15,16]. This approach is still widely used in practice (e.g., Google claims to apply a threshold of 30 min in their Web analytics application[3]), but an important limitation relates to the application of the same threshold for all contexts (e.g., different users may behave differently, and different query logs may reflect particular system and user characteristics that affect the typical duration of the sessions).

---

[1] https://www.nytimes.com/2006/08/09/technology/09aol.html.

[2] https://github.com/PedroG1515/Segmenting-User-Sessions.

[3] https://support.google.com/analytics/answer/2731565.

Mehrzadi and Feitelson [9] proposed an approach which deals with the afore-mentioned limitation, adapting the temporal threshold based on the activity of each user. The proposed approach leverages temporal gaps between consecutive queries and binning on a logarithmic scale. First, for each user, the authors extract the time gap between all consecutive queries, and then they create a histogram with basis on these values. The bins in the histogram are built based on powers of 2, starting with the interval from 0 to 32 s. The authors also restrict the bins to be analyzed in the subsequent steps, ranging from 512 s in the lower value to 8192 s in the upper value. Each candidate bin is finally scored, based on how much lower its count value is than the maximal count value on its two sides. The upper value for the bin with a higher score is chosen as the user threshold, to be used when segmenting user sessions. In case of a tie, the upper value from the bin closest to 1,200 s is chosen.

Instead of relying on temporal thresholds, other studies have proposed to use lexical similarity heuristics. For instance, Bernard et al. [17] proposed an approach to detect session boundaries based on query reformulations, considering that two queries do not belong to the same session if they do not have query terms in common. Lucchese et al. [18] proposed, among other approaches, a clustering method that leverages the Jaccard similarity coefficient [19] computed from character 3-grams, to assess the similarity between queries. Despite yielding high accuracy, these methods are slower and can also introduce several problems, namely (i) they are limited to sub-string matches and cannot detect semantic similarity between queries, and (ii) they directly assign similar queries to the same session, independently of the time separating these queries.

Considering the aforementioned limitations, Gayo-Avello [10] proposed a method that combines temporal and lexical heuristics. The temporal compo-nent $f_t$ can be calculated as shown in Eq. 1 [7], where $t_i$ and $t_{i+1}$ correspond to the timestamps for the consecutive queries:

$$f_t = \max\left\{0, 1 - \frac{t_{i+1} - t_i}{24\,\mathrm{h}}\right\} \qquad (1)$$

The lexical component $f_l$ is based on representing queries as sets of character 3-grams and assessing the overlap between these representations. To decide if two queries belong to the same session, the author proposed a geometric interpreta-tion for how temporal and lexical similarity measurements, both in the interval $[0, 1]$, can be combined. The method corresponds to computing the area enclosed by positive semi-axes and a unit circle centered at $(1, 1)$, as shown in Eq. 2:

$$\sqrt{f_t^2 + f_l^2} \geq 1 \qquad (2)$$

Hagen et al. [7] proposed a cascade method (i.e., an incremental procedure based on a sequence of heuristics), which also combines temporal and lexical components. This method relies first on more efficient features (i.e., query re-formulation patterns), and then progressively on more complex features with higher effectiveness and lower efficiency, only using the more complex features if strictly necessary to obtain reliable results. Query reformulation patterns (e.g., query repetition, as well as query generalization or specialization through the inclusion/removal of terms) are first used to detect the similarity of two consecutive queries, regardless of the time between them. Although this step is very efficient, it has a low efficiency because it does not detect misspellings or other vocabulary mismatches. The second step uses the aforementioned geometric method from Gayo-Avello [10] to refine the results, being invoked only when Step 1 decided for a new session (i.e., when no query repetition or reformulation was detected). In this case, the authors used Eq. 1 to compute the temporal component, but the lexical component was instead based on the cosine similarity between vector representations encoding 3- to 5-grams. The third step uses Explicit Semantic Analysis (ESA) as a refinement over lexical similarity [20], capturing the semantic similarity between the new query and all the keywords of the queries in the session to which the previous query belongs. ESA is applied on the cases having a high temporal similarity (i.e., greater than 0.8) but a low lexical similarity (i.e., less than 0.4), thus being incorrectly classified by the geometric method. ESA does not compare representations for the texts under analysis directly, instead building representations from a background collection (e.g., a large random sample of Wikipedia articles) so that each term is represented as a column vector in the TF-IDF matrix of the background corpus, and a text (i.e., a set of terms) is represented as the centroid of the vectors representing the terms. The ESA vectors are compared through the cosine similarity and if the result is greater than a threshold (i.e., 0.35 in the experiments reported by Hagen et al. [7]), the two queries belong to the same session. In the final step, which is computationally more demanding, the authors use Web search results to detect semantically similar queries, comparing the top retrieved documents for two consecutive queries. If there is at least one URL in common in the sets of top documents, then the queries are considered to be in the same session.

The authors compared the cascade method with the geometric method from Gayo-Avello [10], obtaining improvements in terms of recall and in the F1-score, although also a lower precision. In general, the cascade method is very reliable, although the final step is an important bottleneck in terms of performance. The authors concluded that it may be preferable to ignore the last step, this way achieving a better trade-off between efficiency and effectiveness.

Several previous studies have also advanced supervised methods for query session segmentation, in some cases leveraging user activity during a search (e.g., clicks or dwell time on search results) for extending existing lexical and time features. For instance, Ozmutlu et al. [21] proposed a method based on thresholding the results from a linear regression with two-factor interactions, using features corresponding to search patterns, time between consecutive queries, and the sequential position of the query within the session. Jones and Klinkner [8] proposed to learn a binary classifier for inferring whether two queries belong to the same task, leveraging temporal features, lexical similarity features based on words or characters, query co-occurrence features, and features derived from the search results. Despite the interesting results, supervised approaches require training data, thus being harder to generalize to new application domains. We aim to detect sessions in the query logs of different systems, using suitable heuristics that operate directly on the logs, and avoiding the training of a classifier.

# 3   Unsupervised Segmentation of User Sessions

To address the problem of segmenting user sessions in search logs, we propose a new unsupervised approach combining multiple heuristics, evaluating it against a set of baselines that covers the current state-of-the-art. An ablation analysis was also considered, checking the impact of temporal, lexical, and semantic similarity heuristics, in the overall method that integrates them.

In the rest of this section, we first describe the individual heuristics that we considered for the ablation tests, and which are also the main components of the complete method. Then, we describe the complete method, detailing some of the components that are involved (e.g., the use of word embeddings).

## 3.1   Individual Heuristics and Ablated Approaches

In terms of temporal heuristics, our tests with baselines and ablated models considered two different approaches. The first relies on a global threshold, in which two consecutive queries belong to the same session if the elapsed time is less than a pre-defined threshold. With basis on previous studies, we tested the standard values of 5 [13], 15 [14], and 30 min [15]. The second approach considers a user-specific threshold, defined with basis on the user distribution of intervals between consecutive queries, as proposed by Mehrzadi and Feitelson [9].

In terms of lexical and semantic heuristics, our ablation tests considered three different approaches. The first is based on the Jaccard similarity coefficient between the sets of 3- and 4-grams extracted from the new query, and from all the queries in the session of the previous query. The second is based on pre-trained FastText embeddings [11], computing the cosine similarity between averaged embedding vectors for the words present in the consecutive queries. Finally, the third approach also relies on FastText embeddings, but in this case we use the word mover's distance [22] to assess the similarity between sets of embeddings, respectively for words in the new query, and for words in all the queries in the session of the previous query. We used an existing implementation[4] for the earth mover's distance between word embeddings. In all three approaches, we tested different thresholds (i.e., between 0.1 and 0.9) in the obtained similarity value. The lexical similarity computations did not involve language-specific lists of stop-words or stemming algorithms, although we ignored punctuation symbols and sub-strings such as `www.` or `.com` (i.e., queries often contain URLs, and we ignored common URL tokens from the similarity computations).

---

[4] https://radimrehurek.com/gensim/models/keyedvectors.html#gensim.models. keyedvectors.WordEmbeddingsKeyedVectors.wmdistance.

In terms of combinations between multiple heuristics, besides our complete approach, we also tested three different methods. The first was the geometric method from Gayo-Avello [10], with the same parameters proposed by the author. The second corresponds to an improved version of the geometric method, which instead of using the overlap between character 3-grams, in the lexical component, uses the Jaccard similarity coefficient between sets of character $n$-grams of lengths 3 and 4, extracted from the last query and from all the queries in the session of the previous query. In the improved version of the geometric method, we also changed the temporal component in Eq. 1, using a normalization constant equal to the minimum between twice the maximum time between consecutive queries for the user under analysis and 24 h, instead of the fixed normalization constant of 24 h. Finally, the third method corresponds to a slightly different procedure from the complete method described in Sect. 3.2, using only the cosine similarity between averaged word embeddings for consecutive queries, instead of using the word mover's distance.

In the methods combining multiple heuristics that use a threshold over the Jaccard similarity coefficient between character $n$-grams (although not on the lexical baselines that use the Jaccard coefficient alone), we used a simple two-step approach to improve the computational performance, based on the intuition that a fast lower-bound for the similarity can be computed from the length of common prefixes and/or suffixes. First, notice that for a string of size $k$, the maximum number of distinct $n$-grams is given by $k - (n - 1)$. For two strings in which one is a prefix or a suffix of the other (i.e., strings resulting from a typical reformulation pattern, corresponding to the addition or removal of terms from the search query), in which the size of the common sub-string is $k_1$ and the length of the longer string is $k_2$, the number of $n$-grams in common cannot be higher than $k_1 - (n - 1)$, and the number of distinct $n$-grams cannot be lower than the number of $n$-grams in common, or higher than $k_2 - (n - 1)$. The ratio between these two quantities gives us an approximation on the Jaccard similarity coefficient, that we can use as a lower-bound. This procedure will, in some cases, lead to wrong lower-bound estimates when there are many $n$-grams appearing repeated in the strings. However, in such cases, the strings under comparison will still have a significant match in their contents, and we can use the estimate in a way that is similar to the query reformulation patterns in the cascade method [7].

In the combined methods, when checking if the Jaccard similarity coefficient is above a given threshold, we first check if the lower-bound (computed with basis on the similarity towards the last query) is greater than the threshold, and only if this is not enough to reach a decision do we compute the actual similarity coefficient. Notice that Eq. 2 from the geometic method corresponds to a minimum threshold of $\sqrt{1 - f_t^2}$ on the (lower-bound to the) Jaccard similarity.

## 3.2 The Proposed Approach

Our complete method corresponds to a cascade approach, extending the geometric method and the approach from Hagen et al. [7] through the use of word

**Algorithm 1.** The Proposed Session Segmentation Method

1: Sort the log using the userID as a first criterion, and then using the timestamp
2: Initialize each query in the log as belonging to a separate session
3: **for each** user $u$ **do**
4:     $t_{\max_u}$ = Maximum time between consecutive queries for user $u$
5:     **for each** pair of consecutive sessions $i$ and $i+1$ from the same user $u$ **do**
6:         $f_t = \max\left\{0, 1 - \dfrac{t_{i+1}-t_i}{\min\{24\,\mathrm{h}, 2\times t_{\max_u}\}}\right\}$
7:         $f_{l_1}$ = Lower-bound on the Jaccard similarity coefficient
8:         **if** $f_{l_1} > \sqrt{1 - f_t^2}$ **then**
9:             Merge the two consecutive sessions
10:        **else**
11:            $f_{l_2}$ = Jaccard similarity based on character $n$-grams ($n \in \{3, 4\}$)
12:            **if** $\sqrt{f_t^2 + f_{l_2}^2} > 1$ **then**
13:                Merge the two consecutive sessions
14:            **else**
15:                **if** $f_t > 0.7$ and $f_{l_2} < 0.5$ **then**
16:                    $f_{s_1}$ = Cosine similarity from averaged word embeddings
17:                    **if** $f_{s_1} > 0.5$ **then**
18:                        Merge the two consecutive sessions
19:                    **else**
20:                        $f_{s_2}$ = Word mover's distance [22] from sets of embeddings
21:                        **if** $f_{s_2} < 0.1$ **then**
22:                            Merge the two consecutive sessions
23:                        **else**
24:                            **if** $\sqrt{f_{s_1}^2 + f_{s_2}^2} > 1$ **then**
25:                                $f_u$ = Similarity from largest common URL sub-sequence
26:                                **if** $f_u > 0.7$ **then**
27:                                    Merge the two consecutive sessions

embeddings. The method consists of the following three steps, and it can also be summarized through the pseudo-code shown in Algorithm 1.

First, we use the aforementioned improved version of the geometric method, relying on a per-user maximum threshold for the temporal component, using the fast lower-bound on the Jaccard similarity coefficient, and using character 3- and 4-grams in the lexical component. A new query will belong to the previous session if an adapted version of Eq. 2 (i.e., using the condition greater than one, instead of greater or equal to one, thus ensuring that equal queries separated by very large time spans are not merged) is satisfied, and otherwise different sessions will be considered. Although effective on its own, this step fails at capturing semantic similarities (i.e., it incorrectly classifies many cases involving queries in close temporal proximity, but with a low lexical similarity). Adapting the cascade method from Hagen et al. [7], if the temporal proximity is above the threshold of 0.7, and the lexical similarity is below the threshold of 0.5, we attempt to merge the queries into the same session according to the results of the second step.

In the second step, starting on Line 16 from Algorithm 1, we use pre-trained FastText embeddings [11] to quickly assess the semantic similarity of two consecutive queries/sessions. The FastText approach has been shown to perform well in representing words (e.g., in sentence classification as a down-stream task leveraging word embeddings), especially in the case of rare words, by making use of character level information. Each word is seen as a bag of character $n$-grams, in addition to the word itself. During model training, FastText learns weights for each of the $n$-grams, as well as for the entire word token. Rare words can be properly represented, since it is highly likely that some of their $n$-grams also appear in other words, and even out-of-vocabulary words can be represented, by taking the average of the embeddings for the corresponding $n$-grams.

We start by measuring the cosine similarity between averaged word embeddings for the consecutive queries. If the similarity is above the threshold of 0.5, then the queries are defined to belong to the same session. Otherwise, we compare the set of embeddings for the words in the query, against the set of embeddings corresponding to words in all the queries belonging to the session of the previous query. In this second case, a fast algorithm for computing the word mover's distance [22] is used to compare the sets of embeddings and, if the resulting distance is lower than 0.1, we assume that the two consecutive queries belong to the same session (otherwise different sessions will be considered). The Word Mover's Distance (WMD) is a special case of the well-studied earth mover's distance transportation problem, measuring the dissimilarity between two sets of embeddings as the minimum amount of distance that the embeddings of one set need to travel to reach the embeddings of another set.

**Table 1.** Results for a sample of queries taken from the 2006 AOL query log [12].

**A. Segmentation from Human Annotator**

| Query | URL | Time |
|---|---|---|
| teeth like god's shoeshine lyrics | www.selyrics.com | 1142351220 |
| grills lyrics | | 1142369580 |
| grills lyrics nelly | www.lyrics07.com | 1142369580 |
| blink 182 lyrics | www.azlyrics.com | 1142371620 |
| edit the sad parts lyrics | www.azlyrics.com | 1142372820 |
| my lips are cold the truth is told lyrics | www.lyricsdepot.com | 1142375940 |
| the authority song | | 1142449620 |
| the authority song lyrics | www.selyrics.com | 1142449680 |
| black dresses by spill canvas | www.selyrics.com | 1142449980 |
| playing for keeps lyrics | www.lyrics07.com | 1142450040 |
| rhyming dictionary | www.rhymer.com | 1142452560 |
| monstr in a wheelchair | | 1142465880 |

**B. Segmentation Resulting from Step 1**

| Query | URL | Time |
|---|---|---|
| teeth like god's shoeshine lyrics | www.selyrics.com | 1142351220 |
| grills lyrics | | 1142369580 |
| grills lyrics nelly | www.lyrics07.com | 1142369580 |
| blink 182 lyrics | www.azlyrics.com | 1142371620 |
| edit the sad parts lyrics | www.selyrics.com | 1142372820 |
| my lips are cold the truth is told lyrics | www.lyricsdepot.com | 1142375940 |
| the authority song | | 1142449620 |
| the authority song lyrics | www.selyrics.com | 1142449680 |
| black dresses by spill canvas | www.azlyrics.com | 1142449980 |
| playing for keeps lyrics | www.lyrics07.com | 1142450040 |
| rhyming dictionary | www.rhymer.com | 1142452560 |
| monstr in a wheelchair | | 1142465880 |

**C. Segmentation Resulting from Step 2**

| Query | URL | Time |
|---|---|---|
| teeth like god's shoeshine lyrics | www.selyrics.com | 1142351220 |
| grills lyrics | | 1142369580 |
| grills lyrics nelly | www.lyrics07.com | 1142369580 |
| blink 182 lyrics | www.azlyrics.com | 1142371620 |
| edit the sad parts lyrics | www.selyrics.com | 1142372820 |
| my lips are cold the truth is told lyrics | www.lyricsdepot.com | 1142375940 |
| the authority song | | 1142449620 |
| the authority song lyrics | www.selyrics.com | 1142449680 |
| black dresses by spill canvas | www.azlyrics.com | 1142449980 |
| playing for keeps lyrics | www.lyrics07.com | 1142450040 |
| rhyming dictionary | www.rhymer.com | 1142452560 |
| monstr in a wheelchair | | 1142465880 |

**D. Segmentation Resulting from Step 3**

| Query | URL | Time |
|---|---|---|
| teeth like god's shoeshine lyrics | www.selyrics.com | 1142351220 |
| grills lyrics | | 1142369580 |
| grills lyrics nelly | www.lyrics07.com | 1142369580 |
| blink 182 lyrics | www.azlyrics.com | 1142371620 |
| edit the sad parts lyrics | www.selyrics.com | 1142372820 |
| my lips are cold the truth is told lyrics | www.lyricsdepot.com | 1142375940 |
| the authority song | | 1142449620 |
| the authority song lyrics | www.selyrics.com | 1142449680 |
| black dresses by spill canvas | www.azlyrics.com | 1142449980 |
| playing for keeps lyrics | www.lyrics07.com | 1142450040 |
| rhyming dictionary | www.rhymer.com | 1142452560 |
| monstr in a wheelchair | | 1142465880 |

In the third step, if the decision remains unreliable (i.e., if the similarity scores from the previous step are within particular thresholds, also according to a geometric interpretation) we will compare clicked URLs through the longest sub-strings in common. We assume that the query log under analysis contains information on clicked URLs (i.e., for each query, if the user accessed one of the URLs in the search results, then the corresponding URL is registered on the log). We first normalize the URLs by removing redundant information, including prefixes corresponding to protocol specifications (e.g., `http://` or `https://`), sub-strings corresponding to top-level domain names (e.g., `.com`, `.org` or `.edu`), or suffixes corresponding to popular file extensions (e.g., `.html`, `.jsp` or `.php`). Then, we compute the longest common sub-strings between the normalized URL associated with the new query, and any of the normalized URLs associated to queries in the same session as the previous query. If any of these longest common sub-strings has a length that is at least 70% of the length of the URL for the new query, then the queries are considered to belong to the same session (and otherwise a different session will be considered for each of the queries).

Tables 1A to D illustrate the obtained results at the different steps of the algorithm, for a sample of queries taken from the AOL query log (i.e., a sequence of queries for the same user, that made system interactions generally related to the topic of music). Table 1A shows the segmentation boundaries made by a human annotator, whereas Tables 1B to D show the boundaries resulting from each step of the algorithm, progressively reconstructing the same decisions as the human annotator. For instance, Table 1C shows that by considering semantic similarity based on word embeddings, one can almost reconstruct the first session from Table 1A. Step 3 effectively refines the results by leveraging URLs, although the method still failed at joining the last two iterations on the table.

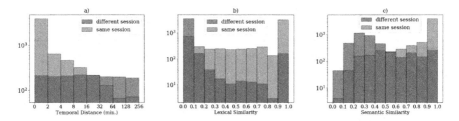

**Fig. 1.** Distribution for the number of consecutive queries, according to (a) temporal proximity, (b) lexical similarity, and (c) semantic similarity.

## 4    Experimental Evaluation

This section describes the experimental evaluation of the proposed method. We first present a statistical characterization of the AOL dataset that supported our tests, together with the considered experimental methodology. Then, Subsect. 4.2 presents and discusses the obtained results.

## 4.1   Dataset and Experimental Methodology

The dataset used in our experiments corresponds to a subset of the AOL query log released on August 2006 [12]. To ensure a meaningful comparison against previously published results, we used the subset of the AOL query log, with ground-truth annotations regarding session segmentation, made available by Gayo-Avello [10] and used in several previous studies in the area. This subset has a total of 10,235 queries of 215 unique users, which are divided into 4,253 sessions with an average of 2.4 queries per session.

In the dataset, each record contains the following attributes: (i) userID (i.e., a unique user identifier); (ii) query text (i.e., the set of keywords submitted by the user); (iii) URL (i.e., the URL that the user clicked after receiving the results for the query, or empty if no clicks were made); (iv) timestamp (i.e., the instant when the user submitted the query); and (v) session boundary (i.e., a Boolean indicator for whether the query marks the beginning of a new session, according to the ground-truth annotations). The records (i.e., the user queries) are first sorted according to userID (i.e., joining together queries from the same user), and then sorted according to the timestamp, prior to analysis.

To better understand the dataset, we first looked at consecutive queries from the same users, judged by the human annotators as belonging or not to the same session. The distributions for several characteristics associated to these consecutive queries are depicted in Fig. 1, which shows side-by-side the distribution for (a) the temporal proximity in minutes, (b) the lexical similarity according to the Jaccard coefficient between character $n$-grams (i.e., 3- and 4-grams) from consecutive queries, and (c) the semantic similarity according to the cosine similarity between averaged word embeddings of consecutive queries. The figure shows that all three heuristics have different distributions for the consecutive queries in each of the two classes (i.e., same versus different sessions), although the three heuristics seem to capture different cases. Through our experiments, we attempted to assess the contribution of each heuristic, in the overall results.

The evaluation methodology relied on the same metrics considered by Gayo-Avello [10], corresponding to notions of precision and recall. Precision is defined as the ratio between the number of consecutive queries when there is a change of session in which the algorithm has agreed with the ground-truth, and the number of consecutive queries when the algorithm predicted a change of session. Recall, on the other hand, is defined as the ratio between the number of consecutive queries when there is a change of session in which the algorithm agreed with the ground-truth, and the number of consecutive queries corresponding to a session change in the ground truth. We also computed an F1-score, corresponding to the harmonic mean between precision and recall. Besides assessing the quality of the predictions, we also measured the time involved in processing the entire subset of the AOL query log. The measurements for the different approaches were all made in a standard PC with an Intel Core i7 8700K (3.7 GHz) CPU, an SSD drive where the log file was stored, and 64 Gb of RAM.

**Table 2.** Performance metrics for different user session segmentation methods.

| Component | Method | | Quality Metrics | | | Execution Time (m.sec) |
|---|---|---|---|---|---|---|
| | | | Precision | Recall | F1-Score | |
| Temporal | Global Threshold | $T = 5$ | 77.00 | 87.54 | 81.93 | 1615 |
| | | $T = 15$ | 84.91 | 80.04 | 82.40 | |
| | | $T = 30$ | 89.00 | 75.12 | 81.47 | |
| | Threshold per User | | 90.68 | 71.15 | 79.74 | 1846 |
| Lexical or Semantic | Jaccard Coefficient | $>= 0.1$ | 83.67 | 92.50 | 87.86 | 2970 |
| | | $>= 0.3$ | 75.42 | 94.59 | 83.93 | |
| | | $>= 0.5$ | 69.49 | 95.18 | 80.33 | |
| | | $>= 0.7$ | 64.26 | 95.67 | 76.88 | |
| | | $>= 0.9$ | 60.62 | 96.10 | 74.34 | |
| | Word Embeddings Cosine | $>= 0.1$ | **95.87** | 7.64 | 14.16 | 5101 |
| | | $>= 0.3$ | 90.58 | 54.03 | 67.69 | |
| | | $>= 0.5$ | 84.82 | 88.53 | 86.63 | |
| | | $>= 0.7$ | 76.05 | 93.98 | 84.07 | |
| | | $>= 0.9$ | 65.16 | 95.65 | 77.52 | |
| | Word Embeddings WMD | $<= 0.1$ | 61.49 | 95.79 | 74.90 | 6049 |
| | | $<= 0.3$ | 64.82 | 92.23 | 76.47 | |
| | | $<= 0.5$ | 69.45 | 92.55 | 79.35 | |
| | | $<= 0.7$ | 74.42 | 90.24 | 81.57 | |
| | | $<= 0.9$ | 79.25 | 87.11 | 83.00 | |
| Temporal + Lexical and Semantic | Geometric Method (GM) | | 88.24 | 88.90 | 88.57 | 3542 |
| | Improved GM | | 83.93 | **97.60** | 90.25 | 2287 |
| | Proposed Method | | 88.06 | 95.20 | 91.49 | 4983 |
| | Proposed Method WMD | | 88.19 | 95.13 | **91.53** | 5771 |

## 4.2   Experimental Results

We compared the different approaches listed in Sect. 3.1, against the complete procedure given in Sect. 3.2. Table 2 presents the obtained results, showing that the complete procedure outperforms all the considered baselines in terms of the F1-score, although also with a higher computation time.

Methods based on a global temporal threshold already achieve a very satisfactory performance (i.e., an F1-score of 82.40, when using a threshold of 15 min), at the same time also being faster. Relying on user-specific temporal thresholds is not much slower, although we failed to outperform the results obtained with a global threshold of 15 min. When using a lexical heuristic alone, the results are slightly better than those obtained with a temporal threshold, although the semantic heuristics (i.e., both methods relying on word embeddings) alone perform slightly worse. The lexical and semantic approaches are also much slower.

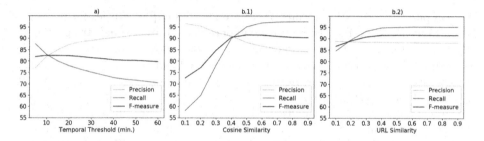

**Fig. 2.** Variation in precision, recall, and F1-scores, as a function of thresholds.

In terms of the combined methods, the proposed approach outperforms all individual baselines, the simpler geometric method, and the variants that were considered, although at the cost of a higher computation time. The improved geometric method, and a variation of the proposed method that does not use the word mover's distance, both offer a good compromise between result quality and computation time.

Figure 2 further details the results, plotting the variation on precision, recall, and the F1-score, (a) for a baseline corresponding to a global temporal threshold, as a function of that threshold, and (b) for the complete method, as a function of the threshold (b.1) on the cosine similarity between sets of word embeddings, or (b.2) on the similarity between URLs. Chart (a) confirms that a temporal threshold of approximately 15 min corresponds to the best trade-off in terms of the F1-score, while Charts (b.1) and (b.2) show that the thresholds that were given in Sect. 3.2, in connection to the proposed method, are also adequate.

## 5  Conclusions and Future Work

Segmenting user sessions in search engine query logs is a fundamental task in the context of several applications. The task is particularly challenging, involving the detection of query reformulations involving a variety of factors: misspellings (e.g., *gogle* versus *google*), co-referential expressions (e.g., *CEO Facebook* versus *Mark Zuckerberg*), acronyms (e.g., *John Fitzgerald Kennedy* versus *JFK*), generalizations and specializations (e.g., *Jaws* versus *Jaws the movie*), etc.

This paper presented a new unsupervised procedure for session segmentation, improving upon current methods [7,10] through the usage of pre-trained word embeddings. Our experiments confirmed the effectiveness of the proposed method, which achieves a higher segmentation accuracy than competing unsupervised approaches, while not significantly expanding on the computational effort. The algorithm's performance, together with the fact that it does not require training data or significant parameter tuning, makes it ideal for processing very large query logs from real-world search systems, independently of the domain (e.g., we plan to use this method to analyze the query log of a national search engine for legislative contents, in the context of an ongoing project).

Despite the interesting results, there are also many possibilities for improvement in future work. For instance, instead of relying on traditional string similarity metrics (e.g., the Jaccard similarity coefficient between character $n$-grams), we can perhaps experiment with the use of learned similarity functions [23–25], which have been shown to achieve significantly better results in other types of string matching problems. One such similarity function could be pre-trained on general data from other domains besides query logs (e.g., on large collections of alternative names for Wikipedia entities), and then used in our segmentation procedure. Another idea relates to the inclusion of additional steps in the proposed procedure, improving on the computational performance by first relying on simple string similarity metrics with a very permissive threshold, and later using increasingly more reliable, although more compute-intensive, string similarity functions with more restrictive thresholds.

One particular challenge that we plan to tackle in future work (i.e., in an ongoing project related to a search engine for legislative contents) relates to the fact that query logs often do not feature unique user identifiers, instead containing only cookie identifiers in a fraction of the records, plus information on source IP addresses and user-agents (i.e., identifiers for the type of Web browser in which the query was submitted). In these cases, the logs may feature queries from different users (and consequently also from different sessions) appearing interleaved in chronological order, all associated to the same IP address (e.g., from a common Internet proxy). We plan to adapt the proposed procedure to this specific scenario, not only by first sorting the records according to the combination of user cookie, IP address, and user-agent (instead of sorting records according to userID), but also by adding a post-processing step that merges different non-consecutive sessions that are temporally and thematically coherent.

**Acknowledgements.** This work was supported by Fundação para a Ciência e Tecnologia (FCT), through project GoLocal (CMUP-ERI/TIC/0046/2014) and also through the INESC-ID multi-annual funding from the PIDDAC program (UID/CEC/50021/2019).

# References

1. Feild, H., Allan, J., Jones, R.: Predicting searcher frustration. In: Proceedings of the ACM Conference on Research and Development in Information Retrieval (2010)
2. Hassan, A., Shi, X., Craswell, N., Ramsey, B.: Beyond clicks: query reformulation as a predictor of search satisfaction. In: Proceedings of the ACM Conference on Information and Knowledge Management (2013)
3. Jiang, J., Awadallah, A.H., Shi, X., White, R.W.: Understanding and predicting graded search satisfaction. In: Proceedings of the ACM Conference on Web Search and Data Mining (2015)
4. Kim, Y., Hassan, A., White, R.W., Zitouni, I.: Modeling dwell time to predict click-level satisfaction. In: Proceedings of the ACM Conference on Web Search and Data Mining (2014)
5. Mehrotra, R., et al.: Deep sequential models for task satisfaction prediction. In: Proceedings of the ACM on Conference on Information and Knowledge Management (2017)

6. Mayr, P., Kacem, A.: A complete year of user retrieval sessions in a social sciences academic search engine. In: Kamps, J., Tsakonas, G., Manolopoulos, Y., Iliadis, L., Karydis, I. (eds.) TPDL 2017. LNCS, vol. 10450, pp. 560–565. Springer, Cham (2017). https://doi.org/10.1007/978-3-319-67008-9_46

7. Hagen, M., Stein, B., Rüb, T.: Query session detection as a cascade. In: Proceedings of the ACM Conference on Information and Knowledge Management (2011)

8. Jones, R., Klinkner, K.L.: Beyond the session timeout: automatic hierarchical segmentation of search topics in query logs. In: Proceedings of the ACM Conference on Information and Knowledge Management (2008)

9. Mehrzadi, D., Feitelson, D.G.: On extracting session data from activity logs. In: Proceedings of the Annual International Systems and Storage Conference (2012)

10. Gayo-Avello, D.: A survey on session detection methods in query logs and a proposal for future evaluation. Inf. Sci. **179**(12), 1822–1843 (2009)

11. Bojanowski, P., Grave, E., Joulin, A., Mikolov, T.: Enriching word vectors with subword information. Trans. Assoc. Comput. Linguist. **5**, 135–146 (2017)

12. Pass, G., Chowdhury, A., Torgeson, C.: A picture of search. In: Proceedings of the International Conference on Scalable Information Systems (2006)

13. Downey, D., Dumais, S.T., Horvitz, E.: Models of searching and browsing: languages, studies, and application. In: Proceedings of the International Joint Conference on Artificial Intelligence (2007)

14. He, D., Göker, A.: Detecting session boundaries from web user logs. In: Proceedings of the BCS-IRSG Annual Colloquium on Information Retrieval Research (2000)

15. Radlinski, F., Joachims, T.: Query chains: learning to rank from implicit feedback. In: Proceedings of the ACM SIGKDD Conference on Knowledge Discovery and Data Mining (2005)

16. Catledge, L.D., Pitkow, J.E.: Characterizing browsing strategies in the world wide web. Comput. Network ISDN Syst. **27**(6), 1065–1073 (1995)

17. Jansen Bernard, J., Spink, A., Blakely, C., Koshman, S.: Defining a session on web search engines. J. Am. Soc. Inform. Sci. Technol. **58**(6), 862–871 (2007)

18. Lucchese, C., Orlando, S., Perego, R., Silvestri, F., Tolomei, G.: Identifying task-based sessions in search engine query logs. In: Proceedings of the ACM Conference on Web Search and Data Mining (2011)

19. Jaccard, P.: The distribution of the flora in the alpine zone. New Phytol. **11**(2), 37–50 (1912)

20. Gabrilovich, E., Markovitch, S.: Computing semantic relatedness using Wikipedia-based explicit semantic analysis. In: Proceedings of the International Joint Conference on Artificial Intelligence (2007)

21. Ozmutlu, S., Cenk Ozmutlu, H., Spink, A.: Automatic new topic identification in search engine transaction logs? Using multiple linear regression. In: Proceedings of the Hawaii International Conference on System Sciences (2008)

22. Kusner, M., Sun, Y., Kolkin, N., Weinberger, K.: From word embeddings to document distances. In: Proceedings of the International Conference on Machine Learning (2015)

23. Santos, R., Murrieta-Flores, P.: Learning to combine multiple string similarity metrics for effective toponym matching. Int. J. Digit. Earth **11**(9), 913–938 (2018)

24. Santos, R., Murrieta-Flores, P., Calado, P., Martins, B.: Toponym matching through deep neural networks. Int. J. Geographical Inf. Sci. **32**(2), 324–348 (2018)

25. Gan, Z., et al.: Character-level deep conflation for business data analytics. In: Proceedings of the IEEE International Conference on Acoustics, Speech and Signal Processing (2017)

# A Human-Friendly Query Generation Frontend for a Scientific Events Knowledge Graph

Said Fathalla[1,3]([⊠]), Christoph Lange[1,2], and Sören Auer[4,5]

[1] Smart Data Analytics (SDA), University of Bonn, Bonn, Germany
{fathalla,langec}@cs.uni-bonn.de
[2] Fraunhofer IAIS, Sankt Augustin, Germany
[3] Faculty of Science, Alexandria University, Alexandria, Egypt
[4] Computer Science, Leibniz University of Hannover, Hannover, Germany
[5] TIB Leibniz Information Center for Science and Technology, Hannover, Germany
soeren.auer@tib.eu

**Abstract.** Recently, semantic data have become more distributed. Available datasets should serve non-technical as well as technical audience. This is also the case with our EVENTSKG dataset, a comprehensive knowledge graph about scientific events, which serves the entire scientific and library community. A common way to query such data is via SPARQL queries. Non-technical users, however, have difficulties with writing SPARQL queries, because it is a time-consuming and error-prone task, and it requires some expert knowledge. This opens the way to natural language interfaces to tackle this problem by making semantic data more accessible to a wider audience, i.e., not restricted to experts. In this work, we present SPARQL-AG, a human-Friendly front-end that automatically generates and executes SPARQL queries for querying EVENTSKG. SPARQL-AG helps potential semantic data consumers, including non-experts and experts, by generating SPARQL queries, ranging from simple to complex ones, using an interactive web interface. The eminent feature of SPARQL-AG is that users neither need to know the schema of the knowledge graph being queried nor to learn the SPARQL syntax, as SPARQL-AG offers them a familiar and intuitive interface for query generation and execution. It maintains separate clients to query three public SPARQL endpoints when asking for particular entities. The service is publicly available online and has been extensively tested.

**Keywords:** Scientific events · SPARQL endpoint · Query builder · User Interaction · EVENTSKG dataset

## 1 Introduction

Nowadays, large amounts of semantic data have become widely available on the Web. This plethora of semantic data and the wide range of domains this

© Springer Nature Switzerland AG 2019
A. Doucet et al. (Eds.): TPDL 2019, LNCS 11799, pp. 200–214, 2019.
https://doi.org/10.1007/978-3-030-30760-8_18

data belongs to make it difficult to query this data. In addition, querying such data is a ponderous process, not only because of the syntax barrier, but mainly because of data heterogeneity and diversity. Semantic data is queried by means of the widely-adopted W3C-standardized SPARQL query language [20]. SPARQL queries are executed against SPARQL endpoints, i.e., standardized query interfaces for semantic data stores. The advantages of SPARQL come from its expressivity and scalability, however, people spend a large part of their time to learn how to write a SPARQL query to fulfill their needs and, in many cases, they fail. In this article, we present SPARQL-AG, a semantic web frontend that assists users in generating SPARQL queries for querying the EVENTSKG [7] knowledge graph [6], a comprehensive knowledge graph for scientific events in computer science. The rationale to develop SPARQL-AG is to help potential semantic data consumers, including both SPARQL experts and non-experts, by automatically generating SPARQL queries, ranging from simple to complex ones, using an interactive web interface. It helps SPARQL experts by reducing the time required to write queries by modifying the generated query (*modify-before-execution*), i.e., removing the need to write the query from scratch. The generated query is displayed in a readable way to make it easier to understand when a modification is needed before execution. The ultimate goal behind this work is to widen the access to semantic data available on the Web by making it easier to generate and execute SPARQL queries with prior knowledge of neither the schema of the data being queried nor the SPARQL syntax. The architecture of SPARQL-AG is composed of six components: user interface, components selection, query composer, SPARQL clients manager, query validator, and query executor. This architecture integrates aspects of four research paradigms: query building (QB), semantic search (SS), human-computer interaction (HCI), and SPARQL query federation. Most of the SPARQL 1.1 specification [20] is covered, such as optional graph patterns, filters, aggregations, restricting aggregations, ordering, and limiting the number of results. SPARQL-AG maintains three SPARQL clients to query three public SPARQL endpoints (DBpedia SPARQL endpoint[1], the Scientific Events Ontology (SEO) SPARQL endpoint[2], and the EVENTSKG SPARQL endpoint[3]), asking for particular entities. Hence, there is no need to precisely know externally-defined entities; for instance, it is not required to know the DBpedia identifier for a country, some of which cannot be guessed trivially (e.g., http://dbpedia.org/page/Georgia_(country)). Querying external SPARQL endpoints is transparent to the user. A list of all currently existing countries is retrieved and cached by running a query against the DBpedia SPARQL endpoint. This list is periodically updated to obtain new updates, if there are any. It is worth to mention that no special configurations for SPARQL endpoints are needed. Currently, SPARQL-AG is tailored to generate and execute queries over the EVENTSKG knowledge graph. This follows the motivation "*the more a system is tailored to a domain, the better its retrieval performance is*" [13]. However,

---

[1] https://dbpedia.org/sparql.

[2] http://kddste.sda.tech/SEOontology/sparql.

[3] http://kddste.sda.tech/sparql.

the approach is easily transferable to other datasets and domain representations. Our research aims at answering the following questions:

- How can users query semantic data without knowing the schema of this data?
- How can users query semantic data without learning RDF, OWL, or SPARQL?
- How can we combine data from several SPARQL endpoints to formulate a SPARQL query?

SPARQL-AG is a web-based user interface, which allows end users to create and execute both simple and complex SPARQL queries over scholarly knowledge bases. Generally, we believe that SPARQL-AG closes an important gap between researchers outside the semantic web community, or even within the community but not being SPARQL experts, and the semantic data available on the Web. The service is publicly available online at http://kddste.sda.tech/SER-Service/ SPARQL-AG/SPARQL-AG.php. It has been tested by several SPARQL experts by creating a large number of successful queries. The source code is available on GitHub (see Table 1). The remainder of this article is organized as follows: Sect. 2 gives an overview on related work. Section 3 presents the design principles considered when developing SPARQL-AG. Section 4 outlines the methodology we used. Section 5 presents a use case. Section 6 discusses the implementation and results of the evaluation. Finally, Sect. 7 concludes with an outline of future work.

## 2   Related Work

The origins of query builders go back to preliminary research works in the 1990s [3]. Natural language interfaces (NLIs) are widely used to ease the process of querying semantic data [5,13,15,17]. Many contributions have been made for this purpose; below, we present the state of the art. Most of these contributions use NLIs in two different ways: generating SPARQL queries based on User Interactions (UI), and answering user queries using a Question Answering system (QA). The latter completely hides SPARQL queries from the user, allowing them to directly submit their question, e.g., NLP-Reduce [14] and PowerAqua [17], whereas the former focuses on generating SPARQL queries using a visual interface, e.g., Semantic Crystal [13], Querix [15], and SPARQL Views [5].

*UI-Based Systems.* NLI-based systems are often tailored to a specific application and require exceptional design and implementation efforts. Below we present some of the state-of-the-art efforts in SPARQL query building using NLIs. Semantic Crystal [13] is a graphically-based query tool that can be used for querying OWL knowledge bases by generating SPARQL queries. The generated query is composed by clicking on ontology elements from the ontology graph displayed on a screen and selecting elements from menus. Querix [15] is an NLI-based tool that translates natural language questions, written in English, to SPARQL queries with little user interactions. One drawback of Querix is that it does not resolve ambiguities in the input text, but asks the user for clarification. SPARQL Views [5] is an NLI-based tool that supports visual query building via drag and drop over RDF data in a Drupal CMS[4]. Via an autocomplete search box, users can filter predicates, which can be used in the query pattern. QUaTRO2 [1] provides a graphical user interface to formulate complex queries based on an abstract domain-driven query language. QUaTRO2 tool has been used to query the UniProt[5] protein database. QueryVOWL [12] is a visual query language tool for creating SPARQL queries using GUI controls. This tool is developed based upon the VOWL [16] ontology visualization.

In contrast to much of the existing work on building SPARQL queries, which tends to focus on translating natural language queries to SPARQL, such as Crystal and SPARQL Views, which is still far from efficient, SPARQL-AG completely uses graphical interface controls to generate SPARQL queries, requiring prior knowledge neither about the schema being queried nor the SPARQL syntax. On the other hand, one of the limitations of our previous work on analyzing scholarly data [8,9] is that the analysis was based on predefined queries. These analyses cannot be flexibly extended by changing the parameters of these queries. Therefore, more work is needed regarding the use of NLIs for facilitating the process of querying distributed semantic data, for both end users and SPARQL experts, and further comprehensive usability studies to investigate the end users' perspective are required.

## 3   Design Principles

*System Design.* When designing SPARQL-AG, we integrate different research paradigms in the system architecture, illustrated in Fig. 1. (1) *query building (QB):* to build error-free SPARQL queries based on user selections from a visual interface. Query builders have the advantage of allowing for high expressivity while assisting users by listing eligible query elements without prior knowledge about the syntax of the language. This helps to completely avoid syntax errors, (2) *semantic search (SS):* for entities in various knowledge graphs that match the query pattern, (3) *Human Computer Interaction (HCI):* to make the user's interaction as simple and efficient as possible, in terms of accomplishing user goals, i.e., facilitating the task of querying semantic data without writing any piece of code, and (4) *Federated Query:* SPARQL 1.1 Federated Query is a technique that is used for executing queries distributed over different SPARQL endpoints.

*Portability.* To promote portability, SPARQL-AG is a fully web-based service following web standards. A public SPARQL endpoint is used for querying knowledge graphs using HTTP requests, PHP and JavaScript for the application code, and HTML5/CSS3 (Bootstrap) for designing and styling the user interface (more details in Sect. 6).

---

[4] https://www.drupal.org/.
[5] https://www.uniprot.org/.

*Availability.* SPARQL-AG has been available online at http://kddste.sda.tech/ SER-Service/SPARQL-AG/SPARQL-AG.php since December 2018. Users only need the URL of the service to be able to use it, i.e., no configuration or prerequisites are required.

*Maintainability and Sustainability.* SPARQL-AG is developed and maintained by the first author and hosted on the server mentioned above. To ensure the sustainability of SPARQL-AG, we use the issue tracker on its GitHub repository (cf. Table 1) in order to make it easier for users to request new features, e.g., features not covered in the initial release, and to report any problems/bugs.

**Table 1.** SPARQL-AG-related resources

| Resource | URL |
| --- | --- |
| EVENTSKG | http://kddste.sda.tech/EVENTSKG-Dataset/ |
| SEO Ontology | https://w3id.org/seo# |
| SPARQL-AG URL | http://kddste.sda.tech/SER-Service/SPARQL-AG/ SPARQL-AG.php |
| GitHub repository | https://github.com/saidfathalla/SPARQL-AG |
| Issue Tracker | https://github.com/saidfathalla/SPARQL-AG/issues |

## 4    Architecture

The architecture of SPARQL-AG is composed of six components (see Fig. 1): user interface, components selection, query composer, SPARQL clients manager, query validator, and query executor. Later in this section, we denote the set of SPARQL variables with $V$, the set of predicates used in the query pattern with $P$, the set of RDF resources with $R$, the set of query restrictions with $QR$, and the set of RDF literals with $L$.

*User Interface.* The role of the user interface component is to (1) provide end-users a Graphical User Interface (GUI) through which they can select different query components using a web form, (2) display the generated query (GQ) to the user, who can then modify it before it is submitted to the SPARQL endpoint for execution, and (3) submit the queries to the EVENTSKG SPARQL endpoint and display the results in a human-readable format (HTML table). SPARQL-AG features are: (1) generating and executing simple SPARQL queries, (2) generating SPARQL queries with aggregation, and (3) executing predefined query templates. Users are able to (1) select columns they want to appear in the result using checkboxes, (2) restrict the results by selecting the checkbox corresponding to each predicate and by entering/selecting possible object values for these predicates by – depending on the datatype – direct input of numeric values, selecting from a list, or picking a date from a calendar. This avoids the problem of resolving the ambiguity that might arise when processing natural language queries and irrelevant queries.

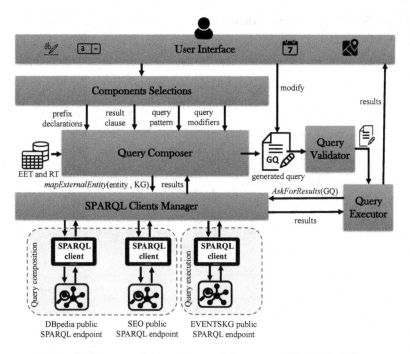

**Fig. 1.** The complete system architecture of SPARQL-AG.

*Components Selections.* User selections of the different SPARQL query components, listed below, are bypassed to the Query Composer (QC) in order to formulate the SPARQL query based on these selections. (1) *Prefix declarations:* the set of namespace prefixes used in the query, (2) *Dataset definition:* we omit the *dataset definition* part of the SPARQL query from user selections, because it is implicitly given, i.e., the EVENTSKG URI, (3) *Result clause:* identifying what information to return from the query, (4) *Query patterns:* specify the query's graph pattern that matches the data, such as UNION, MINUS, FILTER, and OPTIONAL, and (5) *Query modifiers:* a set of modifiers for the query results, such as order, projection, distinct, offset, and limit. Each selection is mapped to a query element in the generated query. To address scalability issues, users can limit the number of results retrieved using the LIMIT modifier.

*Query Composer.* The query composer is the core component of SPARQL-AG, as it formulates the SPARQL query based on user selections and data received from the SPARQL Clients Manager, which collects data from external SPARQL endpoints. The main steps carried out by the Query Composer are summarized in Algorithm 1, where "+" denotes string concatenation. First, users should define the namespaces used in the query in the prefix set ($P$). Currently, as SPARQL-AG is provided for the EVENTSKG dataset, the prefix declaration is automatically generated with the required predicates, i.e., seo and conference-ontology. For future purposes, if a namespace mapping

## 1. Simple SPRQL query generation

**1.1 Declare prefix:** each Name space SHOULD be in a new line and SHOULD be like: *vcard: <http://www.w3.org/2001/vcard-rdf/3.0#>*

```
PREFIX seo: <http://purl.org/seo/>
PREFIX conference-ontology: <https://w3id.org/scholarlydata/ontology/conference-
ontology.owl#>
```

**1.2 Select column(s):**

☑ all , ☑ URI, ☐ event type, ☐ series, ☐ country, ☐ city, ☐ field, ☐ acceptance rate, ☐ accepted papers, ☐ submitted papers, ☐ start date, ☐ end date, ☐ website, ☐ publisher.

☑ DISTINCT

**1.3 Query pattern:**

| | | |
|---|---|---|
| ☐ event type | Conference ▼ | |
| ☐ series | ISWC | |
| ☐ country | Germany ▼ | |
| ☐ city | Berlin | |
| ☐ field | Artificial Intelligence ▼ | |
| ☐ acceptance rate | > ▼ | 0.20 | |
| ☐ accepted papers | > ▼ | 50 | ☐ OPTIONAL |
| ☐ submitted papers | > ▼ | 100 | ☐ OPTIONAL |
| ☐ start date | > ▼ | 08/01/2013 | ☐ OPTIONAL -- format *YYYY-MM-DD* |
| ☐ end date | > ▼ | 08/01/2013 | ☐ OPTIONAL -- format *YYYY-MM-DD* |

**Fig. 2.** A part of the User interface of SPARQL-AG.

is not available in the system, then the user should add this namespace to the prefix declaration. Each selection in the result clause (RC) (upper part in Fig. 2) is mapped to a new variable in the SPARQL query (call `mapResultClause`). For instance, when *country* is selected, it represented by the variable ?*country*. Formally, the mapping is defined as follows: Each RC selection is assigned a unique variable via the function $mapResultClause : RC \mapsto V$. Each query pattern is represented as a tuple of $(prop, op, val)$, where *prop* is the property being restricted, *op* is the operation, and $val \in L$ is the value. For example, $(acceptanceRate, \geq, 0.25)$ represents the results with an acceptance rate greater than or equal to 0.25. A query pattern might contain externally defined entities, such as countries and cities (defined in DBpedia), and the research field which the events belong to (defined in the SEO ontology [10]). Here, the External Entities Table (EET) plays its role, in which all external entities are stored along with the URL of the public SPARQL endpoint of the knowledge graph in which these entities can be found. Therefore, these entities should be identified (call `isExternallyDefined`). The function *isExternallyDefined* $: P \mapsto \mathbb{B}$ is defined

---

**Algorithm 1.** QueryGeneration

---

query = *null*;
**foreach** *namespace* $n_i \in PS$ **do**
  $\lfloor$ query+="PREFIX "+ $n_i$ ;

query+="SELECT ";
**while** *rc is not empty* **do**
  $\lfloor$ //add result clause elements query+="?"+$mapResultClause(rc)$;

query+="WHERE { ";
**foreach** *pattern* $P_i \in QP$ **do**
  $|$ **if** $uri=isExternallyDefined(P_i)$ **then**
  $|$ $|$ value=$mapExternalEntity(P_i)$;
  $|$ **else**
  $|$ $\lfloor$ value=UI.control.value;
  $|$   // to get literal values, e.g. numeric values from the UI
  $|$ query+= "?e " + $mapToPredicate(P_i.prop)$ + $mapToVariable(P_i.prop)$ + "
  $\lfloor$ FILTER ( $mapToVariable(P_i.prop)$ + $P_i.op$ + $P_i.val$ +")";

query+="}";

---

as: $isExternallyDefined(p) := true$ if $p$ is found in $EET$, and *false* otherwise. The URIs of these external entities should be retrieved as well by sending requests to the SPARQL Clients Manager via the function: $mapExternalEntity : P \mapsto R$. Each request is assigned a unique number via the function $reqID : RR \mapsto \mathbb{N}$, where $RR$ is the set of requests made by the Query Composer component. After successful retrieval of the requested data, all these requests are stored in the requests table ($RT$) for answering further requests, instead of sending them to the Clients Manager, i.e., caching requests. Therefore, after a period of time, when all external entities have been requested, there is no more need to query external endpoints for these entities. This reduces the workload of querying external knowledge graphs for every request. In addition, it performs results aggregations when more than one client returns a result. In order to map query restriction ($QR$) to the corresponding predicate in the dataset, the function $mapToPredicate : QR \mapsto P$ is used. For instance, when the user wants to filter results by, e.g., country, then he/she should select the country checkbox (Fig. 2), which should be mapped to the corresponding predicate in the dataset, i.e., `seo:heldInCountry`. Each variable in the result clause must be bound in the query pattern, therefore the function $mapToVariable : P \mapsto V$ is used to obtain these variables, which are defined in the result clause to be bound in the query pattern. For example, when users want to display events along with their start and end dates, these attributes are bound to two variables in the result clause, which are `?SD` and `?ED` respectively. Mapping query modifiers is straightforward, e.g., the *order by* modifier specifies columns (currently limited to one or two) to order the results by, using the `ORDER BY` keyword.

*Query Validator.* This component is responsible for validating the generated query before sending it to the SPARQL endpoint for execution. In addition, when users modified the generated query before execution, they can validate the modified query using the *"Validate"* button. *SPARQL Clients Manager.* This component is responsible for managing SPARQL clients in order to be able to query external SPARQL endpoints, DBpedia and SEO in this case. SPARQL clients allow executing SPARQL queries against remote SPARQL endpoints using the SPARQL protocol [11]. After a successful connection to the endpoint, the SPARQL client sends the SPARQL query to the endpoint and waits for the result. When requests are received from the Query Composer, asking for the resource URI of an externally defined entity, e.g., Germany, the Clients Manager formulates a SPARQL query and sends it to the SPARQL client responsible for this type of request and waits for the requested resource URI, e.g., http://dbpedia.org/resource/Germany.

*Query Executor.* This component is responsible for sending the validated query to the Clients Manager (call `AskForResults`) and displaying the results in a human-readable format. Since the query results are returned as an array of variable bindings, which are difficult to understand for end-users who are not familiar with SPARQL, we decided to display the results as an HTML table.

*Generating SPARQL with Aggregation Functions.* Aggregation functions are useful when users want to study data in an analytical fashion, e.g., finding the total number of publications of all events in each research field. Results are grouped using the `GROUP BY` clause, and these groups can be restricted using the `HAVING` clause. Here, it is worth to mention that SPARQL-AG enforces some SPARQL rules to be applied while users select different query elements. For instance, a group column is added to the `GROUP BY` clause when aggregation functions are used, and aggregation functions are automatically restricted using `HAVING`. For example, when the user selects a column in an aggregation function, this column must be added to the `GROUP BY` clause; this is a SPARQL restriction.

## 5   Use Cases

In this section, we present two use cases for SPARQL-AG for supporting scholarly communication stakeholders by providing figures about computer science events in the context of eight computer science communities. Listing 1 shows the SPARQL query generated for the query *"Q1: List the top-10 events with topics related to Artificial Intelligence with an acceptance rate lower than 0.20, which have been held in Germany, order the results by ascending acceptance rate."*. Listing 2 shows the SPARQL query generated for a query with an aggregation: Q2:*"List the subfields of computer science whose events have a large number of submissions, i.e., greater than 10,000. Order the results by ascending field name"*.

**Listing 1.** SPARQL query generated for Q1.

```
PREFIX seo: <http://purl.org/seo/>
PREFIX conference-ontology:
<https://w3id.org/scholarlydata/ontology/conference-ontology.owl#>
SELECT DISTINCT ?event ?acceptance ?field WHERE {
  ?event rdf:type ?type .
    FILTER (?type = conference-ontology:Conference ||
      ?type = conference-ontology:Workshop || ?type = seo:Symposium) .
  ?event seo:heldInCountry ?country .
    FILTER (?country = <http://dbpedia.org/resource/Germany>) .
  ?event seo:field ?field .
    FILTER (?field = <http://purl.org/seo#ArtificialIntelligence>) .
  ?event seo:acceptanceRate ?acceptance .
    FILTER (?acceptance < 0.20) .
} ORDER BY ?acceptance LIMIT 10
```

**Listing 2.** SPARQL query generated for Q2.

```
SELECT ?field SUM(?submissions) AS ?SP_SUM WHERE {
  ?event seo:submittedPapers ?submissions .
  ?event seo:field ?field .
} GROUP BY ?field
HAVING (SUM(?submissions) > 10000)
ORDER BY ?field
LIMIT 10
```

# 6  Implementation and Evaluation

This section describes the implementation and the evaluation of SPARQL-AG, and discusses the results of a usability study for testing it.

*Implementation.* SPARQL-AG is implemented in PHP as a web-based service, using a client-server architecture. We have implemented all functions described in Sect. 4 using PHP 7.2.10 and the RAP[6] (RDF API for PHP) toolkit. In addition, JavaScript is used to validate input data and to enforce some rules, such as GROUP BY rules, as mentioned in Sect. 4. SPARQL-AG only needs the URL of an endpoint to explore it, without any further required configuration. Thus the approach is easily transferable to other datasets by just changing the components selections and the dataset URL. Queries to SPARQL endpoints are sent directly from the client browser, using HTTP requests, which makes SPARQL-AG independent from a server.

*Experimental Setup.* Usability testing is a technique used in user-centered inter-action design to evaluate a product by testing it by letting real users use the system [18]. Nielsen and Landauer [18] argue that the best usability evaluation

---

[6] http://wifo5-03.informatik.uni-mannheim.de/bizer/rdfapi/index.html.

results come from testing no more than five users and running as many small tests as possible. This type of evaluation was performed by several Semantic Web query interfaces [5,13] since it gives direct insight into how real users use the system. The goal is to improve the usability of the system being tested.

In this experiment, casual end-users should test and assess the usability of the service. To apply the usability test for SPARQL-AG with real-world end-users, we promoted the usability study on its web site, several mailing lists and between colleagues. A total of 12 participants were recruited for this study. They are distributed over a wide range of backgrounds and professions. In addition, we ensure the anonymity of the participants in order to obtain unbiased results. The participants were split into two groups (six users each) based on their SPARQL experience: (1) experienced SPARQL users (all are computer scientists), and (2) casual end-users from other fields and professions, such as dentistry and engineering. To assure the usefulness of SPARQL-AG, we confirm that it is able to answer a number of competency queries listed in Table 2. These queries were thoroughly selected to assure that they cover all features provided by SPARQL-AG. In the beginning, we informed all participants that the query interfaces were being tested and not the users themselves. This is an important issue that can severely influence the test results. Inexperienced users are confused when given

**Table 2.** Queries used in evaluating SPARQL-AG. Each variable, such as X and Y, is a placeholder for any appropriate replacement.

| No. | # Query |
| --- | --- |
| Q1 | List events related to field X that took place in country X |
| Q2 | List events related to field X with an acceptance rate less than Y along with their sponsors, publishers, website and start date |
| Q3 | List events that took place in a particular month X along with their publishers and the field of research |
| Q4 | List conference series that have been held in country X in a particular month Y |
| Q5 | List the number of submitted and accepted papers of a series X in a particular time period |
| Q6 | List the top-X countries that hosted the most events in CS overall |
| Q7 | List the subfields of CS for which a country X has hosted most events since a particular date Y |
| Q8 | Compare the popularity of different computer science research communities, in terms of the number of submissions to the respective events |
| Q9 | List the top-X research fields, in terms of the number of events they have |
| Q10 | Find the average acceptance rate for events in each computer science research community |

too many interaction options. Therefore, at the beginning of each experimental run, we gave each participant all information and instructions concerning the experiment either in a face-to-face meeting or in a call (for remote participants). Most of the users found that the experiment can be easily understood by casual end-users and does not require expert knowledge. After testing the service, experienced users were explicitly asked to fill in a satisfaction questionnaire (accessible through the link https://goo.gl/55TbRU) in which they were asked about their assessment of the interface, generated query, the presentation of the results, and the usefulness of SPARQL-AG for both casual and experienced users. In addition, casual users were explicitly asked to fill in the System Usability Scale (SUS) questionnaire [4] (available at https://goo.gl/Mxj9Uu). SUS is a standardized usability test, which contains ten questions with five possible responses ranging from 1 (strongly disagree) to 5 (strongly agree). The best way to interpret one's results is by normalizing the scores to produce a percentile ranking. We also asked experienced SPARQL users for further qualitative feedback, including positive and negative aspects, and suggestions for future improvements.

*Results.* Five (out of six) experts strongly agreed that SPARQL-AG is helpful for users with no prior knowledge of SPARQL and they are satisfied with the design of the user interface. For the analysis of results, the SUS scoring method [19] has been used for the casual end user questionnaire. The average SUS score falls into seven adjective ratings, ranging from *Best Imaginable* (above 90.9) to *Worst*

**Table 3.** Statistics for questions of the SUS Questionnaires for casual end-users.

| Metrics | Q1 | Q2 | Q3 | Q4 | Q5 | Q6 | Q7 | Q8 | Q9 | Q10 |
|---------|------|------|------|------|------|------|------|------|------|------|
| Mean | 4.57 | 4.14 | 4.71 | 4.57 | 4.57 | 4.00 | 4.86 | 4.43 | 4.29 | 3.86 |
| SD | 0.53 | 1.46 | 0.49 | 0.53 | 0.53 | 1.00 | 0.38 | 1.13 | 0.76 | 0.90 |
| Median | 5.00 | 5.00 | 5.00 | 5.00 | 5.00 | 4.00 | 5.00 | 5.00 | 4.00 | 4.00 |
| Mod | 5.00 | 5.00 | 5.00 | 5.00 | 5.00 | 4.00 | 5.00 | 5.00 | 5.00 | 3.00 |

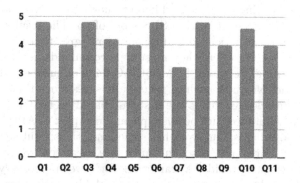

**Fig. 3.** The mean of experts response in the satisfaction questionnaire.

*Imaginable* (below 12.5) [2]. Most strikingly, findings showed that SPARQL-AG scored a high SUS satisfaction score of 93, i.e., Best Imaginable, thus reaching excellent usability. Table 3 contains the statistics for each question of the SUS questionnaires for casual end-users. Since all questions measure positive agreement, notably, the mode of almost every response is 5, which means that most participants responded with *strong agree* for most questions. As shown in Fig. 3, the mean of expert responses to the expert questionnaire falls into the range of 3.2–4.8, which is rather high. This implies a fair satisfaction of all experts for all questions, since all questions measure positive satisfaction. Q7 ("Do you agree that the the translation of SPARQL queries to natural language is useful?") has the lowest score of 3.2, which means that there is no need to translate SPARQL queries to natural language to let casual users confirm their actual intention.

## 7  Conclusions and Future Work

This work presents SPARQL-AG, which aims at improving data access to semantic knowledge graphs by generating SPARQL queries for users who may be challenged by a lack of schema or data knowledge regarding a knowledge graph. The architecture of SPARQL-AG can be used for generating SPARQL queries for any semantic data. It combines research techniques from different disciplines in an integrated fashion. We highlight the importance of using NLIs to make semantic data accessible to a wider community. One aim of this study is to show the potentials of NLIs that give a chance to casual users to benefit from the Semantic Web's capabilities without having to study them. In fact, SPARQL-AG also significantly lowers the barrier of writing SPARQL queries from scratch, by providing additional support for SPARQL experts. It generates SPARQL queries of three kinds: simple query generation, SPARQL query generation with aggregation, and parameterized execution of predefined queries. We believe that we are on the way towards increasing users' understanding of SPARQL by lowering the syntax barrier, since generating queries using user interactions will increase the understanding of the syntax itself, enabling users to incrementally improve their understanding of the query language. Our usability study with twelve participants using a list of 21 different questions showed that the usability of the system is excellent, with a SUS score of 93. The results of our evaluation show that both experienced and casual users agree that writing SPARQL queries in a blank sheet, where they must type commands, is cumbersome and time-consuming. As anticipated, SPARQL-AG enables successful generation of error-free and readable queries which potentially saves much time and effort. To the best of our knowledge, this is the first web-based user interface that allows end users to create and execute both simple and complex SPARQL queries over scholarly knowledge bases. Our work has some limitations. Still not all SPARQL 1.1 specifications are covered. Also, currently, it is restricted to only one dataset. Nevertheless, our work provides a framework for developing query builders for querying scholarly data, making such data available for further analysis and improvement.

There are several directions for future work along three dimensions: (1) *Extension:* extend SPARQL-AG's functionality, especially with respect to expressiveness, and interface robustness. For expressiveness, we are planning to cover almost all SPARQL 1.1 features (as suggested by experts involved in the evaluation), in particular, subqueries, multidimensional queries, nested aggregations for rich analytics, and graphs as results for CONSTRUCT queries and updates. For interface robustness, we are planning to adopt the interface to let the user select the knowledge base to be queried, and improve the interface based on participants feedback. (2) *Evaluation:* a comprehensive evaluation of the services will be done after the implementation of the new features by considering more complex queries in different domains. (3) *Data visualization:* present results using graphical visualizations, e.g., charts and graphs.

**Acknowledgement.** This work was co-funded by the European Research Council for the project ScienceGRAPH (Grant agreement ID: 819536).

# References

1. Balis, B., Grabiec, T., Bubak, M.: Domain-driven visual query formulation over RDF data sets. In: Wyrzykowski, R., Dongarra, J., Karczewski, K., Waśniewski, J. (eds.) PPAM 2013. LNCS, vol. 8384, pp. 293–301. Springer, Heidelberg (2014). https://doi.org/10.1007/978-3-642-55224-3_28
2. Bangor, A., Kortum, P., Miller, J.: Determining what individual SUS scores mean: adding an adjective rating scale. J. Usability Stud. **4**(3), 114–123 (2009)
3. Bechhofer, S., Stevens, R., Ng, G., Jacoby, A., Goble, C.: Guiding the user: an ontology driven interface. In: Proceedings of User Interfaces to Data Intensive Systems. IEEE (1999)
4. Brooke, J., et al.: SUS-A quick and dirty usability scale. Usability Eval. Ind. **189**(194), 4–7 (1996)
5. Clark, L.: SPARQL views: a visual SPARQL query builder for Drupal. In: 9th International Semantic Web Conference, ISWC (2010)
6. Fathalla, S., Lange, C.: EVENTSKG: a knowledge graph representation for top-prestigious computer science events metadata. In: Nguyen, N.T., Pimenidis, E., Khan, Z., Trawiński, B. (eds.) ICCCI 2018. LNCS (LNAI), vol. 11055, pp. 53–63. Springer, Cham (2018). https://doi.org/10.1007/978-3-319-98443-8_6
7. Fathalla, S., Lange, C., Auer, S.: EVENTSKG: A 5-Star Dataset of Top-Ranked Events in Eight Computer Science Communities. In: Hitzler, P., Fernández, M., Janowicz, K., Zaveri, A., Gray, A.J.G., Lopez, V., Haller, A., Hammar, K. (eds.) ESWC 2019. LNCS, vol. 11503, pp. 427–442. Springer, Cham (2019). https://doi.org/10.1007/978-3-030-21348-0_28
8. Fathalla, S., Vahdati, S., Lange, C., Auer, S.: Analysing scholarly communication metadata of computer science events. In: Kamps, J., Tsakonas, G., Manolopoulos, Y., Iliadis, L., Karydis, I. (eds.) TPDL 2017. LNCS, vol. 10450, pp. 342–354. Springer, Cham (2017). https://doi.org/10.1007/978-3-319-67008-9_27
9. Fathalla, S., Vahdati, S., Auer, S., Lange, C.: Metadata analysis of scholarly events of computer science, physics, engineering, and mathematics. In: Méndez, E., Crestani, F., Ribeiro, C., David, G., Lopes, J.C. (eds.) TPDL 2018. LNCS, vol. 11057, pp. 116–128. Springer, Cham (2018). https://doi.org/10.1007/978-3-030-00066-0_10

10. Fathalla, S., Vahdati, S., Lange, C., Auer, S.: The scientific events ontology of the OpenResearch curation platform. In: Proceedings of the Symposium on Applied Computing. ACM (2019)
11. Feigenbaum, L., Williams, G.T., Clark, K.G., Torres, E.: SPARQL 1.1 Protocol. Recommendation, W3C (2013)
12. Haag, F., Lohmann, S., Siek, S., Ertl, T.: QueryVOWL: a visual query notation for linked data. In: Gandon, F., Guéret, C., Villata, S., Breslin, J., Faron-Zucker, C., Zimmermann, A. (eds.) ESWC 2015. LNCS, vol. 9341, pp. 387–402. Springer, Cham (2015). https://doi.org/10.1007/978-3-319-25639-9_51
13. Kaufmann, E., Bernstein, A.: How useful are natural language interfaces to the semantic web for casual end-users? In: Aberer, K., et al. (eds.) ASWC/ISWC - 2007. LNCS, vol. 4825, pp. 281–294. Springer, Heidelberg (2007). https://doi.org/10.1007/978-3-540-76298-0_21
14. Kaufmann, E., Bernstein, A., Fischer, L.: NLP-Reduce: a naive but domain independent natural language interface for querying ontologies. In: ESWC 2007 (2007)
15. Kaufmann, E., Bernstein, A., Zumstein, R.: Querix: a natural language interface to query ontologies based on clarification dialogs. In: ISWC (2006)
16. Lohmann, S., Negru, S., Haag, F., Ertl, T.: VOWL 2: user-oriented visualization of ontologies. In: Janowicz, K., Schlobach, S., Lambrix, P., Hyvönen, E. (eds.) EKAW 2014. LNCS (LNAI), vol. 8876, pp. 266–281. Springer, Cham (2014). https://doi.org/10.1007/978-3-319-13704-9_21
17. Lopez, V., Motta, E., Uren, V.: PowerAqua: fishing the semantic web. In: Sure, Y., Domingue, J. (eds.) ESWC 2006. LNCS, vol. 4011, pp. 393–410. Springer, Heidelberg (2006). https://doi.org/10.1007/11762256_30
18. Nielsen, J., Landauer, T.K.: A mathematical model of the finding of usabilityproblems. In: INTERACT/CHI. ACM (1993)
19. Sauro, J., Lewis, J.R.: When designing usability questionnaires, does it hurt to be positive? In: SIGCHI. ACM (2011)
20. World Wide Web Consortium. SPARQL 1.1 overview (2013)

# User Interface for Interactive Scientific Publications: A Design Case Study

Camila Wohlmuth[1(✉)] and Nuno Correia[2]

[1] FCT, Universidade Nova de Lisboa, Lisbon, Portugal
cw.silva@campus.fct.unl.pt
[2] NOVA-LINCS, FCT, Universidade Nova de Lisboa, Lisbon, Portugal

**Abstract.** Scientific publications have been gradually changing and innovating, offering new possibilities to access scientific content, such as visual and interactive features. This paper provides a discussion, contextualization and improvements of scientific publishing within a case study that presents a user interface design based on a cognitive framework. The study combined usability methods to evaluate the application of the cognitive framework in an interactive prototype. The user evaluation centered on usability, think-aloud, a questionnaire as well as an expert reviewer evaluation. The paper concludes with considerations to guide practices for interactive multimedia publishing design.

**Keywords:** Electronic publishing · User interface · Cognitive models

## 1 Introduction

The scientific content can be more dynamic and offers additional relationships to the reading process. In this sense, scientific journals are starting to engage in a more fluid form, presenting new viewing possibilities [1]. Meanwhile, the Multimedia Design principles [2] can properly attempt to complement information effectively. Accordingly, design principles and cognition studies around publications are becoming a more relevant aspect. Due to the complexity of the content, the challenge is to design new ways of presenting scientific content as more interactive and engaging.

This paper exhibits a user interface design for scientific publishing with interactive multimedia features that have been tested and evaluated using several methods. Thus, the research questions that provide the scope for this work are: R1. Does a design based on the cognitive framework improve interaction with multimedia content? R2. Does interactivity engage content comprehension? R3. What usability issues most affect user interaction with the interface? R4. Which parts of the interface require more attention when designing interactive scientific publications?

The following sections present the background with related work. Subsequently, a case study reveals the user interface design based on a cognitive framework as an interactive prototype, along with an assessment through usability testing, observations and questions as well as an expert review evaluation, reaching the results of this case study; and discussing considerations for the design of interactive scientific publications.

© Springer Nature Switzerland AG 2019
A. Doucet et al. (Eds.): TPDL 2019, LNCS 11799, pp. 215–223, 2019.
https://doi.org/10.1007/978-3-030-30760-8_19

## 2  Background and Related Work

The transformation of conventional scientific content increasingly stimulates the creation of visual and interactive enrichments that affect the layout of the publications [3]. However, the even more recurring solution for communicating multimedia data and related materials depends on the creation of supplementary files that are linked for download through the publisher's site or other platforms. Conversely, the correlation between actual publishing and multimedia data support becomes more complex, as coherency is needed, and crucial information is shared across different supports [4].

The vast majority of published research papers still are a linear reading path [5, 6]. Nonetheless, some related projects attempted to incorporate enrichments into scientific publishing, through the creation of software and tools [5, 7–10], or by adding dynamic content along with the text. For instance, the National Library of Medicine has partnered with Elsevier to identify interactive improvements in articles from print-based journals [9]. The project's hypothesis was that the enhanced article would produce more knowledge acquisition than the original article because of interactivity aspects, increasing reader acceptance [9]. The findings prove the hypothesis and suggest the need for further study to include a greater focus on interactivity, encouraging the advances of this research.

In addition, other publishers, e.g., Wiley[1] and Elsevier[2] redesigned their user interface for a three-panel, non-linear reading exploration. Elsevier correspondingly conducted a study using eye-tracking to identify and analyze visual user attention. As a result, the users first examine the central area, then the left and followed by the right [10], leading the user to different levels of attention [11], and consequently, may cause cognitive overload [12], which is what the study intends to avoid. Furthermore, it is important to note that most interactive visualization tools are available on the right, not directly related to the content that supports the knowledge as is the aim of our proposal.

On the other hand, there are open access journals, such as Plos One [11] that offer integrated multimedia content in the article's central area. Although these enhancements are expected to influence the knowledge acquisition, they do not have the necessary interactivity to become more dynamic. In essence, the integration of multimedia and interactivity in a central area, demand to build a more participatory user relationship with the content, where the user becomes engaged in the narrative. Generally, this narrative is driven by interactive features that enable different levels of navigation [13].

In this study, interactivity is operationally defined as a purposeful action from the user, which causes a directional change or a meaningful response by the system with regard to the content [11]. The results of these investigations are incorporated throughout this study as a guide for questioning improvements to interactive scientific publishing. It was perceived that the design approaches that can assist in the creation of

---

[1] http://olabout.wiley.com/WileyCDA/Section/id-819787.html.

[2] https://www.elsevier.com/connect/designing-the-article-of-the-future.

more active participatory interaction with multimedia content. Hence, there are theories and guides concerning multimedia and cognition to integrate with design processes (see Sect. 3).

## 3   Case Study

The case study was established by considering scientific publishing as well as the related work. Studies related to cognitive theories, construct a framework that is related to the interactivity concepts and design principles that were prototyped.

### 3.1   User Interface Design Based on a Cognitive Framework

The theories and cognitive studies were combined and correlated to design principles [14], attempting to reduce processing and cognitive load that complements or reinforces information through interactive multimedia integration, making interactivity the focal point of scientific learning. It defines how content is organized and the way in which it engages interactive actions to create user experiences. According to Miller [15], the human cognitive system can process from 5 to 9 elements simultaneously. In order to promote effective comprehension, a balance between the loads was applied to increase the efficiency of the content, e.g., the information disclosed is limited to one item at a time in sequential elements within the dialog boxes of the sections (Fig. 1A).

The user has a limited capacity of information processing in each channel. Thus, the Dual Code Theory precepts [16] try to give equal weight to verbal and non-verbal processing. As Paivio [16] points out, interactions with multimedia publications can establish any or all types of processing. Hence, to establish the equity of the cognitive load and processing, some of the Mayer [12] principles were included to construct the prototype. It consists of five principles for reducing extraneous processing, principles for managing the essential processing, principles for fostering generative processing and boundary conditions for design principles (individual differences) [12].

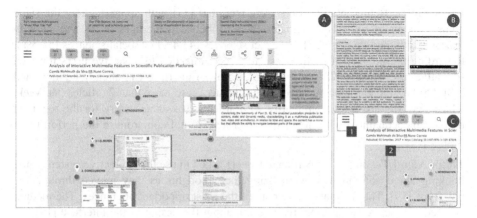

**Fig. 1.** Prototype's first (A) and second (B) page. In detail (C) the menu (1) and the points (2).

**The Prototype Interface Design.** The interface design illustrates the approach of the user interface design based on the cognitive framework. Design problems include how to organize and unify multimedia to enhance interactivity and support usability requirements [14]. Furthermore, preventing users from making too many mistakes through design principle defaults, such as feedback, visibility, mapping, consistency and constraints [14]. In this way, five basic types of interactivity are presented: stimulus and response, navigation, control objects, communication and exchange information. The prototype has an interactive overview map as the main focus (Fig. 1A).

The overview map was chosen to visually synthesize the article in strategic points related to its sections trying to deepen the user experience. Constraints [14] imposed on navigation limit the interaction to guide the user. Likewise, it is segmented to achieve a user-paced multimedia presentation [15]. The applied elements form symbolic associations, which are present in user associative and referential processing [16] (Fig. 1C). In relation to visual design, the points received different colors and sizes for their segregation [14]. Correspondingly, the selected spatial hierarchy map the points according to the Gestalt principles [14].

According to the temporal contiguity principle, the decision was made to synchronize the dynamic content to the textual narrative of the article [12]. Text and dynamic images on the interface are physically integrated, following the spatial proximity/contiguity and multimedia principle. The organization of the dynamic media within the interface is related to the user's knowledge that occurs most significantly with combining words and images, instead of words alone. In addition, when the user interacts with a dynamic or static image, a specific part of the text will be underlined (Fig. 1B).

### 3.2    Method

There are six main research steps of the study: (1) participants were introduced to a designed interface, (2) required to experience the interface, (3) encouraged to think aloud, (4) invited to join the usability test, (5) requested to answer the questionnaire, and (6) an expert review evaluation.

**Participants.** Representative users were recruited [17] with approximately the same number of males (N = 4) as females (N = 5), between the ages of 28 and 43 with master's or doctorate degrees from exact sciences (44.4%) or social sciences (55.5%). Regarding the number of participants, it is recommended to have five users for each formative test, because 80% of the problems of an interface can already be identified [18]. Of the nine participants, seven indicated access to more than 2 articles per week, which may suggest a user familiarity with articles. It was necessary for the recruited users to be acquainted with interactive interfaces to not compromise the performance results [17].

**Think-Aloud Testing.** Test participants were asked to use the interactive system while thinking aloud continuously, verbalizing their thoughts as they moved through the prototype [19]. The facilitator took note of the most important utterances. The method allowed to discover what users really think about the design of the interface [17].

**System Usability Scale Evaluation.** After participants' interaction with the prototype for measuring attitudes toward system usability, 10 items were evaluated and divided into 2 types of statements interspersed, according to the System Usability Scale (SUS) [17, 20]. The average SUS score has a 100-point scale of their percentile ranking.

**Questionnaire.** Q1. Did the interactive multimedia features in the publication help you understand what the article is about? Explain. Q2. Do you think that the way the information was arranged in the article makes you understand more quickly compared to other types of scientific publishing you have already encountered? Explain. Q3. What would you like to see modified in the interface? Please give some suggestions.

**Expert Review Evaluation.** A group of four usability experts conducted the prototype review. The experts were recruited based on academic background (Computer Science), current Human-Computer Interaction research and the years of experience in usability studies. The specialized review approach attended to the context, nature and interaction objectives [1]. A list was created to maintain evaluation parameters with the following sections: occurrence, usability strengths, usability problem, usability guidelines violated and severity rating score, along with recommendations and examples of best practices. The review evaluation began with the understanding of system users and their objectives [17]. Severity ratings by Nilsen [21] were adopted to address the greatest problems and add a rough estimate of the need for additional usability efforts.

## 4   Results and Discussion

The results are discussed in the next two subsections (1) lessons learned from user evaluation and, (2) expert review evaluation lessons and recommendations.

### 4.1   Lessons Learned from User Evaluation

The participants interacted with the prototype, which included briefly reporting their learning aloud. At first contact, many of the thoughts about the overview map were related to their mental models (linear flow) still anchored to the table of contents [24]. On the other hand, some thought aloud: *"I like how we can see the whole article... I can click on the section name and go directly to the subject.... this is interesting"* [P7]. It was observed that the focus of the users was related to the map, this occurred because a balance between the loads [12] applied to limit the disclosure of content to one item at a time. However, some users also reported usability issues with the map as a result of the highest interactive component to support feedback of the user expectations.

Moreover, in association to participants' usability feedback, figure (Fig. 2) shows the relation of the participants with scored corresponding statements of positive (green) and negative (red). "Strongly Agree" was reached in four positive statements [S1, S3, S5, S7 and S9], green cells indicate an overall favorable rating, it represents an increased incremental usability perceived by the user [20]. Regarding [S1] "I think that I would like to use this type of interactive multimedia publication frequently" received the maximum score from three participants as well as a score of 4 from five participants. Concerning [S7] "I would imagine that most researchers would learn to use this type of publication quickly", which received four maximum scores and four scores of 4 demonstrating an inclination to quickly learn the flow of navigation and interaction.

In relation to the negative statements [S2, S4, S6, S8 and S10] in red (Fig. 2), a score of two to three on average was observed in the data collected, which leads to lower overall values per participant statements. [S4] received the lowest score, revealing that participants did not require assistance to use this type of publication, most of them did not find inconsistencies in their interactions. In the end, the average SUS score obtained from the participants was 68.1 on a 100-point scale [17, 20], giving it a C grade, which corresponds 50% to an upward average for the usability of the interface design tested.

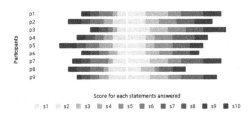

**Fig. 2.** The results of usability evaluation. (Color figure online)

Overall, the answers about whether interactive multimedia features helped the user understand the article subject [Q1] represent a scholar acceptance to the interactivity as facilitation to the content understanding, such as, *"Yes, a tool like this is a resource when you need to look up miscellaneous articles (and learn about them) in a short time."* [P2]; *"Visualization helps you understand the parts that make up the articles. Quick access to sections is interesting."* [P3]. The second question [Q2] related to the organization of the information and consequently, a faster understanding of the article were *"Yes, I think it made it easier than other types of publications. However, at first, I needed to adapt to the context of the interaction and then understand the content."* [P4]; *"Since I'm more used to the usual type, I would say that this one does not make it easier for me right now. But maybe with more use, yes."* [P6]. Referring to the last question [Q3], the participants had given some suggestions, mainly associated with the hierarchy of the article sections (an improved color usage, sizes and spatial axes in the interactive points). [P7] expressed this well *"... a more explicit order from where I should click first. Because the elements are arranged in a circular way, the relationship of animated images to the topic referred to is not so clear... using more of the hierarchy and proximity to the related content can help."*.

## 4.2    Reviewer's Evaluation Lessons and Recommendation

The reviewers evaluated four main occurrence areas of possible usability issues, as well as usability strengths, namely: (1) related articles menu, (2) top menu bar, (3) overview map, (4) article structure and menu collapse, represented below. The minor usability problem was related to the menu of related articles, which needs to be corrected but with low priority. The reviewers recommended removing the button inserted inside the information boxes as well as increasing size with the hovering mouse. Already in the article structure, the top menu bar and the menu collapse have major usability problems. The expert review has shown a reevaluation of menu collapse mapping and visibility, minimizing the user's memory load, aligning the menu as well as following the sections of the article. The advice related to usability issues found in the top bar menu are related to affordance, aesthetics, legibility, feedback, and metaphors [14].

The significant issue found is associated with the overview map, which received a value of four, indicating a usability problem that is mandatory to fix. In the overview map, it is recommended to add an accessible shrink icon to allow the user's back action. In relation to the overview points, it is vital to review the hierarchy [14] of elements as well as simplify the interaction possibilities for the next action to be appropriate. It is also crucial to organize the distribution of points at a greater distance between sections. Reshaping the size and color of the points indicates the path to be followed by the user.

## 5    User Interface Design Considerations and Conclusion

Multimedia presentations can encourage scientific readers to engage in active learning by mentally representing the article in words and images; making connections between pictorial and verbal representations [22]. In this way, the cognitive framework transforms the complexity of textual content in a visual and interactive way. It seeks to establish a relationship between users' demand and the available features on the publication. Accordingly, the lessons learned demonstrate the usefulness and importance of applying the design principles of the cognitive framework. Users are more likely to understand scientific content when they can participate in active learning as well as relevant cognitive processing [22]. Coordination of the usability results along with the answers from the study prove which of the decisions from the cognitive framework did not support usability, becoming an obstacle to user's comprehension and interactions.

The interface with the symbolic association to two visualization modes of articles are considered: simplified and interactive visualization can activate user associative processing [16] and provide accessibility options for interactive multimedia content. In addition, it provides an overview in the article central area, directly influencing the interactive process with the interested parties through a more active role of the reader. The reading experience is supported by segmenting the multimedia presentation as user-paced and synchronizing the textual narrative with a suitable time. Besides, offering a content replacement tool to analyze and compare data, motivates user engagement in the content flow and reduces cognitive overload [12, 15]. Moreover, guiding the view progression by color or icons, indicating what was viewed and what is currently being displayed helps minimize the user's memory load.

In conclusion, the study combined usability methods to evaluate the application of the cognitive framework in the prototype. Usability is directly linked to the quality of interaction and efficient use of interactive features, indicating improvement to the user experience. The experts pointed their criticisms to issues not perceived by users, whose proposed best practices were extremely valuable. Thus, a complete result of the prototype evaluation is achievable through the selected methodologies. According to participants' reports, this type of publication provides quick access to sections through the amplified view of the entire article, and the multimedia features help to understand the information more objectively. Likewise, they expose outputs for design decisions, taking into account the organization of the elements and content within the publication in a structured way. Finally, the limitations found in this work are related to a deeper understanding of user's desires, designing an interface and elements as imagined by them. For this reason, the study will focus on participatory design for future directions.

# References

1. Fyfe, A., Steven, H.: The journal article: is the end in sight? Is the journal fit for purpose? In: The Future of Scholarly Scientific Communication, pp. 28–29. Session 1A. The Royal Society Conference (2015)
2. Moreno, R., Mayer, R.: Interactive multimodal learning environments. Educ. Psychol. Rev. **19**, 309–326 (2007). https://doi.org/10.1007/s10648-007-9047-2
3. Cope, B., Phillips, A.: The Future of the Academic Journal, 2nd edn. Chandos Publishing, Oxford (2014)
4. Ziegler, A., Mietchen, D., Faber, C., et al.: Effectively incorporating selected multimedia content into medical publications. BMC Med. **9**(17), 1–6 (2011)
5. Lancaster, F.W.: The evolution of electronic publishing. Ser. Rev. **21**(1), 518–527 (1995)
6. Shum, S.B., Summer, T.: JIME: an interactive journal for interactive media. Learn. Publ. **14**, 273–285 (2001)
7. Ackerman, M.J.: The educational value of truly interactive science publishing. J. Electr. Publ. **18**(2), 1–8 (2015). New Forms of Expression
8. Ackerman, M.J., Siegel, E., Wood, F.: Interactive Science Publishing: a joint OSA-NLM project. Inf. Serv. Use **30**, 39–50 (2010)
9. Siegel, E.R., Lindberg, D.A.B., Campbell, G.P., et al.: Defining the next generation journal: the NLM-Elsevier interactive publications experiment. Inf. Serv. Use **30**, 17–30 (2010)
10. Zudilova-Seinstra, E., Klompenhouwer, M., Heeman, F., Isbrand J.A.: The Elsevier Article of the Future project: a novel experience of online reading. In: The Future of the Academic Journal, 2nd edn., pp. 357–377. Chandos Publishing, Oxford (2014)
11. da Silva, C.W., Correia, N.: Analysis of interactive multimedia features in scientific publication platforms. In: Kamps, J., Tsakonas, G., Manolopoulos, Y., Iliadis, L., Karydis, I. (eds.) TPDL 2017. LNCS, vol. 10450, pp. 525–530. Springer, Cham (2017). https://doi.org/10.1007/978-3-319-67008-9_41
12. Mayer, R.E.: Multimedia learning. Psychol. Learn. Motiv. **41**, 85–139 (2002)

13. Owen, J.M.: The Scientific Article in the Age of Digitization (Information Science and Knowledge Management), 1st edn. Springer, Heidelberg (2006). https://doi.org/10.1007/1-4020-5340-1
14. Norman, D.A.: The Design of Everyday Things. Revised and Expanded Edition. Basic Books, New York (2013)
15. Miller, G.A.: The magical number seven, plus or minus two: some limits on our capacity for processing information. Psychol. Rev. **101**(2), 343–352 (1994)
16. Paivio, A.: Dual coding theory. Can. J. Psychol. **45**(3), 255–287 (1991)
17. Barnum, C.M.: Usability Testing Essentials. Morgan Kaufmann, Burlington (2011)
18. Barnum, C., Polytechnic, S., Pky, S.M., et al.: The "Magic Number 5": is it enough for web testing? In: CHI 2003 Ext. Abstr. Hum. factors Comput. Syst., vol. 5, pp. 698–699 (2003)
19. NN/g Nielsen Norman Group. https://www.nngroup.com/articles/thinking-aloud-the-1-usability-tool/. Accessed 05 Jan 2019
20. Brooke, J.: SUS, A quick and dirty usability scale. Usability Eval. Ind., 4–7 (1996). https://doi.org/10.1002/hbm.20701
21. NN/g Nielsen Norman Group. https://www.nngroup.com/articles/how-to-rate-the-severity-of-usability-problems/. Accessed 12 Jan 2019
22. Clark, R.C., Mayer, R.E.: E-Learning and Science of Instruction, 3rd edn. Pfeiffer, San Francisco (2008)

# Stable Word-Clouds for Visualising Text-Changes Over Time

Elisa Herold$^{(\boxtimes)}$ , Marcus Pöckelmann , Christian Berg , Jörg Ritter ,
and Mark M. Hall

Martin-Luther-University Halle-Wittenberg, Halle, Germany
`elisa.herold@student.uni-halle.de`, {`marcus.poeckelmann,christian.berg,`
`joerg.ritter,mark.hall`}`@informatik.uni-halle.de`

**Abstract.** Word-clouds are a useful tool for providing overviews over
texts, visualising relevant words. Multiple word-clouds can also be used
to visualise changes over time in a text. This requires that the words
in the individual word-clouds have stable positions, as otherwise it is
very difficult so see what changed between two consecutive word-clouds.
Existing approaches have used coordinated positioning algorithms, which
do not allow for their use in an online, dynamic context. In this paper
we present a fast word-cloud algorithm that uses word orthogonality
to determine which words can share the same space in the word-clouds
combined with a simple, but fast spiral-based layout algorithm. The evaluation shows that the algorithm achieves its goal of creating series of
word-clouds fast enough to enable use in an online, dynamic context.

**Keywords:** Text analysis · Visualisation · Visual analysis ·
Word-clouds · Optimisation

## 1 Introduction

Word-clouds, such as Wordle [7], have long been used to generate overviews over
texts, visualising the most frequently occurring or most relevant words, generally
using font size to visualise the words' frequency or importance and optionally
adding colour or transparency to visualise further attributes [17].

While word-clouds work well as overview visualisations for individual texts
or larger text corpora [8,22], one of the main limitations of basic word-clouds
is that they only show a static view of the text. In contrast to this, for text
analysis it is often desired to be able to visualise part of the text and then
move the visualisation window over the text to see how the text changes [18].
While it is possible to generate individual word-clouds for each time-slice the
user moves the visualisation window to, the word locations in the word-clouds
will change each time, making it difficult to track changes. While algorithms
such as Word Storm [3] can generate multiple word-clouds that have relatively
stable word locations, the process of creating these coordinated word-clouds is
time consuming.

© Springer Nature Switzerland AG 2019
A. Doucet et al. (Eds.): TPDL 2019, LNCS 11799, pp. 224–237, 2019.
https://doi.org/10.1007/978-3-030-30760-8_20

The LERA[1] tool provides an environment for this kind of inter-textual analysis. The user can select a range within the text and then gets a word-cloud for that text range. They can then move the range through the text and observe the changes, which means that the word-clouds have to be generated very quickly. While the text itself is static and thus would be amenable to using pre-calculation of the word-clouds using the existing, slower algorithms, the user is provided with a range of parameters to tune what exactly they see in the word-cloud. The range of parameters make pre-calculation unfeasible, it is thus necessary to have a fast word-cloud algorithm that generates stable word-clouds.

In this paper we present a novel algorithm for fast generation of coordinated word-clouds in which all words have a completely fixed location. The remainder of the paper is structured as follows: Sect. 2 discusses previous approaches to creating comparable word-clouds, Sect. 3 provides an overview over the data we are working with, Sect. 4 presents our algorithm for stable word-clouds, which is evaluated in Sect. 5 and in Sect. 6 we conclude with future work.

## 2   Background

The most commonly used word-cloud algorithm is the Wordle algorithm [7]. It positions words both horizontally and vertically and generally uses the word frequency to scale each word's size. When positioning the words, the algorithm uses a very compact representation of each word's outline, which ensures that words do not overlap and are spaced out as little as possible. This creates a very dense visualisation, but the use of vertical text and the placement of words within the outline of other words can make reading the visualisations harder for the user. In the algorithm presented here we thus only place text horizontally and also utilise more white-space between individual words.

In addition to this relatively common word-cloud layout, there have been a number of other layout approaches, including layouts for even less white-space [12,19], the ManiWordle approach [13], rolled-out word-clouds [21], or TagPies [10]. As will be described below, due to our focus on layout stability, we will use a very simple spiral-based layout algorithm. However, this could in the future be adapted to combine improved layouts with our high-performancy, stability-focused algorithm.

The main limitation motivating the work presented here is that these algorithms are static and are not designed to incorporate links between different word-clouds. Work on integrating temporal aspects has generally focused on approaches such as the SparkClouds [15] or Fish-Eye Clouds [23], where additional temporal information is integrated into the basic word-cloud layout. Alternatives have also used word-clouds as part of a more complex visual interface [24] or developed alternatives for comparing changes between two time-slices [6]. However, none of these address the requirement for adapting the actual word-cloud content over time.

---

[1] Locate, Explore, Retrace and Apprehend complex text variants https://lera.uzi.uni-halle.de.

One of the earliest approaches for coordinated word-clouds was the Parallel Tag Clouds approach [4], which simplified the word-clouds' layout to a set of vertical columns, one per word-cloud. By using just one dimension in the layout algorithm and sorting the words alphabetically, Parallel Tag Clouds help the user in comparing multiple word-clouds, particularly since interactive visual clues were used to highlight the same word across all word-clouds. However, the word locations are not stable across the individual clouds.

Cui et al. [5] demonstrate taking one word-cloud's layout into account when generating the next in their context-preserving dynamic word-clouds. Their approach combines a time-line graph with multiple word-clouds. Each word-cloud uses a force-directed layout to factor in the layout from the previous word-cloud. This ensures that their word-clouds are semantically coherent and word locations are spatially relatively stable. However, the dynamic nature of the force-driven layout cannot ensure complete layout stability, only that the rough layout is preserved across word-clouds.

The Word Storm algorithm [3] produces coordinated word-clouds, by combining an iterative placement algorithm that averages word locations across all word-clouds with a gradient method inspired by multi-dimensional scaling that compacts the locations generated by the iterative algorithm. This creates coordinated word-clouds in which the word locations are very similar across the clouds. The clouds are then placed in a grid structure to allow for comparison. The core concept is expanded in the Word Flock algorithm [14], where not only exact words, but also semantic relatedness are used to place semantically similar words together. Instead of treating it as an optimisation problem, the COWORDS algorithm [20] uses a probabilistic sampling approach to pick a visual distribution that is both compact and retains stable word positions. While the approach produces word-clouds that are just as compact [1] as those in Word Storm, the probabilistic model allows for the integration of additional constraints, making the system more flexible.

A different approach is taken in the ConcentriCloud visualisation [16], which visualises the word-clouds in a set of concentric circles. In the inner-most circle they place those words that appear in all word-clouds, while the outer circle has those words that only appear in specific word-clouds. The circles inbetween show words that appear in some, but not all word-clouds. This gives the user a good overview over the shared and distinguishing concepts. However, it also limits the number of word-clouds that can be compared, before the visualisation becomes unreadable.

All of these approaches are focused primarily on generating word-clouds to be shown together for comparison, a scenario in which small positional changes between the layouts do not present an issue. However, in our use scenario the system generates a large number of word-clouds that are shown sequentially and where even small positional changes between consecutive word-clouds generate a lot of visual noise, which would distract and potentially mask the actual changes. Additionally, as stated above, the user has full control over a large number of parameters (visualised segment size, which words to include, what statistics to use for the word sizes, number of words to visualise, ...), thus pre-calculation is not viable. The algorithm we developed is thus designed to create word-clouds where the word locations are completely fixed and which can be generated very quickly.

## 3   Project & Data

The work presented here was developed based on the requirements of the LERA tool. The tool is used to support humanities researchers in the inter-textual analysis of texts in a variety of contexts, with the aim of identifying similarities and differences between multiple versions of the same text. To do this the tool automatically segments and aligns the texts, the result of which can then be manually modified and corrected if so desired [2].

To analyse the texts the tool provides three linked visualisations (Fig. 1): an overview visualisation that shows the identified segments and their alignment; the detailed text view that shows the actual text in each segment for all texts, and the word-clouds that visualise the relevant words in a section of the text. Multiple relevance metrics (frequency, Term-Frequency Inverse-Document-Frequency [TFIDF], ...) and filters (word length, part-of-speech tags, number of words to display, ...) can be applied to control what the word-clouds show.

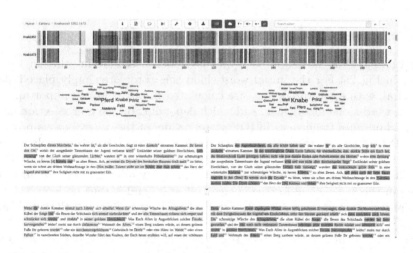

**Fig. 1.** Screenshot of the LERA user-interface, showing the overview visualisation at the top with a range of segments selected, the word-clouds below, and two versions of the source text with differences highlighted at the bottom.

To visualise the words in the word-clouds, the user selects a range of segments in the overview and the word-clouds are immediately re-calculated for the selection range. The user can then move the selection range across the full length of the text and the word-clouds are updated in real-time to reflect the content of the newly selected range. This allows the researcher to develop an understanding of how the content of the text changes over the course of the text. In order to support the researcher in correctly interpreting the changes, it is necessary that the word locations remain stable as the selection range moves and words are added, removed, or change in importance. Otherwise after each step the researcher has to hunt for the changes.

The LERA system holds a number of different texts for analysis, the examples shown here are taken from a work by the nineteenth century author Karl Gutzkow "Aus der Knabenzeit". The text exists in two versions (1852 and 1873) consisting of 81695 and 75941 tokens, respectively, which after alignment produce 236 aligned segments, with the length of each segment ranging from single words to full paragraphs. For the word-cloud examples shown here we use the most relevant words identified via TFIDF and filtered to only include nouns. However, this filtering is undertaken before the data is passed to the word-cloud algorithm and the word-cloud algorithm does not make any specific demands of the tokens it is asked to visualise.

## 4    Stable Word-Clouds

To support the need for fast, stable word-clouds an initial naive approach was implemented, based on which the novel algorithm presented here was developed.

### 4.1    Naive Stable Word-Clouds

An initial fast, but naive approach was developed based around the fixed spiral layout in Fig. 2a. For the initial word-cloud the words are simply placed along the spiral, with each word's font size calculated from the word's importance, as in most word-cloud algorithms, and which depending on the user selection might be based on pure frequency, TFIDF score, or any of the other metrics provided by LERA. Then, as the user moves the selection, new words are placed into available slots on the spiral. The big question is at what point to free up those slots in the spiral for which the word that was originally placed there no longer occurs in the word-cloud for the current selection and is thus no longer shown. If no re-use is undertaken, then the spiral keeps expanding and the word-cloud becomes very sparse and hard to read.

To address this, the algorithm tracks how many steps the slot has remained empty. A step here is defined as the user moving the selection one segment. Thus if a slot has been empty for five steps, this means that the word that was originally placed there has not appeared as relevant in the last five segments. The problem lies in how to determine the number of steps $s$ after which to flag a slot as free, so that it can be re-used with a different word. A low value drastically reduces the word-cloud's stability, as words first disappear and then re-appear in different locations, as their original slot has been re-used for a different word. At the same time a high value does not make good use of the available space, as spaces are not re-used for a long period of time.

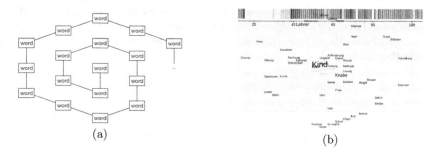

(a)                                                      (b)

**Fig. 2.** (a) Fixed spiral-based layout used to position words in the word-cloud. (b) Example of a word-cloud that has degenerated into a very sparse display after the user has moved the selection range a few times.

Due to its naive nature, the algorithm's performance is very high and runs in the browser without any pre-processing. However, after extensive experimentation, we have concluded that the local-information approach is not able to provide the kind of stable and compact clouds (see Fig. 2 for an example of how the word-clouds degenerate and become sparse) that are required.

## 4.2  Stable Placement via Pairwise Orthogonality

As demonstrated by the existing work, the difficulty with finding stable word-cloud configurations is the large number of potential word placements, from which the most stable one needs to be selected. To circumvent this problem, the approach presented here is not based on finding stable word placements, but on determining which words never co-occur across the range of word-clouds that are generated. The words that never co-occur are grouped together and can then share the same location in the word-cloud. This allows us to re-use the word spiral for the final placement of words, but at the same time make it significantly more compact.

To determine which words can be grouped together the algorithm first constructs the word-segment occurrence matrix $A$, in which each row represents one aligned segment and each column one word. The matrix values are then set to the frequency with which a given word occurs in a given segment. Table 1 shows an example matrix for four segments and six words taken from the full matrix for the data-set. The columns are ordered by the increasing frequency with which the words occur over the whole text.

To determine which words can be grouped together we test which columns are pairwise orthogonal. Two columns $a$ and $b$ are orthogonal if their vector multiplication results in the zero vector (Eq. 1) and each such pair is a candidate for grouping. In the example in Table 1 the columns "Herr" and "Baum", "Herr" and "Meister", "Herr" and "Gott", "Baum" and "Kind", "Baum" and "Knabe", "Meister" and "Kind", and "Meister" and "Knabe" are all pairwise orthogonal, because they do not share any rows where they have values greater than zero. Each of these pairs is thus a candidate for grouping together into a group.

**Table 1.** Example word-segment occurrence matrix $A$ for the four segments with the words "Knabe, Kind Gott" (#1), "Gott, Gott, Meister, Baum" (#2), "Knabe" (#3), and "Knabe, Kind, Herr" (#4). In this example the user has selected to only include nouns in the word-cloud.

| Segment | Herr | Baum | Meister | Kind | Gott | Knabe |
|---------|------|------|---------|------|------|-------|
| #1 | 0 | 0 | 0 | 1 | 1 | 1 |
| #2 | 0 | 1 | 1 | 0 | 2 | 0 |
| #3 | 0 | 0 | 0 | 0 | 0 | 1 |
| #4 | 1 | 0 | 0 | 1 | 0 | 1 |

$$a \cdot b^\top = \vec{0} \tag{1}$$

Determining which columns to group together to minimise the total number of groups is an NP-hard problem [11], thus we have developed the greedy Algorithm 1 to determine which columns to group together. The algorithm iterates over each column and, as long as the column has not already been assigned to a group, is added to a new group (lines 4–6). Then a new group occurrence vector is initialised with the current column's occurrences (line 7). Next the algorithm iterates over the remaining columns that have not yet been added to groups. Each of these columns is first checked for whether it has already been merged into another group (line 9) and then checked for orthogonality against the group vector (line 10). If the two are orthogonal, then the column is assigned to the current group, marked as merged, and the group's vector is updated by adding the column vector (lines 11–13). At the end of the outer loop each column has been assigned to a group and each group has at least one column in it.

For the example in Table 1 the first group would initially contain the column "Herr". Then the algorithm would iterate through the remaining columns and the first orthogonal column is "Baum", which would be added to the group. Next, the group would be compared to "Meister", but while "Herr" is orthogonal to "Meister", the merged group no longer is, thus neither "Meister" nor any of the other columns is not merged into the group. Table 2 shows how over four iterations the algorithm greedily merges together the columns into groups, adding the "Meister" and "Kind" group in the second iteration, while the words "Gott" and "Knabe" each get their own group as they are not orthogonal to each other.

The word-cloud visualisation generation then works based on the groups (Fig. 3), rather than on individual words, but still uses the spiral to generate the placements. For the initial word-cloud the groups are placed along the spiral as in the naive approach, with individual words' font-size still determined by each word's relevance. The difference is that as the user moves the selection range, when a word is no longer displayed, because it no longer occurs in the selection range, that word's slot can immediately be re-used and re-filled with another word that has been allocated to the same group. This has two main benefits. First, as the number of groups is generally smaller than the number of words,

```
1   merged_columns = []
2   groups = []
3   for i in 0 .. |columns|
4       if i not in merged_columns
5           group = [i]
6           merged_columns.push(i)
7           group_v = columns[i]
8           for j in i + 1 .. |columns|
9               if j not in merged_columns:
10                  if orthogonal(group_v, columns[j])
11                      merged_columns.push(j)
12                      group.push(j)
13                      group_v = group_v + columns[j]
14                  end
15              end
16          end
17          groups.push(group)
18      end
19  end
```

**Algorithm 1.** Greedy algorithm that constructs the merged groups based on the pairwise orthogonality of the individual columns. The algorithm's worst-case performance is $O(n^2 \cdot m)$ where $n$ is the number of columns and $m$ the number of rows.

**Table 2.** Example of the greedy Algorithm 1 processing the example data-set from Table 1. In each iteration one group is added, containing one or more word columns in that group. The fourth iteration represents the final set of groups to visualise.

| Iteration | Groups | Words Columns in the Group |
|-----------|--------|----------------------------|
| 1         | 1      | "Herr", "Baum"             |
| 2         | 1      | "Herr", "Baum"             |
|           | 2      | "Meister", "Kind"          |
| 3         | 1      | "Herr", "Baum"             |
|           | 2      | "Meister", "Kind"          |
|           | 3      | "Gott"                     |
| 4         | 1      | "Herr", "Baum"             |
|           | 2      | "Meister", "Kind"          |
|           | 3      | "Gott"                     |
|           | 4      | "Knabe"                    |

overall the word-clouds are more compact. Second, because the number of groups is known before visualising, the visualisation as a whole can be scaled to ensure that the word-cloud is always visible as a whole, regardless of where the selection range is moved.

Gott                              **Gott**

Knabe          Kind                        Meister    Knabe                    Knabe              Kind

Baum                                              Herr

(#1)                           (#2)                    (#3)                    (#4)

**Fig. 3.** Four word-clouds generated for the four segments in Table 1, but using the groups identified in Table 2 to place words on the spiral. Words in the same group appear in the same location, as can be seen when comparing the words "Kind" and "Meister" or "Herr" and "Baum". Also visible is the scaling of the word "Gott" in the word-cloud for the second segment in which the word appears twice

### 4.3    Multi-segment Selection Ranges

As the user is free to select ranges that cover multiple segments, the matrix A has to be updated to represent the multi-segment selection. In the updated matrix each row represents a series of segments and the matrix values are updated to show the frequency of each word across all selected segments. Table 3 shows the matrix $A$ for a selection range of two segments. As the example shows, the number of rows is reduced by $|selection range| - 1$, in this case to 3 segments. This matrix is then fed into the grouping and layout algorithms as above.

**Table 3.** Example word-segment occurrence matrix $A$ for the three two-segments-selected segments derived from the four original segments "Knabe, Kind Gott", "Gott, Gott, Meister, Baum", "Knabe", and "Knabe, Kind, Herr". The new segment #1 contains the words from the original segments #1 and #2, new segment #2 from the original segments #2 and #3, and new segment #3 from the original #3 and #4.

| Segment | Herr | Baum | Meister | Kind | Knabe | Gott |
|---------|------|------|---------|------|-------|------|
| #1      | 0    | 1    | 1       | 1    | 1     | 3    |
| #2      | 0    | 1    | 1       | 0    | 1     | 2    |
| #3      | 1    | 0    | 0       | 1    | 2     | 0    |

## 5    Evaluation

As stated above, the two core requirements for our algorithm were positional stability and high performance, both of which we evaluate here. A user-focused evaluation is planned in the context of evaluating the LERA system as a whole.

### 5.1    Stability of the Layout Algorithm

Looking at the positional stability, we undertook a qualitative and technical evaluation. For the qualitative we used ten-segment wide selection ranges and then visually inspected the results to verify that slots were being consistently filled and re-used. Figure 4 demonstrates the stability of the algorithm. For the two selection ranges the words "Hand", "Prinz", and "Tod" occur in both selections (highlighted in green) and stay in the same location. On the other hand the words "Fähnrich" and "Mäßigung" (highlighted in blue) are orthogonal and thus can share the same location.

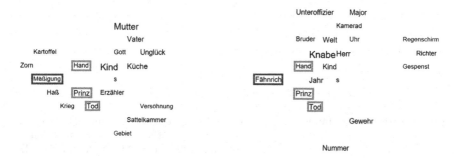

**Fig. 4.** Word-clouds showing two sets of 10 segments, demonstrating the stability of the positions for the words "Hand", "Prinz", and "Tod" (green) and the re-use of a position for the words "Mäßigung" and "Fähnrich" (blue). (Color figure online)

Additionally we manually tested a wide range of selection ranges and then repeatedly moved the selection range across the text length. In our naive approach this would lead to the word-cloud degenerating as illustrated above (Fig. 2b). In our tests the novel algorithm always maintained a stable cloud and compact word-cloud.

One recurring issue the testing identified is that the simple spiral layout in some cases has issues with word-overlap in the final display (Fig. 5). This is because the spiral does not take into account the final, rendered size of the words and instead uses static distances between the word centres, which assume a relatively even size distribution. For future work there is thus a clear need to improve this by using an overlap-free layout algorithm.

## 5.2 Performance

To test the algorithm's performance we automatically generated word-clouds for a range of selection sizes and measured the time needed for this. The algorithm was implemented in Ruby 2.4.5 and run on an Intel Core i7-3770 CPU with 16 GB of RAM running a Sabayon Linux with Kernel version 4.4.39. Table 4 shows the results from averaging ten runs of each configuration.

The main results in Table 4 clearly show that the algorithm's performance allows for running it on-demand without any pre-calculation. As is to be expected, the slowest run-time is for the single-segment word-clouds, where generating 146 groups from 2552 unique words takes approximately 6.35 s. For the largest practical selection size of 90 segments, run-time reduces to on average 3.74 s. The most common selection scenario is for a size of 40 and here the generation takes on average 4.11 s.

**Fig. 5.** Example of overlapping words in the final layout.

**Table 4.** Performance timings for a range of selection ranges. The number of groups is deterministic, but the run-time is reported as *average (standard deviation)* calculated from ten runs for each configuration displaying 100 words. The selection sizes have been determined based on feedback from LERA users.

| Selection size | # Groups | Time |
|---|---|---|
| 1 | 146 | 6.35 s (0.18 s) |
| 40 | 151 | 4.11 s (0.28 s) |
| 70 | 121 | 3.65 s (0.13 s) |
| 90 | 117 | 3.74 s (0.17 s) |

The other result is that through the orthogonality calculation the algorithm can substantially reduce the number of groups from 2552 unique input words to between 117 and 146 groups. As the examples show this number of groups can easily be visualised, but we are also investigating other space-filling curves [9] to create a denser layout that utilises all of the rectangular space and avoids overlaps.

As part of the performance testing we also assessed an optimisation based on the hypothesis that by reversing the direction of the inner loop (Algorithm 1, line 8–16), the overall performance would improve. The hypothesis behind the optimisation was that by starting with a column from the beginning of $A$, where the columns are generally sparse, and then trying to merge it with the more dense columns at the end of $A$, determining when two columns were not orthogonal would be faster, as it would take less row comparisons until a row was found where both columns had values.

Table 5 shows the results of running the algorithm with the inner loop direction reversed. It shows that for selection sizes of 1 and 40 it has little impact on the number of groups generated, but it does improve run time. In the case of a selection size of 1, the improvement is over 1 s. However, for the larger selection sizes, the performance is lower and it generates significantly more groups. The results confirm our basic hypothesis that merging very sparse with dense columns increases efficiency. However, when there are few sparse columns, as is the case for the larger selection sizes, by not letting the algorithm merge medium density columns first, the greedy approach is not as successful at reducing the total number of generated columns.

**Table 5.** Performance timings for a range of selection ranges and reversing the order of the inner loop. The number of groups is deterministic, but the time is reported as *average (standard deviation)* calculated from ten runs for each configuration displaying 100 words. The selection sizes have been determined based on feedback from LERA users.

| Selection size | # Groups | +/− | Time | +/− |
|---|---|---|---|---|
| 1 | 145 | −1 | 4.99 s (0.39 s) | −1.36 s |
| 40 | 153 | +2 | 4.03 s (0.53 s) | −0.08 s |
| 70 | 138 | +17 | 3.86 s (0.12 s) | +0.21 s |
| 90 | 128 | +11 | 3.73 s (0.12 s) | +0.01 s |

However, as the optimisation requires only minimal change to the algorithm, it is possible to dynamically change the inner loop's direction based on the selection size. While the exact breakpoint where the increased number of groups is no longer worth the time savings is likely to vary depending on the actual text, this can be determined automatically and the algorithm can then dynamically switch the inner loop's direction.

## 6    Conclusion & Future Work

Word-clouds are a useful tool for visualising text changes over time, but the generation of a series of word-clouds in which words remain in stable positions and which are nevertheless compact, is a highly time-consuming process. In this paper we have presented a novel word-cloud algorithm that uses word-occurance orthogonality to determine which words never cooccur and can thus share a location in the generated word-clouds. This compacts the clouds and allows the use of a simple spiral-based layout algorithm to create the a series of positionally stable word-clouds.

We have evaluated the algorithm and it successfully produces positionally stable series of word-clouds fast enough (between 4 and 6 s for the tested configurations) to allow for dynamic, online generation based on user selections. After this initial build time, the user can then instantaneously scroll through the generated word-clouds and easily see the changes over time.

For future work we propose further improvements in the performance and quality of the final word-clouds. While for the texts that we have used in the system dynamic generation is viable, for very long text further speed improvements are likely required, in particular for the orthogonality calculation. Two optimisations we are considering are the use of a heuristic that quickly determines whether it is at all possible for two columns to be independent, based on keeping track of the number of rows a column has values in, as if the sum of the number of non-zero rows of the two columns is greater than the total number of rows, the columns cannot be independent. The other planned optimisation is to use bitvectors to represent the columns, which would enable the use of fast bit-wise operations to check for orthogonality, rather than the current row-wise comparisons. Together these should allow the algorithm to scale to even very large texts.

As shown above, the layout algorithm currently has issues with word-overlap. To address this we plan to use a space-filling curve approach that takes into account the maximum size required for all the words in a group. This should only have a minimal impact on the generation time, but will further improve the ease with which the word-clouds can be interpreted and with which changes in the word-clouds can be visually tracked.

Finally, while the word-cloud algorithm has been deployed in the LERA system and has been used successfully by researchers, we have not yet formally evaluated its usability. In particular there are questions concerning whether colour- or animation-based cues are needed to indicate to users which words have appeared, been replaced, or changed in importance. We are planning to conduct such a user-study in the context of evaluating the LERA system as a whole.

# References

1. Barth, L., Kobourov, S.G., Pupyrev, S.: Experimental comparison of semantic word clouds. In: Gudmundsson, J., Katajainen, J. (eds.) SEA 2014. LNCS, vol. 8504, pp. 247–258. Springer, Cham (2014). https://doi.org/10.1007/978-3-319-07959-2_21

2. Bremer, T., Molitor, P., Pöckelmann, M., Ritter, J., Schütz, S.: Zum einsatz digitaler methoden bei der erstellung und nutzung genetischer editionen gedruckter texte mit verschiedenen fassungen. In: Editio, vol. 29, pp. 29–51. Nutt-Kofoth, R. and Plachta, B. (2015). https://doi.org/10.1515/editio-2015-004

3. Castella, Q., Sutton, C.: Word storms: multiples of word clouds for visual comparison of documents. In: Proceedings of the 23rd International Conference on World Wide Web, pp. 665–676. ACM (2014)

4. Collins, C., Viegas, F.B., Wattenberg, M.: Parallel tag clouds to explore and analyze faceted text corpora. In: 2009 IEEE Symposium on Visual Analytics Science and Technology, pp. 91–98. IEEE (2009)

5. Cui, W., Wu, Y., Liu, S., Wei, F., Zhou, M.X., Qu, H.: Context preserving dynamic word cloud visualization. In: 2010 IEEE Pacific Visualization Symposium (PacificVis), pp. 121–128. IEEE (2010)

6. Dodds, P.S., Harris, K.D., Kloumann, I.M., Bliss, C.A., Danforth, C.M.: Temporal patterns of happiness and information in a global social network: hedonometrics and twitter. PloS one 6(12), e26752 (2011)

7. Feinberg, J.: Wordle. In: Steele, J., Iliinsky, N. (eds.) Beautiful Visualization Looking at Data Through the Eyes of Experts. O'Reilly Media, Newton (2010)

8. Heimerl, F., Lohmann, S., Lange, S., Ertl, T.: Word cloud explorer: text analytics based on word clouds. In: 2014 47th Hawaii International Conference on System Sciences, pp. 1833–1842. IEEE (2014)

9. Hilbert, D.: Über die stetige Abbildung einer Linie auf Flächenstück. Math. Ann. **38**, 459–460 (1891)
10. Jänicke, S., Blumenstein, J., Rücker, M., Zeckzer, D., Scheuermann, G.: Tagpies: comparative visualization of textual data. In: VISIGRAPP (3: IVAPP), pp. 40–51 (2018)
11. Karp, R.M.: Reducibility among combinatorial problems. Complexity of Computer Computations. The IBM Research Symposia Series, pp. 85–103. Springer, Boston (1972). https://doi.org/10.1007/978-1-4684-2001-2_9
12. Kaser, O., Lemire, D.: Tag-cloud drawing: Algorithms for cloud visualization. arXiv preprint cs/0703109 (2007)
13. Koh, K., Lee, B., Kim, B., Seo, J.: Maniwordle: providing flexible control over wordle. IEEE Trans. Vis. Comput. Graph. **16**(6), 1190–1197 (2010)
14. Le, T., Lauw, H.W.: Word clouds with latent variable analysis for visual comparison of documents (2016)
15. Lee, B., Riche, N.H., Karlson, A.K., Carpendale, S.: Sparkclouds: visualizing trends in tag clouds. IEEE Trans. Vis. Comput. Graph. **16**(6), 1182–1189 (2010)
16. Lohmann, S., Heimerl, F., Bopp, F., Burch, M., Ertl, T.: Concentri cloud: word cloud visualization for multiple text documents. In: 2015 19th International Conference on Information Visualisation, pp. 114–120. IEEE (2015)
17. Lohmann, S., Ziegler, J., Tetzlaff, L.: Comparison of tag cloud layouts: task-related performance and visual exploration. In: Gross, T., Gulliksen, J., Kotzé, P., Oestreicher, L., Palanque, P., Prates, R.O., Winckler, M. (eds.) INTERACT 2009. LNCS, vol. 5726, pp. 392–404. Springer, Heidelberg (2009). https://doi.org/10.1007/978-3-642-03655-2_43
18. Schütz, S., Pöckelmann, M.: Lera - explorative analyse komplexer textvarianten in editionsphilologie und diskursanalyse. In: Digital Humanities im deutschsprachigen Raum 2016 - Konferenzabstracts, pp. 249–253. Leipzig (2016), http://dhd2016.de/boa.pdf
19. Seifert, C., Kump, B., Kienreich, W., Granitzer, G., Granitzer, M.: On the beauty and usability of tag clouds. In: 2008 12th International Conference Information Visualisation. pp. 17–25. IEEE (2008)
20. Silva e Silva, L.G., Assunção, R.M.: Cowords: a probabilistic model for multiple word clouds. J. Appl. Stat. **45**(15), 2697–2717 (2018)
21. Strobelt, H., Spicker, M., Stoffel, A., Keim, D., Deussen, O.: Rolled-out wordles: a heuristic method for overlap removal of 2D data representatives. In: Computer Graphics Forum. vol. 31, pp. 1135–1144. Wiley Online Library (2012)
22. Vuillemot, R., Clement, T., Plaisant, C., Kumar, A.: What's being said near "martha"? exploring name entities in literary text collections. In: 2009 IEEE Symposium on Visual Analytics Science and Technology, pp. 107–114. IEEE (2009)
23. Wang, J., Dent, K.D., North, C.L.: Fisheye word cloud for temporal sentiment exploration. In: CHI 2013 Extended Abstracts on Human Factors in Computing Systems, pp. 1767–1772. ACM (2013)
24. Wanner, F., Jentner, W., Schreck, T., Stoffel, A., Sharalieva, L., Keim, D.A.: Integrated visual analysis of patterns in time series and text data-workflow and application to financial data analysis. Inf. Vis. **15**(1), 75–90 (2016)

# A Hierarchical Label Network
# for Multi-label EuroVoc Classification
# of Legislative Contents

Danielle Caled[(✉)], Miguel Won, Bruno Martins, and Mário J. Silva

INESC-ID, Instituto Superior Técnico, Universidade de Lisboa, Lisbon, Portugal
{dcaled,mjs}@inesc-id.pt, {miguelwon,bruno.g.martins}@tecnico.ulisboa.pt

**Abstract.** EuroVoc is a thesaurus maintained by the European Union Publication Office, used to describe and index legislative documents. The Eurovoc concepts are organized following a hierarchical structure, with 21 domains, 127 micro-thesauri terms, and more than 6,700 detailed descriptors. The large number of concepts in the EuroVoc thesaurus makes the manual classification of legal documents highly costly. In order to facilitate this classification work, we present two main contributions. The first one is the development of a hierarchical deep learning model to address the classification of legal documents according to the EuroVoc thesaurus. Instead of training a classifier for each level, our model allows the simultaneous prediction of the three levels of the EuroVoc thesaurus. Our second contribution concerns the proposal of a new legal corpus for evaluating the classification of documents written in Portuguese. Our proposed corpus, named EUR-Lex PT, contains more than 220k documents, labeled under the three EuroVoc hierarchical levels. Comparative experiments with other state-of-the-art models indicate that our approach has competitive results, at the same time offering the ability to interpret predictions through attention weights.

**Keywords:** Extreme multi-label classification ·
Classification of legal documents · Deep neural networks · EuroVoc

## 1 Introduction

EuroVoc is a multilingual thesaurus translated in all official languages of the European Union (EU). It has more than 6,700 detailed descriptors, hierarchically related to 127 micro-thesauri terms and 21 general domains. EuroVoc is maintained by the EU Publications Office, which is responsible for the publication of all legal documentation produced by the institutions of the EU. The thesaurus is mainly used as an indexing tool for the common needs of archiving and searching legal documentation. Given the importance of EuroVoc in the European legal context, several EU national parliaments also index their legislation according to the EuroVoc thesaurus. The classification of this documentation is generally carried out manually or semi-automatically with the

© Springer Nature Switzerland AG 2019
A. Doucet et al. (Eds.): TPDL 2019, LNCS 11799, pp. 238–252, 2019.
https://doi.org/10.1007/978-3-030-30760-8_21

help of software such as JEX [18]. Since the manual classification can be costly, several research studies have addressed the problem of automatically classifying legal documents according to the EuroVoc thesaurus [3,16,18].

This work advances this line of research, reporting on an initial assessment on the viability of using modern neural models for legal text classification. Specifically, we propose a hierarchical deep neural network that works simultaneously at three levels: domains, micro-thesauri, and descriptors. The proposed method outputs, for each document, a set of three multi-label classifications, one for each level. Our main goal was to create a EuroVoc classifier for the Portuguese language, envisioning the application to contents published in *Diário da República Eletrónico*, i.e., the official Portuguese gazette. Besides the neural model, an additional contribution of this work is the development of a new corpus, named EUR-Lex PT, for supporting the evaluation of methods for multi-label classification of legal documents. The EUR-Lex PT corpus is composed by more than 220k documents written in Portuguese and labeled under the three EuroVoc hierarchical levels. Previous studies addressing legal document classification according to EuroVoc have mostly focused on the English language, despite the interest in applying these methods also to other languages. The English datasets used in support of previous methods are also slightly smaller.

The next section gives a brief description of related work. The data collection that lead to the EUR-Lex PT corpus is explained in Sect. 3. Section 4 describes our hierarchical approach to handle EuroVoc classification. Section 5 reports the experimental methodology and the obtained results, contrasting the proposed method against several strong baselines. Finally, Sect. 6 presents conclusions and possible directions for future work.

## 2   Related Work

We considered two types of research studies related to the present work: (i) studies dedicated exclusively to the development of text classifiers according to EuroVoc descriptors; and (ii) previous work related to the field of Extreme-Multi-Label-Classification (XML), which deals with the task of classifying documents according to a high number of classes, possibly with more than one class per document (i.e., multi-label classification).

### 2.1   EuroVoc Classifiers

Several authors have described classifiers focused exclusively in the EuroVoc thesaurus. This is the case of the JRC EuroVoc Indexer (JEX), a publicly available software that can help users to classify legal documents with EuroVoc descriptors [18]. JEX first aggregates training documents per class and estimates heuristically a category embedding vector with the ranked list of typical word tokens for this class. Each new document is then classified according to the rank resulting from a cosine distance between each class embedding vector and the document embedding, obtained by counting the relative frequency of each word.

Boella et al. used Support-Vector-Machines (SVM), training one SVM for each class in a one-vs-all strategy [3]. Since most of the documents are classified with more than one descriptor, the authors propose to replicate each document among its labeled classes, in order to obtain a corpus of *mono-labeled* documents. At prediction time, a probability distribution is generated for each class, allowing the selection of the top-$k$ most likely classes. Šaric et al. used the same procedure to create an EuroVoc classifier for Croatian legal documents [16]. A fourth example is the work by Mencía et al. [11], which tested the use of perceptron-based classifiers, using several training strategies (e.g., pairwise one-versus-one, where one classifier is trained for each pair of classes).

## 2.2    Extreme Multi-label Classification

The eXtreme Multi-Label (XML) classification task has the main objective of predicting a subset of labels from a very large set of categories, possibly with a hierarchical arrangement. For text classification, XML traditionally works with corpora such as Wikipedia-500K ($\approx$500k labels), AmazonCat-13K ($\approx$13k labels), or EURLex-4K, a small set of Eur-Lex legal documents classified according to the EuroVoc thesaurus. These corpora are available at the Extreme Classification Repository[1]. One can also find several strategies to the problem in the literature, with the most common methods being divided into four main groups: one-vs-all linear models, tree ensembles, embedding-based approaches, and more recent methods that use deep learning. Next, we present a short description of each methodology, together with state-of-the-art approaches.

**One-vs-all approaches**, such as PD-Sparse [21] or DiSMEC [1], train an independent classifier (e.g., a linear model based on SVMs or logistic regression, leveraging bag-of-words representations for the documents) per label. These methods have high computational complexity both for training and predicting. PD-Sparse was proposed based on the assumption of sparse learning, using a margin-maximizing loss function combined with a $\ell_1$ penalty, to obtain a sparse solution both in the primal and in the dual spaces inherent to the XML problem. DiSMEC is a large-scale distributed model which takes advantage of parallelization for learning a linear classifier for each label. DiSMEC implements a two-layer parallelization architecture to gain significant training and predicting speedup: labels are separated into batches and sent to separate nodes consisting of sets of the available cores. This approach also controls the size of the generated models by removing spurious parameters in order to make fast predictions.

**Tree-based approaches** adopt the strategy of recursively partitioning the instance space by features at non-leaf nodes within a decision tree, and associating each leaf node to a simple classifier that is used to predict the active labels assigned to that node. These methods generally learn decision boundaries based on feature combinations to split the instance space at each node, thus making more robust predictions for sparse feature spaces [10]. Ensemble approaches,

---

[1] http://manikvarma.org/downloads/XC/XMLRepository.html.

combining multiple decision trees, are also common [15]. For instance, Pfas-treXML [9] creates trees by recursively partitioning nodes until the trees are fully grown. Then, the nodes are split in two by a hyperplane learned by opti-mizing a propensity scored objective function, which gives rewards according to correct tail label predictions. Each PfastreXML leaf contains a classifier based on a probabilistic model over labels. Although generally classified as tree-based, Parabel [15] is a hybrid method. It starts by learning an ensemble of labeled trees, which are further recursively partitioned into balanced groups. For each label contained by the node leaf, Parabel creates a one-vs-all classifier. For pre-dicting labels, Parabel traverses different paths to reach the one-vs-all classifiers in the leaves. The classifiers evaluate the probability of the labels being relevant, and then the ensemble makes predictions by averaging these probabilities.

**Embedding-based approaches** assume a correlation between labels and try to reduce the number of labels by projecting label vectors onto a low dimen-sional space. The labels are compressed for training and later decompressed for prediction. The main difference among the embedding methods is the strategy used for compression and decompression. SLEEC [2] is an embedding approach that learns non-linear label correlations by preserving the pairwise distances between only the closest label vectors. This method conducts the training by first partitioning the instances into clusters and learning a projection matrix for each partition in the label space. Predictions are then performed with a $k$-nearest neighbor classifier in the embedding space. However, SLEEC does not guarantee the assignment of similar labels to the same partition, and it also fails to consider the value of the distance between partitions in the prediction step. AnnexML [19] addresses these problems through a $k$-nearest neighbour graph-based app-roach, which considers training instances as vertices. AnnexML partitions the generated graph preserving its structure, and the sub-graphs are then divided into individual embedding spaces. XML is finally treated as a ranking problem.

**Deep learning approaches** explore a new way to represent documents. Instead of the simplistic bag-of-word representation from the previous meth-ods, most deep learning methods extract context-sensitive features from text. XML-CNN [10] was the first attempt to apply deep learning to XML prob-lems. This model uses a Convolutional Neural Network (CNN) with dynamic pooling for identifying multi-label co-occurrence patterns. XML-CNN, however, has two deficiencies: it does not take into account long-distance dependencies among words, and it attributes all words the same level of importance for dif-ferent labels. AttentionXML [22] handles these deficiencies by using a Recurrent Neural Network (RNN) instead of a CNN, also combining RNN representations through a multi-label attention mechanism.

## 3 Data Collection

For supporting the present work, we created a new corpus of European legal documents, which we called EUR-Lex PT. The corpus was extracted from the

EUR-Lex webportal[2], where documents are classified according to the EuroVoc thesaurus. As our main objective was to create a classifier for Portuguese contents, we only collected EU legal documentation written in Portuguese. We collected data published from 1987 up to 2018, given that Portugal became a member of EU in 1986, but during this year only a small number of documents was published in EUR-Lex. Besides the main text data (document title and body) and the EuroVoc concept descriptors, we have additionally extracted other relevant information such as publication date, authors, relationship with other documents, and CELEX unique identifiers. This last information is particularly relevant, since CELEX identifiers can allow the creation of a parallel corpus of the same legal publications written in different EU official languages.

We also obtained the EuroVoc thesaurus version 4.9, released on December the 20th of 2018 in the European Union Open Data Portal[3]. The EuroVoc follows a concept-based approach, having a vocabulary based on concepts which are language-independent of the terms representing them. The EuroVoc data not only contains the descriptors and respective codes, but also the micro-thesauri and domains. The domains in EuroVoc are divided into micro-thesauri, which correspond to concept schemes with subsets of concepts. The EuroVoc descriptors are lexical representations of concepts in a given language. Each detailed descriptor belongs to one or more micro-thesauri, and each micro-thesaurus term is assigned to a specific domain. For instance, for the descriptor *France*, we have as micro-thesauri identifiers *Europe*, *political geography* and *economic geography*. These three micro-thesauri identifiers belong to the domain *geography*. Thus, from each EuroVoc descriptor, we extracted all possible hierarchical micro-thesauri and the corresponding domains.

Besides the EuroVoc descriptors, we have included in the training process the hierarchical and more general information of the corresponding descriptors from the micro-thesauri and domains, also available in EuroVoc. Figure 1 shows the distribution of the number of EuroVoc identifiers per document, and Fig. 2 shows the number of documents per identifier for the domain and micro-thesaurus levels. Notice that only a small fraction of documents are mono-labeled, for which reason we have considered modeling the task as a multi-label classification problem. Figure 2 shows that the classification task is also hampered by the fact that the labels are highly unbalanced in the collected corpus. Thus, the traditional corpus division in training, validation, and test sub-sets must be done carefully. A simple split without considering the label's distributions could result in a highly an unrepresentative set, in respect to the original corpus. Therefore, splittings were performed according to an iterative stratification respecting the original label's distributions, as proposed by Sechidis et al. [17]. The test set contains 20% of the data, and we additionally split the development data (80%) into training (64%) and validation (16%) splits. Accordingly, the training, validation and test sets have 140,883; 35,189 and 44,254 documents, respectively, and the entire corpus has a vocabulary with 42,556 words. Table 1 presents descriptive statistics for the EUR-Lex PT corpus.

---

[2] http://eur-lex.europa.eu/homepage.html.

[3] http://data.europa.eu/euodp/data/dataset/eurovoc.

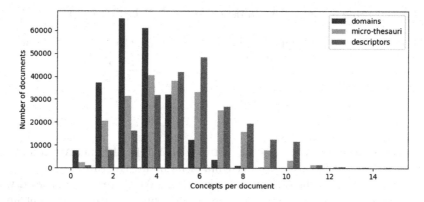

**Fig. 1.** Distribution for the number of EuroVoc concepts per document.

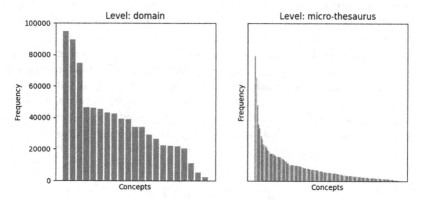

**Fig. 2.** Distribution for the number of documents per concept. *European Union, Geography* and *Trade* are the most frequent domains. At the micro-thesaurus level, *Economic Geography* and *Political Geography* are the most frequent.

## 4    Hierarchical Label Attention Neural Network

We propose the use of a deep neural network to simultaneously predict three levels of the EuroVoc thesaurus: domain, micro-thesauri and descriptors. Some previous XML methods, such as SLEEC or AnnexML, construct an embedding space based on the fact that many classes are correlated. These embedding spaces are constructed by clustering training samples into a label space, and correlated classes will end in clusters related to their co-occurrence frequency. We take advantage of the label correlation knowledge, within a neural network, by hierarchically including the broader EuroVoc levels of domain and micro-thesaurus. For example, the descriptor *rail transport* is more likely to co-occur with the descriptor *railway carriage* and both these descriptors are assigned to the micro-thesaurus *land transport*. For this reason, we have designed a network with three hierarchical outputs, where each output is used as input in the

Table 1. Descriptive statistics for the EUR-Lex PT corpus.

| Level | #concepts | Documents per concept | Concepts per document |
|---|---|---|---|
| Domain | 21 | ≈37,638.95 | ≈3.59 |
| Micro-thesaurus | 127 | ≈8,813.24 | ≈5.08 |
| Descriptor | 5,797 | ≈224.03 | ≈5.89 |

following deeper layer. We name the network Hierarchical Label Attention Network (HLAN), and Fig. 3 shows a schema of its main structure.

The main input is the original tokenized text. We represent each word with a word embedding [12] and then encode each document with a recurrent layer, followed by a context attention network. For the recurrent layer, we used a bidirectional Long Short-Term Memory (LSTM) [8] unit with a final concatenation of both directions, resulting in a final hidden representation $h$. For each word token $i$ from a sequence with $T$ tokens: $h_i = \overrightarrow{h}_i \oplus \overleftarrow{h}_i$, $i = 1, ..., T$.

The attention mechanism is the same used in several previous studies [4,20]. First, a word context vector $u_t$ is extracted from the LSTM hidden representation $h_i$, through the use of a fully-connected layer. This step is followed by the measurement of each word's importance, given by a softmax evaluation of the direct product of the word context by a general context vector, learned during training. The resulting weights are then used in a final weighted average of the hidden representation vectors $h_i$, that results in a single attention representation vector $d_i$. We show the full attention mechanism in Eqs. 1–3:

$$u_t = \tanh\left(W_w h_t + b_w\right) \tag{1}$$

$$\alpha_t = \frac{\exp\left(u_t . u_w\right)}{\sum_t \exp\left(u_t . u_w\right)} \tag{2}$$

$$d_i = \sum_t \alpha_t h_t. \tag{3}$$

In the previous equations, $t = 1, ..., T$ and $i = 1, ..., N$, with $T$ equaling the sequence length and $N$ corresponding to the total number of documents. We additionally note that we have included a dropout of 30% between the LSTM and the attention layer, and used the penalized hyperbolic tangent [5] as the LSTM activation function, and as the activation function for the LSTM recurrent step, given that previous studies have shown consistently better results for this particular choice, in several different NLP tasks.

To perform multi-label classification, we first include a fully-connected layer. This will produce a summarized representation from which we predict the vector domain label. For the following levels, we use the same representation produced by the fully-connected layer, concatenated with the higher level output prediction. For the micro-thesaurus level, we use the domain level prediction together with the original representation and for the descriptor level, we use the original representation together with the domain and micro-thesaurus

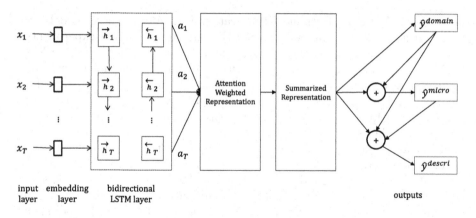

**Fig. 3.** General architecture for the HLAN classification model.

level predictions. In all three level predictions, we use a sigmoid activation function and the binary cross-entropy loss function, which is beneficial in the case of multi-label tasks [13]. The full classification structure is formalized in Eqs. 4–7:

$$I_i = W_1 d_i + b_1 \tag{4}$$

$$\hat{y}_i^{domain} = \sigma(W_{2,d} I_i + b_{2,d}) \tag{5}$$

$$\hat{y}_i^{micro} = \sigma(W_{2,m}(I_i \oplus \hat{y}_i^{domain}) + b_{2,m}) \tag{6}$$

$$\hat{y}_i^{descri} = \sigma(W_{2,de}(I_i \oplus \hat{y}_i^{domain} \oplus \hat{y}_i^{micro}) + b_{2,de}). \tag{7}$$

In the previous equations, $\hat{y}_i^{level}$ is the vector of prediction probabilities for the respective level, and $(W_{1,l}, b_{1,l})$ and $(W_{2,l}, b_{2,l})$ are the parameters matrix and bias terms of the first and second fully-connected layers, respectively. For each level of prediction, as stated earlier, we use a binary cross-entropy loss function, formulated for each document $i$ as follows:

$$L^l = \frac{1}{N}\frac{1}{L}\sum_i^N \sum_j^L [y_{ij}^l \log(\hat{y}_{ij}^l) + (1 - y_{ij}^l)\log(1 - \hat{y}_{ij}^l)]. \tag{8}$$

In the equation, $l$ runs over the three levels, $i$ by the number of instances, and $j$ by the number of classes for each level. The main loss is a weighted average of all individual losses, with the weights related to the complexity of the prediction task, as follows:

$$L = w_1 L^{domain} + w_2 L^{micro} + w_3 L^{descri}. \tag{9}$$

## 5  Experimental Evaluation

Through a set of experiments, we compared the proposed approach against an extensive set of baselines. The implementations of PD-Sparse, DiSMEC, PfastreXML, Parabel, AnnexML and XML-CNN were provided by the authors and made available in the Extreme Classification Repository. These models were tested with default parameters. The SLEEC version used on our experiments is publicly available as the Python package named `sleec_python`[4]. For the XML-CNN, instead of using the original English pre-trained 300-dimensional Glove embeddings, we employed the 300-dimensional Word2Vec CBOW model [7], trained on a large Portuguese corpus. This same pre-trained embedding model was employed for the proposed HLAN approach. We also tried to run experiments with the AttentionXML model. However, an implementation for this model is not publicly available and we were not able to reproduce it correctly.

In respect to the HLAN setup, we used an embedding layer with a vocabulary size of 30k and a maximum document length of 500 words (i.e., documents were clipped to this length). We used LSTM units with a hidden size of 256, and the fully-connected layer of Eq. 4 has an output size of 512. The experimental results were obtained for the test set, after 6 epochs of training using an Adam optimizer with a learning rate of 0.001 (i.e., the number of 6 iterations was based on an early-stopping criteria based on the loss function over the validation set). The final loss was estimated through the weighted sum of Eq. 9 with $w_1 = 0.001$, $w_2 = 0.01$ and $w_3 = 1$.

## 5.1 Evaluation Metrics

The literature generally evaluates extreme multi-label classification results using ranked-based evaluation metrics. This is due to the fact that each instance normally has few relevant labels. Thus, we evaluated the performance of the analyzed methods with precision at $k$ (P@k) and the normalized discounted cumulative gain at $k$ (nDCG@k), having $k \in \{1, 3, 5\}$.

$$P@k = \frac{1}{k} \sum_{l \in r_k(\hat{y})}^{k} y_l \tag{10}$$

$$DCG@k = \sum_{l \in r_k(\hat{y})}^{k} \frac{y_l}{\log(l+1)} \quad nDCG@k = \frac{DCG@k}{\sum_{l=1}^{\min(k,||y||_0)} \frac{1}{\log(l+1)}} \tag{11}$$

In the previous equations, $y \in \{0,1\}^L$ is the binary vector of true labels of a given document, $\hat{y} \in \mathbb{R}^L$ is the predicted score vector, $r_k(\hat{y})$ refers to the $k$ largest indices of $y$ ranked in descending order, and $||y||_0$ is the number of truly relevant labels. Both the P@k and the nDCG@k metrics are computed for each document in the test set and averaged over all the documents.

## 5.2 Results and Discussion

We carried experiments considering the three hierarchical levels of the EuroVoc thesaurus. The results are presented in Table 2 for the domain, micro-thesaurus,

---

[4] http://github.com/xiaohan2012/sleec_python.

**Table 2.** Results for EUR-Lex PT classification.

(a) Domains

| Model | nDCG@1 | nDCG@3 | nDCG@5 | P@1 | P@3 | P@5 |
|---|---|---|---|---|---|---|
| PD-Sparse | 0.956 | 0.887 | 0.886 | 0.956 | 0.795 | 0.598 |
| DiSMEC | 0.963 | 0.902 | 0.905 | 0.963 | 0.812 | 0.616 |
| PfastreXML | 0.954 | 0.892 | 0.899 | 0.954 | 0.803 | 0.613 |
| Parabel | 0.960 | 0.902 | 0.905 | 0.960 | 0.812 | 0.616 |
| SLEEC | 0.819 | 0.746 | 0.755 | 0.819 | 0.671 | 0.519 |
| AnnexML | 0.962 | 0.902 | **0.907** | 0.962 | 0.811 | **0.618** |
| XML-CNN | 0.918 | 0.876 | 0.878 | 0.918 | 0.792 | 0.598 |
| HLAN | **0.967** | **0.905** | **0.907** | **0.967** | **0.813** | 0.617 |

(b) Micro-thesauri

| Model | nDCG@1 | nDCG@3 | nDCG@5 | P@1 | P@3 | P@5 |
|---|---|---|---|---|---|---|
| PD-Sparse | 0.897 | 0.818 | 0.785 | 0.897 | 0.761 | 0.627 |
| DiSMEC | 0.938 | **0.873** | **0.907** | 0.938 | **0.820** | **0.687** |
| PfastreXML | 0.918 | 0.851 | 0.825 | 0.918 | 0.799 | 0.670 |
| Parabel | 0.934 | 0.871 | 0.845 | 0.934 | 0.819 | 0.686 |
| SLEEC | 0.734 | 0.665 | 0.641 | 0.734 | 0.623 | 0.522 |
| AnnexML | 0.934 | 0.867 | 0.840 | 0.934 | 0.814 | 0.681 |
| XML-CNN | 0.901 | 0.837 | 0.813 | 0.901 | 0.786 | 0.659 |
| HLAN | **0.940** | 0.872 | 0.843 | **0.940** | 0.818 | 0.682 |

(c) Descriptors

| Model | nDCG@1 | nDCG@3 | nDCG@5 | P@1 | P@3 | P@5 |
|---|---|---|---|---|---|---|
| PD-Sparse | 0.699 | 0.642 | 0.600 | 0.699 | 0.611 | 0.513 |
| DiSMEC | **0.885** | **0.815** | **0.907** | **0.885** | **0.780** | **0.659** |
| PfastreXML | 0.806 | 0.735 | 0.683 | 0.806 | 0.701 | 0.586 |
| Parabel | 0.867 | 0.799 | 0.747 | 0.867 | 0.765 | 0.645 |
| SLEEC | 0.596 | 0.530 | 0.485 | 0.596 | 0.502 | 0.410 |
| AnnexML | 0.864 | 0.786 | 0.729 | 0.864 | 0.749 | 0.624 |
| XML-CNN | 0.816 | 0.729 | 0.670 | 0.816 | 0.690 | 0.566 |
| HLAN | 0.865 | 0.784 | 0.723 | 0.865 | 0.746 | 0.617 |

and descriptor levels, respectively. A bootstrapping approach [6] was used to assess the statistical significance of the difference between HLAN and the (second) best method, for each EuroVoc level and evaluation metric. The results for the HLAN classifier were not found to be significantly different from those from the (second) best method, as in all cases we observed $p$-values above 0.1.

As shown in Table 2a, for domain classification, HLAN slightly outperforms the state-of-the-art methods in all settings, except at the P@5 metric. Particularly, HLAN achieved better results than the XML-CNN approach, i.e. the original deep learning model. Among the one-vs-all methods, the latest approach, DiSMEC, outperforms the original model (PD-Sparse). As expected, Parabel outperformed both the original one-vs-all (PD-Sparse) model and the tree-based classifier (PfastreXML), having similar results to DiSMEC, except at nDCG@k and P@k for $k = 1$. The model with the worst results was SLEEC, which might be because of the unsuccessful partition of the labels due to the small number of domains. By tackling SLEEC's deficiencies, AnnexML obtained a competitive performance, achieving similar results to the leading method. XML-CNN was easily outperformed by the other competitors (except SLEEC).

Table 2b presents the results for the micro-thesauri classification. We can observe a deterioration on the results of all methods, when compared to the domains classification. DiSMEC is the best classifier, overcoming the competitors in four of the six settings. HLAN was the second leading approach, being the best at nDCG@k and P@k for $k = 1$. Once again the original approaches were outperformed by the latest ones: PD-Sparse was outperformed by DiSMEC and Parabel, PfastreXML was also outperformed by Parabel, SLEEC was outperformed by AnnexML, and XML-CNN was outperformed by HLAN.

The results for the experiments on the descriptor level are reported in Table 2c. In this set of results we can notice a greater difference in the performance of the evaluated methods. Once again, DiSMEC is the best approach, outperforming the other classifiers at the descriptor level. Parabel, AnnexML and HLAN had slightly inferior performance than DiSMEC. PD-Sparse, PfastreXML, SLEEC, and XML-CNN had worse results, with a P@5 inferior to 60%.

Despite the slightly worse results in some settings, our HLAN approach has some interesting advantages. Our task was to classify a corpus according to three different levels of specificity. For each state-of-the-art model, we run the model three times in order to classify the domain, micro-thesaurus and descriptor levels. Alternatively, we could have returned the domain and micro-thesaurus terms that correspond to EuroVoc ancestors for the predicted descriptors, with a single model execution, but this would ignore other potentially relevant domains and micro-thesaurus terms. With HLAN, we can predict these three levels in a single execution, with a model that was directly trained to explore co-occurrences between class labels at the multiple levels of the EuroVoc hierarchy. Although the HLAN model could not significantly outperform all classifiers tested in all configurations, it still has competitive results and was able to beat the state-of-the-art deep learning baseline at all EuroVoc levels in all settings.

Perhaps even more interestingly, by leveraging neural attention, the proposed model can also offer result interpretability, by allowing users to see which parts of the input (i.e., which words) are attended to when making predictions. Figure 4 illustrates the attention weights calculated as shown in Eq. 2, for the contents of two documents (respectively with weights shown in red or in blue) from the testing set of EUR-Lex PT. The first example document was correctly assigned to EuroVoc descriptors *sunflower* and *oil seed rape*, and the figure shows the words *girassol* (sunflower) and *colza* having a significant impact. Our classification model also predicted the label *common organisation of markets* for this document, which although is not given in the EUR-Lex PT ground-truth, seems to closely related to the contents. In turn, the second document in Fig. 4 was correctly assigned to EuroVoc descriptors *cocoa* and *international agreement*. In this example, the words *cacau* (cocoa), *internacional* (international) and *conselho* (council) have significant weights.

REGULAMENTO (CEE) N° 91/87 DA COMISSÃO de 14 de Janeiro de 1987 que altera o coeficiente relativo aos montantes diferenciais para as sementes de colza, de nabita e de girassol REGULAMENTO (CEE) N° 91/87 DA COMISSÃO de 14 de janeiro de 1987 que altera o coeficiente relativo aos montantes diferenciais para as sementes de colza, de nabita e de girassol A COMISSÃO DAS COMUNIDADES EUROPEIAS, Tendo em conta o Tratado que institui a Comunidade Económica Europeia, Tendo em conta o Regulamento n° 136/66/CEE do Conselho de, 22 de Setembro de 1966, que estabelece organização comum de mercado no sector das matérias gordas (1), com a última redacção que lhe foi dada pelo regulamento (CEE) n° 1454/86 (2), Tendo em conta o Regulamento (CEE) n° 1569/72 do Conselho, de 22 de Julho de 1972, que prevê medidas especiais para as sementes de colza, de nabita e de girassol, (3) com a última redacção que lhe foi dada pelo regulamento (CEE) n° 1474/84 (4), e, nomeadamente, o n° 2 do seu artigo 2° A, Considerando que, com efeitos partir de 12 de Janeiro de 1987, as taxas centrais das diferentes moedas que fazem parte do sistema monetário europeu foram alteradas; que o coeficiente referido no n° 2 do artigo 2° A do Regulamento (CEE) n° 1569/72 deve ser, em consequência, alterado; que esta alteração deve ser aplicável partir de 15 de Janeiro de 1987; Considerando que as medidas previstas no presente regulamento estão em conformidade com parecer do Comité de Gestão das Matérias Gordas, ADOPTOU O PRESENTE REGULAMENTO: Artigo 1° O valor do coeficiente referido no n° 2 do artigo 2° A do Regulamento (CEE) n° 1569/72 é fixado em 1,125696. Artigo 2° O presente regulamento entra em vigor na data da sua publicação no Jornal Oficial das Comunidades Europeias. O presente regulamento é aplicável partir de 15 de Janeiro de 1987. O presente regulamento é obrigatório em todos os seus elementos e directamente aplicável em todos os Estados-membros. Feito em Bruxelas, em 14 de Janeiro de 1987. Pela Comissão Frans ANDRIESSEN

87/166/CEE: Decisão do Conselho de 16 de Janeiro de 1987 relativa à aplicação provisória do Acordo International de 1986 sobre o Cacau Decisão do Conselho de 16 de Janeiro de 1987 relativa à aplicação provisória do Acordo International de sobre Jornal Oficial n° L 069 de 12/03/1987 p. 0024 - 0024 Edição especial finlandesa: Capítulo 11 Fascículo 11 p. 0404 Edição especial sueca Capítulo 11 Fascículo 11 p. 0404 DECISÃO DO CONSELHO de 16 de Janeiro de 1987 relativa à aplicação provisória do Acordo Internacional de 1986 sobre Cacau (87/166/CEE) O CONSELHO DAS COMUNIDADES EUROPEIAS, Tendo em conta o Tratado que institui a Comunidade Económica Europeia e, nomeadamente, os seus arti- gos 113 e 116, Considerando que o Acordo internacional de 1980 sobre Cacau expirou em 30 de Setembro de 1986 e que foram tomadas disposições a fim de assegurar a manutenção do funcionamento do depósito regulador e dos seus recursos até 31 de Janeiro de 1987 ; considerando que, em aplicação da decisão do Conselho de 30 de Setembro de 1986, o Acordo Internacional de 1986 sobre Cacau foi assinado pela Comunidade e pelos seus Estados-membros em 30 de Setembro de 1986 ; Considerando que é conveniente assegurar a entrada em vigor, a título provisório, do Acordo de 1986 o mais tardar em 1 de Fevereiro de 1987 ; que, para o efeito, é necessário que a Comunidade e os seus Estados-membros, de acordo com os seus procedimentos internos necessários e logo após a sua conclusão, notifiquem Secretariado- -Geral da Organização das Nações Unidas da sua intenção de aplicarem o novo Acordo a título provisório, DECIDE: Artigo 1 A Comunidade e os Estados-membros, após a conclusão dos procedimentos internos necessários para o efeito, notificam o Secretariado-Geral da Organização das Nações Unidas da sua intenção de aplicarem Acordo Internacional de 1986 sobre Cacau, a título provisório, em conformidade com o seu artigo 70 O texto do Acordo vem anexo à presente decisão. Artigo 2 O Presidente do Conselho fica autorizado a designar a pessoa habilitada a depositar a notificação da aplicação provisória por parte da Comunidade. Feito em Bruxelas, em 16 de Janeiro de 1987. pelo Conselho O Presidente G. VERHOFSTADT

**Fig. 4.** Attention weights for two example documents from EUR-Lex PT.

# 6    Conclusions and Future Work

This paper presented a new corpus, EUR-Lex PT, for supporting the training and evaluation of models for the classification of legal documents according to the

EuroVoc thesaurus. EUR-Lex PT is classified with respect to the three EuroVoc hierarchical levels, namely, domains, micro-thesauri and descriptors. Due to the nature of the corpus, it can be used both in multi-label and in XML classification. We also proposed a hierarchical deep learning model to perform XML classification. Our proposed method, named HLAN, takes advantage of the hierarchical structure of the EUR-Lex PT corpus to make predictions. Unlike other traditional models, requiring three stages of training and prediction for each of the levels of the EuroVoc thesaurus, our model can be trained once and then process instances simultaneously for the three classification levels. In addition, we evaluated the performance of HLAN against several state-of-the-art XML methods. Experiments revealed that HLAN is suited for XML classification and can achieve competitive results to the other extreme models. The EUR-Lex PT corpus, HLAN source code, and additional supporting resources used in this study are available from a GitHub repository[5].

Despite the interesting results, there are also many possibilities for future improvements. For instance, instead of the Word2Vec embeddings used in our tests, we also plan to experiment with pre-trained contextual embeddings [14], which have achieved state-of-the-art results on several NLP benchmarks. Another possible extension relates to using multiple attention heads, e.g. one for each EuroVoc classification level instead of one per class as in the AttentionXML [22] neural network architecture, separately capturing the parts that are more relevant to each level.

**Acknowledgements.** This research was partially supported by grant UID/CEC/50021/2019 from Fundação para a Ciência e Tecnologia (FCT). We also gratefully acknowledge the support from NVIDIA Corporation, for the donation of the Titan Xp GPU used in our experiments, and the support from Imprensa Nacional-Casa da Moeda (INCM).

# References

1. Babbar, R., Schölkopf, B.: DiSMEC: distributed sparse machines for extreme multi-label classification. In: Proceedings of the ACM International Conference on Web Search and Data Mining (2017)
2. Bhatia, K., Jain, H., Kar, P., Varma, M., Jain, P.: Sparse local embeddings for extreme multi-label classification. In: Proceedings of the Conference on Neural Information Processing Systems (2015)
3. Boella, G., Di Caro, L., Lesmo, L., Rispoli, D., Robaldo, L.: Multi-label classification of legislative text into EuroVoc. In: Proceedings of the International Conference on Legal Knowledge and Information Systems (2012)
4. Duarte, F., Martins, B., Pinto, C.S., Silva, M.J.: Deep neural models forICD-10 coding of death certificates and autopsy reports in free-text. J. Biomed. Inform. **80**, 64–77 (2018)
5. Eger, S., Youssef, P., Gurevych, I.: Is it Time to Swish? Comparing Deep Learning Activation Functions Across NLP tasks. arXiv preprint arXiv:1901.02671 (2019)

---

[5] http://github.com/dcaled/EUR-Lex-PT.

6. Hall, P.: Theoretical comparison of bootstrap confidence intervals. Ann. Stat. **16**, 927–953 (1988)
7. Hartmann, N., Fonseca, E., Shulby, C., Treviso, M., Silva, J., Aluísio, S.: Portuguese word embeddings: evaluating on word analogies and natural language tasks. In: Proceedings of the Brazilian Symposium in Information and Human Language Technology (2017)
8. Hochreiter, S., Schmidhuber, J.: Long short-term memory. Neural Comput. **9**, 1735–1780 (1997)
9. Jain, H., Prabhu, Y., Varma, M.: Extreme multi-label loss functions for recommendation, tagging, ranking & other missing label applications. In: Proceedings of the ACM SIGKDD International Conference on Knowledge Discovery and Data Mining (2016)
10. Liu, J., Chang, W.C., Wu, Y., Yang, Y.: Deep learning for extreme multi-label text classification. In: Proceedings of the International ACM SIGIR Conference on Research and Development in Information Retrieval (2017)
11. Loza Mencía, E., Fürnkranz, J.: Efficient multilabel classification algorithms for large-scale problems in the legal domain. In: Francesconi, E., Montemagni, S., Peters, W., Tiscornia, D. (eds.) Semantic Processing of Legal Texts. LNCS (LNAI), vol. 6036, pp. 192–215. Springer, Heidelberg (2010). https://doi.org/10.1007/978-3-642-12837-0_11
12. Mikolov, T., Sutskever, I., Chen, K., Corrado, G.S., Dean, J.: Distributed representations of words and phrases and their compositionality. In: Proceedings of the Conference on Neural Information Processing Systems (2013)
13. Nam, J., Kim, J., Loza Mencía, E., Gurevych, I., Fürnkranz, J.: Large-scale multi-label text classification — revisiting neural networks. In: Calders, T., Esposito, F., Hüllermeier, E., Meo, R. (eds.) ECML PKDD 2014. LNCS (LNAI), vol. 8725, pp. 437–452. Springer, Heidelberg (2014). https://doi.org/10.1007/978-3-662-44851-9_28
14. Peters, E., et al.: Deep contextualized word representations. In: Proceedings of the Conference of the North American Chapter of the Association for Computational Linguistics (2018)
15. Prabhu, Y., Kag, A., Harsola, S., Agrawal, R., Varma, M.: Parabel: partitioned label trees for extreme classification with application to dynamic search advertising. In: Proceedings of the Conference on World Wide Web (2018)
16. Šaric, F., Bašic, B.D., Moens, M.F., Šnajder, J.: Multi-label classification of croatian legal documents using EuroVoc thesaurus. In: Proceedings of the Workshop on Semantic Processing of Legal Texts (2014)
17. Sechidis, K., Tsoumakas, G., Vlahavas, I.: On the stratification of multi-label data. In: Gunopulos, D., Hofmann, T., Malerba, D., Vazirgiannis, M. (eds.) ECML PKDD 2011. LNCS (LNAI), vol. 6913, pp. 145–158. Springer, Heidelberg (2011). https://doi.org/10.1007/978-3-642-23808-6_10
18. Steinberger, R., Ebrahim, M., Turchi, M.: JRC EuroVoc Indexer JEX - A freely available multi-label categorisation tool. arXiv preprint arXiv:1309.5223 (2013)
19. Tagami, Y.: AnnexML: approximate nearest neighbor search for extreme multi-label classification. In: Proceedings of the ACM SIGKDD International Conference on Knowledge Discovery and Data Mining (2017)
20. Yang, Z., Yang, D., Dyer, C., He, X., Smola, A., Hovy, E.: Hierarchical attention networks for document classification. In: Proceedings of the Conference of the North American Chapter of the Association for Computational Linguistics: Human Language Technologies (2016)

21. Yen, I.E.H., Huang, X., Ravikumar, P., Zhong, K., Dhillon, I.S.: PD-sparse: a primal and dual sparse approach to extreme multiclass and multilabel classification. In: Proceedings of the International Conference on Machine Learning (2016)
22. You, R., Dai, S., Zhang, Z., Mamitsuka, H., Zhu, S.: AttentionXML: Extreme Multi-Label Text Classification with Multi-Label Attention Based Recurrent Neural Networks. arXiv preprint arXiv:1811.01727 (2018)

# Can Language Inference Support Metadata Generation?

José María González Pinto$^{(\boxtimes)}$ (iD), Janus Wawrzinek (iD), Suma Kori, and Wolf-Tilo Balke (iD)

IFIS TU-Braunschweig, Mühlenpfordstrasse 23, 38106 Brunswick, Germany
{pinto, wawrzinek, balke}@ifis.cs.tu-bs.de,
kori@tu-braunschweig.de

**Abstract.** As more papers get included in Digital collections satisfying information needs is becoming harder. In particular, when the user searches for information beyond bibliographic metadata. The situation is even worse when the information need requires *a key aspect* of a paper that first needs to be annotated for indexing purposes and thus, allow searching. For instance, in the biomedical field this might apply to structured abstracts, e.g. 'background', 'objectives', 'results', 'methods' and 'conclusion'. Current state-of-the-art deep learning approaches can only succeed if a sufficiently large amount of annotated data is available for training purposes. However, annotating several thousands of documents is not only expensive, but due to the limited availability of experts often even infeasible. To alleviate this problem, we explore the use of *Language Inference* as a *universal feature* that once applied to a limited number of annotated documents can help to achieve high accuracy to generate the desired metadata. We show through our experiments the degree of success on the difficult task of generating the *structured metadata* of biomedical papers and its performance stability as we increase the number of examples. We compare our suggested approach with deep learning approaches such as Doc2Vec and show that language inference is up to two orders of magnitude better achieving up to 0.82 F1 scores.

**Keywords:** Digital libraries · Metadata generation · Language inference

## 1 Introduction

To help users satisfy complex information needs and explore the richness contained in the knowledge of Digital collections, information providers rely on indexing mechanisms using high-quality metadata. Furthermore, as more critical aspects of scientific manuscripts are discovered and used by the community, for instance, scientific claims [7, 8] to ensure high-quality content in Digital collections or structured abstracts in the biomedical field [9, 10, 12], the need to annotate documents with such first-class citizens increases. However, annotating documents is an expensive and time-consuming process. Current state-of-the-art deep learning approaches [13, 26] have succeeded in related tasks such as document classification but with one major caveat common to most of them: they require several thousands of annotated examples to

A. Doucet et al. (Eds.): TPDL 2019, LNCS 11799, pp. 253–264, 2019.
https://doi.org/10.1007/978-3-030-30760-8_22

learn useful features to deliver high-quality results. It is excellent that manual feature engineering with these deep learning models is not needed anymore. However, as resources are scarce annotating several thousands of documents is just unfeasible. However, current advances in the natural language community may help to solve this need in our community. In particular, language inference [2]. Language inference aims at instantiating computational models that help machines to learn useful general representations of language that can be used in different tasks. For instance, the case of InferSent [4] trained to distinguish whether a given pair of sentences contradict, are related, or one entails the other, have shown promising results. The question is whether this *universal representation of sentences* that were not explicitly trained on the biomedical domain can indeed be used as *features to generate high-quality biomedical metadata*?

Although some studies on using Language Inference to classification tasks exist see for instance [4], we still know little about its applicability in Digital libraries and in particular in scientific collections where the language complexity is higher with many acronyms and terminology variations. Furthermore, can language inference help when the number of examples is limited? In this paper, we shed new light into the suitability of language inference for metadata generation. In particular, we show in the biomedical field how InferSent can be used to generate high-quality structured abstracts using a handful of examples. In contrast, other deep learning approaches, such as Doc2Vec show lower performance. For information providers, our findings show promising results to alleviate the burden of not having enough annotated examples to deliver high-quality metadata.

In this paper, we explore *the potential of language inference, a computational model that learns general representations of natural language sentences,* as a useful feature extractor for metadata generation given a limited amount of labeled examples. In a nutshell, we provide through our work an interesting lens through which to look at the significant potential of Language Inference to benefit both information providers and users of scientific digital collections.

The rest of the paper is structured as follows: Sect. 2 is devoted to related work. Then we will introduce InferSent and our baseline Doc2Vec in more details. In Sect. 3, we describe the data used in our experiments where we empirically prove the potential of language inference for metadata generation. Finally, in Sect. 4, we provide a summary of our findings and point and future work.

## 2   Related Work

The successful semantics learned by word embeddings such as word2vec Mikolov, et al. [17], Glove by Pennington, et al. [19], FastTex by Bojanowski, et al. [1] and more recently a model called ELMo by Peters, et al. [20] have motivated a growing body of scientific literature to develop model representations to account for longer sequences of text such as sentences. One of the first attempts to perform such a task was relying on word embeddings and applying a simple average of the sentence's word vectors, some examples of this idea are the work of [16, 21]. Recent efforts have taken two different approaches to learn sentence embeddings, $d$-dimensional continuous vector representations of sentences, unsupervised, and supervised. One representative example of such efforts that use an unsupervised approach is the work of Kiros, et al. [14] called Skip-thought. Skip-thought builds on the core idea presented by Mikolov, et al. in [17] but instead of words as a core unit of information, Kiros, et al. use sentences. At its core, the model uses the current sentence to predict the sentence before and after it. Formally, Skip-thought uses the framework of encoder-decoder. Encoder-decoder models have shown a lot of success in neural machine translation [11, 22]. Thus, Skip-thought builds on these ideas to do the following: an encoder maps words to a sentence vector, and a decoder is used to generate the surrounding sentences. Another model inspired by Skip-thought is the work of [6] that instead of a recurrent neural model (RNN) used in Skip-thought uses a convolutional neural network as an encoder. Then, reconstruct the input sentence and its neighbor sentences using RNNs. The main problem with both approaches is that these models are prolonged to train in massive amounts of data. Thus, researches started to focus on methods that introduced important supervised tasks in the hope that the models will learn general representations of sentences that could be used on several tasks. An instantiation of these approaches is InferSent [4] and Google Universal Embeddings [3]. Both approaches were trained using the Stanford Natural Language Inference (SNLI) dataset (more details in the description of InferSent). The main difference between the two is that Google Universal Embeddings also uses unsupervised training. In particular, web sources such as Wikipedia, web news, web question-answer pages, and discussion forums. Secondly, the model that encodes the sentence uses an encoding sub-graph architecture. What is interesting about their sub-graph architecture is that it uses an attention mechanism to compute context-aware representations of words in a sentence that considers both the ordering and identity of other words. We decided to focus on InferSent because Google Universal Embeddings incorporate sources that go beyond our goal in this paper: to explore whether Language Inference can support metadata generation even when we have limited number of annotated documents.

In the rest of this section and for self-containment, we describe the two core models used in our experimental section. To do so, we provide a summary of the terminology used on the original papers. We will first describe InferSent [4] and then Doc2vec [15].

**InferSent.** The work of Conneau, et al. [4] introduces an approach called InferSent that aims at providing a universal sentence representation trained on the Stanford Natural Language Inference (SNLI) dataset [2]. Inspired by the success of word embeddings, where pre-trained word embeddings over a large corpus have been used to tackle other tasks, Conneau, A. et al. introduced a supervised task to learn sentence embeddings also from a large corpus. In particular, they used the SNLI dataset that comprises 570 K human-generated English sentence pairs that were manually labeled with one of three categories: entailment, contradiction, and neutral. The idea behind this dataset is to capture language inference, previously known as Textual Entailment (TE). The hypothesis of the work of Conneau, et al. is that the semantic nature of Natural Language Inference can help computational models to learn sentence embeddings in a supervised way [4]. Similar to the idea of learning word embeddings by learning $d$-dimensional vectors of a target word predicting its context words, the authors argue that sentence embeddings can be learned using Language Inference at its core. Afterward, the sentence embeddings model could be used in some general classification tasks such as sentiment on movies, product review, opinion polarity, among others. To discover a sentence encoder suitable for the task, they tried several different deep learning architectures including LSTM, GRU, BiLSTM with mean/max pooling, self-attentive network, and hierarchical convnet. Through a series of experiments, the BiLSTM with max pooling was found to outperform the other variants. Thus, the model that we used in our experiments is the one based on BiLSTM with max pooling. In a nutshell, InferSent is a model that once trained on a high-quality language inference supervised machine learning task, learns to represent sentences in $d$-dimensional semantic space with the potential to be used as a universal feature representation. More details about the model can be found in the paper that introduced the model [4]. In our work, we aim at providing insights about the potential of this model for metadata generation when we have a limited number of samples and how a given algorithm can be affected once it has more samples available.

**Doc2Vec.** The work of Le and Mikolov [15] introduced a model known as Paragraph Vector, popularized as Doc2Vec due to its connection with its predecessor word2vec, see [18]. The idea behind Doc2Vec is to learn in an unsupervised way, fixed-length feature representations from variable-length pieces of texts, such as sentences, paragraphs, and documents [15]. At the heart of the model is the idea of learning the paragraph vectors by predicting the surrounding words in contexts sampled from the paragraph.

In a nutshell, Doc2Vec introduces the idea of mapping each paragraph as a vector, and its incorporation with the concatenation of the word vectors within the paragraph are used to predict the next word in context. Thus, the paragraph vector is shared across all contexts generated from the same paragraph but not across paragraphs. However, the word vectors are shared across paragraphs [15].

Two models were proposed by the authors of Doc2Vec to learn paragraph vectors, building on the ideas mentioned above: the Distributed memory version (PV-DM) that uses the concatenation of the paragraph vector with the word vectors to predict the next word in a text window.

The second model named Distributed Bag of Words (PV-DBOW) does not preserve word order. In other words, it ignores the context words in the input, and instead, the model is trained to predict words randomly sampled from the paragraph output.

More details of the model can be found in the paper [15]. In our experiments, we use both models and compare them with InferSent.

## 3   Experimental Setting

First, we describe the Evaluations Corpus followed by presenting our Evaluations Datasets. Hereafter we explain our algorithm which we use to determine a class label using Doc2Vec and InferSent. Finally, we compare different models and present the results followed by a discussion.

## 3.1   Experimental Set-up

*Corpus.* With 29 million citations, PubMed is one of the largest digital libraries in the biomedical field of which 4,226,200 are structured abstracts. Structured abstracts, as stated by the US National Library of Medicine[1], have several advantages for authors and readers. Structured abstracts assist health professionals in selecting clinically relevant and methodologically valid journal articles. They also guide authors in summarizing the content of their manuscripts precisely, facilitate the peer-review process for manuscripts submitted for publication, and enhance computerized literature searching [9, 10]. Each structured abstract consists of five different metadata classes and each class are labeled either with the class Background, Methods, Objective, Results, or Conclusions. Also, each section can consist of several sentences. In our evaluation, we use only the structured PubMed abstracts.

*Evaluation-Datasets.* We aim to assign one of the five section metadata classes to the individual sentences of an unstructured abstract, e.g., sentence s belongs to the metadata class Methodology. Therefore, our datasets generally consist of the pair $\langle s, c \rangle$ where $s$ is a sentence and $c$ is the metadata class. Our focus in the investigations is on the use case that only a few labeled data may be available, and this may affect the classification accuracy. Therefore, we examine the different approaches with data sets of different sizes. Thus, by sampling the $\langle s, c \rangle$ pairs from the corpus we generate a total of 6 datasets of the following sizes: (1) 4000 pairs, (2) 24,000 pairs, (3) 48,000 pairs, (4) 100,000 pairs, (5) 200,000 pairs, and (6) 400,000 pairs. The datasets are disjoint and balanced for each metadata class.

*Sentence-Embedding Models.* In our evaluation, we compare the accuracy of Doc2-Vec with the results that can be achieved with InferSent. Furthermore, we train Doc2Vec with a DBOW as well as with a DM architecture. For InferSent, we use the pre-trained models from [3] where one model was trained using Glove, and the second Model was trained using FastText.

*Model Optimization.* InferSent models are already optimized regarding hyperparameters. In order to allow a fair comparison between the different approaches, we have investigated in our experiments with Doc2Vec the hyperparameters window-size and dimension-size using grid search. We achieved the best values with a window size of 15 and a dimension size of 300. Therefore, we used in all our experiments this setting for Doc2Vec training.

## 3.2   Evaluation of the Models

The steps that we used to evaluate the models can be divided into the following four steps (Fig. 1):

---

[1]   https://www.nlm.nih.gov/bsd/policy/structured_abstracts.html

**Fig. 1.** Summarization of the different evaluation steps for Doc2Vec and InferSent models.

1. Text Pre-Processing: Our pre-processing of the individual sentences of a dataset is limited to the removal of (default) stop words using the Natural Language Tool Kit (NLTK). Also we lowercase all words before training.
2. Model Training: InferSent models are already pre-trained so that we only have to train the Doc2Vec models (DBOW, DM) on our datasets. For the Doc2Vec training, we divide the described datasets into a training and a test dataset. In our experiments, we train the Doc2Vec models on 75% of the data and use the remaining data for later testing.
3. Vector Extraction: In the next step, we extract the vector representations for each sentence as well as from each model. In the case of the Doc2Vec models, we extract the sentence vectors using sentence-ids. Since the Doc2Vec models were trained with 75% of a dataset, we also need a vector representation of the remaining 25% of the dataset's records for later testing. Thus, to get a vector representation from Doc2Vec model after training, we use the *infer_vector* function. In the case of InferSent since we use pre-trained model, we rely on the *encoder* function to get a vector representation for all the sentences.
4. Logistic Regression Model Training: Next, we use the extracted sentence-vectors to train a regression model. The goal is for the model to learn a metadata class from the extracted vectors. In our experiments, we train one regression model for each Sentence Embedding Model we described, using 75% of the data set for training and the remaining 25% for testing of the regression model. For each dataset and model, we measure the precision, recall, and F1 score.

We have performed the steps described above on all data sets, and show a summary of the results in Fig. 2. As expected, the quality, measured by F1 scores, for all models increases with the size of the dataset. What surprised us, however, was how much better the InferSent models perform in comparison to Doc2Vec models, although Doc2Vec was trained on the medical abstracts and InferSent was not. The pre-trained InferSent models seem to have learned a universal and inherent sentence semantics, which is also reflected in the abstracts' sentences and in which the metadata classes can be determined with a certain degree of success (F1 score up to 82%). This makes these models interesting as an alternative approach for complex classification tasks for metadata generation if only a few training data is available.

*Why does Doc2Vec trained with DBOW lead to better results compared to DM?* The DBOW model performs much better than the DM model, although it was shown in [15] that the DM architecture on average leads to better results because the order of the words is preserved. How can this be reconciled with our results? In [15], the documents used for training consist not of single sentences but instead of many paragraphs. In our case, the document size seems to be the decisive factor for the rather poor performance of the DM architecture.

### Doc2Vec vs. InferSent Analysis

We contrast the results of the best Doc2Vec model (DBOW) and the best InferSent model (InferSent 2) in Tables 1 and 2. Let us first consider Table 1, where we show the performance of the models per metadata class using the smallest dataset. We can observe that DBOW is outperformed in every metadata class by a large margin. In average, the InferSent model achieves 16 points above the DBOW model. When contrasting per metadata class we can observe that both models achieved the lowest F1 score in the 'Background' metadata class. However, even in this case the differences are interesting to discuss: InferSent 2 achieving a 0.53 F1 score while DBOW fifteen points below. Indeed, the differences that we can observe are remarkable.

Furthermore, both models achieve the highest F1 score in the 'Methods' metadata class. However, InferSent 2 with an F1 score of 0.76, thirteen points above DBOW. We can observe similar behavior in Table 2, where we show the results of the models using the biggest dataset available. Once more, the 'Background' metadata class was the most difficult one for both models. However, InferSent 2 performed up to 25 points better than DBOW achieving an F1 score of 0.80. We observe the same behavior when comparing the metadata class with the highest F1 score: InferSent 2 with more than 20 points above DBOW.

What is also remarkable is that DBOW obtained an F1 score average of 0.66 with the biggest dataset while InferSent 2 was already able to obtain the same average but with the smallest dataset and that means with 1% of the data that DBOW had to use to reach 0.66. This finding reveals the impact of Language Inference and its potential to help ongoing efforts for metadata generation in different fields.

In summary, we can observe that models using Language Inference outperformed Doc2Vec models by a large margin no matter the size of the dataset used. To assess the statistical significance of the differences between DBOW and InferSent 2 over all the datasets, we used a t-test. With a p-value of 1.7397E-17 ($p < 0.001$) we can conclude that differences between the models are significant. Furthermore, we also performed a t-test analysis over the two InferSent models because we observed small differences and even no differences in F1 scores, for instance, in Dataset 4. With a p-value of 0.0735 ($p > 0.001$) we can conclude that differences observed are not significant. Thus, using a pre-trained model with Glove vectors or FastText vectors resulted in negligible margin differences.

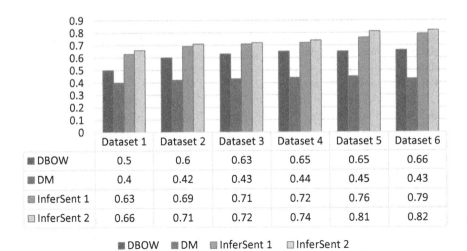

**Fig. 2.** Overall F1 score summary

**Table 1.** Results with DBOW and InferSent 2 using dataset 1

|  | Precision | Recall | F1 |
|---|---|---|---|
| Background | | | |
| -DBOW | 0.37 | 0.38 | 0.38 |
| -InferSent 2 | 0.54 | 0.52 | 0.53 |
| Conclusions | | | |
| -DBOW | 0.45 | 0.50 | 0.47 |
| -InferSent 2 | 0.64 | 0.70 | 0.67 |
| Methods | | | |
| -DBOW | 0.61 | 0.65 | 0.63 |
| -InferSent 2 | 0.74 | 0.79 | 0.76 |
| Objective | | | |
| -DBOW | 0.48 | 0.45 | 0.47 |
| -InferSent 2 | 0.65 | 0.56 | 0.61 |
| Results | | | |
| -DBOW | 0.59 | 0.50 | 0.54 |
| -InferSent 2 | 0.72 | 0.73 | 0.73 |
| AVG | | | |
| -DBOW | 0.50 | 0.51 | 0.50 |
| -InferSent 2 | 0.66 | 0.66 | 0.66 |

For completeness of our analysis, we also calculated a t-test between DBOW and DM, and with a p-value of 3.0975E-16, we can conclude that differences between the two models are indeed statistically significant.

**Table 2.** Results with DBOW and InferSent 2 using Dataset 6

|  | Precision | Recall | F1 |
|---|---|---|---|
| Background |  |  |  |
| -DBOW | 0.57 | 0.52 | 0.55 |
| -InferSent 2 | 0.81 | 0.79 | 0.80 |
| Conclusions |  |  |  |
| -DBOW | 0.68 | 0.68 | 0.68 |
| -InferSent 2 | 0.83 | 0.84 | 0.84 |
| Methods |  |  |  |
| -DBOW | 0.72 | 0.77 | 0.75 |
| -InferSent 2 | 0.84 | 0.88 | 0.86 |
| Objective |  |  |  |
| -DBOW | 0.67 | 0.62 | 0.64 |
| -InferSent 2 | 0.79 | 0.84 | 0.80 |
| Results |  |  |  |
| -DBOW | 0.67 | 0.74 | 0.70 |
| -InferSent 2 | 0.85 | 0.85 | 0.83 |
| AVG |  |  |  |
| -DBOW | 0.66 | 0.67 | 0.66 |
| -InferSent 2 | 0.82 | 0.83 | 0.82 |

Despite an average of 0.66 F1 score in the smallest dataset with the InferSent model, the result obtained look promising. Indeed, the model could be a valuable alternative in cases where getting more annotated data is unrealistic.

One way to improve our current results is to enhance the InferSent model by adding concept embeddings from the Unified Medical Language System UMLS, such as in [24] but constraining them to maintain the semantic associations that exist. This strategy is known in the community as retrofitting, see [5], and it has been shown to improve word embeddings in general.

Our proposed enhancement constitutes part of our current efforts in our attempt to tune the model and assess the impact on its performance.

## 4    Conclusions and Future Work

In this paper, we have shown the potential of Language Inference for metadata generation. In particular, we evaluated InferSent considering the limited availability of annotated data. We focus on the biomedical field in the challenging task of annotating abstracts with distinct labels such as 'background', 'objective', 'methods', 'results', and 'conclusions'.

We showed the stability of performance of language inference as we vary the number of samples that a classification algorithm can have compared to the deep learning model Paragraph vector to assess the value. To our surprise, the language inference model outperformed Doc2Vec by a significant margin in the experiments that we performed. Even with a handful of examples using a logistic regression model trained using language inference vector representations, we were able to achieve promising results. These findings suggest the value of the role language inference as the basis for metadata generation, opening a new opportunity for information providers to support users and their complex information needs.

To further assess the quality of language inference in our task, we will conduct a user study with our experts to evaluate a representative sample of manuscripts that currently do not have structured metadata. To do so, we will contrast the level of agreement between our experts and the results of the different models trained using different sizes of samples. As another future line of work, we will also explore the potential of language inference to generate descriptive summaries of our ongoing efforts on semantic facettation in Pharmaceutical Collections [25].

Finally, we believe we have just started to see the potential of Language Inference for Digital Libraries using metadata generation in biomedicine as a use case. However, some other tasks relevant to our Digital library community could also benefit and may be worth investigating. For instance, consider the task of ranking documents or assessing the semantic similarity between documents.

We hypothesize that Language Inference could also have an impact on some other relevant, challenging tasks within our community, such as advancing ongoing efforts for automatic subject indexing of shorts texts [23].

# References

1. Bojanowski, P., et al.: Enriching word vectors with subword information. Trans. Assoc. Comput. Linguist. **5**, 135–146 (2016)
2. Bowman, S.R., et al.: A large annotated corpus for learning natural language inference. In: Proceedings of the 2015 Conference on Empirical Methods in Natural Language Processing (EMNLP). Association for Computational Linguistics (2015)
3. Cer, D., et al.: Universal sentence encoder. In: Proceedings of the 2018 Conference on Empirical Methods in Natural Language Processing, pp. 169–174. Association for Computational Linguistics, Brussels, Belgium (2018)
4. Conneau, A., et al.: Supervised learning of universal sentence representations from natural language inference data. In: Proceedings of the 2017 Conference on Empirical Methods in Natural Language Processing, pp. 670–680. Association for Computational Linguistics, Copenhagen, Denmark (2017)
5. Faruqui, M., et al.: Retrofitting word vectors to semantic lexicons. In: Proceedings of the 2015 Conference of the North American Chapter of the Association for Computational Linguistics: Human Language Technologies, pp. 1606–1615. Association for Computational Linguistics (2015)
6. Gan, Z., et al.: Learning generic sentence representations using convolutional neural networks. In: Proceedings of the 2017 Conference on Empirical Methods in Natural Language Processing, pp. 2390–2400. Association for Computational Linguistics, Copenhagen, Denmark (2017)
7. González Pinto, J.M., Balke, W.-T.: Can plausibility help to support high quality content in digital libraries? In: TPDL 2017 – 21st International Conference on Theory and Practice of Digital Libraries, pp. 169–180. Springer International Publishing, Thessaloniki, Greece (2017)

8. González Pinto, J.M., Balke, W.-T.: Assessing plausibility of scientific claims to support high-quality content in digital collections. Int. J. Digit. Libr. **19**(59), 1–14 (2018)

9. Haynes, R.B., et al.: More informative abstracts revisited. Ann. Intern. Med. **113**(1), 69–76 (1990)

10. Hayward, R.S.A., et al.: More informative abstracts of articles describing clinical practice guidelines. Ann. Intern. Med. **118**(9), 731–737 (1993)

11. Kalchbrenner, N., Blunsom, P.: Recurrent continuous translation models. In: Proceedings of the 2013 Conference on Empirical Methods in Natural Language Processing, pp. 1700–1709. Association for Computational Linguistics, Seattle, Washington, USA (2013)

12. Kilicoglu, H., et al.: SemMedDB: a PubMed-scale repository of biomedical semantic predications. J. Bioinform. **28**(23), 3158–3160 (2012)

13. Kim, Y.: Convolutional neural networks for sentence classification. In: Proceedings of the 2014 Conference on Empirical Methods in Natural Language Processing (EMNLP), pp. 1746–1751. Association for Computational Linguistics, Doha, Qatar (2014)

14. Kiros, R., et al.: Skip-thought vectors. In: Cortes, C., et al. (eds.) Advances in Neural Information Processing Systems, 28, pp. 3294–3302. Curran Associates Inc, Red Hook (2015)

15. Le, Q., Mikolov, T.: Distributed representations of sentences and documents. In: Jebara, E.P. X. (ed.) International Conference on Machine Learning - ICML 2014, pp. 1188–1196. PMLR, Bejing, China (2014)

16. Lev, G., et al.: In defense of word embedding for generic text representation. Lect. Notes Comput. Sci. (including Subser. Lect. Notes Artif. Intell. Lect. Notes Bioinformatics) **9103**, 35–50 (2015)

17. Mikolov, T., et al.: Distributed representations of words and phrases and their compositionality. In: Proceedings of the 26th International Conference on Neural Information Processing Systems, pp. 3111–3119. Curran Associates Inc., Lake Tahoe, Nevada (2013)

18. Mikolov, T., et al.: Efficient estimation of word representations in vector space. In: Proceedings of the International Conference on Learning Representations (ICLR 2013), pp. 1–12. arXiv, Scottsdale, Arizona USA (2013)

19. Pennington, J., et al.: Glove: global vectors for word representation. In: Proceedings of the 2014 Conference on Empirical Methods in Natural Language Processing (EMNLP), pp. 1532–1543. Association for Computational Linguistics, Doha, Qatar (2014)

20. Peters, M., et al.: Deep contextualized word representations. In: Proceedings of the 2018 Conference of the North American Chapter of the Association for Computational Linguistics: Human Language Technologies, vol. 1 (Long Papers), pp. 2227–2237. Association for Computational Linguistics, New Orleans, Louisiana (2018)

21. Arora, S., Liang, Y., Tengyu, M.: A simple but tough-to-beat baseline for sentence embeddings. In: 5th International Conference on Learning Representations (ICLR 2017), Toulon, France (2017)

22. Sutskever, I., et al.: Sequence to Sequence Learning with Neural Networks. NIPS, 9 (2014)

23. Toepfer, M., Seifert, C.: Content-based quality estimation for automatic subject indexing of short texts under precision and recall constraints. In: Méndez, E., et al. (eds.) Digital Libraries for Open Knowledge (TPDL 2018), pp. 3–15. Springer International Publishing, Cham (2018). https://doi.org/10.1007/978-3-030-00066-0_1

24. De Vine, L., et al.: Medical semantic similarity with a neural language model. In: Proceedings of the 23rd ACM International Conference on Information and Knowledge Management, pp. 1819–1822. ACM, New York, NY, USA (2014)

25. Wawrzinek, J., Balke, W.-T.: Semantic facettation in pharmaceutical collections using deep learning for active substance contextualization. In: Choemprayong, S., Crestani, F., Cunningham, S.J. (eds.) ICADL 2017. LNCS, vol. 10647, pp. 41–53. Springer, Cham (2017). https://doi.org/10.1007/978-3-319-70232-2_4
26. Zhang, Y., Wallace, B.: A sensitivity analysis of (and practitioners' guide to) convolutional neural networks for sentence classification. In: Proceedings of the 8th International Joint Conference on Natural Language Processing, pp. 253–263. Asian Federation of Natural Language Processing, Taipei, Taiwan (2017)

# Information Governance Maturity Assessment Using Enterprise Architecture Model Analysis and Description Logics

Diogo Proença[1]([envelope]) [iD] and José Borbinha[1,2] [iD]

[1] INESC-ID - Instituto de Engenharia de Sistemas e Computadores Investigação
e Desenvolvimento, Lisbon, Portugal
{diogo.proenca, jlb}@tecnico.ulisboa.pt
[2] Instituto Superior Técnico, Universidade de Lisboa, Lisbon, Portugal

**Abstract.** A Maturity Model represents a path towards an increasingly organized and systematic way of doing business. It is therefore a widely used
technique valuable to assess certain aspects of organizations, as for example
business processes. A maturity assessment can enable stakeholders to clearly
identify strengths and improvement points, and prioritize actions in order to
reach higher maturity levels. Doing maturity assessments can range from simple
self-assessment questionnaires to full-blown assessment methods, such as those
recommended by the ISO/IEC TS 33030 or the SEI SCAMPI. A main caveat of
these assessments is the resources they encompass. In addition, many times the
lack of automation renders benchmarks not possible. Assuming that the widespread of Enterprise Architecture practices is making the modeling of business
domains a fact, and considering the recent state of the art on the representation
of those models as ontologies, this paper proposes how existing semantic
technology can be used to automate Information Governance maturity assessment of real organizations by automating the analysis of enterprise architecture
models in ArchiMate.

**Keywords:** Information governance · Enterprise architecture ·
Maturity model · Ontology · Description Logics · ArchiMate · OWL

## 1 Introduction

A Maturity Model (MM) is a technique that, when applied to relevant aspects of the
organizations, can provide: (1) A measuring for auditing and benchmarking; (2) A
measuring of progress assessment against objectives; (3) An understanding of
strengths, weaknesses and opportunities (which can support decision making concerning strategy and project portfolio management).

Usually a MM consists of a number of "maturity levels", from the lowest to the
highest, often five (for example Initial, Managed, Defined, Quantitatively Managed and
Optimizing. However, the number of levels can vary, depending on the domain and the
concerns motivating the model).

This technique goes back to [1], having great visibility with the Software Engineering Institute Capability Maturity Model Integration (CMMI) [2, 11] and the

© Springer Nature Switzerland AG 2019
A. Doucet et al. (Eds.): TPDL 2019, LNCS 11799, pp. 265–279, 2019.
https://doi.org/10.1007/978-3-030-30760-8_23

ISO/IEC 15504 [3]. Both these key references were born in the Software Engineering domain, culminating decades of development and refinement of the corresponding models. Moreover, there is certification for these two references, as they are the de facto assessment techniques used when benchmarking organizations for their software engineering process implementation and maturity. As such, in order for the results to be comparable, there is a detailed maturity assessment method behind each of these MMs. These methods detail how to plan and conduct an assessment, how the maturity levels are calculated and how to present the results to the organization. These methods make each assessment repeatable and comparable with results from other organizations, allowing for benchmarking.

In the computer science domain, we can find several definitions for ontologies. One of the most widely used definitions describes ontologies as a "formal, explicit specification of a shared conceptualization" [4]. Conceptualization refers to an "abstract, simplified view of the world" [5], containing "the objects, concepts, and other entities that are assumed to exist in some area of interest and the relationships that hold among them" [6]. The Web Ontology Language (OWL) is a "semantic web language designed to represent rich and complex knowledge about things, groups of things, and relations between things" [7]. Moreover, the use of ontologies and computational inference mechanisms for representing and analyzing Enterprise Architecture (EA) models has already been proven in [8], and the use of such mechanisms for the purpose of supporting maturity assessment methods has been demonstrated in [10].

This paper discusses how to use Description Logics (DL) and EA models expressed as ontologies for the automation of the assessment of a maturity model for information governance already proposed in [9] named A2MIGO. For that purpose, it introduces the related work on ontologies and DL. Then, based on the findings provided by such analysis, it proposes an architecture template for A2MIGO including the ArchiMate models and DL queries necessary to perform the assessment. It then demonstrates the use of such constructs, following the application methods proposed in [10], in real scenarios by performing a maturity assessment to seven organizations and detailing the results, which takes advantage of the expressive power of DL for enterprise architecture model analysis and maturity level determination.

The structure of paper is as follows. Section 2 presents related work in the domain of Ontologies and DL. Then, Sect. 3 describes a proposal in terms of how to use EA models analysis and DL to automate MM assessments. A demonstration of the proposal in compliance analysis of specific information governance implementations using seven organizational scenarios is in Sect. 4. Finally, Sect. 5 presents conclusions on this work.

# 2 Background

In this section, we describe relevant related work in Ontologies and DL.

## 2.1 Ontologies

The term ontology originates on the Greek language, being a combination of "ontos" (being) and "logos" (word) [12]. From the perspective of philosophy, ontology is the "systematic explanation of existence" [13]. In the computer science domain, there are several definitions for the term. One of the most widely used definitions is in [4], building upon earlier definitions provided in [14] and [15]. Such definition describes ontologies as a "formal, explicit specification of a shared conceptualization" [4]. According to [5], "conceptualization" refers to an "abstract, simplified view of the world", containing "the objects, concepts, and other entities that are assumed to exist in some area of interest and the relationships that hold among them" [6]. "Explicit" refers to the explicit definition of the "type of concepts used, and the constraints on their use" [4]. "Formal" refers to the fact that the conceptualization "should be machine readable" [4]. "Shared", reflects that the ontology "captures consensual knowledge" shared between several parties [4].

We can classify the uses of ontologies into three categories [16]: human communication, interoperability, and systems engineering. In human communication, ontologies reduce conceptual and terminological confusion and enable shared understandings between "people with different needs and viewpoints arising from their particular contexts" [16]. When used for interoperability ends, it can support the exchange of data with success among heterogeneous sources. When engineering systems, informal (simple) ontologies can be the basis for manual checking of designs against specifications, to improve systems reliability; ontologies can also foster reusability, enabling the reuse of knowledge models in new applications (in this case, ontologies are used to make the underlying assumptions of software component design explicit [12, 16]). An overview of research domains making use of ontologies is in [17], listing for example: "knowledge engineering, knowledge representation, qualitative modelling, language engineering, database design, information modelling, information integration, object-oriented analysis, information retrieval and extraction, knowledge management and organization, and agent-based systems design".

## 2.2 Description Logics

DL is "a family if knowledge representation formalisms that represent the knowledge of an application domain (the "world") by first defining the relevant concepts of the domain (its terminology), and then using these concepts to specify properties of objects and individuals occurring in the domain (the world description)" [18] and can be seen as a "decidable fragment of first-order logic" [19]. Using this technique, the description of a domain consists of concepts, roles and individuals. Logical statements named axioms make possible to declare relations between roles and concepts. There are several types of DL, which differ on their expressivity. The DL language is $\mathcal{AL}$ which stands for attributive language. $\mathcal{AL}$ is a minimal language which can be seen as a family of languages which are deemed extensions of $\mathcal{AL}$. One example is $\mathcal{ALC}$ which stands for attributive language with complements. $\mathcal{ALC}$ is the most widely used DL in reasoners and is obtained by adding a negation complement operator ($\neg$) to $\mathcal{AL}$.

Axioms in DL can be of two kinds, terminological or assertional. Terminological axioms describe concepts and properties for the concepts, while assertional axioms are statements compatible with the terminological axioms about individuals belonging to the concepts. A TBox is any finite set of terminological axioms, while an ABox is a finite set of assertional axioms. The TBox and ABox statements make up a knowledge base (KB) and has semantics that make it equivalent to a set of axioms in first-order predicate logic. The most used form of TBox axioms are called general concept inclusions [20]. ABox can contain two kinds of axioms, "one for asserting that an individual is an instance of a given concept, and the other for asserting that a pair of individuals is an instance of a given role" [20].

## 3   Automated Maturity Model Assessment

Current maturity assessment methods focus on highly complex and specialized tasks performed by competent assessors in an organizational context. These tasks mainly focus on manually collecting evidence to substantiate the maturity level calculation. Because of the complexity of these methods, maturity assessment becomes an expensive and burdensome activity for organizations.

These methods usually start by creating an assessment plan, which describes how to conduct the assessment, as well as, the schedule, people involved, necessary documents and how to collect evidence. Then a group of assessors, denominated assessment team follows the assessment plan, they collect all the necessary evidence, calculate the maturity levels and assemble the assessment report, which details the findings and maturity levels of the assessment. Then, based on the assessment results, the organization can plan for improvement by following an improvement plan.

As such, the objective is to develop methods and techniques to automate maturity assessment. There are several examples of models used to represent an organization architecture, such as, ArchiMate, BPMN or UML. These models are descriptive and can be detailed enough to allow to perform, to some extent, maturity assessment. For example, the collected evidence from an organization can be synthetized into a set of model representations that to use when analyzing and calculating the maturity levels.

However, in order for these models to become relevant for maturity assessment there should be a formal representation for both MMs and model representations.

One hypothesis is that it is possible to represent them as ontologies. Then, by representing MMs and EA models of real organizational scenarios using ontologies we can verify if the organizational models, as represented, match the requirements to reach a certain maturity level using ontology query and reasoning techniques, such as SPARQL and DL inference.

The final objective is thus to identify how these methods and techniques can be used in existing maturity assessment methods, so that they can be relevant to enable the automation of certain aspects of maturity assessment, such as, the maturity level determination. In order to do this, there should be an exploration of what types of analysis can be performed using the information on model representations that is relevant in a maturity assessment effort.

However, in the scope of this paper we focus on the analysis of EA models, modelled in ArchiMate [23], using DL inference. In order to use these techniques there are two perspectives to take into consideration. The MM developer and assessor perspective.

Regarding the developer perspective, we can find several development methods, procedures and design principles, some quite popular among scholars based on their respective citation counts. For example, the general design principles from Roglinger et al. [24], the Design Science Research (DSR) perspective on MMs by Mettler [25], the development guidelines from Maier et al. [26], and he procedure model based on DSR from Becker et al. [27]. For the purpose of this paper, we decided to focus on the development procedure of Becker et al. [27], based on DSR, which, as result, offers a sound methodological foundation, suitable for application in the research approach. This development procedure gives a stringent and consistent approach to the DSR guidelines of Hevner et al. [28].

As depicted in the procedure model in Fig. 1 the first steps focus on the problem identification. First, is the identification and detailing of the research problem, with the specification of the practical relevance of the problem and the justification the value of the artifact. Then follows the comparison with existing MMs. This must use the problem identification of the first step and analysis of existing MM in the domain, which leads to the identification of weaknesses in these models.

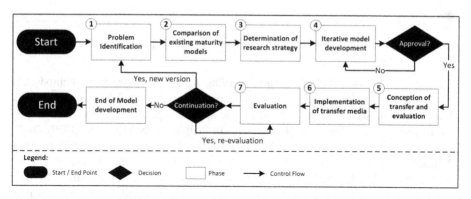

**Fig. 1.** Procedure model of the research approach (adopted from Becker et al. [27])

The next step deals with the determination of the research strategy outlined in this section of the paper. Then follows the iterative MM development. The following steps (5 and 6) is where MM developers can incorporate the type of analysis detailed in this paper. Step 5, conception of transfer and evaluation is where developers develop the assessment criteria to use for the assessment of the MM. During this step, and in order to be able to use these techniques, developers should identify all the criteria possible to assess through EA model analysis. Then, in step 6, implementation of transfer media, developers can develop software tools that will incorporate the criteria identified in step 5 as suitable for assessment using DL inference to automate, in part or fully, the assessment. The last step evaluates the MM against the requirements.

Finally, regarding the MM assessor perspective, we can find two main assessment methods in literature. The first is the Software Engineering Institute Standard CMMI Appraisal Method for Process Improvement (SEI SCAMPI [29]) and the ISO/IEC TS 33030 Assessment Method [30]. SCAMPI as the name suggests is the appraisal method used by CMMI to perform assessments and is depicted in the top half of Fig. 2. It contains three main tasks (1) Plan and Prepare for Assessment, (2) Conduct Appraisal, and (3) Report Results. It is possible to decompose these steps into several sub-steps not relevant for the purpose of this paper. The ISO/IEC TS 33030 assessment method is composed of seven main steps as depicted in the bottom half of Fig. 2. As can be seen in Fig. 2 there is a correlation between the steps of both assessment methods as these have a common background behind their development [2].

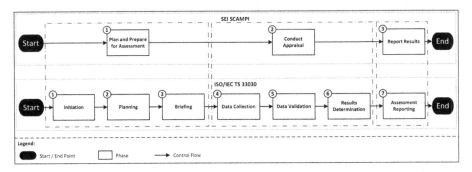

**Fig. 2.** Maturity models assessment methods (SEI SCAMPI [29] and ISO/IEC TS 33030 [30])

From an assessor perspective and regarding these two assessment methods, the technique proposed by this paper regarding the use of EA models analysis and DL inference can be useful while conducting the appraisal (in SCAMPI) and while performing the Data Validation and Results Determination (in ISO/IEC TS 33030). In the Data Validation step assessors can benefit from this technique to validate if a certain EA model developed during the data collection is sound and complete to calculate the maturity levels. Finally, in the Results Determination assessors can benefit from these techniques as a way to automate the determination of the maturity levels and as way to substantiate the maturity levels determination.

One aspect to take into consideration is that the best scenario is that MM developers begin planning to use this technique right when the MM is in the development stage. In this way, MM developers can guarantee that the assessment criteria are verifiable by analyzing EA models and using DL inference.

In order to use the techniques proposed in this paper we created two possible methods for governing the instantiation of the artefacts presented in this paper. From a MM developer viewpoint, these methods have the purpose of translating existing maturity assessment questionnaires into an ontology and then translating the assessment questions into DL queries which answers will be provided by reasoning engines over the ontology. From a MM assessor viewpoint, these methods enable them to instantiate a specific MM ontology and collect the assessment results for a given MM.

The roles associated with these methods activities are the following: (1) *Maturity Model Developer* is responsible for developing the MM and creating the assessment questionnaire that will be used by the architect to develop a template architecture model; (2) *Architect* is responsible for formalizing the assessment questionnaire into a template architecture model, to make sure that the template faithfully represents the assessment questionnaire and to verify the ontology converted from the architecture models is complete and correct; (3) *Ontology Engineer* is responsible for converting the architecture models into an ontology and translating the assessment questions into DL Queries over the ontology; and (4) *Assessor* is responsible for performing a maturity assessment, instantiate the architecture model template, executing the DL queries over the instantiated architecture models, execute reasoners over populated ontologies of specific MMs, analyze and collecting the assessment results.

In the first method (Method 1), depicted in Fig. 3, the goal is to develop the Architecture Model Template and DL Queries for a specific MM for use when assessing real organizational scenarios. This method can either be used when developing a new MM or by using an existing MM. It starts with Identification of the Assessment Questions by the MM Developer. An Architect can then use these questions to develop the Architecture Model Template, which must be fully aligned with the language used in the Assessment Questions and must be enough to satisfy all the assessment criteria. The Architecture Model Template is then converted to an ontology by an Ontology Engineer. Finally, follows the development of the DL Queries to assess a given scenario according to the assessment questions and the Architecture Model Template.

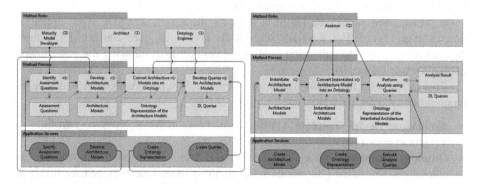

**Fig. 3.** Instantiation methods (Method 1 on the left and Method 2 on the right)

In the second method (Method 2), the goal is to support the assessment of specific organizational scenarios using the Architecture Model Template and DL Queries developed with the specific purpose of supporting the assessment of a MM. This method starts with assessor instantiating the Architecture Model Template. Then follows the conversion of the Instantiated Architecture Models into an ontology. Then, using the DL Queries already developed for this MM and the Architecture Model

Template, the Assessor performs an analysis of the results and determines the one or more maturity levels according to the MM definition.

## 4    Demonstration Using an Information Governance Maturity Model

This section demonstrates the use of the computational inference mechanisms that can be used together with ontologies for assessing the information governance maturity in organizations according to the assessment criteria defined by the A2MIGO maturity model proposed in [9]. Information Governance (IG) is defined by Gartner is the "specification of decision rights and an accountability framework to encourage desirable behavior in the valuation, creation, storage, use, archival and deletion of information. Includes the processes, roles, standards and metrics that ensure the effective and efficient use of information in enabling an organization to achieve its goals" [21]. In the context of this maturity model Information Governance is seen from the digital preservation perspective. Moreover, in the context of this maturity model the perspective of Digital Preservation consists of an archive that follows the recommendation and architecture detailed in the OAIS specification.

In order to demonstrate the utility of this proposal, first we applied the instantiation method 1 previously described in Sect. 3. This means that we developed the ArchiMate template (examples of the template are provided in Figs. 5 and 6) used for the assessment of a given organizational scenario, as well as, the translation of the assessment questions into DL queries to use to gather the final assessment results. Examples of the DL Queries are depicted in Table 2.

It presents the ArchiMate template used for the assessment of a given organizational scenario, as well as, the translation of the assessment questions into DL queries that can then be used to gather the final assessment results, following the instantiation methods proposed in [10].

This section uses the following resources (available at http://web.tecnico.ulisboa.pt/ diogo.proenca/TPDL2019.zip):

- **ArchiMate model template** – Which can be used by a given organization to instantiate their scenario;
- **Ontology template** – The translation of the ArchiMate model template into an ontology in OWL, the DL queries detailed in this section can then be executed over this ontology to get the assessment results;
- **DL Queries** - DL queries used to assess each assessment criterion for the each of the three maturity dimensions and general questions.

Figure 4 details the business process overview of all the maturity dimensions. In the middle is the archive business function which contains the business functions for the management, processes and infrastructure maturity dimensions. The archive business function is associated with the four business functions that are used to assess maturity levels 4 and 5 according to the general assessment questions.

Figure 5 details the business process view for the infrastructure and dimension. Then, Fig. 6 details business process view for the processes dimension and provides an

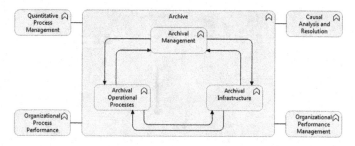

**Fig. 4.** A2MIGO overview ArchiMate template.

example of the template for the ingest sub-dimension. The management maturity dimension, the other four sub-dimensions of the processes dimension and the general questions used to assess maturity levels 4 and 5 for all dimensions of the maturity model can be found in the ArchiMate model template available at the URL provided earlier. It contains all the business processes, business objects and relations deemed necessary to assess that specific maturity dimension according to the assessment questionnaire detailed by the A2MIGO information governance maturity model [9].

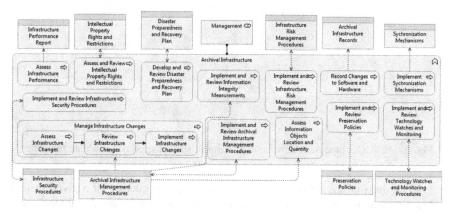

**Fig. 5.** A2MIGO infrastructure dimension ArchiMate template.

Table 1 provides examples of the DL queries used to assess each assessment criterion for the each of the three maturity dimension and general questions. In case any of these queries cannot be executed this means that specific assessment criterion is not achieved. For a complete collection of the DL Queries please check the PDF file available at the URL detailed previously.

For each assessment criterion there is an identifier that is defined as "Maturity Dimension (First Letter)" "Maturity Level". "Criterion ID", as an example the second criterion for maturity level 3 of the management dimension would be "M3.2". In this sense, "M" stands for the management dimension, "P" stands for the processes dimension, and "I" stands for the infrastructure dimension.

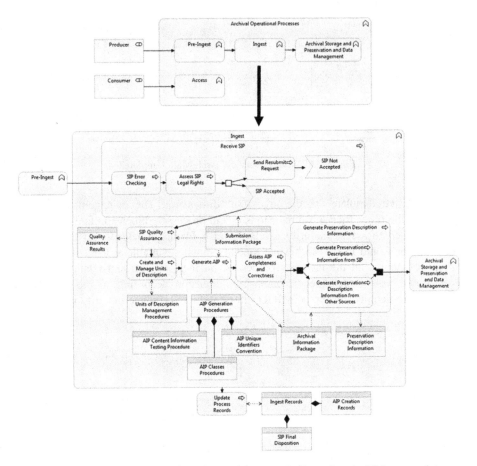

**Fig. 6.** A2MIGO processes dimension and ingest sub-dimension ArchiMate template.

This means, that for a given dimension, if all the DL queries for a given maturity level and the levels below return a result, the organization achieves that maturity level in that dimension. For example, if an organization is compliant with all the criteria for maturity levels 2 and 3 in the processes dimension it will achieve maturity level 3 for the processes dimension. This also means that the DL queries for maturity levels 2 and 3 for the processes dimension were correctly executed over the ontology representation of the enterprise architecture models of the organization.

In order to demonstrate the utility of the proposal, first we applied the instantiation method 1 previously described in Sect. 3. This means that we developed the ArchiMate template (examples provided in Figs. 5 and 6) used for the assessment of a given organizational scenario, as well as, the translation of the assessment questions into DL queries to use to gather the final assessment results. Examples of the DL Queries are depicted in Table 1.

Following this first step, we assessed seven organizations by following the instantiation method 2. Each organizational scenario was instantiated in ArchiMate

**Table 1.** Examples of DL queries for maturity assessment of information governance.

| Criterion | DL query |
|-----------|----------|
| Dimension: Management | |
| M2.1 | BusinessProcess and {Define_Mission_Statement} and hasAccessTypeWrite value Mission_Statement and componentOf value Archival_Management |
| M3.9 | BusinessProcess and {Implement_and_Review_Financial_Practices_and_Procedures} and hasAccessTypeRead_Write value Management_Practices_and_Procedures and componentOf value Archival_Management |
| M5.2 | BusinessProcess and {Dissemination_of_Practices_and_Procedures} and hasAccessTypeWrite value Research_Papers and componentOf value Archival_Management |
| Dimension: Processes | |
| Sub-dimension: Ingest | |
| P2.3 | BusinessObject and {AIP_Generation_Procedures} and inverse (hasAccessTypeRead) some (BusinessProcess and {Generate_AIP} and componentOf some (BusinessFunction and {Ingest} and componentOf value Archival_Operational_Processes)) |
| P3.13 | BusinessProcess and {Assess_AIP_Completeness_and_Correctness} and hasAccessTypeRead value Archival_Information_Package and componentOf some (BusinessFunction and {Ingest} and componentOf value Archival_Operational_Processes) |
| Sub-dimension: Access | |
| P3.22 | BusinessObject and {Access_Policies} and inverse(hasAccessTypeRead) some (BusinessProcess and {Verify_Access_Compliance} and componentOf some (BusinessFunction and {Access} and componentOf value Archival_Operational_Processes)) |
| P3.23 | BusinessProcess and {Verify_Access_Compliance} and hasAccessTypeRead value Access_Policies and componentOf some (BusinessFunction and {Access} and componentOf value Archival_Operational_Processes) |
| Dimension: Infrastructure | |
| I2.3 | BusinessProcess and {Implement_Sychronization_Mechanisms} and hasAccessTypeWrite value Sychronization_Mechanisms and componentOf value Archival_Infrastructure |
| I3.3 | BusinessProcess and {Implement_and_Review_Technology_Watches_and_Monitoring} and hasAccessTypeRead_Write value Technology_Watches_and_Monitoring_Procedures and componentOf value Archival_Infrastructure |
| I4.1 | BusinessProcess and {Assess_Infrastructure_Performance} and hasAccessTypeWrite value Infrastructure_Performance_Report and componentOf value Archival_Infrastructure |

using this maturity model's architecture model template, which was then converted into an ontology in OWL that resulted in one ArchiMate model and one OWL ontology for each scenario which are available at http://web.tecnico.ulisboa.pt/diogo.proenca/ TPDL2019.zip.

Organization Alpha ($\alpha$) is the national archive of Denmark. Among its collection are the archives of the Danish overseas trading companies and the Sound Toll Records which are inscribed in the UNESCO's Memory of the World Register.

Organization Beta ($\beta$) is the organization that is responsible for the preservation of objects from Norwegian state institutions. It preserves court sentences, surveys, censuses, church records, among many other objects.

Organization Gamma ($\gamma$) is the organization that handles all the archival administration in Estonia since 1999. It collects and preserves records that document culture, history and social aspects in Estonia.

Organization Delta ($\delta$) is an Estonian private archive that provides archival services, which specializes in the professional management, organization and maintenance of information based on documents.

Organization Omega ($\omega$) are the archives of the Republic of Slovenia. Its main goals are to collect, preserve, arrange and facilitate access to the national archive heritage of the Republic of Slovenia. It archives objects created by the government and other entities under the public law.

Organization Epsilon ($\varepsilon$) is a Portuguese organization which specializes in providing services for archiving and preserving digital information. Among its customers are Portuguese Municipalities, public higher education institutions, museums and archives.

Organization Zeta ($\zeta$) is the organization responsible for preserving Hungary's valuable records and make them available to public. It contains records going back to the $10^{th}$ century which include, maps, diplomas, charters, seals, corporations, associations, among many others.

For each of these seven organizations we took the role of assessors, instantiated the Architecture Model template to its organizational scenario, then used a converter to create the ontology representation of that architecture model, which resulted in an OWL file for each organization. Then, in each ontology representation of the organizations, the DL queries were executed and the results analyzed which resulted in the assessment results depicted in Table 2.

**Table 2.** Maturity assessment results - final maturity levels.

| Dimension | $\alpha$ | $\beta$ | $\gamma$ | $\delta$ | $\omega$ | $\varepsilon$ | $\zeta$ | $\varnothing$ |
|---|---|---|---|---|---|---|---|---|
| Management | 2 | 1 | 2 | 1 | 2 | OS | 1 | **1.5** |
| Processes | 2 | 1 | 2 | 1 | 2 | 1 | 2 | **1.6** |
| Infrastructure | 5 | 1 | 4 | 2 | 1 | 1 | 2 | **2.3** |
| $\varnothing$ **(Average)** | **3** | **1** | **2.7** | **1.3** | **1.7** | **1** | **1.7** | **1.8** |

Table 2 details the final enterprise architecture maturity levels determined through the analysis of the results of DL queries and the maturity level determination rules defined by the maturity model. "OS" means that maturity dimension is out of the scope of the assessment.

These scenarios showed the utility of the constructs proposed by this work as a technique that can be used to assess information governance maturity in organizational scenarios. The assessment criteria defined in the maturity model were translated to DL queries that can then be used over architecture models of specific scenarios, with the use of computational inference, to gather the assessment results for that scenario.

## 5 Conclusion

This paper presented an approach for maturity assessment of information governance using EA model analysis and DL. For that purpose, we present an analysis of the related work in ontologies and DL reasoning, concluding that such techniques are in fact relevant for our purpose.

Based on those findings, a proposal is presented for taking advantage of ontologies in the representation, extension, and analysis of EA models for the purpose of supporting the assessment of information governance maturity based on an existing maturity model for this purpose. An EA model template, expressed in ArchiMate, with the purpose of assessing the information governance maturity in organizations is presented, as well as, the set of DL queries used to assess a given organization that must be executed over an ontology representation of that EA model template. This demonstrates the proposal of how to formalize the assessment criteria in an existing maturity model and how to verify the compliance to those assessment criteria. Next, we detailed how to use this template and DL queries in real scenarios, by assessing seven organizations and detailing the assessment criteria that was satisfied and the final maturity levels for each organization.

Despite the capabilities brought to table by ontologies, we must acknowledge limitations. There are different types of analysis that rely on different types of techniques that offer features not always possible with ontologies. One example of such limitation is that the quality of the analysis is dependent on the quality of the information captured in the EA model. By quality of the information we refer to the detail, amount, accuracy, or others, depending on the objective and scope of the MM assessment, this provides an insight on the effectiveness of the approach.

Future work will focus on developing a system that allows MM developers to upload their MMs as well as, the assessment criteria, expressed in DL queries to verify the compliance of an organizational scenario against the MM assessment criteria. Users can then log into this system select the MM which they which to assess their organization against and provide the EA models deemed necessary by the MM developer to get an assessment report that can then be used as an input for an improvement plan.

Work is already ongoing and a first version of this system, named Maturity Model Architect (MMArch) [22] is available at http://web.tecnico.ulisboa.pt/diogo.proenca/MMArch/ (Username: "TestUser"/Password: "TestUser_pwd!").

This first version was developed using the Microsoft .NET framework, and SQL Server and supports the instantiation methods proposed in [10].

The developed solution is a web application that provides: an interface to create maturity models, define maturity levels and assessment criteria. It also allows to export a maturity model to OWL. It allows to perform assessments using the assessment criteria in the maturity model or by using DL queries and export that assessment into OWL.

**Acknowledgement.** This work was supported by national funds through Fundação para a Ciência e a Tecnologia (FCT) with reference UID/CEC/50021/2019.

# References

1. Nolan, R.L.: Managing the computer resource: a stage hypothesis. Commun. ACM **16**, 399–405 (1973)
2. Ahern, D.M., Clouse, A., Turner, R.: CMMI Destilled: A Practical Introduction to Integrated Process Improvement, 3rd edn. Addson Wesley Professional, Boston (2008)
3. ISO/IEC 15504:2004: Information technology - Process assessment. International Organization for Standardization and International Electrotechnical Commission Std. (2004)
4. Studer, R., Benjamins, R., Fensel, D.: Knowledge engineering: principles and methods. Data Knowl. Eng. **25**, 161–198 (1998)
5. Guarino, N., Oberle, D., Staab, S.: What is an ontology? In: Staab, S., Studer, R. (eds.) Handbook on Ontologies, pp. 1–17. Springer, Heidelberg (2009). https://doi.org/10.1007/978-3-540-92673-3_0
6. Genesereth, M.R., Nilsson, N.J.: Logical Foundations of Artificial Intelligence. Morgan Kaufmann, Los Altos (1987)
7. W3C: OWL 2 Web Ontology Language Structural Specification and Functional-Style Syntax (Second Edition). World Wide Web Consortium Recommendation (2012). http://www.w3.org/TR/owl2-syntax/. Accessed Jan 2015
8. Antunes, G.: Analysis of Enterprise Architecture Models: An Application of Ontologies to the Enterprise Architecture Domain. Ph.D. thesis, University of Lisbon (2015)
9. Proença, D., Vieira, R., Borbinha, J.: Information governance maturity model final development iteration. In: Kamps, J., Tsakonas, G., Manolopoulos, Y., Iliadis, L., Karydis, I. (eds.) TPDL 2017. LNCS, vol. 10450, pp. 128–139. Springer, Cham (2017). https://doi.org/10.1007/978-3-319-67008-9_11
10. Proença, D., Borbinha, J.: Using enterprise architecture model analysis and description logics for maturity assessment. In: The 33rd ACM/SIGAPP Symposium on Applied Computing, SAC 2018, Pau, France (2018)
11. CMMI Product Team: CMMI for development, version 1.3. Software Engineering Institute - Carnegie Mellon University, Technical report. CMU/SEI-2010-TR-033 (2010)
12. Breitman, K., Casanova, M.A., Truszkowski, W.: Semantic Web: Concepts, Technologies and Applications. Springer, London (2007). https://doi.org/10.1007/978-1-84628-710-7
13. Gomez-Perez, A., Benjamins, R.: Overview of knowledge sharing and reuse components: ontologies and problem-solving methods. In: Proceedings of IJCAI-99 Workshop on Ontologies and Problem Solving Methods (KRR5), Stockholm, Sweden (1999)
14. Gruber, T.R.: A translation approach to portable ontology specifications. Knowl. Acquis. **5**, 199–220 (1993)
15. Borst, W.N.: Construction of engineering ontologies. Ph.D. thesis, University of Twente, Enschede (1997)

16. Uschold, M., Gruninger, M.: Ontologies: Principles, Methods and Applications. Knowl. Eng. Rev. **11**, 93–136 (1996)
17. Guarino, N.: Formal ontology in information systems. In: Proceedings of the First International Conference, FIOS 1998, Trento, Italy, 6–8 June (1998)
18. Baader, F., Calvanese, D., McGuiness, D., Nardi, D., Patel-Schneider, P.: The Description Logic Handbook: Theory, Implementation, and Applications, 1st edn. Cambridge University Press, New York (2003)
19. Vaculin, R.: Process mediation framework for semantic web services. Ph.D. thesis, Department of Theoretical Computer Science and Mathematical Logic, Faculty of Mathematics and Physics, Charles University (2009)
20. Baader, F., Horrocks, I., Sattler, U.: Chapter 3: Description Logics (2007). http://www.cs.ox.ac.uk/ian.horrocks/Publications/download/2007/BaHS07a.pdf
21. Gartner: Information Governance Definition (2019). https://www.gartner.com/it-glossary/information-governance/
22. Proença, D., Borbinha, J.: Maturity model architect - a tool for maturity assessment support. In: 20th IEEE Conference on Business Informatics, CBI 2018, Vienna, Austria (2018)
23. The Open Group: Archimate 3.0.1 Specification (2017). http://pubs.opengroup.org/architecture/archimate3-doc/
24. Röglinger, M., Pöppelbuß, J.: What makes a useful maturity model? A framework for general design principles for maturity models and its demonstration in business process management. In: Proceedings of the 19th European Conference on Information Systems, Helsinki, Finland, June 2011
25. Mettler, T.: A design science research perspective on maturity models in information systems. Institute of Information Management, Universtiy of St. Gallen, St. Gallen (2009)
26. Maier, A., Moultrie, J., Clarkson, P.: Assessing organizational capabilities: reviewing and guiding the development of maturity grids. IEEE Trans. Eng. Manag. **59**(1), 138–159 (2012)
27. Becker, J., Knackstedt, R., Pöppelbuß, J.: Developing maturity models for IT management: a procedure model and its application. Bus. Inf. Syst. Eng. **3**, 213–222 (2009)
28. Hevner, A., Ram, S., March, S., Park, J.: Design science in information systems research. MISQ **28**, 75–105 (2004)
29. CMMI Product Team: Standard CMMI Appraisal Method for Process Improvement (SCAMPI) A, Version 1.3: Method Definition Document. Software Engineering Institute - Carnegie Mellon University, Technical report. CMU/SEI-2011-HB-001 (2011)
30. ISO/IEC TS 33030:2017: Information technology — Process assessment — An exemplar documented assessment process, International Organization for Standardization and International Electrotechnical Commission Std. (2017)

# Finding Documents Related to Taiwan in the Veritable Records of Qing Using Relevance Feedback

Hsin-Hsuan Sung, Jou-An Chen, and Jieh Hsiang[✉]

Department of Computer Science and Information Engineering, National Taiwan
University, No. 1, Sect. 4 Roosevelt Rd, Taipei 10617, Taiwan
{sunghsinhsuan, chenjouan0708, jhsiang}@ntu.edu.tw

**Abstract.** In this paper we describe a method for finding relevant texts in historical documents. Instead of using keyword search, it computes the level of relevance between texts. Using a subset of documents that are known to be relevant, our method computes the degree of relevance between the pre-selected texts and the remaining texts in the document set. The potential texts of interest obtained from the computation are listed by their ranks and given to historians to confirm their relevance. The marked results are then fed back to the system to start the next iteration. We applied our method to find Taiwan-related entries in the Veritable Records of Qing, and discovered an additional 988 related entries which were not included in the volume of Veritable Records of Qing – Taiwan Collection (which contains 2989 entries).

## 1 Introduction

The *Veritable Records of Qing* [1] (*VRQ*) is a chronologically arranged collection of important events associated with the daily activities of the Qing emperors (1616CE to 1912CE). It is divided into 11 dynastic eras, each corresponding to an emperor. *VRQ* is among the most valuable primary sources for Qing historians. However, due to its large volume (totally 4,433 volumes, which includes 325,941 entries and 35,057,506 characters), finding information that are relevant can be a problem. The full-text of *VRQ* described in this study was obtained from the Institute of History and Philology of Academia Sinica [3]. The dates mentioned in the entries were annotated and standardized [4] and person/place names tagged [5]. In 1990 s, a group of (mainland Chinese) scholars extracted 2,994 entries from *VRQ* that they deemed relevant to Taiwan and compiled a volume entitled *Veritable Records of Qing - Taiwan Selection* [2] (*VRQTS*). *VRQTS* spans from the 18th year of Shunzhi (順治) (1661) to the 30th year of Guangxu (光緒) (1904). Its full-text was transcribed and included in THDL (Taiwan History Digital Library) [6, 13], an extensive collection of primary historical documents about Taiwan, also with annotation of dates and person/place names.

The editorial of *VRQTS* states that "This album recorded Qing's eleven dynasties, of which relevant local historical materials about Taiwan were all compiled. According to this principle of catching-all, any Taiwan-related document exists in *VRQ*, regardless of their length and relevancy, will be recorded and included". However, even a simple

© Springer Nature Switzerland AG 2019
A. Doucet et al. (Eds.): TPDL 2019, LNCS 11799, pp. 280–287, 2019.
https://doi.org/10.1007/978-3-030-30760-8_24

search of *VRQ* using keyword "Taiwan" yielded 412 entries that were not included in *VRQTS*. We would, therefore, like to design an automated method to see what additional entries related to Taiwan can be discovered.

## 2  Relevance Feedback Algorithms and Evaluations

The approach we used is relevance feedback. Using the entries in *VRQTS* as ground truth, we designed a learning algorithm to identify entries that are (potentially) related to Taiwan. The entries were then given to two historians to check if they were indeed relevant. Their inputs were fed back to the system to start another iteration. This process terminates when the historians think that no more can be added.

The first task was to decide which relevance feedback algorithm to employ. We tested three such algorithms, including Naïve Bayes Classifier [7], TF-IDF with Rocchio's Algorithm [8] and Okapi BM25 algorithm [9]. We treat each entry as a bag of bi-grams. By using 80% of the entries in *VRQTS* as ground truth and the rest 20% as test data, we produced the following 11-point interpolated recall-precision average curve [10] (Fig. 1).

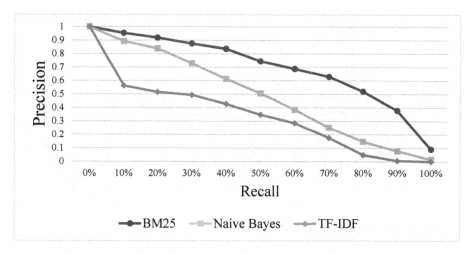

**Fig. 1.** Recall-precision averages curve of the three relevance feedback algorithms

The results showed that BM25 algorithm is clearly superior than the other two. Even when reaching 90% recall, the precision of BM25 is still nearly 0.4. This means when the tester (a historian) had found 90% of relevant entries from the test data set, the number of entries she had to read from the recommendations were only 2.5 times the number of those 90% relevant entries. Moreover, we have also conducted tests using other standard evaluation methods such as the Average Precision (AP) [10] and R-Precision [10]. They also showed the superiority of BM25 (Table 1).

**Table 1.** The average precision and r-precision of the three relevance feedback algorithms

| AP | | | R-Precision | | |
|---|---|---|---|---|---|
| BM25 | TF-IDF | Naïve Bayes | BM25 | TF-IDF | Naïve Bayes |
| 0.69 | 0.47 | 0.31 | 0.63 | 0.48 | 0.35 |

One reason why BM25 is so effective is because of its document length normalization effect. The length of entries in *VRQ* varies from a few words to 5,000. Normalization reduces biases caused by such discrepancies.

We also designed a friendly interface for the historians to choose relevant entries from those generated by the system. The user can click "relevant", "irrelevant", or "undecided" when viewing the content (Figure 2).

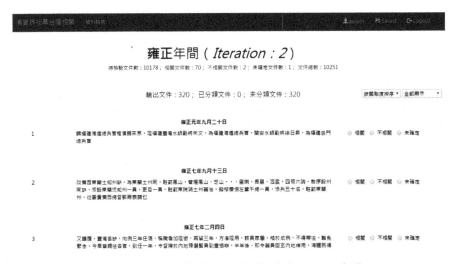

**Fig. 2.** The user interface of relevance feedback documents finding system

## 3    System and Experiments

Let *C* denote the entire set of *VRQ* entries. *C* is divided into 4 mutually exclusive sets: *D*, the target entries set, contains the entries whose relevance are to be decided; *R*, the relevant entries set, contains the entries that are considered relevant to Taiwan; *NR*, the non-relevant set, contains those that are considered not relevant; *P*, the pending set, contains those that the historian cannot decide their relevance.

At the beginning of the experiment, *R* is set to be *VRQST*, *D* is *C-R*, and both *P* and *NR* are empty. (Actually, we ran each dynastic era separately. We treat the process as one for simplicity in explanation.) The goal of our system is for the two historians participating in the experiments to find as many relevant entries as possible while examining at most 15%, a relatively small amount, of the entries. The way we achieve this is as follows. We run the system and return the most relevant 3% of the entries to the two historians. Each of them then marks each entry as relevant, irrelevant, or pending. They then put the results together, resolve their differences and decide on the relevance of the pending entries (some entries may remain "pending"). The resulting entries are then added to the respective sets, and the system will start again. This process will continue for 5 iterations or if no more entries is added to the set *R*. The system workflow is shown in Fig. 3.

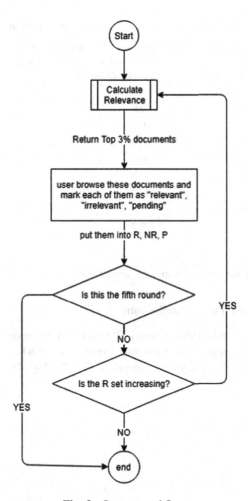

**Fig. 3.** System workflow

## 4   Some Results and Observations

After the above experiment, we identified 988 additional entries of *VRQ* that are relevant to Taiwan. The newly found Taiwan-related entries in *VRQ* are hereinafter referred to as "Supplement Edition". They have also been added to THDL (Table 2). (The Shunzhi (順治) era, which has only 5 entries in *VRQTS*, was bypassed.)

**Table 2.** Number of entries relevant to Taiwan

|  | Number of Entries in *The Veritable Records of Qing* | Number of Matching Entries in *Veritable Records of Qing-Taiwan Selection* | Newly Found Entries Using Proposed Method |
|---|---|---|---|
| Kangxi | 32142 | 300 | 213 |
| Yongzheng | 10251 | 68 | 26 |
| Qianlong | 84630 | 977 | 402 |
| Jiaqing | 25689 | 228 | 149 |
| Daoguang | 41558 | 408 | 47 |
| Xianfeng | 23644 | 89 | 15 |
| Tongzhi | 22889 | 170 | 74 |
| Guangxu | 55452 | 749 | 62 |
| **Total** | **296255** | **2989** | **988** |

In the following we present some observations:

### 4.1   Observation on Time Distribution

We found 24 new entries in 1664 (Kangxi 3rd year), 17 new entries in 1796 (Jiaqing 1st year), and 30 new entries in 1862 (Tongzhi 1st year), each of which exceeds the original number of entries of the same year recorded in *VRQTS* (Fig. 4).

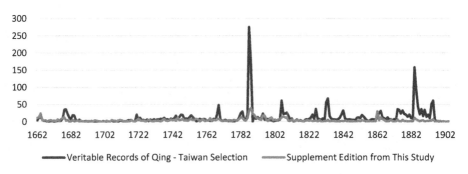

**Fig. 4.** The comparison of number of entries based on time distribution

We give some explanations as follow:

1. 1664 (Kangxi 3rd year): Many subordinates of Koxinga (鄭成功, ruler of Taiwan at the time and a Ming loyalist) defected to Qing after Koxinga's son, Zheng Jing, took over in 1863. The newly found entries reflected these events.
2. 1796 (Jiaqing 1st year): The 1st year of Jiaqing marks the emergence of a notorious pirate, Cai Qian (蔡牽), who eventually invaded Taiwan, caused great harm to the coastal regions, and even established a short-lived kingdom. But before Cai Qian ventured into Taiwan, he ravaged the Chinese coastal provinces of Fujian and Zhejiang. Our historians considered Cai's early activities in China as relevant to Taiwan, since he might not have invaded Taiwan had he been successful in coastal China.
3. 1862 (Tongzhi 1st year): Two important events occurred during this time: Dai Chaochun (戴潮春) Rebellion, and the enlistment of the army of General Lin Wencha (林文察) to help fighting Taiping Rebellion in Zhejiang. The latter was grossly underreported in *VRQTS*.

## 4.2   Observation on Person Names

We have also used the person and place name lists from THDL to compare the differences of names in VRQTS and Supplement Edition. The most significant was Lin Wencha, a Taiwanese general who was sent to China to fight the Taiping Rebellion (thrice) and eventually died in battlefield. Lin appeared in only 24 entries in VRQTS while we added an additional 28 entries about Lin into the Supplement Edition. This brings to the question of what is deemed as "relevance". Lin Wencha's demise lead to local power struggle in Taiwan with lasting effect. We therefore consider his military expeditions in China as relevant, while the editors of *VRQTS* might not have.

   Similar phenomena can be observed on other names. For instance, Lin Weiyuan (林維源), who was the head of one of the wealthiest families in Taiwan, donated an unprecedented large sum of money to the government in 1879 and was rewarded an important official title accordingly. This entry was also missing from *VRQTS*.

## 4.3   Observation on Place Names

The most significant was the 412 entries which can be retrieved from *VRQ* with a simple keyword search of "Taiwan" but were conspicuously missing from *VRQTS*. We observed certain somewhat interesting phenomena. For instance, during Qianlong (乾隆), the emperor gave banquets to "Taiwanese savages" (臺灣生番), together with other dignitaries from Mongolia, Muslim regions, and Burma, 12 times, but none of which were included in *VRQTS*. The editors of *VRQTS* might have thought of these feasts as inconsequential events. But in fact these banquets, which spanned from 1788 to 1790, involve two separate groups of indigenous Taiwanese. The first were 30 chiefs of indigenous villages that helped putting down the Lin Shuangwen Rebellion. The second group of 12 was invited to celebrate the 80th birthday of Qianlong. During the entire Qing reign, indigenous Taiwanese were only invited to the imperial court three times (the other time was 1734). This might have something to do with the change of policy of Qing court towards the indigenous Taiwanese [12].

## 5   Discussion

In this paper we presented a relevance feedback method based on Okapi BM25 and used it to extract entries from *VRQ* which are considered relevant to Taiwan but not included in *VRQTS*. To this end, we have discovered an additional 988 entries and have included them in THDL. Our method is quite general and has been incorporated into DocuSky [11], a personal DH platform, for recommending relevant documents in other corpuses.

The notion of "relevance" is quite subjective. A major portion of our new addition that were omitted in *VRQTS* has to do with events occurred in Chinese mainland that had indirect yet significant impact on Taiwan. Of the 412 new entries with the conspicuous keyword "Taiwan" but bypassed *VRQTS*, 287 appeared during the first 3 dynastic era (Kangxi, Yunzheng, Qianlong), with Qianlong leading the group with 227 entries. We closely examined these entries, and found them all rather relevant to Taiwan. For instance, the earliest such new entry, dated 1667, discussed how to cultivate Taiwanese land once it is conquered. Considering that Qing did not occupy Taiwan until 1683, we thought this entry is quite significant. Many of the remaining (and later) 125 entries were appointments of Taiwanese officials or the reports of taxes collected. They, collectively, should also be meaningful. In addition to obvious factors such as depth of knowledge or academic training, the current trend of historical research or political climate could also be factors. Another possibility is that *VRQTS* was collected manually, without the help of IT. It is therefore conceivable that certain entries were missed due to human error. In any case, while historical narratives vary from generation to generation, the collection of primary sources never loses its significance.

**Acknowledgement.** We would like to thank the anonymous referees for their useful comments.

## References

1. The Veritable Records of Qing, Zhonghua Book Company (1986)
2. Zhang, B.-Z.: Veritable Records of Qing - Taiwan Selection. Fujian People's Publishing House, Fuzhou (1993)
3. The Institute of History and Philology, Academia Sinica, Scripta Sinica database (1984)
4. Hu, R.-A.: The construction of a searching system of the veritable records of the ming and Qing dynasties and annals of the Joseon Dynasty. Master's Thesis, National Taiwan University (2014)
5. Chen, P.-Y.: A Preliminary Textual and Temporal Analysis of the Veritable Records of the Qing Dynasty. Master's Thesis, National Taiwan University (2011)
6. Hsiang, J., Chen, S.-P., Tu, H.-C.: On building a full-text digital library of land deeds of Taiwan. In: Digital Humanities 2009 University of Maryland, College Park, 22–25 June, 2009, Conference Abstracts, pp. 85–90 (2009)
7. Domingos, P., Pazzani, M.: On the optimality of the simple bayesian classifier under zero-one loss. Mach. Learn. **29**(2), 103–130 (1997)

8. Joachims, T.: A probabilistic analysis of the Rocchio algorithm with TFIDF for text categorization. In: Proceedings of the Fourteenth International Conference on Machine Learning, San Francisco, CA, USA, pp. 143–151 (1997)
9. Robertson, S.E., Walker, S., Jones, S., Hancock-Beaulieu, M.M., Gatford, M.: Okapi at TREC-3. Nist Special Publication Sp **109**, 109 (1995)
10. Manning, C.D., Raghavan, P., Schütze, H.: Introduction to Information Retrieval, vol. 39. Cambridge University Press, Cambridge (2008)
11. Hsiang, J., Tu, H.-C.: DocuSky Collaboration Platform. National Taiwan University, Research Center for Digital Humanities, 2017. https://docusky.digital.ntu.edu.tw
12. Chen, Z.: Visits of indigenous Taiwanese to the Qing court during early Qing Dynasty. Indigenous Arch. **17**, 47–58 (2014)
13. Hsiang, J., Chen, S.P., Ho, H.I., Tu, H.C.: Discovering relationships from imperial court documents of qing dynasty. Int. J. Hum. Arts Comput. Edinb. Univ. Press **6**(1-2), 22–41 (2012)

# Fake News Detection with the New German Dataset "GermanFakeNC"

Inna Vogel[(⊠)] and Peter Jiang

Fraunhofer Institute for Secure Information Technology SIT,
Rheinstrasse 75, 64295 Darmstadt, Germany
{Inna.Vogel,Peter.Jiang}@SIT.Fraunhofer.de
https://www.sit.fraunhofer.de/de/

**Abstract.** The spread of misleading information and "alternative facts" on the internet gained in the last decade considerable importance worldwide. In recent years, several attempts have been made to counteract fake news based on automatic classification via machine learning models. These, however, require labeled data. The scarcity of available corpora for predictive modeling is a major stumbling block in this field, especially in other languages than English. Our contribution is twofold. First, we introduce a new publicly available German dataset "German Fake News Corpus" (GermanFakeNC) for the task of fake news detection which consists of 490 manually fact-checked articles. Every false statement in the text is verified claim-by-claim by authoritative sources. Our ground truth for trustworthy news consists of 4,500 news articles from well-known mainstream news publishers. With regard to the second contribution, we choose a Convolutional Neural Network (CNN) ($\kappa = 0.89$) and the widely used SVM ($\kappa = 0.72$) technique to detect fake news. Thus we hope that our approach will stimulate the progress in fake news detection and claim verification across languages.

**Keywords:** Fake news detection · Fake statement ·
Deception detection · German corpus

## 1 Introduction

Although the term "Fake News" is a new phenomenon in the media vocabulary, the spread of misinformation, rumors and lies have always tarnished the media sectors by swaying the public opinion and manipulating millions of people. Fake news can crush reputations of corporations, push the stock price down, and topple political figures. Fraudsters use journalistic formats like news, reports and interviews because this genre serves the readers in terms of high credibility and acceptance. According to Rubin et al. [11], different sub-types of fake news exist such as satire, hoax and serious fabrications. While satire is written to entertain the reader with irony and sarcasm, hoax and serious fabrications try to persuade the reader of the truthfulness of the content. Serious fabrications, which

© Springer Nature Switzerland AG 2019
A. Doucet et al. (Eds.): TPDL 2019, LNCS 11799, pp. 288–295, 2019.
https://doi.org/10.1007/978-3-030-30760-8_25

are strongly presented in yellow press and tabloids, use eye" catching headlines ("clickbaits"), scandal–mongering and sensationalism to increase traffic on a website [12] in order to maximize the profit with advertising revenue. Rashkin et al. [9] extend the categories of fake news by the format "propaganda". This genre uses true news and mixes them often with false information to make the readers believe a certain political or social agenda.

As false content is written with different intentions and uses different news types and formats, there exists no agreed definition of the term fake news. In this paper, we define this term as (online) publications which imitate journalistic genres and formats for spreading intentionally and verifiable false or misleading information [3,12]. As satire and reporting mistakes are not written to mislead readers, we exclude these journalistic types from the concept of fake news.

Digital libraries store, represent and disseminate data that offers an enormous cultural, scientific, educational, artistic, and social value. Such libraries have the advantage that they can be updated on a daily basis and can be accessed easily and instantly by users. Fact-checking websites such as PolitiFact.com, Snopes.com or FactCheck.org take the technology advantage of digital libraries by storing, managing, and providing factual assertions in non-fictional texts by determining the veracity and correctness of the factual statements of the content. Such websites correct misperception of events among citizens, they can discourage politicians from spreading misinformation [6] and can help researchers to develop tools to validate the content of news articles.

Most of the scientific work and proposed methods in the field of deception detection is based on English language datasets. However, to keep up with the spread of misinformation in Germany, we need tools and techniques which are trained for the German language to automatically detect and classify false and misleading information. The scarcity of labeled German datasets prevents developing and training classifiers to automatically detect fraudulent reporting. To address these issues, we investigate in this paper the topic of fake news detection for the German language. Our first contribution is to introduce our new manually fact-checked and verified "German Fake News Corpus" (GermanFakeNC). As far as we know, this is the first German reference corpus for fake news detection of its kind. The ground truth for truthful news was retrieved from German well-known mainstream news media websites. With regard to the second contribution, we choose a Convolutional Neural Network (CNN) ($\kappa = 0.89$) and the widely used SVM ($\kappa = 0.72$) technique to detect fake news.

The paper is organized as follows: After a review of related work, Sect. 3 details the newly corpus and how it was constructed. Section 4 introduces our classification techniques. Section 5 shows that good results on detecting potentially misleading information can be achieved with the selected classifiers. The last Sect. 6 concludes this paper.

## 2   Related Work

A lot of approaches for fake news detection rely on fact-checking websites such as PolitiFact.com [9,14] and Snopes.com [7], or on satirical news sources such as "The Onion" [10]. Less popular are Wikipedia datasets. In "FEVER" [13] Thorne et al. introduced 2018 a fact extraction and verification dataset. The 185.4 K claims were generated by altering sentences from Wikipedia pages and manually verified against introductory sections of the online encyclopedia. Human annotators mutated artificially the extracted claims by providing additional knowledge, by negating, paraphrasing the claim or by substituting the relation or entity with a similar or dissimilar one.

Wang [14] introduced in 2017 the "LIAR" dataset. The texts were collected from the fact-checking website PolitiFact.com and include 12.8K hand-labeled, fact-checked short statements approved by experts. Although LIAR is bigger than other datasets it focuses just on the false claims rather than the full-text.

Potthast et al. [8] enriched the BuzzFeed[1] fact-checked news corpus with ratings, linked articles and other relevant metadata and presented the BuzzFeed-Webis Fake News Corpus[2] in 2018. The authors analyzed the writing style of fake, mainstream, hyperpartisan and satire news using the unmasking method. The method was originally conceptualized for authorship verification [4]. They showed that hyperpartisan (extremely one-sided) news and satire can be distinguished from mainstream news by their writing style. Fake news, on the other hand, cannot be detected by their style alone.

## 3  The "German Fake News Corpus" 2019: GermanFakeNC

Many authors presented datasets, which are not suitable for fake news detection since falsifications were old-dated or not verified by experts. This is due to the fact that fact-checking is very time-consuming and costly. Additionally, major resources and datasets for deception detection are based on English language datasets. Since fake news is a worldwide phenomenon and affects almost every language, we present the publicly available "German Fake News Corpus" (GermanFakeNC)[3]. We will detail its construction and annotation, and we will give some key statistics from the dataset.

### 3.1  Corpus Construction

GermanFakeNC was constructed, fact-checked claim-by-claim, and annotated by eleven students of the Hochschule der Medien (HdM) in Stuttgart. To ensure the reliability of the corpus, the students were trained by coaching experts of fact-checking initiatives, through extensive pre-tests and regular exchanges with the group and the project management. After the annotation work was completed, inter-coder reliability tests among the data collectors were performed

---

[1] https://github.com/BuzzFeedNews/2016-10-facebook-fact-check.

[2] https://zenodo.org/record/1239675#.W6tIy2gzY-V.

[3] Our "German Fake News Corpus Dataset" (GermanFakeNC) is available under: https://doi.org/10.5281/zenodo.3375714.

to document the reproducibility and reliability of the corpus. The inter-coder reliability for localizing false statements in the text (up to 3 false statements could be annotated) exhibits an overall APPA between 97.6% and 100%[4] demonstrating consistency among observational ratings provided by the eleven annotators.

The dataset includes 490 texts which were retrieved from German alternative online media sources (such as www.allesroger.at, www.compact-online.de, www. rapefugees.net etc.). The texts can be assigned to the category propaganda of Rashkin et al. [9] as they combine truths, falsehoods, and ambiguities to mislead the readers and make them believe a certain political or social agenda. In order to ensure the reliability and validity of the corpus, detailed annotation guidelines were elaborated. Every fake statement in the text was verified claim-by-claim with reports from authoritative sources (e.g. from local police authorities, scientific studies, the police press office, the constitutional law, annual reports or verified press releases). The extracted statements are provided with the news texts in the corpus[5]. The time interval for most of the news is established from December 2015 to March 2018.

The dataset was rated in two ways. First, a fine-grained rating (Overall_Rating) was considered in the range between [0.1; 1.0] where the lower boundary value 0.1 can be interpreted as mostly true with nearly no disinformation. Texts with the rating 1.0 are strongly disinformative. The second rating (Ratio_of_Fake_Statements) expresses the ratio of fake statements in the news texts. It provides the proportion of false statements in the article compared to the whole text.

- "1" means the text is based on true information with up to 25% false claims in the text.
- "2" means that half of the statements in the text are factually not accurate.
- If up to 75% of the claims in the text are fabricated, the overall rating is "3".
- Pure fabrications (100% untrue) are rated with the number "4".
- "9" means the reporting lacked a claim.

The ground truth for genuine articles, we retrieved in a semiautomatic way. We used a web crawler to collect press releases from German well-known mainstream news organizations such as Frankfurter Allgemeine Zeitung (FAZ) and Süddeutsche Zeitung. The crawler searched the media web pages for topics which are related to those that occurred in the fake news corpus (e.g. migration, internal security, European policy, the presidential election in the USA 2016, etc.) and which were published in the same period of time. About 4,500 of the crawled articles were used for our classification task. We rely on the truthfulness of the mainstream news texts as Potthast et al. [8] showed in their study that none of

---

[4] Inter-coder reliability (APPA - average pairwise percent agreement) detecting fake statement 1 = 97.6%, fake statement 2 = 98.2%, fake statement 3 = 100%.

[5] Unfortunately, we cannot share the sources of verification as natural persons and public authorities (e.g. local police authorities) were contacted and therefore must be protected.

the fact-checked articles from mainstream online sources were completely false. Only 0.97% of the manually annotated true news texts contained some elements or claims which were factually not accurate. We have accepted this deviation in our corpus for true news.

### 3.2 Corpus Statistics

The distribution of the ratings in the corpus shows that less than a quarter of the phony press releases are completely false. 384 out of 490 texts are either based on true information (not less then 75% of the content of the text is true) or are a mix of true and false statements (up to 50% of the text is factually accurate). 82 of the texts in the dataset are for the most part (up to 75% of the content) incorrect. 20 reports are pure fabrications with up to 100% lack of factual claims[6]. 65% of the texts contain two false statements and 33% up to three distinct incorrect statements. The corpus is aligned along the news topics: internal security (41%) (related to the refugee crisis from 2015 in Germany), migration (13%), justice (8.6%) and media policy (6.5%). The sub-topic migration is overrepresented with 36.5%. In most of the news articles (more than 80%) the tone is negative and the frequency of spelling mistakes indicates that the texts were not written by professional journalists.

## 4   Methodology for Baseline Classifiers

Empirically, we have evaluated two popular classification methods on our dataset. The first one is based on SVM and the second one on a CNN. To train the classifiers, we selected articles not shorter than 200 words. This reduced the fake news corpus from 490 to 300 articles. As true news we used 4,500 news texts. This overrepresented class resulted in an imbalanced corpus. But the ratio is intrinsic to the problem as we assume that most newspaper reports on the Internet are based on facts and are not written to mislead readers. On the other hand, machine learning algorithms can "focus" on the majority class and ignore the smaller one [1]. In our application, the ratio of the small to the large class is 1 to 15. According to Chawla et al. [1], the problem of imbalanced data is prevalent in applications like fraud and intrusion detection.

As demonstrated in the work of Wang [14], Convolutional Neural Networks achieved state-of-the-art performance in fake news detection compared to other neural networks like BLSTM (bidirectional long short-term memory network models). Based on the work of Wang [14], we choose CNN to detect misleading information in articles and compare the results to the widely used SVM technique. We applied both methods on the GermanFakeNC dataset.

For the SVM implementation and data vectorization, we used the open source machine learning package scikit-learn and a 50% split of our datase. Both the training and test texts were converted to tf-idf feature vectors. This information

---

[6] 4 texts lacked a factual claim (Ratio_of_Fake_Statements = 9).

retrieval technique multiplies the relative frequency (tf) of a word with its inverse frequency (idf) over the entire corpus.

For training and evaluation of the CNN model we used a 50% training, 25% validation and 25% test split. For the implementation we used the open source neural network framework Keras. Our model architecture is a CNN with a single convolutional layer, followed by a standard max-pooling layer. Then, the max-pooled text representations were transferred to two fully-connected dense layers. The first layer uses ReLU as activation function. The last dense layer generates the final predictions with a sigmoid activation function. To train the CNN architecture, we used as input pre-trained German word embeddings trained on Wikipedia using fastText[7]. This simple model achieved good results (discussed in the next section) suggesting that the pre-trained word vectors are universally applicable and can be utilized for various text classification tasks.

## 5 Experimental Evaluation

Although accuracy is a common measure for binary classification tasks and a valid performance measure, it is not suitable for corpora with unequal class distribution. The overrepresented class (in our case true news) benefits from this measure when a method solely predicts this class [2]. Therefore, we chose Cohen's Kappa to evaluate out classifiers as an alternative metric to $F_1$.

Cohen's Kappa is a robust and well-known statistical measure of inter-rater agreement (agreement of two individuals) for categorical items. Cohen's Kappa discards the agreement by chance out of the equation which means: the higher TP[8] and TN, the higher Cohen's Kappa (highest $\kappa = 1$). If FP and FN are high, the model will be penalized with a low Cohen's Kappa (lowest $\kappa = -1$). 0 corresponds to the amount of agreement that can be expected from random chance. While Cohen's Kappa values below 0 are possible, they are unlikely in practice and indicate great disagreement[9] [5]. Using a confusion matrix to reflect counts of matching and mismatching agreements, $\kappa$ is calculated as follows:

$$\kappa = \frac{P_0 - P_e}{1 - P_e}$$

$P_0$[10] refers to the observed agreement and is calculated equivalent to the accuracy measure with n = classification samples. $P_e$[11] is the proportion of observations for which the agreement was predicted by chance. The coefficient of $\kappa$ is a metric after chance agreement was removed [2].

The empirical results of our trained classifiers are outlined in Table 1. The best classification Cohen's Kappa of 0.89 on the holdout test set and an $F1$-score

---

[7] https://fasttext.cc/docs/en/crawl-vectors.html.
[8] TP - True Positive, TN - True Negative, FP - False Positive, FN - False Negative.
[9] $-1 < \kappa < 0$ indicates a systematically wrong classification.
[10] $P_0 = n^{-1}(TP + TN)$.
[11] $P_e = n^{-2}(TP + FN)(TP + FP) + (FP + TN)(FN + TN)$.

of 0.90 was achieved by the CNN, outperforming the SVM classifier ($\kappa = 0.72$). The evaluation results show that a high Cohen's Kappa is harder to obtain in comparison to a high accuracy. While accuracy indicates almost perfect classification results, as expected, the confusion matrix reveals that mainly the overrepresented class true news contributes to these measures.

**Table 1.** The evaluation results on the GermanFakeNC dataset with the metrics Cohen's Kappa ($\kappa$), Accuracy (Acc.), Precision (P), Recall (R), and $F_1$

| Method | Confusion matrix | | | | | Performance measure | | | |
|--------|------|------|------|-------|----------|------|------|------|------|
|        | TP   | FN   | FP   | TN    | $\kappa$ | Acc. | P    | R    | $F_1$ |
| SVM    | 118  | 32   | 50   | 2,200 | 0.72     | 0.96 | 0.71 | 0.78 | 0.74 |
| CNN    | 62   | 13   | 1    | 1,124 | 0.89     | 0.98 | 0.98 | 0.81 | 0.90 |

## 6   Conclusion and Future Work

We introduced GermanFakeNC, our new publicly available corpus for fake news detection. To the best of our knowledge, this is the first German fact-checked dataset of its kind. As the German language is underrepresented in the field of fake news research, we hope that our corpus will foster research in this area. Our dataset consists of fine-grained rated news excerpts and up to three false statements verified as false by authoritative sources. To demonstrate the usefulness of our corpus we established two competitive baselines, we chose CNN in comparison to the widely used SVM technique to detect misleading information. The CNN could achieve a $\kappa$ of 0.89 outperforming the SVM classifier ($\kappa = 0.72$). Our results prove that the classification of truthful articles is possible by selecting suitable features and algorithms.

To increase the reliability of our work, we want to improve the ground truth for our true news data. As we retrieved topics corresponding to those that occurred in the fake news corpus and which were published in the same period of time, articles on the presidential election in the USA are overrepresented. In our future work, we want to correlate every misleading article to the corresponding fact-checked article by applying, e.g. a lexical (cosine) similarity measure to guarantee topic concordance. Furthermore, it is crucial to develop a larger fake news corpus to improve our approach based on an SVM classifier and a CNN.

## References

1. Chawla, N.V., Japkowicz, N., Kotcz, A.: Special issue on learning from imbalanced data sets. ACM SIGKDD Explor. Newsl. **6**(1), 1–6 (2004)
2. Halvani, O., Graner, L.: Rethinking the evaluation methodology of authorship verification methods. In: Bellot, P., et al. (eds.) CLEF 2018. LNCS, vol. 11018, pp. 40–51. Springer, Cham (2018). https://doi.org/10.1007/978-3-319-98932-7_4

3. Horne, B., Adali, S.: This just in: fake news packs a lot in title, uses simpler, repetitive content in text body, more similar to satire than real news. In: International AAAI Conference on Web and Social Media, pp. 759–766 (2017). https://aaai.org/ocs/index.php/ICWSM/ICWSM17/paper/view/15772/14898

4. Koppel, M., Schler, J.: Authorship verification as a one-class classification problem. In: Proceedings of the Twenty-first International Conference on Machine Learning, p. 62. ACM (2004)

5. Marston, L.: Introductory Statistics for Health and Nursing Using SPSS. SAGE Publications, Thousand Oaks (2010)

6. Nyhan, B., Reifler, J.: The effect of fact-checking on elites: a field experiment on us state legislators. Am. J. Polit. Sci. **59**(3), 628–640 (2015)

7. Popat, K., Mukherjee, S., Strötgen, J., Weikum, G.: Credibility assessment of textual claims on the web. In: Proceedings of the 25th ACM International on Conference on Information and Knowledge Management, CIKM 2016, pp. 2173–2178. ACM, New York (2016). https://doi.org/10.1145/2983323.2983661, http://doi.acm.org/10.1145/2983323.2983661

8. Potthast, M., Kiesel, J., Reinartz, K., Bevendorff, J., Stein, B.: A stylometric inquiry into hyperpartisan and fake news. In: The 56th Annual Meeting of the Association for Computational Linguistics (Long Papers). Association for Computational Linguistics (2018)

9. Rashkin, H., Choi, E., Jang, J.Y., Volkova, S., Choi, Y.: Truth of varying shades: Analyzing language in fake news and political fact-checking. In: Proceedings of the 2017 Conference on Empirical Methods in Natural Language Processing, pp. 2931–2937. Association for Computational Linguistics (2017). http://aclweb.org/anthology/D17-1317

10. Rubin, V., Conroy, N., Chen, Y., Cornwell, S.: Fake news or truth? Using satirical cues to detect potentially misleading news. In: Proceedings of the Second Workshop on Computational Approaches to Deception Detection, pp. 7–17. Association for Computational Linguistics (2016). https://doi.org/10.18653/v1/W16-0802, http://www.aclweb.org/anthology/W16-0802

11. Rubin, V.L., Chen, Y., Conroy, N.J.: Deception detection for news: three types of fakes. In: Proceedings of the 78th ASIS&T Annual Meeting: Information Science with Impact: Research in and for the Community, ASIST 2015, pp. 83:1–83:4. American Society for Information Science, Silver Springs, MD, USA (2015). http://dl.acm.org/citation.cfm?id=2857070.2857153

12. Shu, K., Sliva, A., Wang, S., Tang, J., Liu, H.: Fake news detection on social media: a data mining perspective. ACM SIGKDD Explor. Newsl. **19**(1), 22–36 (2017)

13. Thorne, J., Vlachos, A., Christodoulopoulos, C., Mittal, A.: Fever: a large-scale dataset for fact extraction and verification. In: Proceedings of the 2018 Conference of the North American Chapter of the Association for Computational Linguistics: Human Language Technologies, Volume 1 (Long Papers), pp. 809–819. Association for Computational Linguistics (2018). http://aclweb.org/anthology/N18-1074

14. Wang, W.Y.: Liar, liar pants on fire: a new benchmark dataset for fake news detection. In: Proceedings of the 55th Annual Meeting of the Association for Computational Linguistics (Volume 2: Short Papers), pp. 422–426. Association for Computational Linguistics (2017)

# The CSO Classifier: Ontology-Driven Detection of Research Topics in Scholarly Articles

Angelo A. Salatino[✉], Francesco Osborne,
Thiviyan Thanapalasingam, and Enrico Motta

Knowledge Media Institute, The Open University,
MK7 6AA Milton Keynes, UK
{angelo.salatino,francesco.osborne,thiviyan.
thanapalasingam,enrico.motta}@open.ac.uk

**Abstract.** Classifying research papers according to their research topics is an important task to improve their retrievability, assist the creation of smart analytics, and support a variety of approaches for analysing and making sense of the research environment. In this paper, we present the CSO Classifier, a new unsupervised approach for automatically classifying research papers according to the Computer Science Ontology (CSO), a comprehensive ontology of research areas in the field of Computer Science. The CSO Classifier takes as input the metadata associated with a research paper (title, abstract, keywords) and returns a selection of research concepts drawn from the ontology. The approach was evaluated on a gold standard of manually annotated articles yielding a significant improvement over alternative methods.

**Keywords:** Scholarly data · Digital libraries · Bibliographic data · Ontology · Text mining · Topic detection · Word embeddings · Science of science

## 1 Introduction

Classifying scholarly papers according to the relevant research topics is an important task that enables a multitude of functionalities, such as: (i) categorising proceedings in digital libraries, (ii) enhancing semantically the metadata of scientific publications, (iii) generating recommendations, (iv) producing smart analytics, (v) detecting research trends, and others [1, 2]. Typically, this is done by either classifying the papers in pre-existent categories from domain vocabularies, such as MeSH[1], PhySH[2], and the STW Thesaurus for Economics[3], or by means of topic detection methods, such as probabilistic topic models [3, 4]. The first solution has the significant advantage of relying on a set of formally-defined research topics associated with human readable labels, but

---

[1] Medical Subject Headings: https://www.nlm.nih.gov/mesh/.

[2] PhySH - Physics Subject Headings: https://physh.aps.org.

[3] STW Thesaurus for Economics: http://zbw.eu/stw.

© Springer Nature Switzerland AG 2019
A. Doucet et al. (Eds.): TPDL 2019, LNCS 11799, pp. 296–311, 2019.
https://doi.org/10.1007/978-3-030-30760-8_26

requires a good vocabulary of research topics in the domain. Conversely, the latter approaches tend to produce noisier and less interpretable results [5].

We recently released the Computer Science Ontology (CSO) [6], a large-scale, granular, and automatically generated ontology of research areas which includes more than 14 K research topics and 162 K semantic relationships. CSO has been adopted by Springer Nature editors to classify proceedings in the field of Computer Science, such as the well-known LNCS series [2]. We published this resource to make available to all the relevant communities an open knowledge-base for supporting the development of further applications. However, many users interested in adopting CSO for character-izing their data have limited understanding of semantic technologies and how to use an ontology for annotating documents. Hence, the natural next step was to develop a classifier that allows all the relevant stakeholders to annotate research papers according to CSO.

In this paper, we present the CSO Classifier, a new approach for automatically classifying research papers according to the Computer Science Ontology (CSO). Since the Computer Science Ontology is not yet routinely used by researchers, it is not possible to adopt supervised machine learning algorithms that would require a good number of examples for all the relevant categories. For this reason, we focused instead on an unsupervised solution that does not require such a gold standard. Similarly to Song and Roth [7] and other relevant literature [8], we consider this approach unsu-pervised because it does not require labelled examples, even if it uses word embeddings produced by processing a large collection of text.

The CSO Classifier takes as input the metadata associated with a scholarly article (usually title, abstract, and keywords) and returns a selection of research topics drawn from CSO. It operates in three steps. First, it finds all topics in the ontology that are explicitly mentioned in the paper. Then it identifies further semantically related topics by utilizing part-of-speech tagging and world embeddings. Finally, it enriches this set by including the super-areas of these topics according to CSO.

The CSO Classifier was evaluated on a gold standard of manually annotated research papers and demonstrated a significant improvement over alternative approa-ches, such as the classifier previously used by Springer Nature editors to support the annotation of Computer Science proceedings [9].

In summary, our main contributions are:

1. A new unsupervised approach for classifying papers according to the topics in a domain ontology;
2. An application based on this approach which automatically annotates papers with the 14 K research topics in CSO;
3. A novel gold standard including 70 papers in the field of "Semantic Web", "Natural Language Processing", and "Data Mining" annotated by 21 domain experts.

The data produced in the evaluation, the Python implementation of the approaches, and the word embeddings are publicly available at http://w3id.org/cso/cso-classifier.

The rest of the paper is organised as follows. In Sect. 2, we review the literature regarding the topic detection in research papers, pointing out the existing gap. In Sect. 3, we discuss the Computer Science Ontology. In Sect. 4 we describe the new approach adopted by the CSO Classifier. In Sect. 5 we explain how we generated the gold standard and in Sect. 6 we evaluate the CSO Classifier against several alternative methods. Finally, in Sect. 7 we summarise the main conclusions and outline future directions of research.

## 2 Literature Review

The task of characterising research papers according to their topics has traditionally been addressed either by using classifiers for assigning to the articles a set of pre-existent categories, or by topic detection methods [3, 4], which generate topics from the text in a bottom-up style.

The first approach has the advantage to produce clean and formally-defined research topics, and thus is usually preferred when a good characterization of the research topics within a domain is available. For instance, Decker [10] introduced an unsupervised approach that generates paper-topic relationships by exploiting keywords and words extracted from the abstracts in order to analyse the trends of topics on different timescales. Mai et al. [11] developed an approach to subject classification using deep learning techniques and they applied it on a set of paper annotated with the STW Thesaurus for Economics ($\sim 5$ K classes) and MeSH ($\sim 27$ K classes). Similarly, Chernyak [12] presented a supervised approach for annotating papers in Computer Science with topics from ACM.

The second class of approaches are based on topics detection methods. One of the first studies to provide a systematic approach to identifying topics was the Topic Detection and Tracking (TDT) program developed by DARPA [13]. In the literature we can find several approaches that apply clustering techniques to identify topics within a collection of scientific documents [3, 14]. Some approaches rely on just one type of information, e.g., citations [15] or titles [11], while other approaches combine multiple types, e.g., abstract and keywords [2, 10], textual content and citation networks [16]. Several other methods exploit Latent Dirichlet Analysis (LDA) [17], which is a three-level hierarchical Bayesian model that retrieves latent patterns in texts, to model their topics [4]. For instance, Griffiths et al. [4] designed a generative model for document collections, the author-topic model, that simultaneously modeled the content of documents and the interests of authors. A main issue of the approaches that rely on LDA is that they represent topics as a distribution of words and it is often tricky to map them to topics in a classification, although some approaches have been proposed to do so [18].

Another set of methods rely just on keywords. For instance, Duvvuru et al. [19] built a network of co-occurring keywords and subsequently perform statistical analysis by calculating degree, strength, clustering coefficient, and end-point degree to identify clusters and associate them to research topics. Some recent approaches use word embeddings, aiming to quantify semantic similarities between words based on their distributional properties in samples of text. For example, Zhang et al. [20] applied K-means on a set of word represented as embeddings. However, all these approaches to topic detection need to generate the topics from scratch rather than exploiting a domain vocabulary or ontology, resulting in noisier and less interpretable results [5].

In sum, we still lack practical unsupervised approaches for classifying papers according to a granular set of topics. Indeed, most available repositories of scholarly articles, such as Scopus[4], Dimensions[5], and Semantic Scholar[6] adopt keywords or use rather coarse-grained representations of research topics. The CSO Classifier was designed to precisely address this gap and enable high quality automatic classification of research papers in the domain of Computer Science.

## 3  The Computer Science Ontology

The Computer Science Ontology is a large-scale ontology of research areas that was automatically generated using the Klink-2 algorithm [21] on a dataset of 16 million publications, mainly in the field of Computer Science [22]. Differently from other solutions available in the state of the art, CSO includes a much larger number of research topics, enabling a granular characterisation of the content of research papers, and it can be easily updated by running Klink-2 on recent corpora of publications.

The current version of CSO[7] includes 14 K semantic topics and 162 K relationships. The main root is Computer Science; however, the ontology includes also a few secondary roots, such as Linguistics, Geometry, Semantics, and others.

The CSO data model[8] is an extension of SKOS[9]. It includes four main semantic relations:

- *superTopicOf*, which indicates that a topic is a super-area of another one (e.g., Semantic Web is a super-area of Linked Data).
- *relatedEquivalent*, which indicates that two topics can be treated as equivalent for the purpose of exploring research data (e.g., Ontology Matching and Ontology Mapping).
- *contributesTo*, which indicates that the research output of one topic contributes to another.
- *owl:sameAs*, this relation indicates that a research concepts is identical to an external resource. We used DBpedia Spotlight to connect research concepts to DBpedia.

The Computer Science Ontology is available through the CSO Portal[10], a web application that enables users to download, explore, and provide granular feedback on CSO at different levels. Users can use the portal to rate topics and relationships, suggest missing relationships, and visualise sections of the ontology.

---

[4] Scopus - https://www.scopus.com.

[5] Dimensions - https://www.dimensions.ai.

[6] Semantic Scholar - https://www.semanticscholar.org.

[7] CSO is available for download at https://w3id.org/cso/downloads.

[8] CSO Data Model - https://cso.kmi.open.ac.uk/schema/cso.

[9] SKOS Simple Knowledge Organization System - http://www.w3.org/2004/02/skos.

[10] Computer Science Ontology Portal - https://cso.kmi.open.ac.uk .

CSO currently supports a range of applications including Smart Topic Miner [2], a tool designed to assist the Springer Nature editorial team in classifying proceedings, Smart Book Recommender [23], an ontology-based recommender system for selecting books to market at academic venues, and several others [6]. It has been used in several research efforts and proved to effectively support a wide range of tasks such as forecasting new research topics, exploration of scholarly data, automatic annotation of research papers, detection of research communities, and ontology forecasting. More information about CSO and how it was developed can be found in [6].

## 4   CSO Classifier

The CSO Classifier is a novel application that takes as input the text from abstract, title, and keywords of a research paper and outputs a list of relevant concepts from CSO. It consists of two main components: (i) the syntactic module and (ii) the semantic module. Figure 1 depicts its architecture.

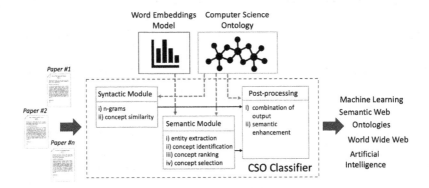

**Fig. 1.**  Workflow of the CSO Classifier.

The *syntactic module* parses the input documents and identifies CSO concepts that are explicitly referred in the document. The *semantic module* uses part-of-speech tagging to identify promising terms and then exploits word embeddings to infer semantically related topics. Finally, the CSO Classifier combines the results of these two modules and enhances them by including relevant super-areas. To assist the description of our approach, we will use the sample paper showed in Table 1 [24] as a running example.

**Table 1.** Sample paper that will be analysed by the CSO Classifier [24].

**De-anonymizing Social Networks**

**Authors:** A.Narayanan and V. Shmatikov

**Abstract:** Operators of online social networks are increasingly sharing potentially sensitive information about users and their relationships with advertisers, application developers, and data-mining researchers. Privacy is typically protected by anonymization, i.e., removing names, addresses, etc. We present a framework for analyzing privacy and anonymity in social networks and develop a new re-identification algorithm targeting anonymized social-network graphs. To demonstrate its effectiveness on real-world networks, we show that a third of the users who can be verified to have accounts on both Twitter, a popular microblogging service, and Flickr, an online photo-sharing site, can be re-identified in the anonymous Twitter graph with only a 12% error rate. Our de-anonymization algorithm is based purely on the network topology, does not require creation of a large number of dummy "sybil" nodes, is robust to noise and all existing defenses, and works even when the overlap between the target network and the adversary's auxiliary information is small.

**Keywords:** social networks, anonymity, privacy

## 4.1 Syntactic Module

The syntactic module maps n-grams in the text to concepts within CSO. First, the algorithm removes English stop words and collects unigrams, bigrams, and trigrams. Then, for each n-gram, it computes the Levenshtein similarity with the labels of the topics in CSO. Research topics having similarity equal or higher than a threshold (i.e., the constant *msm*) with an n-gram, are selected for the final set of topics, i.e., the *returned topics*. In the prototype *msm* was empirically set to 0.94. This value allows us to recognize many variations of CSO topics and to handle hyphens between words, i.e., "knowledge based systems" and "knowledge-based systems", and plurals, i.e., "database" and "databases".

In Table 2 we report the list of topics returned by the syntactic module for the running example. In contrast with the keyword field, which contains only three terms ("social networks", "anonymity", and "privacy"), the classifier is able to identify a wide range of pertinent topics, such as "microblogging", "data mining", "twitter", and "network topology".

**Table 2.** Topics returned from the syntactic module when processing the paper in Table 1.

microblogging, real-world networks, data privacy, sensitive informations, social networks, anonymization, anonymity, online social networks, privacy, twitter, data mining, network topology, graph theory

## 4.2 Semantic Module

The semantic module was designed to find topics that are semantically related to the paper but may not be explicitly referred to in it. It utilizes word embeddings produced by word2vec to compute the semantic similarity between the terms in the document and the CSO concepts.

The semantic module follows four steps: (i) entity extraction, (ii) CSO concept identification, (iii) concept ranking, and (iv) concept selection.

In the following sections, we will describe how we trained the word embedding model and illustrate the algorithm.

### 4.2.1  Word Embedding Generation

We applied the word2vec approach [25, 26] to a collection of text from the Microsoft Academic Graph (MAG)[11] for generating word embeddings. MAG is a scientific knowledge base and a heterogeneous graph containing scientific publication records, citation relationships, authors, institutions, journals, conferences, and fields of study. It is the largest dataset of scholarly data publicly available, and, as of December 2018, it contains more than 210 million publications.

We first downloaded titles, and abstracts of 4,654,062 English papers in the field of Computer Science. Then we pre-processed the data by replacing spaces with under-scores in all n-grams matching the CSO topic labels (e.g., "digital libraries" became "digital_libraries") and for frequent bigrams and trigrams (e.g., "highest_accuracies", "highly_cited_journals"). These frequent n-grams were identified by analysing com-binations of words that co-occur together, as suggested in [26] [12]. Indeed, while it is possible to obtain the vector of a n-gram by averaging the embedding vectors of all its words, the resulting representation usually is not as good as the one obtained by considering the n-gram as a single word during the training phase. Finally, we trained the word2vec model, after testing several combinations of parameters[13].

### 4.2.2  Entity Extraction

We assume that research concepts can be represented either by nouns or adjectives followed by nouns. Considering only these n-grams reduces the number of text chunks to be analysed, speeds up computation and avoids combinations that usually result in false positives. Therefore, the classifier tags each word according to its part of speech (e.g., nouns, verbs, adjectives, adverbs) and then applies a grammar-based chunk parser to identify chunks of words, expressed by the following grammar:

$$< \mathbf{JJ}.* > * < \mathbf{NN}.* > + \tag{1}$$

where JJ represents adjectives and NN represents nouns.

### 4.2.3  CSO Concept Identification

At this stage, the classifier processes the extracted chunks and uses the word2vec model to identify semantically related topics. First, it decomposes the returned chunks in unigrams, bigrams and trigrams. Then, for each gram, it retrieves from the word2vec model its top 10 similar words (having cosine similarity higher than 0.7). The CSO

---

[11] Microsoft Academic Graph - https://www.microsoft.com/en-us/research/project/microsoft-academic-graph/ .

[12] In particular, for the collocation analysis, we used *min-count* = 5 and *threshold* = 10.

[13] The final parameters of the word2vec model are: *method* = skipgram, *embedding-size* = 128, *window-size* = 10, *min-count-cutoff* = 10, *max-iterations* = 5.

topics matching these words are added to the result set. Figure 2 illustrates this process more in detail.

When processing bigrams or trigrams, the classifier joins their tokens using an underscore, e.g., "web_application", in order to refer to the corresponding word in the word2vec model. If a n-gram is not available within the vocabulary of the model, the classifier utilizes the average of the embedding vectors of all its tokens.

A specific CSO concept can be identified multiple times due to two main reasons: (i) multiple n-grams can be semantically related to the same CSO concept, and (ii) the same n-gram can appear multiple times within the title, abstract and keywords. For example, the concept "social_media" can be inferred by several semantically related n-grams, such as: "social_networking_sites", "microblogging", "twitter", "blogs", "on-line_communities", "user-generated_content", and others.

### 4.2.4 Concept Ranking

The previous step may produce a large number of topics (typically more then 70), some of which only marginally related to the research paper in question. For instance, when processing the paper in Table 1, some n-grams triggered concepts like "malicious_behaviour" and "gateway_nodes", that may be considered unrelated. For this reason, the semantic module weighs the identified CSO concepts according to their overall relevancy to the paper. The relevance score of a topic is computed as the product between the number of times it was identified (frequency) and the number of unique n-grams that led to it (diversity). For instance, if a concept has been identified five times, from two different n-grams, its final score will equal 10. In addition, if a topic is directly mentioned in the paper, its score is set to the maximum score found. Finally, the classifier ranks the topics according to their relevance score.

### 4.2.5 Concept Selection

The relevance score of the candidate topics typically follow a long-tailed distribution. In order to automatically select only the relevant topics, the classifier adopts the elbow method [27]. This technique was originally designed to find the appropriate number of clusters in a dataset. Specifically, it observes the cost function for varying numbers of clusters. The best number of clusters is then located at the elbow of the resulting curve. This point provides a good trade-off between the number of clusters and the percentage improvement of the cost function.

Figure 3 shows an example of how the elbow method automatically identifies the best cut in the curve of relevance scores, selecting the first 18 topics. In Table 3 we report the list of topics obtained using the semantic module on the running example. In bold are the topics that were detected by the semantic module but not by the syntactic module.

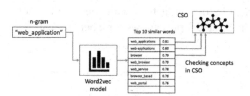

**Fig. 2.** Identification of CSO concepts semantically related to n-grams.

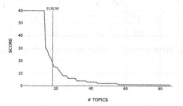

**Fig. 3.** Distribution of the CSO topic scores associated to a paper (blue line), and its elbow (red line). (Color figure online)

**Table 3.** Topics returned from the semantic module when processing the paper in Table 1. In bold the topics missing from the syntactic module in Table 2.

| |
|---|
| social networks, anonymity, topology, twitter, anonymization, sensitive informations, data privacy, online social networks, data mining, privacy, **social media**, social networking sites, graph theory, **network architecture**, **micro-blog**, **online communities**, **social graphs** |

### 4.3   Combined Output and Enhancement

The CSO Classifier combines the topics returned by the two modules. In this phase, it first discards the topics returned by the semantic module that appear among the first $n$ most occurring words in the vocabulary of the embeddings ($n=3,000$ in the proto-type). This is done because these very generic terms (e.g., 'language', 'learning', 'component') tend to have a good similarity value with a large number of n-grams, typically resulting in too many false positives. It then enriches the combined set of topics by inferring all their direct super topics, exploiting the *superTopicOf* relationship within CSO [6]. For instance, when the classifier extracts the topic "machine learning", it will infer also "artificial intelligence". By default, the CSO Classifier includes only the direct super topics, but it is also possible to infer the list of all their super topics up to the root, i.e., Computer Science.

In Table 4 we report the list of topics inferred from the topics returned by the syntactic and semantic module. As we can see there are several other topics that are pertinent to the paper in Table 1, such as: "security of data", "authentication", "world wide web", and others.

**Table 4.** Topics obtained from the enhancement process when processing the running paper

| |
|---|
| authentication, theoretical computer science, world wide web, privacy preserving, access control, network protocols, complex networks, online systems, network security, security of data, computer science |

We take the union of the result sets of the two modules, since this solution max-imizes the f-measure according to the evaluation (see Sect. 6). However, it is possible to adopt different strategies to combine the topics produced by the two modules, resulting in various trade-offs between precision and recall. Intuitively, the topics that get explicitly referred to in the text, returned by the syntactic module, tend to be more accurate, but including also the semantically related topics allows for a better recall. We will further discuss this in Sect. 6.1.

# 5   Creation of the Gold Standard

Since the CSO ontology was only released a few months ago, we lacked a dataset of manually annotated papers that could be used as gold standard. Therefore, we built such a gold standard by asking 21 domain experts to classify 70 papers in terms of topics drawn from the CSO ontology. This new gold standard has two objectives. First, it allows us to evaluate the proposed classifier against baseline methods, and, second, it provides a resource which will facilitate further evaluations in this area from other members of the research community.

## 5.1   Data Preparation

We queried the MAG dataset and selected the 70 most cited papers published in 2007-2017 within the fields of *Semantic Web* (23 papers), *Natural Language Processing* (23 papers), and *Data Mining* (24 papers)[14].

We then contacted 21 researchers in these fields, at various levels of seniority, and asked each of them to annotate 10 of these papers. We structured the data collection in order to have each paper annotated by at least three experts, using majority vote to address disagreements. The papers were randomly assigned to experts, while minimising the number of shared papers between each pair of experts.

## 5.2   Data Collection

We designed a web application to support the domain experts in annotating the papers. For each paper, the application displayed to the users: title, abstract, keywords (when available), and the set of candidate topics. The experts were asked to carefully read all the information and assess a set of candidate topics by dragging them in two different baskets: *relevant* and *not relevant*. They also could input further CSO topics that according to their judgment were missing from the candidate topics. Each paper was assigned with an average of $18 \pm 9$ topics.

We created the initial set of candidate topics by aggregating the output of three classifiers: the syntactic module (Sect. 4.1), the semantic module (Sect. 4.2), and a third approach, which was introduced for reducing the bias towards the first two methods. The latter first splits the input document into overlapping windows of size 10 (same as the training window of the word2vec model), each of them overlapping by 5 words. Then, for each window, it computes the average of the embedding vectors of all its words, creating an embedding representation of the window, and uses the word2vec model to identify the top 20 similar words with similarity above 0.6. It then assigns to each CSO concept a score based on the number of times it is found in the list of similar words and on the embedding similarity (cosine similarity between the vector representation of the window and word embedding). Finally, it sorts them in descending

---

[14] These three fields are well covered by CSO, which includes a total of 35 sub-topics for the Semantic Web, 173 for Natural Language Processing, and 396 for Data Mining.

order and prunes the result set using the elbow method [27]. The combination of these approaches produced a very inclusive set of $41.8 \pm 17.5$ candidate topics for each paper.

### 5.3   Gold Standard

The data collection process produced 210 annotations (70 papers times 3 annotations per paper). In order to consider the taxonomic relationships of CSO, the resulting set of topics were semantically enriched by including also their direct super-areas as in [1, 2].

We computed the Fleiss' Kappa to measure the agreement among the three annotators on each paper. We obtained an average of $0.451 \pm 0.177$ indicating a moderate inter-rater agreement, according to Landis and Koch [28].

We created the gold standard using the majority rule approach. Specifically, if a topic was considered relevant by at least two annotators, it was added to the gold standard. Each paper in the gold standard is associated with $14.4 \pm 7.0$ topics.

## 6   Evaluation

We evaluated the CSO Classifier against thirteen alternative approaches on the task of classifying the papers in the gold standard according to CSO topics. Table 5 summarizes their main features and reports their performance.

**TF-IDF** returns for each paper a ranked list of words according to their TF-IDF score. The IDF of the terms was computed on the dataset of 4.6 M papers in Computer Science, introduced in Sect. 4.2.1. **TF-IDF-M** maps these terms to CSO by returning all the CSO topics having Levenshtein similarity higher than 0.8 with them.

The following six classifiers use the Latent Dirichlet Allocation (LDA) [17] over the same corpus and then produce a number of keywords extracted from the distribution of terms associated to the LDA topics. **LDA100** was trained on 100 topics, **LDA500** on 500 topics, and **LDA1000** on 1000 topics. These three classifiers select all LDA topics with a probability of at least $j$ and return all their words with a probability of at least $k$. **LDA100-M**, **LDA500-M**, and **LDA1000-M** work in the same way, but the resulting keywords are then mapped to the CSO topics. In particular, they return all CSO topics that have Levenshtein similarity higher than 0.8 with the resulting set of terms. We performed a grid search for finding the best values of $j$ and $k$ on the gold standard and report here the best results of each classifier in term of f-measure.

**W2 V-W** is the classifier described in Sect. 5.2 in order to produce further candidate topics for the domain experts. It processes the input document with a sliding window and uses the word2vec model to identify concepts semantically similar to the embedding of the window.

**STM** is the classifier originally adopted by Smart Topic Miner [2], the application used by Springer Nature for classifying proceeding in the field of Computer Science. It works similarly to the syntactic module described in Sect. 4.1, but it detects only exact matches between the terms extracted from the text and the CSO topics. **SYN** is the first version of the CSO classifier, originally introduced in [9], and it is equivalent to the syntactic module as described Sect. 4.1. **SEM** consists of the semantic module described in Sect. 4.2. **INT** is a hybrid version that returns the intersection of the topics produced by the syntactic (**SYN**) and semantic (**SEM**) modules. Finally, **CSO-C** is the default implementation of the CSO Classifier presented in this paper. As described in Sect. 4, it produces the union of the topics returned by the two modules.

We assessed the performance of these fourteen approaches by means of precision, recall and f-measure. When classifying a given paper $p$, the value of precision $pr(p)$ and recall $re(p)$ are computed as shown in Eq. 3:

$$pr(p) = \frac{|cl(p) \cap gs(p)|}{cl(p)} \qquad re(p) = \frac{|cl(p) \cap gs(p)|}{gs(p)} \tag{3}$$

where $cl(p)$ identifies the topics returned by the classifier, and $gs(p)$ the gold standard obtained for that paper, including the super-areas of the gold standard used to enrich the user annotations as mentioned in Sect. 5.3. In order to obtain a better comparison between the different classifiers, we enhanced the results of each method with their direct super-concepts. The overall precision and recall for a given classifier are computed as the average of the values of precision and recall obtained over the papers. The f-measure (F1) is the harmonic mean of precision and recall.

**Table 5.** Values of precision, recall, and f-measure for the classifiers. In bold the best results.

| Classifier | Description | Prec. | Rec. | F1 |
|---|---|---|---|---|
| TF-IDF | TF-IDF | 16.7% | 24.0% | 19.7% |
| TF-IDF-M | TF-IDF mapped to CSO concepts | 40.4% | 24.1% | 30.1% |
| LDA100 | LDA with 100 topics | 5.9% | 11.9% | 7.9% |
| LDA500 | LDA with 500 topics | 4.2% | 12.5% | 6.3% |
| LDA1000 | LDA with 1000 topics | 3.8% | 5.0% | 4.3% |
| LDA100-M | LDA with 100 topics mapped to CSO | 9.4% | 19.3% | 12.6% |
| LDA500-M | LDA with 500 topics mapped to CSO | 9.6% | 21.2% | 13.2% |
| LDA1000-M | LDA with 1000 topics mapped to CSO | 12.0% | 11.5% | 11.7% |
| W2V-W | W2V on windows of words (Sect. 5.2) | 41.2% | 16.7% | 23.8% |
| STM | Classifier used by STM, introduced in [2]. | **80.8%** | 58.2% | 67.6% |
| SYN | Syntactic module (Sect. 4.1) [9] | 78.3% | 63.8% | 70.3% |
| SEM | Semantic module (Sect. 4.2) | 70.8% | 72.2% | 71.5% |
| INT | Intersection of SYN and SEM | 79.3% | 59.1% | 67.7% |
| CSO-C | The CSO Classifier | 73.0% | **75.3%** | **74.1%** |

## 6.1  Results

We ran the fourteen classifiers and evaluated their results against the gold standard. In Table 5 we report the resulting values of precision, recall and f-measure.

The approaches based on LDA and TF-IDF performed poorly and did not exceed 30.1% of f-measure. It should be noted that while a tighter threshold on the Levenshtein similarity used for matching terms with CSO topics may further raise the precision, the low recall makes these approaches mostly unfit for this task. An analysis on the LDA topics showed that these tend to be mostly noisy and coarse-grained. They are thus unable to return several of the most specific CSO topics and often cluster together distinct CSO topics (e.g., "databases" and "search engines") in the same LDA topic. For instance, the LDA topic characterizing papers about Social Networks includes as top words many generic terms such as *users, online, social, profile, trust*, and so on. In general, LDA works quite well at identifying the main topics characterizing large collection of documents, but it is typically less suitable when trying to infer more specific research topics, which may be associated with a low number of publications (50–200), as discussed in [21]. **W2V-W** performed also poorly in term of both precision (41.2%) and recall (16.7%).

**STM** and **SYN** yielded a very good precision of respectively 80.8% and 78.3%. Indeed, these methods are good at finding topics that get explicitly mentioned in the text, which tend to be very relevant. However, they failed to detect some more subtle topics that are just implied, suffering from a low recall of 58.2% and 63.8%. The method used to map the terms from the text to the CSO topics plays a key role in the difference of performance between these two classifiers. Indeed, **STM** identifies only concepts that match exactly at least one of the terms extracted from the text. Conversely, **SYN** finds also partial matches, reducing precision but increasing recall.

The semantic module (**SEM**) lost some precision in comparison with **SYN**, but provided a better recall and f-measure. This suggests that it is able to identify further topics that do not directly appear directly in the paper, but naturally this may also produce some more false positives. **INT** yielded a higher precision (79.3%) compared to the syntactic and the semantic modules (78.3% and 70.8%), but it did not perform well in term of recall, which dropped from 63.8% and 72.2% to 59.1%.

Finally, the CSO Classifier (**CSO-C**) outperformed all the other methods in terms of both recall (75.3%) and f-measure (74.1%).

We compared the performance of the approaches using the McNemar's test for correlated proportions. The **CSO-C** performed significantly better ($p < 10^{-7}$) than all the other approaches. In addition, STM [2], SYN [9], SEM, and INT were also significantly different from all the other baselines based on TF-IDF and LDA ($p < 10^{-7}$). In summary, the CSO Classifier yielded the best overall results. However, it is possible to obtain a better precision by adopting a purely syntactic method that focus on the topics that are explicitly referred to in the text.

Another way to obtain a specific trade-off between precision and recall is changing the method used for selecting the returned topics from the ranked list produced by the semantic module. Intuitively, selecting the ones with the highest weights will yield a high precision, while being more inclusive will result in a higher recall. Figure 4 shows the value of precision, recall, and f-measure obtained by taking the first $n$ topics in the ranked list. The precision (blue line) decreases while the recall (orange line) increases. The intersection of these two curves determines the highest value of f-measure (green line), with a peak of 63.6% when selecting the first 10 topics. It is useful to note that the elbow method, yielding a f-measure of 71.5%, clearly outperforms this solution based on a fixed number of returned topics.

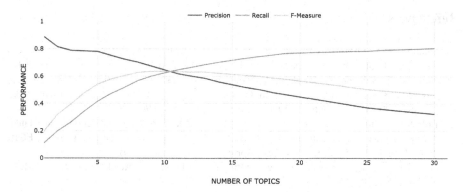

**Fig. 4.** Average values of precision, recall, and f-measure according to the different sizes of candidate topic set returned for each paper. (Color figure online)

As final step of the analysis, we treated the CSO Classifier as another expert and we observed how this influenced the inter-rater agreement. The general agreement when including CSO Classifier slightly lowers to $0.392 \pm 0.144$ yielding a moderate agreement with the majority of human experts.

## 7 Conclusions and Future Work

In this paper, we introduced the CSO Classifier, an application for classifying academic documents according to the Computer Science Ontology (CSO). The CSO Classifier analyses the text associated with research papers (title, abstract, and keywords) both on a syntactic and semantic level and returns a set of pertinent research topics drawn from CSO. This solution was evaluated on a gold standard of 70 manually annotated articles and outperformed the alternative approaches in terms of recall and f-measure. The code of the CSO Classifier and all the relevant material is freely available to the wider research community.

The approach presented in this paper opens up several interesting directions of work. On the research side, we will investigate further solutions combining natural language processing, machine learning, and semantics to improve the performance of the CSO Classifier. We also plan to explore the application of this approach to other research fields. In particular, we are currently working on a topic ontology for the Engineering field and we plan to produce a version of the classifier tailored to this area. We are also planning to extend it to the field of Medicine, in which we can take advantage of MeSH as ontology of subjects and the Medline dataset[15] for training our word2vec model.

On the technology transfer side, we will include the CSO Classifier within the pipelines of the Smart Topic Miner [2] and Smart Book Recommender [23], two applications we developed to support editorial processes at Springer Nature.

---

[15] Medline dataset: https://www.nlm.nih.gov/bsd/medline.html .

# References

1. Salatino, A.A., Osborne, F., Motta, E.: AUGUR: forecasting the emergence of new research topics. In: Joint Conference on Digital Libraries 2018, Fort Worth, Texas, pp. 1–10 (2018)
2. Osborne, F., Salatino, A., Birukou, A., Motta, E.: Automatic classification of springer nature proceedings with smart topic miner. In: Groth, P., et al. (eds.) ISWC 2016. LNCS, vol. 9982, pp. 383–399. Springer, Cham (2016). https://doi.org/10.1007/978-3-319-46547-0_33
3. Bolelli, L., Ertekin, Ş., Giles, C.L.: Topic and trend detection in text collections using latent dirichlet allocation. In: Boughanem, M., Berrut, C., Mothe, J., Soule-Dupuy, C. (eds.) ECIR 2009. LNCS, vol. 5478, pp. 776–780. Springer, Heidelberg (2009)
4. Griffiths, T.L., Steyvers, M.: Finding scientific topics. Proc. Natl. Acad. Sci. U. S. A. **101**(1), 5228–5235 (2004)
5. Osborne, F., Motta, E.: Mining semantic relations between research areas. In: Cudré-Mauroux, P., et al. (eds.) ISWC 2012. Lecture Notes in Computer Science, vol. 7649, pp. 410–426. Springer, Heidelberg (2012). https://doi.org/10.1007/978-3-642-35176-1_26
6. Salatino, A.A., Thanapalasingam, T., Mannocci, A., Osborne, F., Motta, E.: The computer science ontology: a large-scale taxonomy of research areas. In: Vrandečić, D., et al. (eds.) ISWC 2018. LNCS, vol. 11137, pp. 187–205. Springer, Cham (2018). https://doi.org/10.1007/978-3-030-00668-6_12
7. Song, Y., Roth, D.: Unsupervised sparse vector densification for short text similarity. In: Human Language Technologies: Annual Conference of the North American Chapter of the ACL, pp. 1275–80 (2015)
8. Lilleberg, J., Zhu, Y., Zhang, Y.: Support vector machines and Word2vec for text classification with semantic features. In: 2015 IEEE 14th International Conference on Cognitive Informatics & Cognitive Computing (ICCI*CC), pp. 136–140. IEEE (2015)
9. Salatino, A.A., Thanapalasingam, T., Mannocci, A., Osborne, F., Motta, E.: Classifying research papers with the computer science ontology. In: ISWC-P&D-Industry-BlueSky 2018 (2018)
10. Decker, S.L., Aleman-meza, B., Cameron, D., Arpinar, I.B.: Detection of Bursty and Emerging Trends towards Identification of Researchers at the Early Stage of Trends (2007)
11. Mai, F., Galke, L., Scherp, A.: Using deep learning for title-based semantic subject indexing to reach competitive performance to full-text. In: JCDL 2018 Proceedings of the 18th ACM/IEEE on Joint Conference on Digital Libraries. pp. 169–178. ACM, New York (2018)
12. Chernyak, E.: An approach to the problem of annotation of research publications. In: Proceedings of the Eighth ACM International Conference on Web Search and Data Mining - WSDM '15, pp. 429–434. ACM Press, New York (2015)
13. Allan, J., Carbonell, J., Doddington, G., Yamron, J., Yang, Y.: Topic Detection and Tracking Pilot Study Final Report (1998)
14. Osborne, F., Scavo, G., Motta, E.: Identifying diachronic topic-based research communities by clustering shared research trajectories. In: Presutti, V., d'Amato, C., Gandon, F., d'Aquin, M., Staab, S., Tordai, A. (eds.) ESWC 2014. LNCS, vol. 8465, pp. 114–129. Springer, Cham (2014). https://doi.org/10.1007/978-3-319-07443-6_9
15. Small, H., Boyack, K.W., Klavans, R.: Identifying emerging topics in science and technology. Res. Policy **43**, 1450–1467 (2014)
16. Caragea, C., Bulgarov, F., Mihalcea, R.: Co-Training for Topic Classification of Scholarly Data. Association for Computational Linguistics (2015)
17. Blei, D.M., Ng, A.Y., Jordan, M.I.: Latent Dirichlet allocation. J. Mach. Learn. Res. **3**, 993–1022 (2003)

18. Bhatia, S., Lau, J.H., Baldwin, T.: Automatic labelling of topics with neural embeddings. In: Proceedings of COLING 2016, the 26th International Conference on Computational Linguistics: Technical Papers, Osaka, Japan, pp. 953–963. The COLING 2016, December (2016)

19. Duvvuru, A., Radhakrishnan, S., More, D., Kamarthi, S.: Analyzing structural & temporal characteristics of keyword system in academic research articles. Procedia - Procedia Comput. Sci. **20**, 439–445 (2013)

20. Zhang, Y., Lu, J., Liu, F., Liu, Q., Porter, A., Chen, H., Zhang, G.: Does deep learning help topic extraction? A kernel k-means clustering method with word embedding. J. Informetr. **12**, 1099–1117 (2018)

21. Osborne, F., Motta, E.: Klink-2: integrating multiple web sources to generate semantic topic networks. In: Arenas, M., et al. (eds.) ISWC 2015. LNCS, vol. 9366, pp. 408–424. Springer, Cham (2015). https://doi.org/10.1007/978-3-319-25007-6_24

22. Osborne, F., Motta, E., Mulholland, P.: exploring scholarly data with rexplore. In: Alani, H., et al. (eds.) ISWC 2013. LNCS, vol. 8218, pp. 460–477. Springer, Heidelberg (2013). https://doi.org/10.1007/978-3-642-41335-3_29

23. Thanapalasingam, T., Osborne, F., Birukou, A., Motta, E.: Ontology-based recommendation of editorial products. In: Vrandečić, D., et al. (eds.) ISWC 2018. Lecture Notes in Computer Science, vol. 11137. Springer, Cham (2018). https://doi.org/10.1007/978-3-030-00668-6_21

24. Narayanan, A., Shmatikov, V.: De-anonymizing social networks. In: 30th IEEE Symposium on Security and Privacy, pp. 173–187. IEEE (2009)

25. Mikolov, T., Chen, K., Corrado, G., Dean, J.: Efficient estimation of word representations in vector space (2013)

26. Mikolov, T., Chen, K., Corrado, G., Dean, J.: Distributed representations of words and phrases and their compositionality. In: Advances in Neural Information Processing Systems, pp. 3111–3119 (2013)

27. Satopää, V., Albrecht, J., Irwin, D., Raghavan, B.: Finding a "Kneedle" in a haystack: detecting knee points in system behavior. In: ICDCSW 2011 Proceedings of the 2011 31st International Conference on Distributed Computing Systems, pp. 166–171. IEEE Computer Society Washington (2011)

28. Landis, J.R., Koch, G.G.: The measurement of observer agreement for categorical data. Biometrics **33**, 159–174 (1977)

# Non-Parametric Subject Prediction

Shenghui Wang[1]([✉]), Rob Koopman[1], and Gwenn Englebienne[2]

[1] OCLC Research, Schipholweg 99, 2316XA Leiden, The Netherlands
{shenghui.wang,rob.koopman}@oclc.org
[2] University of Twente, Hallenweg 19, 7522NH Enschede, The Netherlands
g.englebienne@utwente.nl

**Abstract.** Automatic subject prediction is a desirable feature for modern digital library systems, as manual indexing can no longer cope with the rapid growth of digital collections. This is an "extreme multi-label classification" problem, where the objective is to assign a small subset of the most relevant subjects from an extremely large label set. Data sparsity and model scalability are the major challenges we need to address to solve it automatically. In this paper, we describe an efficient and effective embedding method that embeds terms, subjects and documents into the same semantic space, where similarity can be computed easily. We then propose a novel Non-Parametric Subject Prediction (NPSP) method and show how effectively it predicts even very specialised subjects, which are associated with few documents in the training set and are not predicted by state-of-the-art classifiers.

**Keywords:** Random projection · Subject prediction · Non-parametric method · Semantic embedding

## 1 Introduction

Because of the ever-increasing number of documents that information systems deal with, automatic subject indexing, i.e., identifying and describing the subject(s) of documents to increase their findability, is one of the most desirable features for many such systems. Subject index terms are normally taken from knowledge organization systems (e.g., thesauri, subject headings systems) and classification systems (e.g., dewey decimal classification) which easily contain tens or hundreds of thousands terms or codes. Automatically assigning a small set of most relevant subjects from the huge label space – the Extreme Multi-label Text Classification (XMTC) problem – is therefore very difficult. Data sparsity and scalability are the major challenges.

In this paper, we solve this in two steps. First, we propose a novel embedding method which extends random projection by weighting and projecting raw term embeddings orthogonally to an average language vector, thus improving the discriminating power of resulting term embeddings, and build more meaningful document embeddings by assigning appropriate weights to individual terms.

A. Doucet et al. (Eds.): TPDL 2019, LNCS 11799, pp. 312–326, 2019.
https://doi.org/10.1007/978-3-030-30760-8_27

Subjects are treated as special terms which get embedded into the same semantic space where terms and documents live. Secondly, we propose a novel Non-Parametric Subject Prediction (NPSP) method to predict subjects for unseen documents. We compare this method with the state-of-the-art deep learning method and the direct subject-document-similarity based method.

## 2    Related Work

*Automatic Subject Indexing.* According to [9], there are three groups of approaches: text categorisation, where supervised machine learning is used to predict subjects from features extracted from documents [24]; document clustering, where unsupervised machine learning is used to group documents and the resulting groups are then associated with certain topics [6]; and document classification, where no training data is (necessarily) used but string matching relates the subjects to the documents [2,7,8]. In this paper, we focus on data-driven text categorisation, and it is still an open research question how this problem should best be approached.

*Extreme Multi-label Text Classification.* The goal of automatic subject prediction is to assign a small subset of relevant subject labels (subjects) to a document, taken from tens or hundreds of thousands target labels. This remains a difficult problem and is a form of Extreme Multi-label Text Classification (XMTC) [3,17,23], where the prediction space often consists of hundreds of thousands to millions of labels. Data sparsity and scalability are the major challenges. Unlike traditional binary or multi-class classification problems, in multi-label classification the target labels are neither independent nor mutually exclusive, thus making the modelling of the relationship between the documents and the labels challenging.

There are four categories of solutions: (1) 1-vs-All classification [22], (2) Embedding-based [3,25], (3) Tree-based [23], and (4) Deep learning methods [12,17].[1]. Each of these approaches has pros and cons. In 1-vs-all classification, a separate classifier is trained for each subject and is used to decide whether that particular subject is applicable for a given document: such an approach ignores the correlation between subjects and does, therefore, not make optimal use of the available data. Furthermore, this is not practical for extreme multi-label classification, because of the number of classifiers that need to be trained and evaluated for prediction is too high. Tree-based methods and Deep-learning methods can model the correlation between labels and can be extremely powerful given enough training data, but they are hard to interpret and suffer from the inevitable lack of data for the rare labels that make up so much of the heavy tail of the label distribution.

Embedding-based approaches [3,25] aim to address the data sparsity issue by projecting the high-dimensional label vectors to their low-dimensional embeddings during training. When classifying a new sample, a decompression process

---

[1]  http://manikvarma.org/downloads/XC/XMLRepository.html.

is used to map the predicted embedding back to the original high-dimensional space. These methods are powerful, relatively fast and well understood, but they either rely on low-rank assumptions on the inter-subject distance matrix [27] or require clustering of the data which, in turn, depends on an arbitrarily chosen number of clusters and their initial cluster parameters [3].

In contrast, our approach does not make any assumptions on the rank of the inter-subject distance matrix. Instead, we use random projection to embed the co-occurrence matrix of the terms that constitute the documents and the subjects we try to predict. By modeling terms in function of their relationship with subjects, we obtain a very flexible embedding that also allows us to embed single documents (by considering which terms occur in them), directly incorporate the statistical relationship between terms and subjects and avoid needing to arbitrarily cluster the documents to resolve the high rank of the global inter-subject distance matrix.

## 3   Method

We propose to apply a Random Projection based embedding method to embed both terms and subjects in a semantic space as described in Sect. 3.1. This allows us to compute a vector representation of any document, seen or unseen. When classifying an unseen document, we propose two methods: first to compute its vector representation and compute that vector's similarity to the vector representations of all subjects, thus allowing us to rank subject candidates in order of decreasing similarity, to find the most appropriate ones for that document, as described in Sect. 3.2. Second, we propose computing similarities between the query document and documents from the training set: these are annotated with subjects and provide us with a way to better assess the validity of a subject to the query document, as explained in Sect. 3.3.

### 3.1   Ariadne Semantic Embedding

Let a document be a set of words for which term co-occurrence is relevant[2] and which can be meaningfully annotated with a subject. Let $n_D$ be the total number of documents in the training set, $n_S$ the number of subjects, $n_V$ the number of *frequent* terms,[3]. A term is considered frequent when it occurs in more than $k$ documents in the corpus, where $K$ is flexible depending on the size of the corpus. In addition, let $n_E$ be the total number of entities we want to embed (in our case $n_E = n_S + n_V$) and $D$ the chosen dimensionality of the embedding vectors.

Building on our previous work [13–15], we embed the relevant entities by Random Projection [1,11] of their weighted co-occurrence:

$$\mathbf{C}'_{[n_E \times D]} = \mathbf{C}_{[n_E \times n_S]} \mathbf{R}_{[n_S \times D]} \tag{1}$$

---

[2] In general, a document could therefore be a sentence, a paragraph, a fixed-size window, a bibliographic record, *etc.*; in our case, documents are scientific publications.

[3] Terms could be words, n-grams or phrases. In our work, common phrases are automatically detected using the method described in [19].

where $\mathbf{C}'$ is the matrix of embedding vectors, $\mathbf{C}$ is the weighted co-occurrence matrix of different terms and $\mathbf{R}$ is a random matrix. In this work, we focus on subjects, and in this particular use case we observe that it is useful to use co-occurrence of the entities with the subject labels only. In general, term-term co-occurrences are more common and well-suited, in which case we would have $n_V$ columns to the matrix $C$ and $n_V$ rows to $\mathbf{R}$.

**Weighted Co-occurrence Counts.** To improve the robustness of the approach, we weight the co-occurrence matrix $\mathbf{C}$ to reduce the effect of terms that are extremely common in certain documents and of terms that occur in the vast majority of documents. We use the terms' average TFIDF score in the training documents, modified as follows. Let each element $c_{t_i,s_j}$ of $C$ be the weighted co-occurrence count of entity $t_i$ and subject $s_j$. For notational simplicity, we will use $s \in d$ to indicate that document $d$ is annotated with subject $s$ and $t \in d$ to indicate the document contains word $t$. Further, let $d_t$ be the total number of documents that term $t$ occurs in; $r_s$ a $D$-dimensional "random vector" for subject $s$, i.e., $r_s$ is a row of $\mathbf{R}$ (In our implementation, this vector is binary and contains an equal number of $+1$ and $-1$, thus making computations very efficient [13]). Experimentally, we verified that the traditional IDF weighting factor of $\log \frac{N}{d_t}$ suppresses frequent terms too much, and replace it by a factor of $\sqrt{N/d_t}$, which has a similar effect but a longer tail and can also be seen as the normalisation constant of the t-test statistic [18]. For the TF factor, we use a factor of $1 + \log c_t(d)$, where $c_t(d)$ is the term count of term $t$ in document $d$, and ignore the constant $N$ which cancels out in the subsequent normalisation. The co-occurrence counts $c_{t,s}$ are, therefore, replaced with weighed counts so that the elements of $\mathbf{C}$ become:

$$c_{t,s} = \sum_d I(t \in d)\, I(s \in d)\, \frac{1 + \log c_t(d)}{\sqrt{d_t}} \tag{2}$$

where $I(t \in d)$ is an indicator function which is 1 if entity $t$ occurs in document $d$, and zero otherwise. After projection, each row of $\mathbf{C}'$, denoted $v_t$ in the remainder of this document, is a vector embedding of term $t$.

**Orthogonal Projection.** Traditional models discard both very infrequent words (because they are too rare for the model to be able to capture their semantics from the training data) and very frequent words (so-called "stop words" because they do not provide any semantically useful information). In our approach, we give a continuous weight to terms based on how frequently they occur and compute the average "language vector" of the corpus, $v_a$, the sum of all the rows of $\mathbf{C}'$. Unsurprisingly, this vector is very similar to the average vector of stop words. Intuitively, words are increasingly more informative as they differ more from the average vector. By this reasoning, we project[4] word vectors on the

---

[4] We use projection rather than subtracting $v_a$ to prevent orthogonal vectors from gaining undue importance.

orthogonal hyperplane to $v_a$: $v_t^* = v_t - (v_t \cdot v_a)v_a$, resulting in a representation where the uninformative component of terms is eliminated, and normalise the vectors to have unit length. When computing document vectors, we down-weight terms according to their similarity to $v_a$ (see Eq. 3). This step is crucial to get distinctive document embeddings.

As a nice side effect, projection makes it possible to handle multilingual corpora. The vocabulary of one language tends to be largely orthogonal to that of other languages (since words of one language tend to co-occur almost exclusively with words of the same language), so that projection using one language's average vector does not have much effect on the terms in other languages. This makes it possible to handle different languages effectively, within the same vector space.

**Term Weight Assignment and Document Embedding.** Using the projection described above, the component that differentiates a term from the average vector is kept as its final embedding. Similarly, how different a term is from $v_a$ also indicates how much that term contributes to the semantics of a document it is part of. In fact, we can interpret the cosine similarity as a lower bound on the mutual information (MI) between the two vectors [5]. In order to give a higher weight to the most informative terms, we assign a higher weight to words with lower MI to $v_a$ by setting the final weight of each term to be $w_t = 1 - \cos(v_t, v_a)$.

With the frequent terms' embedding vectors and their proper weights, we can compute document embedding as the weighted average of its component terms' embeddings. For a document $d$, we obtain a set of normalised vectors $v_{t_1}^*, \ldots, v_{t_n}^*$, where $n$ is the number of terms in document $d$ and $v_{t_i}^*$ is the final embedding vector for term $t_i$. The embedding of document $d$ is calculated as follows:

$$v_d = \frac{\sum_{i=1}^n w_{t_i} \cdot v_{t_i}^*}{\sum_{i=1}^n w_{t_i}}. \tag{3}$$

where $w_{t_i}$ is the weight for term $t_i$ and out-of-vocabulary words are ignored. Note how term and document vectors all have unit length, making similarity computations elegant and effective.

## 3.2 Prediction by Subject-Document Similarity

Once subjects and documents are embedded in the same semantic space, it is straightforward to calculate the similarity between any subject and any document. Notice how we can interpret $w_{t_i}/\sum_t w_t$, as the document-conditional probability distribution over the terms, and $v_d$ as the expectation of the embedding of the query document by marginalising out its component terms, while the subject embedding corresponds to the empirical mean of the training documents that were annotated by that subject. If we assume an isotropic distribution for documents annotated by a given subject, then the most related subjects to a document are simply the ones closest to the document, $i.e.$, the subjects with the highest cosine similarities to the document itself.

---

**Algorithm 1.** Non-Parametric Subject Prediction (NPSP)

---

1: **function** SUBJECT_PREDICTION(training documents $\mathcal{D}$, unseen document $u$, $k$)
2:     $D \leftarrow \text{sort}_{S(v_d, v_u)}(\mathcal{D})$    ▷ Order the document embeddings by decreasing similarity to the unseen document $u$
3:     $\forall s : w_s \leftarrow S(v_s, v_u)$ ▷ Initialise the weight $w_s$ with the similarity between the subjects and $u$
4:     **for all** documents $d \in D_{1...k}$ **do**                    ▷ For the $k$ documents closest to $u$
5:         **for all** subjects $s$ of document $d$ **do**
6:             $w_s \leftarrow w_s + S(v_d, v_u)$         ▷ Add the similarity of the documents to $w_s$
7:     **return** $\text{sort}_{w_s}(\{s\})$     ▷ Return a ranked list of subjects according to their weights

---

### 3.3   NPSP: Non-Parametric Subject Prediction

In practice, the distribution of documents annotated by a subject is quite complex, and we can discard the assumption we made in Sect. 3.2 by computing similarities between the query document and training documents only, and using these as supporting evidence for their subjects.

Algorithm 1 describes how we rank the subjects for a given new document $u$. The algorithm returns a ranked list of subjects, where the subjects are sorted according to a summation of (1) the similarity of each subject to the document and (2) the similarity of those of the $k$ most similar documents from the training set which are annotated with the subject. This combination provides us with a robust ranking measure, which combines the direct embedding of the subject in the semantic space where the documents also live and an extra component which lets the $k$ nearest neighbour documents of the new document vouch for the validity of the subject. The idea is that the embedding of each document is more precise than the embedding of the subjects (since that is done based on a combination of many documents), making the similarity computation more trustworthy and the subjects those documents are annotated with reflect more likely to fit the target document.

## 4   Datasets and Experiments

Our experiments were carried out on a subset of the MEDLINE database ($10^6$ articles for training and $10^4$ for testing), randomly selected from WorldCat.[5] Written in English and published between 1984 and 2012, each article has a title and an abstract, to ensure sufficient textual information for computing the word embeddings. This dataset is interesting as it contains an above-average proportion of technical terms and jargon. Very rare terms carry critical meaning and make the task of word and document embedding particularly challenging.

There are in total 324,619 unique MeSH subjects in the training set, and in average each article is indexed by 16 subjects. These subjects are used in an extremely unbalanced way. On one hand, 222,135 subjects are used to index less than 10 articles, among which 95,218 subjects are used to index only one

---

[5] http://www.worldcat.org/.

single article. On the other hand, 7 subjects are each used to index more than 100K articles, and the most frequently used subject "Humans" indexes nearly 58% of the whole corpus (see Table 1). Similar statistics of the subject headings in the testing set is shown in Fig. 2.

We first computed embeddings for frequent terms[6] and MeSH subjects using the training set. For each article in the training set, we computed its document embedding based on the terms in its title and abstract. When classifying an unseed article in the testing set, we first computed its document embedding and then either looked for the most similar subjects directly or applied the NPSP method to predict the subjects (here, we took the top 25 closest neighbours, i.e., $k = 25$ in Algorithm 1). The actual MeSH subjects of this article were used as the target subjects for the evaluation.

We also applied fastText [12] which is a state-of-the-art multi-label text classifier to our dataset, and compared our predictions with those from fastText.

## 5    Evaluation Metrics

The goal of subject prediction is to provide a shortlist of potentially relevant subjects to describe the document at hand. It is important to present a ranked shortlist of candidate subjects and to evaluate the quality of the prediction with an emphasis on the relevance of the top portion of such lists. Therefore, we use rank-based evaluation metrics against the existing human annotations.

For a test document, let $\mathbf{y} \in \{0,1\}^L$ be its *annotated* ground truth label vector and $\hat{\mathbf{y}} \in R^L$ be the predict score vector. Traditionally, we compute the precision, recall and the normalised Discounted Cumulative Gain (nDCG) up to the top $n$ predictions

$$P@n = \frac{1}{n} \sum_{l \in r_n(\hat{\mathbf{y}})} \mathbf{y}_l, \tag{4}$$

$$R@n = \frac{1}{\|\mathbf{y}\|_0} \sum_{l \in r_n(\hat{\mathbf{y}})} \mathbf{y}_l, \tag{5}$$

$$DCG@n = \sum_{l \in r_k(\hat{\mathbf{y}})} \frac{\mathbf{y}_l}{\log(l+1)}, \tag{6}$$

$$nDCG@n = \frac{DCG@k}{\sum_{l=1}^{\min(k,\|\mathbf{y}\|_0)} \frac{1}{\log(l+1)}} \tag{7}$$

where $r_n(\hat{\mathbf{y}})$ is the set of rank indices of the annotated relevant labels among the top-$n$ portion of the predicted ranked list for a document, and $\|\mathbf{y}\|_0$ counts the number of labels in the annotated ground truth label vector $\mathbf{y}$. P@n, R@n and nDCG@n are calculated for each test document and then averaged over all the documents.

---

[6] We extracted terms from titles and abstracts and removed those that occurred in less than 10 articles.

However, the complete set of ground truth labels is not obtainable, and infrequently occurring tail labels might be more informative and rewarding, Jain et al. proposed to use propensity scored measures to avoid the popularity bias and in favour rare/novel labels [10]:

$$\text{PSP@}n = \frac{1}{n} \sum_{l \in r_n(\hat{\mathbf{y}})} \frac{\mathbf{y}_l}{p_l}, \tag{8}$$

$$\text{PSR@}n = \frac{1}{1^T \mathbf{y}^*} \sum_{l \in r_n(\hat{\mathbf{y}})} \frac{\mathbf{y}_l}{p_l}, \tag{9}$$

$$\text{PSDCG@}n = \sum_{l \in r_n(\hat{\mathbf{y}})} \frac{\mathbf{y}_l}{p_l \log(l+1)} \tag{10}$$

$$\text{PSnDCG@}n = \frac{\text{PSDCG@}n}{\sum_{l=1}^{n} \frac{1}{\log(l+1)}} \tag{11}$$

where $p_l$ is the propensity score for label $l$, which could be modelled as a sigmoidal function of the frequency of label $l$:

$$p_l = P(y_l = 1 | y_l^* = 1) = \frac{1}{1 + Ce^{-A \log(d_l + B)}} \tag{12}$$

where $d_l$ is the number of documents that are indexed with the label $l$ in the training set of size $N$. $A$ and $B$ depend on the specific dataset and $C = (\log(N) - 1)(B + 1)^A$. Jain et al. suggested $A = 0.55$ and $B = 1.5$. $\mathbf{y}^*$ is the complete (but unobtainable) ground truth label vectors and $1^T \mathbf{y}^*$ can be approximated as the sum of the propensity of the labels in the annotated ground truth, that is, $\sum_{l \in \mathbf{y}} \frac{\mathbf{y}_l}{p_l}$.

## 6   Evaluation Results

Previous studies [13,26] have shown that Ariadne semantic embedding is highly efficient and competitive with the state-of-the-art word and document embedding methods, such as Word2Vec [19], Doc2Vec [16], GloVe [21], fastText [4] and Sent2Vec [20]. Figure 1 shows the comparison of our two subject prediction methods to the state-of-the-art fastText method in terms of Precision, Recall and nDCG for varying values of $n$. In these graphs, *Ariadne* represents the straightforward predictions based on subject-document similarities. If we look at the standard precision, recall and nDCG (leftmost graphs), we can see that the quality of the predicted subjects from our similarity-based prediction are comparable with those generated by fastText. The precision of fastText is higher than our Ariadne method for low values of $n$ while it quickly decreases to be worse than ours. Up to top 20 candidates, the recall for both Ariadne and fastText are more or less the same, but our method is able to predict more actual subjects at lower ranks, where the recall outperforms fastText. This is reflected in the propensity-weighted metrics (rightmost graphs), where even the basic Ariadne method outperforms fastText for all but the lowest values of $n$.

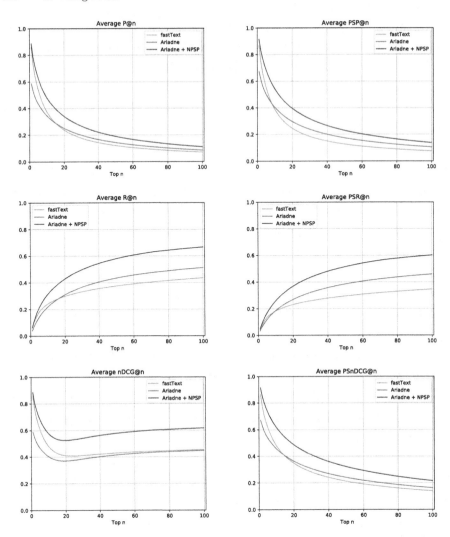

**Fig. 1.** Precision, Recall, nDCG comparison with and without propensity

The clear winner is the NPSP method. The precision and recall are both consistently higher than the other two methods. At $n = 100$, the recall is nearly 20% higher than the fastText predictions. More correct subjects are predicted at lower ranks, which explains the much slower decrease of precision with increasing rank.

Overall, we can note how well our method performs in the tail of the distribution of the subjects. This is somewhat reflected in the propensity-weighted metrics, but can also be observed directly. Figure 2 shows a histogram of subjects, binned according to the number of documents they are assigned to in the training set. For example, there were 849 unique subjects in the training data

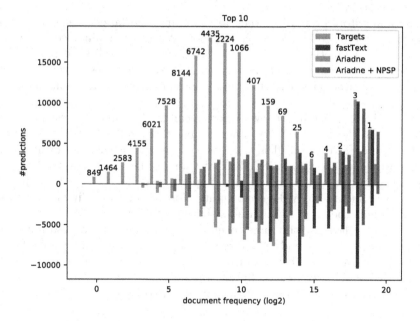

**Fig. 2.** Predictions vs subjects' document frequencies

that were assigned to exactly one (that is, $2^0$) document, 1464 subjects that were assigned to two documents, etc. We then made label predictions for the documents in the test set, and report the true positive predictions (positive bars) and false positive predictions (negative bars) grouped by the assignment frequency of those subjects in the training set. The total number of documents of the test set that were annotated with each category of subjects (the annotated ground truth) are indicated by the grey bars, while the predictions are indicated by the coloured bars: the number of true positive predictions as positive bars and the number of false positive predictions as negative bars, so that the false negatives are indicated by the difference between the grey and the positive coloured bars.

As we can see from this graph, the subjects that are infrequently assigned are harder to predict (since there is less training data to train the model on). It is also noteworthy that commonly assigned subjects are broad terms that cover many documents and very much at the forefront of the annotators' mind, and so we can be confident that these subjects are correctly assigned: their presence may not be very informative but should be trusted. Their absence, on the other hand, is much more meaningful and should also be treated as trustworthy. In other words: for these subjects, false negatives are rare and have little practical relevance, while false positives are much more problematic. Conversely, when they are present, very rare subjects are much more informative and should be treated as both important and trustworthy, but predicting them is much harder: the true positives of rare subjects are very valuable. At the same time, when they are absent, we should allow for the fact that these subjects are often overlooked by the annotators even when they are relevant: the false negatives for these subjects should be considered with suspicion. With this in mind, we can see how much better our method performs when compared to FastText: it has far fewer false positives for the common subjects, far more true positives for the uncommon subjects, and although it does have more false positives for uncommon subjects, these may well still be relevant subjects.

Notice how, unlike in retrieval where recall is of limited interest in practice because only the few most relevant documents would be actually looked at, in the case of XMTC recall is the more important metric, especially for the more obscure subjects for which lack of training data makes it hard to build comprehensive models. A high recall is important as it would greatly reduce the search space and also provides opportunities for cataloguers to find more suitable subjects which they may otherwise not have considered.

Also notice how, by the same token, higher values of $n$ are also important. Highly ranked subjects tend to be very frequent terms: at best, they are relatively uninformative, at worst they are incorrect. Lower-ranked subjects which tend to be less frequently used terms, by contrast, are at best informative, at worst incorrect and more likely relevant but unannotated.

*A Closer Look.* To illustrate these points, Table 1 lists the 23 actual MeSH subjects for an arbitrary article, titled "Cumulative probability of neodymium: YAG laser posterior capsulotomy after phacoemulsification.", which is about laser-based eye surgery.[7] The MeSH terms that reflect the major subjects of this article, as annotated by the indexers, are marked with an asterisk (*). The 25 most relevant MeSH subjects predicted by our two methods and fastText are also listed.

It is not surprising that subjects such as "Humans" and "Female" are predicted first by fastText, because they are the most frequent in the dataset. In fact, many of the subjects predicted by fastText are very common (see their document counts in Table 1), which leads to higher precision and recall at the low values of $n$. However, as argued above, a P@5 of 100% is actually uninformative about the real topic of this article, therefore, less valuable. FastText has trouble finding subjects which describe the articles more precisely (also illustrated in Fig. 2).

The raw subject-document similarity is able to rank infrequent actual subjects such as "Phacoemulsification," "Lens Capsule, Crystalline/Surgery" high in the list. We believe these infrequent subjects are more informative and valuable in terms of subject indexing. Common subjects such as "Female" and "Male" tend to be ranked lower though. The NPSP method effectively boosts these common subjects to the front (such as "Human" is recovered and ranked at the top), while the correct specific subjects still stay relatively high in the list. The previously-missed subjects such as "Acrylic Resins" and "Silicone Elastomers" get into the top 25. Unfortunately the highly relevant but extremely infrequent subject "Capsulorhexis" drops out of the top 25 list now.

---

[7] https://www.ncbi.nlm.nih.gov/pubmed/14670424.

**Table 1.** An example of actual MeSH subjects versus the top 25 predicted ones by our two methods and fastText, where the ones in bold match the actual subjects. The raw document counts ($d_t$) of the MeSH subjects in the training dataset are also given.

| Actual MeSH subjects (alphabetical order) | $d_t$ | Ariadne | $d_t$ | Ariadne + NPSP | $d_t$ | fastText | $d_t$ |
|---|---|---|---|---|---|---|---|
| Acrylic Resins | 920 | Lenses, Intraocular | 434 | **Humans** | 579975 | **Humans** | 579975 |
| Aged | 118655 | **Lens Implantation, Intraocular** | 317 | **Male** | 336647 | **Female** | 328885 |
| Aged, 80 and over | 40642 | **Phacoemulsification** | 225 | **Female** | 328885 | **Middle Aged** | 168714 |
| Capsulorhexis | 24 | **Visual Acuity** | 2026 | **Aged** | 118655 | **Male** | 336647 |
| Female | 328885 | **Lens Capsule, Crystalline/Surgery** | 79 | Lenses, Intraocular | 434 | **Risk Factors** | 34538 |
| Humans | 579975 | **Lens Capsule, Crystalline/Pathology** | 65 | **Lens Implantation, intraocular** | 317 | Adult | 194200 |
| Laser therapy* | 847 | Visual Acuity/Physiology | 949 | **Visual Acuity** | 2026 | **Aged** | 118655 |
| Lens Capsule, Crystalline/Pathology | 65 | Lens Implantation, Intraocular/Methods | 90 | **Phacoemulsification** | 225 | **Retrospective Studies** | 32642 |
| Lens Capsule, Crystalline/Surgery* | 79 | Cataract Extraction/Methods | 136 | **Middle Aged** | 168714 | Follow Up Studies | 27911 |
| Lens Implantation, Intraocular | 317 | Phacoemulsification/Methods | 106 | Prospective Studies | 25714 | **Aged 80 and over** | 40642 |
| Male | 336647 | **Retrospective Studies** | 32642 | **Lens Capsule, Crystalline/Surgery** | 79 | Incidence | 11468 |
| Middle Aged | 168714 | **Aged** | 118655 | Follow Up Studies | 27911 | Adolescent | 75361 |
| Phacoemulsification* | 225 | Prospective Studies | 25714 | **Acrylic Resins** | 920 | Young Adult | 27991 |
| Polymethyl Methacrylate | 392 | **Aged 80 and Over** | 40642 | **Lens Capsule, Crystalline/Pathology** | 65 | Prospective Studies | 25714 |
| Postoperative Complications/Pathology | 351 | **Middle Aged** | 168714 | Postoperative Complications | 32642 | Time Factors | 50339 |
| Postoperative Complications/Surgery* | 823 | **Male** | 336647 | **Aged 80 and Over** | 40642 | Logistic Models | 7258 |
| Probability | 2914 | Cataract Extraction | 350 | Cataract Etiology | 3961 | Case Control Studies | 13306 |
| Retrospective Studies | 32642 | Lenses, Intraocular/Adverse Effects | 62 | Adult | 194200 | Cohort Studies | 12275 |
| Risk Factors | 34538 | Adolescent | 75361 | **Retrospective Studies** | 32642 | Treatment Outcome | 40496 |
| Sex Factors | 10203 | **Female** | 328885 | Visual Acuity/Physiology | 949 | Child | 53738 |
| Silicone Elastomers | 294 | Intraocular Pressure | 712 | Treatment Outcome | 40496 | Survival Rate | 7975 |
| Survival Analysis | 7046 | **Capsulorhexis** | 24 | Cataract Extraction | 350 | Prognosis | 17160 |
| Visual Acuity | 2026 | Pseudophakia Physiopathology | 56 | Lens Implantation, Intraocular/Adverse Effects | 45 | Risk Assessment | 9271 |
| | | Adult | 194200 | **Silicone Elastomers** | 294 | Reoperation | 3355 |
| | | **Risk Factors** | 34538 | Prosthesis Design | 2096 | Proportional Hazards Models | 3403 |

We realise that this evaluation has its limitations. As shown in Table 1, highly related MeSH subjects such as "Lenses Intraocular" and "Phacoemulsification Methods" are predicted as good candidates for this article, both of which are reasonable and potentially useful, but since they are not the subject headings that the professional taxonomists have chosen, their value cannot be easily assessed. As discussed previously, such false negatives should be treated critically.

That being said, we believe our predictions are useful in practice and can be presented to cataloger as candidate subjects to choose from. Consider, for example, "Cataract Extraction," "Intraocular Pressure," etc. in our example. Again, we need to get subject specialists involved to conduct such qualitative evaluations.

## 7   Conclusion

In this paper, we have shown that a similarity-based subject prediction based on a suitable semantic space that allows for the embedding of both subjects and documents is very competitive with the state-of-the-art subject-prediction method based on a classifier. We have described such an embedding and have shown how effective this specific semantic space really is, both with quantitative and with qualitative evaluations. In addition, we have shown how our embedding-based method is particularly effective at correctly predicting very specialised subjects, which are associated with few documents in the training set and are more problematic for a classifier, as is reflected in our method's much slower decrease of precision with increasing rank. In addition, we proposed a novel, non-parametric, similarity-based method with the documents instead of the subjects. We have shown that this method substantially improves the quality of the predictions, both in comparison to the state-of-the-art and to the bare similarity-based method.

## References

1. Achlioptas, D.: Database-friendly random projections: Johnson-Lindenstrauss with binary coins. J. Comput. Syst. Sci. **66**(4), 671–687 (2003). https://doi.org/10.1016/S0022-0000(03)00025-4
2. Arash, J., Abdulhussain, E.M.: Classification of scientific publications according to library controlled vocabularies: a new concept matching-based approach. Libr. Hi Tech **31**, 725–747 (2013). https://doi.org/10.1108/LHT-03-2013-0030
3. Bhatia, K., Jain, H., Kar, P., Varma, M., Jain, P.: Sparse local embeddings for extreme multi-label classification. In: Cortes, C., Lawrence, N.D., Lee, D.D., Sugiyama, M., Garnett, R. (eds.) Advances in Neural Information Processing Systems 28, pp. 730–738. Curran Associates, Inc. (2015)
4. Bojanowski, P., Grave, E., Joulin, A., Mikolov, T.: Enriching word vectors with subword information. Trans. Assoc. Comput. Linguist. **5**, 135–146 (2017). https://doi.org/10.1162/tacl_a_00051
5. Foster, D.V., Grassberger, P.: Lower bounds on mutual information. Phys. Rev. E **83**, 010101 (2011). https://doi.org/10.1103/PhysRevE.83.010101

6. Frommholz, I., Abbasi, M.K.: Automated text categorization and clustering. In: Golub, K. (ed.) Subject Access to Information: An Interdisciplinary Approach: An Interdisciplinary Approach, pp. 117–131. ABC-CLIO (2014)

7. Godby, J., Reighart, R.: The wordsmith indexing system. J. Libr. Adm. **34**(3–4), 375–385 (2001). https://doi.org/10.1300/J111v34n03_18

8. Godby, J., Smith, D.: Scorpion. https://www.oclc.org/research/activities/scorpion.html. Accessed Apr 2019

9. Golub, K.: Automatic subject indexing of text. In: ISKO Encyclopedia of Knowledge Organization. http://www.isko.org/cyclo/automatic. Version 07 Mar 2019

10. Jain, H., Prabhu, Y., Varma, M.: Extreme multi-label loss functions for recommendation, tagging, ranking & other missing label applications. In: Proceedings of the 22nd ACM SIGKDD International Conference on Knowledge Discovery and Data Mining, KDD 2016, pp. 935–944. ACM, New York (2016). https://doi.org/10.1145/2939672.2939756

11. Johnson, W., Lindenstrauss, J.: Extensions of Lipschitz mappings into a Hilbert space. Contemp. Math. **26**, 189–206 (1984)

12. Joulin, A., Grave, E., Bojanowski, P., Mikolov, T.: Bag of tricks for efficient text classification. arXiv preprint arXiv:1607.01759 (2016)

13. Koopman, R., Wang, S., Englebienne, G.: Fast and discriminative semantic embedding. In: Proceedings of the 13th International Conference on Computational Semantics - Long Papers, Gothenburg, Sweden, 23–27 May 2019, pp. 235–246. ACL (2019)

14. Koopman, R., Wang, S., Scharnhorst, A.: Contextualization of topics: browsing through the universe of bibliographic information. Scientometrics **111**(2), 1119–1139 (2017). https://doi.org/10.1007/s11192-017-2303-4

15. Koopman, R., Wang, S., Scharnhorst, A., Englebienne, G.: Ariadne's thread: interactive navigation in a world of networked information. In: Proceedings of the ACM Conference Extended Abstracts on Human Factors in Computing Systems, pp. 1833–1838 (2015)

16. Le, Q.V., Mikolov, T.: Distributed representations of sentences and documents. In: International Conference on Machine Learning - ICML 2014, vol. 32, pp. 1188–1196, March 2014. https://doi.org/10.1145/2740908.2742760

17. Liu, J., Chang, W.C., Wu, Y., Yang, Y.: Deep learning for extreme multi-label text classification. In: Proceedings of the 40th International ACM SIGIR Conference on Research and Development in Information Retrieval, SIGIR 2017, pp. 115–124. ACM, New York (2017). https://doi.org/10.1145/3077136.3080834

18. Manning, C.D., Schütze, H.: Foundations of Statistical Natural Language Processing. MIT Press, Cambridge (1999)

19. Mikolov, T., Sutskever, I., Chen, K., Corrado, G., Dean, J.: Distributed representations of words and phrases and their compositionality. In: Proceedings of the 26th International Conference on Neural Information Processing Systems - Volume 2, NIPS 2013, pp. 3111–3119. Curran Associates Inc., USA (2013)

20. Pagliardini, M., Gupta, P., Jaggi, M.: Unsupervised learning of sentence embeddings using compositional n-gram features. In: Proceedings of the 2018 Conference of the North American Chapter of the Association for Computational Linguistics: Human Language Technologies, Volume 1 (Long Papers), pp. 528–540. Association for Computational Linguistics (2018). https://doi.org/10.18653/v1/N18-1049

21. Pennington, J., Socher, R., Manning, C.D.: GloVe: global vectors for word representation. In: Empirical Methods in Natural Language Processing (EMNLP), pp. 1532–1543 (2014). https://doi.org/10.3115/v1/D14-1162

22. Prabhu, Y., Kag, A., Harsola, S., Agrawal, R., Varma, M.: Parabel: partitioned label trees for extreme classification with application to dynamic search advertising. In: Proceedings of the International World Wide Web Conference, April 2018

23. Prabhu, Y., Varma, M.: FastXML: a fast, accurate and stable tree-classifier for extreme multi-label learning. In: Proceedings of the 20th ACM SIGKDD International Conference on Knowledge Discovery and Data Mining, KDD 2014, pp. 263–272. ACM, New York (2014). https://doi.org/10.1145/2623330.2623651

24. Sebastiani, F.: Machine learning in automated text categorization. ACM Comput. Surv. **34**(1), 1–47 (2002). https://doi.org/10.1145/505282.505283

25. Tagami, Y.: AnnexML: approximate nearest neighbor search for extreme multi-label classification. In: Proceedings of the 23rd ACM SIGKDD International Conference on Knowledge Discovery and Data Mining, KDD 2017, pp. 455–464. ACM, New York (2017). https://doi.org/10.1145/3097983.3097987

26. Wang, S., Koopman, R.: Semantic embedding for information retrieval. In: Proceedings of the Fifth Workshop on Bibliometric-enhanced Information Retrieval, pp. 122–132 (2017)

27. Weston, J., Bengio, S., Usunier, N.: WSABIE: Scaling up to large vocabulary image annotation. In: Proceedings of the Twenty-Second International Joint Conference on Artificial Intelligence - Volume Three, IJCAI 2011, pp. 2764–2770. AAAI Press (2011). https://doi.org/10.5591/978-1-57735-516-8/IJCAI11-460

# Visual Summarization of Scholarly Videos Using Word Embeddings and Keyphrase Extraction

Hang Zhou[1], Christian Otto[2]($\boxtimes$) (iD), and Ralph Ewerth[1,2] (iD)

[1] L3S Research Center, Leibniz Universität Hannover, Hannover, Germany
zhhz417@gmail.com
[2] Leibniz Information Centre for Science and Technology (TIB), Hannover, Germany
{christian.otto,ralph.ewerth}@tib.eu

**Abstract.** Effective learning with audiovisual content depends on many factors. Besides the quality of the learning resource's content, it is essential to discover the most relevant and suitable video in order to support the learning process most effectively. Video summarization techniques facilitate this goal by providing a quick overview over the content. It is especially useful for longer recordings such as conference presentations or lectures. In this paper, we present a domain specific approach that generates a visual summary of video content using solely textual information. For this purpose, we exploit video annotations that are automatically generated by speech recognition and video OCR (optical character recognition). Textual information is represented by semantic word embeddings and extracted keyphrases. We demonstrate the feasibility of the proposed approach through its incorporation into the TIB AV-Portal (http://av.tib.eu/), which is a platform for scientific videos. The accuracy and usefulness of the generated video content visualizations is evaluated in a user study.

**Keywords:** Video summarization · Word embeddings · Scientific videos

## 1 Introduction

The massive growth of online video platforms underline the role of audiovisual content as one of the most commonly used sources of information not only for entertainment, but also in learning related scenarios. Exploring a large collection of videos in order to find the most relevant candidate for a specific learning intent can be overwhelming and therefore inefficient. This is especially true for longer videos if the title alone does not capture all parts and aspects of the content. Approaches for *video summarization* address this problem by analyzing the visual content and generating an overview by the combination of identified key sequences and frames. However, such approaches struggle with videos where the visual content lacks variance or is mostly comprised of concepts with low

© Springer Nature Switzerland AG 2019
A. Doucet et al. (Eds.): TPDL 2019, LNCS 11799, pp. 327–335, 2019.
https://doi.org/10.1007/978-3-030-30760-8_28

*visualness* [16], e.g., abstract concepts. Scientific and educational videos often share this characteristic, for example, tutorials or lecture recordings of the STEM subjects (Science, Technology, Engineering, and Mathematics) like chemistry or computer science.

In this paper, we propose an interactive visualization approach in order to summarize the content of scientific or educational videos using solely textual information. The goal is to provide a tool that facilitates the exploratory search capabilities of respective video portals and thus, making learning for the end user more efficient and satisfying. Our approach makes use of automatically extracted video annotations and entities, which significantly enrich the usually available, conventional metadata. These entities are generated from the (1) speech transcript, (2) visual concept classification, and (3) text extracted using optical character recognition (OCR). Such kind of metadata is available for videos of the TIB AV-Portal (https://av.tib.eu), which is run by the Leibniz Information Centre for Science and Technology (TIB). The metadata are provided to the public as open data as well. For these reasons, we choose the TIB AV-Portal as the basis platform and incorporate the proposed system there. Our system utilizes these data and generates a comprehensive, interactive visualization by combining semantic word embeddings and keyphrase extraction methods. We demonstrate how to display the visualization on the actual website with a *GreaseMonkey* script, which is also a pre-requisite for our user study that investigates the usefulness of the proposed approach for video content visualization.

The paper is structured as follows. Section 2 discusses the related work for video summarization and other related areas, while Sect. 3 introduces the different components of our system and the utilized dataset. Section 4 describes the experimental setup and discusses the results. Finally, Sect. 5 concludes the paper and briefly outlines areas of future work.

## 2   Related Work

**Video Summarization.** Most of the video summarization approaches rely on visual features and are very domain specific (e.g., movies, sports, news, documentary, surveillance), resulting in a large number of different algorithms. The focus of these approaches can be dominant concepts [12], user preferences [9], query context [15], or user attention [10]. A typical result of these approaches is a sequence of keyframes or a video excerpt comprising the most important parts of a video. More recent methods treat video summarization as an optimization problem [5] or they utilize recurrent neural networks [17] based on, for instance, long short-term memory cells (LSTMs), which can capture temporal or sequential information well. Chang et al. [4] combine image processing, text summarization, and keyword extraction techniques resulting in a multimodal surrogate. A word cloud is generated, where more important words are displayed with a bigger font size, supplememted by a set of three to four thumbnails with a short transcription.

In this paper, we go one step further and show how to summarize the content solely based on textual information. The core techniques to create a video summary utilized in this paper are keyphrase extraction and measures for semantic text similarity. The related work in these areas is subsequently described.

**Keyphrase Extraction.** Hasan and Ng [7] describe that keyphrase extraction techniques are generally comprised of two steps. First, a list of possible candidate phrases is identified, and then these candidates are ranked according to their importance. This is realized by a wide range of approaches that can be categorized into supervised and unsupervised methods. Supervised techniques share the drawback that the training data require manual labeling, which in general is time-consuming and resource-intensive. Unsupervised approaches, however, automatically discover the underlying structure of a dataset without human-labeled keyphrases. To summarize, the two most popular methods are *graph-based ranking* and *topic-based clustering*. The idea behind graph-based algorithms is to construct a graph of phrases, which are connected with weighted edges that describe their relation derived from the frequency of their co-occurrences. Topic-based clustering methods use statistical language models, which contain the probability of all possible sequences of words. Recently, the fusion of these two directions has gained attention, namely PositionRank [6] and MultiPartiteRank [3]. The latter one, which is also used in our approach, first builds a graph representation of the document and then ranks each keyphrase with a relevance score. In addition, in an intermediate step edge weights are adjusted to capture the information about the word's position in the document.

**Semantic Text Similarity.** Corpus-based similarity algorithms determine the semantic relation between two textual phrases based on information learned from large corpora like Wikipedia. Particularly neural network approaches benefit greatly from huge amounts of data, leading to the current success of methods such as Word2Vec [11], GloVe [14], and fastText [1]. They all create word-vector spaces that cover a desired vocabulary size and embed semantically similar words close to one another, while they also allow for mathematical operations on these vectors to unveil relationships. For instance, when applying fastText, the difference vectors between Paris - France and Rome - Italy are almost identical, indicating the vectors describe the relation "capital".

## 3   Visual Summarization of Scientific Video Content

In this section, we describe our approach for video content summarization solely based on textual information. The necessary process to summarize a scientific video and display this information in an efficient way consists of four steps: (1) pre-processing, (2) semantic embedding of content related information to generate a bubble diagram, (3) creation of a keyphrase table from the speech transcript, and (4) combining diagram and table to form a visualization.

The utilized video dataset of the TIB AV-Portal is available at https://av.tib. eu/opendata, including the associated metadata as Resource Description Framework (RDF) triples (under Creative Commons License CC0 1.0 Universal). To build the RDF graph we use Python 3.6 and the *rdflib* library. Next, we use the query language SPARQL to select videos that contain automatically extracted metadata. This is the case for videos that belong to one of TIB's six core subjects (engineering, architecture, chemistry, computer science, mathematics, physics).

This yields a list of 1756 videos. fastText does not allow for multi-lingual support so we choose the biggest subset of videos from a single language, which is German. We then query further the embedded metadata, in particular the **key entities** which are the result of visual concept classification, optical character recognition, and automated speech recognition. In addition, we crawl the unfiltered speech transcript from the website using the *BeautifulSoup* library.

**Semantic Embedding of Key Entities.** We use fastText to generate word embeddings from the extracted key entities. fastText's tri-gram technique embeds words by their substrings instead of the whole word, for instance, the word *library* would be decomposed into the following tri-grams: <li, lib, ibr, bra, rar, ary, ry>. This is a valuable feature for multiple reasons. First, it enables the system to encode misspelled or unknown words. Secondly, the quality of embeddings of the generally longer or compound words of the German language is improved, too. We use the pre-trained model for German, which contains the vocabulary of the German Wikipedia and encodes each word $w$ in a 300-dimensional vector $f_w$. The visualization of the embedded feature vectors requires dimension reduction to project data onto a two-dimensional space. We apply a linear algorithm (principal component analysis) from Python's scikit-learn library instead of a non-linear one like t-SNE, since we intend to keep the semantic arrangement laid out by fastText and refrain from clustering the keywords further.

**Keyphrase Extraction.** Input for the keyphrase extraction process is the unfiltered speech transcript, which is already divided into time segments in the TIB AV-Portal. The required format of the textual information is given by the *pke* toolkit [2]. Requirements are a tokenization and part-of-speech tagging (POS tagging), that is the assignment of lexical categories such as noun, verb and so on. For this process we use the Python *Natural Language Toolkit (NLTK)*, in particular, the Stanford POS-Tagger which also comes with a pre-trained model for the German language[1]. Results of the POS tagging process are then passed to the Multipartite Rank [3] algorithm of the *pke* library in order to perform keyphrase extraction. As stated in Sect. 2, this technique models topics and phrases in a single graph, and their mutual reinforcement together with a specific mechanism to select the most import keyphrases to generate candidate rankings. We only consider nouns, adjectives, personal pronouns, and verbs

---

[1] https://nlp.stanford.edu/software/tagger.shtml.

('NOUN','ADJ','PROPN','VERB') and dismiss all words given by *NLTK*'s collection of German stop words. The remaining parameters are $alpha = 1$, which controls the weight adjustment mechanism, and the $threshold = 0.4$ for the minimum similarity for clustering (default: 0.25). We decide to set this value to 0.4 due to the high similarity of topics in a single video. The linkage method was set to *average*. Finally, we choose to retrieve the 20 highest ranked keyphrases of every time interval for our keyphrase table that will become part of the visualization.

Table 1. Overview of the visualization properties.

| Components | Meaning | Approach |
|---|---|---|
| Circle | Key topics | Entity recognition |
| Size of a circle | Importance of the topic | Entity's frequency |
| Arrangement | Similarity between topics | Word embeddings |
| Table | Timestamp based summary | Keyphrase extraction |

**Visualization of Results.** Finally, we display the recognized, embedded entities in an interactive graph with the properties shown in Table 1 and combine it with the keyphrase table generated in the last section. We choose a bubble diagram as opposed to Chang et al.'s [4] word cloud. This allows us to illustrate and emphasize also on the distance, between related or unrelated keywords, which reflects (dis)similarity. In addition, smaller differences in area sizes are visually easier to perceive than font sizes. We decided against other alternative implementations such as TextArc [13] since we aimed for a more intuitive approach. The inclusion of the temporal dimension using ThemeRiver [8] did not deliver consistent results for videos that were short, or contained only few keywords.

The actual implementation is realized in Javascript and the *Plot.ly* API[2]. As displayed in Fig. 1, the visualization is comprised of circles of different sizes each representing a topic and its importance. An interactive toolbar is displayed on the upper right allowing the user to easily explore the graph. At the bottom, a keyphrase table indicates the main topic of each time segment.

---

[2] https://plot.ly/api/.

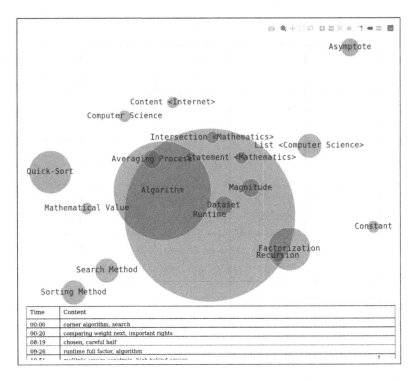

**Fig. 1.** Visualization of video https://av.tib.eu/media/9557 titled "Bubblesort, Quicksort, Runtime" incorporated via GreaseMonkey in the live website as portrayed during the user study comprised of the visualization itself, a toolbar, and the keyphrase table. Note: Translated to English for better comprehensibility.

## 4    Experimental Results

We conducted a user study to evaluate the quality and usefulness of the proposed visualization approach. Ten volunteers were recruited, of which eight participants were male and two female. Their age was between 21 and 30, and their educational levels between high-school and master. Eight participants study computer science, one mechanical engineering and one mathematics. All of them are fluent in German, four of them are native speakers. **Task I** of the study investigates how precisely the visual summary represents the video content. Therefore, 10 videos with a duration between five and 30 min were randomly assigned to each participant. Then, the user had to rate how well the presented visualization matches the video content, based on the following options: "0" - no correlation, "1" - slight match, "2" - good match, "3" - exact match. **Task II** evaluates if the visualization is a useful tool to provide a quick overview of the video content, or if it is no improvement over the current state of the website. The participants could choose one of the following options: "0" - not helpful at all, "1" - slightly helpful, "2" - moderately helpful, "3" - very helpful, "4" - extremely helpful, and had to give a statement about their reasoning. We received nine valid user evaluations for Task II. Figure 2 shows the distribution of the 100 gathered ratings, while Fig. 2 shows the results of Task II.

(a)

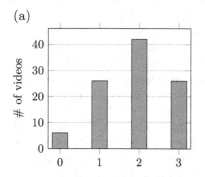

(b)

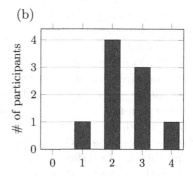

Results of Task I of the user study evaluating the correlation of the visualization to the video content. From "0" - no correlation to "3" - exact match.

Results of Task II of the user study showing the perceived helpfulness of the visualization. From "0" - not helpful at all to "4" - extremely helpful.

**Fig. 2.** (a) Accuracy and (b) Helpfulness.

**Discussion.** Figure 2 shows that 68% of the visualizations were good or better, while 26% only provided a slight match or did not correlate at all to the video content (6%). Positive examples, as can be seen in Fig. 1, successfully provide the user with a summarization of the video content. The first example, video 9557, explains the runtime behavior of the sorting algorithms Bubblesort and Quicksort. The largest circle in the visualization is Runtime ("Laufzeit") and represents well the main topic. Also related topics from computer science covered in the video like sorting methods ("Sortierverfahren"), algorithm ("Algorithmus"), and Quick-Sort itself are closely arranged on the left, while related topics from mathematics like factorization ("Faktorisierung"), asymptote ("Asymptote"), and statement ("Aussage <Mathematik>") are grouped on the right. Another positive example (video 10234), which talks about eigenvalues and eigenvectors, is mainly represented by the entity matrix multiplication ("Matrizenmultiplikation") and vector ("Vektor"), but also shows more detailed aspects of that topic, namely vector algebra ("Vektorrechnung"), inverse matrix, gradient and of course, eigenvector and eigenvalue. The results of the keyphrase extraction, as can be also seen in Fig. 1, were less helpful. The main reason is most likely the nature of the automatic speech transcripts, which usually differs from written text. They often consist of incomplete sentences, misspelled words, missing punctuation, and falsely recognized words which can change interpretations of a sentence completely. Since common keyphrase models are suited for proper textual content, there is still room for improvement in our scenario. The six videos rated "uncorrelated" came from the subject of engineering and had very application-specific content. One video, for instance, discusses the cause, consequences, and solutions of driftwood accumulation on bridges leading to overflowing rivers (https://av.tib.eu/media/11442). A lot of technical terms, switching contexts from real world to model, testing to technical, considerations paired with topic specific phrases yielded a visualization which was only marginally helpful. Finally, the reason that more results present a "good match" instead of an exact match is most likely due to the nature of the entities extracted from the speech transcript. For example, videos and tutorials from the field of mathematics contain a lot of terms that are important when explaining a concept, but are rather general and not closely related to the topic itself. That includes words like "square", "point" and "integral". Yet, these words are captured by the system and are present in the dataset, but they contribute only marginally to the comprehension of the video even though they appear very frequently. This circumstance is also reflected in the results of Task II, where our participants agreed in their statements that the visualization would be more helpful if the redundant keywords were omitted.

## 5   Conclusion and Future Work

In this paper, we have presented a system that summarizes the content of scholarly videos in order to support semantic search. Based on automatic video analysis in the TIB AV-Portal, we have proposed a solely text-based approach that leverages automatically extracted metadata, which are utilized to generate an interactive visualization and a keyphrase table to outline a video's content. The usefulness of the visualization was evaluated in a user study that demonstrated the feasibility of the proposed summarization, but also indicated areas for future work. For instance, we plan to implement reliable filters for keywords that are not closely related to the content to provide a better user experience.

**Acknowledgments.** Part of this work is financially supported by the Leibniz Association, Germany (Leibniz Competition 2018, funding line "Collaborative Excellence", project SALIENT [K68/2017]).

## References

1. Bojanowski, P., Grave, E., Joulin, A., Mikolov, T.: Enriching word vectors with subword information. TACL **5**, 135–146 (2017)
2. Boudin, F.: PKE: an open source python-based keyphrase extraction toolkit. In: International Conference on Computational Linguistics, Conference System Demonstrations, pp. 69–73. Osaka, Japan (2016)
3. Boudin, F.: Unsupervised keyphrase extraction with multipartite graphs. In: Conference for Computational Linguistics: Human Language Technologies, New Orleans, Louisiana, USA, pp. 667–672 (2018)
4. Chang, W., Yang, J., Wu, Y.: A keyword-based video summarization learning platform with multimodal surrogates. In: International Conference on Advanced Learning Technologies, Athens, Georgia, USA, pp. 37–41 (2011)

5. Elhamifar, E., Kaluza, M.C.D.P.: Online summarization via submodular and convex optimization. In: Conference on Computer Vision and Pattern Recognition, Honolulu, HI, USA, pp. 1818–1826 (2017)
6. Florescu, C., Caragea, C.: Positionrank: an unsupervised approach to keyphrase extraction from scholarly documents. In: Annual Meeting of the Association for Computational Linguistics, Vancouver, Canada, pp. 1105–1115 (2017)
7. Hasan, K.S., Ng, V.: Automatic keyphrase extraction: a survey of the state of the art. In: Meeting of the Association for Computational Linguistics, 22–27 June 2014, Baltimore, MD, USA, pp. 1262–1273 (2014)
8. Havre, S., Hetzler, E.G., Whitney, P., Nowell, L.T.: Themeriver: visualizing thematic changes in large document collections. IEEE Trans. Vis. Comput. Graph. **8**(1), 9–20 (2002)
9. Lu, Z., Grauman, K.: Story-driven summarization for egocentric video. In: Conference on Computer Vision and Pattern Recognition, Portland, OR, USA, pp. 2714–2721 (2013)
10. Ma, Y., Hua, X., Lu, L., Zhang, H.: A generic framework of user attention model and its application in video summarization. IEEE Trans. Multimedia **7**(5), 907–919 (2005)
11. Mikolov, T., Sutskever, I., Chen, K., Corrado, G.S., Dean, J.: Distributed representations of words and phrases and their compositionality. In: Conference on Neural Information Processing Systems, Lake Tahoe, Nevada, USA, pp. 3111–3119 (2013)
12. Over, P., Smeaton, A.F., Awad, G.: The TRECVid 2008 BBC rushes summarization evaluation. In: ACM Workshop on Video Summarization, Vancouver, British Columbia, Canada, pp. 1–20 (2008)
13. Paley, W.B.: Textarc: showing word frequency and distribution in text. In: Poster presented at IEEE Symposium on Information Visualization, vol. 2002 (2002)
14. Pennington, J., Socher, R., Manning, C.D.: Glove: global vectors for word representation. In: Conference on Empirical Methods in Natural Language Processing, Doha, Qatar, pp. 1532–1543 (2014)
15. Wang, M., Hong, R., Li, G., Zha, Z., Yan, S., Chua, T.: Event driven web video summarization by tag localization and key-shot identification. IEEE Trans. Multimedia **14**(4), 975–985 (2012)
16. Yanai, K., Barnard, K.: Image region entropy: a measure of "visualness" of web images associated with one concept. In: ACM International Conference on Multimedia, Singapore, pp. 419–422 (2005)
17. Zhao, B., Li, X., Lu, X.: HSA-RNN: hierarchical structure-adaptive RNN for video summarization. In: Conference on Computer Vision and Pattern Recognition, Salt Lake City, UT, USA, pp. 7405–7414 (2018)

# Posters and Demonstrations

# Towards Serendipitous Research Paper Recommender Using Tweets and Diversification

Chifumi Nishioka[1(✉)], Jörn Hauk[2], and Ansgar Scherp[3]

[1] Kyoto University Library, Kyoto, Japan
nishioka.chifumi.2c@kyoto-u.ac.jp
[2] Kiel University, Kiel, Germany
[3] University of Essex, Colchester, UK

**Abstract.** In this paper, we examine whether a user's tweets can help to a generate more serendipitous recommendations. In addition, we investigate whether the use of diversification applied on a list of recommended items further improves serendipity. To this end, we conduct an experiment with $n = 22$ subjects. The result of our experiment shows that the subject's tweets did not improve serendipity, but diversification results in more serendipitous recommendations.

**Keywords:** Recommender system · Scientific publication · User study

## 1 Introduction

Various works have developed recommender systems for research papers to overcome the information overload problem. Most of the previous works have focused on the accuracy of recommendations. However, several works argue that there are important aspects other than accuracy [4]. One of these aspects is *serendipity*, which is concerned with the novelty of recommendations and in how far recommendations positively surprise users [2].

In this paper, we study a research paper recommender system focusing on serendipity. Specifically, this paper conducts an experiment to investigate the influence of user's tweets and diversification to deliver serendipitous recommendations. The experiment is composed of three factors. In the first factor *User Profile Source*, we compare the two sources of a user's own papers vs. the user's tweets. We assume that user's tweets produce recommendations that cannot be generated based on papers, since researchers tweet about very recent developments and interests that are yet not reflected in their papers. In the second factor *Text Mining Method*, we apply three different methods for computing profiles of candidate items (i.e., research papers) and user profiles. In the third factor *Ranking Method*, we compare two ranking methods: classical cosine similarity and the established diversification algorithm IA-Select [1]. IA-Select ranks candidate items with the objective to diversify recommendations in a list. Since it

© Springer Nature Switzerland AG 2019
A. Doucet et al. (Eds.): TPDL 2019, LNCS 11799, pp. 339–343, 2019.
https://doi.org/10.1007/978-3-030-30760-8_29

broadens the coverage of topics in a list, we assume that IA-Select delivers more serendipitous recommendations. The result of the experiment reveals that users' tweets did not improve the serendipity, but IA-Select delivers more serendipitous recommendations.

## 2  Experimental Factors

In this paper, we build a content-based recommender system along with the three factors *User Profile Source*, *Text Mining Method*, and *Ranking Method*. It works as follows: (a) Candidate items of the recommender system (i.e., research papers) are processed by a text mining methods and paper profiles are generated. (b) A user profile is generated based on his/her user profile source by the same text mining method, which is applied to generate paper profiles. (c) One of the ranking methods determines the order of recommended papers. In the following paragraphs, we describe the details of each factor. The three factors described above result in total in $2 \times 3 \times 2 = 12$ strategies.

*User Profile Source.* In this factor, we compare the following two data sources that are used to build a user profile.

- **Own papers:** As baseline, we use the own papers of the users as Sugiyama and Kan [8] did.
- **Twitter:** In contrast to the user's papers, we assume that using tweets provide more serendipitous recommendations, since researchers tweet about their most recent interests.

*Text Mining Method.* For data sources, we apply a profiling method using one of three text mining methods:

- **TF-IDF:** We use TF-IDF since it is often used in recommender systems as baseline [3].
- **CF-IDF:** Concept Frequency Inverse Document Frequency (CF-IDF) [3] is an extension of TF-IDF, which replaces terms with semantic concepts from a knowledge base.
- **HCF-IDF:** Hierarchical Concept Frequency Inverse Document Frequency (HCF-IDF) [6] is an extension of CF-IDF. It applies a propagation function [5] over a hierarchical structure of a knowledge base to give a weight to concepts in higher levels. Thus, it identifies concepts that are not mentioned in a text but highly relevant.

*Ranking Method.* Finally, we rank all candidate items to determine which items are recommended to a user. In this factor, we compare two ranking methods: cosine similarity and diversification with IA-Select [1].

- **Cosine similarity:** As baseline, we employ a cosine similarity. Top-$k$ items with largest cosine similarities are recommended.

- **IA-Select:** We employ IA-Select [1] for serendipitous recommendations. IA-Select diversifies recommendations in a list to avoid suggesting similar items together. The basic idea of IA-Select is that it lowers iteratively the weights of features in the user profile, which are already covered by papers already selected for recommendation.

## 3  Evaluation

*Procedure.* Along with the previous work [7], we have implemented a web application where human subjects evaluate the twelve recommendation strategies described above. First, subjects input their Twitter handle and their name. Based on their name, we obtain the content of their papers by mapping them to the ACM-Citation-Network V8 dataset (see below). The top-5 recommendations are computed for each strategy. Thus, each subject evaluates $5 \cdot 12 = 60$ items as "interesting" or "not interesting". Subjects can directly access and read the research paper by clicking the link.

*Datasets.* As research papers, we use the ACM citation network V8 dataset[1]. From the dataset, we use 1,669,237 papers with title, author, year, venue, and abstract. As a knowledge base for CF-IDF and HCF-IDF, we use the ACM Computing Classification System (CCS) [2].

*Subjects.* Overall $n = 22$ subjects were recruited. The subjects published on average 1256.97 tweets (SD: 1155.8). Regarding research papers for user profiling, on average a subject has 11.41 own papers (SD: 13.53).

*Metric.* To evaluate the serendipity of recommendations, we use the Serendipity Score (SRDP) [2]. It takes into account both unexpectedness and usefulness of candidate items, which is defined as: $SRDP = \sum_{d \in UE} \frac{rate(d)}{|UE|}$. $UE$ denotes a set of unexpected items that are recommended to a user. An item is considered as unexpected, if it is not included in a recommendation list computed by the primitive strategy. We use the strategy Own Papers $\times$ TF-IDF $\times$ Cosine Similarity as a primitive strategy. The function $rate(d)$ returns an evaluation rate of an item $d$ given by a subject. If a subject evaluates an item as "interesting", it returns 1. Otherwise, it returns 0.

## 4  Result and Discussion

Table 1 shows the results of the twelve strategies in terms of SRDP. Since we use the strategy Own Papers $\times$ TF-IDF $\times$ Cosine Similarity as a primitive strategy, mean is .00 for the strategy. An ANOVA is conducted to detect significant differences between the strategies. The significance level is set to $\alpha = .05$. Applying a

---

[1] https://lfs.aminer.org/lab-datasets/citation/citation-acm-v8.txt.tgz.
[2] https://www.acm.org/publications/class-2012.

Muchly's test detects a violation of sphericity ($\chi^2(54) = 80.912$, $p = .01$). Thus, a Greenhouse-Geisser correction with $\epsilon = 0.58$ is applied. The ANOVA reveals significant differences between the strategies ($F(5.85, 122.75) = 3.51$, $p = .00$). Shaffer's modified sequentially rejective Bonferroni procedure reveal significant differences between the primitive strategy and one of the other strategies.

The results of our experiment showed that tweets do not improve the serendipity. As shown at the rightmost column in Table 1, tweets deliver unexpected recommendations to users. However, only a small fraction of these serendipitous recommendations were interesting to the users. The results show further that the IA-Select algorithm produces serendipitous recommendations. Thus, IA-Select can be used in a research paper recommender to improve serendipity.

Table 1. SRDP and the number of unexpected items of the twelve strategies.

| | Strategy | | | SRDP | \|UE\| |
|---|---|---|---|---|---|
| | Text mining method | Profiling source | Ranking method | M (SD) | M (SD) |
| 1 | TF-IDF | Own Papers | IA-Select | .45 (.38) | 2.95 (1.05) |
| 2 | CF-IDF | Twitter | CosSim | .39 (.31) | 4.91 (0.29) |
| 3 | TF-IDF | Twitter | IA-Select | .36 (.29) | 4.91 (0.43) |
| 4 | CF-IDF | Twitter | IA-Select | .31 (.22) | 4.95 (0.21) |
| 5 | CF-IDF | Own Papers | CosSim | .26 (.28) | 4.91 (0.29) |
| 6 | CF-IDF | Own Papers | IA-Select | .25 (.28) | 4.91 (0.29) |
| 7 | HCF-IDF | Own Papers | IA-Select | .24 (.22) | 4.95 (0.21) |
| 8 | HCF-IDF | Twitter | CosSim | .22 (.28) | 5.00 (0.00) |
| 9 | TF-IDF | Twitter | CosSim | .20 (.24) | 4.95 (0.21) |
| 10 | HCF-IDF | Twitter | IA-Select | .18 (.21) | 5.00 (0.00) |
| 11 | HCF-IDF | Own Papers | CosSim | .16 (.18) | 5.00 (0.00) |
| 12 | TF-IDF | Own Papers | CosSim | .00 (.00) | 0.00 (0.00) |

## 5  Conclusion

We have investigated whether tweets and IA-Select deliver more serendipitous recommendations. Our online experiment reveals that tweets do not improve the serendipity of recommendations, but IA-Select does. This insight contributes to the development of future recommender systems in such a sense that a provider can make more informed design choices for the systems and services developed.

## References

1. Agrawal, R., Gollapudi, S., Halverson, A., Ieong, S.: Diversifying search results. In: WSDM, pp. 5–14. ACM (2009)

2. Ge, M., Delgado-Battenfeld, C., Jannach, D.: Beyond accuracy: evaluating recommender systems by coverage and serendipity. In: RecSys, pp. 257–260. ACM (2010)
3. Goossen, F., IJntema, W., Frasincar, F., Hogenboom, F., Kaymak, U.: News personalization using the CF-IDF semantic recommender. In: WIMS, ACM (2011)
4. Herlocker, J.L., Konstan, J.A., Terveen, L.G., Riedl, J.: Evaluating collaborative filtering recommender systems. TOIS $22(1)$, 5–53 (2004)
5. Kapanipathi, P., Jain, P., Venkataramani, C., Sheth, A.: User interests identification on twitter using a hierarchical knowledge base. In: Presutti, V., d Amato, C., Gandon, F., d Aquin, M., Staab, S., Tordai, A. (eds.) ESWC 2014. LNCS, vol. 8465, pp. 99–113. Springer, Cham (2014). https://doi.org/10.1007/978-3-319-07443-6_8
6. Nishioka, C., Große-Bölting, G., Scherp, A.: Influence of time on user profiling and recommending researchers in social media. In: i-KNOW, ACM (2015)
7. Nishioka, C., Scherp, A.: Profiling vs. time vs. content: what does matter for top-k publication recommendation based on Twitter profiles? In: JCDL, pp. 171–180. ACM (2016)
8. Sugiyama, K., Kan, M.Y.: Scholarly paper recommendation via user's recent research interests. In: JCDL, ACM (2010)

# Enriching the Cultural Heritage Metadata Using Historical Events: A Graph-Based Representation

Ilie Cristian Dorobăț[(⊠)] and Vlad Posea[(⊠)]

Politehnica University of Bucharest, Bucharest, Romania
ilie.dorobat@stud.acs.upb.ro, vlad.posea@cs.pub.ro

**Abstract.** Due to the fact that the presentation as accurate and as wide as possible of the events in which cultural heritage is involved play an essential role in understanding the past, the metadata aggregators must use representation models that satisfy the demands of information. Unfortunately, even if, besides the object orientated approach, the Europeana Data Model also makes available a more complex approach, oriented towards the events in which the object is involved, no data aggregator, uses the latter approach. Therefore, we propose a framework for translation of the represented metadata using the LIDO XML Schema, in sets of semantic data represented in conformity with the Europeana Data Model, using the event-oriented approach, so that users have the possibility to interconnect the events to cultural heritage objects and the other way around.

**Keywords:** Cultural heritage · Digital libraries · Linked data · Europeana Data Model · RDF graph transformation

## 1 Data Challenges

Europeana is the largest digital library in Europe encompassing over 58 million descriptions of cultural heritage objects (CHO's), aggregating metadata acquired from more than 3,000 museums, galleries, libraries and archives of the EU member states. For this, Europeana uses an own ontology, the Europeana Data Model (EDM) [1], that allows specialist both to implement a simple approach (*object-centric approach*), in which the main focus is on the CHO itself, and a more complex one (*event-centric approach*), which allows the emphasize of the relationships between the CHO's described. Unfortunately, the direction of data aggregators towards the object-centric approach [2] only diminishes the power of digital representation of the CHO's.

By analysing the cultural heritage spectrum from the region, we have identified that for representing CHO's, besides using the object-centric approach of the EDM conceptual model, a wide series of data aggregators (National Heritage Institute of Romania, National Digital Library of Finland, Athena Plus, German Digital Library, Partage Plus and others), it also uses one of the most popular standard in the area, LIDO XML Schema [3, 4]. Even though the LIDO XML Schema is a standard which can be used to represent metadata regarding the museum objects, an ontology offers more advantages in the presentation and reuse of the data. Thus, our attention is

A. Doucet et al. (Eds.): TPDL 2019, LNCS 11799, pp. 344–347, 2019.
https://doi.org/10.1007/978-3-030-30760-8_30

focused on the implementation of the EDM event-centric approach, approach which allows us to create a more thorough description of CHO's, including not only their physical description, but also the description of the events in which they have been involved in. Below, we are going to highlight the main challenges which have influenced the Framework architecture.

- **first-come, first-served basis:** the cardinality constraints imposed by EDM forces us to extract a single value [5] even if the LIDO XML Schema allows the existence of several values for the same property;
- **assigning the URIs for resources:** one of the fundamental principles of publishing in Linked Data is the using of URIs for representing the resources [6, 7], so that the former will be easily accessible both for humans and for machines;
- **the extension of the EDM vocabulary:** in some cases, the EDM vocabulary does not cover the needs of detailing of the resources, which urges us to extend the property sphere of the data model.

## 2   The Framework Architecture

This section is destined to the presentation of the architecture in concordance with the data challengers mentioned in the previous section. As can be seen in Fig. 1, the first part of this process is represented by the translation of the analysed LIDO files using the LIDO Parser component, which allows users the translation and storage in the internal memory for a successive processing of any of the data sets structures according to the LIDO data model. In the second part of the process, which represents the main component of the Framework [8], the previously generated dataset, will be mapped in a RDF tree according to the EDM data structure. Finally, users will be able to charge the set of triplet's *subject-predicate-object* in the semantic data store.

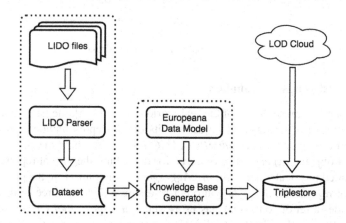

**Fig. 1.** Framework architecture.

## 2.1   Cardinality Constraints

The mapping of data from one model to another may have implications in the presentation of the data. Therefore, there are cases when, for certain properties, the EDM
conceptual model allows the registration a single value, but the LIDO XML Schema
can accept more values for the equivalent properties. For example, in the case of the
creation of a resource which identifies an organization, we will create an instance of the
foaf:Organization class, which, according to the EDM, must have a single identifier
(the property dc:identifier must have just one value per language), but the corresponding LIDO XML Schema record (lido:legalBodyID) allows the existence of an
undetermined number of such identifiers. Therefore, we will apply the *"first-come,
first-served"* principle and we will extract only the first value, ignoring the rest.

## 2.2   URI's Assignment

As far as the method of assigning of the URIs, if the LIDO record possesses a certain
property for the described element, it will be considered the use of the URIs already
existing, otherwise, a new URI will be created. In Fig. 2 it can be observed that for
creating an URI, the resource namespace must be concatenated to the following elements: (i) the country's code; (ii) the type of resource; (iii) an optional description
element which can be used for disambiguation a real-world object of another one (for
agents we can use their role; for events we can use the type of event etc.) and (iv) the
name of the represented object; thus generating an unique URI in the namespace. At the
same time, for the name of the objects, their sanitization will also be considered by
replacing all spaces and special characters with the underscore character ("_").

**Fig. 2.** Example of resource address.

## 2.3   Knowledge Base Vocabulary

For the semantic representation of the real-world objects [1, 5], the EDM considers the
differences between the physical object and its digital representations, providing the
following three core classes: (i) *edm:ProvidedCHO* for describing the characteristics of
the physical objects; (ii) *edm:WebResource* for describing the virtual representation of
the represented physical object; (iii) *ore:Aggregation* for connecting the physical object
to its digital representations. Also, in order to assure a higher degree of detailing, the
EDM provides a set of contextual classes as well (*edm:Agent, foaf:Organization, edm:
Event, edm:Place, edm:TimeSpan, skos:Concept*) and allows the extension of the data
model with user own terms.

# 3   Conclusions and Further Development

The usefulness of digital libraries can be found in the behaviour of regular users who needs to be informed about some certain CHO's that have caught their attention, as well as experts, who need more complex and more accessible information sources. Unfortunately, even though Europeana, the largest digital library in Europe, provides users for the data publications both an object-centric approach and a more complex approach, the event-centric approach, data aggregators prefer the first one, decreasing the power of digital representation of the CHO's, which, by their specific feature, present historical connections which might be useful for the understanding of the past.

The automatic Framework [8] proposed by us, allows data aggregators to increase the level of representation of knowledge by changing the perspective of the description of the objects towards the characterization of the various events in which the agents and the objects have been involved in. For this, data aggregators have at their disposal both a full-featured parser useful for the translation and storage of the LIDO files, and a feature for mapping the data generated through the parsing component into semantic data structured according to the EDM conceptual model. Further work which we are going to focus on is to determine a better way of dealing with the cardinality constraints and to identify an automatic or semi-automatic way of separating the organizational concept from the persons, because at the moment there is no distinction between those two types of agents involved in the production, finding and collecting of CHO's.

# References

1. Europeana Data Model Primer Documentation. https://pro.europeana.eu. Accessed 19 June 2019
2. Meghini, C., Bartalesi, V., Metilli, D., Benedetti, F.: Introducing narratives in europeana: a case study. Int. J. Appl. Math. Comput. Sci. **29**(1), 7–16 (2019). https://doi.org/10.2478/amcs-2019-0001
3. de Boer, V., Wielemaker, J., van Gent, J., Oosterbroek, M., Hildebrand, M., Isaac, A., van Ossenbruggen, J., Schreiber, G.: Amsterdam museum linked open data. Semantic Web **4**(3), 237–243 (2013). https://doi.org/10.3233/SW-2012-0074
4. Simou, N., Tsalapati, E., Drosopoulos, N., Stein, R.: Evolving LIDO-based aggregations into linked data. In: CIDOC 2012 Annual Conference "Enriching Cultural Heritage", Helsinki (2019). http://network.icom.museum/fileadmin/user_upload/minisites/cidoc/ConferencePapers/2012/simou.pdf. Accessed 19 June 2019
5. Charles, V., Manguinhas, H., Isaac, A., Freire, N., Gordea, S.: Designing a multilingual knowledge graph as a service for cultural heritage – some challenges and solutions. In: International Conference on Dublin Core and Metadata Applications 2018 (DCMI 2018), pp. 29–40. The Porto (2018)
6. Berners-Lee, T.: Linked Data: Design issues. https://www.w3.org/DesignIssues/LinkedData.html. Accessed 19 June 2019
7. Haslhofer, B., Isaac, A.: data.europeana.eu - the europeana linked open data pilot. In: International Conference on Dublin Core and Metadata Applications 2011 (DC 2011), pp. 94–104. The Hague, National Library of The Netherlands (2011)
8. CHO Enrichment Framework Github page. https://github.com/iliedorobat/enriching-cultural-heritage-metadata. Accessed 19 June 2019

# Open Research Knowledge Graph: A System Walkthrough

Mohamad Yaser Jaradeh[1,2]([✉]), Allard Oelen[1,2], Manuel Prinz[2],
Markus Stocker[2], and Sören Auer[1,2]

[1] L3S Research Center, Leibniz University of Hannover, Hanover, Germany
{jaradeh,oelen}@l3s.de
[2] TIB Leibniz Information Centre for Science and Technology, Hanover, Germany
{manuel.prinz,markus.stocker,auer}@tib.eu

**Abstract.** Despite improved digital access to scholarly literature in the last decades, the fundamental principles of scholarly communication remain unchanged and continue to be largely document-based. Scholarly knowledge remains locked in representations that are inadequate for machine processing. The Open Research Knowledge Graph (ORKG) is an infrastructure for representing, curating and exploring scholarly knowledge in a machine actionable manner. We demonstrate the core functionality of ORKG for representing research contributions published in scholarly articles. A video of the demonstration [7] and the system (https://labs.tib.eu/orkg/) are available online.

**Keywords:** Digital libraries · Information science · Knowledge graph · Research infrastructure · Scholarly communication

## 1 Introduction

Documents are central to scholarly communication. Virtually all research findings are nowadays communicated by means of electronic scholarly articles. Scholarly knowledge communicated in such form is hardly accessible to computers and the primary machine-supported tasks are largely limited to traditional full-text search. As such, the current scholarly infrastructure does not exploit modern information systems and technologies to their full potential [6].

We argue that there is an urgent need for a more flexible, fine-grained, context sensitive representation of scholarly knowledge and thus corresponding infrastructure for knowledge curation, publishing and processing. Furthermore, we suggest that representing scholarly knowledge as structured, interlinked, and semantically rich knowledge graphs is a key element of a technical infrastructure [3].

While some important conceptual foundations have been developed over several decades [1,6], knowledge graph infrastructure for science has recently gained momentum in the literature and community. The Research Graph [2] is a prominent example of an effort that aims to link publications, datasets, and researchers.

© Springer Nature Switzerland AG 2019
A. Doucet et al. (Eds.): TPDL 2019, LNCS 11799, pp. 348–351, 2019.
https://doi.org/10.1007/978-3-030-30760-8_31

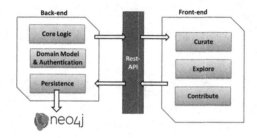

**Fig. 1.** The ORKG architecture showing the main infrastructure components.

The Scholix project [4] standardized the information about the links between scholarly literature and data exchanged among (primarily) publishers and data repositories. More recently, the FREYA H2020 project[1] has released information on their work towards a PID Graph [5]. The key distinguishing factor between these systems and the ORKG is the granularity of captured scholarly knowledge (article bibliographic metadata vs. materials, methods, and results communicated in articles).

## 2 Architecture and Features

The ORKG leverages knowledge graph technologies to represent, store, link, and process scholarly knowledge. It has two main components: The back end, which contains the logic to handle requests by client applications and the front end through which users create, curate or explore scholarly knowledge.

The concept of `ResearchContribution` is central to the ORKG as it represents key aspects of scholarly knowledge in structured, machine actionable form. A `ResearchContribution` is an information object which relates the `ResearchProblem` addressed by the contribution with a `ResearchMethod` and at least one `ResearchResult`.

The ORKG back end represents descriptions by means of a graph data model. Similarly to the Research Description Framework[2] (RDF), the data model is centered around the concept of a statement, a triple consisting of two nodes (resources) connected by a directed edge. In contrast to RDF, it allows annotating edges and statements. As metadata of statements, provenance information, e.g. when and by whom a statement was created, is a concrete and relevant application of such annotations.

ORKG users interact with the front end (UI), which guides users through the process of creating research contribution descriptions in a step by step manner. More advanced features of the infrastructure include the ability to directly find similar contributions (and related papers), thus enabling efficient state-of-the-art comparison and literature review. Figure 1 depicts the ORKG system architecture.

---

[1] https://project-freya.eu.

[2] https://www.w3.org/RDF/.

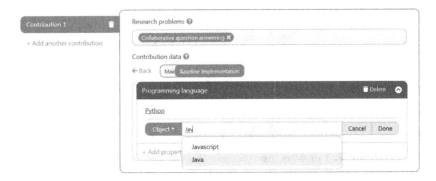

**Fig. 2.** ORKG UI curation wizard step (3) depicting the auto-completion feature that enables linking existing resources (here, Java).

## 3 Use Case

Consider the following research contribution: *FRANKENSTEIN* [8] *is a collaborative question answering (QA) framework written in Java and Python. It generates QA pipelines based on predictions for the best performing pipelines obtained via a supervised learning model. FRANKENSTEIN evaluates the results against QALD and LC-Quad datasets using the f1-score and accuracy@k metrics.* We can identify the following instances of relevant concepts:

- **Problem**: Collaborative question answering
- **Programming Language**: Python, Java
- **Approach**: Generate optimal QA pipelines
- **Datasets**: QALD, LC-Quad
- **Evaluation Metrics**: f1-score, accuracy@k.

Using the "Add paper" wizard (Fig. 2), we can create structured descriptions that encode, in machine actionable manner, the key information of research contributions. This process is straightforward also for non-technical users. Firstly, bibliographic metadata is collected, either via DOI lookup using the Crossref API or manually. Secondly, users can classify their paper according to the research domain. Finally, the research contributions described in the paper are collected using a flexible and dynamic interface.

## 4 Conclusion and Future Work

We presented the Open Research Knowledge Graph, an infrastructure that makes the first steps of a larger research and development agenda that aims to transition document-based scholarly communication to a knowledge-based information representation. In future work, we will include additional techniques from machine support to content creation and curation (such as NLP tools to suggest/annotate relevant concepts on behalf of users). Furthermore, we will further develop novel features such as state-of-the-art comparisons (Fig. 3). Such features will underscore the possibilities enabled by machine actionable scholarly knowledge and corresponding infrastructure.

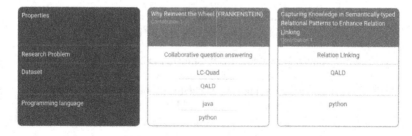

**Fig. 3.** ORKG UI state-of-the-art comparison for research contributions, showing a subset of shared properties between two articles.

**Acknowledgment.** This work has received funding from the European Research Council (ERC) under the European Union's Horizon 2020 Research and Innovation Programme (Grant agreement No. 819536).

# References

1. Allen, R.: Model-oriented scientific research reports. D-Lib Mag. **17**(5/6) (2011). https://doi.org/10.1045/may2011-allen
2. Aryani, A., Wang, J.: Research graph: building a distributed graph of scholarly works using research data switchboard. In: Open Repositories CONFERENCE (2017)
3. Auer, S., Kovtun, V., Prinz, M., Kasprzik, A., Stocker, M., Vidal, M.E.: Towards a knowledge graph for science. In: Proceedings of the 8th International Conference on Web Intelligence, Mining and Semantics, p. 1. ACM (2018)
4. Burton, A., et al.: The Scholix framework for interoperability in data-literature information exchange. D-Lib Mag. **23**(1/2) (2017)
5. Fenner, M., Aryani, A.: Introducing the PID Graph (2019). https://doi.org/10.5438/JWVF-8A66
6. Hars, A.: Designing scientific knowledge infrastructures: the contribution of epistemology. Inf. Syst. Front. **3**(1), 63–73 (2001)
7. Jaradeh, M.Y.: A demo of the open research knowledge graph. Technische Informationsbibliothek *TIB*, Leibniz Universität Hannover *LUH*, L3S Research Center (2019). https://doi.org/10.5446/42537. Accessed 21 Jun 2019
8. Singh, K., et al.: Why reinvent the wheel: let's build question answering systems together. In: Proceedings of the 2018 World Wide Web Conference, WWW 2018 (2018)

# The Biodiversity Heritage Library: Unveiling a World of Knowledge About Life on Earth

Martin R. Kalfatovic[1]([⊠]) [iD], Grace Costantino[1] [iD],
and Constance A. Rinaldo[2] [iD]

[1] Smithsonian Libraries, Washington DC 20013, USA
kalfatovicm@si.edu
[2] Ernst Mayr Library, Museum of Comparative Zoology, Harvard University,
Cambridge 02138, MA, USA

**Abstract.** The Biodiversity Heritage Library (BHL) is an international consortium making research literature openly available to the world as part of a global biodiversity community. Through its extensive network of Members, Affiliates, and Reciprocal Partners, over 56 million pages of biodiversity literature are openly available through the BHL portal. Created in 2006, the BHL was a direct response to the needs of the taxonomic community for access to early literature. The original BHL organizational model, based on United States and United Kingdom partners, provided a template for what is now over 80 global partners. In the international digital library world, BHL collaborates with, and aggregates content to national and pan-national digital libraries including Europeana and the Digital Public Library of America.

Now a cornerstone of biodiversity infrastructure, BHL is integral to key databases and data aggregators (e.g. World Registry of Marine Species, Tropicos, Global Biodiversity Information Facility, and the Encyclopedia of Life), and has engaged the research community in tool development and content reuse. Data contained in the Biodiversity Heritage Library (BHL) describes collections held in the world's major museums and botanical garden libraries. Finding those collections data, however, remains a challenge. BHL is actively engaging in incorporating tools and services (including digital object identifiers, full-text-search, and application programming interface) to make finding and linking to collection specimen information better.

**Keywords:** Knowledge discovery in digital libraries ·
Research infrastructures · Digital libraries · Biodiversity · Life sciences ·
Biodiversity heritage library · BHL

## 1 Overview

Operating as a consortium of natural history, botanical gardens, research institutions, and related organizations, the Biodiversity Heritage Library (BHL), founded in 2006, is administered via a Secretariat located at the Smithsonian Libraries in Washington, DC, and operates via global network of staff at participating institutions. BHL collections, spanning the 15th century through yesterday, contain over 56 million pages from over 244,000 volumes, approaching the size of many libraries in typical natural history or

© Springer Nature Switzerland AG 2019
A. Doucet et al. (Eds.): TPDL 2019, LNCS 11799, pp. 352–355, 2019.
https://doi.org/10.1007/978-3-030-30760-8_32

botanical collections. Importantly, the BHL data is both human-readable via the BHL portal, but accessible through open APIs that allow use and reuse of BHL data directly by other data systems.

The BHL's open access collections and services enable scientists to find the information they need to identify, describe, and conserve the world's species and habitats. The services in the BHL were developed directly in response to the research needs of the scientific community. BHL remains an integral part and responsive to the needs of a growing global biodiversity community.

## 2 Global Digital Library Partnerships

The BHL is an inaugural and key science data content provider to the Digital Public Library of America in the United States and also to the Europeana, the European Union's portal to museum and library collections. Natural History books and archives provide information that is critical to the study of biodiversity. The species data, ecosystem profiles, distribution maps, illustrations, behavioral, and inter-dependency observations, and geological and climatic records contained in this literature reinforces current scientific research and provides an historical perspective on species abundance, habitat alteration, and human exploration, culture, and discovery. Scientists have long considered lack of access to biodiversity literature a major impediment to the efficiency of scientific research.

## 3 Open Access and Scientific Impact

Illustrative of the BHL's commitment to open data, the BHL is a charter signatory of the Bouchout Declaration for Open Biodiversity Knowledge Management. BHL's commitment to open access extends beyond making scanned pages available through BHL. Content is available via Internet Archive, the Digital Public Library of America, and Europeana, and BHL's suite of APIs brings BHL data directly to users. BHL metadata is licensed as CC0 to allow for the widest dissemination of the data.

As noted in the Bouchout Declaration: "Collaborative Open Biodiversity Knowledge Management can bring together the achievements of many independent biodiversity projects, yet will allow them to retain their identity and missions. The resulting virtual pool of information will allow new services to emerge for everyone who relies on information about life on Earth. Awareness of, access to, preservation, and curation of information will be enhanced by a shared and seamless network of infrastructures" [1].

As noted by Hobern, et al., BHL is an important part of the global biodiversity ecosystem: "As an example of an existing collaboration, which might serve as a proof-of-concept project and which would benefit from increased exposure and openness, Catalogue of Life, GBIF, Encyclopedia of Life, Barcode of Life Data Systems and Biodiversity Heritage Library are currently working to develop a new collaborative model for building a shared taxonomic framework, under the project name, Catalogue of Life Plus (CoL+)" [2].

## 4  Technology

The BHL portal is located at the Smithsonian and runs under a .Net environment. BHL offers various web APIs, downloads, and other services for export and download of BHL data and content. BHL partners with the Internet Archive for file staging and storage. Additionally, BHL has developed software service, MACAW that simplifies ingest of partner content into BHL. MACAW is an open source tool with all code available on GitHub [3].

Looking forward, the BHL is in the planning stages of the next iteration of the BHL portal, dubbed BHL EVO, that will provide a number of enhancements and redesign elements, including the following:

- **Platform Transformation.** A total revamping of the BHL back-end will move the platform to the latest proven technologies. Funding will allow for the contracting of two developers/programmers to rewrite the underlying BHL code-base and transition the hardware to new open source technologies. Modularizing the BHL code will enable more rapid development in the future and create opportunities to co-develop with other major digital libraries such as the HathiTrust, Digital Public Library of America, etc.

- **Metadata Model Revision.** The fundamental recommendation is to create a concept of derivative digital objects (DDOs) that are first-class citizens, and to make it easy to create both individual DDOs and new classes of them. DDOs might eventually represent such diverse objects as ebooks, articles (including born-digital articles that are not part of an Item), chapters, snippets, annotations, plates, lists, tables, interesting flies squashed between two pages, and more. Once a DDO has been created, it must be easy to enrich it and to manage links to it and from it, and to have them form part of larger wholes within or outside of the BHL.

- **Semantic and Linked Data.** Enhancing existing BHL data and metadata through linked data and sematic web technologies will allow for more machine-to-machine use of deep BHL content. This data, which includes key facets such as habitat, diet, and author, and biomorphic data, will be exposed for researchers to integrate it into their own tools and publications. This data enhancement will created expanded links to key biodiversity resources such as the existing links to Tropicos, GBIF, and the Encyclopedia of Life.

- **Enhanced Platform.** The BHL platform excels at delivery of books. Funding will allow for improvements to the platform to enhance current field book content discovery and display; provide better support for Arabic and Asian-language texts; provide the capabilities to delivery new types of content including maps, visual resources, and related biodiversity content held in partner collections. Additionally, this will include integrated search and discovery of the rich illustrations and visual treasures included in the BHL corpus and deliver this content to new communities. Additional human interface improvements will include multilingual support and personal customization of the interface by users and the ability to save searches.

- **Dimensions of Biodiversity Literature and Gaps in BHL.** Finding a number to describe the quantity of biodiversity literature available is elusive. As BHL evolves into BHL Version 2 and content continues to become more robust, it is important to identify what is missing from the BHL collections. Identifying gaps will provide targets for prioritization and funding. Users have requested the incorporation of more in-copyright content providing another option to pursue for adding collections.
- **Engagement with a Wider Community Through Social Media**. Science is hard. The BHL has created multi-channel streams to tell the story of biodiversity to new and under-served communities. The rebooted BHL platform will enable wider sharing through linked data and other methods of core data to help people understand their world and its fellow inhabitants. These award winning social media platforms will democratize the delivery of understandable science to a wider community.

## 5    Conclusion

The BHL has been a successful model for digital library development and collaboration for a variety of reasons. Chief among these has been the BHL focus on a specific use case, namely, providing access to a core constituency of taxonomists. Expanding beyond this core group in carefully planned stages (e.g. those interested in the visual images within BHL) and partner growth (e.g. the global growth via targeted institutions) has broadened both the participant and user base. Likewise, the integration of BHL into core functions of its participating institutions has put BHL on the path to financial sustainability. BHL looks to the future with planned and sustainable growth, enriched content, and appropriate services.

## References

1. The Bouchout Declaration for Open Biodiversity Knowledge Management. http://www.bouchoutdeclaration.org/declaration/. Accessed 23 Apr 2019
2. Hobern D., et al.: Connecting data and expertise: a new alliance for biodiversity knowledge. Biodivers. Data J. **7**(e33679) (2019). https://doi.org/10.3897/BDJ.7.e33679
3. macaw-book-metadata-tool. https://github.com/gbhl/macaw-book-metadata-tool. Accessed 24 Apr 2019

# Clipping the Page – Automatic Article Detection and Marking Software in Production of Newspaper Clippings of a Digitized Historical Journalistic Collection

Kimmo Kettunen$^{(\boxtimes)}$ ⓘ, Tuula Pääkkönen ⓘ, and Erno Liukkonen

The National Library of Finland, DH Research, University of Helsinki,
Saimaankatu 6, 50100 Mikkeli, Finland
{Kimmo.kettunen, Tuula.paakkonen,
Erno.liukkonen}@helsinki.fi

**Abstract.** This paper describes utilization of article detection and extraction on the Finnish Digi (https://digi.kansalliskirjasto.fi/etusivu?set_language=en) newspaper material of the National Library of Finland (NLF) using data of one newspaper, *Uusi Suometar* 1869–1918. We use PIVAJ software [1] for detection and marking of articles in our collection. Out of the separated articles we can produce automatic clippings for the user. The user can collect clippings for own use both as images and as OCRed text. Together these functionalities improve usability of the digitized journalistic collection by providing a structured access to the contents of a page.

**Keywords:** Article extraction · Digitized historical newspaper collections · PIVAJ software · Content marking and distribution

## 1 Introduction

It is a common practice that historical newspaper collections are digitized on page level: pages of the physical newspapers are scanned and OCRed and the page images serve as the basic browsing and searching unit of the collection. Searches to the collection are made on page level and results are shown on page level to the user. Page, however, is not any kind of basic informational unit of a newspaper, only a typographical or printing unit. Pages consist of articles or news items (and advertisements or notices of different kind, too), although length and form of them can be quite variable. Thus, separation of the article structure of digitized newspaper pages is an important step to improve usability of digital newspaper collections. As the amount of digitized historical journalistic information grows, also good search, browsing and exploration tools for harvesting the information are needed, as these affect usability of the collection. Contents of the collections are one of the key elements of usefulness of the collections, but also presentation of the contents for the user is important [2, 3]. According to Dengel and Shafait [4] "availability of logical structure facilitates navigation and advanced search inside the document as well as enables better presentation of the document in a possibly restructured format." Possibility to use article structure

A. Doucet et al. (Eds.): TPDL 2019, LNCS 11799, pp. 356–360, 2019.
https://doi.org/10.1007/978-3-030-30760-8_33

will also improve further analysis stages of the content, such as topic modeling or any other kind of content analysis. Several digitized historical newspaper collections have implemented article extraction on their pages. Good examples are for example Italian La Stampa[1], British Newspaper Archive[2], and Australian Trove[3].

The historical digital newspaper archive environment of the NLF is based on commercial docWorks[4] software. The software is capable of article detection and extraction, but our material does not seem to behave well in the system in this respect. We have not been able to produce good article segmentation with docWorks, although such work has been accomplished e.g. in the Europeana Newspaper framework [5]. However, we have recently produced article separation and marking on pages of one newspaper, *Uusi Suometar,* by using article extraction software named PIVAJ developed in the LITIS laboratory of University of Rouen Normandy [1, 6, 7]. In this paper we describe intended use of the extracted articles in our digital library presentation system, digi.kansalliskirjasto.fi (Digi), as newspaper clippings which can be collected by the user out of the markings of the article extraction software.

## 2   Article Extraction

We have described results of article extraction using PIVAJ software in a recent conference paper [7]. The results we achieved with our training and evaluation collection were at least decent, if not remarkable, and we believe that they provide a useful

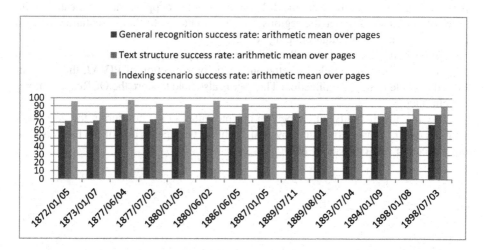

**Fig. 1.** Area weighted success rates for the three evaluation scenarios. Mean average figures for the issues.

---

[1]  http://www.archiviolastampa.it/.

[2]  https://www.britishnewspaperarchive.co.uk/.

[3]  https://trove.nla.gov.au/.

[4]  https://extranet.content-conversion.com/dW/_layouts/15/start.aspx#/SitePages/Home.aspx.

way to introduce articles for users, too. Figure 1 describes evaluation results of a 14 issue and 56 page evaluation collection with three evaluation scenarios described in [8]. On average the three evaluation scenarios get success rates of 67.9, 76.1, and 92.2 for the whole data set of 56 pages. Same evaluation schema is used in the bi-annual digitized journalistic data evaluation campaign ICDAR [9].

## 3   Providing Articles for the User

Users of our digital presentation system Digi have been able to mark and collect so called clippings for several years [10]. The clipping feature has been quite popular and many users have collected hundreds and even thousands of clippings for their own collections on their user accounts[5]. The clippings can also be seen by other users. Researchers have used the clipping function to collect their data, too. So far the feature has been totally manual: the user has marked on the pdf representation of the page the textual area he/she is interested in and the image of the clipping has been stored with bibliographical information. The user can also add keywords, topic and title to the clippings. There has not been possibility of storing the OCRed text of the clipping so far, only an image file [10].

The procedure of creating articles automatically for the user utilizes the existing clipping functionality of Digi. PIVAJ uses the defined newspaper models of Uusi Suometar for article extraction, and it provides as its output an XML file (regions.xml) which contains the coordinates of the article regions for each recognized article on a page. In Digi's context these are the different parts of the clipping that are created in the order of the creation. After the regions have been entered to the presentation system, they are shown as individual clippings on the page.

Figure 2 illustrates the overall work flow of clipping production.

After choosing the article from the automatic pre-selection of PIVAJ, the user can store the article in his/her collection. The user is also able to store the OCRed text along the clipping.

The new functionality will appear in our presentation system during the year 2019 with the data of Uusi Suometar 1869–1918. This newspaper is one of the most used in our collection and consists of 86 068 pages.

---

[5] In early June 2019 the number of stored clippings in our system was 165 494.

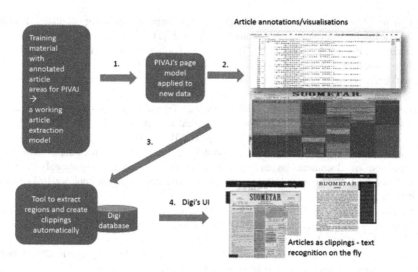

**Fig. 2.** Flow of article and clipping creation

# 4  Conclusion

This paper has described utilization of automatic article extraction on one historical Finnish newspaper, Uusi Suometar, in the journalistic collection of The National Library of Finland. The new enhanced functionality of the digital presentation system has been implemented by using an article detection and extraction tool PIVAJ and a clipping functionality already available in the user interface of our presentation system. The user can collect automatically marked articles for his/her own use both as images and OCRed text.

**Acknowledgment.** This work is funded by the European Regional Development Fund and the program Leverage from the EU 2014-2020. We thank LITIS laboratory of The University of Normandy Rouen for the possibility of using PIVAJ software.

# References

1. Hebert, D., Palfray, T., Nicolas, T., Tranouez, P., Paquet, T.: PIVAJ: displaying and augmenting digitized newspapers on the web experimental feedback from the "Journal de Rouen" collection. In: Proceeding DATeCH 2014 Proceedings of the First International Conference on Digital Access to Textual Cultural Heritage, pp. 173–178 (2014). http://dl.acm.org/citation.cfm?id=2595217
2. Fuhr, N., et al.: Evaluation of digital libraries. Int. J. Digit. Libr. **8**(1), 21–38 (2007)
3. Xie, H.I.: Users' evaluation of digital libraries (DLs): their uses, their criteria, and their assessment. Inf. Process. Manag. **44**(3), 1346–1373 (2008)
4. Dengel, Andreas, Shafait, Faisal: Analysis of the logical layout of documents. In: Doermann, David, Tombre, Karl (eds.) Handbook of Document Image Processing and Recognition, pp. 177–222. Springer, London (2014). https://doi.org/10.1007/978-0-85729-859-1_6

5. Willems, M., Atanassova, R.: Europeana Newspapers: searching digitized historical newspapers from 23 European countries. Insights **28**(1), 51–56 (2015)
6. Hebert, D., Palfray, T., Nicolas, T., Tranouez, P., Paquet, T.: Automatic article extraction in old newspapers digitized collections. In: Proceeding DATeCH 20114 Proceedings of the First International Conference on Digital Access to Textual Cultural Heritage, pp. 3–8 (2014). http://dl.acm.org/citation.cfm?id=2595195
7. Kettunen, K., Ruokolainen, T., Liukkonen, E., Tranouez, P., Antelme, D., Paquet, T.: Detecting articles in a digitized finnish historical newspaper collection 1771–1929: early results using the PIVAJ software. In: DATeCH 2019 (2019)
8. Clausner, C., Pletshacher, S., Antonacopoulos, A.: Scenario driven in-depth performance evaluation of document layout analysis methods. In: 2011 International Conference on Document Analysis and Recognition (ICDAR) (2011). https://doi.org/10.1109/icdar. 2011.282
9. Antonacopoulos, A., Clausner, C., Papadopoulos, C., Pletschacher, S.: ICDAR2013 competition on historical newspaper layout analysis – HNLA2013 (2013). https://doi.org/ 10.1109/icdar.2013.293
10. Pääkkönen, T.: Crowdsourcing metrics of digital collections. Liber Quarterly (2015). https:// www.liberquarterly.eu/article/10.18352/lq.10090/

# Document Recommendations in Slovenian Academic Digital Libraries

Mladen Borovič[(✉)] and Milan Ojsteršek

University of Maribor, Maribor, Slovenia
{mladen.borovic,milan.ojstersek}@um.si

**Abstract.** With the aim to improve the overall visibility of Slovenian research, one of the main features in the Slovenian open-access infrastructure is providing recommendations of similar documents to researchers, students and other interested parties across all included digital libraries, and other digital archives and journal repositories. In this work we describe the architecture of our hybrid recommender system along with observations of its use in the years after inclusion on real-world data between 2015 and 2018 by investigating which types of recommended documents get recommended the most.

**Keywords:** Hybrid recommender systems ·
Real-world recommender systems · Open-access · Digital libraries

## 1 Introduction

The use of recommender systems in academia has recently been on the rise. Students and researchers use them in digital libraries to find relevant theses, articles, studies, datasets and other documents. As an important feature of digital libraries, quite a few recommender systems have been developed for use in academia. Recommender systems such as presented in [1,3,5] were developed specifically for use in academic digital libraries and repositories to aid researchers in finding relevant publications. Moreover, such recommender systems can also be found in academic social networks like Mendeley [6]. In Slovenia, research regarding recommending documents in the Slovenian language for academic purposes is very scarce. The reason for this was the lack of a structured dataset of documents. This has improved since the introduction of the Slovenian Open-Access Infrastructure [4] which provided a large structured dataset with approximately 200,000 documents[1]. As a part of the infrastructure, a hybrid recommender system has been developed with the aim to improve the visibility of research in Slovenia and encourage researchers from all Slovenian universities to collaborate. This work presents the architecture of our hybrid recommender system included in the Slovenian Open-Access Infrastructure and some observations we made on the digital libraries that are using our recommender system.

---

[1] Open Science Slovenia Dataset, https://www.openscience.si/OpenData.aspx.

© Springer Nature Switzerland AG 2019
A. Doucet et al. (Eds.): TPDL 2019, LNCS 11799, pp. 361–364, 2019.
https://doi.org/10.1007/978-3-030-30760-8_34

## 2    Slovenian Open-Access Infrastructure

In 2013, the Slovenian Open-Access Infrastructure was established and has provided researchers, students and the public with access to the publications of Slovenian educational and research institutions. The infrastructure consists of a national web portal, institutional repositories for each of the four Slovenian universities, a repository for research institutions and a repository for colleges and higher education institutions. Metadata from other digital archives are also aggregated within the infrastructure. By type, the infrastructure contains diploma, master's and doctoral theses, journal and conference articles, proceedings, datasets, scientific and technical reports, books, lecture materials and videos of lectures. Because a great majority of publications are in Slovenian, an extensive full-text corpus of Slovenian language in different research domains was created. Currently it represents the largest corpus of texts in Slovenian language [2].

## 3    Method

We use a cascade approach in our hybrid recommender system (Fig. 1) with content-based filtering acting as a primary recommendation technique and collaborative filtering as its cascading re-ranking method. Documents are represented with titles, keywords, abstracts, typologies and year of publication. We use $tf$-$idf$ weights that are the basis for the calculation of BM25 similarity values for each document pair, forming a document similarity index. New documents are periodically processed as they are included to the system daily. Finally, the user activity data and the calculated similarities between documents are also considered before ranking the documents into a list that is presented to the end-user. The ranking process is where the hybridization occurs, applying content-based filtering and collaborative filtering in cascade.

In our content-based filtering method, we use a collection of metadata, which describes the documents with titles, keywords and abstracts, document typology [8], issue year, authors, repository and the language of the document. Our content-based filtering method uses two scores to return an initial ranking of the documents. A BM25 score is used as a relevance measure between the documents multiplied by a Jaro-Winkler [7] distance score (Eq. 1) acting as a document typology similarity.

$$Score_{CBF} = BM25(d_A, d_B) \cdot d_{jw}(t_{d_A}, t_{d_B}) \tag{1}$$

In our collaborative filtering method, we use the user activity for a document $a_d$. As actions include views and downloads, the counts of these actions are stored for each document and regularly updated as users use the digital libraries. A feedback value $f(a_d)$ is calculated with the sum of all values of actions on each document. A similar feedback value $f(a_r)$ is calculated with the sum of all values of action on each clicked recommended document. The final score for this method

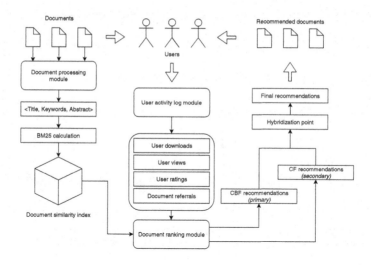

**Fig. 1.** Architectural diagram of the hybrid recommender system.

is calculated with the sum of feedback values $f(a_d)$ and $f(a_r)$ multiplied by the respective download to view ratios $h_d$ and $h_r$ as shown in Eq. 2.

$$Score_{CF} = f(a_d) \cdot \frac{downloads(d)}{views(d)} + f(a_r) \cdot \frac{downloads(d_r)}{views(d_r)} \tag{2}$$

The hybrid recommender system is implemented in two phases. The content-based method is first used to obtain an initial relevant set of documents which can be recommended. At this stage, an additional exponential temporal decay is applied to increase the ranks of recently published documents. The resulting set of ranked documents is then re-ranked using the feedback values of user actions obtained with our collaborative filtering method.

## 4    Observations and Conclusions

The goal of the recommender system was to provide recommendations in repositories across the national open-access infrastructure and encourage collaboration of researchers from different Slovenian universities. We investigated the types of documents which get recommended the most. This ties into the logic of the recommender system, which is configured to recommend similar types of documents and it reflects what types of documents are the most popular among our users.

We found that two groups of documents emerged as the most recommended. The first group consists of undergraduate theses, followed by master's theses and doctoral dissertations. The second group consists of scientific articles, review articles, professional articles and other reviews. An increase of recommendations through the years for these two groups can also be observed from Fig. 2. This is due to natural accumulation of new documents in our digital repositories which

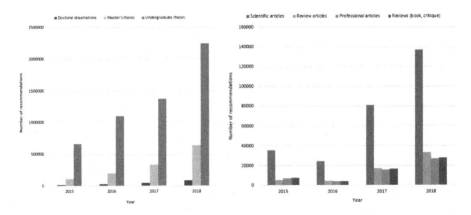

**Fig. 2.** Recommendations per year (left: group 1; right: group 2).

is on average approximately 13000 per year. We conclude that recommendations in digital libraries have a positive effect on students and researchers looking to broaden their research or acquire different views on the same topic. A unified framework is to be developed in the future in order to perform a more extensive evaluation of our recommender system's contribution to knowledge exchange.

# References

1. Beel, J., Aizawa, A., Breitinger, C., Gipp, B.: Mr. DLib: recommendations-as-a-Service (RaaS) for academia. In: 2017 ACM/IEEE Joint Conference on Digital Libraries (JCDL), pp. 1–2, June 2017. https://doi.org/10.1109/JCDL.2017.7991606
2. Erjavec, T., Fišer, D., Ljubešić, N., Logar, N., Ojsteršek, M.: Slovenska znanstvena besedila: prototipni korpus in načrt analiz. In: Proceedings of the Conference on Language Technologies & Digital Humanities, 29th September–October 1st 2016, pp. 58–64. Faculty of Arts, University of Ljubljana, Ljubljana, Slovenia (2016)
3. Knoth, P., et al.: Towards effective research recommender systems for repositories. In: Proceedings of the 12th International Conference on Open Repositories. Brisbane, Australia, June 2017. https://arxiv.org/abs/1705.00578
4. Ojsteršek, M., et al.: Establishing of a Slovenian open access infrastructure: a technical point of view. Program **48**, 394–412 (2014)
5. Porcel, C., Moreno, J., Herrera-Viedma, E.: A multi-disciplinar recommender system to advice research resources in University Digital Libraries. Expert. Syst. Appl. **36**(10), 12520–12528 (2009). https://doi.org/10.1016/j.eswa.2009.04.038. http://www.sciencedirect.com/science/article/pii/S0957417409003698
6. Vargas, S., Hristakeva, M., Jack, K.: Mendeley: recommendations for Researchers. In: RecSys 2016 Proceedings of the 10th ACM Conference on Recommender Systems, Boston, MA, USA, p. 365 (2016)
7. Winkler, W.: String comparator metrics and enhanced decision rules in the Fellegi-Sunter model of record linkage. In: Proceedings of the Section on Survey Research Methods, pp. 354–359 (1990)
8. Typology of documents/works for bibliography management in COBISS. https://home.izum.si/COBISS/bibliografije/Tipologija_eng.pdf. Accessed 10 Apr 2019

# An Evaluation of the Effect of Reference Strings and Segmentation on Citation Matching

Behnam Ghavimi[✉], Wolfgang Otto, and Philipp Mayr

GESIS – Leibniz Institute for the Social Sciences, Köln, Germany
{behnam.ghavimi,wolfgang.otto,philipp.mayr}@gesis.org

**Abstract.** In this paper, three different possible inputs (reference strings, reference segments and a combination of reference strings and segments) were tested to find the best performing strategy for citation matching. Our evaluation on a manually curated gold standard showed that the input data consisting of the combination of reference segments and reference strings lead to the best result. In addition, the usage of the probabilities of the segmentation improve the result when only features based on reference segments are considered.

**Keywords:** Citation matching · Reference segments · Reference strings · Evaluation

## 1 Introduction

The process of mapping an extracted reference string from a publication to one entity of a given Digital Library (DL) is called citation matching. Proper citation matching is an essential step for every citation analysis [7] and the improvement of citation matching leads to a higher quality of bibliometric studies. Christen et al. [2] reviewed different matching approaches and based on their study, they suggested general steps for the record linkage process: input pre-processing, blocking technique, feature extraction and classification. We also followed these steps for citation matching in this experiment and consider different input configurations to investigate their effects. In the pre-processing step the reference strings are segmented. Our used segmentation tool was Exparser [1] which includes a probability for each predicted segment. The next step is the blocking technique in order to decrease the number of pairs required to be compared. We used the search engine Solr for blocking. Koo et al. tried to find the best combination of citation record fields [6] that helps increase citation matching performance. We used a similar approach to shrink the number of queries in the blocking step. In the final step of the citation matching process, each candidate record pair (i.e, reference string and related segments paired with each retrieved item of the DL) are compared using a variety of attributes and comparison functions to generate a vector of features. Each candidate record pair is

© Springer Nature Switzerland AG 2019
A. Doucet et al. (Eds.): TPDL 2019, LNCS 11799, pp. 365–369, 2019.
https://doi.org/10.1007/978-3-030-30760-8_35

classified into one of the classes *match* and *non-match* based on their vector of features. Wellner et al. [8] investigated the effect of extraction probabilities on citation matching by the consideration of more than one of the top segmentation sequence probabilities based on the Viterbi algorithm. Our approach considers only the most probable segmentation. The probability of each segment is used in additional features that are utilized by the binary classifier for the citation matching task.

## 2  Evaluation Setup

For each reference, our matching algorithm[1] in this experiment retrieves the corresponding block with the help of blocking queries. Queries are formulated with the help of the parsed segments and reference strings by using the operators OR and AND from the Solr query syntax[2]. Additional we use fuzzy search (~-operator) which reflects a fuzzy string similarity search based on the Levenshtein distance. The threshold for this score was defined as 0.7 experimentally. The output of the blocking step is a ranked lists of retrieved items from the target database. The items are ranked by the tf/idf[3]-based Lucene score. To get the best trade off between retrieving all possible matching items and the reduction of necessary comparisons in the following classification task we identified two opportunities for influence. One is varying the query and select the best query formulation. The other is the selection of a cut off threshold which determines how many of the retrieved items per query are used for further processing. To exclude not well performing segment combinations for query generation we measured the 'precision@1' of the queries on our gold data. We only select segment combinations where at least 60% of the retrieved items are a correct match. This reduces the number of maximum combinations we consider for query generation by 25%. As an alternative strategy we generated queries from the reference strings. For this we consider all token of the reference string as potentially including title information. The idea is to formulate a bigram search of the whole reference string. The resulting query leads to results which at least need to include one bigram of the reference string in the title field. But the more bigrams of the reference string are included in the title, the more preferred results are. In addition, to increase the precision, a query based on year and bigrams of the reference string will also be considered. For this, the year information is taken into account which is extracted with a regular expression. After retrieving candidates for matches with our blocking procedure we need to decide which of the found candidates our system identifies as a match. We used features generated from the raw reference string and from the segmentation. Also we tried to find the effect of utilizing the certainty of our parser for the detected segments as an additional input feature for our classifier. The first group of features is

---

[1] https://github.com/exciteproject/EXmatcher.

[2] https://lucene.apache.org/solr/guide/6_6/query-syntax-and-parsing.html.

[3] https://lucene.apache.org/core/7_4_0/core/org/apache/lucene/search/similarities/ TFIDFSimilarity.html.

based on the comparison of the reference segments and the retrieved items in the blocking step: 1. Features based on the author segment (e.g., A. Levenshtein score (phono-code and exact) and B. Segmentation probability of first author (surname)), 2. Features based on titles (e.g., A. Jaccard score (including segmentation probabilities) and B. Levenshtein score (token and character level)), and some other feature which for reasons of space are not listed here [3]. The second feature group are based on the comparison of the raw reference string with the information of the retrieved record. Examples features for this group are the longest common sub-string of title and reference string, and the occurrence of the abbreviation of the source field (e.g., journal abbreviation) of retrieved item in the reference string.

# 3   Evaluation

The matching target DL used in this paper is Sowiport [4] which contains bibliographic metadata records of more than 9 million references. A manually checked gold standard was generated for this evaluation. This corpus include the information about 816 reference strings (randomly selected from EXCITE corpus which contains about 300K publications in PDF format) and all their corresponding items in Sowiport. 517 of these items have at least one matched item. We published this corpus and a part of sowiport data (18,590 bibliographic items) openly in our Github repository[4]. Three different configurations for the input of blocking were examined. In addition, the effect of the consideration of different numbers of top items from the blocking step was checked. The result shows that the precision of blocking based on reference strings is higher than the two other configurations. The highest recall has been achieved using the combination of reference strings and segments. The consideration of more top items shrinks the recall gap between different input configurations. Since we have another step after blocking which improve the precision, the important point in blocking is to keep the recall score high and at the same time shrinking the number of items for comparison. The precision of these three curves were not significantly different, therefore, the combination of reference strings and segments is picked in blocking step to generate input for the evaluation of classification step. For the number of top items in blocking, which are used for further processing in our experience, five is selected. This value is chosen because considering more items doesn't have a significant improvement on the recall score of using the combination of reference strings and segments as input but it generates much more false pairs. For the 816 references of the gold standard 10,997 match candidates are generated with our selected configuration in blocking. These candidates are based on top 5 retrieved items of all considered queries for each reference. In these 10,997 pairs, 1,026 (9.3%) are correct matches and 9,971 (90.7%) are no matches. After blocking, the number of reference strings which have at least one correct match is 507, and 302 references are without any correct pair. It means,

---

[4] https://github.com/exciteproject/EXgoldstandard/.

for only ten references (1.2%) which have at least one match in the gold standard could not pass blocking successfully. We applied ten-fold cross validation for testing two classifiers (SVM and Random Forest) and feature combinations. Table 1 contains precision, recall and f-measure for our compared configurations.

**Table 1.** Evaluation macro-metrics of different classifiers.

| Ref_String | Ref_Segments | Seg_probability | SVM | Random forest | Precision | Recall | F1 |
|---|---|---|---|---|---|---|---|
| ✓ | ✓ | ✓ | ✓ | – | 0.947* | 0.904 | 0.925* |
| ✓ | ✓ | ✓ | – | ✓ | 0.938 | 0.906 | 0.921 |
| ✓ | ✓ | – | ✓ | – | 0.941 | 0.908* | 0.924 |
| ✓ | ✓ | – | – | ✓ | 0.923 | 0.899 | 0.910 |
| – | ✓ | ✓ | ✓ | – | 0.942 | 0.865 | 0.901 |
| – | ✓ | ✓ | – | ✓ | 0.918 | 0.874 | 0.895 |
| – | ✓ | – | ✓ | – | 0.836 | 0.869 | 0.852 |
| – | ✓ | – | – | ✓ | 0.876 | 0.883 | 0.879 |
| ✓ | – | – | ✓ | – | 0.843 | 0.903 | 0.871 |
| ✓ | – | – | – | ✓ | 0.879 | 0.855 | 0.866 |

* refers to the highest value.

## 4    Discussion and Conclusions

We analyzed the impact of different inputs (i.e., reference strings, segments and the combination of both) on citation matching procedure. The segmentation probabilities are considered directly and as weights for creating specific features for classifiers. Segments probabilities have a good impact on the precision score when the citation matching algorithm uses segments as input. Using the combination of reference strings and segments as input outperforms the other configurations. The effect of different classifiers on the result are very depended on other parameters in the citation matching configuration such as input types and the consideration of segment probabilities. The citation matching approach which has been described and evaluated in this paper is implemented in a demonstrator which connects all important steps from reference extraction, reference segmentation and matching in the EXCITE toolchain (see [5] http://excite.west.uni-koblenz.de/excite).

## References

1. Boukhers, Z., et al.: An end-to-end approach for extracting and segmenting high-variance references from PDF documents. In: Proceedings of JCDL 2019. ACM (2019). https://doi.org/10.1109/JCDL.2019.00035
2. Christen, P.: Data Matching: Concepts and Techniques for Record Linkage, Entity Resolution, and Duplicate Detection. Springer, Heidelberg (2012). https://doi.org/10.1007/978-3-642-31164-2

3. Ghavimi, B., Otto, W., Mayr, P.: EXmatcher: combining features based on reference strings and segments to enhance citation matching. arXiv preprint (2019). arXiv:1906.04484
4. Hienert, D., et al.: Digital library research in action — supporting information retrieval in sowiport. D-Lib Mag. **21**(3/4) (2015). https://doi.org/10.1045/march2015-hienert
5. Hosseini, A., et al.: EXCITE - a toolchain to extract, match and publish open literature references. In: Proceedings of JCDL 2019 (2019). https://doi.org/10.1109/JCDL.2019.00105
6. Koo, H.K., et al.: Effects of unpopular citation fields in citation matching performance. In: Proceedings of ICISA 2011 (2011)
7. Moed, H.F.: Citation Analysis in Research Evaluation, vol. 9. Springer, New York (2006). https://doi.org/10.1007/1-4020-3714-7
8. Wellner, B., et al.: An integrated, conditional model of information extraction and coreference with application to citation matching. AUAI Press (2004)

# À la Carte: Turning Historical Menu into Menu Network

Hui Li[1]([✉]), Junming Hou[2], Yuanyuan Chen[3], and Keven Liu[1]

[1] Shanghai Library, Shanghai 200031, China
lhjulie@gmail.com, kevenlw@gmail.com
[2] Zhonghua Book Company, Beijing 100073, China
junminghou@hotmail.com
[3] Fudan University, Shanghai 200433, China
nightingale0612@126.com

**Abstract.** Confronted with the digitization of historical menus and motivated by the potentially valuable insights into history, researchers have recently focused on the content analysis of historical menus. Inspired by previous research, our objective is to reassemble and interpret historical menu network. In this paper, we develop a comprehensive historical menu network model, which integrates temporal, geographical, economic, and textual information into a graph representation. We conduct experiments on the basis of the menu collection of New York Public Library to uncover the interesting structures and patterns embedded in the network.

**Keywords:** Historical menu · Menu network · Signature dish

## 1 Introduction

Historical menus provide abundant information about changing regional tastes, the ingredients of popular dishes, the arrangements of different meals, and fascinating stories behind the menu, to name but a few. These menus constitute a significant aspect of the culture of diet [1]. Most preserved and digitized menus comprise two parts: menu metadata and menu content. The metadata of most menus usually contain a restaurant name, the location of the restaurant, the date on which a certain menu was used, and so on. The content of most menus usually consists of dish names and dish prices. The availability of such metadata and texts reveals details about the popular cuisine of restaurants and shows us certain trends of tastes and flavors over space and time.

Recently network analysis has been applied in the field of digital humanities, e.g., kinship analysis [2] and correspondence network [3], to explore a variety of relations among different entities effectively and efficiently. However, research upon the modeling, measurement, and analysis of menu network is still at its very beginning. In this paper, we aim to propose a menu network that closely resembles today's social network based on the metadata and content of menus. It is our hypothesis that such a menu network provides a more holistic view

A. Doucet et al. (Eds.): TPDL 2019, LNCS 11799, pp. 370–374, 2019.
https://doi.org/10.1007/978-3-030-30760-8_36

of that period of time than what would be perceivable through single menu sheet only.

## 2    Literature Review

An increasing number of libraries and institutes, e.g., New York Public Library [8], Los Angeles Public Library [9], and Cornell University Library [10], devote to digitizing the menu collections and making them accessible to not only academic, but also the general public who are interested in the history of dining. Researchers are curious to explore more beyond the words on the menu. For instance, Jurafsky et al. [4,5] investigated the origin of Sushi and employed state-of-art statistical methods such as linear regression to compare the differences between the language used by low-cost restaurants and expensive ones on their menus. Turnwald et al. [6] used log-likelihood ratio to illustrate that restaurants described healthy dishes with significant less appealing words but more health-related words. Chahuneau et al. [7] built a statistical model to predict price and sentiment for restaurants based on menus and customer reviews. But they did not take the temporal or geographical information of menus into account, which makes their modeling less comprehensive.

## 3    Menu Networks

We start with the definition of our menu network model and then introduce corresponding network measurements. Our model and measurements will later be applied to the experiments and reveal interesting patterns that contribute to our understanding of the historical menus.

**Definition 1. Menu.** *A menu is represented as a tuple $m = \{r, l, t, f, p\}$. $r \in R$ denotes the restaurant name. $l \in L$ denotes the restaurant location and $t \in T$ specifies the date when the menu was used. $f \in F$ specifies a dish on the menu. $p \in P$ corresponds to the dish price.*

**Definition 2. Menu Network.** *A menu network is represented as an undirected graph $G = (V, E)$, in which nodes $V \subseteq M$ correspond to menus and labeled edges $E$ correspond to the co-occurrence of dishes on the menus.*

We define an attribute function atn for each node $atn : N \to M_n$. $M_n$ is the set of four types of entities, i.e., restaurants, locations, dates, and dishes: $M_n = \{R, L, T, F\}$. Each node has associated attributes $\{(r, l, t, fd) \mid r \in R, l \in L, t \in T\}$. we define a "dish" function $fd : V \to F$ as an attribute for each node to mark the dishes on each menu.

Similarly, we define an attribute function ate for each edge $ate : E \to M_e$. $M_e$ is the set of three types of entities, i.e., id, dishes and prices: $M_e = \{N, F, P\}$. Each edge has associated attributes $\{(d, f, p) \mid d \in \mathbb{N}, f \in F, p \in P\}$. Considering that there might be more than one dish appearing on both menus, we use an index number $d$ to differentiate each element in the edge attribute set.

Thus we can represent the menu network by an adjacency matrix $A$ with entries that are not simply zero or one, but which are associated with the number of triplets in the edge attribute set. We define the weight of an edge as the corresponding value in the adjacency matrix $A$ that quantifies the relation between two menus.

$$A_{ij} = \left| \{(1, f_{ij}^1, p_{ij}^1), (2, f_{ij}^2, p_{ij}^2), ..., (k, f_{ij}^k, p_{ij}^k)\} \right| \tag{1}$$

**VIP Menu.** In order to capture the most important menu in the network, i.e., the menu that has largest overlap on dishes with other menus, we adopt degree centrality to measure how important a node $i$ is within a given (undirected) weighted network:

$$D_c(i) := \sum_{i \neq j} A_{ij}, \tag{2}$$

where $\sum_{i \neq j} A_{ij}$ represents the sum of the weights of all edges incident to node $i$.

**Signature Dish.** In order to know which particular dish is most popular among different menus in the network, we propose a measurement named signature dish. The signature dish $f$ within the whole network is calculated as,

$$Sig(f) := \{|f| \geq \eta \mid f \in ate(e_{ij}), i, j \in V, i \neq j, e \in E\}. \tag{3}$$

## 4    Experiments

In this section, we present our initial experimental results with an empirical dataset. The dataset used in this paper is a subset of the historical menus collected and transcribed by the New York Public Library (NYPL), which has one of the largest menu collections in the world [8]. We construct a menu network with 1473 nodes and 578,100 edges accordingly. We highlight the important menus, their latent communities, and signature dishes embedded in the resulting graphs.

**VIP Menu.** We calculate the degree for each node in order to find the central menu in the network. We find that the menu, which has most connections with others, comes from Cafe St. Denis. And the items on this menu, which shared most by others are oranges, chicken salad, and bananas. We suppose all these three were popular, cheap, low-cost, and easy to prepare in New York around 1900s. This might be the reason why most restaurants have them on the menus.

**Signature Dish.** Our focus here concerns the most popular dishes within the whole menu network. Most of these popular dishes are beverages, fruits, snacks, or desserts. However, there exist still large variances among their prices in the network. We suppose these dishes were frequently ordered by people at that time, thus many restaurants, no matter economic or luxury ones, prefer to put them on the menus with their own price budgets.

**Menu Communities.** In order to investigate the potential groups of menus, we apply the Louvain algorithm to our menu network based on NYPL dataset. The largest community contains 569 nodes (menus) and restaurant names of these menus are longest in average (ca. 20.885 characters). These names are highly related to rail transportations, e.g., railroad and railway, while in the second largest community words are highly related to person names and entertainments, e.g., antoinette, club, and park (Fig. 1).

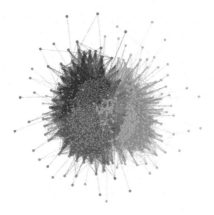

**Fig. 1.** Community structures in the menu network of NYPL dataset.

## 5   Conclusion

For future work, more investigations into the temporal and geographical dimensions such as regional influence and evolving patterns will be implemented with the intention of enriching the exploration of menu networks.

## References

1. Menus: the Art of Dining. http://digital.library.unlv.edu/collections/menus/early-restaurants-america. Accessed 23 Nov 2018
2. Kindred Britain. http://kindred.stanford.edu/. Accessed 23 Nov 2018
3. Mapping the Republic of Letters. http://republicofletters.stanford.edu/. Accessed 23 Nov 2018
4. Jurafsky, D.: The Language of Food: A Linguist Reads The Menu. W. W. Norton & Company, New York (2015)
5. Jurafsky, D., Chahuneau, V., Routledge, B., Smith, N.: Linguistic markers of status in food culture: Bourdieu's distinction in a menu corpus. J. Cult. Anal. (2016). https://doi.org/10.31235/osf.io/j9tga
6. Turnwald, B.P., Jurafksy, D., Conner, A., Crum, A.J.: Reading between the menu lines: are restaurants' descriptions of "healthy" foods unappealing? J. Health Psychol. **36**(11), 1034–1037 (2017)

7. Chahuneau, V., Gimpel, K., Routledge, B.R., Scherlis, L., Smith, N.A.: Word salad: relating food prices and descriptions. In: Proceedings of the 2012 Joint Conference on Empirical Methods in Natural Language Processing and Computational Natural Language Learning, pp. 1357–1367. Association for Computing Machinery, New York (2012)
8. What's on the Menu. http://menus.nypl.org/. Accessed 23 Nov 2018
9. Menu Collection. https://www.lapl.org/collections-resources/visual-collections/menu-collection. Accessed 23 Nov 2018
10. Menu Collection. https://rare.library.cornell.edu/collections/food-wine/menus. Accessed 23 Nov 2018

# Semantic Representation of Scientific Publications

Sahar Vahdati[1], Said Fathalla[1,3(✉)], Sören Auer[4,5], Christoph Lange[1,2],
and Maria-Esther Vidal[4,5]

[1] Smart Data Analytics (SDA), University of Bonn, Bonn, Germany
{vahdati,fathalla,langec}@cs.uni-bonn.de
[2] Fraunhofer IAIS, Sankt Augustin, Germany
[3] Faculty of Science, Alexandria University, Alexandria, Egypt
[4] TIB Leibniz Information Centre for Science and Technology, Hannover, Germany
[5] L3S Research Centre, Leibniz University of Hannover, Hanover, Germany
{maria.vidal,soeren.auer}@tib.eu

**Abstract.** In this work, we tackle the problem of generating comprehensive overviews of research findings in a structured and comparable way. To bring structure to such information and thus to enable researchers to, e.g., explore domain overviews, we present an approach for automatic unveiling of realm overviews for research artifacts (Aurora), an approach to generate overviews of research domains and their relevant artifacts. Aurora is a semi-automatic crowd-sourcing workflow that captures such information into the OpenResearch.org semantic wiki. Our evaluation confirms that Aurora, when compared to the current manual approach, reduces the effort for researchers to compile and read survey papers.

**Keywords:** Metadata extraction · Semantic publishing ·
Knowledge graphs

## 1 Introduction

The goal of preparing survey articles is to summarize the benefits and limitations of the existing research work in a specific research topic by producing, for example, tables of comparisons for state-of-the-art tools [3]. However, creating such document-based overviews requires significant effort from the researchers to not only describe the main characteristics of the examined approaches but also to compare and position them. We tackle the problem of semantically describing scientific papers using overviews that represent the *main characteristic* of a paper. We present Aurora, a semi-automatic crowd-sourcing workflow that captures information about research contributions in the *OpenResearch.org* semantic wiki; it facilitates the description of the scientific papers with the SemSur ontology [1] into a knowledge graph. Further, Aurora enables the generation of surveys comprising comprehensive analytics which cover different research domain overviews by querying the knowledge graph. Fathalla et al. [1,2] define an ontology that contains core concepts for describing scholarly documents, whereas

© Springer Nature Switzerland AG 2019
A. Doucet et al. (Eds.): TPDL 2019, LNCS 11799, pp. 375–379, 2019.
https://doi.org/10.1007/978-3-030-30760-8_37

Aurora facilitates the usage of ontologies. SemSur ontology is employed as the reference ontology for modeling research findings in scientific articles [2]. Knowledge encoded in document-oriented scientific publications reveals the *main characteristic* of the approach defined in a paper; they correspond to the results of multiple steps of the research methodology, e.g., problem statement, proposed approach, and evaluation methods. Exploiting semantic representations of scientific papers involves: Fig. 1 depicts the pipeline of Aurora based on the aforementioned required steps. Aurora receives a set of scholarly artifacts and annotations provided by the crowd, and outputs a knowledge graph representing the main parts of the artifacts. Traversing and exploring the generated knowledge graph facilitates to analysis and comparison of the existing approaches in a particular domain. In order to demonstrate the descriptive capability of the Aurora knowledge graph, several complex questions are evaluated. The observed results suggest that representing research artifacts in terms of domain overviews facilitates the exploration of related approaches. Our contributions are summarized as follows: (1) An ontology for creating a scholarly knowledge graph representing research contributions in a semantic way, (2) Aurora, a framework implemented on top of the crowd-sourcing platform *OpenResearch.org* which relies on extraction and curation methods for a scholarly knowledge graph, and (3) Providing domain overviews and suggestions such as which publication to read, which tools to use, where to publish similar results on sub-networks of the knowledge graph.

## 2    The Proposed Solution

This work focuses on facilitating scholarly communication by semantically representing elements of regular research articles and other types of scholarly artifacts, e.g., tools and frameworks. As mentioned initially, writing survey articles is a traditional but still the most widespread way of creating a systematic overview about scholarly artifacts. Survey articles summarize and organize the state of the art and emphasize the classification of the existing developments, frameworks, or evaluation methods. Despite legal and technical improvements to the access to scientific publications and despite a number of services developed for supporting scholarly communication, such as research repositories, search engines and digital libraries, it is often a time-consuming task to find information such as: papers containing certain information about a topic of interest, a comparison of state of the art tools, and Overview of approaches addressing a particular research problem. To support scholars who want to find and learn from such overviews about a domain or those researchers attempting to create such overviews, we aim at representing such information in a research knowledge graph underlying our *OpenResearch.org* (OR) platform.

## 3    Metaresearch Queries

In this section, we describe the design and expectation procedure of a set of metaresearch queries on top of the Aurora knowledge graph. The goal of this

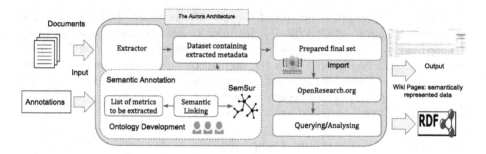

**Fig. 1.** Aurora Pipeline.

representation is to evidence the descriptive capability of the Aurora knowledge graph in terms of complex queries. The queries are relatively hard to directly answer using existing scholarly search engines ad other services e.g., Google Schoolar, DBLP, Semantic Scholar. The answer for such queries requires content of scholarly publications, particularly survey papers which include summaries and comparisons. For instance, the table on the left side in Fig. 2 is one of these tables, extracted from the survey paper "Querying over Federated SPARQL Endpoints–A State of the Art Survey" [4]. Creating such a table takes considerable time and effort [2] for a researcher providing a survey paper for the community. This evaluation aims at illustrating how Aurora enables the execution of complex queries that requires information from different sources about various artifacts. To answer such queries, normally researchers are required to do a comprehensive literature review on a specific topic by being able to conclude such comparison tables. Figure 2 shows a comparison between a table in a survey paper and a corresponding table generated by our approach.

Table II: The Existing Frameworks Supports Federation over SPARQL Endpoints without reformulating query to SPARQL 1.1.

| Framework | Catalogue | Platform | Source Selection | Cache | Query Execution | Source Tracking | GUI |
|---|---|---|---|---|---|---|---|
| DARQ | Service Description | Jena | Statistic of Predicate | ✓ | Bind Join or Nested Loop Join | Static | ✗ |
| ADERIS | Predicate List during setup phase | ✗ | Predicate List | ✗ | Nested Loop Join | Static | ✓ |
| FedX | ✗ | Sesame | ASK | ✓ | Bind Join parallelization | Dynamic | ✓ |
| Splendid | VoID | Sesame | Statistic + ASK | ✗ | Bind Join or Hash Join | Static | ✗ |
| GDS | Service Description | Jena | Statistic of Predicate | ✓ | Bind Join or Semi Join | Dynamic | ✗ |
| Avalanche | Search Engine | Avalanche | Statistic of predicates and ontologies | ✓ | Bind join | Dynamic | ✗ |
| Distributed SPARQL | ✗ | Sesame | ✗ | ✗ | Bind join | ✗ | ✗ |

| Tool/Ontology | Data Catalogue | Platform | GUI |
|---|---|---|---|
| ANAPSID | Predicate list and endpoint status | ANAPSID | Yes |
| SemWIQ | RDF stats + VoID | Jena | Yes |
| Avalanche | Search Engine | Avalanche | No |
| FedX | - | Sesame | Yes |
| DARQ | Service Description | Jena | No |
| GDS | Service Description | Jena | No |
| WoDQA | VoID stores | Jena | Yes |
| SPLENDID | VoID | Sesame | No |
| ADERIS | Predicate List during setup phase | - | Yes |
| Distributed SPARQL | - | Sesame | No |

Table generated by human in a survey paper               Table *automatically* generated by OpenResearch.org

**Fig. 2.** A table included in a survey paper (left-side) is compared to the table generated (right-side) by querying the knowledge graph.

Aurora is implemented on top of the OpenResearch.org platform which is built upon Semantic MediaWiki [5]. In order to obtain sample queries to be implemented by Aurora, five researchers brainstormed (authors of this paper– three senior and two junior) from the domain of Linked data and Knowledge Engineering and Data Management. A set of ten predefined natural language queries has been finalized to be implemented as *ASK* queries. To demonstrate the efficiency of our proposed approach, we used a set of four survey papers and extracted information of 36 papers surveyed, as a seed in order to create a knowledge graph representing research findings in these papers referenced by the four survey papers. Assume that a researcher wants to answer these queries using the current scholarly search engines, how much time and effort does it take to answer these queries? These ten queries are currently implemented and made available on *OpenResearch.org*[1]. These queries cover essential findings presented in the four survey articles; they are chosen in increasing order of complexity.

For getting an overview of a certain topic, we prepared a query: *Query 1*: get an overview of the Tools addressing the research problem "SPARQL Query Federation". The results of such query are available at http://openresearch.org/wiki/Papers_query1.

## 4   Discussion

We presented Aurora for representing research findings in computer science in a semantic way and crowd-sourcing the creation of these semantic representations using a semantic wiki. We evaluated the approach with a number of competency questions, which can now be answered using Aurora and simple queries, instead of long-term survey compilation. We believe that Aurora is a one of the initial steps towards transforming the current document-based information flows in scholarly communication into knowledge-based ones. Aurora follows the problem-approach-implementation-evaluation methodological pattern, which is widespread in computer science and other engineering fields.

## References

1. Fathalla, S., Vahdati, S., Auer, S., Lange, C.: SemSur: a core ontology for the semantic representation of research findings. In: Proceedings of the 14th International Conference on Semantic Systems. ACM (2018, in press)
2. Fathalla, S., Vahdati, S., Auer, S., Lange, C.: Towards a knowledge graph representing research findings by semantifying survey articles. In: Kamps, J., Tsakonas, G., Manolopoulos, Y., Iliadis, L., Karydis, I. (eds.) TPDL 2017. LNCS, vol. 10450, pp. 315–327. Springer, Cham (2017). https://doi.org/10.1007/978-3-319-67008-9_25
3. Kitchenham, B.: Procedures for performing systematic reviews. In: Keele, UK, Keele University 33(2004), pp. 1–26 (2004)

---

[1] https://www.openresearch.org/wiki/Papers.

4. Rakhmawati, N.A., Umbrich, J., Karnstedt, M., Hasnain, A., Hausenblas, M.: Querying over federated SPARQL endpoints - a state of the art survey. CoRR abs/1306.1723 (2013)
5. Vahdati, S., Arndt, N., Auer, S., Lange, C.: OpenResearch: collaborative management of scholarly communication metadata. In: EKAW (2016)

# Determining How Citations Are Used in Citation Contexts

Michael Färber[1](✉) and Ashwath Sampath[2]

[1] Karlsruhe Institute of Technology (KIT), Karlsruhe, Germany
michael.faerber@kit.edu
[2] University of Freiburg, Freiburg, Germany
ashwath92@gmail.com

**Abstract.** Citations have been classified based on their textual contexts w.r.t. their worthiness, function, polarity, and importance. To the best of our knowledge, so far citations have not automatically been classified by their grammatical role, that is, whether the citation (1) is grammatically integrated in the sentence, (2) is annotated directly after the occurrence of author names, (3) backs up a concept, (4) backs up a claim, or (5) is not appropriate because the context is incomplete or noisy. We argue that determining such classes for citation contexts is useful for a variety of tasks, such as improved citation recommendation and scientific impact quantification. In this paper, we propose this classification scheme, as well as a machine-learning-based approach to determine the classes automatically. Our evaluation reveals that the classification performance varies significantly between the citation types.

**Keywords:** Citations · Scholarly data · Bibliometrics · Classification

## 1 Motivation

Citing sources has always been an integral part of academic research. Scientific works need to contain appropriate citations to other works due to several reasons [1]. Most notably, all claims written by an author need to be backed up to ensure transparency, reliability, and truth. Furthermore, mentions of methods, data sets and important domain-specific concepts need to be linked via references to help the reader properly understand the text and to give attribution to the corresponding publications and authors.

Citation contexts have been classified in several respects so far. Noteworthy to mention is the classification of citation contexts (e.g., sentences) concerning the cite-worthiness [2]. Apart from that, citation contexts have been classified according to their citation function using some annotation scheme [1,3] (i.e., determining the "role" of a citation in its pragmatic context; e.g., that the author mentions a weakness of an approach). Similar tasks to the citation function determination are the polarity determination (i.e., if the author speaks in a positive, neutral, or negative way about the cited paper) [4,5] and

© Springer Nature Switzerland AG 2019
A. Doucet et al. (Eds.): TPDL 2019, LNCS 11799, pp. 380–383, 2019.
https://doi.org/10.1007/978-3-030-30760-8_38

**Table 1.** Examples for citation types taken from our data set.

| Citation type | Example sentence |
|---|---|
| IN-TEXT | "The approaches of [7] and [1] allow to plug an advisor system in a scenario from the environments Telos and ExploraGraph" |
| AUTHOR | "Gibson et al. [12] used hyperlink for identifying communities" |
| CONCEPT | "To this end, SWRL [14] extends OWL-DL and OWL-Lite with Horn clauses" |
| CLAIM | "In the traditional hypertext Web, browsing and searching are often seen as the two dominant modes of interaction (Olston and Chi 2003)" |
| INCOMPLETE | "see [16, 15]" |

the determination of the citation importance [6]. Redi et al. [7] proposed reasons why citations are used and needed in Wikipedia texts. However, to our knowledge, citation contexts have not been classified automatically by grammatical functions, that is, whether the citation (1) is grammatically integrated in the sentence, (2) is mentioned directly after the occurrence of author names, (3) backs up a concept, (4) backs up a claim, or (5) is not appropriate due to incomplete or noisy context. Determining such classes for citation contexts can be seen as a prerequisite for a variety of tasks, such as for improved citation recommendation and for creating alternative measurements of the scientific impact other than citation counts.

## 2    Citation Types

Based on the findings gained by manually examining various citation contexts and previous works on citation classification [8], we introduce five classes of citation types (see also the examples in Table 1):

1. IN-TEXT: The citation marker is part of the sentence. Citations are then "weaved" into the grammar of the sentence.
2. AUTHOR: The citation marker is set directly after the occurrence of author names.
3. CONCEPT: The citation marker follows a concept. This can be a named entity (e.g., a specific data set, method, or project) or an abstract scientific concept.
4. CLAIM: A claim made by the author is backed up by the citation.
5. INCOMPLETE: The citation does not need to be considered because the citation context is incomplete or noisy (e.g., containing only formulas or references from the reference section if extracted automatically) and, thus, not fully understandable.

## 3    Citation Type Classification Approach

To determine the citation types for a given citation context (including the citation markers), we develop a classifier based on a multi-label (one vs. the rest) gradient boosting classifier.[1] We use the following features, each extracted from the given citation context:

1. the number of words;
2. the normalized number of nouns, verbs, proper nouns, numbers, and prepositions;
3. the normalized number of citation markers;
4. the normalized number of mentioned people's names, using the named entity recognition implementation of the Python library Spacy;
5. the citation positions sum, which is calculated by adding the normalized word positions of all the citation markers in the citation context;
6. the sum of the distance of each of the citation markers in the citation context to the nearest noun, nearest proper noun, nearest preposition, and nearest verb, respectively.
7. the sum of the distance of each of the citation markers to the nearest person mentioned;
8. the TF-IDF values of the words in the context;
9. the average of the fastText vectors of all citation context's words.[2]

## 4    Evaluation

### 4.1    Data Set

We manually created a ground truth data set for the citation type classification task. To that end, we manually labeled 500 citation contexts that were written in English and extracted from the Microsoft Academic Graph where the cited document is tagged by the Microsoft Academic Graph with "semantic web". To create a test data set, we annotated 100 English citation contexts retrieved from the Microsoft Academic Graph where the cited document is tagged as "natural language processing." The data set is freely available online.[3]. Note that we used different domains for the training and test data sets to keep our machine learning model generic enough and to avoid overfitting. The domains were chosen based on the expertise of the authors as assessors.

---

[1] See https://github.com/michaelfaerber/citation-type-classifier for our source code. Note that each citation context can belong to one or several citation types. This makes our classification task a multi-label classification task.

[2] See https://fasttext.cc/. The pretrained vectors were trained on Common Crawl and Wikipedia using the CBOW model of fastText. fastText operates at the character level, and therefore can generate vectors for words not seen in the training corpus.

[3] See https://github.com/michaelfaerber/citation-type-classifier.

**Table 2.** Evaluation results.

| Class | IN-TEXT | AUTHOR | CONCEPT | CLAIM | INCOMPLETE |
|---|---|---|---|---|---|
| *precision* | 0.50 | 1.00 | 0.46 | 0.57 | 0.50 |
| *recall* | 0.45 | 0.06 | 0.59 | 0.72 | 0.40 |
| *F1* | 0.47 | 0.11 | 0.52 | 0.64 | 0.44 |

### 4.2 Evaluation Results

Table 2 shows the performance of our classifier. Overall, we can observe that automatically determining all classes for a citation context is a difficult task. However, the classifier seems to work significantly better for some classes than others. The CLAIM and AUTHOR classes lie at the extremes, while the other three classes are around average. We obtain an accuracy over all classes (defined as the proportion of samples in which all the predicted labels match all the true labels) of 0.4. The Hamming loss, a more suitable metric than accuracy for multi-label classification tasks (as it allows partial mismatches), is 0.216.

## 5 Conclusion

In this paper, we presented a novel classification scheme for in-text citations. We then proposed a machine-learning-based approach to determine these citation types automatically for given citation contexts. In the future, we will analyze the citation types for various scientific disciplines. We also plan to incorporate the citation type classifier into citation recommendation systems.

## References

1. Teufel, S., Siddharthan, A., Tidhar, D.: An annotation scheme for citation function. In: Proceedings of SIGdial 2009, pp. 80–87 (2009)
2. Färber, M., Thiemann, A., Jatowt, A.: To cite, or not to cite? Detecting citation contexts in text. In: Pasi, G., Piwowarski, B., Azzopardi, L., Hanbury, A. (eds.) ECIR 2018. LNCS, vol. 10772, pp. 598–603. Springer, Cham (2018). https://doi.org/10.1007/978-3-319-76941-7_50
3. Teufel, S., Siddharthan, A., Tidhar, D.: Automatic classification of citation function. In: Proceedings of EMNLP 2007, pp. 103–110 (2006)
4. Abu-Jbara, A., Ezra, J., Radev, D.R.: Purpose and polarity of citation: towards NLP-based bibliometrics. In: Proceedings of NAACL-HLT 2013, pp. 596–606 (2013)
5. Ghosh, S., Das, D., Chakraborty, T.: Determining sentiment in citation text and analyzing its impact on the proposed ranking index. CoRR abs/1707.01425 (2017)
6. Valenzuela, M., Ha, V., Etzioni, O.: Identifying meaningful citations. In: Proceedings of SBD 2015 (2015)
7. Redi, M., Fetahu, B., Morgan, J.T., Taraborelli, D.: Citation needed: a taxonomy and algorithmic assessment of Wikipedia's verifiability. In: Proceedings of WWW 2019 (2019)
8. Petrić, B.: Rhetorical functions of citations in high-and low-rated master's theses. J. Engl. Acad. Purp. **6**(3), 238–253 (2007)

# Dendro: A FAIR, Open-Source Data Sharing Platform

Lázaro Costa$^{(\boxtimes)}$ ⓘ and João Rocha da Silva ⓘ

INESC TEC/Faculdade de Engenharia da Universidade do Porto, Porto, Portugal
`lazaroosta@hotmail.com`, `joaorosilva@gmail.com`

**Abstract.** Dendro, a research data management (RDM) platform developed at FEUP/INESC TEC since 2014, was initially targeted at collaborative data storage and description in preparation for deposit in any data repository (CKAN, Zenodo, ePrints or B2Share). We implemented our own data deposit and dataset search features, consolidating the whole RDM workflow in Dendro: dataset exporting, automatic DOI attribution, and a dataset faceted search, among other features. We discuss the challenges faced when implemented these features and how they make Dendro more FAIR.

**Keywords:** Research data · Repositories · Data citation · FAIR · Dendro

## 1 Introduction

Research data management (RDM) is essential for science, enabling the reproducibility of research results [8] and credit attribution [1,3,4]. Data citation requires data search, access, sharing and reuse, being a widely recognized practice in many research areas [1].

The FAIR principles [9] assist in RDM, both by humans and machines [5,6], and help steer the design of adequate RDM workflows and software.

The Dendro platform [7][1] is an RDM platform under development at FEUP's InfoLab since 2014. It supports the collaborative management of research data within research groups, in preparation for their deposit in a data repository.

We made Dendro more FAIR by enabling the deposit and cataloguing of research datasets in Dendro itself, no longer requiring (but still allowing) the export to an external repository for long-term sharing of finished datasets. The new version also integrates with DataCite for automatic DOI attribution.

## 2 New Deposit and Citation Features

Starting from the user requirements, we outline a new workflow for data deposit and citation and present several new features.

---

[1] https://github.com/feup-infolab/dendro.

© Springer Nature Switzerland AG 2019
A. Doucet et al. (Eds.): TPDL 2019, LNCS 11799, pp. 384–387, 2019.
https://doi.org/10.1007/978-3-030-30760-8_39

- **From researcher requirements to new Dendro features**. The implementation of this new deposit and citation functionality in Dendro derives from several researcher requirements. These features are partially present in some of the platforms (CKAN[2], Dataverse[3], Zenodo[4], DSpace[5] or ePrints[6]), but no single software solution implements them all [2].
- **Flexible, domain-specific metadata** Since not all repository platforms support generic and domain-specific metadata, these would have to be translated via crosswalking or embedding (e.g. specific metadata descriptors such as `Sample Size` from the Social Sciences or `Reactor Type` from Hydrogen Generation would become part of a Dublin Core `Description`). With our own deposit features, all metadata is kept intact in the published dataset.
- **History of metadata changes** Dendro also maintains a complete history of changes made to metadata records. After exporting to an external repository, this important provenance information would be separated from the finished dataset record; it is now maintained if the dataset is published in the Dendro instance.
- **Structured datasets** Since all other platforms represent their datasets as a flat list of files with metadata associated the root dataset record only, Dendro datasets (which are hierarchies of files and folders) had to be exported as BagIt files containing RDF metadata in order to preserve the structure and metadata associated to every node. Now the structure is kept intact.
- **Citation snippets** Zenodo and Dataverse already provide citation snippets. We have added this feature to Dendro, providing a BibTeX citation snippet for every dataset. The snippets are provided by DataCite upon minting of the DOI, which is done automatically by Dendro.
- **More refined access management** We now support embargo, the ability to specify terms of use when accessing a data and an on-demand dataset access workflow for creators to approve data requests.
- **Automatic DOI attribution** With this new implementation, Dendro can now mint persistent identifiers (DOI) via DataCite. These identifiers are now added to the metadata record of each published dataset, while a metadata record is automatically translated into the DataCite Schema 4 at the time of DOI minting. This way, even if that Dendro becomes unavailable, the metadata remains accessible via DataCite.
- **Faceted Search** Figure 1 shows our new faceted search, powered by SPARQL and available as an API. Facets include: dataset visibility (public, private or embargoed), dataset creator, creation date, and a logical combination (`OR` or `AND`) of descriptors-value pairs to filter datasets.

---

[2] https://ckan.org/.
[3] https://dataverse.org/.
[4] https://zenodo.org/.
[5] https://duraspace.org/dspace/.
[6] https://www.eprints.org/uk/.

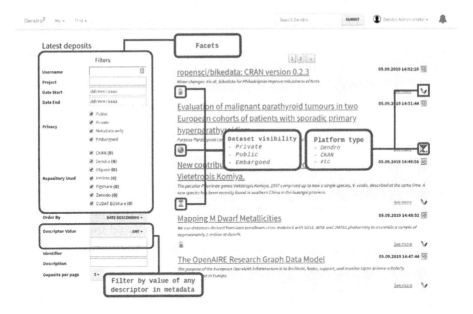

**Fig. 1.** Faceted dataset search in Dendro

## 2.1 A Revised Workflow

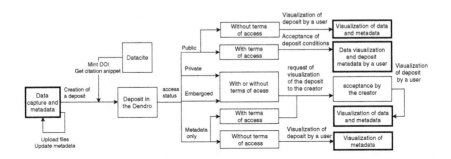

**Fig. 2.** New deposit workflow implemented in Dendro

Figure 2 shows our new workflow. Upon data deposit, the user can pick the visibility of the new dataset and, optionally, add access terms that any user wanting to access the data must accept. Visibility can be private (the dataset appears in the search but will not be accessible without author approval), public (data and metadata will be accessible), metadata only (dataset metadata will be visible when accessing the dataset, but not the data) and embargoed, which is private until after a certain date specified by the creator, and then becomes public. If terms of access are specified, they have to be accepted by users when accessing the data. In the case of private datasets, users can request access to the data creator. In that case, the creator is notified to approve or reject the request, and the requester is then notified of the result. Dataset creators retain the power to revoke access permissions at any time.

## 3    Conclusions

Dendro now supports storage, description and retrieval of research data over the entire data lifecycle. It also facilitates data citation by both a DOI and a BibTeX citation snippet for datasets, fostering credit attribution.

The platform is now more FAIR, closely following the FAIR Guiding principles for scientific data management: persistent identifiers for datasets; rich, domain-specific metadata that complies with FAIR ontologies and faceted search, accessible to both humans and machines. Metadata is still accessible even if the data is not as the DataCite metadata record and DOIs will remain.

**Acknowledgements.** This work is financed by the ERDF – European Regional Development Fund through the Operational Programme for Competitiveness and Internationalisation - COMPETE 2020 Programme and by National Funds through the Portuguese funding agency, FCT - Fundação para a Ciência e a Tecnologia within project POCI-01-0145-FEDER-016736.

## References

1. Altman, M., Crosas, M.: The evolution of data citation: from principles to implementation. IASSIST Q. **37**, 62–70 (2013)
2. Amorim, R., Castro, J., Rocha da Silva, J., Ribeiro, C.: A comparison of research data management platforms: architecture, flexible metadata and interoperability. Universal Access in the Information Society **16**(4) (2017). https://doi.org/10.1007/s10209-016-0475-y
3. Costello, M.J.: Motivating online publication of data. Bioscience (2009). https://doi.org/10.1525/bio.2009.59.5.9
4. Leonelli, S., Spichtinger, D., Prainsack, B.: Sticks and carrots: encouraging open science at its source. Geo: Geography and Environment (2015). https://doi.org/10.1002/geo2.2
5. Pontika, N., Knoth, P., Cancellieri, M., Pearce, S.: Fostering open science to research using a taxonomy and an eLearning portal. In: Proceedings of the 15th International Conference on Knowledge Technologies and Data-driven Business - i-KNOW 2015 (2015). https://doi.org/10.1145/2809563.2809571
6. Ross-Hellauer, T., Deppe, A., Schmidt, B.: Survey on open peer review: attitudes and experience amongst editors, authors and reviewers. PLoS ONE (2017). https://doi.org/10.1371/journal.pone.0189311
7. da Silva, J.R., Ribeiro, C., Lopes, J.C.: Ranking Dublin Core descriptor lists from user interactions: a case study with Dublin Core Terms using the Dendro platform (2018). https://doi.org/10.1007/s00799-018-0238-x
8. Silvello, G.: Theory and practice of data display. CoRR abs/1706.0 (2017). https://doi.org/10.1088/0305-4624/9/3/409, http://arxiv.org/abs/1706.07976
9. Wilkinson, M.D.: The FAIR Guiding Principles for scientific data management and stewardship, pp. 1–9 (2016)

# User's Behavior in Digital Libraries: Process Mining Exploration

Marwa Trabelsi[1]([⊠]), Cyrille Suire[2], Jacques Morcos[1], and Ronan Champagnat[1]

[1] L3i Laboratory, University of La Rochelle, La Rochelle, France
{marwa.trabelsi,jacques.morcos,ronan.champagnat}@univ-lr.fr
[2] CHCSC Laboratory, University of Versailles Saint-Quentin en Yvelines,
Paris Saclay, Versailles, France
cyrille.suire@uvsq.fr

**Abstract.** In digital libraries, users have diverse ways to perform their research according to their objectives. In order to have access to target documents, users almost make sequences of activities that can be considered as processes. It would be useful to represent the behavior of users in their information seeking processes in order to have a global view on users' interactions with digital libraries and to effectively answer to their requirements. Discovered processes in digital libraries are almost self-defined that may vary in term of significance, structure and results. It is therefore important to automatically build a model that describe users' behaviors. In this paper, we tested six state-of-the-art process discovery techniques on two datasets collected from users' interactions with a cultural heritage digital library. Our preliminary evaluation presents the best performing model that can be used to optimize the exploration of documents in digital libraries.

**Keywords:** Digital library · User's behavior · Process discovery

## 1 Introduction

In the context of cultural heritage digital library, the challenge for users, especially for researchers or students, is to be able to easily discover and exploit stored digitized documents. The accessibility to these documents usually starts by queries and is followed by various interactions with the search engine and the documents themselves. The generation of process models encoding user's interactions will be prominent to represent the behavior of users and their information seeking to respond to their requirements. However, information seeking in digital libraries usually presents unstructured processes where the execution is not always basically repeated in the same way. Handling unstructured processes almost reflects a real challenge since instances do not represent many similar execution behavior [4]. In particular, users' interactions of digital libraries provide many examples; they strongly depend to users' requirements, their levels

© Springer Nature Switzerland AG 2019
A. Doucet et al. (Eds.): TPDL 2019, LNCS 11799, pp. 388–392, 2019.
https://doi.org/10.1007/978-3-030-30760-8_40

of knowledge, types of information handling strategies, as well as the way how data are indexed.

This paper aims to study the contribution of process mining to analyze users' behaviors and thus to generate effective models from such unstructured processes. We executed the most-known techniques of process discovery through two sets of event logs produced by users researching documents in a Digital Library. We evaluated then their effectiveness to finally present in more detail the model generated by the best performing technique. The rest of the paper is organized as follow: Sect. 2 introduces process mining techniques used in this work. Section 3 is devoted to describe data sets that we have used. In Sect. 4, we present the best performing process discovery algorithm. Finally, Sect. 5 concludes the paper.

## 2 Process Mining

An Information Retrieval System is a set of resources and tools permitting users to search for information in a given domain. In order to optimize the use of such systems, we generally take advantage from the user execution log history. From these logs *Process Mining* techniques generate models to build an accurate view on how the process is executed. In the context of a search engine of digital library, a lot of features can be defined to help users in accomplishing their requirements. For instance, instead of exploring documents that are archived as images, an Optical Character Recognition (OCR) system that extract texts from images can be suggested to user seeking for an information inside documents. An effective model is therefore necessary in order to specify and anticipate required features for any user according to his behavior.

There are two main artifacts that are used in process mining: event logs and process models [1]. An event log corresponds to the set of execution traces (*i.e.* process instances) that delivers a specific service or product. For example, to make an online purchase, a user have to subscribe, select a product and proceed to payment. All of these activities constitute a particular trace for the main process (online purchase). Process models are destined to represent the whole of event logs. Several models can be used for this purpose such as Petri nets or BPMN models [1]. There are many process discovery methods that have been proposed in the literature in order to automatically generate process models. In this work, we tested six well known process discovery methods: the alpha algorithm ($\alpha^{++}$), the Heuristic Miner (HM), the Inductive Miner (IM), the Regions Based algorithms (SBR and ILP) and the Genetic Miner (GM) [1,5]. In order to evaluate the quality of the resulting process models of each method, we used three typical metrics [2]: [F]itness which determines how well the model covers the event logs. [P]recision that corresponds to the rate of activities in the event logs compared to the total of activities enabled in the process model. [G]eneralization: it is related to the unseen behavior. This criteria aims to measure the ability of the model to generalize the behavior seen in the logs. A suitable model has to find a balance between these metrics [3].

## 3   Datasets Extraction

Our event logs come from experimentation conducted with forty master students who are at the beginning of their specialization in the Cultural Heritage field of study [7]. They have a medium level of topic knowledge and are able to adapt their behavior to the task type. The experimental corpus must be precise enough to allow participants to perform realistic tasks. It contains documents related to the Cultural Heritage field of study which the students are relatively familiar with. The resources of the corpus are heterogeneous: general works, scientific articles, iconographic documents, multimedia resources and even primary documents. To carry out our experiment, we chose to make the students perform tasks in two overall categories defined by Marchionini [6] and designed by a specialist of the Cultural Heritage field of study. The lookup category consists of information seeking tasks from *fact retrieval* and *known item search* Marchionini's subcategories. Participants had to successively find the date of a particular event, where an event took place and had to retrieve a precise document using given information. The exploratory category refers to *learn and investigate* Marchionini's subcategory. Participants had to identify and write a research problem on the Cultural Heritage topic in one if its aspect covered by the corpus. All these tasks required users to search the corpus and access documents in their original form or in full text.

Two databases have therefore been collected: the first database consists in a set of event logs for simple lookup tasks while the second focuses on exploratory search tasks. The lookup database contains 102 traces, 1655 events and 34 users while the exploratory database includes 29 traces, 1472 events and 29 users.

## 4   Results and Discussion

As we mentioned in Sect. 2, we used six algorithms to discover process models over our two databases. We employed ProM's packages in order to evaluate obtained models (cf. Table 1).

**Table 1.** Evaluation metrics obtained on graphs mined from the used datasets

|           | Lookup |        |        | Exploratory |        |        |
|-----------|--------|--------|--------|-------------|--------|--------|
|           | F      | P      | G      | F           | P      | G      |
| HM        | 0.00   | 0.00   | 0.00   | 0.00        | 0.00   | 0.00   |
| IM        | **0.9886** | 0.2391 | 0.9994 | **0.9315** | 0.1437 | 0.9992 |
| GM        | 0.9992 | 0.1800 | 0.9938 | 0.6232      | 0.8053 | 0.9963 |
| ILP       | 0.6163 | 0.3825 | 0.9793 | 0.7835      | 0.1919 | 0.9622 |
| SBR       | 0.8995 | 0.4233 | 0.9957 | 0.9560      | 0.2942 | 0.9918 |
| $\alpha^{++}$ | 0.00   | 0.00   | 0.00   | 0.00        | 0.00   | 0.00   |

As shown in Table 1, the fitness measure in the Inductive Miner algorithm reaches the best scores for both datasets. The good quality of the IM model is also observed in term of readability. The IM algorithm applies a divide and conquer approach, by splitting event logs into smaller parts and recursively finds models for these sub-logs, which are later combined. In addition, it has the particularity to handle infrequent behaviors, which are not representative for the typical behavior of the process. The resulting two models are hierarchically structured under the form of a Process Tree which will be converted into a Petri Net [5]. The strength of the Inductive Miner consists in its ability to detect the starting and the ending points of the process (Fig. 1). It removes the less important arcs and gives a very clear idea of the process followed by users of digital libraries. The intermediate steps and the arcs presented in the model make easier the understanding of different paths followed by users to accomplish their task. However, it is not possible to measure the frequency of each of the navigation options chosen by users and therefore their importance in the process.

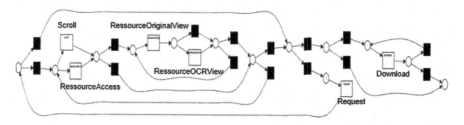

**Fig. 1.** Process model generated from Inductive Miner algorithm: lookup dataset

## 5    Conclusion

In this paper we experimented many process discovery techniques and tested them with two datasets encoding user's interactions with a digital library. We underline the benefits of using process mining for evaluating user's behavior in a digital library exploration process. The work is linked to practical need of using digital libraries.

Future works will firstly consist in exploring more generic process discovery methods. Secondly we plan to explore more databases linked to the use of digital libraries in order to build more robust models able to present a set of recommendations to all users of digital libraries.

## References

1. Van der Aalst, W.: Process Mining: Data Science in Action. Springer, Heidelberg (2016). https://doi.org/10.1007/978-3-662-49851-4
2. Adriansyah, A.: Aligning observed and modeled behavior. Ph.D. thesis, Technische Universiteit Eindhoven (2014)

3. Buijs, J.C.A.M., van Dongen, B.F., van der Aalst, W.M.P.: On the role of fitness, precision, generalization and simplicity in process discovery. In: Meersman, R., et al. (eds.) OTM 2012. LNCS, vol. 7565, pp. 305–322. Springer, Heidelberg (2012). https://doi.org/10.1007/978-3-642-33606-5_19
4. Cole, M.J., Hendahewa, C., Belkin, N.J., Shah, C.: User activity patterns during information search. ACM Trans. Inf. Syst. 33(1), 1:1–1:39 (2015)
5. Leemans, S.J., Fahland, D., van der Aalst, W.M.: Discovering block-structured process models from event logs containing infrequent behaviour. In: Lohmann, N., Song, M., Wohed, P. (eds.) BPM 2013. LNBIP, vol. 171, pp. 66–78. Springer, Cham (2013). https://doi.org/10.1007/978-3-319-06257-0_6
6. Marchionini, G.: Exploratory search: from finding to understanding. Commun. ACM 49(4), 41–46 (2006)
7. Suire, C., Jean-Caurant, A., Courboulay, V., Burie, J.C., Estraillier, P.: User activity characterization in a cultural heritage digital library system. In: Proceedings of the 16th ACM/IEEE-CS on Joint Conference on Digital Libraries, JCDL 2016, pp. 257–258. ACM, New York (2016)

# SciTo Trends: Visualising Scientific Topic Trends

Serafeim Chatzopoulos[1,2], Panagiotis Deligiannis[1], Thanasis Vergoulis[2(✉)],
Ilias Kanellos[2,3], Christos Tryfonopoulos[1], and Theodore Dalamagas[2]

[1] Department of Informatics and Tel/tions, University of the Peloponnese,
22100 Tripoli, Greece
{cst11017,trifon}@uop.gr
[2] IMSI - "Athena" Research & Innovation Center, 15125 Athens, Greece
{schatz,vergoulis,ilias.kanellos,dalamag}@athenarc.gr
[3] School of Electrical and Computer Engineering, NTUA, 15780 Athens, Greece

**Abstract.** Monitoring trends in scientific disciplines is a common task
for researchers and other professionals in the broad research and academic community, like research and innovation policy makers and
research fund managers. We demonstrate SciTo, a powerful tool that
assists in the monitoring of trends in scientific disciplines. SciTo supports keyword-based search for the identification of scientific topics of
interest and comparison of interesting topics to each other in terms of
their popularity inside the academic community.

**Keywords:** Information retrieval · Scientific impact · Topic modeling

## 1 Introduction

Monitoring trends in scientific disciplines, comparing different scientific topics in
terms of their popularity in the academic community, or identifying new areas
that will attract much attention in the near future, are useful tasks for researchers
drafting their research plans for the next months or years. However, apart from
scientists, such tasks are also of great interest for other professionals in the broad
research and academic community, like research fund managers trying to develop
new calls for research projects.

Although many tools to explore scientific literature have been introduced
in recent years (e.g., Google Scholar[1], AMiner[2] [4], Semantic Scholar[3], Cite-
SeerX[4] [5]), most of them focus solely on the keyword-based publication retrieval
and do not provide advanced topic trend monitoring options. Even those providing such features either give insights about the evolution of topics based solely on

---

[1] https://scholar.google.com/.
[2] https://aminer.org/.
[3] https://www.semanticscholar.org.
[4] https://citeseerx.ist.psu.edu.

© Springer Nature Switzerland AG 2019
A. Doucet et al. (Eds.): TPDL 2019, LNCS 11799, pp. 393–396, 2019.
https://doi.org/10.1007/978-3-030-30760-8_41

the number of relevant publications (e.g., AMiner's Trend[5] and Scholar Plotr[6]), or provide trends for particular keywords or predefined topics (e.g., Scholar Plotr, Dimensions[7]). Providing trends for keywords is not very convenient since users often ignore important keywords that would facilitate or expand their searches (e.g., in the case of very recently created or alternative technical terms). Finally, relying on predefined topics is not sustainable since it requires curation of topic lists by domain experts since domain-specific research topics evolve.

We introduce "SciTo trends"[8] (Scientific Topics trends), a Web-based tool for topic trend monitoring and comparison, addressing the previous issues. It is built on top of a very large, interdisciplinary dataset containing information (abstracts, citations, etc.) for more than $12M$ scientific articles. Our main contributions are the following:

- SciTo automatically extracts topics from the abstracts of the articles it stores avoiding the need for manual curation.
- It provides a powerful keyword-based search on the stored scientific topics.
- Apart from trends based on the number of publications, it also provides trends based on citation counts and the average short-term impact of the topics (based on RAM [2] scores of its papers).

## 2 Functionality

Figure 1 illustrates SciTo's search interface where a user can enter keywords that describe an interesting topic. Upon submitting a query on these keywords, SciTo returns the set of tag clouds, each representing a related topic. The user can select to review the popularity trends for any of the displayed topics (clicking on the "information button"), or to compare the trends for 2–4 different topics (clicking on the "comparison button" for each topic to be part of the comparison).

The page that displays the popularity trends of a particular topic contains two different types of infographics (top-left corner of Fig. 1): (a) the *pyramid infographic* and (b) the *trend infographics*. Both visualise the information related to the topic popularity according to three indicators (number of publications, number of citations, average short-term impact). The former informs if the topic is among the top (1% or 20%) according to each popularity indicator. The latter displays (a) yearly numbers of topic-related articles published, (b) yearly numbers of citations attracted by topic-related articles, and (c) the average short-term impact for topic-related articles published each year. The topic comparison page (top-right corner of Fig. 1) contains only the trend infographics, however displaying the time series for all topics under comparison.

---

[5] https://trend.aminer.org/.
[6] https://www.csullender.com/scholar/.
[7] https://app.dimensions.ai.
[8] http://scito.imsi.athenarc.gr.

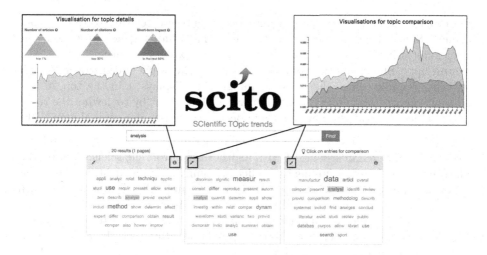

**Fig. 1.** SciTo's search interface.

## 3  Data Collection and Processing

SciTo's database stores (a) paper citation data, (b) article impact scores, and (c) article abstracts. The citation data is collected from the latest version of the OpenCitations COCI dataset[9] ($\sim$450$M$ citations for >45$M$ articles). Based on this data, SciTo calculates and stores paper citation counts and RAM [2] scores, used to measure overall and short-term paper impact, respectively.

Since COCI does not provide article abstracts, SciTo collects abstracts for those papers also indexed by the Crossref API[10] and Open Academic Graph[11] [3, 4] (about $\sim$12$M$ papers). Based on these abstracts it trains an LDA [1] model, using the gensim[12] topic modelling library. All extracted topics are indexed by a full-text search engine powered by Apache Solr[13] and running on a 3 VM cluster (8 cores & 16 GB RAM/node) to facilitate keyword-based search.

Finally, SciTo's Web UI was implemented using PHP under the MVC architecture (Yii2 framework was used). Custom JS code, based on third-party libraries, was used for SciTo's visualisations (e.g., *D3.js*).

## 4  Demonstration

At the conference, the audience will have the opportunity to interact with SciTo to examine its full capabilities. However, we will also demonstrate some interesting scenarios we have identified, two of which are described below:

---

[9] http://opencitations.net/download.
[10] https://www.crossref.org/services/metadata-delivery/rest-api/.
[11] https://www.openacademic.ai/oag/.
[12] https://radimrehurek.com/gensim/.
[13] http://lucene.apache.org/solr/.

**Scenario 1:** An audience member explores topic trends relevant to the keyword "gene". Since she is interested in the field that studies gene expression, she finds interesting a topic containing the terms "express", "mrna", "rna", and "transcript". She opens the details of this particular topic and discovers that it is rather popular, since the pyramid infographic displays it in the top 20% of all topics according to all indicators provided. Moreover, by reviewing the trend infographics she realises that this topic became very popular after the mid 80s.

**Scenario 2:** The same audience member wants to compare the "gene"-related topic she discovered in scenario 1 with another topic from life sciences, in particular, the research field studying drug effects. Using SciTo she identifies a relevant topic containing the terms "drug", "treatment", and "effect". She selects both this topic and the "gene"-related topic for comparison. In the comparison page the trend infographics reveal that, although the "drug"-related topic was traditionally more popular than the "gene"-related one, after 1995 the latter started to become equally or, even, more popular (depending on the indicator used).

## 5   Conclusion and Future Work

We demonstrated SciTo, a Web-based tool that assists monitoring trends in scientific disciplines. It supports (a) keyword-based search for the identification of interesting scientific topics and (b) comparison of topics in terms of their popularity inside the academic community. These features make SciTo a powerful tool for professionals in the broad research and academic community. In the future, we plan to extend SciTo to include topics of different levels of granularity (more and less generic in comparison to the current ones) that will be organised in hierarchies. Moreover, we plan to capture and exploit topic history (evolution).

**Acknowledgments.** We acknowledge support of this work by the project "Moving from Big Data Management to Data Science" (MIS 5002437/3) which is implemented under the Action "Re-inforcement of the Research and Innovation Infrastructure", funded by the Operational Programme "Competitiveness, Entrepreneurship and Innovation" (NSRF 2014–2020) and co-financed by Greece and the European Union (European Regional Development Fund).

## References

1. Blei, D.M., Ng, A.Y., Jordan, M.I.: Latent Dirichlet allocation. JMLR **3**, 993–1022 (2003)
2. Ghosh, R., Kuo, T.T., Hsu, C.N., Lin, S.D., Lerman, K.: Time-aware ranking in dynamic citation networks. In: IEEE ICDMW, pp. 373–380. IEEE (2011)
3. Sinha, A., et al.: An overview of Microsoft Academic Service (MAS) and applications. In: WWW, pp. 243–246 (2015)
4. Tang, J., Zhang, J., Yao, L., Li, J., Zhang, L., Su, Z.: ArnetMiner: extraction and mining of academic social networks. In: ACM SIGKDD, pp. 990–998 (2008)
5. Wu, J., et al.: CiteSeerX: AI in a digital library search engine. AI Mag. **36**(3), 35–48 (2015)

# Off-the-shelf Semantic Author Name Disambiguation for Bibliographic Data Bases

Mark-Christoph Müller[1]([✉])[iD], Adam Bannister[2][iD], and Florian Reitz[3][iD]

[1] Heidelberg Institute for Theoretical Studies gGmbH, Heidelberg, Germany
`mark-christoph.mueller@h-its.org`
[2] Mathematics Department, FIZ Karlsruhe, Berlin, Germany
`adam.bannister@fiz-karlsruhe.de`
[3] Schloss Dagstuhl LZI, Wadern, Germany
`florian.reitz@dagstuhl.de`

**Abstract.** The demo presents a minimalist, off-the-shelf AND tool which provides a fundamental AND operation, the comparison of two publications with ambiguous authors, as an easily accessible HTTP interface. The tool implements this operation using standard AND functionality, but puts particular emphasis on advanced methods from natural language processing (NLP) for comparing publication title *semantics*.

**Keywords:** Author name disambiguation · Semantic similarity · Word embeddings · API · Open source software

## 1 Introduction and Motivation

Institutions where bibliographic data is collected, processed, and stored on a large scale – like e.g. digital libraries – frequently encounter the **author name ambiguity** problem: two or more identical, or highly similar, author *names* appear in the headers of different publications, but it is uncertain whether these names refer to the same author *individual*. Author name ambiguity mainly results from a combination of the following: 1. very common names, 2. publishers' practice of abbreviating first names, and 3. lack of consistency on the part of the authors [9].

Author name disambiguation (AND) attempts to resolve the referential uncertainty of author names by automatically distinguishing them on the basis of a wide range of properties, and assigning to them a collection-wide unique identifier.[1] The difficulty of correctly disambiguating two ambiguous author names in two publications ranges from *trivial* to *virtually impossible*, and mainly depends on the following factors: – the availability of general **author and publication**

---

[1] In contrast, the non-technical, *organizational* approaches of orcid.org or researcherid.com attempt to *prevent* referential uncertainty, by having authors use globally unique identifiers in their publications.

© Springer Nature Switzerland AG 2019
A. Doucet et al. (Eds.): TPDL 2019, LNCS 11799, pp. 397–400, 2019.
https://doi.org/10.1007/978-3-030-30760-8_42

**meta data**, e.g. complete author names, email addresses, affiliations, and publication venues; – the type of publication, e.g. **single- or multi-author**; and – the degree of specialization of the publication **topic**, normally observable in its **title**. At one extreme end of the spectrum, both author names are accompanied by matching email addresses, which are almost perfect author identifiers. At the other extreme, each of the two publications features a run-off-the-mill title and a single author with a very common name[2].

In this demo, we present our open-source Python implementation of a simple, lightweight, and extensible AND tool. Its functionality – which currently consists of one elementary AND operation – is exposed via an HTTP API and can be used in isolation (e.g. via a web browser), or as the basis for implementing higher-level AND workflows in practically every modern programming language. Due to the tool's minimalist approach, it is runnable off-the-shelf, i.e. without extensive configuration, let alone training. A specific back-end data base is not required, either, since all author and publication meta data needed for disambiguation are provided by the user in the API function call. The tool and pre-trained resources are available and will continue to be maintained at github.com/nlpAThits/scad-tool.

In recent years, many different AND systems have been proposed and published (cf. [1,2]), but as far as we can see none of them has been accepted as a standard or *best practice* by the community. One problem is that existing AND systems implement the task in different ways, e.g. incrementally vs. non-incrementally, record- vs. profile-based, grouping- vs. assignment-based [1], or online (i.e. processing *one new* record at a time) vs. batch (i.e. processing *a whole block* of records at once) [4]. Also, systems are often solely applied to, and sometimes even tailored towards, particular bibliographic data bases (like e.g. PubMed, MEDLINE, CiteSeerX, or dblp), or they are tested and optimized on particular AND test collections (cf. Müller et al. [9] for an overview), which also limits their broader applicability. Another problem is that in many cases, complete, well-maintained source code is either not available at all, or apparently outdated, as Kim et al. [5] observe with CiteSeerX[3] and AMiner[4]. However, Kim et al. do not provide source code for their system, either. In contrast, our tool is completely agnostic to particular data bases, research disciplines, and AND workflow implementations, and the source code is freely available.

Many existing AND systems strongly rely on **coauthor information** for disambiguation, which is a reasonable strategy in those research disciplines where publications commonly have multiple authors. Actually, the popularity of coauthor-based AND and the high prevalence of multi-author publications in AND test collections [9] can be seen as mutually affecting each other. However, there are also many research disciplines in the real world where author collaboration is much less common, and for which most existing AND systems will fail to produce acceptable results.

---

[2] See e.g. dblp.uni-trier.de/pers/hd/w/Wang:Wei.

[3] github.com/SeerLabs/CiteSeerX.

[4] github.com/askerlee/namedis.

**Semantic similarity** between two publications, on the other hand, is a domain-independent potential indicator for author identity, whose usefulness has been demonstrated already [7]. However, with only a few exceptions (e.g. [5–7]), the majority of currently existing AND systems recognizes similarity between two publications' titles, keywords, or abstracts on the *surface* level only, i.e. by simple string matching over lists of white-space-separated tokens, word stems, or character n-grams. In natural language processing (NLP), **word embeddings** are now the generally accepted standard method for quantifying semantic similarity beyond the string level.[5] Since word embeddings can be trained with comparably little effort on large collections of raw text, they can be employed as resources for computing **domain-specific semantic similarity**. Our tool supports this flexible use of different word embeddings by accepting word embedding identifiers as *parameters* in the API function call.

## 2    `match_authors` as an Atomic AND Procedure

Our tool currently provides the atomic procedure `match_authors`, which analyses the meta data of two publications with ambiguously named authors, and returns *True* if it classifies the authors as identical, and *False* otherwise. The classification is accompanied by a confidence score. The procedure is similar to the 'record-based query' of Kim et al. [5], but with the important difference that `match_authors` expects *both* publications to be provided by the user, while the system of Kim et al. tries to match *one* user-provided publication against pre-existing publications in its back-end data base. The API expects the meta data for the two publications as one JSON object each. We use a simple and straightforward JSON format which can be easily extended, e.g. to cover publications from sources which provide richer meta data. The following is an example of a publication from the KISTI data set [3], which is based on data from dblp.org.

```
{'id':        'dblp:journals/taslp/KarmakarKP06',
 'title':     'A Multiresolution Model of Auditory Excitation Pattern and
              Its Application to Objective Evaluation of Perceived Speech Quality',
 'authors': [
              {'name': 'A. Karmakar',   'shortname': 'A. Karmakar'},
              {'name': 'A. Kumar',      'shortname': 'A. Kumar', 'id': 'A.Kumar_8'},
              {'name': 'R. K. Patney',  'shortname': 'R. Patney'}],
 'year':      2006,
 'venue':     'journals/taslp',
 'pages':     '1912-1923',
 'classifications': {} }
```

The second example comes from the SCAD-zbMATH AND data set [9], which is based on data from zbmath.org. This publication features some additional meta data, incl. keywords, which are particularly relevant for semantic AND.

```
{'id':        'zbmath:0614.93069',
 'title':     'Positional modeling of stochastic control in dynamical systems',
 'authors': [
              {'name': 'Osipov, Yu.S.',      'shortname': 'Osipov, Yu.',      'id': 'osipov.yuri-s'},
              {'name': 'Kryazhimskij, A.V.', 'shortname': 'Kryazhimskij, A.', 'id': 'kryazhimskii.arkadii-v'}],
 'year': 1986,
 'venue': 'Stochastic optimization, Proc. Int. Conf., Kiev/USSR 1984, Lect. Notes Control Inf. Sci. 81, 696-704 (1986).',
 'classifications': {
              'msc-codes': ['93E20', '34A55', '93C10', '91A23', '93C15'],
              'keywords': ['inverse dynamical problems', 'stochastic controls']}}
```

---

[5] E.g.    github.com/tmikolov/word2vec,    github.com/facebookresearch/fastText, github.com/allenai/allennlp/blob/master/tutorials/how_to/elmo.md.

`match_authors` is called with two publications' JSON strings and the ambiguous author position in each (as an index into the authors JSON array). In addition, it can accept a word embedding identifier in WOMBAT format [10]. WOMBAT is used for efficient word-level retrieval of vector representations, which are the main input for computing semantic similarity scores. The use of WOMBAT allows the system to dynamically select a word embedding resource for a particular domain (e.g. computer science, math, chemistry, etc.) when publications from a corresponding venue are processed. In order to increase the transparency and acceptability of the automatic classification, semantic similarity scores are computed in such a way that they yield both a numerical value and a compact, human-interpretable representation of what exactly went into the computation [8]. This way, sanity checking by a human expert is easily implemented.

Since the whole design of our tool is open and extensible, the implementation details can change as long as the method signature and its in- and output requirements are observed.

**Acknowledgements.** The work described in this paper was conducted in the project *SCAD – Scalable Author Disambiguation*, funded in part by the Leibniz Association (grant SAW-2015-LZI-2), and in part by the Klaus Tschira Foundation.

# References

1. Ferreira, A.A., Gonçalves, M.A., Laender, A.H.: A brief survey of automatic methods for author name disambiguation. SIGMOD Rec. **41**(2), 15–26 (2012)
2. Hussain, I., Asghar, S.: A survey of author name disambiguation techniques: 2010–2016. Knowl. Eng. Rev. **32**, 1–24 (2017)
3. Kang, I.S., Kim, P., Lee, S., Jung, H., You, B.J.: Construction of a large-scale test set for author disambiguation. Inf. Process. Manag. **47**(3), 452–465 (2011)
4. Khabsa, M., Treeratpituk, P., Giles, C.L.: Large scale author name disambiguation in digital libraries. In: BigData, pp. 41–42. IEEE Computer Society (2014)
5. Kim, K., Sefid, A., Weinberg, B.A., Giles, C.L.: A web service for author name disambiguation in scholarly databases. In: ICWS, pp. 265–273. IEEE (2018)
6. Müller, M.-C.: Semantic author name disambiguation with word embeddings. In: TPDL, pp. 300–311 (2017). https://doi.org/10.1007/978-3-319-67008-9_24
7. Müller, M.-C.: On the contribution of word-level semantics to practical author name disambiguation. In: JCDL, pp. 367–368. ACM (2018). https://doi.org/10.1145/3197026.3203912
8. Müller, M.-C.: Semantic matching of documents from heterogeneous collections: a simple and transparent method for practical applications. In: RELATIONS, pp. 34–41 (2019). https://www.aclweb.org/anthology/W19-0804
9. Müller, M.-C., Reitz, F., Roy, N.: Data sets for author name disambiguation: an empirical analysis and a new resource. Scientometrics **111**(3), 1467–1500 (2017). https://doi.org/10.1007/s11192-017-2363-5
10. Müller, M.-C., Strube, M.: Transparent, efficient, and robust word embedding access with WOMBAT. In: COLING (System Demonstrations), pp. 53–57 (2018). https://aclweb.org/anthology/papers/C/C18/C18-2012

# Re-finding Behaviour in Educational Search

Arif Usta[1]([✉]), Ismail Sengor Altingovde[2], Rifat Ozcan[3], and Özgür Ulusoy[1]

[1] Bilkent University, Ankara, Turkey
{arif.usta,oulusoy}@bilkent.edu.tr
[2] Middle East Technical University, Ankara, Turkey
altingovde@ceng.metu.edu.tr
[3] Microsoft, Oslo, Norway
rifatozcan1981@gmail.com

**Abstract.** One of the search tasks in Web search is repeat search behaviour to find out documents that users once visited, which is called *re-finding*. Although there have been several works in the context of general-purpose Web search addressing the latter phenomena, the problem is usually overlooked for vertical search engines. In this work, we report *re-finding* and *newfinding* behaviours of users in an educational search context and compare results with the findings in the literature for general-purpose web search. Our analysis shows that re-finding pattern of students differs from web search drastically as only 26% of all queries indicate *re-finding* behaviour compared to 40% in Web.

**Keywords:** Vertical search · Educational search · Query log analysis · Re-finding

## 1 Introduction

In the literature, analysis of query logs is widely applied to detect search patterns and identify user intents. One of the most common user activities during search is *re-finding*, which constitutes average of 4 out of 5 page visits being to previously seen pages [2]. There have not been many works on analyzing re-finding behavior, until it is noted in [3] that, 17% of the users reports "Not being able to find out a page once visited" as one of the biggest problems to be solved in web search.

One of the large-scale re-finding behavior analysis was done by Teevan et al. [6] through queries issued to Yahoo!. They demonstrate that 40% of query issues lead users into repeat behaviour. Sadeghi et al. [5] analyzed features for detecting a re-finding session in different verticals such as news and movies.

In education domain, which is another popular application area of search, Usta et al. [7] studied general search characteristics of students and compared them with the findings in the literature for general Web. Bilal and Gwizdka [1] analyzed query types and reformulations of students in Google. To the best of our knowledge, none of these works address re-finding behaviour in the context of educational search.

© Springer Nature Switzerland AG 2019
A. Doucet et al. (Eds.): TPDL 2019, LNCS 11799, pp. 401–405, 2019.
https://doi.org/10.1007/978-3-030-30760-8_43

**Table 1.** Categorization of query types in education vertical

| All queries: 64078 (100%) | Overlapping click queries - 16676 (26%) | | | No common clicks 47402 (74%) |
|---|---|---|---|---|
| | Equal click queries 5010 (8%) | | Some common clicks 11666 (18%) | |
| | Single click 3982 (6%) | Multi click 1028 (1,6%) | | |
| Equal query 22591 (35%) | Navigational queries 2863 (4,4%) | 681 (1%) | 7355 (11,5%) | 11692 (18%) |
| Different query 41487 (65%) | 1119 (1,7%) | 347 (<1%) | 4311 (7%) | 35710 (56%) |

In this paper, we explore re-finding behavior of students at K-12 level through analyzing the query logs of a commercial educational search engine, called *Vitamin*. We also report the similarities and differences between educational and general web search in the context of re-finding by comparing our findings to those in [6]. Our findings help understanding re-finding pattern of students in educational search and provide possible new directions to further improve educational verticals.

## 2    Re-finding Analysis

For this analysis, we focus on the so-called *re-finding* queries as stated in [6]. Specifically, re-finding query is the query in which user clicks a document that was clicked as a result of another past query issue by again that particular user.

We use a query log consisting of 64,078 queries issued by 18,534 unique users extracted from *Vitamin*. There are also 165,587 learning objects that we refer as documents for the rest of the paper. Other characteristics of query log we use in this paper can be found in [7].

In web, re-finding behavior is observed in 40% of all search sessions, while in our case, only around 26% of queries exhibit re-finding behavior. An analysis of clicked documents also shows differences in comparison to web search. Among all clicked documents, 28% of documents are clicked multiple times by the same user at different search sessions on the web, which indicates Refinding. In contrary, out of all documents clicked at least once in our query log, only 20,594 documents are clicked multiple times by the same user, which roughly corresponds to only 12%.

We categorized query types using the same methodology in [6]. Queries are categorized according to their texts (*Equal vs Different*) and click sets. Overlapping click query results in Table 1 represent re-finding behaviour. Considering query texts, the ratio between *Equal-Query* and *Different-Query* is almost the

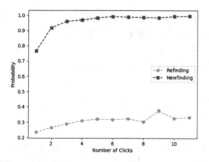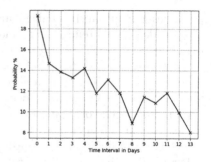

**Fig. 1.** Probability of a query session being Refinding and Newfinding given number of clicks (left plot) and Probability of Repeat Queries Having Common Click Depending on Time Intervals (right plot).

same with Web, which is two to one. However, the behavior is quite different than Web for click characteristics. In Web, 29% of queries have equal click sets. In our query log, we only have 8% of queries categorized as *Equal-Click*. One of the reasons for different behavior in education context is that students tend to click more documents [7] than users in Web, which decreases the chance of click-through sets of queries being exactly same even if query texts are the same. Due to this search behavior, the results for navigational queries also differ, constituting only 4% of all queries compared to 24% in Web. Other radical difference between education context and Web is that although there are much less documents available in our query log, the volume of queries having no common clicks is higher than the Web. The result is mostly due to having *Equal-Queries* with no common clicks as 18% of all queries compared to 4% in Web.

## 2.1   Student Click Patterns for Re-finding

Students have different click characteristics than users in Web [7]. They tend to click more which eventually alters re-finding behavior. We examine repeat queries that have overlapping clicks in terms of time intervals between pairs. Unlike Web, highest probability for a repeat query to have common clicks is when queries are issued in the same day, which can be seen in Fig. 1. The probability decreases drastically as time interval between issued queries gets bigger.

Another analysis made in the paper [6] is whether re-finding behavior depends on the number of clicks user made. Among all query issues made, 29% of the search issues which result in single click on a document have re-finding behavior. The results for this analysis on our query log are similar to Web. Students prefer re-finding document 23% of time in a search with a single click.

We also examine queries with multiple clicks for comparison. In web, among all query instances including multiple clicks on documents, only 5.3% of them include re-finding behavior. 30% of queries including multiple clicks lead students to click on a document they once visited. We believe that there are two reasons for this behavior. First, the educational vertical considered in our analysis includes a significantly smaller number of documents in comparison to Web. Hence, students who tend to click more documents in the educational context, eventually end up with clicking some of the documents they have visited before. The second reason would be that students are less likely to remember the documents they visited before in a successful search [4], therefore for a re-finding intent, they have to click more documents than general Web users.

Apart from single or multi-click query instances, we also explore the correlation between the number of clicks in a search and the probability of the query instance being re-finding or newfinding. The results can be seen in Fig. 1. As the number of clicks increases, the probability of query being re-finding increases until certain click number. Newfinding probability is lowest for single click queries as expected.

## 3   Conclusion

In this work, we presented an in-depth analysis of re-finding pattern of students at K-12 level using a query log extracted through a commercial educational search engine. We also compared our findings with Web and reported similarities and differences. Our analysis shows that educational search differs from the Web in terms of re-finding Behavior. We believe there are two different aspects to consider when explaining difference. First, search characteristics of students differ from users in the Web as they may fail in expressing their search intents clearly and tend to click more documents in result lists [7]. Second, searching for an educational document for learning purpose definitely changes user behavior. In educational search environment, students periodically study different materials related to the subjects listed in curriculum. For re-finding, it is understandable to access the same learning object in order to reinforce their knowledge. On the other hand, in terms of learning aspect, it might be rational and wise to choose a document they have never visited to explore what that particular material can offer for them to learn the subject better.

**Acknowledgments.** This research is supported by The Scientific and Technological Research Council of Turkey (TUBITAK) under the grant no 113$E$065. I.S. Altingovde is supported by Turkish Academy of Sciences Distinguished Young Scientist Award (TUBA-GEBIP 2016).

## References

1. Bilal, D., Gwizdka, J.: Children's query types and reformulations in google search. Inf. Process. Manag. **54**(6), 1022–1041 (2018)
2. Cockburn, A., Greenberg, S., Jones, S., McKenzie, B., Moyle, M.: Improving web page revisitation: analysis, design, and evaluation (2003)
3. iProspect: Search engine user behavior study. http://district4.extension.ifas.ufl.edu/Tech/TechPubs/WhitePaper_2006_SearchEngineUserBehavior.pdf. Accessed 20 May 2019

4. Rutter, S., Ford, N., Clough, P.: How do children reformulate their search queries? Inf. Res. Int. Electron. J. **20** (2015)
5. Sadeghi, S.S., Blanco, R., Mika, P., Sanderson, M., Scholer, F., Vallet, D.: Re-finding behaviour in vertical domains. ACM Trans. Inf. Syst. **35**(3), 21:1–21:30 (2017)
6. Teevan, J., Adar, E., Jones, R., Potts, M.A.S.: Information re-retrieval: repeat queries in Yahoo's logs. In: Proceedings of SIGIR, pp. 151–158 (2007)
7. Usta, A., Altingovde, I.S., Vidinli, I.B., Ozcan, R., Ulusoy, O.: How k-12 students search for learning?: analysis of an educational search engine log. In: Proceedings of SIGIR, pp. 1151–1154 (2014)

# Qatar Digital Library as a Platform for Digital Repatriation of Qatar's Cultural Heritage

Marcin Werla$^{(\boxtimes)}$ ⓘ

Qatar National Library, Education City, Doha, Qatar
mwerla@qnl.qa

**Abstract.** Digital repatriation is a process in which cultural heritage objects, physically located outside of countries or communities of their origin, are "returned" where they belong in a digital form. The aim of this paper is to present challenges related to digital repatriation, basing on the experiences of Qatar National Library. Qatar's complex history caused that its tangible heritage is distributed in over a dozen countries on at least three continents. The library undertakes a number of efforts to locate and digitize such heritage materials, in order to present them online in a digital form and preserve for the future. The main online platform for that is Qatar Digital Library, which is described in this paper from organizational, technical and end-user perspectives.

**Keywords:** Qatar Digital Library · Digital repatriation ·
Large scale digitization projects

## 1 Concept of Digital Repatriation

It's probably impossible to find a country or a community in the world, which would not lose parts of its cultural heritage at some point in time. In the worst cases, the heritage is physically destroyed, but sometimes it leaves the originating country and is moved to a different part of the world. Reasons for that may be different, including political and border changes, military conflicts, mass migrations or simply looting. Sometimes the immediate change of location of heritage objects is the only way to protect them from destruction.

When the negative circumstances finally disappear, it may come out that (again, for different reasons) it's not possible to bring lost or moved heritage objects back. In such cases, modern digitization technologies can help to at least provide a high-quality digital surrogate of the physical item. The digital form in such case, of course, cannot fully substitute the physical presence of the heritage. On the other hand, it allows building and presenting unique collections of objects which could not be gathered together by physical means, providing a wide context for the nation's heritage and history.

Digital repatriation projects already have a history reaching at least to 2000s, when National Museum of American Indian, part of the Smithsonian Institute, developed a website utilizing QuickTime Virtual Reality technology to provide online access to museum's exhibitions [1].

A. Doucet et al. (Eds.): TPDL 2019, LNCS 11799, pp. 406–409, 2019.
https://doi.org/10.1007/978-3-030-30760-8_44

With the progress of technology, the development of the internet and the increasing role of digitization and online access in the cultural heritage sector, more possibilities appear. One widely known example of such international initiatives is Europeana.eu, but there are more portals like that with various geographical or subject focus and features specific to the type of aggregated cultural heritage [2].

The next section of this paper describes, how the concept of digital repatriation is being implemented in practice by the Qatar National Library and how it supports the library's mission to "preserve the nation's and region's heritage and enable the people of Qatar to positively influence society by creating an exceptional environment for learning and discovery".

## 2  Digital Repatriation at Qatar National Library

Qatar gained independence in 1971, after a few centuries of turbulent colonial history, which started in the early 16th century, when the control over mainland Qatar territory was seized by Portuguese. Once independent and very well equipped in natural resources, Qatar began very intense development in many areas, starting from the most crucial areas of infrastructure and economy. To foster the social development of Qatar, in 1995 a non-profit organization called Qatar Foundation (QF) was established. The aim of the Foundation was defined as "to support Qatar on its journey from a carbon economy to a knowledge economy by unlocking human potential". The Foundation quickly became very active in the areas of education, science, research and social development. In 2012 QF announced a project to create Qatar National Library, institution crucial for all the areas of Foundation's activity.

One of the important conditions for the country's development is the strong feeling of its own identity shared by the citizens. It is even more important for a very ambitious and rapidly progressing country like Qatar [3]. Therefore in parallel to the development of Qatar National Library as a physical space, in 2012 intense works began to enable online access to Qatar's cultural heritage. The outcome of that was the Qatar Digital Library portal which was made publicly accessible in 2014 at https://www.qdl.qa/.

This portal was one of the outcomes of a partnership between Qatar National Library and British Library, and currently it contains mostly archival documents related to Qatar and the Gulf region from the collections of BL. According to the research done by the QNL's Historical Research and Partnerships Directorate [4], besides the UK, archival documents related to the history of Qatar can be found in many other countries, such as India, Turkey, USA, France, Portugal, Iran or the Netherlands. One of the key tasks of this directorate is to locate the most valuable collections interesting for QNL and establish partnerships leading to digital repatriation of these heritage objects. If these objects are not yet digitized, the partnership agreements cover also the digitization process with emphasis on high-quality outcomes suitable for long-term digital preservation.

In order to effectively manage a number of worldwide partnerships and have the same rules for use and re-use of digitally repatriated content, QNL defined a set of partnership principles that have to be followed in each undertaken cooperation. By defining and publishing such shared principles, the library also hopes to reach a wider understanding and acceptance of these principles among current and future partners.

These principles define the main aim of partnerships ("increased access to and preservation of heritage material related to Qatar, the Gulf and wider region, and to promote its use") and stress that the partnership modes can vary, but should be based on shared values and commitments related to preservation and provisioning of access to cultural heritage, as well as openness, transparency and bi-directional knowledge transfer. They also balance the rights of partners regarding the online presence of materials covered by the partnership. The principles assume that even if the content is for the first time digitized for the partnership, using QNL funds, the owner of the physical content is not limited (by the partnership) regarding the platforms which can be used to present the digitized material, including commercial platforms. So, for example, this content can be used to provide commercial high-quality print on demand. At the same time partners acknowledge that the (selection of) digitized content will be also made available online via the Qatar Digital Library portal, on a license which will at least allow free reuse for non-commercial purposes. So users interested in a high-quality printout of a specific object can choose whether they to download the image from QNL and do the printout on their own, or if they prefer to use the commercial service provided by the owner of the physical content. Partners are also encouraged not to assert copyright over digital copies of materials which entered Public Domain.

Besides, the partnership principles emphasize the need for a professional approach to all technical aspects of the cooperation, including selection, conservation and preservation of the physical materials, the integrity of physical collections and digital images, high-quality standards of digitization and metadata, including the creation of at least bi-lingual metadata (Arabic and English).

While the principles focus on the part of digital repatriation which is related to acquiring the digital content, an equally important aspect is how the content is digitally preserved and presented online, once acquired. The next section of this paper outlines the core aspects of the Qatar Digital Library as QNL's platform for digital repatriation.

## 3 Qatar Digital Library Overview

Qatar Digital Library is available online at https://www.qdl.qa. The main functionality of the portal is browsing and searching through the archival collections. These collections are accompanied by over 150 expert articles, which provide additional context for the archival material and are useful entrance or discovery point to the archive for users, which are not looking for very specific items but are rather interested in more general topics. The system is fully bilingual (English and Arabic) in terms of user interface labels, metadata and expert articles.

The data model behind the QDL archival collections is currently based on METS and EAD standards and allows to store and present hierarchical archival objects with the distinction of logical and physical items. For example, a book of letters is a logical item, which has its own metadata and nested logical items. These nested items are single letters, which again have their own metadata and nested physical items. These physical items are particular pages of a letter, which can also have their own metadata and include links to IIIF interface to access the digital content.

From a technical perspective, Qatar Digital Library is a complex service consisting of several components hosted in a public cloud. The frontend part is based on the Drupal CMS system and it is used to present a combination of data from three sources: backend relational database of the CMS, Solr search engine index and IIIF image server. The image server provides access to high-resolution images. The Solr index serves as the basis for search functionality and as a database for metadata. The relational database behind the CMS stores all the data which is necessary for the CMS to work and also the content of expert articles.

## 4   Future Works

The current interface of QDL was developed mainly in the first phase of partnership between QNL and BL. During the few years which have passed since QDL launch, QNL significantly developed the number of digital repatriation partnerships and now collections from several other institutions are ready or soon will be ready to appear in QDL. Because of that, the web interface has to be redesigned to be able to emphasize the institutional provenance of items presented to QDL users. The design challenge will be to keep the institutional provenance visible while integrating and connecting the distributed heritage at the same time. Another direction of development for QDL is coming from the user-centred approach taken by the library. Each key element of the interface was analysed using web analytic tools. Conclusions from that research will inform the planned redesign process, to make sure that the new interface will meet end users needs and will make the interaction and discovery of the archive easier and more engaging, event for accidental visitors.

## References

1. Roy, L., Christal, M.: Digital repatriation: constructing a culturally responsive virtual museum tour. J. Libr. Inf. Sci. **28**(1), 14–18 (2002)
2. Burrows, T.: Connecting medieval and renaissance manuscript collections. Open Libr. Hum. **4**(2), 32 (2018). http://doi.org/10.16995/olh.269
3. Exell, K., Rico, T.: 'There is no heritage in Qatar': orientalism, colonialism and other problematic histories. World Archaeol. **45**(4), 670–685 (2013). https://doi.org/10.1080/00438243.2013.852069
4. Shaon, A.: Digital Preservation to Support Large-Scale Digital Repatriation Initiative of Qatar National Library. Digital Preservation Coalition Blog. https://www.dpconline.org/blog/large-scale-digital-repatriation-qnl. Accessed 20 May 2019

# Correcting and Redesigning Metadata for the Excavation of an Archaeological Site

Sarantos Kapidakis$^{(\boxtimes)}$ (iD)

Laboratory on Digital Libraries and Electronic Publishing, Department of Archive, Library and Museum Sciences, Faculty of Information Science and Informatics, Ionian University, 72, Ioannou Theotoki Street, 49100 Corfu, Greece
sarantos@ionio.gr

**Abstract.** Libraries have a long tradition on cataloging with consistency. Other domains try to follow their paradigm, but there are many challenges to be addressed. In this paper we examine the metadata design and implementation for the excavation of an archaeological site. We start by discussing with the excavation personnel, to understand the procedures and the metadata involved. We examine the current metadata scheme and the way it was used to fill in all metadata element values and we classify the obvious errors found in them. We reveal additional required functionality and propose an improved scheme. In the poster we expose our methodology and findings.

**Keywords:** Metadata scheme · Controlled vocabularies · Authority files · Controlled terms · Documentation · Excavation · Values · Errors

## 1 Introduction and Related Work

Good quality metadata is essential. The evaluation and quality of metadata is examined as one dimension of the digital library evaluation frameworks and systems in the related literature, like [1,2]. Additionally, Fuhr et al. in [3] and Vullo et al. In [4] propose a quality framework for digital libraries that deal with quality parameters. In [5] Kapidakis studies the presence and the repetitions of the values of the metadata elements from many harvested metadata.

Unfortunately, archaeologists avoid sharing excavation and findings information, especially before publishing them, and even if the documentation of the findings is organized in a database, it is only accessible to the excavation personnel. Therefore, there are very few publicly accessible excavation data available, and each excavation organizes its data in a different way.

In this work we examine the metadata design and implementation for the excavation at the archaeological site of Amykles, an important political and religious center of ancient Sparta. Our first step was to discuss with the excavation personnel and to reveal and understand the excavation procedures and the metadata design.

© Springer Nature Switzerland AG 2019
A. Doucet et al. (Eds.): TPDL 2019, LNCS 11799, pp. 410–414, 2019.
https://doi.org/10.1007/978-3-030-30760-8_45

The initial documentation of the excavation is kept on a diary, that records the excavation procedures and findings. Additional documentation for each finding is later added from the related bibliography.

Since 2017, appropriate forms have been created and used to describe the metadata of the findings at the archaeological site of Amykles, forming a small collection with 5 main categories of findings, each with its own sub schema, that has many common elements.

Additionally, the data entry is not accompanied by any written rules, guidelines, or tools for assisting using controlled vocabularies or preventing errors in values. It is difficult to consistently enforce oral guidelines when the documentation lasts a few weeks each year, and sometimes may has to be continued by different personnel.

We examine the filled in metadata element values, we locate and examine metadata errors and classify the obvious errors found in them in groups with common properties.

## 2   Examining Values for Errors

We examine the metadata value syntax for obvious errors, like values of different type or not following the (oral or trivially assumed) guidelines. A general issue we found was the many empty values on described elements.

**Table 1.** Top 10 values of element *color*.

| Frequency | Value |
|---|---|
| 171 | 5YR 6/6 |
| 108 | 2.5YR 6/6 |
| 93 | 2.5YR 6/8 |
| 52 | 5YR 6/4 |
| 49 | 7.5YR 6/4 |
| 47 | 7.5YR 6/6 |
| 37 | 7.5YR 7/6 |
| 35 | 10R 6/8 |
| 22 | 2.5YR 5/8 |
| 22 | 2.5YR 5/6 |

The element *color* is used to describe the main color of a finding. It was one of the few elements with (oral) instructions on its use: All color values have to follow the Munsell[1] scheme, that define color syntax rules. We found 307 discrete values for the element *color*, in 1197 findings. In Table 1 we can see the

---

[1] https://munsell.com/.

top ten values of element *color* (column *value*) with its number of occurrences (column *frequency*). Only 21 values have a frequency greater than 10 and 53 values have a frequency between 2 and 10. The rest 233 values appear only once! This distribution is unusual for an element with values formed by following rules.

**Table 2.** Remarks on the 233 unique *color* values.

| Frequency | Remark | Example values |
|---|---|---|
| 112 | 2–3 Comma separated multi-color values | 7.5YR 6/4, 2.5YR 6/8 <br> 5YR 6/4, 10R 6/8 <br> 5YR 6/6, 5Y 5/1, 2.5YR 6/8 |
| 40 | Hyphen separated multi-color values | 7.5YR 6/4 - 2,5YR 5/6 <br> 2.5YR 6/8- 5/8 <br> 5YR 6/6-2.5YR 5/4-2.5Y 5/1 |
| 30 | Using extra words | GREY 13/N <br> BURN 10YR 5/2 <br> 5 YR IN THE CORE, 10R 5/6 |
| 15 | Variation of syntax: using "," instead of "." | 2,5YR 6/8 <br> 5YR 6/4, 7,5YR 7/6 <br> 7.5YR 6/4 - 2,5YR 5/6 |
| 50 | Wrong syntax from other reasons | 7.5YR, 6/6 <br> 5.YR 6/6, 7.5YR 4/1 <br> 5YR 5/6 AND 10R 6/8 |
| 8 | Unusual spacing | 7.5 YR 6/4 <br> 10R 6/8 - 2.5YR 5/6 <br> GLEY1 5/N |

In Table 2 we classify the 233 unique *color* values showing representatives (column *example values*) a description of the class property (column *remark*), and how many finding/filled values, fall under this category (column *frequency*).

The element *coating* represents the color of a specific part of the findings and is designed to take the same values as the element *color*. Despite having similar issues with those in Table 2, there are 15 more values that do not even resemble the Munsell scheme.

Element *grid* represents the horizontal coordinates that each finding was found, in $5\,\mathrm{m}^2$, and is designed to take values like "A2", "H11" or "K5". Some findings had no assigned values and we found 74 discrete values for 605 findings. Nevertheless, ignoring spacing into the values, we also found many inappropriate values, as we see and comment in Table 3. Column *findings*, denotes how many finding/filled values, fall under this category, column *values* denotes how many discrete values fall under this category, and column *example value* contains an example value, which we often translate to English to make it more understandable.

**Table 3.** Remarks on the 74 unique *grid* values.

| Findings | Values | Remark | Example value |
|---|---|---|---|
| 478 | 54 | OK | B8 |
| 8 | 2 | Extra dash | A-8 |
| 14 | 5 | Text | Remain of the Tsounda excavation 1890 |
| 1 | 1 | Complex range | B4/B3-G3 |
| 66 | 7 | Range | A2-A8 |
| 8 | 2 | Unusual letter | OM1 |
| 1 | 1 | Unusual range | P3,4 |
| 23 | 1 | Text and range | INTERSECTION A2-A8 |
| 6 | 1 | Unusual syntax for range | G2-3 |
| 605 | 74 | *Total* | |

Variation on the syntax and separation of the values is highly undesirable because it makes machine reading and understanding of the values much harder or impossible.

## 3   Conclusions and Future Work

Most metadata element values were not designed to be descriptive text but encoded information. We studied and classified the most common value errors and developed a methodology to locate and count unusual metadata values that constitute *obvious errors*. It can be applied to many small collections, maintained sporadically. We examined the current metadata scheme, the way it was used to fill in all metadata element values and also the new required functionality, to propose an improved scheme.

Many values in the collection need to conform to rules. In many cases we found unique values because of unusual value syntax, misuse of the element semantics, including text in various languages or containing too much detail.

We conclude that we need more standardization on the values. Values with invalid syntax should be corrected. More metadata elements are needed, to improve the information granularity. Some existing metadata elements should use controlled vocabularies. Variations in the element values that include supplementary information or uncertainty on the value should be inserted in other, possibly *comment*, elements and the original element must have more agreed values.

More information will be demonstrated on the body of the poster. Our analysis and methodology can be used to investigate the quality of other collections.

**Acknowledgment.** This research has been co-financed by the European Union and Greek national funds through the Operational Program Competitiveness, Entrepreneurship and Innovation, under the call RESEARCH – CREATE – INNOVATE (project code: T1EDK- 02168-15.6.2017).

# References

1. Moreira, B.L., Gonçalves, M.A., Laender, A.H., Fox, E.A.: Automatic evaluation of digital libraries with 5SQual. J. Informetrics **3**(2), 102–123 (2009)
2. Zhang, Y.: Developing a holistic model for digital library evaluation. J. Am. Soc. Inform. Sci. Technol. **61**(1), 88–110 (2010)
3. Fuhr, N., et al.: Evaluation of digital libraries. Int. J. Digit. Libr. **8**(1), 21–38 (2007)
4. Vullo, G., et al.: Quality interoperability within digital libraries: the DL.org perspective. In: 2nd DL.org Workshop in conjunction with ECDL 2010, pp. 9–10, September 2010
5. Kapidakis, S.: Metadata synthesis and updates on collections harvested using the open archive initiative protocol for metadata harvesting. In: Méndez, E., Crestani, F., Ribeiro, C., David, G., Lopes, J.C. (eds.) TPDL 2018. LNCS, vol. 11057, pp. 16–31. Springer, Cham (2018). https://doi.org/10.1007/978-3-030-00066-0_2

# Topic Modelling vs Distant Supervision: A Comparative Evaluation Based on the Classification of Parliamentary Enquiries

Riza Batista-Navarro[1]([✉]) and Oliver Hawkins[2]

[1] School of Computer Science, University of Manchester, Manchester, UK
riza.batista@manchester.ac.uk
[2] House of Commons Library, Parliament, London, UK
hawkinso@parliament.uk

**Abstract.** We investigate two different approaches to text classification, by categorising enquiries submitted to the House of Commons Library from elected Members of the UK Parliament. One is an unsupervised approach, i.e. topic modelling, and the other is a supervised approach based on weakly labelled data, i.e. distant supervision. Models were trained on two types of feature sets: one based only on bag of words, and the other combining bag of words with structured metadata attached to enquiries. Our results show that topic modelling obtains superior performance on this task, and that the incorporation of structured metadata as learning features contributes insignificantly to improved model performance.

**Keywords:** Text classification · Topic modelling ·
Distant supervision · Parliamentary enquiries ·
House of Commons Library

## 1 Introduction

The House of Commons Library is the research service for elected Members of the UK Parliament (MPs). The Library produces independent and impartial research for MPs and their staff on a wide range of public policy issues. Some of this research exists as publicly available briefing material, including in-depth research briefings, short online articles, and interactive data tools. MPs are also able to commission research directly from the Library through a confidential enquiry service. Responding to these enquiries forms the bulk of the Library's day-to-day research work.

MPs' offices can submit enquiries to the Library in person, by phone, by email, or by post. Each enquiry is received by a member of the House of Commons (HoC) staff and is recorded in the Enquiries Database, an internally accessible platform for searching and tracking enquiries. The Enquiries Database has

Supported by an EPSRC Impact Acceleration Account awarded to the University of Manchester.

A. Doucet et al. (Eds.): TPDL 2019, LNCS 11799, pp. 415–419, 2019.
https://doi.org/10.1007/978-3-030-30760-8_46

existed in some form since the 1990s, but data has been recorded using the current structure since 2005. For every enquiry, the following fields are recorded: date, title, description, the name of the MP whose office has submitted the enquiry, the name of the individual who submitted the enquiry, the purpose or reason for the enquiry, the names of the Library researchers who will respond to the enquiry and their research sections within the Library[1].

The title and description fields allow for free-text input and are thus written in natural language. The database does not currently support the manual categorisation or tagging of each enquiry according to any taxonomy of subjects or topics. While the user interface allows for searching by exact keyword matching against words in the free-text fields of the enquiry (i.e. title and description), there is no way to search the database for enquiries by specifying topics of interest. For example, if a database user is interested in retrieving enquiries pertaining to the topic of the European Union, only enquiries that mention "European Union" verbatim will be retrieved (and miss those that use alternative terms, e.g. "Brexit", "EU Exit", "EU").

In this work, we seek to enrich the information stored in the Enquiries Database by automatically tagging each enquiry using the 20 highest-level topics in the UK Parliamentary topic taxonomy[2]. To this end, we explore and compare two approaches to text classification, one unsupervised and the other supervised, namely, topic modelling and distant supervision.

## 2   Methodology

In this section, we first provide details of the Enquiries Corpus that we constructed for the purposes of developing our text classification methods. This is then followed by an overview of how our machine learning-based models were developed.

### 2.1   The Enquiries Corpus

From the Enquiries Database, we retrieved enquiries recorded over 10 years, i.e. from the 1st January 2008 up to the 31st December 2017. Out of these enquiries, only those that were allocated to research sections of the Library were retained. This was to eliminate enquiries that could not be classified under topics that typically require research (e.g. simple reference enquiries for things like telephone numbers and addresses, or library book loans). The final corpus contains a total of 125,071 enquiries.

---

[1] There are eight research sections in the Library: Business and Transport Section (BTS), Economic Policy and Statistics (EPAS), Home Affairs Section (HAS), International Affairs and Defence Section (IADS), Parliament and Constitution Centre (PCC), Science and Environment Section (SES), Social and General Statistics (SGS), Social Policy Section (SPS).

[2] https://www.parliament.uk/topics/topical-issues.htm.

Each enquiry comes with free-text fields (i.e. enquiry title and description) and the following metadata: date, a unique identifier corresponding to the MP whose office submitted the enquiry, a unique identifier corresponding to the person who submitted the enquiry, the reason for the enquiry (any of Frontbench Duties, Backbench Duties, Constituent Issue and Unknown), and the names of the Library staff to which the enquiry was allocated (subject specialists who are tasked with responding to the enquiry).

## 2.2   Topic Modelling

We firstly developed topic models based on Latent Dirichlet Allocation [1]. Here, we explored various values for the number of topics (from $k = 20$ to $k = 45$ in increments of 5), taking into consideration that we are aiming to classify enquiries according to the 20 highest-level topics in the Parliamentary taxonomy. We made use of the Structural Topic Modelling (STM) package [4] in R[3], which allowed us to investigate the effect of incorporating enquiry metadata as additional features for learning into the topic models.

The resulting topics, each of which is represented as a list of the 20 most frequently occurring keywords within that topic, were then manually assigned labels from the Parliamentary taxonomy by an expert (the second author of this paper), who is a long-time member of the Library's research staff. This step was done with the topics generated using $k = 45$, as these provided the best coverage of the 20 topics in the taxonomy (i.e. some topics were missing when lower values of $k$ were specified for modelling).

## 2.3   Distant Supervision

In investigating supervised approaches to text classification, we employed distant supervision, which involves the assignment of 'weak labels' to originally unlabelled data [3]. In this case, we obtained weak labels by making use of the Library's Subject Specialists Directory. This contains a mapping between the names of Library researchers (to whom enquiries are allocated) and their subject areas of specialisation, which in turn can be mapped to the Parliamentary taxonomy. Casting the problem as a multi-class, multi-label classification task, we trained support vector machine (SVM) models [2] with a linear kernel[4], using a one-vs-all setting. Here, we trained models based on bag of words (BoW), with and without enquiry metadata as additional features for learning.

## 3   Results

In this section, we present the results of the evaluation of our two proposed approaches. The evaluation was performed against a validation corpus containing

---

[3] http://www.structuraltopicmodel.com/.
[4] http://topepo.github.io/caret/index.html.

500 enquiries submitted in 2018, which were manually labelled with topics in the taxonomy by our expert[5]. To allow us to assess the reliability of these labels, a subset of 200 enquiries were also manually labelled independently by the first author of this paper. The inter-annotator agreement on this subset is satisfactory, i.e. 85% in terms of F-score.

The results obtained by our methods on the validation corpus are summarised in Table 1. In training our models, two different feature sets were used: one using only bag of words (BoW) and the other combining bag of words with metadata attached to enquiries; namely, reason for enquiry and political party[6], which are both represented as categorical features (BoW+Metadata).

**Table 1.** Comparison of topic modelling and distant supervision results

|  | Features | Precision | Recall | F-score |
|---|---|---|---|---|
| Topic modelling | BoW | 50.25 | 59.80 | 54.61 |
|  | BoW+Metadata | 49.92 | 60.80 | 54.82 |
| Distant supervision | BoW | 46.69 | 56.80 | 51.07 |
|  | BoW+Metadata | 47.66 | 55.00 | 51.25 |

Our results show that in general, topic modelling obtained superior performance over distant supervision, in terms of all of the metrics: precision, recall and F-score. Specifically, the topic models trained on features that incorporated not only textual features (BoW) but also enquiry metadata, yielded optimal performance, although the improvement over using only BoW is insignificant.

A similar observation can be made when it comes to the models trained using distant supervision: there is only a slight improvement in the performance of SVM models trained on BoW+Metadata, compared with models trained only on BoW.

## 4   Conclusion

In this paper, we describe our investigation into the application of one unsupervised and one supervised approach to a text classification task; specifically, the categorisation of MPs' enquiries according to a 20-class topic taxonomy. In particular, we trained topic models (unsupervised) and support vector machine models (supervised), while examining the effect of incorporating structured metadata as additional features for learning. Our results demonstrate that for the task of classifying enquiries: (1) topic modelling obtains better performance over distant supervision, and (2) the incorporation of structured metadata as features contributes very little to the improvement of model performance.

---

[5] Each enquiry was assigned at most two labels or topics from the taxonomy.
[6] The political affiliation of the MP's office at the time they submitted an enquiry, which was obtained from the UK Parliament's data platform using the pdpr R package: https://github.com/olihawkins/pdpr.

# References

1. Blei, D.M., Ng, A.Y., Jordan, M.I.: Latent Dirichlet allocation. J. Mach. Learn. Res. **3**, 993–1022 (2003)
2. Joachims, T.: Text categorization with Support Vector Machines: learning with many relevant features. In: Nédellec, C., Rouveirol, C. (eds.) Machine Learning: ECML 1998. LNCS, pp. 137–142. Springer, Heidelberg (1998). https://doi.org/10.1007/BFb0026683
3. Mintz, M., Bills, S., Snow, R., Jurafsky, D.: Distant supervision for relation extraction without labeled data. In: Proceedings of the Joint Conference of the 47th Annual Meeting of the ACL and the 4th International Joint Conference on Natural Language Processing of the AFNLP: Volume 2, ACL 2009, pp. 1003–1011. Association for Computational Linguistics, Stroudsburg (2009)
4. Roberts, M.E., Stewart, B.M., Tingley, D., et al.: STM: R package for structural topic models. J. Stat. Softw. **10**, 1–40 (2014)

# Author Index

Printed in the United States
By Bookmasters